# The International Handbook of
# Organizational Culture and Climate

# The International Handbook of Organizational Culture and Climate

*Editors*

**Cary L. Cooper**

*University of Manchester Institute of Science and Technology, UMIST, UK*

**Sue Cartwright**

*University of Manchester Institute of Science and Technology, UMIST, UK*

*and*

**P. Christopher Earley**

*Indiana University, IN, USA*

JOHN WILEY & SONS, LTD
Chichester · New York · Weinheim · Brisbane · Singapore · Toronto

National        01243 779777
International   (+44) 1243 779777
e-mail (for orders and customer service enquiries): cs-books@wiley.co.uk
Visit our Home Page on http://www.wiley.co.uk
or http://www.wiley.com

*Other Wiley Editorial Offices*

John Wiley & Sons, Inc., 605 Third Avenue,
New York, NY 10158-0012, USA

WILEY-VCH GmbH, Pappelallee 3,
D-69469 Weinheim, Germany

John Wiley & Sons Australia Ltd, 33 Park Road, Milton,
Queensland 4064, Australia

John Wiley & Sons (Asia) Pte Ltd, 2 Clementi Loop #02-01,
Jin Xing Distripark, Singapore 129809

John Wiley & Sons (Canada) Ltd, 22 Worcester Road,
Rexdale, Ontario M9W 1L1, Canada

***British Library Cataloguing in Publication Data***

A catalogue record for this book is available from the British Library

ISBN 0-471-49126-8

Typeset in 10/12 Times by Deerpark Publishing Services Ltd
Printed and bound in Great Britain by Bookcraft (Bath) Ltd, Midsomer Norton, Somerset
This book is printed on acid-free paper responsibly manufactured from sustainable forestry, in which at least
two trees are planted for each one used for paper production.

# Contents

# About the Editors

**Cary L. Cooper** is currently BUPA Professor of Organizational Psychology and Health in the Manchester School of Management, and Pro-Vice-Chancellor (External Activities) of the University of Manchester Institute of Science and Technology (UMIST). He is the author of over 80 books (on occupational stress, women at work and industrial and organizational psychology), has written over 300 scholarly articles for academic journals, and is a frequent contributor to national newspapers, TV and radio. He is currently Founding Editor of the *Journal of Organizational Behavior*, Co-Editor of the medical journal *Stress Medicine*; Co-Editor of the *International Journal of Management Review*. He is a Fellow of the British Psychological Society, The Royal Society of Arts, The Royal Society of Medicine and The Royal Society of Health. Professor Cooper is the President of the British Academy of Management, is a Companion of the (British) Institute of Management and one of the first UK-based Fellows of the (American) Academy of Management (having also won the 1998 Distinguished Service Award for his contribution to management science from the Academy of Management). Professor Cooper is the Editor (jointly with Professor Chris Argyris of Harvard Business School) of the international scholarly *Blackwell Encyclopedia of Management* (12 volume set). He has been an advisor to the World Health Organization, ILO, and recently published a major report for the EU's European Foundation for the Improvement of Living and Work Conditions on "Stress Prevention in the Workplace".

**Sue Cartwright** is a Chartered Psychologist and Senior Lecturer in Organizational Psychology at the Manchester School of Management, UMIST, UK. She is also Editor of the *Leadership & Organization Development Journal* and Book Review Editor for *Stress Medicine*. She has published widely in international journals on organizational culture and change and is co-author with Cary L. Cooper of *HR Know-How in Mergers and Acquisitions* (2000) published by the Institute of Personnel Development.

**P. Christopher Earley** is the Randall L. Tobias Chair of Global Leadership at the Kelley School of Business, Indiana University, USA. His research interests include cross-cultural and international aspects of organizational behavior such as the relationship of cultural values to workgroup dynamics, the role of face and social structure in organizations, and motivation across cultures. He is the author of seven books and numerous articles and book chapters. His recent publications include *Culture, Self-identity, and Work* and *The Transplanted Executive: Managing in Different Cultures* (both with Miriam Erez), Oxford University Press, *Face, Harmony, and Social Structure: An Analysis of Behavior in Organizations*, Oxford University Press, and "Creating Hybrid Team Cultures: An Empirical Test of International Team Functioning" with E. Mosakowski, *Academy of Management Journal*. He is the Editor of *Group and Organization Management* as well as former associate editor of *Academy of Management Review* and a member of several other editorial boards. He received his PhD in Industrial and Organizational Psychology from the University of Illinois, Urbana-Champaign, USA. He has taught on the faculties of London Business School, University of Arizona, University of Minnesota, University of California, Irvine, and has taught executives and consulted for companies in England, Hong Kong, Israel, People's Republic of China, Singapore, South Korea, and Thailand, among others.

# List of Contributors

Ramon J. Aldag, *University of Wisconsin, School of Business, 975 University Avenue, Madison, WI 53706, USA*

Philippe Baumard, *IAE Aix-en-Provence, BP 33 Clos Guiot – BD des Camus, 13540 Puyricard, France*

Christina L. Butler, *London Business School, Sussex Place, Regent's Park, London SW1 4SA, UK*

Glenn R. Carroll, *Graduate School of Business, Stanford University, Stanford, CA 94305, USA*

Sue Cartwright, *Manchester School of Management, University of Manchester Institute of Science and Technology (UMIST), P.O. Box 88, Manchester, M60 1QD, UK*

Jennifer A. Chatman, *Haas School of Business, 545 Student Services Building, University of California, Berkeley, CA 94720-1900, USA*

Marie-Thérèse Claes, *Institut Catholique des Hautes Etudes Commerciales, Université Catholique de Louvain, Boulevard Brand Whitlock 2, 1150 Brussels, Belgium*

Cary L. Cooper, *Manchester School of Management, University of Manchester Institute of Science and Technology (UMIST), P.O. Box 88, Manchester, M60 1QD, UK*

Tom Cummings, *Department of Management and Organization, Marshall School of Business, University of Southern California, Los Angeles, CA 90089-1421, USA*

Daniel Denison, *International Institute for Management Development, Chemin de Bellerive 23, Lausanne 1001, Switzerland*

Roger Dunbar, *Stern School of Business, Tisch Hall # 79, New York University, New York, NY 10012, USA*

P. Christopher Earley, *Kelley School of Business, Indiana University, Bloomington, IN 47405, USA*

Gerhard Fink, *Vienna University of Economics and Business Administration, Althanstrasse 39-45/2/3, 1090 Vienna, Austria*

Francis J. Flynn, *Columbia Business School, Columbia University, New York, USA*

Raghu Garud, *Stern School of Business, Tisch Hall # 79, New York University, New York, NY 10012, USA*

Cristina B. Gibson, *Center for Effective Organizations, University of Southern California, Los Angeles, CA, USA*

Kate Gilbert, *Management Research Centre, Wolverhampton Business School, University of Wolverhampton, Priors Lee, Telford TS2 4NT, UK*

Robert Goffee, *London Business School, Sussex Place, Regent's Park, London, NW1 4SA, UK*

J. Richard Harrison, *School of Management, University of Texas at Dallas, Richardson, TX 75983, USA*

Bo Hedberg, *Research Programme on Imaginary Organizations, School of Business, Stockholm University, S-106 92 Stockholm, Sweden*

Benjamin E. Hermalin, *Haas School of Business, 545 Student Services Building, University of California, Berkeley, CA 94720-1900, USA*

Nigel J. Holden, *Department of Intercultural Communication and Management, Copenhagen Business School, Dalgas Have 15, 2000 Frederiksberg, Denmark*

Karen A. Jehn, *The Wharton School, University of Pennsylvania, 200 Steinberg/Dietrich Hall, Philadelphia, PA 19104-6370, USA*

Gareth Jones, *BBC, Room 203, 6 Langham Street, London, W1A 1AA, UK*

Craig C. Lundberg, *Cornell University, Ithaca, NY, USA*

Kate Mackenzie Davey, *Department of Organizational Psychology, Birkbeck College, University of London, Mallett Street, Bloomsbury, London WC1E 7HX, UK*

Elizabeth A. Mannix, *Johnson Graduate School of Management, Cornell University, 452 Sage Hall, Ithaca, NY, USA*

Christian Maravelias, *Research Programme of Imaginary Organizations, School of Business, Stockholm University, S-106 92 Stockholm, Sweden*

Wolfgang Mayrhofer, *Vienna University of Economics and Business Administration, Augasse 2-6, A-1090, Vienna, Austria*

D. Harrison McKnight, *Information and Management Sciences Department, Florida State University, Tallahassee, FL 32306-1110, USA*

David A. Nadler, *Mercer Delta Consulting, LLC, 1177 Avenue of the Americas, New York, NY 10036, USA*

Mark B. Nadler, *Mercer Delta Consulting, LLC, 1177 Avenue of the Americas, New York, NY 10036, USA*

Narayan Pant, *Department of Business Policy, NUS Business School, National University of Singapore, FBA-1, 15 Law Link, Singapore 115591*

Roy L. Payne, *Curtin University of Technology, School of Psychology, G.P.O. Box U 1987, Perth, Western Australia 6845, Australia*

Sonja Sackmann, *Institüt für Personal- und Organisationalsforschung, Universität BW München, Werner-Heinsenberg-Weg 39, 85779 Neubiberg, Munich, Germany*

Dorte Salskov-Iversen, *Department of Intercultural Communication and Management, Copenhagen Business School, Dalgas Have 15, 2000 Frederiksberg, Denmark*

Kulwant Singh, *Department of Business Policy, NUS Business School, National University of Singapore, FBA-1, 15 Law Link, Singapore 115591*

Iva Smit, *E&E Consultants Inc, Slawijkseweg, 7077 AM Netterden, The Netherlands*

Paul R. Sparrow, *Sheffield University Management School, 9 Mappin Street, Sheffield, S1 4DT, UK*

William H. Starbuck, *Leonard N. Stern School of Business, New York University, Henry Kaufman Management Center, 44 West Fourth Street, 7-52, New York 10012, USA*

Gillian Symon, *Department of Organizational Psychology, Birkbeck College, University of London, Mallett Street, Bloomsbury, London WC1E 7HX, UK*

Charles T. Tackney, *Japan Studies Program, Department of Intercultural Communications and Management, Copenhagen Business School, Dalgas Have 15, DK-2000 Frederiksberg, Denmark*

Sherry Thatcher, *Eller College of Business and Public Administration, University of Arizona, 430 McLelland Hall, Tucson, AZ 85721, USA*

Peter K. Thies, *Mercer Delta Consulting, LLC, 1177 Avenue of the Americas, New York, NY 10036, USA*

Jan Ulijn, *Department of Organisation and Management Science, Faculty of Technology Management, Eindhoven University of Technology, P.O. Box 513, 5600 MB Eindhoven, The Netherlands*

Jane Webster, *Department of Management Sciences, University of Waterloo, 200 University Ave West, Waterloo, Ontario, Canada N2L 3B1*

M. Weggeman, *Department of Organisation and Management Science, Faculty of Technology Management, Eindhoven University of Technology, P.O. Box 513, 5600 MB Eindhoven, The Netherlands*

Anna Zarkada-Fraser, *School of International Business, Faculty of International Business and Politics, Griffith University, Nathan Campus, Queensland 4111, Australia*

Mary E. Zellmer-Bruhn, *University of Minnesota, Carlson School of Management, 321 19th Avenue South, Minneapolis, MN 55406, USA*

# Introduction

**Cary L. Cooper**
*University of Manchester Institute of Science and Technology,*
*UMIST, UK*

**Sue Cartwright**
*University of Manchester Institute of Science and Technology,*
*UMIST, UK*

*and*

**P. Christopher Earley**
*Indiana University, IN, USA*

The concept of organizational culture has been around a long time. Jacques (1951) described the changing culture of a factory, defining it as: 'The customary or traditional ways of doing things, which are shared to a greater or lesser extent by all members of the organization and which new members must learn and at least partially accept in order to be accepted into the service of the firm'. Schein (1985) provided a more complex definition: 'Organizational culture is the pattern of basic assumptions that a given group has invented, discovered or developed in learning to cope with its problems of external adaptation and internal integration, and that have worked well enough to be considered valid, and therefore, to be taught to new members as the correct way to perceive, think and feel in relation to these problems'. Morgan and Smircich (1980) discussed concepts of people as responding mechanisms or as adaptive mechanisms. Powell (1985) provides a general overview of the publishing industry in his institutional analysis of organizational culture and social structure. In the popular press, organizational culture received a great deal of emphasis with the publication of Peters and Waterman's (1982) popular work, *In Search of Excellence* detailing a number of case organizations that depict effective organizational cultures. At this time, a number of scientifically-based studies and discussions of organizational culture were presented by Martin (1982), Jaeger (1983, 1986), Martin and Siehl (1983), Trice and Beyer (1984) and Harris and Sutton (1986), More recently, organizational culture has been the focus of many scholars including seminal work by Smircich and Calas (1986), Martin (1992), Schneider (1990) and Chatman and Barsade (1995), just to name a few. Despite this exemplary work, organizational culture remains a difficult phenomenon to study and assess.

Research suggests that national, or societal-level, culture and other contextual variables (DiMaggio and Powell, 1983; Scott and Meyer, 1994) must be considered along with organizational culture in order to fully understand the relation of an organization's culture to organizational functioning (England, 1983). For example, Lincoln et al. (1981) found that matching organizational culture with societal culture results in high job satisfaction. Ferris and Wagner (1985) found that a congruence of Japanese organization structure with Japanese values was positively related to the effectiveness of quality circles. A similar idea is forwarded by Ouchi (1980) and his Theory Z analysis (Ouchi and Jaeger, 1983). Another good example of this awareness of societal and organizational cultures is presented by Misumi (1984) concerning the embeddedness of participatory decision-making and Japanese values. He argued that decision styles such as the *ringi* system are consistent with the early Meiji era of Japan.

There are a number of issues related to a full analysis of organizational culture. The first issue is best expressed by Benedict (1934) who cautioned the field of anthropology that "topical studies" of particular institutions (e.g. marriage, initiation, or economic) were potentially misguided since the significant unit is not the institution but is the general cultural configuration. This concern was echoed by Tyler (1969: 3) who said "Cultures then are not material phenomena; they are cognitive organizations of material phenomena. Consequently, cultures are neither described by mere arbitrary lists of anatomical traits and institutions such as house type, family type, kinship type, economic type, and personality type, nor are they necessarily equated with some over-all integrative pattern of these phenomena".

Second, the study of organizational culture may be misleading in the sense that organizations do not possess their own cultures independent of the social context in which they operate and function. As Schneider (1975: 203) points out, "Where norms tell the actor how to behave in the presence of ghosts, gods, and human beings, culture tells the actor what ghosts, gods, and human beings are and what they are all about". Organizational culture reflects the norms that regulate action within a firm and those myths and rituals underlying the sense-making that individuals engage in.

Third, much controversy remains concerning the general nature of organizational culture as a construct. Martin (1992) describes several different views that can be used to operationalize organizational culture. She presents a characterization of three general forms of organizational culture, namely, integration, differentiation, and fragmentation. Briefly, an integration view posits culture as shared meanings held in common. The differentiation view points out that there exist subgroups within any given organization that differ in their shared meanings from one another. Finally, a fragmentation perspective suggests that culture is a differential network of meanings that are interrelated and reciprocally related but ill-defined and inconsistent.

Fourth, the most effective way to measure and assess organizational culture remains unclear with a plethora of methods available to the researcher. O'Reilly, Chatman and their colleagues have developed a promising approach to assessing organizational culture (e.g. O'Reilly and Chatman, 1994; Chatman and Barsade, 1995) using a variation on a Q-sort method. Others have chosen to describe organizational cultures using typologies derived from Durkheim's discussion of society (e.g. Goffee and Jones, Section I, Chapter 1). However, it remains unclear what method yields the best results under various circumstances.

Thus, over the last 50 years organizational culture has become a more important part of the behavioral landscape of the organizational sciences. Its centrality to business activities including mergers and acquisitions, joint ventures, total quality management and the like, where organizational or corporate fit and change have become the staple diet of regionalization and globalization, is quite obvious. The purpose of this volume is to bring together the issues, constructs and research in the field of organizational culture and climate to help understand and inform future changes in organizations as we move toward ever larger and larger businesses across the world.

The book is divided into six sections, with an Associate Editor responsible for each section and leading scholars from across the world writing on specific topics of immense importance to organizational behavior. Our purpose in organizing the edited volume with Section/Associate Editors was to stimulate diverse thinking and writing. We imposed upon these Associate Editors (themselves experts in the field of organizational culture) to invite scholars of their own choosing to address the critical general categories that we had identified earlier through our own discussions. Associate Editors were invited to represent cutting-edge research from across the globe and we wished to avoid authors simply rehashing existing work in the field. Thus, our emphasis in this edited volume is not merely a review of the existing literature rather, it is to provide the field with new directions for the future. The strong contributions made by the various authors in this volume make us optimistic that such a lofty goal has been attained.

We begin the volume by exploring (Section I – Associate Editor, P. Christopher Earley) conceptual issues and perspectives in organizational cultures. This section examines an overview of the field of differentiation of culture and climate, a sociological perspective on organizational culture, temporal aspects of cultures, and multinational groups and the structure of organizational culture. Section II (Associate Editor, Paul R. Sparrow) highlights assessment and research methods in the organizational culture field. The issues explored deal with cultural complexity, recent approaches to qualitative analysis, assessment of cultures, a three-dimensional framework for assessing culture and individuals and an exploration of high performance cultures. Section III (Associate Editor, Jennifer A. Chatman) explores the implications of cultures for individuals and the organization itself, particularly its impact on influence networks, economics, innovation and information and group consensus. Section IV (Associate Editor, Tom Cummings) examines one of the most important issues, culture and change. Here the authors examine culture change in the strategic enterprise, social rules and emotions in cultures and organizational cultures as the key to organizational change. Section V (Associate Editor, Nigel J. Holden) highlights the international dimensions of organizational culture and climate. This aspect is particularly important in terms of the globalization of business, from understanding Japanese management practice to change in central and eastern Europe, as well as stereotyping in international business, communications between and within cultures, inter-cultural issues in business and innovation and managing globalization. Finally, Section VI (Associate Editor, William H. Starbuck) examines organizational cultures in the future. The authors attempt to answer questions like where are organizational cultures going, what will be there impact in "telework" settings, what will be the impact on diversity, will there be collaborative insight or privacy invasion in organization climates in the future.

As might be imagined, this volume was not merely the product of the editors' efforts alone. We would not only like to thank the various contributors to this book, but we would like to reiterate our appreciation for the hard work of the Associate Editors (Chatman, Cummings, Holden, Sparrow, and Starbuck) without whom the book would not have been completed. On behalf of all the editors, I would also like to thank Margaret Cannon for her diligent and systematic work on this volume. We have also been working very closely with the John Wiley's editor, Karen Weller, and we would like to thank her for her patience and perseverance on this major project.

In addition, the third editor would like to thank the support that he received from the Randall L. Tobias Chair of Global Leadership as well as the Kelley School of Business, Indiana University and special thanks to Ms. Kathy Sparks whose persistence and understanding concerning last minute "emergencies" were invaluable.

# REFERENCES

Benedict, R. (1934) Patterns of Culture. Boston: Houghton Mifflin.

Chatman, J. A. and Barsade, S.G. (1995) Personality, organizational culture, and cooperation: evidence from a business simulation. Administrative Science Quarterly, 40: 423–443.

DiMaggio, D.J. and W.W. Powell (1983) The iron cage revisited: institutional isomorphism and collective rationality in organizational fields. American Sociological Review, 48: 147–160

England, G.W. (1983) Japanese and American management: theory Z and beyond. Journal of International Business Studies, 14: 131–141.

Ferris, G.R. and Wagner, J.A. (1985) Quality circles in the United States: a conceptual reevaluation. Journal of Applied Behavior Science, 21: 155–167.

Harris, S.G. and Sutton, R.I. (1986) Functions of parting ceremonies in dying organizations. Academy of Management Journal, 29: 5–30.

Jaeger, A. (1983) The transfer of organizational culture overseas: an approach to control in the multinational corporation. Journal of International Business Studies, 14: 91–114.

Jaeger, A.M. (1986) Organizational development and national culture: where's the fit? Academy of Management Review, 11: 178–190.

Lincoln, J.R., Hanada, Mr.R. and Olson, J. (1981) Cultural orientation and individual reactions to organizations: a study of employees of Japanese armed forces. Administrative Science Quarterly, 26: 93–115.

Martin, J. (1982) Stories and scripts in organizational settings. In A.H. Hastorf and A.M. Isen (Eds.), Cognitive Social Psychology, pp. 255–306. New York: Elsevier.

Martin, J. (1992) Cultures in Organizations: Three Perspectives. New York: Oxford University Press.

Martin, J. and Siehl, C. (1983) Organizational culture and counterculture: an uneasy symbiosis. Organizational Dynamics, 12: 52–64.

Misumi, J. (1984) Decision-making in Japanese groups and organizations. In B. Wilpert and A. Sorge (Eds.), International Perspectives on Organizational Democracy. New York: Wiley.

Morgan, G. and Smircich, L. (1980) The case for qualitative research. Academy of Management Review, 5: 491–500.

O'Reilly, C. and J. Chatman (1994) Working smarter and harder: a longitudinal study of managerial success. Administrative Science Quarterly, 39: 603–627

Ouchi, W.G. (1980) Markets, bureaucracies and clans. Administrative Science Quarterly, 25: 129–141.

Ouchi, W.G. and Jaeger, A.M. (1978) Type Z organization: stability in the midst of mobility. Academy of Management Review, 5: 305–314.

Powell, W. (1985) Institutional forces in the publishing industry. Unpublished paper.

Peters, T.J. and Waterman, R.H. (1982) In search of excellence. New York: Harper & Row.

Schein, E.H. (1985) Organizational culture and leadership: a dynamic view. San Francisco, CA: Jossey-Bass.

Schneider, B. (1975). Organizational climate: an essay. Personnel Psychology, 28: 447–479.

Schneider, B. (1990) Organization climate and culture. San Francisco, CA: Jossey-Bass.

Scott, W.R. and Meyer, J.W. (1994) Institutional Environments and Organizations: Structural Complexity and Individualism. Thousand Oaks, CA: Sage.

Smircich, L. and Calas, M.B. (1986) Organizational culture: a critical assessment. Annual Review of Sociology, 228–263.

Trice, H.M. and Beyer, J.M. (1984) Studying organizational cultures through rites and ceremonials. Academy of Management Review, 9: 653–669.

Tyler, S.A. (1969) Cognitive Anthropology. New York: Holt, Rinehart and Winston.

# Section I

# Conceptual Issues and Perspectives

**Editor: P. Christopher Earley**

In Chapter 1 of our volume, Gareth Jones and Robert Goffee examine the nature of organizational culture from a sociological perspective focusing on various relationships. They argue that despite the importance of these relationships, they have remained underexplored in contemporary organizational analysis. How do networks vary? How does the nature of reciprocity differ between contrasting organizational contexts? They offer a framework as a means to understand different *social architectures* that characterize distinctive organizational cultures. They examine how various values, attitudes, behaviors and assumptions are shaped by different sets of organizational relationships. The model they develop rests upon two distinctive types of social relations – those of sociability and solidarity. They illustrate their model largely within the context of the large scale corporation and argue that it can be applied to other organizational settings including small business enterprises, occupational networks, and professional associations.

Chapter 2 focuses on a relatively recent area of interest in the management literature, the importance of time concepts to business practice and organizational culture. Time to market has become a critical issue in many industries with ever shortening new product development times. Mary E. Zellmer-Bruhn, Cristina B. Gibson, and Ramon J. Aldag focus on various new ideas concerning timing and pacing in work industry such as ideas of "clockspeed" (the pace at which innovation occurs) or "high velocity" (the need to make decisions in less time). They illustrate the importance of time considerations in an organization's culture with time horizons for "dot com" companies and other high-tech organizations as they face increasing competitive pressures. The authors take the ideas concerning time concepts in industry and illustrate its impact on various organizational cultures.

   Chapter 3 of this section presents the nature of organizational culture from a psychological and sociological perspective drawing on Giddens' Structuration Theory. The focus is on how multiculturally diverse groups of employees relate to the nature of organizational culture. The authors suggest that an increased understanding of how best to make use of multinational management teams contributes critically to competitive advantage and to take advantage requires an understanding of how these teams relate to the general organizational culture. The overarching link that the authors use is a key element of Giddens' Structuration Theory (1979, 1984), that of "colonization of the future". The authors use this concept to consider how colonization links important research findings in the areas of micro status structures and group performance, providing insights into the challenges of managing organizational culture, and finally make recommendations as to promising lines of research in the area of organizational culture.

# Chapter 1

# Organizational Culture: a Sociological Perspective

**Robert Goffee**
*London Business School, London, UK*

*and*

**Gareth Jones**
*Department of Human Resources and Internal Communications,
BBC, London, UK*

## INTRODUCTION

The 1980s marked the beginning of a resurgence of research into organizational culture. The interest was driven by a number of factors. First, business school academics and consultants became increasingly interested in co-ordination issues raised by the globalization of large scale business and the challenges it posed for conventional means of structural integration (Ghoshal and Bartlett, 1988, 1997). Second, there was the argument that levels of organizational performance could be explained by distinctive types of culture, and that "strong" cultures characterized by clearly expressed and widely practised values predicted corporate achievement (Peters and Waterman, 1982). Finally, there was the related claim that distinctive organizational cultures (unlike technologies, for example) could represent a source of long-term competitive advantage because they were not quickly or easily replicated by competitors (Kay, 1995).

The growing interest in corporate culture reflected a rejection of narrow "rational-analytic" approaches to the study of organizational structure and strategy. It was impossible to understand the design of structures or the implementation of strategies, it was argued, without reference to the cultural context within which they were embedded (Schein, 1995). A related view suggested that as reliance upon conventional formal mechanisms for organizational integration diminished, so the significance of corporate culture as "glue" increased (Evans, 1993). Processes of decentralization, devolution and delayering were undermining conventional organizational structures and breaking apart the climbing frame for long-term career-related attachments between individuals and their employing organizations (Peiperl et al., 2000). At the same time, the growth of lateral integration mechanisms – cross-functional teams, project groups, networks – together with tighter customer–supplier links, joint ventures and alliances, accelerated the dissolution of intra- and inter-organizational boundaries.

As the vertical and lateral contours of organizations altered so the language of organizational analysis changed. Culture – or sometimes community – became the preferred metaphors and organizational relationships were increasingly mapped through "networks" or "clusters" rather than hierarchies. What held the modern, "flexible" organization together were not reporting relationships, functions or depart-ments but more fluid, shifting relationships of collaboration, interdependence and reciprocity (Goffee and Scase, 1995).

Yet the nature of these relationships has remained underexplored in contemporary organizational analysis. How do networks vary? How does the nature of reciprocity differ between contrasting organizational contexts? (Parker and Arthur, 2000). We offer the framework in this chapter as a means to understand different *social architectures* that characterize distinctive organizational cultures. Our focus, then, is upon the manner in which shared values, attitudes, behaviours and assumptions may be shaped by different sets of organizational relationships. The model we develop rests upon well established traditions of sociological analysis which identify two distinctive types of social relations – those of sociability and solidarity. We illustrate our model largely within the context of the large scale corporation but it can be applied to other organiza-tional settings: for example, smaller enterprises, occupational networks, professional associations and regional industrial communities.

## ANALYZING SOCIAL ARCHITECTURES

*Sociability* is an aspect of social life central to the concerns of classic sociological analysis. It refers primarily to affective, non-instrumental relations between individuals who are likely to see one another as "friends". Friends tend to share certain ideas, attitudes, interests and values and to be inclined to associate on equal terms. So defined, friendship groups frequently constitute a primary unit in sociological analysis of status groups and of social class (Gerth and Mills, 1948). In its pure form, sociability repre-sents a type of social interaction which is valued for its own sake (Simmel, 1971). It is frequently sustained through continuing face-to-face relations typically characterized by high levels of unarticulated reciprocity; there are no "deals" prearranged. Indivi-duals help each other "with no strings".

*Solidarity*, by contrast, describes task focused co-operation between *unlike* indivi-duals and groups (Durkheim, 1993). It does not, in other words, depend upon close friendship or even personal acquaintance, nor is it necessarily sustained by continuous social relations. Solidarity is demonstrated instrumentally and discontinuously – as and when the need arises. In contrast to sociability, then, its expression is both intermittent and contingent.

Although sociability and solidarity may be distinguished conceptually in this way, many discussions of organizational relations confuse the two. Clearly, social interaction within organizations may constitute the sociability of friends, the solidarity of colleagues, both, or – sometimes – neither. Equally, when colleagues socialize outside organizations, this may represent an extension of workplace solidarity, rather than an expression of intimate or close friendships. Few descriptions of organizational social life explicitly address these distinctions, though some provide sufficient ethnographic material to enable an informed guess about the nature of particular social architectures.

Clearly, to co-operate in the instrumental pursuit of common goals it is not necessary for individuals to like one another. Indeed, solidarity may often be exhibited amongst those who strongly dislike each other. Equally, intimate forms of sociability may actually be less likely amongst those who feel constrained to act solidaristically as work colleagues.

The intensity of sociability may vary directly, independently or inversely with the intensity of solidarity. As a starting point, it is useful to distinguish organizations as exhibiting high or low levels of sociability and solidarity. In effect, this suggests four distinctive corporate forms (Figure 1.1): the *networked*, the *mercenary*, the *fragmented* and the *communal* (Goffee and Jones, 1996, 1998). The examples we use below are intended to illustrate each type of organization and are drawn from recent field

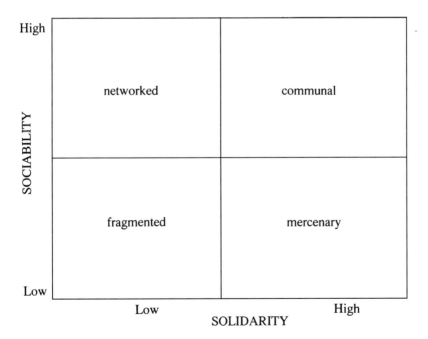

**Figure 1.1** Four organizational archetypes.

research. For purposes of illustration the organizational unit of analysis is the firm, but the model can be applied at various levels – the division or business unit, the function or the team, for example.

*Networked* organizations exhibit high levels of sociability but relatively low levels of solidarity. Such organizations are often characterized by loyalty, a "family ethos" and work routines regularly punctuated by social events and rituals of one kind or another. These serve to sustain a strong sense of intimacy, loyalty and friendship. Patterns of sociability within the workplace often extend beyond it, via leisure and sporting clubs and informal social contacts amongst families.

Levels of solidarity, however, are low. Relationships of personal affection do not automatically translate into high levels of intra-organizational co-operation. Indeed, although social networks are characterized by well established friendships, the culture of networked organizations can sometimes become "gossipy" and "political". Indeed, it is a mistake to assume that well established patterns of sociability will form the basis for solidaristic co-operation. In fact, the reverse may be true. Close friendships, for example, may constrain open expression of difference which can be a necessary condition for developing and maintaining a shared sense of purpose.

At the level of the firm, the *networked* form may be indicated where:

- Knowledge of local markets is a critical success factor.
- Corporate success is an aggregate of local success (interdependencies are minimal).
- There are few opportunities for transfer of learning between divisions or units.
- Strategies are long-term (sociability maintains strategic intent when short-term calculations of interest would not).

Business organizations with *networked* cultures often benefit from informal social relations which, in turn, facilitate flexible responses to problems, swift and easy communication between members and a generalized preparedness to help others. Those drawn to such cultures report satisfaction with the friendship and empathy of work colleagues and the relaxed, "easygoing" atmosphere.

Our data indicate that the person–organization fit works best for *networked* cultures where individuals:

- are extrovert and energized by relationships;
- possess good social skills, empathy and situation sensing abilities;
- are tolerant of ambiguity and difference;
- are affable and loyal to others;
- are patient (not always expecting immediate action);
- are prepared to build long-term relationships.

But our field data indicate that such organizations can also suffer from "negative" politics. To some extent, this may be inevitable – at least in large-scale organizations. As we have indicated, sociability tends to be sustained by face-to-face relationships – but clearly there are limits to the number of people that any one person can know. As a result, networks can degenerate into cliques. Similarly, informal information exchange can easily become disruptive "gossip", and meetings between "friendly" people may produce much talk but little action. More than other cultures, it is the informality of the *networked* culture which sanctions political game playing: for example, manipulation of communication (by copying e-mails), high rates of job mobility (to avoid performance measures and extend networks), and advanced impression management (by slick presentations and managing relationships upwards in the hierarchy rather than managing performance-related outcomes).

In *mercenary* organizations, a heightened sense of competition and a strong desire to succeed – or at least survive – is often a central feature of corporate culture. Dominant values may be built around competitive individualism and personal achievement but these do not preclude co-operative activity where this demonstrably produces benefits for both individuals and their organizations. In other words, colleagues display a solidarity which does not depend upon close friendships or ties of affection. Good teamwork can sometimes be described by members of mercenary cultures as "eagles flying in formation". Day-to-day relationships in such organizations are rarely characterized by high levels of collective co-operation – quite the reverse may be true. As we have pointed out, solidarity may be both *intermittent* and *contingent*.

The *mercenary* form is indicated where:

- Capacity to act swiftly in a highly co-ordinated way is a critical source of competitive advantage.
- Economies of scale and competitive advantage can be gained from creating corporate centres of excellence which can impose processes and procedures on operating units.
- The nature of the competition is clear – external enemies help to build internal solidarity.
- Corporate goals are clear and measurable and there is little need for consensus building.

Organizations which have a predominantly *mercenary* culture typically benefit from a clear understanding of purpose and the ability to mobilize resources swiftly in order to achieve ends. Members of these cultures are attracted by their meritocratic intolerance of poor performance, the preparedness to openly address conflict, and the relentless drive to measurably improve standards.

Our evidence suggests that individuals who fit best with *mercenary* cultures tend to be:

- goal-oriented;
- keen to complete tasks once started;
- motivated by clarity and structure rather than ambiguity;
- instrumental rather than affective in their work relations;
- energized by competition and success;
- able to address rather than avoid conflict.

The benefits of a *mercenary* culture for business organizations operating within competitive market economies are clear (Hamel and Prahalad, 1995). But we have also collected examples of behaviour within such contexts which suggest that high solidarity relationships may breed peculiar managerial problems. The tendency to focus upon measurable performance neglects the unmeasurable – and since co-operative behaviour

is not always easily assessed mercenary cultures can easily become internally competitive. The bias towards means–ends relationships also means that the management of
uncertainty and ambiguity is difficult – alliance management, for example, can be
particularly difficult for members of a *mercenary* culture. Finally, low levels of sociability indicate limited emotional involvement and, therefore, a relatively brittle psychological contract. Even a momentary misalignment of individual and organizational
interests can be enough to produce disaffection and the loss of organizational members.
In knowledge-based businesses, for example, this can prove extremely expensive
(Morris, 2000).

But what of organizations which exhibit low levels of both sociability and solidarity?
Can these *fragmented* organizations survive or succeed? Although it seems implausible
there is evidence that, at least in some contexts, these "disintegrated" corporate
cultures can survive and grow. For example, organizations which rely heavily on
outsourcing and homework and those which rely largely upon the contribution of
individual, non-interdependent experts and professionals may be predominantly fragmented.

Thus, the major contingencies which indicate the *fragmented* form are where:

- Innovation is produced primarily by individuals not groups.
- Standards are achieved primarily through input (e.g. professional qualifications)
  rather than process controls.
- There are few learning opportunities between individuals (or when professional
  pride prevents knowledge transfer).
- There are low levels of work interdependence.

Organizations with predominantly *fragmented* cultures can derive substantial benefits from the autonomy and freedom which are granted to members. University
academics or partners in a law firm, for example, possess considerable discretion to
set their own work agendas and develop their professional talents without external
"interference". Under such conditions individual creativity can flourish and resources
may flow to those with proven track records.

It is perhaps not surprising to find that those who best fit *fragmented* cultures tend to
be:

- introvert, learning best through self-contained reflection;
- motivated by autonomy and independence;
- analytical rather than intuitive;
- capable of managing their own development;
- able to separate idea evaluation from personal relationships.

Despite these apparent advantages in certain contexts, *fragmented* cultures can sometimes become so individualized that they may literally fall apart. Freedoms may be
abused by selfish and secretive behaviour, organizational identification can be reduced
to levels where it is virtually forgotten, and simple attempts at co-operation – meetings,
for example – are undermined by disruptive behaviours or even absenteeism.

Although, then, it is clearly possible for corporations to survive and prosper largely
in the absence of either sociability or solidarity, it is perhaps not surprising that some

see the *communal* organization – with high levels of both – as the ideal. Solidarity alone may suggest an excessively instrumental organizational orientation; co-operation may be withdrawn the moment that it is not possible for members to identify shared advantage. In such organizations, scope for "goodwill" and general "flexibility" may be absent. By contrast, organizations which are characterized primarily by sociability may lose their sense of purpose. Critics claim that such organizations tend to be overly tolerant of poor performance and possibly complacent.

No doubt, the *communal* organization has much appeal. Indeed, this model informs much of the literature on innovative, "high performance" business organizations (Kanter, 1990). However, it may be an inappropriate and unattainable ideal in many corporate contexts. Those businesses which are able to achieve the communal form frequently find it difficult to sustain. There are a number of possible explanations. High levels of sociability and solidarity are often formed around particular founders or leaders whose departure may weaken either or both forms of social relationship. Similarly, the communal corporation may be difficult to sustain in the context of growth, diversification and internationalization. More profoundly, there may be a fundamental tension between relationships of sociability and solidarity which makes the communal corporation inherently unstable. In effect, friendships can undermine collective interests or vice versa (Homans, 1951).

The *communal* form is indicated where:

- Innovation requires extensive teamworking across functions and locations.
- There are measurable synergies and opportunities for teamworking across organizational sub-units.
- Strategies are long-term and emergent rather than the sum of measurable stages.
- The business environment is dynamic and complex – requiring multiple interfaces with the environment and high capacity for internal organizational information synthesis.

Organizations with *communal* cultures become almost like a "cult". Members tend to be passionate about the "cause" and so are able to expend high levels of energy over long time periods in proving their case – or "converting" others. *Communal* cultures can often sustain complex teams apparently divided by geography, nationality and function, for example, but united in a common purpose and close ties between espoused values and embedded practices.

Individuals who fit best in communal cultures tend to be:

- idealist and obsessive;
- prepared to make sacrifices for the greater good;
- attracted to teams;
- able to wholeheartedly identify with the organization;
- prepared to place the organization above private and family life.

Many successful business start-ups and fast growth enterprises have exploited the benefits of a *communal* culture. But such cultures may be particularly prone to what has become known as the "paradox of success": the tendency to persist with behaviours even when they have ceased to be appropriate to context (Audia et al., 2000). Members of (successful) *communal* cultures often develop an inappropriate sense of invulnerability. Competitors are dismissed and customers seen to be in need of education. New ideas are crushed by unquestioning adherence to values or principles which may have ceased to serve their purpose. In this way, a *communal* organization such as IBM is undermined by new rivals such as Apple who then paradoxically fall foul of the same collective sense of invulnerability as their original target.

## OBSERVING SOCIAL ARCHITECTURES

We have used this model to inform our observations in a range of private and public organizations across different industrial sectors. To illustrate this we include a checklist for the main cultural types in four areas (Table 1.1). First, the use of physical space: for example, whether it is shared or defended, how it is allocated, the way it is decorated, and its functionality. Second, patterns of communication: for example, the extent to which ideas or information are shared face-to-face or electronically, the degree to which communication networks are inclusive, or the "availability" of certain individuals. Third, how time is managed: for example, how long people stay at work, what people do with their time and how time is measured, how long people stay in their jobs, and how long it takes to "get to know" someone. Fourth, how people express their personal identities: for example, the extent to which there are common dress codes or manners of speech, the rituals which mark joining or leaving, what it is that people identify with (traditions, each other or the corporate vision for example), and the relative strength of this identification.

Of course, it is likely that large, complex organizations will be characterized by more than one culture. Given different work performed in different parts of an organization, different technologies, customers, competitive environments and so on, uniformity in culture would be exceptional. Indeed, we share the view that the clarity, consistency and consensus attributed to so-called "strong" culture businesses has been regularly exaggerated (Martin, 1992).

Although, then, a *networked* culture might pervade a multinational organization such as Unilever, for example – cutting across many divisions, functions and territories – it is quite possible to find local subcultures at business unit level (Calvin Klein in New York, for instance) with distinctive "local" cultural identities. Similarly, although several of the largest professional service firms may be conceived as *fragmented* at the macro-global level, local offices may be deliberately developed as a series of almost identical *communal* "cells", or allowed to develop quite different cultural characteristics according to local environmental contingencies.

The fact that organizations may occupy more than one quadrant in our model poses interface management issues. Two examples may illustrate this point. First, in highly innovative pharmaceutical companies, for instance, we might expect the R&D function to be *communal*, and the Sales & Marketing function to be *mercenary*. In such organizations a perennial issue is "how and why, in the innovation process, should marketing be involved?". Turf battles often follow as the *communal* R&D function protects its cherished "values" from the perceived "ruthlessness" of the *mercenary* marketeers.

**Table 1.1**  Checklist for the main cultural types

## Physical space
### Networked
Office doors are open or unlocked; people move freely into and out of each other's rooms. Offices may be decorated with pictures of family, postcards, cartoons, humorous notes/pictures of colleagues. Large allocations of space are for social activity: bars, coffee lounges, sporting facilities, etc. "Privileged" space (larger offices, car parking) is linked to the formal hierarchy but there are also "deals" favouring some rather than others. There may be corporate logos but in negatively networked organizations these may be a source of amusement. Similarly, different territories within a building may be decorated and defended in ways that set them apart from others; the marketing department may become effectively a "no-go" zone for the finance people and vice versa. Outsiders are likely to be spotted – they will knock on doors before they enter, will be dressed differently, etc.

### Mercenary
Space is allocated "functionally" – in ways that help to get the job done. Open plan or flexible desk use is possible – but in order to assist with simple, efficient and cost effective methods of means of task achievement, not "chatting". Uninvited visitors/people that "drop by" are likely to be shooed away if someone is busy. Little space is wasted in work areas, although entrances may be designed to underline fearsome reputation. Office decorations may be dominated by awards, recognitions of achievement, etc. Space allocation is linked to achievement and there are no favours in the car park; indeed, the priority may be the customer.

### Fragmented
Space is designed to help individuals work without interruption. Office doors are closed and offices are well equipped so that employees are effectively self-contained. Much of the time these offices may be empty (people are on the road, working from home, at a conference, etc.) but it is hard to tell if they are there or not. Some individuals may make their elusiveness a trademark (a common joke in this context: "What's the difference between Jo and God? God is everywhere; Jo is everywhere but here!") In the virtual/fragmented organization there is very little corporate space – work is conducted from home, the car, etc.

### Communal
Much space is shared either formally (open plan) or informally (lots of movement in and out of offices). It may sometimes be difficult to determine whose office you are in, and there are few barriers between departments or functions. There are unlikely to be big differences in space allocation between people. Formal social facilities are supported by extensive informal socializing; food and drink spreads into "work" space. The corporate logo is everywhere; office decoration will improvise around, extend or adapt the language of the company values, mission or credo.

**Table 1.1** (*continued*)

**Communication**

*Networked*

There is a lot of talk. Although there are formal hierarchies and processes, much communication takes place around the formal systems in face-to-face conversation, on the phone, in "meetings before meetings". Paper-based documents may be annotated by hand before being passed on to some others in the network. E-mail may be used to gossip. In highly politicized networked cultures papers may be copied routinely to key players. Skilfully managed, the networks span the business and assist integration, but often cliques and factions form around functions, levels, businesses, or countries, which impedes communication. On the other hand, because there is a lot of talk, there is the possibility of rapid information exchange and increased creativity. Considerable attention may be paid to communicating in the "right" way; to style, manner, and presentation rather than content.

*Mercenary*

Communication is swift, direct, and work-focused. Terse memos and data-laden reports leave little room for "idle" conversation. Conflicts are unlikely to be resolved by gentlemen's agreement; face-to-face confrontation or legalistic duelling (speak to my lawyer) are more common. Communication across boundaries (hierarchy, geography, etc.) is expected and accepted if it is task-focused. Meetings are business-like – well planned and with a premium on actionable outcomes. The expression of personal problems is discouraged.

*Fragmented*

Talk is limited to brief one-to-one exchanges in the corridor or on the phone. Meetings are resisted (what's the point?), difficult to arrange, hard to manage for any length of time without boredom, acrimony or people simply walking out. Individuals will talk only to those who are "worth" talking to (to get rid of a problem; to pick their brains; to ask for resources); otherwise the deal is "I leave you alone if you leave me alone". Key individuals may be difficult to find, even within your own department. Documents may replace talk but there is no guarantee that they will be read. Much communication is directed outside the organization to clients and professional peers.

*Communal*

There is communication in every channel, but oral, face-to-face methods are likely to dominate. Non-verbal communication is, nevertheless, important; dress, colour, and symbolism may all help individuals to feel close to others. Communication flows easily inside between levels, departments, and across national cultures (the cult encompasses all), but outsiders may feel excluded. Talk is littered with the private company language reaffirming the bonds between "us" and the difference from "them". It is difficult *not* to talk, and there are few secrets – private or professional. Guilt and shame are used to correct "closed" behaviour.

**Table 1.1** (*continued*)

**Time**

*Networked*

People use work time to socialize and they are not penalized for doing so. To some extent, the reverse applies – "all work and no play makes Jack a dull boy". In addition, social activities are often extensions to the working day. This may make the "working day" long but some part of it may be in the bar, on the golf course, or at the social club. People get to know each other quickly, and many have known each other for a long time.

*Mercenary*

Long hours are the norm, although it is acceptable to leave once the job is done. This is clearly signalled, since time and performance measures are explicit. Private time is precious and, where possible, protected (it is what's left if you don't cut it at work). It takes a long time to know people other than in their work roles; "idle chat" is regarded as a waste of time.

*Fragmented*

People go to the office only when they need to; absence is the norm. Achievement, not time, is the measure (and the achievements may take a long time to deliver). Most time is devoted to the pursuit of individual professional and technical excellence; anything which interferes with this – colleagues, administrative chores, even clients/customers – can be considered a waste of time. It is possible for individuals to work "together" for many years without knowing each other (a common gaffe is for colleagues to reveal their ignorance of each other in front of clients at, admittedly rare, social events). Careful time management is a key skill – often involving complex schedule control.

*Communal*

People live at work; professional life is so engaging that "conventional" time is ignored. Work and non-work life dissolve into one; even when at home work can be a pre-occupation. Close working relationships may be reflected in friendship groups, marriage, affairs, etc. Work becomes a way of life; social activity that is disconnected from professional interests may be regarded as a waste of time (work is relaxation and vice versa).

**Identity**

*Networked*

People identify with each other; close ties of sociability heighten feelings of similarity as individuals. Differences are understated and if expressed at all they are seen in subtle variations of dress code or speech patterns. Excessive displays of personal difference are resisted, and some store is set by long-established social rituals which tie people in even after they have left (social clubs, pensioners associations, alumni associations). Personal loyalties persist; although in some contexts the company may

*Mercenary*

People identify with winning. Although norms of behaviour emerge here as anywhere, differences between individuals are acceptable and encouraged if they assist in achieving the result. What draws people together are shared experiences, goals, and interests rather than shared sentiments or feelings. Ultimately, attachments are instrumental – the enemy may eventually be the next employer if it suits personal interests. There is no shame in shifting allegiance or ruthlessly exploiting

**Table 1.1** (*continued*)

be criticized, this is often manifested in dark humour because its a little like criticizing yourself.

knowledge of business weaknesses once employees move on.

*Fragmented*

People identify with values of individualism and freedom, with personal technical excellence, and with organizations that minimize interference. There are significant personal differences between individuals, but these are unlikely to impede achievement (there are low levels of interdependence), and they confirm values of freedom. Allegiance will be professional rather than organizational. Private lives are often a mystery; frequently a strong compensation for the loneliness of working in the fragmented.

*Communal*

People identify with the values and mission of their company. The credo is lived; the words are played out, enacted, debated, applied, developed. Work becomes a way of life. Logos, symbols, war cries abound. Excessive identification (combined with a track record of success) can lead to a loss of perspective, intolerance of criticism and complacency. The company attracts fierce loyalty. When individuals leave they continue to be supporters. Indeed, their fervent identification can be disabling in their subsequent careers. Work identity is carried over into private life – logos on clothes, trying out company products at home, visiting company stores on weekends, etc.

Reproduced from Goffee and Jones (1998).

Similar interface issues arise in companies with "cultural products" – music, books and television programming, for example. Again there are frequent clashes (rarely productive) in our experience between functions and activities with different social architectures.

## THE FRAMEWORK APPLIED

### Understanding Organizational Innovation and Change

Clearly organizational cultures are neither uniform nor static. They evolve over time and change. How change occurs within organizations has been the subject of a large though often disappointing literature – often uninformed by theory, failing to track change over time and, in accounts of planned change, typically exaggerating the potential of managers to "control", "engineer" or "transform" culture (Bate, 1994). Our own view is that in so far as organizations are designed to repeat activities and cultures are underpinned by "deep" assumptions which are patterned and shared, then we should expect persistence to be the norm rather than swift or radical change (Schein, 1995).

In terms of the model, cultural change may often be best understood as a subtle shift *within rather than between quadrants* in the mix of elements – as reviewed above – which characterize a particular culture. These elements, as we have argued, may have positive or negative outcomes in terms of business performance or member motivation, for example. In a sense, "good" *networked* cultures which appear to deliver business performance, for example, are rather more likely to slip and turn "bad" than be transformed into another cultural form. Transformations may only be achievable via relatively dramatic interventions such as merger or acquisition.

In a similar vein, innovation processes may occur within every culture but they are likely to be initiated by different triggers and enacted in distinctive ways (Robinson and Stern, 1997). The trigger for creativity and innovation in the *networked* culture is likely to be informal relationships and "fun", in the *communal* culture it is more often intensive teamwork, in the *mercenary* culture it is sensitivity to market pressure, and in the *fragmented* culture it is productive cognitive conflict.

Innovation processes may be similarly differentiated. It is more reasonable to expect innovation to be characterized by unplanned connections and relatively slow implementation given the slack often available (or skilfully created) in *networked* organizations. By contrast, the *mercenary* organization is more typically characterized by planned, measured (and often incremental) innovation processes and fast implementation. Innovation in the *communal* form is likely to involve complex teamwork over lengthy periods – often driven by visionary leadership intent on achieving major breakthroughs. Finally, it is often (highly trained) individuals working with considerable autonomy and resources which characterize innovation processes in *fragmented* cultures.

It is with some caution, given our comments on cultural persistence, that we offer the following tentative suggestions about the way in which movement *between* quadrants may be patterned (Goffee and Jones, 1998). One pattern starting in the *communal* quadrant – either as a new or established organization – suggests a reversed z movement through *networked* and *mercenary* to *fragmented*. In this migration the move from *communal* to *networked* may be triggered by the fact that, as we have argued, the behaviours of sociability may undermine relations of solidarity. Alternatively, *communal* enterprises which succeed in business terms can become complacent – especially if the founding mission appears to have been accomplished and the major competitive threat defeated. Relationships persist but a shared sense of purpose diminishes: the culture drifts to a more *networked* form. To compensate, managers may attempt to rebuild solidarity by more explicit targets and clear financial objectives – with reward systems appropriately aligned. But in the process, long established – and delicate – ties of sociability are unintentionally severely damaged. A shift intended to build a more *mercenary* culture succeeds only in creating a *fragmented* organizational culture.

A second pattern of unintentional cultural change involves a move from *networked* to *mercenary* and back to *networked*. In this process, senior managers within *networked* cultures are typically driven to build solidarity (and reduce sociability) by severe competition and associated performance pressures. But the informal networks, in effect, "hide" covert resistance to the change process; long established ties of sociability explain the organizational inertia which repeatedly drags the culture back to the *networked* form.

A third pattern sees organizations move direct from *communal* to *fragmented*. As we have argued, the *communal* culture is fragile because of the inherent tension between relations of sociability and solidarity. The culture of many successful entrepreneurial start-ups, for example, effectively implodes when the founder-owner retires or when the company is acquired (Goffee and Scase, 1995). Other founding members leave and those who remain talk fondly of "the good old days" and remain detached from the present.

## The Psychological Contract and "Work–Life" Relationships

The distinctive social architectures identified by our model also offer a useful means for understanding different individual–organization linkages and their place within the context of more widely conceived lifestyles and social relations.

The relationship between individuals and the organizations to which they "belong" has been usefully conceptualized in terms of the psychological contract (Argyris, 1964; Schein, 1978; Rousseau, 1995): the exchange which, explicitly or implicitly, is negotiated when individuals join, remain with and perform in organizations. How, then, might the distinctive social architectures which we have described help to predict differences in the psychological contract? Focusing upon managers and professionals for the purposes of this discussion we might predict that in the *networked* form the psychological contract will be predominantly implicit – with substantial elements of the relationship neither written down nor precisely articulated. Close social ties between individuals are likely to have been built up gradually and provide the basis for relatively high levels of interpersonal trust. Heavy emphasis is placed upon relationships which are nurtured over long periods and are flexible; the assumption is that immediate actions may have consequences that emerge much later.

It is within the *networked* form that the traditional contract of employment security in exchange for loyalty and obedience has come under the most sustained attack. Under pressure to reduce costs, demonstrate "value" from acquisitions and focus on core capabilities, many business organizations have acted opportunistically to exploit the discretion granted by these largely implicit contracts to gain short-term competitive advantage. In the process, long-term trust relationships have been undermined.

In effect, organizational change processes in many larger corporations in the 1990s have involved a deliberate attempt to move from a *networked* to *mercenary* social architecture – high in solidaristic pursuit of clearly defined, shared interests ("strategic intent") but rather lower in terms of sociability. In the *mercenary* context we would expect the psychological contract to be more explicit, specific and transaction/project-related. This process of change can be understood by reference to an expectancy theory type analysis of the motivational links between effort, performance and reward. Large scale corporate restructuring – downsizing, delayering and so on – is an attempt to do more with less: to reduce labour costs and maximize work intensity or "effort". At the same time there has been an increasing emphasis upon the monitoring and measurement of "performance". The nature of "rewards" has also shifted: two significant (and often implicit) rewards, job security and promotion, have been reduced and replaced by differing mixes of intrinsic (challenge, growth, autonomy) and extrinsic (money, share options) alternatives. Whatever the mix, the trend is clear – rewards are more clearly contingent upon current, measurable contribution. This is a world where contracts are more closely defined and, apparently, "equal" parties stay together for as long as it serves their respective interests and then renegotiate or break apart when it no longer works.

Gains in terms of clarity and mutual responsibility (rather than dependence) must be set against losses in terms of flexibility, rapid information flows and more open-ended preparedness to help – all of which can characterize the networked culture at its best. It is also clear, as we have suggested already, that the intended transition from *networked* to *mercenary* is not always successfully achieved. Whereas the latter form's explicit contract of "interests" may be entirely consistent with the expectations of certain professional groups – those employed within highly competitive investment banks or consultant surgeons in hospitals, for example – it can appear as a peculiarly soulless place for those more used to high sociability workplaces.

In effect, when employers opportunistically exploit relational contracts they may provoke a similar response from employees. Some individuals, for example, denied the job security and hierarchical progression implicitly promised at the beginning of their careers may develop more calculative orientations to their work, their careers and their employing organizations. Under these circumstances, they may deliver sufficient performance to ensure their jobs – but little more. Little time is wasted on building relationships with colleagues or expending energy promoting the organization. Again, as we have pointed out, the *fragmented* form may be appropriate in work contexts – particularly where there are low levels of interdependence between tasks – but organizations where the culture drifts towards fragmentation may have produced a psychological contract which severely damages their performance.

The psychological contract of the *communal* form is often promoted as the ideal in much of the management literature. In this form there is a powerful alignment of individual and organizational behaviour. Members become completely immersed in their organizations; there are high levels of "identification" (Etzioni, 1961). Here reciprocity is generalized – individuals give with no expectation of return (as in blood-giving) and they do so because it is good for the organization. By contrast, reciprocity is balanced in the networked culture (a return is expected but not immediately), negotiated in the mercenary culture (the exchange is both more immediate and explicit), and negative in the fragmented form (members attempt to get help without giving anything in return). Such relationships may be more sustainable in not for profit or smaller organizations; there are few instances of larger business corporations which have maintained this social architecture over time.

The broader relationships between work, family and private life are also played out in the context of the social architecture of the organization. We would expect the clearest separation between organizational and private life to occur in the mercenary culture. Again, focusing upon managers and professionals, we would anticipate that individuals would devote as much time as it takes to succeed at work, pursuing measured targets in exchange for tangible rewards. The clarity of the psychological contract, it is alleged, allows an equally clear separation between work and private life. Managers in *mercenary* organizations may work hard but when they stop their time is their own; efforts expected at work are perceived as primarily instrumental – allowing material possessions to be consumed in their private or domestic lives. However, this idealized portrayal may conceal as much as it reveals. Even if there is a sharp separation of work and non-work lives, pressured executives are likely to carry with them work obsessions and anxieties into their domestic lives. The large body of research on executive stress is ample testimony to this (Quick et al., 1992). If separation is to be achieved it clearly requires considerable psychological work to insulate one world from another. But such strategies do not always succeed. There are at least two other relationships which might arise. Firstly, the demands of the *mercenary* context may require so much of the executive that their work and domestic lives become severely in conflict, so much so that negative consequences are generated for either or both spheres of life. Secondly, to use Evans and Bartolomé's terms (Evans and Bartolomé, 1980), home may be seen as *compensation* for the rigours of employment. Evenings and weekends become periods of intensive rest and recreation before re-entering the "combat zone".

By contrast, in *networked* cultures the division between organizational and personal life is more blurred. As we have already mentioned *networked* organizations are characterized by high levels of sociability which typically entails an inquisitiveness about colleagues' personal lives. Indeed, in order to operate successfully in such a context it may be "required" that individuals reveal aspects of their private lives to colleagues. Further, organizational rituals, like retirement parties, sales conferences and birthday celebrations, may involve interaction including both "work" and "private" partners. In this context, relationships "spill-over" so that "one affects the other in a positive or negative way". In some contexts partners may add to the resources at an individual's disposal in their organizational lives; they may confirm positive attributes, complement weaknesses or add required social capital (see Bourdieu). Indeed, in highly *networked* contexts access to senior positions may depend upon not just the individual but their partner and wider family. When this happens the organization culture may develop family qualities but at the same time family life is never quite separate from work. On the other hand, partnerships established early in life may prove to be a considerable impediment later on.

In the *communal* quadrant it is possible to see some of the same patterns driven to their extreme. Here the organization is so powerful that it subsumes everything – values, norms, rituals, obsessions. Individuals may derive all of the satisfactions that they need from their employed life – material, emotional and intellectual. Some have argued that in this context work relationships take on many of the characteristics of familial relationships (Kanter, 1990) with all of the dysfunctions this may imply. For example, little account is taken of time spent at work; it is simply assumed that all time at work is well spent. Even in recreation, the best people to be with, it is typically claimed, are work colleagues. This obsessive quality may help to explain why maintaining commercial organizations in the *communal* quadrant is rather difficult. Similarly, such organizations face difficulties when they downsize: since the organization is all embracing, anything which threatens the membership of a colleague undermines the psychological infrastructure of the whole organization.

In the *fragmented* culture the relationship between work and private life may be characterized as entirely independent. Since an individual's value at work is entirely dependent on both outcome measures and the value of individual human capital there is little or no interest in life away from the organization. In the *fragmented* culture individuals typically know little about the domestic or private lives of their colleagues. However, there is a complication. Even though individuals may have little concern for their organizational presence they may have considerable concern for their occupational careers. This, in turn, may require that their partners exhibit the requisite social skills. The established professions of medicine and law are good examples; here occupational mobility may be dependent not just on individual output but also on the occupational networks which are often maintained through social relationships involving family and friends. It is perhaps paradoxical that the organizational culture which offers the most apparent freedom may still implicate family and partners in processes of occupational mobility.

## CONCLUSIONS

In this chapter we have developed a framework for differentiating organizational cultures by their distinctive social architectures. The framework draws upon two dimensions at the heart of much sociological analysis: sociability and solidarity. Despite the rich theoretical traditions which underlie these concepts, their application to the study of organizations generally and organizational culture in particular has been limited. We have attempted to illustrate how these dimensions might provide insight into processes of organizational innovation and change as well as distinctive psychological contracts and related patterns of work/life balance. Our focus has been upon relatively large scale, complex organizations at the macro-level of analysis. But clearly the dimensions are applicable to different units of analysis including, for example, the team, the function and the business unit. Further, following the traditions of classical sociology, these concepts may be fruitfully applied to our understanding of, for example, families, social classes, regions and nation states and the manner in which these intersect with complex organizations (Fukuyama, 1995).

## REFERENCES

Audia, P.G., Locke, E.A. and Smith, K.G. (in press) The paradox of success: an archival and a laboratory study of strategic persistence following a radical environmental change. Academy of Management Journal.

Barlett, C. and Ghoshal, S. (1988) Managing Across Borders: the Transnational Solution. Boston, MA: Harvard Business School Press.

Bate, P. (1994) Strategies for Cultural Change. Oxford: Butterworth Heineman.

Evans, P. (1993) Dosing the glue: applying human resource technology to build the global organisation. Research in Personnel and Human Resource Management, 3: 21–54.

Fukuyama, F. (1995) Trust: the Social Virtues and the Creation of Prosperity. London: Penguin Books.

Ghoshal, S. and Bartlett, C.A. (1997) The Individualized Corporation. New York: Harper Business.

Goffee, R. and Jones, G. (1998) The Character of a Corporation. New York: Harper Business.

Goffee, R. and Scase, R. (1995) Corporate Realities. New York: Routledge.

Hamel, G. and Prahalad, C.K. (1995) Competing for the Future. Boston, MA: Harvard Business School Press.

Kanter, R.M. (1990) When Giants Learn to Dance. London: Unwin.

Kay, J. (1995) Foundations of Corporate Success. Oxford: Blackwell.

Martin, J. (1992) Cultures in Organisations: Three Perspectives. New York: Oxford University Press.

Morris, T. (2000) Promotion policies and knowledge bases in the professional service firm. In M. Peiperl, M.

Arthur, R. Goffee and T. Morris (Eds), Career Frontiers, New Conceptions of Working Lives. New York: Oxford University Press.

Parker, P. and Arthur, M. (2000) Careers, organizing, and community. In M. Peiperl, M. Arthur, R. Goffee and T. Morris (Eds), Career Frontiers, New Conceptions of Working Lives. New York: Oxford University Press.

Peiperl, M., Arthur, M., Goffee, R. and Morris, T. (2000) Career Frontiers, New Conceptions of Working Lives. New York: Oxford University Press.

Peters, T.J. and Waterman, R.H. (1982) In Search of Excellence: Lessons from America's Best Run Companies. New York: Harper and Row.

Robinson, A.G. and Stern, S. (1997) Corporate Creativity. San Francisco, CA: Berrett Koehler.

Schein (1995) Organization, Culture and Leadership. San Francisco, CA: Jossey Bass.

# Chapter 2

# Time Flies Like an Arrow: Tracing Antecedents and Consequences of Temporal Elements of Organizational Culture

**Mary E. Zellmer-Bruhn**
*University of Minnesota, Carlson School of Management,
Minneapolis, MN, USA*

**Cristina B. Gibson**
*Center for Effective Organizations, University of Southern California,
Los Angeles, CA, USA*

*and*

**Ramon J. Aldag**
*University of Wisconsin, School of Business, Madison, WI, USA*

## INTRODUCTION

Time has recently become a more central focus in management research and practice. Time to market has become a critical issue in many industries, with ever shortening new product development times. New terms are being coined in organizational research like industry "clockspeed" (Carrillo, 2000; Fine, 1996; Mendelson and Pillai, 1999), referring to the pace at which innovation occurs, and "high velocity" (Eisenhardt and Bourgeois, 1988), referring to the need to make decisions in less time. In the popular press, references to "Internet time" and "doing business the dot-com way" fill the pages. Time horizons for "dot-coms" and other high-tech organizations are ever more contracted in the face of competitive pressures.

Although little direct attention to time in organizational research occurred until relatively recently, the recognition of the impact of time pressure and speed on organizational life has a long history, as noted by W.R. Greg (1877, p. 263) in "Life at High Pressure":

> Beyond doubt, the most salient characteristic of life in this latter portion of the 19$^{th}$ century is its SPEED – what we call its hurry, the rate at which we move, the high-pressure at which we work – and the question to be considered is, first, whether this rapid rate is in itself a good; and, next, whether it is worth the price we pay for it – a price reckoned up, and not very easy to ascertain.

More specifically, recognizing the importance of time and timing to organizations over a decade ago, researchers began calling for greater attention to temporal variables in organizational research (Ancona and Chong, 1996; Bluedorn and Denhardt, 1988; McGrath and Rotchford, 1983).

Despite the potentially potent impact time can have on organizational behavior, and the increasing awareness of the importance of time in organizational behavior research, surprisingly little direct attention has been paid to temporal elements of organizational culture (notable exceptions include Bluedorn, 2000; Bluedorn et al., 1999; Onken, 1999; Schein, 1992; Schriber and Gutek, 1987). Schein (1992, p. 114) made clear the connection between time and organizational culture when he commented that "there is probably no more important category for cultural analysis than the study of how time is conceived and used in a group or organization". Time has often been an implicit element in models and descriptions of organizational culture, but is rarely the focus of cultural analysis at the organizational level.

In this chapter we examine how organizational cultures reflect different assumptions about time. As Bluedorn (2000) noted, so little has been written about time and organizational culture, and so much has been left unsaid, that it is prohibitive to cover all aspects of this issue in a single chapter. So here we contribute by developing a framework of antecedents to temporal aspects of organizational culture and examine a few key consequences. We address two questions. First, "What temporal assumptions characterize organizational cultures?" And second, "What impact do these assumptions have on work behaviors?" We begin with a brief general review of time in organizational research. Then we review the limited research on time and organizational culture. Based on this review, we propose a refined conceptualization of temporal elements in organizational culture. We then develop a model of potential antecedents to temporal aspects of organizational cultures. Next, we discuss the potential impact of organizational assumptions concerning time. We conclude with suggestions for future research.

# TIME IN ORGANIZATIONAL RESEARCH

Over the past decade and a half, time has become a more prominent feature in organizational behavior research; this fact is reflected in the assertion by Bluedorn and Denhardt (1988, p. 299) that "Issues of time and timing are absolutely central to modern management", and the definitive statement by Schriber and Gutek (1987, p. 642) that "Time is a basic dimension of organizations". Although often not a central theme, time has been examined in prior organizational research. This includes research about norms relating to time (e.g. Roy, 1952), time as a contingency variable in the choice of leadership style (Vroom and Jago, 1978; Vroom and Yetton, 1973), time orientation across units as a key element of differentiation (e.g. Lawrence and Lorsch, 1967), timing of feedback and time aspects of goal setting, including the motivational aspects of deadlines (e.g. Locke and Latham, 1984), time issues in agenda setting (Pfeffer, 1992), and time and choice of conflict handing mode (Farmer and Roth, 1998). A full review of this literature is prohibitive here; however, research in three general areas – decision making, group performance, and new product development – illustrates recent trends and highlights the importance of time in organizational research.

## Temporal Aspects of Decision Making

Time is an important factor in decision making, and we will later suggest that temporal aspects of decision making, which have been explored primarily at the individual and group levels, may have important consequences at the organizational level. For example, there is substantial evidence that time constraints influence decision mode. Janis and Mann (1977), for instance, argued that decision mode depends, among other things, on time available for decision making. In cases with little stress and ample time, decision makers are likely to engage in unconflicted modes, making "easy" decisions to maintain the status quo, resulting in complacency and ineffectiveness. Alternatively, under high levels of stress individuals are likely to engage in defensive avoidance with an emphasis on confirmatory behavior if sufficient time is available, or in hypervigilance (panic) if it is not. Vigilance, resulting in effective search and processing of information, is likely only under moderate stress.

In addition, script-based behavior (behavior that is well-rehearsed and "automatic" rather than consciously considered) may be chosen in the face of time constraints since it is faster than vigilant processing (e.g. Brewer, 1988; Gioia and Poole, 1984; Shiffrin and Schneider, 1977). Related work suggests a bias toward short-term thinking in the face of threat (e.g. Gray, 1999). Further, the literature on temporally-extended choice argues that what is best at a given point in time may conflict with what is best overall, particularly when choices must be enacted over time and outcomes change because they are repeatedly chosen (e.g. Herrnstein, 1990).

Time constraints may influence patterns of information search and use in other ways as well. For example, substantial research suggests that time constraints impact the nature and degree of pre-decisional information search. Time constraints typically cause alternatives to be evaluated on the basis of only a narrow subset of relevant attributes (e.g. Slovic, 1969) and to lead to a focus on negative information to quickly eliminate alternatives. In general, individuals under time constraints use heuristics to reduce cognitive load; those heuristics are generally screening approaches, such as satisficing or elimination by aspects, which eliminate alternatives that do not meet specified hurdles (e.g. Tversky and Kahneman, 1986). Reliance on such screening heuristics, rather than scoring (optimizing) approaches, is generally suboptimal, though consequences may depend on a variety of task and situational factors (Hogarth, 1981).

A final issue relates to the role of individual differences in decision making under time constraints. For example, research has demonstrated that dogmatic individuals are more comfortable than non-dogmatics in making decisions under time constraints, use less information in making a decision, are faster decision makers, and are more reluctant to revise their opinions in the face of disconfirming information (e.g. Long and Ziller, 1965; Taylor and Dunnette, 1974). Similarly, risk seekers make decisions more rapidly than risk averse individuals and use less information in making a decision. Type As feel greater time pressure and engage in polyphasic (multiple phase) behavior, even when such behavior is not required. Type A behavior has also been related to time structure and purpose (Bond and Feather, 1988; Mudrack, 1999). Individuals' circadian rhythms (body clocks) influence when they are at their optimal decision making efficiency; there are many different body clocks, with potentially different time-related implications (Abdulla, 1999; Szuromi, 2000). Cognitively complex individuals, along cognitive dimensions such as dimensional integrative complexity, rule integrative complexity, articulation, and discrimination (e.g. MacNeil, 1974), may be relatively more able to handle complex decision tasks under time constraints.

These individual differences in temporal aspects of decision making are relevant to our discussion in at least two ways. First, they show that temporal elements, and individual differences in interaction with those temporal elements, may influence decision quality. Second, they suggest that some individuals may better fit certain cultures than others based on their own temporal characteristics and those of the organization. In addition, we will later consider some organizational analogues of these individual differences, and associated potential consequences.

## Temporal Effects on Group Performance

In the motivation literature, numerous theories contain a temporal focus. For example, the principle of entrainment (Kelly, 1988; Kelly and McGrath, 1985) suggests that groups become routinized and unable to speed up their progress once they have performed at a slower rate. According to this theory, a given pattern of interaction is entrained to an externally imposed temporal constraint, and that entrained pattern will persist beyond the single task performance, even if the deadline is brought nearer in time. Entrainment predicts that groups become habituated based on an externally imposed deadline. Even if the deadline changes (e.g. time allotted is reduced), their behavior will remain the same.

A second example is Parkinson's Law (Parkinson, 1957), which suggests that work expands to fit the time allotted. When a deadline is extended, rather than finish early, a group will "create" more work for itself in order to appear productive across the entire time available for a given project. A time contraction phenomenon is also evident. That is, it has been argued that work will also contract in the face of time constraints (e.g. McGrath and Kelly, 1986). The overall pattern, then, is one of work quantity "fitting" available time, whether more or less.

Finally, Gersick (1988) describes the role of time as an equilibrium notion, and points to a number of deficiencies in the existing groups literature that emphasizes a standardized process approach to group development (so-called stages of development including forming, storming, norming, etc.). She suggests that for task-performing groups, there is a critical "middle point" of temporal progression (not necessarily the chronological midpoint) that activates a group's progression. At the midpoint of any given time period allotted to a project, groups will leap forward in work progress in order to meet the deadline. In effect, groups will radically change their behavior after the midpoint transition.

Additionally, Gersick (1988) argues that group development is best thought of using a punctuated equilibrium notion that is often used in the physical sciences. A punctuated equilibrium suggests that certain groups will not continue to develop over their history, rather they will reach a particular point and stabilize unless some critical event(s) takes place. For instance, a work team may form and develop norms for behavior but remain at this stage. Only with some dramatic event will the team continue its movement and development.

## New Product Development

In a third domain, organizational research has indicated that introducing a new product or service to the market is a major milestone for most organizations and product innovation is a primary way in which organizations adapt and transform themselves in changing environments (Dougherty, 1992; Eisenhardt and Brown, 1998). The impact of speed in this process is significant. Fast market introductions are important (1) to gain early cash flow for greater financial independence, (2) to gain external visibility and legitimacy as soon as possible, (3) to gain early market share, and (4) to increase the likelihood of survival (Schoonhoven et al., 1990, p. 177). Furthermore, fast adaptation is critical to success in many environments. For example, one study indicated that products that were 6 months late in entering the high-tech market, but were within budget, earned 33% less over a 5 year period than they would have if they were on time (Vessey, 1991). In general, strategic management research has demonstrated that considerable organizational rents can be earned by accelerating adaptation and speeding time to market in the new product development process.

Eisenhardt and colleagues have identified two basic strategies for product innovation, each of which involves very different assumptions about time (Eisenhardt and Tabrizi, 1995). The first is the compression model, which assumes a well-known rational process and relies on compressing the sequential steps of such a process. Acceleration involves planning the steps, simplifying them through supplier involvement, shortening the time that it takes to complete each step in the development process, overlapping the development steps and rewarding designers for speed. The second, referred to as the experiential model, assumes an uncertain process and relies on improvisation, real-time experience and flexibility. In conjunction with this strategy, acceleration involves rapidly building intuition and flexible options to cope with a changing environment, but also involves providing enough structure so that people will create sense making, avoid procrastination, and be confident enough to act quickly in uncertain situations.

Beyond decision making, group performance, and new product development, organizational researchers have only just begun to explore other ways in which time features in organizational life. We move now to a discussion of one key arena, tied to the central theme of this volume – time in organizational culture research.

## ORGANIZATIONAL CULTURE AND TIME

Culture helps us understand the "hidden and complex aspects of organizational life" (Schein, 1992, p. 5). Organizational culture is "a pattern of shared basic assumptions that an [organization] learned as it solved problems of external adaptation and internal integration", and covers emotional, behavioral and cognitive elements (Schein, 1992, p. 12). Shared assumptions in organizations arise from many sources including the context in which the organization exists (e.g. nation and industry), and the organization's founder(s). Cultural assumptions also develop over time as organizational members share common experiences and work together to solve organizational problems. Given this definition, organizational cultures are driven by elements both external and internal to the organization. An important added distinction made by Schein (1992) is that organizational culture consists of multiple, interrelated layers, including artifacts, norms, and underlying assumptions. While organizational culture has received a great deal of research attention, the concepts of time and temporal elements of organizational culture have largely been ignored. In the remainder of this section we review a handful of studies that have addressed time in organizational culture.

Schein (1992) suggested that time is included in a set of a fundamental assumptions on which organizational cultures are built. He argued that at least five aspects of time

**Table 2.1**    Dimensions of time identified in organizational culture research

| Schein (1992) | |
| --- | --- |
| Past, present, near- or far-future orientation | Basic orientation toward the past, present, or future. Past orientation focuses on how things used to be; present orientation focuses on getting the immediate task done; near-future focuses on quarterly results; distant future focuses on long-term investments like R&D and building market share. |
| Monochronicity or polychronicity | Monochronic focuses on doing one thing at a time and dividing time into manageable "chunks"; time is viewed as a valuable commodity that can be spent or wasted. Polychronic focuses on doing several things simultaneously; time is viewed in phases and cycles. |

**Table 2.1** (*continued*)

| | |
|---|---|
| Planning or development time | Planning time involves viewing time as linear, and uses targets like deadlines that are tied to external opportunities. Development time sees the "appropriate" time for the project to emerge as driving planning and development. |
| Discretionary time horizons | The size of relative units in relation to tasks and timetables for various organizational events. |
| Symmetry of temporal activities and pacing | Events sequentially paced to create symmetry and ease coordination. |

**Schriber and Gutek (1987)**

| | |
|---|---|
| Speed versus quality | Norms about importance of speed versus quality. |
| Schedules and deadlines | Importance of meeting deadlines and staying on schedule. Being on time. |
| Allocation | Adequacy of time allocation for tasks. |
| Future orientation | Emphasis on planning and future perspective. |
| Punctuality | Norms about punctuality; perceived effects of arriving late for work from break. |
| Time boundaries between work and non-work | Strength of boundaries between work and non-work. Norms about staying late, taking work home. |
| Awareness of time use | How much people think about and plan their use of time. |
| Work pace | Norms about speed and pace of work. |
| Autonomy of time use | Control over time use. |
| Synchronization | Importance of coordinating time with others. |
| Intraorganizational time boundaries | Whether different time boundaries exist within the organization. |
| Time buffers | Existence of breaks and other buffers in the work day. |
| Sequencing | Temporal dependence of tasks within jobs. |

**Bluedorn (2000)**

| | |
|---|---|
| Polychronicity | Preference to engage in two or more tasks simultaneously, and a belief that this is the correct way to do things. |
| Temporal focus | Degree of emphasis on past, present or future. |
| Temporal depth | How far into the future or past one considers when thinking about events. |

varied across organizational cultures: (1) future, past and present time orientation (Kluckhohn and Strodtbeck, 1961), (2) monochronic and polychronic time perspectives (Hall, 1959, 1976, 1983), (3) planning versus development time (Dubinskas, 1988), (4) time horizons, and (5) pacing. These dimensions are summarized in Table 2.1. We discuss several of these below in the section on antecedents of temporal aspects of organizational culture.

Building upon this work, Bluedorn and colleagues (Bluedorn, in 2000; Bluedorn and Denhardt, 1988; Bluedorn et al., 1999) have also addressed temporal aspects of organizational culture. Focusing specifically on polychronicity, defined as "the extent to which (1) people prefer to engage in two or more tasks or events simultaneously and (2) believe their preference is the correct way to do things" (Bluedorn, 2000, pp. 119–120), Bluedorn et al. (1999) developed and tested a measure of polychronic values and have used this instrument to measure cultural beliefs about polychronicity in organizations. Subsequently moving beyond a singular emphasis on polychronicity, Bluedorn (2000) developed a conceptual approach to time and organizational culture that focused on temporal focus and temporal depth, in addition to polychronicity (see Table 2.1). Temporal focus concerns the direction of temporal emphasis: past, present or future. Temporal depth is similar to time horizon and concerns the "temporal distances into the past or future typically considered when contemplating events that have happened, may have happened or that may happen" (p. 124).

Bluedorn argued that temporal aspects of culture occur at the sociotemporal level, which involves the creation and maintenance of value systems to guide conduct. More specifically, he suggested that the three dimensions may impact efforts to align elements within organizations (e.g. workgroups with wide differences in polychronicity will have difficulty entraining to each other), change attempts, and integration efforts. For example, polychronic organizations may change more readily, and temporal focus and depth may become entrained over time, making it difficult to change these dimensions.

In a third key piece of research Schriber and Gutek (1987, p. 642) conceptualized the role of time in organizational culture as normative, arguing that "norms about time can be viewed as characteristics of culture", and that these norms have "temporal components that help integrate complex work processes and thereby facilitate the flow of work". They developed an instrument to measure several dimensions of time in organizations, including schedules and deadlines, punctuality, future orientation, time boundaries between work and non-work, speed, work pace, and allocation of time. They validated the survey on a sample of 529 respondents from 51 work groups in 23 organizations. Thirteen usable scales (listed in Table 2.1) were extracted.

Based on their results, Schriber and Gutek (1987) offer several interesting avenues for future research, including the comparison of organizations or subunits, the degree of heterogeneity or homogeneity of temporal aspects of organizational culture within organizations, and the impact on employee behaviors and outcomes such as satisfaction or commitment. Unfortunately, to the best of our knowledge, this instrument has not been used in substantive tests, nor did Schriber and Gutek explicitly discuss sources of variation in these dimensions. In addition, reviewing the scales that were extracted in Schriber and Gutek's research, we would argue that they concentrated primarily on cultural manifestations, without addressing the underlying assumptions about time. It is our view that these underlying assumptions are perhaps the most critical, and therefore need to be better understood, as we elaborate upon below.

Onken (1999) provided a rare empirical analysis of the impact of temporal aspects of organizational culture on organizational outcomes. Testing the effects of polychronicity and speed values on organizational performance in the telecommunications and publishing industries, she found marginal support for a positive relationship between polychronicity and organizational performance, and between speed values and organizational performance. She also predicted that the relationship between polychronicity and performance and between speed values and performance would be stronger in hypercompetitive industries. Hypercompetitiveness did moderate the relationship, but opposite the predicted direction. For example, in a hypercompetitive industry (telecommunications) the relationship between polychronicity and performance was negative. While an important step in understanding the impact of temporal aspects of organizational culture, this study is limited by a small sample, and the main effects were tested with simple correlations. It does, however, suggest that further research involving temporal variables and organizational culture is worth pursuing.

Taken together, the existing research on time in organizational cultures suggests that this is an important area deserving of substantial additional research. Existing studies have primarily emphasized the ways in which organizational cultures differ with respect to temporal elements. They have concentrated on identifying multiple dimensions of time and illustrating the differences across these dimensions. These studies have also in some instances (e.g. Bluedorn, 2000; Onken, 1999) suggested ways in which temporal dimensions of organizational culture will influence organizational actions and outcomes.

Thus, the existing research has provided an excellent foundation from which to build a more comprehensive model of time in organizational cultures. We see the need for at least two additional developmental paths of research. First, given that organizational culture has been identified as a multi-layered construct (e.g. Schein, 1992), we will address time across multiple layers of organizational culture. Second, we will focus on antecedents and implications of temporal aspects of organizational cultures. These two issues are discussed in the following sections.

# TIME AS A MULTI-LAYERED ELEMENT OF ORGANIZATIONAL CULTURE

Following the conceptualization of organizational culture by Schein (1992), we argue that time is a key factor in all layers of organizational culture, including artifacts, espoused values and norms, and underlying beliefs and assumptions. Previous empirical research has concentrated on artifacts and norms. Conceptual work has typically considered assumptions. In this section we clarify the distinctions among temporal aspects at each layer of organizational culture.

## Temporal Artifacts

Artifacts are cultural elements at the surface of our perceptions, including rituals, stories, symbols and myths (Martin and Siehl, 1983; Schein, 1992; Trice and Beyer, 1984). Specifically, temporal artifacts are visible structures and processes within the organization concerning time. For example, the Schriber and Gutek (1987) dimensions of deadline setting, allocation, and scheduling are examples of temporal artifacts. As described and measured, these dimensions tap organizational practices at the surface that are easy to perceive and that emerge from underlying beliefs about time.

Other visible artifacts of culture include clothing, physical space, and ceremonies. All of these may exist for temporal elements of culture as well as other elements of culture. For example, a recent *Fortune* article about the best companies to work for identified amenities like "nap tents", on-site banks, stores, dry-cleaners and hairdressers (Useem, 2000). It is noted that the "new workplace" is not a place just to work, but a place to live, saving workers time by encompassing basic life services. At one Internet start-up in Southern California, the organization has contracted a caterer to provide breakfast, lunch and dinner on-site. This "benefit" is provided to employees so they will not have to leave work for meals. Other examples of temporal artifacts are how people react to a ringing phone during a conversation, how they signal impatience, whether clocks are generally visible in the workplace, and whether an effort is made to synchronize clocks. These artifacts suggest underlying beliefs and assumptions about the boundaries between work and non-work and about the need to work long hours in order to accomplish organizational goals.

## Temporal Norms

Temporal norms are conscious, explicitly articulated guidelines that direct behavior in dealing with key situations. An example of a norm is pace, or the rate at which activities are accomplished. Norms underlie artifacts, serving as the driving force for behaviors or symbols. Illustrating the relationship between norms and artifacts, Schriber and Gutek (1987) suggested that underlying norms about pace are related to artifacts such as schedules and deadlines. Another example of a temporal norm provided by Schriber and Gutek is autonomy over the use of time, or the amount of freedom the jobholder has in setting his or her schedule.

A third example is the normative pressure to remain on-site all day at some organizations. This norm was strongly held at the organization mentioned earlier and was evidenced in the temporal artifact of catered meals (breakfast, lunch and dinner). One employee of this organization expressed that though eating the food is not mandated, it is not completely acceptable to leave to get lunch outside the organization (personal communication January, 2000). Employees feel normative pressure to stay on-site and eat the meals. This example demonstrates time-related norms that have developed in this organization.

A final example of temporal norms comes from Japanese organizations. Recent data indicate that while workers in Japan average 15.5 days of authorized vacation time, they take an average of only 8.2 vacation days (Japan External Trade Organization, 1992). Overwork is a growing concern in Japan, seen most dramatically in fears about growing levels of *karoshi* (death by overwork) (Dwyer, 1999; Smith, 1998). As a reflection of the magnitude of those concerns, the Japanese Labor Ministry has undertaken a formal campaign to encourage workers to take more vacation time, with slogans such as "To take a vacation is proof of your competence" (Sanger, 1991). This provides an interesting contrast to earlier Japanese policy relating to vacations; until 1964, there were prohibitions on overseas pleasure travel by Japanese nationals in order to encourage hard work and saving behavior (Sakai et al., 2000).

## Temporal Assumptions

Temporal aspects are also evident in the deepest layer of culture – assumptions. Assumptions are taken-for-granted beliefs of "correct" ways of coping with the environment, and are similar to what Argyris (1976) has identified as "theories-in-use" that tell group members how to perceive, think about, and feel about things (Argyris and Schon, 1974). Temporal assumptions are more stable than manifestations such as norms and artifacts, and are more pervasive (i.e. have less variation). Drawing upon the work of Fishbein and Ajzen (1975) and Kruglanski (1989), social psychologist Daniel Bar-Tal (1990, p. 14) defines this layer of culture as consisting primarily of beliefs, which are "propositions to which a person attributes at least a minimal degree of confidence". From a cognitive perspective, beliefs can be viewed as cognitions, since they are units that represent one's reality. They are encoded, stored and retrieved in long-term memory. The totality of a person's beliefs constitutes his/her total knowledge (Bar-Tal, 1990).

Polychronicity is an example of an underlying assumption about time. Bluedorn (2000, p. 120) describes polychronicity as a "template for behavior that is held largely out of conscious awareness and often so well institutionalized that it is taken for granted as the only way to do things". This definition coincides well with the description of cultural assumptions by Schein (1992).

As another example, we noted earlier that organizations have different assumptions about the need to work long hours in order to accomplish organizational goals. Perlow (1999) has explored such assumptions in a qualitative study of a software development group, focusing on the ways managers control the hours employees work, and therefore the temporal boundary between employees' work and life outside of work. Perlow noted that to "alter a control system so deeply engrained in the work culture requires challenging widely shared assumptions".

Yet another temporal assumption relates to the social value of time. That is, our conception of the timing of activities is not socially neutral; we have assumptions about the "proper" times for particular activities. For example, Cofer et al. (1999) argue that places where the social worth of citizens are measured, such as school and work, generally start in the morning; this results in many problems for "evening types". Using the "Morningness–Eveningness Questionnaire" they found that "evening types" reported more conflicts with parents over childhood rituals of preparation for the day, were more likely to be disaffected from school, and were more likely to engage in night activities that resulted in norm violations and health risks. Evening types may be somewhat marginalized in some societies, as illustrated in Edward Hopper's painting "Nighthawks" (1942) showing three people sitting late at night at the counter of a city diner (Fogel, 1999). The scene exudes loneliness and alienation as these "night people" are out resisting belonging, engaging in activities when "normal people" were home in bed. Organizations may develop similar assumptions about the "appropriate" part of the day for work, meetings, or store hours.

Recent empirical research demonstrated links between various layers of temporal culture. For example, polychronicity is positively related to the pace of work (Onken, 1999), and negatively related to schedules and deadlines (Bluedorn et al., 1999). While it was not the express purpose of these studies to demonstrate relationships across layers of culture, they do demonstrate a link between underlying assumptions and the norms evidenced within organizations.

By way of summary, although previous research has suggested the existence of temporal aspects of organizational culture, no systematic model has been developed to predict antecedents or outcomes of temporal aspects of organizational culture. In the following sections, we propose several potential antecedents. We then discuss the impact of temporal culture on several important work and organizational outcomes.

# ANTECEDENTS TO TEMPORAL ELEMENTS IN ORGANIZATIONAL CULTURE

Time is a socially constructed phenomenon, and as such will vary across different contexts, including societies and organizations (cf. Berger and Luckman, 1966; Hall, 1983). We begin at the macro level and discuss how the social context in which an organization is embedded may influence the conceptualization of time. We then examine industry and professional level antecedents.

## Societal Antecedents

Organizations are embedded in national and societal cultures that likely influence organizational understanding and use of time. Differences in organizational cultures may stem in part from national differences in *time perspective* – also referred to as time orientation (Hofstede, 1993, 1997; Kluckhohn and Strodtbeck, 1961, p. 13). The key distinction in the literature has been between present or future time perspective (Hall, 1983; Jones, 1988; Levine et al., 1980). Future time perspective (FTP) is an overall attitude toward time that focuses on the future (Nuttin, 1985). FTP involves the belief that a behavior performed in the present increases the probability that a desired future goal will be attained and FTP societies tend to value goals whose attainment can only occur in the future (Jones, 1988, p. 23). FTP has US and Western European roots, particularly in the Puritan/Protestant concept of eschewing hedonism in this life in order to attain future rewards. Most Anglo cultures, including the North American culture, tend to be FTP cultures (Erez and Earley, 1992; Jones, 1988; Levine et al., 1980; Spadone, 1992).

Conversely, present time perspective (PTP) supports the idea that behaviors taken today have no more effect on the probability of attaining a future goal than do future behaviors that could be taken as the goal nears. According to Jones (1988, p. 25) "If putting off today does not materially alter the probability of successful goal attainment, there is little reinforcement for anticipatory goal behavior." Similarly, while FTP-oriented societies tend to value future goals more than other goals, PTP-oriented societies often have a generally-held value that enjoying today is more important than worrying about enjoying tomorrow. As such, these societies tend to focus on the immediate social environment, and emphasize expressive behaviors rather than instrumental ones (Jones, 1988). Examples of PTP cultures include Chinese (Erez and Earley, 1992), African-Americans (Jones, 1988), Brazilians (Levine et al., 1980), Latin Americans (Epstein, 1977), and the Thai (Spadone, 1992).

Bluedorn (2000) argues that it is difficult to operationalize the difference between past, present, or future orientation, and also difficult to determine what is short-term past versus long-term past. Temporal extension encompasses both of these aspects and is generally seen as the primary index of time perspective at the societal level (Hulbert and Lens, 1988; Jones, 1988; Lennings et al., 1998; Nuttin, 1985). According to Nuttin, extension occurs because events (goal objects) have signs (past–future) and are also localized (distant–proximate), thus temporal extension is highly related to goal setting and motivation.

Pre-dating Bluedorn's work on organizational culture, the distinction between monochronic and polychronic societies has been made by cultural anthropologists at a national level (Hall, 1983). Monochronic societies are characterized by a pattern of sequential behavior governed by schedules, against which success and failure are measured, processing of one thing at a time; activities are often sequentially performed (Hall, 1983). Viewing time monochronically means that one sees time as divisible into small, objective units, but that only one thing can be scheduled into each unit. Alternatively, polychronic societies are characterized by a pattern of simultaneity, a moment-in-time that stresses involvement with people and completion of transactions, the simultaneous processing of several things at once, and comfort at doing multiple activities at the same time (Hall, 1983). In polychronic cultures, time is measured more by accomplishing wholes rather than by divisible, "spendable" units. People place more value on doing many things at once and this value leads to polychronic behaviors. Hall (1983) found that the US and Northwestern Europe tend to be more monochronic, whereas Southern Europe and Latin America tend to be more polychronic.

The concept of time famine illustrates another difference across national cultures (Linder, 1969). Nations range on a scale from time surplus (e.g. India) to intermediate (e.g. Sweden) to time famine (US, Japan). In time famine cultures the balance between accomplishment in work and leisure has been destroyed as worker productivity has accelerated, "increasing the yield" on an hour of work.

Temporal elements at a societal level will likely influence the temporal elements of organizational culture. For example, typically inhabitants of the US view time as linear, irreversible, objective, measurable, and homogeneous (McGrath and Rotchford, 1983; Schriber and Gutek, 1987). Schein (1992) has suggested that US firms will tend to have organizational cultures assuming a present or future orientation because these are the prevailing assumptions in the US culture. Similarly, US managers tend to have a monochronic approach to work because the US tends to be a monochronic society; however, even within relatively monochronic societies, polychronic organizations exist (Schein, 1992).

In accordance with the above, we argue that time orientation at a societal level will primarily influence norms and assumptions about time in organizational cultures. However, a national sense of "time famine" might also be evidenced in organizational artifacts. Levine and Norenzayan (1999) review literature on the pace of life and present a study comparing the pace of life in large cities from 31 countries around the world in terms of three indicators: average walking speed in downtown locations, the speed at which postal clerks completed a simple request, and the accuracy of public clocks. Their research also considers potential predictors of pace (economic vitality, climate, cultural values, and population size) as well as physical and psychological well-being indices (coronary heart disease, smoking rates, and subjective well-being). Time pace was found to be highest in Japan and Western Europe. As noted by Levine and Norenzayan, "The very slowest were in three countries popularly associated with a relaxed pace of life: Brazil, where the stereotype of *amanha* [literally, "tomorrow"] holds that, whenever it is conceivably possible, people will put off the business of today until tomorrow; Indonesia, where the hour on the clock is often addressed as *jam kerat* ["rubber time"]; and Mexico, the slowest of all, the archetypical land of *mañana* [literally, "tomorrow"]." These artifacts are likely to appear in organizations embedded in these societies.

## Industry Antecedents

In addition to societal context, industry differences are likely to affect organizational culture in general (Gordon, 1991), and assumptions about time in particular. Organizational cultures vary across industries, though within-industry exceptions are also evidenced (Chatman and Jehn, 1994). Recent research has suggested at least three time-related constructs that vary across industries: clockspeed, velocity, and hypercompetitiveness. We briefly review each and suggest ways in which these industry characteristics may influence temporal elements of organizational culture.

Industries vary in the rate of new product development and "clockspeed" captures these differences. In some industries such as pharmaceuticals and biotech, time spans are typically longer, while in other industries, such as computer software, microprocessors, fashion, and Internet-based industries, time spans are typically shorter. Contexts with high rates of new product introductions and short intervals between new product generations have high clockspeed (Carrillo, 2000; Fine, 1996; Mendelson and Pillai, 1999).

Clockspeed may influence organizational assumptions about time. Schein (1992) notes that assumptions develop over time as organizational members have success and begin to internalize cognitions about the reasons for success. In industries characterized by higher clockspeed it is likely that organizations will place more emphasis on pace and coordination over time, because these actions are likely to have led to success. The computer industry is a common example of an industry with high clockspeed. Taken as a whole, the duration of product life cycles has been decreasing at an average rate of 9.4% per year between 1988 and 1995 in the computer industry (Mendelson and Pillai, 1999). In other industries, where clockspeed is lower, basic assumptions about time, such as the importance of speed, are quite different.

Velocity is another industry level characteristic that may influence organizational assumptions about time (Eisenhardt, 1989; Eisenhardt and Bourgeois, 1988). High velocity environments are characterized by discontinuous and rapid change in demand, competitors, technology or regulation. Information is often inaccurate, unavailable, or obsolete (Eisenhardt and Bourgeois, 1988). The microcomputer and airline industries are high velocity. Cyclical industries, where the cycles are regular and predictable (e.g. machine tools), are typically not considered high velocity according to Eisenhardt and colleagues. Velocity is similar to the Lawrence and Lorsch (1967) concept of different time horizons across industries.

Cyclicity may result in "event"-based conceptualization of time (Bluedorn and Denhardt, 1988; Clark, 1978, 1985; Eisenhardt, 1989). Organizations that are event-based act in response to actions of competitors and deviate from plans when important "events" occur (e.g. when something new comes out of the R&D lab) (Eisenhardt, 1989). Event-based time tends to be heterogeneous within organizations and requires more differentiated understanding and use of time. Eisenhardt argued that in high velocity environments, organizations are better off using what she calls "time pacing" or using calendar time and deadlines to move forward.

A third industry characteristic likely to influence organizational assumptions about time is "hypercompetitiveness" (D'Aveni, 1994). Hypercompetitive industries are characterized by "...intense and rapid competitive moves, in which competitors must move quickly to build advantages and erode the advantages of their rivals. This speeds up the dynamic strategic interactions among competitors." (D'Aveni, 1994, p. 218). Sources of competitive advantage in hypercompetitive industries include timing and know-how, with explicit focus on a need to move more rapidly than competitors.

High clockspeed, high velocity, hypercompetitive industries foster pressure for speed. As a result, it is likely that organizations in these industries are likely to develop temporal assumptions about the importance of speed. These assumptions in turn will lead to norms and behavioral practices supporting speed, and finally artifacts representing the value placed on speed. In addition to influencing basic assumptions about the importance of speed, industry clockspeed may also influence organizational assumptions about time orientation. Industries with longer histories have more tradition and collective memory to draw on, suggesting that they may be more likely to engage in past orientation. Furthermore, the longer into the past managers consider, the more likely they will be to take a long-term view of the future (El Sawy, 1983). These findings suggest that in newer, higher clockspeed industries such as Internet and high-tech, orientation may be future focused, but shorter term (less deep) than in other industries.

For example, consider two organizations; one is in a high-tech industry such as computer software while the other is in a low-tech, more stable industry such as furniture manufacturing. New product development timelines and product life cycles are much shorter in the computer industry. These firms are likely to have widely varying beliefs and assumptions about the "appropriate" timeline for basic organizational activities. Internet start-ups also pose another interesting question about timelines. On one hand these firms are notorious for speed and short timelines, however, they also appear to have much longer timelines in terms of acceptable time-to-profit.

## Professional and Functional Antecedents

Previous research suggests that professions, occupations, and functions have distinct elements of culture. Trice and Beyer (1991), for example, argued that occupations and professions are an important "extraorganizational" source of cultural beliefs, assumptions, and artifacts. Essentially, occupations form subcultures, with clusters of understanding, and behaviors that characterize them as distinctive groups within an organization (Trice, 1993). A basic ingredient for the development of a subculture is differential interaction, either on or off the job or both. Subcultures form because their members interact more frequently with one another than with other people. If persons in an interaction cluster share similar problems and uncertainties, an identity as a distinct group with a shared milieu forms (Trice, 1993). Doctors, lawyers, accountants and PhDs are examples of professions with intensive, lengthy socialization processes and strong subcultures.

Employees are often as committed to their occupational cultures as they are to their organizations (Hebden, 1975; Ritzer and Trice, 1969). These subgroups can have a life of their own outside of the organizational setting (Child and Fulk, 1982, p. 156) and can occasionally clash with the organizational culture as a whole. In the 1960s, scholars studying scientists in industry and research laboratories documented the conflicts that arose between the demands of employers and the expectations and values instilled during scientific training (Kornhauser, 1962; Marcson, 1960). Other examples include lawyers in corporations (Smigel, 1964) and physicians and nurses in hospital settings (Strauss, 1972). These same phenomena persist today. Freidson (1977, p. 24) has summarized the ability of occupations such as accounting, engineering and architecture to impact the organizations in which members of these occupations work:

> The effectively organized professional occupation controls even the determination and demarcation of tasks embodied in jobs supported by employees ... the organized progressions are often responsible for writing job descriptions for their members and determining the employer's training and education requirements, as well as the kind of special skill imputed to the qualified worker.

Organizations dominated by particular professions or occupations may come to reflect these subcultures, and therefore the time horizons of the occupational subcultures. For example, Merck is a very "science-driven" firm with an organizational culture that reflects its research scientists' concern with being on the cutting edge, the first to introduce new and innovative pharmaceutical products to the market. Eastman Kodak, on the other hand, has placed particular emphasis on developing its customer service function, and tends to be a service-based organizational culture with less focus on speed and more focus on high quality interpersonal interactions that often require time to develop.

Schein (1992) argued that the dimensions of organizational culture that are less dependent on societal culture – planning versus development time, time horizons and pacing – will vary based on occupational culture. Planning versus development time concerns the different approaches to projects and processes that are taken from people with different backgrounds. For example, Schein (1992, p. 109) cites a study by

Dubinskas (1988) that demonstrated different planning horizon beliefs between biologists and managers. The biologists operated under what Dubinskas calls "development time", in which they felt that things (projects) would take as long as they took. Alternatively, the managers with a business training background operated under what he called "planning time", in which deadlines and external targets drive projects. Schein suggests that development time is open-ended and future focused, whereas planning time inherently seeks closure.

Occupational cultures are likely to affect planning versus development time and time horizons. Furthermore, functional pressures and environmental demands will also influence temporal assumptions. For example, R&D time horizons are often longer than those for other parts of the organization and department managers' temporal orientations tend to reflect the time span for feedback from the environment (Lawrence and Lorsch, 1967). This span of feedback time was related to functional area, and areas with a faster time span for feedback (e.g. sales) led to shorter time orientation than areas with a slower time span for feedback (e.g. R&D). In addition to time horizons and approach to planning, professional socialization and functional area may influence polychronicity. For example, doctors and dentists commonly practice more polychronic work behaviors when juggling multiple patients in several exam rooms.

Having thus described several potential antecedents to temporal aspects of organizational culture, we now consider the implications.

# IMPLICATIONS OF TEMPORAL ASSUMPTIONS IN ORGANIZATION CULTURES

Time-related aspects of organizational culture may have important implications for managers. In this section we explore three important ways that temporal elements of organizational culture affect organizations. First, we describe an extension to person–organization fit research and develop the concept of "temporal fit". Then we consider the influence of temporal elements of organizational culture on decision making. Finally we describe implications for organization culture change efforts.

## Person–Organization Fit Implications of Time in Organizational Culture

Person–culture fit is congruence between organizational values and individual values. Previous research has noted the importance of person–organization fit in predicting individual outcomes such as commitment, job satisfaction, absenteeism and turnover (Chatman and Barsade, 1995; Meglino et al., 1989; O'Reilly et al., 1991). This research takes a cultural approach to fit and examines the congruence between individuals' work-related values and an organization's values. O'Reilly et al. (1991), for example, demonstrated that fit is positively related to organizational commitment and job satisfaction, and negatively related to intent to leave and actual turnover. Several arguments exist for observed outcomes of person–culture fit including identity (Ashforth and Mael, 1989) and attraction–selection–retention (Schneider, 1987; Schneider et al.,

1995). We suggest that "temporal fit" is an extension of person–culture fit. Congruence between time-related values held by individuals and time-related elements of organizational cultures can have important impact on individual outcomes.

As noted earlier, the emphasis on various temporal factors differs across organizations (Schriber and Gutek, 1987), and as such organizations manage time differently. Individuals also manage time differently. As we reviewed earlier, individual differences in personality will likely affect how they allocate time and perceive pace and temporal uncertainty. Given these individual differences, as well as trends in organizational management of time, examining *temporal fit* may be an important extension of person–organization fit theory. We define temporal fit as the congruence between organizational assumptions and norms about time and individual differences in time-related preferences. Temporal fit may have important implications for performance outcomes. For example, organizations vary in the degree to which they allow autonomy over the use of time and setting schedules (Schriber and Gutek, 1987). Organizations also vary in the degree to which they offer flextime, or the ability to have alternative schedules. Furthermore, organizations vary in the amount of "slack time" available to employees. For example, at companies such as 3M employees can use a certain percentage of time for their own purposes, and this is actively encouraged to support innovation.

Individuals also vary in the degree to which they set deadlines for themselves and attempt to self-schedule and coordinate their activities (Conte et al., 1999). Lack of fit may negatively influence important performance-related behaviors. For example, if an individual has low deadline setting and scheduling propensity (Conte et al., 1999), he or she may struggle in environments lacking clear temporal markers. This may be the case because deadlines act as pacing devices, helping individuals and groups to form task strategies and split work to accomplish a task by the deadline. Deadlines and schedules may also act as goals and as such will enhance performance if specific and difficult. In the absence of set schedules or deadlines, individuals who are not likely to set deadlines themselves may have performance problems. Similarly, if an individual tends to set his or her own deadlines and schedules, he or she may experience frustration or dissatisfaction if the organization does not allow freedom to control these activities. Lack of temporal fit may thus impact job satisfaction. Fit between individual temporal preferences and organizational temporal norms may affect important personal and performance outcomes. Lack of fit may result in greater stress, and as a result may increase withdrawal behaviors such as absenteeism and turnover.

Polychronicity is another temporal dimension that may influence person–organization fit. Bluedorn (2000) and others view polychronicity as both a cultural characteristic and an individual difference. As such, polychronicity is likely to play a role in person–culture fit. Slocombe and Bluedorn (1999) found that greater congruence between preferred polychronicity and experienced work-unit polychronicity was associated with dimensions of organizational commitment, the individual's perceived performance evaluation by the supervisor and co-workers, and the individual's perceived fairness of the performance evaluation.

In order to increase temporal fit, individuals are likely to change their behavior and subsequently feel the effects of these changes. Godbey (1981) argues that as time famine increases, people develop "time deepening" skills; some people develop higher rates of "doing" than others. Time deepening can take four forms: (1) shortening the time for each activity; (2) replacing more-time-consuming activities with less-time-consuming alternatives; (3) increasing precision with regard to time, such as planning schedules with only 5 min tolerances; and (4) combining activities to do more than one thing at the same time. Godbey et al. (1998) also provide data on rushing perceptions, behaviors, and consequences in various countries. They write, for example, that time pressures in Japan have led to many signs of stress; one study reported that 124 000 of Toyota's 200 000 workers suffered from chronic fatigue (Rifkin, 1995). Similarly, they cite a 1992 survey (Godbey and Graefe, 1993) showing that 38% of Americans (including 64% of working mothers) "always" felt rushed, up from 22% in 1971 and 32% in 1985. A Hilton Hotel study found that more than 75% of the 1000 workers surveyed rated having more time off, and spending more time with family and friends, higher than the ability to make more money (Babbar and Aspelin, 1998; Matthes, 1992).

## Decision Making Implications of Time in Organizational Culture

In addition to temporal fit, some decision making implications of time in organizational culture flow from our earlier discussion. First, and most obvious, is the need to explicitly address temporal issues in considering decision aspects of organizational culture. Organizational pacing, time constraints, attitudes toward deadlines, and other time-related aspects may influence decision processes and outcomes. This suggests that a full picture of decision making in the context of organizational culture cannot be developed without consideration of temporal elements.

Second, time constraints and other temporal elements may place severe demands on decision making. While such demands are not inherently dysfunctional (they may, for instance, work against complacency) they may nevertheless lead to fundamental changes in the degree and nature of search behaviors, choice making processes, and other aspects of problem solving. These include, but are not limited to, pressures toward limited search, narrowed focus, overweighting of confirming information, and reliance on screening approaches or on scoring approaches that require little cognitive processing.

Third, temporal demands may create and amplify fundamental tensions in organizations. For instance, the same characteristics noted above as products of the current temporal environment may interfere with the ability of the organization to adequately respond to complex environmental issues, to anticipate environmental threats, and to learn. As such, temporal forces may lead to short-term-oriented tendencies that conflict with long-term organizational health (i.e. to overly constricted temporal depth).

Finally, our discussion suggests that it might be useful to consider cultural contingency aspects of decision making. What works when? The fit of decision styles (varying in time requirements) with organizational culture may be an important contingency variable. For example, Type As, risk takers, and dogmatics may have differential advantages and do relatively better in fast-paced cultures than in more leisurely cultures. Type As would seem to ideally fit the decision demands and other attributes of polychronic cultures. We will further explore some of these issues later in the chapter.

## Innovation Implications of Time in Organizational Culture

Differences in organizational cultures with regard to assumptions about time are also likely to impact the ease with which organizations are able to innovate and manage knowledge. Organization researchers have tended to divide the domain of knowledge management into two interrelated elements – (1) knowledge creation and (2) knowledge transfer (Appleyard, 1996; Nonaka, 1994; Szulanski, 1996; Waller et al., 2000). *Knowledge creation* refers generally to the discovery of new knowledge or the combination of old knowledge in new ways. Although the process of knowledge management is referred to at individual, group, organizational, and inter-organizational levels, it is generally acknowledged that ideas themselves are created by individuals, and often by individuals working within teams. Teams that create knowledge can also be described as "communities of interaction" that involve "interaction between individuals [that] typically plays a critical role" in developing new ideas (Nonaka, 1994, p. 15). In contrast to knowledge creation, *knowledge transfer* refers to the cooperative movement of knowledge, often between teams or other organizational units, with the aim of applying it to some strategic problem or question.

In general, time is a central element in knowledge management. Waller et al. (2000), for example, argue that when members in a team have different time perspectives (i.e. within-team heterogeneity), these differences will impact the capacity of the team to create knowledge in a timely fashion. They then propose factors that moderate this relationship, including knowledge characteristics, process characteristics, and location of members. In the second half of the framework, they examine time perspectives and the time necessary to transfer knowledge *between* teams, arguing that when two teams have different time perspectives (i.e. between-team heterogeneity), these differences will impact the time necessary to transfer knowledge between the teams. They then propose factors such as goal congruence, transfer timing, and transfer expectations that moderate this relationship.

Based on this framework, one might expect important implications for cross-organizational teams involving team members that represent organizations with very different assumptions about time that stem from the organizational culture. These heterogeneous teams may be more or less able to both create and transfer knowledge. It may be necessary for them to manage the types of moderators proposed by Waller et al. (2000), or they may need to explicitly select strategies that are consistent with the dominant cultural assumptions. At a much more radical level, they may have to undergo systematic cultural change in order to speed up the process of creation and transfer.

The work of Eisenhardt and Tabrizi (1995) relates to this issue. Examining 36 large computer companies in the US, Europe, and Asia that compete in the personal computer, microcomputer, mainframe and peripherals industry, they demonstrated that in general, the experiential model consisting of improvisation and flexible tactics, rather than sequential and rationalistic compression, led to faster product development.

However, it is important to note that this strategy was best supported by specific configurations of certain elements of organizational cultures, including frequent milestones, powerful leaders, and multifunctional teams. Thus, certain organizational cultures may encourage or impede the development of the compression versus experiential models for new product development.

This phenomenon is perhaps most evident when cross-organizational collaboration occurs during the new product development process. The second author, for example, studied one new product development effort that occurred across four organizations, each of which had very different underlying assumptions regarding time. Members of the organizations involved in the effort reported that the organizations varied dramatically in the degree to which they were able to adopt a concurrent approach involving integrated product development, as compared to a sequential and functional approach. Two of the organizations were already organized in an integrated product development manner – a project manager is in charge and there was easy familiarity with the concurrent approach. This reduces specialization and is faster, but switches relative power from the functional areas to the program or project structure. In contrast, the other two organizations were viewed as much more hierarchical and sequential, following a functional process. This was true even though the explicit objectives of the project were to utilize and develop the concurrent approach. This basic difference in assumptions across the organizations created conflicts between the functional leads and their counterparts in the partner organizations who answered to the project leads. As a result the overall success of the project was questionable.

## Culture Change Implications of Time in Organizational Culture

A related domain that may be impacted by temporal assumptions in organizations is the process of cultural change that occurs when firms are merged or acquired. A recent comprehensive overview of synergy realization in 62 case studies of mergers and acquisitions found that benefits from purchasing, production, marketing, administration, new market access, cross-selling, transfer of current know-how, or creation of new know-how were primarily facilitated by cultural change, as opposed to due diligence, financial incentives, or knowledge transfer (Larsson and Finkelstein, 1999). In fact, most firms reported realizing only about 30% of the potential synergies. A measure of organizational integration was the strongest predictor of synergy realization. Interestingly, there was often less resistance to mergers reported for integration across countries than for integration within countries.

We would argue that a key issue in merging two organizational cultures is the degree to which temporal assumptions are integrated. An excellent example of how temporal assumptions in particular impact synergy realization in a merger has occurred at the newly created Daimler-Chrysler. Coinciding with the merger of German auto manufacturer Daimler-Mercedes-Benz with the US auto manufacturer Chrysler, the company created "post-merger integration teams" consisting of personnel from each company in each country. These teams were charged with the process of integrating the two companies, including creating a unified organizational culture that reflected both the national cultures involved in the merger. Studying one such team, the second author found numerous examples of conflicts that occurred due to different norms regarding time. For example, expectations regarding timeliness in the use of e-mail differed dramatically. The US members of the newly created organization expected an e-mail response from their German counterparts within 24 hours of sending an e-mail message. Focusing on a methodical examination of issues and questions posed in the e-mail, the Germans often waited several days or a week in order to reply. This infuriated the US members of the organization. From the German point of view, the US counterparts were being too quick to respond, often providing top of the mind comments without sufficient examination of the issue in its entirety.

These temporal issues in mergers are also evident in a change effort in which the third author is a participant. The focal organization resulted from the merger of three Midwestern utilities. Interviews, focus groups, and surveys pointed to dramatic differences in temporal orientations across the merged organizations. For instance, in sharp contrast to the largest of the organizations (seen by some as the "acquirer"), the smallest placed heavy emphasis on tradition, and seniority was clearly valued and rewarded. Decision making processes tended to be relatively slow, with emphasis on caution and deliberation. Attempts to impose common "corporate" time perspectives – in effect, those of the largest of the merging firms – were seen by some as cultural genocide. On top of all this, the merged entity has some units that are, and for the foreseeable future will continue to be, heavily regulated and others that are preparing for deregulation. The latter – forced to face the future, to emphasize speed, and to accept many painful changes – see the former as "Neanderthals" that are stuck in the past, and express concerns that if appropriate mechanisms are not put in place, the attitudes of the regulated side will "bleed over" to the nimbler units. The result is a matrix of temporal discontinuities.

While these examples illustrate the difficulties of merging cultures that are temporally quite different, it may be that moderate differences with respect to temporal cultures are most difficult to integrate. A recent study by Earley and Mosakowski (2000) examining teams with varying degrees of cultural homogeneity demonstrated that high homogeneity, as well as high heterogeneity, is advantageous during integration. Homogeneous teams had similarities to draw upon in forming relationships and collaborating. Highly heterogeneous teams were sensitive to differences and tended to create a "hybrid culture". Moderately heterogeneous teams were the worst performers and had dysfunctional group processes.

Another example is when firms competing in the computer industry have merged. Often, a large, traditional multinational organization with monolithic and bureaucratic practices acquires a smaller more agile organization in order to compete in a specific niche and gain access to new markets. The newly acquired firm typically has very different assumptions about time, including a "time is money" and "speed is success" focus, whereas the acquiring firm is slower to react and less able to respond to changing market conditions. This is, of course, the very reason for the merger, but can cause extreme strain as the two firms must restructure, make decisions, and develop and reward employees. Recent examples of this phenomenon include the merger of Time-Warner and America Online, which brought together a traditional media giant with a new Internet start-up, as well as the acquisition by Texas Instruments of numerous smaller "dot-com" companies to expand their electronic commerce.

To bridge these differences, it might be helpful to establish liaison roles across the teams (Mohrman et al., 1995). These roles might be filled by individuals with time horizons that are intermediate between those of other participants (Lawrence and Lorsch, 1967). Similarly, it could be advantageous to select members with the ability to cut across functional boundaries and relate to others from different areas, referred to as "laterality" by Mankin et al. (1996, p. 98). People with this capability (1) can act as a bridge and interpreter between different areas, (2) can rapidly learn the basic language and conceptual framework of their collaborators from other areas, (3) are confident, but not egotistical, about what they know, and (4) are not defensive about their lack of knowledge in other areas and are willing to learn.

# FUTURE DIRECTIONS

In this chapter, we have described the importance of considering temporal elements of organizational culture. Following the work by Schein (1992), we described temporal elements of culture for three different layers: artifacts, norms, and assumptions. We then described three major sources of temporal elements of organizational culture: societal context, industry context and occupations and functions of organizational members. We elaborated on several ways in which temporal elements of organizational culture may influence organizational outcomes such as person–organization fit, decision making, innovation, and cultural change. Figure 2.1 summarizes the antecedents and consequences we discussed. In this final section, we explore directions for future research concerning temporal artifacts, norms and assumptions.

## Testing the Temporal Limits of Current Theories

Our approach to temporal elements of organizational culture and the sources of differences suggests that current theories which demonstrate time-related effects ought to consider moderating implications of differences across organizations in temporal beliefs. For example, many of the approaches to group performance discussed earlier assume a future-oriented approach to time perspective. Theories such as Parkinson's Law (Parkinson, 1957), the punctuated equilibrium model of group development (Gersick, 1989), and entrainment (Kelly and McGrath, 1985) all assume a culture characterized by a future time belief – that is, the belief that present time actions increase the probability of goal attainment in the future – even though such beliefs are not pervasive in all organizations (Jones, 1988; Levine, 1988).

What we believe we know about the impact of time and timing in organizations may not apply to all contexts. For example, perhaps entrainment does not hold in all contexts, given that as we have demonstrated, in some environments, the value of externally imposed deadlines is suspect. Likewise, perhaps Parkinson's Law is culturally dependent. In some organizational contexts, members may be relatively unresponsive to prospects in the future. We may find that when deadlines are extended in

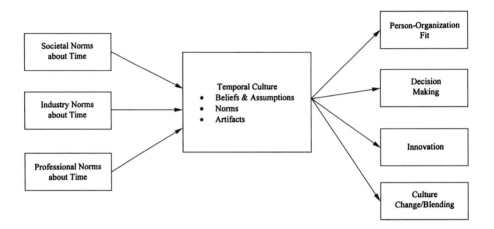

**Figure 2.1**   A summary of antecedents and consequences.

groups characterized by present time perspective, rather than expanding work to fill time allotted, these groups will finish work early. These effects may depend on situational factors, including reward systems. For example, if people are paid by the hour they are more likely to engage in "time-filling" behavior than if they can go home once their quota is met. Similarly, punctuated equilibrium theory of group development may not hold in all organizational contexts; particularly suspect are those in which deadlines are not the focus. Instead, interaction processes and quality of social relations "in-the-moment" are the top priority. In these contexts, regardless of the midpoint transition, we might find that groups are characterized by a relatively steady pace throughout the group's project cycle. These contingencies apply to theories other than group performance (i.e. as our discussion of decision making, innovation, and culture change indicates). Future research should investigate these possibilities.

## Organizational Analogues of Individual Differences

In addition to future research examining the role of cross-organizational differences in temporal artifacts, beliefs and norms, our framework points to additional ways to conceptualize differences in temporal elements of organizational cultures. We suggest that there may be organizational culture analogues of individual differences in temporal aspects of decision making. It might be interesting for future research to explore whether the same differences that matter at the individual level are also important at the organizational level.

Perhaps the most obvious place to begin the search for such analogues is with the Type A–Type B behavior patterns. As noted previously, Type As tend to be polychronic, feel great time pressure, and have other characteristics that appear to neatly parallel temporal elements of culture which we have examined. While some characteristics of

Type As (e.g. impulsiveness and hostility) may appear outside the scope of our discussion, and thus to weaken the parallel, we should note that the Type A behavior pattern is increasingly being viewed as multidimensional. In particular, the hostility dimension of the pattern appears to be relatively distinct, and it is that hostility, rather than polychronic emphasis, that is associated with health problems. As such, we would suggest that closer attention to the literature on Type A versus Type B behavior, focusing specifically on those elements with clear individual–organizational parallels, may prove fruitful.

In addition, consider the fact that dogmatics do relatively well when there are sharp time constraints on decision making. As such, they are likely to do well in cultures facing high speed demands (i.e. clockspeed, velocity, and hypercompetitiveness), and they may be able to make their mark on such cultures (that is, to create "dogmatic cultures" – see Kets de Vries and Insead (1999) for a related discussion). However, since dogmatics tend to discount disconfirming information and to be rigid in their belief structures, such "dogmatic cultures" may hinder organizational learning. Thus, the degree to which a culture is dogmatic may interact with temporal depth to influence organizational outcomes. A short-term focus (i.e. low temporal depth) may, for instance, cause the organization to focus on the benefits to be gained by dogmatism, while higher temporal depth may lead to relatively greater emphasis on the learning-related decrements associated with such a focus.

Finally, the principle of requisite variety states that "the internal regulatory mechanisms of a system must be as diverse as the environment with which it is trying to deal" (Morgan, 1986, p. 47) and that complex situations faced by organization members must be addressed in complex ways (Weick, 1979). Thus, complex environments, rich with temporal variety, will demand "cognitively complex" organizations. As noted earlier, such complexity may be especially critical under conditions of time constraints and stress. What is a cognitively complex culture? It is one with many perspectives, backgrounds, skills, time orientations, and cognitive styles. That is, a complex, temporally diverse environment presents one more case for workforce diversity.

## Measurement and Research Design Issues

As researchers pay more attention to temporal dimensions of organizational cultures, they will face difficult issues surrounding measurement and research design. Measurement of temporal elements of culture presents some intriguing questions. For example, *which* aspects of time – and even which meanings of time – should be considered? There is an old story about three baseball umpires. The first says, "I call 'em as I see 'em." The second says, "I call 'em as they are." The third says, "They ain't nothing till I call 'em." Time and temporal elements, like umpiring, may have perceptual, objective, and socially constructed aspects, each of which may be important. Perception of temporal elements may be most important when the goal is to examine reactions to those elements; for example, our perception of time constraints may be a primary influence on stress. In other cases, objective time, or the accuracy of perception of time, may be more important. In yet other circumstances, social constructions of temporal aspects of culture may be revealing. One thing that is clear is that time and its manifestations are elusive. As just one example, self-reports of time expenditures have "a built-in bias toward over-reporting", with many subjects giving weekly estimates of hours at work that exceed the number of hours in a week (Godbey et al., 1998).

Thus, a key item on the research agenda for temporal researchers is development of valid measures of temporal constructs. As we have discussed, Bluedorn et al. (1999) have developed the Inventory of Polychronic Values (IPV), and Schriber and Gutek (1987) have developed an instrument to measure several dimensions of time in organizations. In addition, the Time Structure Questionnaire (TSQ) (Bond and Feather, 1988) assesses the degree to which individuals perceive their use of time to be structured and purposive. The Inventory of Temporal Experience (Yonge, 1973, 1975) captures such dimensions as Animal Time (negative attitude toward time, with time seen as discontinuous, static, and somewhat overwhelming), Vital Time (measuring the notion of time as connected and unitary, with high scores indicating a liking for planning, working out schemes, and anticipating results), and Physical Time (a neutral attitude toward time).

These measures notwithstanding, time-related measures are often ad hoc, and researchers sometimes do little to demonstrate the construct validity of their measures. It will be important in future research to both show that measures have, for instance, acceptable reliabilities and also that they adequately gauge distinct constructs. For example, we noted earlier that clockspeed, velocity, and hypercompetitiveness each reflect manifestations of speed. Clockspeed relates to product development time, velocity to temporal aspects of environments, and hypercompetitiveness more specifically to temporal elements of competitiveness interaction. Measures that capture the essence of each of these constructs, as well as their degree of domain overlap, could facilitate cumulative understanding of critical temporal issues.

Previous research on culture has suggested several ways in which culture can be identified, and each of those elements may provide temporal clues. Among common visible elements are stories, symbols, rituals, heroes, and rites and ceremonies. In addition, values, sometimes called the "bedrock of culture", may have temporal dimensions. From a measurement perspective, these elements are important in at least two ways. First, they may directly relate to temporal aspects of culture; stories may have temporal elements, symbols may relate to speed, values may address time, and so on. Second, the mere presence of some cultural elements may have temporal implications. For example, rites of passage – whatever their substantive emphasis – may focus attention on the passage of time. Rites of enhancement, such as annual award meetings, may cue attention to particular points in time, as may activities such as annual performance appraisals. As such, it may be useful to gauge both the levels of use of elements and their temporal contents.

Some suggestions for measurement of the temporal dimensions of cultural elements are straightforward. For example, leaders' speeches, annual reports, and company Web pages and newsletters could be coded for attention to time, including references to the past and future, to temporal depth, to resources with temporal elements (such as speed and tradition), and so on. In addition, the physical setting may relate to temporal elements. As noted earlier, for example, are clocks widely evident? Are they placed in positions that permit their unobtrusive observation during meetings and conversations? Have they been synchronized? Further, what mottoes are evident? Does the company's logo relate to speed? What metaphors do employees use when speaking of the company? Do those metaphors have temporal dimensions (e.g. treadmill, sloth, a runaway train, an ostrich, a racetrack)? What cartoons or humorous quotes are taped to walls? Signs such as "You want it *when*?" or Dilbert cartoons showing bosses making unreasonable time demands may be revealing. Further, value scales should include a full complement of temporal values.

A final measurement issue is that of *who* should be asked to provide cultural information. We suggest that researchers should sample as broadly as possible. This might include examination of archival data and surveys, interviews, and focus groups with members of the focal organization. In addition, customers, suppliers, community members, competitors, and others may provide valuable information about temporal elements of culture. Hall noted in his discussion of monochronic and polychronic time that life occurs in a time-frame that we tend to take for granted. Given this, he said, "I came to recognize that pattern through the same method I use in most of my field work: I observed people's responses to cultures other than their own" (cited in Bluedorn, 1998). Thus, those outside the focal organization may provide valuable insights into temporal elements of its culture. Do competitors see the firm as nimble and responsive? Do suppliers feel rushed? Do customers see the firm as temporally responsive? Do industry experts see the firm's actions as short-sighted?

## Conclusion

In this chapter we have attempted to illustrate the importance of considering temporal elements in future organizational culture research. Time is a pervasive element in organizational lives, and as we described, it takes many forms, including artifacts, norms and assumptions. Greater attention has been given to time in organizational research in recent years. This awareness and enthusiasm has begun to spill over into research on organizational culture. The links we made to several research domains suggest that there is much in the way of exciting as well as influential research to be done. It is our hope that our discussion will stimulate future research in these areas.

# REFERENCES

Abdulla, S. (1999) Circadian clocks. Nature, 402: C17.
Ancona, D.G. and Chong, C.L. (1996) Entrainment: pace, cycle, and rhythm in organizational behavior. Research in Organizational Behavior, 18: 251–284.
Appleyard, M. (1996) How does knowledge flow? Interfirm patterns in the semiconductor industry. Strategic Management Journal, 17: 137–154.
Argyris, C. (1976) Theories of action that inhibit individual learning. American Psychologist, 31: 638–651.

Argyris, C. and Schon, D. (1974) Theory in Practice: Increasing Organizational Effectiveness. San Francisco, CA: Jossey-Bass.

Ashforth, B.E. and Mael, E. (1989) Social identity theory and the organization. Academy of Management Review, 14: 20–39.

Babbar, S. and Aspelin, D.J. (1998) The overtime rebellion: symptom of a bigger problem? The Academy of Management Executive, 12(1): 68–76.

Bar-Tal, D. (1990) Group Beliefs. New York: Springer-Verlag.

Berger, P.L. and Luckman, T. (1966) The Social Construction of Reality. New York: Doubleday.

Bluedorn, A.C. (1998) An interview with anthropologist Edward T. Hall. Journal of Management Inquiry, 7: 109–115.

Bluedorn, A.C. (2000) Time and organizational culture. In N. Ashkanasy, C. Wilderom and M. Peterson (Eds), Handbook of Organizational Culture and Climate. Thousand Oaks, CA: Sage.

Bluedorn, A.C. and Denhardt, R.B. (1988) Time and organizations. Journal of Management, 14(2): 299–320.

Bluedorn, A.C., Kalliath, T.J., Strube, M.J. and Martin, G.D. (1999) Polychronicity and the Inventory of Polychronic Values (IPV). Journal of Managerial Psychology, 14: 205–230.

Bond, M.J. and Feather, N.T. (1988) Some correlates of structure and purpose in the use of time. Journal of Personality and Social Psychology, 55: 321–329

Brewer, M. (1988) A dual process model of impression formation. In T.K. Srull and R.S. Wyer (Eds), Advances in Social Cognition, Vol. 1, pp. 1–36. Hillsdale, NJ: Erlbaum.

Carrillo, J.E. (2000) Industry clockspeed and the pace of new product development. Working Paper, John M. Olin School of Business, Washington University.

Chatman, J.A. and Barsade, S.G. (1995) Personality, organizational culture and cooperation: evidence from a business simulation. Administrative Science Quarterly, 40: 423–443.

Chatman, J. and Jehn, K. (1994) Assessing the relationship between industry characteristics and organizational culture: how different can you be? Academy of Management Journal, 37: 522–553.

Child, J.R. and Fulk, J. (1982) Maintenance of occupational control: the case of the professions. Work and Occupations, 9: 155–192.

Clark, P. (1978) Temporal inventories and time structuring in large organizations. In J.T. Fraser, N. Lawrence and D. Park (Eds), The Study of Time, Vol. III, pp. 391–418. New York: Springer-Verlag.

Clark, P. (1985) A review of the theories of time and structure for organizational sociology. Research in the Sociology of Organizations, 4: 35–80.

Cofer, L.F., Grice, J.W., Sethre-Hofstad, L., Radi, C.J., Zimmerman, L.K., Palmer-Seal, D. and Santa-Maria, G. (1999) Developmental perspectives on morning-eveningness and social interactions. Human Development, 42: 169–198.

Conte, J.M., Rizzuto, T.E. and Steiner, D.D. (1999) A construct-oriented analysis of individual-level polychronicity. Journal of Managerial Psychology, 14: 269–287.

D'Aveni, R.A. (1994) Hypercompetition: Managing the Dynamics of Strategic Maneuvering. New York: The Free Press.

Dougherty, D. (1992) Interpretive barriers to successful product innovation in large firms. Organization Science, 3: 179–202.

Dubinskas, F.A. (Ed) (1988) Ethnographies of High Technology Organizations. Philadelphia, PA: Temple University Press.

Dwyer, J. (1999) Hard work never killed anyone? Works Management, 52(9): 52–55.

Earley, P.C. and Mosakowski, E. (2000) Creating hybrid team cultures: an empirical test of transnational team functioning. Academy of Management Journal, 43: 26–49.

Eisenhardt, K.M. (1989) Making fast decisions in high-velocity environments. Academy of Management Journal, 32(3): 543–576.

Eisenhardt, K.M. and Bourgeois, L.J. (1988) Politics of strategic decision making in high-velocity environments. Academy of Management Journal, 32: 543–576.

Eisenhardt, K.M. and Brown, S.L. (1998) Time pacing: competing in markets that won't stand still. Harvard Business Review, March–April: 59–69.

Eisenhardt, K.M. and Tabrizi, B.N. (1995) Accelerating adaptive processes: product innovation in the global computer industry. Administrative Science Quarterly, 40: 84–94.

El Sawy, O. (1983) Temporal perspective and managerial attention: a study of chief executive strategic behavior. Dissertation Abstracts International, 44(05A): 1556–1557 (University Microfilms No. AAI83-20705).

Epstein, J. (1977) Along the Gringo Trail. Berkeley, CA: And/Or Press.

Erez, M. and Earley, P.C. (1992) Culture, Self-Identity, and Work. New York: Oxford University Press.

Farmer, S.M. and Roth, J. (1998) Conflict-handling behavior in work groups: effects of group structure, decision processes, and time. Small Group Research, 29: 669–713.

Fine, C.H. (1996) Industry clockspeed and competency chain design: an introductory essay. Proceedings of the 1996 Manufacturing and Service Operations Management Conference, Dartmouth College, Hanover, NH.

Fishbein, M. (1963) An investigation of the relationship between beliefs about an object and the attitude toward the object. Human Relations, 16: 233–240.

Fishbein, M. and Ajzen, I. (1975) Belief, Attitude, Intention, and Behavior. Reading, MA: Addison-Wesley.

Fogel, A. (1999) Systems, cycles, and developmental pathways. Human Development, 42: 213–216.

Freidson, E. (1977) The future of professionalization. In M. Stacey (Ed), Health and the Division of Labor, pp. 14–38. London: Croom Helm.

Gersick, C.G. (1988) Time and transition in work teams: toward a new model of group development. Academy of Management Journal, 31: 9–41.

Gersick, C.G. (1989) Marking time: predictable transitions in task groups. Academy of Management Journal, 32(2): 274–309.

Gioia, D.A. and Poole, P.P. (1984) Scripts in organizational behavior. Academy of Management Review, 9: 449–459.

Godbey, G. (1981) Leisure in Your Life: an Exploration. Philadelphia, PA: W.B. Saunders.

Godbey, G. and Graefe, A. (1993) Rapid growth in rushin' Americans. American Demographics, 15: 26–28.

Godbey, G., Lifset, R. and Robinson, J. (1998) No time to waste: an exploration of time use, attitudes toward time, and the generation of municipal solid waste. Social Research, 65: 101–140.

Gordon, G.G. (1991) Industry determinants of organizational culture. Academy of Management Review, 16(2): 396–415.

Gray, J.R. (1999) A bias toward short-term thinking in threat-related emotional states. Personality and Social Psychology Bulletin, 25: 65–75.

Greg, W.R. (1877) Literary and Social Judgments. London: Trubner.

Hall, E.T. (1959) The Silent Language. New York: Anchor Books.

Hall, E.T. (1976) Beyond Culture. New York: Anchor Books.

Hall, E.T. (1983) The Dance of Life: the Other Dimension of Time. Garden City, NY: Anchor Press.

Hebden, J.E. (1975) Patterns of work identification. Sociology of Work and Occupations, 2: 107–132.

Herrnstein, R.J. (1990) Behavior, reinforcement, and utility. Psychological Science, 1: 217–224.

Hofstede, G. (1993) Cultural constraints in management theories. Academy of Management Executive, 7(1): 81–94.

Hofstede, G. (1997) Cultures and Organizations: Software of the Mind (revised edition). New York: McGraw-Hill.

Hogarth, R.M. (1981) Beyond discrete biases: functional and dysfunctional aspects of judgmental heuristics. Psychological Bulletin, 90: 197–217.

Hulbert, R.J. and Lens, W. (1988) Time perspective, time attitude and time orientation in alcoholism: a review. International Journal of Addictions, 23: 279–298.

Janis, I.L. and Mann, L. (1977) Decision Making: a Psychological Analysis of Conflict, Choice, and Commitment. New York: The Free Press.

Japan External Trade Organization (1992) Nippon 1992 business facts and figures.

Jones, E.E. and Gerard, H.B. (1967) Foundations of Social Psychology. New York: John Wiley.

Jones, J.M. (1988) Cultural differences in temporal perspectives. In J.E. McGrath (Ed), The Social Psychology of Time: New Perspectives. Beverly Hills, CA: Sage.

Kelly, J.R. (1988) Entrainment in individual and group behavior. In J.E. McGrath (Ed), The Social Psychology of Time: New Perspectives. Beverly Hills, CA: Sage.

Kelly, J.R. and McGrath, J.E. (1985) Effects of time limits and task types on task performance and interaction of four-person groups. Journal of Personality and Social Psychology, 49: 395–407.

Kets de Vries, M.F.R. and Insead, K.B. (1999) Transforming the mind-set of the organization: a clinical perspective. Administration and Society, 30: 640–675.

Kluckhohn, F. and Strodtbeck, F. (1961) Variations in Value Orientations. Westport, CT: Greenwood Press.

Kornhauser, W. (1962) Scientists in Industry: Conflict and Accommodation. Berkeley, CA: University of California Press.

Kruglanski, A.W. (1989) Lay Epistemics and Human Knowledge: Cognitive and Motivational Bases. New York: Plenum.

Larsson, R. and Finkelstein, S. (1999) Integrating strategic, organizational, and human resource perspectives on mergers and acquisitions: a case survey of synergy realization. Organization Science, 10(1): 1–26.

Lawrence, P.R. and Lorsch, J.W. (1967) Organization and Environment. Boston, MA: Harvard Graduate School of Business Administration.

Lennings, C.J., Burns, A.M. and Cooney, G. (1998) Profiles of time perspective and personality: developmental considerations. The Journal of Psychology, 132: 629–641.

Levine, R. (1988) The pace of life across cultures. In J.E. McGrath (Ed), The Social Psychology of Time: New Perspectives, pp. 39–62. Newbury Park, CA: Sage.

Levine, R.V. and Norenzayan, A. (1999) The pace of life in 31 countries. Journal of Cross-Cultural Psychology, 30: 178–205.

Levine, R.V., West, L.J. and Reis, H.T. (1980) Perceptions of time and punctuality in the United States and Brazil. Journal of Personality and Social Psychology, 38(4): 541–550.

Linder, S. (1969) The Harried Leisure Class. New York: Columbia University Press.

Locke, E.A. and Latham, G.P. (1984) Goal Setting for Individuals, Groups, and Organizations. Chicago, IL: Science Research Associates.

Long, B.II. and Ziller, R.C. (1965) Dogmatism and predecisional information search. Journal of Applied Psychology, 49: 376–378.

MacNeil, L.W. (1974) Cognitive complexity: a brief synthesis of theoretical approaches and a concept attainment task analog to cognitive structure. Psychological Reports, 34: 3–11.

Mankin, D., Cohen, S.G. and Bikson, T.K. (1996) Teams and Technology: Fulfilling the Promise of the New Organization. Boston, MA: Harvard Business School Press.

Marcson, S. (1960) The Scientists in American Industry. Princeton, NJ: Industrial Relations Section, Princeton University.

Martin, J. and Siehl, C. (1983) Organizational culture and counterculture: an uneasy symbiosis. Organizational Dynamics, 12(2): 52–65.

Matthes, K.(1992) In pursuit of leisure: employees want more time off. HR Focus, 69: 1–2.

McGrath, J.E. and Kelly, J.R. (1986) Time and Human Interaction: Toward a Social Psychology of Time. New York: Guilford Press.

McGrath, J.E. and Rotchford, N.L. (1983) Time and behavior in organizations. In B. Staw and L. Cummings (Eds), Research in Organizational Behavior, Vol. 5, pp. 57–101. Greenwich, CT: JAI Press.

Meglino, B.M., Ravlin, E.C. and Adkins, C.L. (1989) Work values approach to corporate culture: a field test of the values congruence process and its relationship to individual outcomes. Journal of Applied Psychology, 74: 424–432.

Mendelson, H. and Pillai, R.R. (1999) Industry clockspeed: measurement and operational implications. Manufacturing and Service Operations Management, 1: 1–20.

Mohrman, S.A., Cohen, S.G. and Mohrman, A. (1995) Designing Team-Based Organizations: New Forms for Knowledge Workers. San Francisco, CA: Jossey-Bass.

Morgan, G. (1986) Images of Organization. Beverly Hills, CA: Sage.

Mudrack, P.E. (1999) Time structure and purpose, Type A behavior, and the Protestant work ethic. Journal of Organizational Behavior, 20: 145–158.

Nonaka, I. (1994) A dynamic theory of organizational knowledge creation. Organization Science, 5(1): 14–37.

Nuttin, J. (1985) Future Time Perspective and Motivation. Hillsdale, NJ: Lawrence Erlbaum Associates.

Onken, M. (1999) Temporal elements of organizational culture and impact on firm performance. Journal of Managerial Psychology, 14: 231–243.

O'Reilly, C.A., Chatman, J. and Caldwell, D.F. (1991) People and organizational culture: a profile comparison approach to assessing person-organization fit. Academy of Management Journal, 34(3): 487–516.

Parkinson, C.N. (1957) Parkinson's Law. Cambridge, MA: Riverdale Press.

Perlow, L.A. (1999) The time famine: toward a sociology of work time. Administrative Science Quarterly, 44: 57–81.

Pfeffer, J. (1992) Managing with Power: Politics and Influence in Organizations. Boston, MA: Harvard Business School Press.

Rifkin, J. (1995) The End of Work. New York: Tarcher-Putnam.

Ritzer, G. and Trice, H.M. (1969) An Occupation in Conflict: a Study in Conflict. Ithaca, NY: School of Industrial and Labor Relations, Cornell University.

Roy, D. (1952) Quota restriction and goldbricking in a machine shop. American Journal of Sociology, 57: 430–437.

Sakai, M., Brown, J. and Mak, J. (2000) Population aging and Japanese international travel in the 21$^{st}$ century. Journal of Travel Research, 38: 212–220.

Sanger, D. (1991) …As Japanese work harder to relax. The New York Times: The Week in Review, July 7, p. 2.

Schein, E.H. (1992) Organizational Culture and Leadership, 2nd Edn. San Francisco, CA: Jossey-Bass.

Schneider, B. (1987) The people make the place. Personnel Psychology, 40: 437–453.

Schneider, B., Goldstein, H.W. and Smith, D.B. (1995) The ASA framework: an update. Personnel Psychology, 48: 747–773.

Schoonhoven, C.B., Eisenhardt, K.M. and Lyman, K. (1990) Speeding products to markets: waiting time to first product introduction in new firms. Administrative Science Quarterly, 35: 177–201.

Schriber, J.B. and Gutek, B.A. (1987) Some time dimensions of work: measurement of an underlying aspect of organizational culture. Journal of Applied Psychology, 72(4): 642–650.

Shiffrin, R.M. and Schneider, W. (1977) Controlled and automatic human information processing: II. Perceptual learning, automatic attending, and a general theory. Psychological Review, 84: 127–190.

Slocombe, T.E. and Bluedorn, A.C. (1999) Organizational behavior implications of the congruence between preferred polychronicity and experienced work-unit polychronicity. Journal of Organizational Behavior, 20: 75–99.

Slovic, P. (1969) Analyzing the expert judge: a descriptive study of stockbrokers' decision processes. Journal of Applied Psychology, 53: 255–263.

Smigel, E.O. (1964) The Wall Street Lawyer. New York: Free Press.

Smith, P. (1998) Tougher than the rest. Management, 45(2): 42–47.

Spadone, R.A. (1992) Internal-external locus of control and temporal orientation among Southeast Asians and White Americans. American Journal of Occupational Therapy, 46(8): 713–719.

Strauss, G. (1972) Professionalism and occupational associations. In C. Bryant (Ed), The Social Dimensions of Work, pp. 236–253. Englewood Cliffs, NJ: Prentice-Hall.

Szulanski, G. (1996) Exploring internal stickiness: impediments to the transfer of best practice within the firm. Strategic Management Journal, 17: 27–44.

Szuromi, P. (2000) Picking out the prime suspect. Science, 287: 549–551.

Taylor, R.N. and Dunnette, M.D. (1974) Influence of dogmatism, risk-taking propensity, and intelligence on decision-making strategies for a sample of industrial managers. Journal of Applied Psychology, 59: 420–423.

Trice, H.M. (1993) Occupational Subcultures in the Workplace. Ithaca, NY: ILR Press.

Trice, H. and Beyer, J.M. (1984) Studying organizational cultures through rites and ceremonials. Academy of Management Review, 9: 653–669.

Trice, H. and Beyer, J.M. (1991) The Cultures of Work Organizations. Englewood Cliffs, NJ: Prentice-Hall.

Tversky, A. and Kahneman, D. (1986) Rational choice and the framing of decisions. Journal of Business, 59: 5251–5278.

Useem, J. (2000) Welcome to the new company town. Fortune, January 17: 62–70.

Vessey, J.T. (1991) The new competitors: they think in terms of speed to market. Academy of Management Executive, 5(2): 23–33.

Vroom, V.H. and Jago, A.G. (1978) On the validity of the Vroom-Yetton model. Journal of Applied Psychology, 67: 523–532.

Vroom, V.H. and Yetton, P.W. (1973) Leadership and Decision Making. Pittsburgh, PA: University of Pittsburgh Press.

Waller, M., Gibson, C. and Carpenter, M. (2000) The impact of time perspective diversity on knowledge management in teams. Working paper, University of Illinois.

Weick, K. (1979) The Social Psychology of Organizing. Reading, MA: Addison-Wesley.

Yonge, G.D. (1973) Time experiences as measures of personality. Measurement and Evaluation Guidance, 5: 475–482.

Yonge, G.D. (1975) Time experience, self actualizing values and creativity. Journal of Personality Assessment, 39: 601–606.

# Chapter 3

# Multinational Groups and the Structuration of Organizational Culture: a Sociological Perspective

**Christina L. Butler**
*London Business School, London, UK*

*and*

**P. Christopher Earley**
*Indiana University, IN, USA*

## INTRODUCTION

Managing organizational culture is increasingly important to the success of organizations. At the same time, it has become increasingly difficult to do so. In an environment where forces such as globalization, information technology, intense competition, and mass customization are increasingly salient, successfully managing underlying social architecture is critical.

Increasing complexity and intensity of work have made multiculturally diverse groups of employees of increasing importance to scholars as well as practitioners. The labour force is becoming increasingly diverse. Throughout the developed world, increased labour mobility, encouraged by the development of regional trading blocks (e.g. NAFTA, EU, ASEAN) and passage of equal opportunities legislation in many countries implies that selecting qualified employees for a job requires hiring a diverse workforce on a variety of dimensions including national culture, gender, race and religion. In addition, in the developing world (e.g. China and countries of Central and Eastern Europe), western businesses aim to take advantage of economic and political changes through joint ventures and other forms of co-operation with local organizations. These types of organizational forms result in people from diverse backgrounds working together on a regular, if not always constant, basis. More generally, globalization is bringing into contact people of different backgrounds in a wide range of situations (e.g. expatriate assignments, business travel, video conferences). Importantly, this trend to an increasingly multinational workforce is not expected to abate in the foreseeable future, and can be expected to affect most widely middle/senior management and professional workers.

Concurrent with workforce diversity, a second trend, team-based work, is being implemented within many organizations (Jackson et al., 1991). From the early 1980s onwards, with the success of Japanese manufacturers apparent throughout the developed world, western organizations sought to identify keys to that success and strove to imitate these features in their own organizations. As a consequence, cross-functional team work began to be adopted (Erez and Earley, 1993). Globalization has increased pressure on these teams by requiring them not only to perform at a high level, but to do so "virtually" across several boundaries (e.g. functional, organizational, geographic) simultaneously. Further, with the rapid proliferation of information exchange (e.g. World Wide Web), it is increasingly important, if not inevitable, for employees to co-operate with others in different functions, organizations and regions.

Together the trends we described suggest that an increased understanding of how best to make use of multinational management teams contributes critically to competitive advantage. To take proper advantage of multinational groups requires a good understanding of the impact of such groups on an organization including its culture. Multinational teams, though, only recently have been the subject of intensive empirical study (Canney Davison, 1995; Earley and Mosakowski, 2000; Gibson, 1999; Maznevski and Chudoba, in press; Snow et al., 1996).[1] None of these studies has addressed directly the relationship between groups and the culture of the organization in which those groups operate. It is the aim of this chapter to explore what this relationship looks like by linking groups research with sociological concepts. The overarching link that we propose is a key element of Giddens' structuration theory (Giddens, 1979, 1984), that of "colonization of the future". We begin with an overview of structuration theory including "duality of structure", follow that with a discussion of the consciousness of action incorporating colonization, then consider how colonization links important research findings in the areas of micro-status structures and group performance, providing insights into the challenges of managing organizational culture, and finally make recommendations as to promising lines of research in the area of organizational culture.

---

[1] This contrasts with the growing body of literature on racial, ethnic and gender diversity within national cultures (e.g. Elsass and Graves, 1997; Harrison et al., 1998; Jackson et al., 1995; Lau and Murnighan, 1998).

# STRUCTURATION THEORY AND THE DUALITY OF STRUCTURE

We first outline structuration theory and review key work that has adopted a structuration theory perspective in order to illustrate how structuration theory has been used and to lay the necessary groundwork for further discussion. Structuration theory grew out of a theoretical problem Giddens wrestled with in the 1970s (Giddens, 1981). As a social theorist, he was concerned with how social classes perpetuated themselves across time and space despite shifting individual membership of those social classes across time and the movement of individual members up and down the social ladder. Changes also occur in terms of what is meant by upper, middle or lower class. Notwithstanding both these types of changes, the social classes remain recognizable to members and non-members alike. Until the 1700s, for example, a middle class did not exist in most parts of what is now commonly thought of as the developed or industrialized world (Earle, 1989). Now, however, most people in the West do consider themselves to be middle class. At the same time, the upper and lower classes do still exist, albeit proportionately smaller in size and differently conceived of than three centuries ago. How did a new class emerge while existing ones were maintained?

As the answer to this and other sociological problems, Giddens argued for a duality of structure whereby individual actors both influence and are influenced by social structures. If social classes exist, then they do so because human beings create them; if social classes continue to exist and exert influence, then they do so because human beings act to allow them to continue to exist and exert influence; if they change or indeed cease to exist, then they do so because human beings acted to change them or cause their demise. Within the sociological discipline, this ontological position sets Giddens apart. Sociology focuses on the relationship between the individual and society and the resolution of competing claims. A principal argument has taken place between *social system* sociologists on the one hand and *social action* sociologists on the other. For *social system* sociologists,

> Social actors are pictured as being very much at the receiving end of the social system. In terms of their existence and nature as social beings, their social behavior and relationships, and their very sense of personal identity as human beings, they are determined by it... They are totally manipulable creatures; *tabulae rasae* upon which can be and are imprinted the values and behavioral stimuli necessary for the fulfilment of the functions and, therefore, the maintenance of what is a supra-human, self-generating, and self-maintaining social system, ontologically and methodologically prior to its participants... Social action is thus entirely the product and derivative of social system. (Dawe, 1978, p. 367)

We illustrate this perspective in terms of Giddens' theoretical problem of the perpetuation (i.e. the replication *and* revision) of social classes as follows. An individual from the lower class behaves differently from one from the upper class because he or she is forced to by the pre-existing strictures of the class each belongs to. He or she could simply not do otherwise. This argument, however, fails to account either for the *creation* of social structures in the first place, or for *changes* in classes over time.

*Social action* sociologists propose

> ...the social system as the derivative of social action and interaction, a social world produced by its members, who are thus pictured as active, purposeful, self- and socially-creative beings. The language of social action is thus the language of subjective meaning, in terms of which social actors define their lives, purposes, and situations; of the goals and projects they generate on the basis of their subjective meanings; of the means whereby they attempt to achieve their goals and realize their projects; of the social action upon which they embark in the prosecution of such attempts; of the social relationships into which they enter on the basis of their pursuit of goals and projects; and of social roles, institutions, and the social system conceptualized as the emergent product of their consequent social interaction. (Dawe, 1978, p. 367)

We illustrate this perspective in terms of Giddens' theoretical problem of the perpetuation (i.e. the replication *and* revision) of social classes as follows. Completely unconstrained by social structures, each individual, whether upper, middle, or lower class, acts as he wishes at any given point. This argument fails to account for the *perpetuation* of social structures.

This theoretical social system/social action division of perspectives is a long-standing one and lies at the crux of a sociological debate: the search for a theory of social action. Giddens attempts to address that divide with structuration theory. Most studies adopting a structuration theory perspective have focused exclusively on this duality of structure. Where structuration theory has been equated with the duality of structure, it has been criticized as explaining everything and nothing. The duality of structure is, however, only one important element of the theory. We illustrate here how a focus on duality of structure is incomplete.

Both informal and formal observation show that most of the time people do not change their actions. If only a few individuals in a social system change their actions, then changes overall are likely to be very small or slow. Giddens argued that the reason that change usually happens rarely or only very slowly is that change involves the reduction of personal security, a basic human need. The greater the degree of change, the greater the loss of personal security. Thus, most of the time social structures are replicated, rather than revised, over time. Structuration theory, however, is fundamentally about *order*, not *stability*. There are times when significant individual action, simultaneous action by a larger number of individuals, or cumulative action over time results in social structure revision. Although difficult to define precisely, these critical change events seem most likely to occur when a new or possibly revised social structure from outside a particular social system comes to the attention of the actors within that social system. Under such circumstances these actors are more likely to consider incorporating that social structure into their own social system, than they otherwise would.

A number of organization and management scholars have used structuration theory as the lens through which to explore their change-based research questions. In the main, these questions have revolved around the large scale social phenomena of the type in which Giddens was originally interested. The interested reader is referred to three such examples: (1) the evolution of industries (e.g. Hinings et al., 1991; Ranson et al., 1980); (2) organizational change (e.g. Pettigrew, 1985; Riley, 1983); and (3) the development of the managerial classes (e.g. Sahay and Walsham, 1997; Walgenbach, 1993; Willmott, 1987). As these studies use an organization and/or higher level of analysis, we do not expand further here.

An example of a change more relevant to us is the introduction of new technology as this stream of research often focuses on the group level, sometimes in conjunction with the organization level. Indeed the largest body of empirical research (e.g. Barley, 1986, 1995; DeSanctis and Poole, 1994; Orlikowski, 1992; Poole and DeSanctis, 1992) taking a structuration theory perspective focuses around technological appropriation or change as such changes are comparatively easy to observe and measure. Poole and DeSanctis (1992, p. 30) studied "the degree to which technology can channel structurational processes" in small groups using Group Decision Support Systems (GDSS) for the first time to agree budget allocations. As there were no right answers to the group task, change of consensus was used as a proxy for quality. They found three different patterns of appropriation. "Faithful appropriation", the one with the least process loss (i.e. of "highest" quality), was used by half the groups. In spite of the technology, however, the other half were less efficient in terms of appropriation. These groups acted otherwise than expected by advocates of GDSS. Although this study was focused on technological appropriation, it is rich with theoretical and methodological insights into the application of structuration theory to micro-level processes.

A very relevant area also for which several researchers (Butler, 2001; Maznevski and Chudoba, in press; Weisinger and Salipante, 1999) have adopted a structuration theory perspective to address group level research questions is that of the influence of culture. In their qualitative study of natural multicultural virtual teams, Maznevski and Chudoba (in press) argue that both culture and technology are important social structure characteristics and use the DeSanctis and Poole (1994) Adaptive Structuration Theory to show how effective outcomes in multinational virtual teams are

> ...a function of appropriate interaction incidents and the structuring of those incidents into a temporal rhythm. Within the structure of the technology available, effective interaction incidents match form to function and complexity, which are in turn affected by task and group characteristics. The temporal rhythm is structured by a defining beat of regular, intense face-to-face meetings, followed by less intensive, shorter interaction incidents using various media. [The authors] speculated that the length of time required between the face-to-face meetings depends on the level of interdependence required by the task and the degree of shared view and strength of relationships among members. (p. 42)

Maznevski and Chudoba do not distinguish between degrees or types of "multinational-ness" nor do they directly compare multinational with nationally homogeneous teams. From their study, it is difficult to tease apart culture and technology effects. Further, they studied teams at various stages of their lives whereas the most critical incident from our perspective occurs when the teams are formed, when culture first comes to the attention of the group members and so is at its most salient.

One study (Weisinger and Salipante, 1999) approaches our interests by comparing homogeneous and multicultural subunits in not-for-profit organizations. Both homogeneous and multicultural subunits in their study were comprised of Americans. In the case of the multicultural subunits, membership was differentiated primarily in terms of race. The authors use structuration theory, among other perspectives, to explain how US domestic voluntary organizations can create a pluralistic membership by initiating cross-unit interactions where the focus is on the organization's superordinate identity.

> In the process of interacting repeatedly with each other in a specific context, Giddens claims that people develop "knowledgeability", a practical consciousness that is behavioral and cannot always be discursively stated, or how to "get on" with others in that context. Through processes of individual and collective situated learning (Lave, 1993) a group's members come to produce Giddens' reciprocating action, the taking of action by one person that allows the next person to take a follow-on action. The collective knowledgeability of how to do so produces social integration, in the sense of a group whose members interact effectively.Clearly, these views have implications for integration across diverse groups in society. Through coparticipation, in a setting that encourages situated learning, people can develop practical knowledgeability of skillful, behavioral interaction with differing others... In stark contrast to the contact hypothesis, the emphasis in situated learning, learning that produces social integration, is not on attitudes but on micro-level, repeated, mundane behavior. (Weisinger and Salipante, 1999, pp. 14–15)

Weisinger and Salipante's work demonstrates clearly how actions in a monocultural group are revised successfully and unsuccessfully *once* individuals are placed in multicultural groups, but it does not address *how* the move from mono to multicultural membership takes place. It is to this "oversight" that we will return in the next section. Nonetheless, their work also suggests implications for organizational culture. For example, Goffee and Jones (1998) use two dimensions, solidarity (a measure of shared tasks, interests, goals among members of a community) and sociability (a measure of friendship among members of a community), to categorize organizational culture. Organizations that are, or wish to remain, monocultural have more freedom in the choice of culture practised whereas those that wish to move from a mono to a multicultural membership need to create or maintain a culture high on solidarity.

The research by Butler (2001) compares and contrasts the performance of newly formed multinational and nationally homogeneous groups across time. She focused on *how* multinational and nationally homogeneous groups react differently to critical events that lead to differences in the setting and achieving of goals. Culture is the social structure of interest and a change in the cultural composition of a group is a change in the social structure. To simulate the change in the cultural social structure, her longitudinal quasi-experimental study consisted of a number of executive student groups that were either predominantly British or predominantly multinational in composition. She found that during the initial periods of newly formed multinational groups, individuals are more likely to (1) act "consciously" around critical incidents such as initial group formation and deadlines, and (2) agree on a broader range of action and outcome goals to be replicated across time. One implication of these results is that the two types of teams may be best suited for different types of tasks with varying lifespans. For example, multinational groups may be better suited to longer-term, highly interdependent projects where new learning is required, whereas nationally homogeneous teams may be better suited to shorter-term projects where the task requires less interdependent working and new learning.[2] Implications for organizational culture are that where tasks of the type best suited to multinational teams are either critical to success or dominate the organization, drawing from the Goffee and Jones (1998) framework, a culture high on both solidarity and sociability is required.

In the next section, we argue that what these last three studies show is that duality of structure alone is insufficient to explain change generally, and the impact of cultural composition on organizational culture in particular. This key concept needs to be used in tandem with one that explains *how* new actions are initiated, worked toward, and achieved and *what* those new actions are most likely to be. This involves an understanding of the consciousness of actions, and, as we will show, specifically how such consciousness and change are linked through colonization of the future.

# THE CONSCIOUSNESS OF ACTION AND COLONIZATION OF THE FUTURE

We now discuss the consciousness of actions from a structuration theory perspective, introduce *colonization of the future* and explain how it is an essential and neglected component of structuration theory, after which we propose colonization of the future as an overarching link between group and organizational culture.

In developing structuration theory, Giddens' primary concern was to explain large-scale or macro phenomena (Giddens, 1979, 1981, 1984). He was, nonetheless, fully concerned with micro-processes for, as should be clear by now, both macro- and micro-level activity are integral to the dynamism of the duality of structure. In his work on structuration theory (Giddens, 1979, 1984) as well as in his more recent work on modernity (Giddens, 1991), Giddens wrote in detail about the nature of the self and the role of reflexivity in developing and maintaining the self-identity of actors. This individual-level process is key to the replication and revision of social structures. Giddens characterized the reflexive monitoring of activity, a cognitive process, as:

> ...a chronic feature of everyday action and involves the conduct not just of the individual but also of others. That is to say, actors not only monitor continuously the flow of their activities and expect others to do the same for their own, they also routinely monitor aspects, social and physical, of the contexts in which they move. By the rationalization of action, I mean that actors – also routinely and without fuss – maintain a continuing 'theoretical understanding' of the grounds of their activity (Giddens, 1984, p. 5).

As previously discussed, structuration constitutes a sociological theory of action. In

---

[2] What is longer- and shorter-term has not been definitively determined.

sociology, action is contrasted with behaviour. To use Marx's well-known example, bees and humans both build things; bees build hives and humans build, among other things, buildings. The bee builds hives by instinct. It does not reflect, for example, on what shape of hive is the most attractive, unique, cheapest, or most likely to receive an award, as the human architect does. For sociologists *behaviour* is *instinctual* and *action* is *reflexive* (as discussed in Giddens, 1972). Actors know what they are doing and why, and can usually explain their actions at what Giddens terms the discursive level of consciousness. What knowledgeable actors cannot always do, however, is explain their motives for acting at the discursive level (Giddens, 1984). Motives tend to remain at the unconscious level. In between these two levels lies a third: practical consciousness, a "grey area" of consciousness.

This middle level of consciousness is fundamental to structuration. It is the level of consciousness that links the discursive rationalization of unconscious motives to the replication and revision of social structures. Most cognitive activity leading to routine behaviour is itself routine processing (e.g. Wyer and Srull, 1989), hence the central role of the practical level of consciousness to the replication of structures. When the members of a social system (i.e. group) become aware of a potential change in social structure (e.g. a new technology or cross-cultural contacts), it becomes less likely that cognitive activity will remain routine, and the revision, rather than the replication, of social structures is more likely to occur.[3] The actors introducing change do so more often than not by activating their discursive level of consciousness, and in turn those who experience the change also activate their discursive level of consciousness to make sense of and respond to the change they are experiencing (Barley and Tolbert, 1997).

Further, in his work on modernity, Giddens (1991) makes explicit how reflexivity of action differs in the late modern age from that of traditional societies: individuals now colonize the future to secure a sense of self-identify. Giddens (1991, p. 242) defines colonization of the future as "the creation of territories of future possibilities, reclaimed by counterfactual inference". He expands on this as follows:

> Because of its reflexively mobilised – yet intrinsically erratic – dynamism, modern social activity has an essentially counterfactual character. In a post-traditional social universe, an indefinite range of potential courses of action (with their attendant risks) is at any given moment open to individuals and collectivities. Choosing among such alternatives is always an 'as if' matter, a question of selecting between 'possible worlds'. Living in circumstances of modernity is best understood as a matter of the routine contemplation of counter-factuals, rather than simply implying a switch from an 'orientation to the past', characteristic of traditional societies, towards an 'orientation to the future'. (Giddens, 1991, pp. 28–29)

For example, individuals living in the late modern age (i.e. those alive and living in the industrialized world at the time of writing) now have a choice of what, if any, religion to follow. They are aware of these choices primarily through interaction with people of

---

[3] We must not, however, ever make the mistake of assuming that change will always occur under these circumstances. Active replication may also be the result.

differing faiths and beliefs. Such interaction comes about, because, in contrast to the members of traditional societies, individuals of the late modern age are members of social systems that imperfectly coincide. Membership in social systems that do not strongly coincide means individuals need to make choices about which social practices to adopt. In other words, they need to take risks.

> Individuals seek to colonise the future for themselves as an intrinsic part of their life-planning... [T]he degree to which the future realm can be successfully invaded is partial, and subject to the various vagaries of risk assessment, which may be more or less clearly articulated, well-informed and 'open'; or alternatively may be largely inertial. Thinking in terms of risk becomes more or less inevitable and most people will be conscious also of the risks of refusing to think in this way, even if they may choose to ignore those risks. (Giddens, 1991, pp. 125–126)

In assessing the future risks to self-identity, individuals make decisions about what to do (i.e. set future goals). These future goals link back to each individual's self-identity and the motives (Erez and Earley, 1993) underlying the sense of self. To colonize the future, an individual must visualize himself acting prior to doing so, that is he must see himself acting in the future (i.e. working toward and achieving future goals). In this way, he can do things for the first time, and, equally, do things differently from the way he previously did them. Indeed, he has probably seen others act differently through membership in imperfectly coinciding social systems. Thus, a middle-class actor may work to promote or demote himself by acting in a way that leads others to perceive him or her as upper or lower class. Choice of profession, for example, could lead to a promotion or demotion. The child of middle-class professionals may choose in adulthood to become a manual worker or marry into an upper-class family and, thereby, change his or her position in society (i.e. an individual actor acting to influence existing social structures). At the same time, he may or may not be accepted by the members of the world he wishes to enter (i.e. existing social structures acting on the individual actor). Despite his efforts, society may still view the middle-class person as still middle class despite for example the "new wealth and circumstance". This may be especially true for societies having a more rigid and delineated social structure, and illustrates well the "duality of structure" between individual action and social structures. Equally the middle-class child who remains a middle-class adult chooses to remain so by adopting an occupation and lifestyle commensurate with the middle class. At the time of action, not all risks are known. While not all consequences of an action are intended or foreseen, "in modern social conditions, the more the individual seeks reflexively to forge a self-identity, the more he or she will be aware that current practices shape future outcomes" (Giddens, 1991, p. 129). It is through such reflexive future thought and the setting, working toward, and possible achieving of goals that the social structures are not only maintained, but changes are brought about.

If individuals colonize the future through the setting, working toward, and achieving of goals, then for groups, these individual future goals should also result in the establishment of future goals of some sort. Findings from the groups literature can help us to understand the nature of group goals (Zander, 1977). The two early themes that concerned those interested in group goals were (1) group goals and performance, and (2) personal versus group goals. Conclusions in terms of group goals and performance (see extensive work by Zander (1977)) are similar to those found for individual goals and performance: there is a positive relationship between the existence of goals and performance outcomes. This finding suggests that the establishment of group goals is important to group success. For our purposes, the Zander (1977) synthesis of prior work addressing the issue of personal versus group goals is key. He summarized much of the existing work in three points: "(a) the stronger the group-oriented motives of members, the better the group performs, (b) the desire for group goal attainment often overwhelms the desire for the attainment of personal goals, and (c) the desire for group success increases as a group experiences prior success" (quoted in Guzzo and Shea, 1994, p. 291). Does colonization of the future help us to understand how these findings are likely to manifest themselves in groups, what the likely consequences of those goals are for organizational culture and, conversely, what the likely consequences of organizational culture are for groups and their goals?

The work by Weisinger and Salipante (1999) suggested that newly formed voluntary sector (nationally homogeneous) multicultural groups need the support of an organizational level culture high on solidarity (shared tasks, interests, goals) in order that multicultural groups also begin to develop an organizational culture necessarily high on solidarity where group-oriented motives are strong and the desire for group goal attainment overwhelms that of personal goals. Otherwise, the multicultural groups are likely to fail. The study by Butler (2001) of newly formed multinational and nationally homogeneous groups suggested that multinational groups thrive in a similarly solidaristic organizational level culture, because they initially develop strong group-oriented motives with group goals overwhelming personal goals in order to achieve their wide range of shared goals.[4] However, newly formed nationally homogeneous groups (that are also culturally homogeneous) benefit from a culture that is either high on solidarity or sociability or high on both depending on the nature of the group task and the existing organizational level culture. If there are differences between multinational and nationally homogeneous teams in terms of the setting and achieving of goals, as appears to be the case, then thought and action at the discursive level of consciousness among the members of each type of team is a unifying explanation.

In light of these observations, in the next section we consider the challenges to organizational culture attributable to integrating status structures with group performance through the colonization of the future.

---

[4] As previously discussed, to thrive in the long-term, multinational teams also require a culture high on sociability.

# COLONIZATION OF THE FUTURE: INTEGRATING LINK BETWEEN STATUS STRUCTURES AND GROUP PERFORMANCE

Before reviewing the literature, it is useful to establish what we mean by a real or natural[5] work group or team.[6] The definition by McGrath (1984) of a real group is widely accepted and serves our purposes well. For McGrath, a group is a social aggregate that is distinguished by size, interdependence, and lifespan.[7] More specifically, a group is composed of two or more individuals who are mutually aware and have the potential for mutual interaction. Upper limits on size are thus relatively small, but not specifically stated. Mutual awareness and potential interaction imply at least minimum interdependence whereby members take each other's actions into account. Interdependence in turn implies a lifespan beyond isolated brief encounters. Examples include not only work groups, but families and other social and professional groupings. For the purpose of this chapter, the focus is on work groups. It is with this definition in mind that we now turn to the status literature.

## Status

### American Status Characteristics

With a history of three decades of theoretical and empirical work behind them, the Berger et al. (1974, 1977) theory of status characteristics is now a prominent approach to the study of micro-status structures. Ridgeway and Walker (1995), two scholars in the field, define a status characteristic as:

> An attribute on which individuals vary that is associated in society with widely held beliefs according greater esteem and worthiness to some states of the attribute (e.g. being male or a proprietor) than other states of the attribute (e.g. being female or a laborer). Because it is based in consensual beliefs, the status value of an attribute can change over time and vary among populations... [T]he cultural beliefs that attach status value to a characteristic also associate it with implicit expectations for *competence*. *Worthiness* becomes *presumed competence* (emphasis our own) (p. 292)

Status characteristics can be diffuse or specific. Diffuse characteristics are those which carry general performance expectations that are not limited to the ability to perform one type of task and that are not necessarily rational. Included in this category are such characteristics as gender, race, and age. For example, in many

---

[5] As opposed to groups concocted, for example, for experimental purposes.

[6] In this chapter, the terms group and team are used interchangeably.

[7] Generally other researchers (e.g. Turner et al., 1987) define groups less strictly in terms of one or two of McGrath's three distinguishing dimensions, particularly size.

societies including the US, men are generally believed, rightly or wrongly, to contribute more to, that is, to be more competent on, a whole range of tasks than are women, hence gender is considered a diffuse status characteristic in those societies[8] (Borgatta and Stimson, 1963; Elsass and Graves, 1997; Heiss, 1962; Kenkel, 1957; March, 1953; Ridgeway et al., 1994; Shackelford et al., 1996; Stets, 1997; Walker et al., 1996). Likewise, in the US, whites have traditionally been considered to be more worthy, or competent, than blacks (Elsass and Graves, 1997; Katz and Benjamin, 1960; Katz et al., 1958; Preston and Bayton, 1941). Research on the relationship between whites and other racial/ethnic groups has also shown whites to be perceived as more competent (Kirchmeyer and Cohen, 1992; Ong, 1996; Riches and Foddy, 1989). Specific status characteristics, however, are relevant only to one task, or category of tasks. Computer skills would be an example of a status characteristic of this type as would musical ability, engineering skills, athletic ability, nursing skills, and so on. It is important to emphasize that the assigning of value by individuals in a society to both diffuse and specific characteristics is often not a conscious process with the result that even very consciously ''progressive'' individuals can act otherwise at the micro-behavioural level.

Status characteristics theory's most important postulate is that:

> Once actors have formed expectations for self and other(s), their power and prestige positions relative to the others will be a direct function of their expectation advantage over (or disadvantage compared to) those others. (Berger et al., 1977, p. 130)

The theory makes this prediction within certain scope conditions. It applies only to short-term dyads faced with a task that requires collective effort to reach a goal. Both members of the dyad must also belong to the same society or culture.[9] Only salient characteristics, those with a direct or indirect effect, influence the dyad's interactions. Status characteristics with indirect influence on, that is, not specifically disassociated from, the successful performance of the task must distinguish between the two individuals in order to be salient. The result is that unless both members of the dyad know for certain that an indirect characteristic is not relevant, they will treat that characteristic as if it were. All salient information, whether consistent or inconsistent, is used. The effect of each additional salient characteristic is attenuated. Further, for any individual, a status characteristic with more direct relevance to the task will carry more weight than one that does not. For example, in the case of an American female doctor in a medical setting, her positive characteristic *doctor* will carry greater absolute value than her negative characteristic *female* (West, 1984). This relative ranking of characteristics is consistent with the Hughes (1971) notion of auxiliary status-determining traits as well. Hughes argued that certain characteristics are often associated with others (e.g. in the 1950s American culture, a physi-

---

[8] Recent research (Stewart, 1988) suggests that perception of gender as a diffuse characteristic may be starting to disappear at least among urban university-educated women in Canada.

[9] With a handful of Canadian exceptions (e.g. Stewart, 1988), empirical research has only been conducted in the US.

cian was often associated with the auxiliary characteristic of being male). If these auxiliary status-markers are inconsistent with the primary characteristic, then the primary is somewhat denigrated or discounted.

In general, empirical findings (e.g. Berger and Zelditch, 1985; Webster and Foschi, 1988) support the theoretical predictions outlined here. They also support the work by Bales (1951, 1953) of more than four decades ago. His research showed that experimental groups homogeneous with respect to age, gender, and socio-economic background and with no structure imposed from the outside formed stable participation inequities by the end of the first 1 h session. The status hierarchies that developed reflected the participation inequities of the group members:

- The most talkative member of the group talked considerably more than others.
- Other group members directed their own speech to the most talkative member.
- Other group members rated the most talkative individual as having the best ideas.
- Once these inequities developed, they persisted over remaining group sessions.

Humans seem not only always to rank each other on the basis of physical, social and behavioural characteristics, but carry with them a set of rules for doing so.

Status characteristics play a powerful role in short-lived groups; actors have little else on which to evaluate each other (Earley, 1999). In longer-term groups, one might expect that actors have more opportunity to objectively evaluate each other's skills, and so alter the ranking criteria used over time. A study by Cohen and Zhou (1991) of enduring research and development teams showed that status-organizing processes in these groups nonetheless work much like those in ad hoc groups. Although it is not realistic to generalize from the results of one study, the preliminary conclusion that we draw is that it is difficult for lower status individuals to overcome early impressions. Recent work by Foschi (1996) suggests that it may be difficult for individuals to overturn initial performance expectations, because status characteristics not only influence performance expectations, but also create double standards for the evaluation of that performance.

One of the implications of the theory is that it allows predictions to be made as to which situations will be more egalitarian and which more hierarchical. This is an important prediction, as the more egalitarian the situation, the more the individual talents of the group members should be tapped. Where salient status characteristics are inconsistent or ''cross-cutting'' in the expectations they create (e.g. female doctor and male nurse working together in a medical setting), the group will be more egalitarian. Where salient status characteristics are consistent in this regard, the group will be more hierarchical. Drawing from this, we can infer that the more cross-cutting the heterogeneity in a nationally homogeneous group, the more egalitarian it will be and the better it will achieve goals. What this stream of research suggests is that although these late modern age individuals of which the dyads and groups studied were comprised were colonizing the future, they chose more often than not to replicate rather than revise their actions. Although lower status individuals might have increased the choice of actions available to the group, their ideas either remained unexpressed or were discounted by those of higher status. A look at status across national cultures provides insights into how colonization of the future might operate among the late modern age members of multinational groups.

## *Status Across Cultures*

The cross-cultural literature is rich with explanations as to how one culture differs from other. Often in this literature, culture is crudely equated with national culture or country. Given our interest in multinational groups, we focus on this usage in this section. Depending on the research question, a dimension (e.g. Hall, 1983; Laurent, 1983) or series of inter-related dimensions (e.g. Hofstede, 1980; Trompenaars and Hampden-Turner, 1997) is used to explain cultural differences. The dimension typically used to describe on what basis status is accorded in different cultures is that of ascription versus achievement (McClelland, 1961; Parsons and Shils, 1951; Smith et al., 1996; Stovel et al., 1996; Weber, 1946) which Trompenaars and Hampden-Turner (1997, p. 9) (emphasis in original) describe thus:

> Achievement means that you are judged on what you have recently accomplished and on your record. Ascription means that status is attributed to you, by birth, kinship, gender or age, but also by your connections (who you know) and your educational record (a graduate of Tokyo University or Haute Ecole Polytechnique). In an achievement culture, the first question is likely to be "*What* did you study?", while in a more ascriptive culture the question will more likely be "*Where* did you study?"

The findings by Smith et al. (1996) rank the US very high on achievement. In related research (Trompenaars and Hampden-Turner, 1997), in response to a question about whether respect accorded an individual depends on family background, 87% of American respondents disagreed. In Austria, only 51% responded similarly demonstrating that Austria is a more ascriptive culture than the US. These studies show that it is the English-speaking and Scandinavian countries that rank highest on achievement overall, as Parsons and Shils (1951) and Weber (1946) would have predicted, while the rest of the world is more ascriptive.

Cultures are not simply more or less achievement- or ascription-oriented. Work in the cross-cultural field also demonstrates that not only the actual characteristics on which status is accorded, but also the states of the characteristics themselves vary by culture. For example, while many ascriptive countries value family background as a status characteristic, the Czech Republic, a highly ascriptive nation, is strongly opposed to using such a characteristic as a marker of status (Trompenaars and Hampden-Turner, 1997, p. 106). In the US, youth is accorded status, while in China, elders are. In some countries, having an upper class background (e.g. UK) is revered, whereas in others a middle (e.g. Canada, Sweden) or working (e.g. Cuba, other former Communist states) class background is preferred. Complicating matters, within a culture, status characteristics themselves, as well as which state of a characteristic is positively valued, can change over time (Clarke, 1971; Mateju and Rehakova, 1994; Prandy, 1998; Rallu, 1998; Stovel et al., 1996).

Cross-cultural studies of what makes a good top management team or boss provide valuable insights into how a culture's general set of status characteristics are translated into organizationally useful ones. In cross-cultural organizational culture typologies developed by Hofstede and his associates (Hofstede, 1991; Hofstede et al., 1990) and Trompenaars and Hampden-Turner (1997), the influence of the ascription/achievement dimension is very much in evidence. Drawing on these typologies to characterize top management across cultures, Schneider and Barsoux (1997, p. 83) explain that, in French firms, senior managers provide "a high level of analytical and conceptual ability that need not be industry- or country-specific". In German ones, they have "specific technical competence, but also in-depth company knowledge", while in Chinese ones, they pursue "the Confucian tradition of patriarchal authority". The French preference for general analytical ability is satisfied through the elite system of grandes ecoles at the university level. Entrance to the grandes ecoles is based on achievement excellence in philosophy, mathematics and a range of other subjects in final secondary school exams. It is the graduates of these elite institutions who go on to assume top positions in industry and government. The German system tightly controls the provision of education through a series of achievement hurdles to the end of secondary education. With specific technical knowledge prized, students accepted to the dedicated engineering universities, especially those talented enough to attend the Technical University of Munich, get the top engineering jobs at the start of their careers and ultimately comprise the membership of the powerful company boards. In Chinese-run organizations, ascription is the predominant basis on which status is accorded. Family connections take precedence over academic qualifications with the result that many of the most respected and powerful firms are small in size relative to the top French and German firms as well as family owned and managed. It is the elder family members who make important decisions.

Laurent (1983) argues that managers, like the French, German and Chinese ones portrayed above, conceptualize organizations in one of two basic ways: instrumental, or task-focused, versus social, or relationship-focused. For example, he finds that Italian and French managers consider their roles socially and politically significant. Their energy is focused on the attainment of power rather than on the achievement of goals. British and Danish managers, in contrast, have a low focus on power and a high focus on the achievement of organizational objectives. For *task-focused* individuals, an organization is "...a system of tasks where it is important to know what has to be done, rather than who has power and authority to do so", whereas for *relationship-focused* individuals, an organization is "...a social system, or systems of relationships, where personal networks and social positioning are important. The organization achieves its goals through relationships and how they are managed..." (Schneider and Barsoux, 1997, p. 88). It is striking how two otherwise very similar countries (e.g. as measured by Hofstede's dimensions) can differ when Laurent's definition is considered. We want especially to underline the distinction between this dimension and that of individualism/collectivism (see Earley, 1993). It is tempting to assume that all individualist countries are task-oriented and that all relationship-focused countries are collectivist. Comparing the findings of Hofstede (1980) with those of Trompenaars and Hampden-Turner (1997) shows that this is clearly not the case. We illustrate this point with two examples: Belgium is ranked as moderately individualist and relationship-focused; Venezuela, in contrast, is both highly collectivist and task-focused. Geographical clusters (Ronen and Shenkar, 1985) are also misleading. On the one hand, the US is ranked as one of the most task-oriented nations, together with Norway. On the other hand, Canada and Sweden are two of the more relationship-oriented countries (Trompenaars and Hampden-Turner, 1997). In short, the evidence is clear: different national cultures do accord status differently.

Reports abound on the general challenge of working effectively across cultural boundaries (e.g. Schneider and Barsoux, 1997; Trompenaars and Hampden-Turner, 1997). It is also a specific challenge for the effective working of multinational management teams. Given that, in the achievement-oriented US, status hierarchies develop quickly and remain stable for the lifetime of the dyad or group concerned (Bales, 1951, 1953; Berger and Zelditch, 1985; Berger et al., 1977), it is likely also to be the case in ascriptive-oriented national cultures. Given that status is accorded on such different bases across cultures, can individual members of a multinational group read and accord status in a multinational group in order to develop an effective group culture with strong group goals overwhelming individual ones? And what are the implications for organizational level culture?

As at least some multinational groups do indeed function (Butler, 2000; Canney Davison, 1995; Earley and Mosakowski, 2000; Maznevski and Chudoba, in press), then according status across national cultures must be possible. Finding themselves in a situation where there is no "natural" social hierarchy around which initially to form, individual members of a multinational group, defined as one where none of its members share a nationality, colonize the future through risk assessment of available choices. In such circumstances, heterogeneity is high and so all members of the group are likely to propose ideas regarding how to work together and what their goals should be. A broad range of these ideas is likely to be accepted by the group's members as all are seeking to preserve their positive self-identities through the positive reinforcement of the other group members. A solidaristic culture is likely to develop at the group level that is supported ideally by a solidaristic culture at the organization level. If the organizational level culture is not supportive, then the group will modify their goals and culture, possibly putting their performance at risk. Do the findings from the group performance literature support this argument?

## Group Performance

Although the evidence is mixed (e.g. Abramson, 1992; Adler, 1991; Crossan, 1991; Hackman and Morris, 1975; Levine and Moreland, 1990; Watson et al., 1993), there is a widespread belief that heterogeneous groups, broadly defined, must be "better" than homogeneous ones (e.g. Cox, 1993). A significant problem with making generalizations in this area is the underlying complexity of both "diversity" and "performance". The term diversity has been used to study the effect of a wide range of differences in demographic and other factors. The situation for performance is similar. Work in the area of organizational demography literature, discussed below, illustrates well these issues. Recent research into the study of group mediating processes suggests that it is here that researchers should focus their attention. This issue has been the main focus of recent research in the group diversity literature (again, discussed below). Following our necessarily brief review of the literature, we consider whether colonization of the future explains the relationship between group composition and performance and what the implications are for successfully managing organizational culture.

## Organizational Demography

Organizational demography aims to understand the relationship between characteristics such as age, tenure and education and the achievement of goals such as communication and turnover (e.g. O'Reilly et al., 1989; Zenger and Lawrence, 1989). Demographic researchers originally conceived of "heterogeneity" as an aggregated construct made up of different elements, all of which affected outcomes in the same direction. A group, therefore, that was heterogeneous with respect to age and functional background was "more heterogeneous", and by implication either better or worse off, than a group that was heterogeneous with respect solely to functional area. Little thought appeared to be given to the differential and/or interaction effects of the various demographic indicators. A number of demographic researchers have recently begun to separate out the effects of different types of diversity. An important early study in this vein is that by Zenger and Lawrence (1989). These researchers tested one of the most often cited relationships in the organizational demography field, namely, that demographics are an important determinant of communication. Their results showed a relationship between age and tenure distributions and the frequency of technical communications. Inside project groups, age distributions exert greater influence than tenure distributions on the frequency of technical communication, but the reverse relationship holds for technical communication outside project groups.

Ancona and Caldwell (1992) demonstrated the different effects of functional and tenure diversity in new product development teams. Their results showed that the two demographic characteristics have quite different effects. The greater the functional diversity, the more team members communicate outside team boundaries, and the more external communication, the higher the managerial ratings of team performance. Conversely, tenure diversity impacts internal group dynamics, and is associated with improved task work such as clarifying group goals and setting priorities. In turn, clarity is associated with high team ratings of overall performance. Despite these positive process benefits, the direct effect of diversity on performance is negative. The authors concluded that simply creating diverse groups is not sufficient to obtain improved performance benefits.

Relational demography (Tsui and O'Reilly, 1989; Tsui et al., 1992) considers the relative differences of age, group tenure, and so on, and the effect of those differences on outcomes. Tsui and colleagues' results significantly increased the amount of variance explained over that explained by simple demographic variables alone, suggesting compositional and non-linear effects of diversity. The researchers argued that these results are suggestive of the great deal we still have to learn about "the communication structure, conflict and influence styles, and decision approaches of heterogeneous versus homogeneous groups'' (Tsui et al., 1992, p. 575).

Another important study by Smith et al. (1994) further serves to emphasize this need. The researchers compared three alternative models of the effects of the top management team's (TMT) demography and process on organizational performance: (1) a demography model, in which team demography accounts entirely for performance outcomes, and process has no impact; (2) a process model, in which process contributes incrementally and directly to performance outcomes, over and above the team's demography; and (3) an intervening model, in which the effects of the top management team on performance outcomes are due entirely to the effects of its demography on process. Although direct effects of TMT demography were found, TMT demography was most related indirectly to performance through process, and process was related directly to performance. Social integration and communication were found to be important mediating variables.

Recently organizational demography has been employed in the international management literature to address whether differences in the cultural backgrounds of partners are detrimental for international joint ventures (Barkema and Vermeulen, 1997, 1998). Results show that cultural differences in uncertainty avoidance and long-term orientation are sources of difficulty, while differences around individualism, power distance and masculinity are much more readily resolved (Barkema and Vermeulen, 1997). At the same time, organizations are subject to constraints related to product diversity. Specifically, intermediately product-diversified firms derive little benefit from increases in multinational diversity, suggesting organizational limits on information sharing and learning ventures (Barkema and Vermeulen, 1998).

One concept that can assist with our understanding of diversity in multinational teams is that of ''group faultlines'' described by Lau and Murnighan (1998). Faultlines were defined as ''hypothetical dividing lines that may split a group into subgroups based on one or more attributes'' (p. 328) where the authors limited the attributes to demographic variables, particularly age, gender, race and job tenure. Faultline strength was argued to depend on ''the number of individual attributes apparent to group members; the alignment of the apparent attributes; and the resulting number of subgroups'' (p. 328). The more demographic attributes of group members are correlated, the fewer the number of subgroups, the more homogeneous the subgroups, and the stronger the faultlines. While a group may vary on attributes other than demographic ones, these are argued to remain relatively latent where demographic differences exist. The larger the relative size of a subgroup, the greater the likely status and power of that *majority* subgroup within the group as a whole (Kanter, 1977). Group members from *minority* subgroups are unlikely to contribute to the best of their ability. Lack of, or weak, faultlines in a group should allow minority subgroup members' skills to be fully used.

## Group Diversity

Some work in this literature focuses solely on the direct relationship between demographic factors and performance outcomes. For example, a study by Watson et al. (1993) showed that multicultural groups generally perform as well as or better than homogeneous ones, but take longer to reach the stage of performing. Other studies concentrating on creativity in ethnically diverse groups showed a positive relationship between diversity and creativity outcomes (Cox et al., 1991; McLeod and Lobel, 1992). Two explanations were offered for these results: (1) behavioural correlations with ethnicity; and (2) creative thinking ability correlations with ethnicity. Recent work by Jehn et al. (1999) suggests that team heterogeneity may impact performance differentially through various forms of diversity. In a cross-sectional study, they examine the independent roles of informational (cognitive skills), social (demographic), and value-based diversity on team outcomes along with several moderating variables. As might be expected, they found that various types of diversity differentially impacted various team outcomes. Unfortunately, it is difficult to tease apart these various forms of diversity given that each form is likely linked to the others (e.g. demographic characteristics are tied to values held).

Interest in the relationship between a group's diversity and the interaction of its members began to emerge in the late 1980s. Research by Canney Davison (1995) on intercultural processes in groups found four significant culturally influenced predictor variables on individual and team participation: the culturally influenced style of leadership; being a member of the same nationality as the leadership of the company (i.e. dominant culture); being a mother tongue speaker of the language used for company business; and, if belonging to a non-dominant culture, having previous international experience.

Maznevski (1994) adopted a symbolic interactionist perspective to address the link between group composition and interaction. She developed a model to explain performance in decision-making groups characterized by high diversity in composition, and, with that model, challenged the finding that heterogeneous groups perform less well than homogeneous ones. Her key finding was that a heterogeneous complex decision-making group will perform better than a homogeneous group if the group's diversity is integrated, otherwise a diverse group will perform worse. Her integrating mechanism was communication. The theoretical preconditions she identifies are shared social reality, ability to de-centre, motivation to communicate, ability to negotiate and endorse contracts of behaviour, ability to attribute difficulties appropriately, and confidence.

Earley and Mosakowski (2000) argue that team member characteristics influence the emergence of a shared culture in two general ways. First, team members' personal characteristics shape their expectations of appropriate interaction rules, group efficacy beliefs, and group identity. Second, these personal characteristics affect team members' expectations of how other members should act within the team. Thus, a person's demographic background influences her self construal as a team member and her view of others within the group (Lickel et al., 1998; Markus and Kitayama, 1991). These shared understandings emerging from team interaction have been called alternately a "hybrid culture" (Earley and Mosakowski, 2000), "third culture" (Casmir, 1992), team-based mental models (Klimoski and Mohammed, 1994), or synergy (Adler, 1991). A hybrid team culture refers to an emergent and simplified set of rules and actions, work capability expectations, and member perceptions that individuals within a team develop, share, and enact after mutual interactions. To the extent these rules, expectations, and roles are shared (Rohner, 1987; Shweder and LeVine, 1984), a strong culture exists. Earley and Mosakowski (2000) argue that the relationship of heterogeneity to team performance is curvilinear such that homogeneous and highly heterogeneous teams will outperform moderately heterogeneous ones. Their findings from three studies demonstrate support for this assertion.

Synthesizing findings from the group performance and group diversity literatures suggests that where group diversity enhances the necessary communication and social integration performance or the achievement of group goals is also enhanced. Which factors seem to have a positive effect seems to depend very much on the type of diversity studied, outcome measures used and the context within which the teams work. Drawing from Lau and Murnighan (1998), in assessing this body of work, it would be helpful to know where the faultlines lie in a study, the degree of multiple dimensions of heterogeneity. Nonetheless, the focus of both streams of literature on the importance of social integration and communication to group performance suggests that risk assessment is being used across these studies by their participants in order to produce the results found.

# MULTINATIONAL TEAMS: A CHALLENGE TO THE SUCCESSFUL MANAGEMENT OF ORGANIZATIONAL CULTURE

Using the lens of structuration theory, we have argued that the individual members of a group continuously colonize the future by undertaking risk assessment of the choices apparently open to them. The greater the heterogeneity in a group, the wider the range of choices apparently available. Therefore, multinational[10] and some nationally homogeneous multicultural groups actually assess the widest range of choices leading to groups with a strong task interest and a broad range of group objectives to which the individual members of the group are committed. Performance can be expected to be more than reasonable. Other nationally homogeneous multicultural groups are not sufficiently diverse, and so such groups fail to perform to a reasonable standard. Nationally and culturally homogeneous groups undertake risk assessment across an apparently more limited range of options, leading to groups with shared interests around either the task or friendship or around both of these. Performance can be expected to be reasonable.

While nationally and culturally homogeneous groups can be expected to operate

---

[10] In this section, a multinational group is defined as one where none of its members share a nationality.

successfully within a range of organizational cultures, nationally homogeneous multicultural groups can be expected to need a solidaristic organizational level culture in order to support the development of a solidaristic group level culture and perform to an acceptable standard. Multinational groups can be expected to thrive where the organizational level culture is solidaristic, developing a parallel solidaristic culture and performing above an acceptable level, and where the organizational culture is not solidaristic, performing at a level lower than their combined capabilities.

If the larger organizational cultures within which groups operate are not supportive, then the principles of duality of structure and colonization of the future suggest that these groups are unlikely to create the necessary group culture within which to achieve the goals their organizations have set for them to the detriment of those organizations. Despite the pressures on companies to move to more multinational workforces, not all have or can adopt an organizational culture that successfully supports multinational teams. For example, some companies' primary businesses involve tasks that are highly structured which may constrain the performance (Ilgen and Hollenbeck, 1997) and culture of multinational teams. In weak task situations (Mischel, 1977), however, the reverse should be expected. Given an organization's existing culture, its management clearly needs to think about the consequences of adopting multinational teams on the organization as a whole.

# RECOMMENDATIONS FOR FUTURE RESEARCH

In our analysis of organizational culture and multinational team dynamics, we have used Giddens' notion of colonization of the future and social dynamics as a theoretical lens for understanding these topics. What is unique about a multinational team that is highly diverse is that existing cues and social information useful for determining social structure and rules are largely lacking. That is, such highly diverse teams are more accurately characterized by their dissimilarity rather than similarity. This means that members from these teams must engage in a social "sorting" exercise to create a social consensus concerning who they are as individuals within the team, what is the identity of the team, what its purpose must be, etc. In this sense, much of what we are posing is captured by the social construction reflected by the symbolic interactionists (e.g. Stryker, 1980). Before teams can move forward and reinforce and perpetuate social structure as suggested by Giddens, they must answer fundamental questions concerning personal and team identity. It is this process that we will focus on for some exemplary research that might be conducted using our described framework.

As we stated, our suggestion is that the early phases of team interaction are particularly critical in the development of norms and rules that will subsequently govern the nature of the team and its members. Consistent with the symbolic interactionist view, we argue that individuals are constantly evaluating social settings for cues needed to define and clarify one's role in a social circumstance. These cues are typically derived from fellow team members interpreted using the symbols derived from one's cultural background. However, if these cues are absent, vague, or confused because the social circumstance/setting is dynamic or novel, a search for meaning concerning identity becomes problematic. Even in a simple setting for which cues are clearly defined, the faultline perspective of Lau and Murnighan (1998) suggests that social interpretation is highly complicated. Imagine removing the common symbols and cues that can be relied upon by creating a team of highly heterogeneous nationalities. Many of the status cues that we discussed earlier in the chapter (e.g. ascriptive versus achievement) will still be present such as gender or race, but the relative status perception of these characteristics will vary across individuals. Thus, the American may focus on race and gender while her Thai counterpart may focus on age and education (Earley, 1999).

What role might organizational culture play in helping or hindering the social reconstruction of status and order within a multinational team? We would suggest that a strong and clearly defined organizational culture would aid in helping team members sort themselves out. The cues provided by the organization's culture provide a strong setting for the interpretation required during the early phases of a team's evolution. Specifically, the status cues most directly tied to an organization's culture will be evoked during the ambiguous early phases of a team's interactions. The organization's culture is both shared across team members (presumably, but of varying strength and consistency) and more proximate than other interpretative schemes (e.g. national cultures). Thus, organizational culture becomes a general interpretative frame for members to understand their role identities within a multinational team.

To test such arguments, we can imagine conducting a longitudinal field study of newly formed groups varying the nationality of members and organizational culture. For example, we might look at team member nationality (minimum of two multinational and two nationally homogeneous) in two (or more) organizations of cultures (one high on solidarity, one low on solidarity) holding task, lifespan and the size of the groups constant as much as possible.[11] Observation of critical incidents (initial group formation, deadlines, feedback) can be triangulated with interviews, questionnaires, and personal diaries. Our choice of organizational cultures (solidarity) is based on Goffee and Jones' work on this topic (see Part 1, Chapter 1 in this volume). Once the initial formation of group social structure has been established, a critical question derived from our approach is how (and if) this social structure is perpetuated across generations of the organizational teams. One might examine this question by introducing new memberships into the existing teams (or observing natural attrition) and observing the subsequent transmission of existing norms and status structures.

Our focus in this chapter has been to introduce concepts of social evolution derived from Giddens' viewpoint using specific micro-level characteristics of multinational teams. We have discussed various aspects of status characteristics as a basis for determining relative status in multinational teams. Finally, we recommended some possible research avenues for examining the dynamics we described.

---

[11] Further studies could address the cases of task, lifespan and size.

# REFERENCES

Abramson, N. (1992) Factors influencing the entry of Canadian software manufacturers into the United States market. Unpublished doctoral dissertation, University of Western Ontario.

Adler, N.J. (1991) International Dimensions of Organizational Behavior, 2nd Edn. Boston, MA: PWS-Kent.

Ancona, D.G. and Caldwell, D.F. (1992) Demography and design: predictors of new product team performance. Organization Science, 3(3): 321–341.

Bales, R.F. (1951) Interaction Process Analysis: a Method for the Study of Small Groups. Cambridge, MA: Addison-Wesley Press.

Bales, R.F. (1953) The equilibrium problem in small groups. In T. Parsons, R.F. Bales and E.A. Shils (Eds), Working Papers in the Theory of Action. Glencoe, IL: Free Press.

Barkema, H.G. and Vermeulen, F. (1997) What differences in the cultural backgrounds of partners are detrimental for international joint ventures? Academy of Management Journal, 28(4): 845–864.

Barkema, H.G. and Vermeulen, F. (1998) International expansion through start-up or acquisition: a learning perspective. Academy of Management Journal, 41(1): 7–26.

Barley, S.R. (1986) Technology as an occasion for structuring evidence from observations of CT scanners and the social order of radiology departments. Administrative Science Quarterly, 31: 78–108.

Barley, S.R. (1995) Images of imaging. In G.P. Huber and A.H. Van de Ven (Eds), Longitudinal Field Research Methods: Studying Processes of Organizational Change. Thousand Oaks, CA: Sage.

Barley, S.R. and Tolbert, P.S. (1997) Institutionalization and structuration: studying the links between action and institution. Organization Studies, 18(1): 93–117.

Berger, J. and Zelditch, M. (Eds) (1985) Status, Rewards, and Influence. San Francisco, CA: Jossey-Bass.

Berger, J., Conner, T.L. and Fisek, M.H. (1974) Expectation States Theory: a Theoretical Research Program. Cambridge, MA: Winthrop.

Berger, J., Fisek, M.H., Norma, R.Z. and Zelditch Jr., M. (1977) Status Characteristics and Social Interaction. New York: Elsevier.

Borgatta, E.F. and Stimson, J. (1963) Sex differences in interaction characteristics. Journal of Social Psychology, 60: 89–100.

Butler, C. (2001) Unpublished doctoral dissertation, London Business School.

Canney Davison, S.F. (1995) Intercultural processes in multinational teams. Unpublished doctoral dissertation, London Business School.

Casmir, R. (1992) Third-culture building: a paradigm shift for international and intercultural communication. Communication Yearbook, 16: 407–428.

Clarke, P. (1971) Lancashire and the New Liberalism. Cambridge: Cambridge University Press.

Cohen, B.P. and Zhou, X. (1991) Status processes in enduring work groups. American Sociological Review, 56: 179–188.

Cox, T. (1993) Cultural Diversity in Organizations. San Francisco, CA: Berret-Kohler.

Cox, T., Lobel, S.A. and McLeod, P.L. (1991) Effects of ethnic group cultural differences on cooperative and competitive behavior on a group task. Academy of Management Journal, 34(4): 827–847.

Crossan, M.M. (1991) Organizational learning: a sociocognitive model of strategic management. Unpublished doctoral dissertation, The University of Western Ontario.

Dawe, A. (1978) Theories of social action. In T. Bottomore and R. Nisbet (Eds), A History of Sociological Analysis, pp. 418–456. London: Heinemann.

DeSanctis, G. and Poole, M.S. (1994) Capturing the complexity in advanced technology use: adaptive structuration theory. Organization Science, 5(2): 121–147.

Earle, P. (1989) The Making of the English Middle Class: Business, Society and Family Life in London, 1660-1730. London: Methuen.

Earley, P.C. (1993) East meets west meets mideast: further explorations of collectivistic and individualistic work groups. Academy of Management Journal, 36(2): 319–348.

Earley, P.C. (1999) Playing follow the leader: status-determining traits in relation to collective efficacy across cultures. Organizational Behavior and Human Decision Processes, 80: 1–21.

Earley, P.C. and Mosakowski, E. (2000) Creating hybrid team cultures: an empirical test of transnational team functioning. Academy of Management Journal, 43(1): 26–49.

Elsass, P.M. and Graves, L.M. (1997) Demographic diversity in decision-making groups: the experiences of women and people of color. Academy of Management Review, 22(4): 946–973.

Erez, M. and Earley, P.C. (1993) Culture, Self-identity, and Work. New York: Oxford University Press.

Foschi, M. (1996) Double standards in the evaluation of men and women. Social Psychology Quarterly, 59(3): 237–254.

Gibson, C.B. (1999) Do they do what they believe they can? Group efficacy and group effectiveness across tasks and cultures. Academy of Management Journal, 42(2): 138–152.

Giddens, A. (1971) (reprinted in 1972) Capitalism and Modern Social Theory: an Analysis of the Writings of Marx, Durkheim and Max Weber. London: [s.n.].

Giddens, A. (1979) Central Problems in Social Theory: Action, Structure and Contradiction in Social Analysis. Houndsmill and London: Macmillan.

Giddens, A. (1981) (revised edition) The Class Structure of the Advanced Societies. London: Hutchinson/ New York: Harper and Row.

Giddens, A. (1984) The Constitution of Society: Outline of the Theory of Structuration. Cambridge: Polity Press.

Giddens, A. (1991) Modernity and Self-Identity. Cambridge: Polity Press.

Goffee, R. and Jones, G. (1998) The Character of a Corporation: How Your Company's Culture Can Make or Break Your Business. London: Harper Collins Business.

Guzzo, R.A. and Shea, G.P. (1994) Group performance and intergroup relations in organizations. In M.D. Dunnette and L.M. Hough (Eds), Handbook of Industrial and Organizational Psychology, 2nd Edn. Palo Alto, CA: Consulting Psychologists Press.

Guzzo, R.A., Salas, E. and Associates (Eds) (1995) Team Effectiveness and Decision Making in Organizations. San Francisco, CA: Jossey-Bass.

Hackman, J.R. and Morris, C.G. (1975) Group tasks, group interaction process, and group performance effectiveness: a review and proposed integration. In L. Berkowitz (Ed), Group Processes. New York: Academic Press.

Hall, E.T. (1983) The Dance of Life: the Other Dimension of Time. New York: Anchor Books/Doubleday.

Harrison, D.A., Price, K.H. and Bell, M.P. (1998) Beyond relational demography: time and the effects of surface- and deep-level diversity on work group cohesion. Academy of Management Journal, 41(1): 96–107.

Heiss, J.S. (1962) Degree of intimacy and male-female interaction. Sociometry, 25: 197–208.

Hinings, C.R., Brown, J.L. and Greenwood, R. (1991) Change in an autonomous professional organization. Journal of Management Studies, 28(4): 375–393.

Hofstede, G. (1980) Culture's Consequences. Beverly Hills, CA: Sage.

Hofstede, G. (1991) Cultures and Organizations: Software of the Mind. London: McGraw-Hill.

Hofstede, G., Neuijen, B., Ohayv, D.D. and Sanders, G. (1990) Measuring organizational cultures: a qualitative and quantitative study across twenty cases. Administrative Science Quarterly, 35: 286–316.

Hughes, E.C. (1971) The Sociological Eye: Selected Papers. Chicago, IL: Aldine-Atherton.

Ilgen, D.R. and Hollenbeck, J.R. (1997) Effective decision making in multinational teams. In P.C. Earley and M. Erez (Eds), New Perspectives on International Industrial/Organizational Psychology. San Francisco, CA: The New Lexington Press.

Jackson, S.E., Brett, J.F., Sessa, V.I., Cooper, D.M., Julian, J.A. and Peyronnin, K. (1991) Some differences make a difference: individual dissimilarity and group heterogeneity as correlates of recruitment, promotions and turnover. Journal of Applied Psychology, 76(5): 675–689.

Jackson, S.E., May, K.E. and Whitney, K. (1995) Understanding the dynamics of diversity. In Guzzo, R.A., Salas, E. and Associates (Eds), Team Effectiveness and Decision Making in Organizations. San Francisco, CA: Jossey-Bass.

Jehn, K.A., Northcraft, G.B. and Neale, M.A. (1999) Why differences make a difference: a field study of diversity, conflict, and performance in workgroups. Administrative Science Quarterly, 44(4): 741–763.

Kanter, R.M. (1977) Some effects of proportions on group life: skewed sex ratios and responses to token women. American Journal of Sociology, 82: 965–990.

Katz, I. and Benjamin, L. (1960) Effects of white authoritarianism in bi-racial work groups. Journal of Abnormal and Social Psychology, 671: 448–456.

Katz, I., Goldstone, J. and Benjamin, L. (1958) Behavior and productivity in bi-racial work groups. Human Relations, 11: 123–141.

Kenkel, W.F. (1957) Differentiation in family decision making. Sociology and Social Research, 42: 18–25.

Kirchmeyer, C. and Cohen, A. (1992) Multicultural groups: their performance and reactions with constructive conflict. Group and Organization Management, 17(2): 153–170.

Klimoski, R. and Mohammed, S. (1994) Team mental model: construct or metaphor? Journal of Management, 20: 403–437.

Lau, D.C. and Murnighan, J.K. (1998) Demographic diversity and faultlines: the compositional dynamics of organizational groups. Academy of Management Review, 23(2): 325–340.

Laurent, A. (1983) The cultural diversity of western conception of management. International Studies of Management and Organization, 13(1–2): 75–96.

Lave, J. (1993) The practice of learning. In S. Chaiklin and J. Lave (Eds), Understanding Practice: Perspectives on Activity and Context, pp. 3–32. Cambridge: Cambridge University Press.

Levine, J.M. and Moreland, R.L. (1990) Progress in small group research. Annual Review of Psychology, 41: 585–634.

Lickel, B., Hamilton, D.S., Wieczorkowska, G., Lewis, A., Sherman, S.J. and Uhles, A.N. (1998) Varieties of groups and perceptions of group entitativity. University of California, Santa Barbara, CA (unpublished paper).

March, J.G. (1953) Husband-wife interaction over political issues. Public Opinion Quarterly, 17: 461–470.

Markus, H.R. and Kitayama, S. (1991) Culture and the self: implications for cognition, emotion, and motivation. Psychological Review, 98: 224–253.

Mateju, P. and Rehakova, B. (1994) Une revolution pour qui?: analyse selective de modeles de mobilitie intragenerationnelle entre 1989 et 1992. Reveu d'etudes comparatives Est-Ouest, 4: 15–31.

Maznevski, M.L. (1994) Understanding our differences: performance in decision-making groups. Human Relations, 47(5): 531–552.

Maznevski, M.L. and Chudoba, K.M. (in press) Bridging space over time: global virtual team dynamics and effectiveness. Organization Science.

McClelland, D.C. (1961) The Achieving Society. New York: Free Press.

McGrath, J.E. (1984) Groups: Interaction and Performance. Englewood Cliffs, NJ: Prentice-Hall.

McLeod, P.L. and Lobel, S.A. (1992) The effects of ethnic diversity on idea generation in small groups. Academy of Management Best Paper Proceedings, 227–231.

Mischel, W. (1977) On the future of personality measurement. American Psychologist, 32: 246–254.

Ong, A. (1996) Cultural citizenship as subject-making: immigrants negotiate racial and cultural boundaries in the United States. Current Anthropology, 37(5): 737–762.

O'Reilly, C.A., Caldwell, D.F. and Barnett, W.P. (1989) Work group demography, social integration, and turnover. Administrative Science Quarterly, 34: 21–37.

Orlikowski, W.J. (1992) The duality of technology: rethinking the concept of technology in organizations. Organization Science, 3(3): 398–427.

Parsons, T. and Shils, E.A. (Eds) (1951) Toward a General Theory of Action. Cambridge, MA: Harvard University Press.

Pettigrew, A. (1985) The Awakening Giant: Continuity and Change in ICI. London: Basil Blackwell.

Poole, M.S. and DeSanctis, G. (1992) Microlevel structuration in computer-supported group decision making. Human Communication Research, 19(1): 5–49.

Prandy, K. (1998) Class and continuity in social reproduction: an empirical investigation. The Sociological Review, 46(2): 340–364.

Preston, M. and Bayton, J. (1941) Differential effects of a social variable upon three levels of aspiration. Journal of Experimental Psychology, 29: 351–369.

Rallu, J.-L. (1998) Les categories statistiques utilisees dans les DOM-TOM depuis le debut de la Presencc Francaise. Population, 3: 589–608.

Ranson, S., Hinings, R. and Greenwood, R. (1980) The structuring of organizational structures. Administrative Science Quarterly, 28: 314–337.

Riches, P. and Foddy, M. (1989) Ethnic accent as a status cue. Social Psychology Quarterly, 52(3): 197–206.

Ridgeway, C. and Walker, H.A. (1995) Status structures. In K. Cook, G.A. Fine and J.S. House (Eds), Sociological Perspectives on Social Psychology. Needham Heights, MA: Allyn and Bacon.

Ridgeway, C.L., Johnson, C. and Diekema, D. (1994) External status, legitimacy, and compliance in male and female groups. Social Forces, 72(4): 1051–1077.

Riley, P. (1983) A structurationist account of political culture. Administrative Science Quarterly, 28: 414–437.

Rohner, R. (1987) Culture theory. Journal of Cross-Cultural Psychology, 18: 8–51.

Ronen, S. and Shenkar, O. (1985) Clustering countries on attitudinal dimensions: a review and synthesis. Academy of Management Review, 10: 435–454.

Sahay, S. and Walsham, G. (1997) Social structure and managerial agency. Organization Studies, 18(3): 415–444.

Schneider, S.C. and Barsoux, J.-L. (1997) Managing Across Cultures. Hemel Hempstead: Prentice-Hall.

Shackelford, S., Wood, W. and Worchel, S. (1996) Behavioral styles and the influence of women in mixed-sex groups. Social Psychology Quarterly, 59(3): 284–293.

Shweder, R.A. and LeVine, R.A. (1984) Culture Theory: Essays on Mind, Self, and Emotion. New York: Cambridge University Press.

Smith, K.G., Smith, K.A., Smith, J.D., Sims Jr., H.P., O'Bannon, D.P. and Scully, J.A. (1994) Top management team demography and process: the role of social integration and communication. Administrative Science Quarterly, 39: 412–438.

Smith, P.B., Dugan, S. and Trompenaars, F. (1996) National culture and the values of organizational employees: a dimensional analysis across 43 nations. Journal of Cross-Cultural Psychology, 27(2): 231–264.

Snow, C.C., Snell, S.A., Canney Davison, S. and Hambrick, D.C. (1996) Use transnational teams to globalize your company. Organizational Dynamics, 24: 4.

Stets, J.E. (1997) Status and identity in marital interaction. Social Psychology Quarterly, 60(3): 185–217.

Stewart, P. (1988) Women and Men in Groups: A Status Characteristics Approach to Interaction. In M. Webster Jr. and M. Foschi (Eds), Status Generalization: New Theory and Research. Stanford, CA: Stanford University Press.

Stovel, K., Savage, M. and Bearman, P. (1996) Ascription into achievement: models of career systems at Lloyds Bank, 1890-1970. American Journal of Sociology, 102: 358–399.

Stryker, S. (1980) Symbolic Interactionism: a Social Structural Version. Menlo Park, CA: Benjamin/Cummings.

Trompenaars, F. and Hampden-Turner, C. (1997) Riding the Waves of Culture: Understanding Cultural Diversity in Business. London: Nicholas Brealey.

Tsui, A.S. and O'Reilly III, C.A. (1989) Beyond simple demographic effects: the importance of relational demography in superior-subordinate dyads. Administrative Science Quarterly, 32(2): 402–423.

Tsui, A.S., Egan, T.D. and O'Reilly III, C.A. (1992) Being different: relational demography and organizational attachment. Administrative Science Quarterly, 37: 549–579.

Turner, J.C., Hogg, M.A., Oakes P.J., Riecher S.D. Rediscovering the Social Group: A Self-categorization Theory. Oxford: Blackwell.

Walgenbach, P. (1993) Mittleres Management: Aufgaben, Funktionen, Arbeitsverhalten. Wiesbaden: Gabler.

Walker, H.A., Ilardi, B.C., McMahon, A.M. and Fennell, M.L. (1996) Gender, interaction, and leadership. Social Psychology Quarterly, 59(3): 255–272.

Watson, W.E., Kumar, K. and Michaelsen, L.K. (1993) Cultural diversity's impact on interaction process and performance: comparing homogeneous and diverse task groups. Academy of Management Journal, 36(3): 590–602.

Weber, M. [1921] (1946) Class, status, and party. In H. Gerth and C.W. Mills (Eds and Trans), From Max Weber: Essays in Sociology. New York: Oxford University Press.

Webster Jr., M. and Foschi, M. (Eds) (1988) Status Generalization: New Theory and Research. Stanford, CA: Stanford University Press.

Weisinger, J. and Salipante, P. (1999) A Model of Diversity in Nonprofit Organizations: A Case Study. Paper presented at the 28th annual conference of the Association for Research on Nonprofit Organizations and Voluntary Action, Washington, D.C.

West, C. (1984) When the doctor is a "lady": power, status and gender in physician-patient encounters. Symbolic Interaction, 7(1): 87–106.

Willmott, H. (1987) Studying managerial work: a critique and a proposal. Journal of Management Studies, 24: 249–270.

Wyer Jr., R.S. and Srull, T.K. (1989) Memory and Cognition in its Social Context. Hillsdale, NJ: Erlbaum.
Zander, A.W. (1977) Groups at Work. San Francisco, CA: Jossey-Bass.
Zenger, T.R. and Lawrence, B.S. (1989) Organizational demography: the differentiated effects of age and tenure distributions on technical communications. Academy of Management Journal, 32: 352–376.

# Section II

## Assessment and Research Methods

### Paul R. Sparrow

As various authors in the previous section have noted, culture is a complex construct. Each chapter in this section therefore presents progressively richer forms of quantitative and then qualitative forms of assessments. In the opening chapter of this section Paul R. Sparrow considers some quantitative approaches to diagnosing high performance organizational cultures. The chapter begins by asking why organizations have a need to assess culture from a strategic management and HRM perspective. By pointing to the organizational processes to which assessments of culture are typically applied, it is clear why interest in assessing high performance cultures persists, hence its treatment as a starting point for this section. The chapter raises some of the debates associated with the quest to link culture to organizational performance and reviews some of the main quantitative instruments available. A range of technical and psychometric protocols that accompany assessments of culture are noted, such as issues of aggregation and choice of statistical measures. This is followed by a discussion of practical assessment issues. The question is asked, are cultural assessments just glorified attitude surveys or not? It is argued that they are not, and that they do tap into broad metaphors that are useful for organization analysis. However, there is evidence that the domains assessed by most existing instruments are in fact quite narrow (with an overemphasis on hierarchy, interpersonal relations and rewards). The chapter therefore develops a model of the organizational features that any diagnostic of high performance culture needs to tap. It lays out the linking process between cultural values and climate and organizational effectiveness, via the HRM architecture, mental, emotional and attitudinal states, and resultant organizational behaviours. Work that has picked up specific performance contexts, such as innovative climates, is outlined, along with the latest work on high performance HRM (by making reference to the climate dimensions that they have found the most predictive). The argument is made that items should be designed to reflect all elements of this complex linkage process. Finally, a series of suggestions for the design and implementation of high performance culture diagnostics are made, and a discussion is entered into as to whether such assessment tools need necessarily be quantitative, as is the current preference.

Chapter 5, by Roy L. Payne, reviews the different quantitative traditions that have been used to make assessments of culture and climate. The conceptual overlaps between the two constructs are highlighted and a brief overview of the methodological issues associated with any assessment of climate is presented. Ways in which these may be differentiated and assessed are discussed. The chapter draws upon a three-dimensional model of culture. There have been a number of overlooked features in culture and climate research, such as pervasiveness and psychological intensity of cultures. Ways in which these may be differentiated and assessed are discussed. In asking how close can climate instruments get to culture, and how the issue of consensus might be dealt with, a hypothetical Cultural Intensity Questionnaire is developed. It is argued that assessments must differentiate between the extent to which individuals: publicly express a positive attitude; behave that way (whatever their attitude); hold it as a deep value (whether they behave that way or not); and have it as such a fundamental belief that it is "taken-for-granted" without them necessarily expressing their awareness of it. Strong cultures only exist when most people adopt it and there is consistency of values, beliefs and behaviours. It is concluded that through using climate scales that are designed in collaboration with members of the organization, and by accepting that measures of agreement can be used to reflect integration and fragmentation, the climate approach can be seen to be a useful indicator of culture. Whilst climate is not culture, it is not as different from it as was once thought. If climate instruments can be redesigned along the lines described above they can play a useful role as a research tool. The chapter explores ways in which redesigned climate instruments could also be used as a diagnostic approach to understanding individual organizations, and monitoring change within them.

Having reviewed and presented mainly quantitative methods of assessment in Chapters 4 and 5 of the section, Chapter 6 by Kate Mackenzie Davey and Gillian Symon reviews a range of qualitative methods. This chapter focuses on *how* you can make assessments of culture. It provides an assessment of the strengths and weaknesses of major qualitative methods for assessing culture and examines some of the latest methods that are being used. After a brief description of the concept of organizational culture, a more thorough discussion of what is meant by "qualitative approach" is presented. It is argued that what constitutes a qualitative approach is not self-evident. Attention is therefore given to some fundamental epistemological issues. An overview of the variety of approaches available for exploring culture is produced, highlighting different perspectives and contributions. This overview is illustrated through a detailed and critical analysis of some specific methods, selected to cover a range of perspectives. Techniques considered include repertory grid analysis, twenty statements test, pictorial analysis, story-telling/narrative and ethnography. The chapter concludes with an overall evaluation of current approaches to assessing culture and a series of suggestions for future methodological developments.

Chapter 7 by Sonja Sackmann explores the values and limitations of qualitative methodologies and approaches to organization culture, and considers some future areas of research, especially with regard to assessment issues. The first section argues that definitions of culture influence its assessment and that a given definition of culture should be reflected in its operationalization. The numerous definitions of culture that exist create many different ways to assess it. An argument for a qualitative approach to assessment is made based on the deconstruction of a series of detailed definitions of culture. The chapter explores the values of qualitative methodologies and discusses some limitations to research methodologies. In particular, the problems of comparability, issues of time, problems of subjectivity and objectivity, and the missing links to performance, are examined.

In Chapter 8 Iva Smit asks whether assessing culture gives us a way of solving problems, or presents us with problematic solutions. It is argued that organizational cultures are widely recognized for their considerable influence on the well-being of industrial as well as non-industrial enterprises and their employees. As a pattern of shared beliefs, basic assumptions, it captures well established solutions to recurring problems. Culture is a force that guides the actions of its members during both regular and irregular situations. The outcomes of the actions are usually tangible and measurable with reasonable accuracy, giving us some optimism about its assessability. However, underlying cultural patterns work on more or less unconscious levels and tend to be vague, ambiguous, and characterized by complex interrelations. It is argued that this elusiveness of cultural patterns is reflected in the research methods designed to assess them. Many researchers and practitioners develop their own terminology and define a set of cultural dimensions fitting their specific work perspective, which complicates the comparison of different assessment methods and limits their use. Although many studies stress the relation between organizational culture and performance, very few studies actually explore this relation, as is made clear in the opening chapter of the section. Thus, while culture may be defined as the way in which a group of people solves problems, the ways to understanding cultures can be quite problematic. The chapter combines the knowledge gained by applying various instruments to a method that enables us to systematically assess organizational cultures and their impact on organizational performance and health. The purpose of the method outlined is to both describe and distinguish cultures of various organizations, and to provide information suitable for design of interventions tailored to the particular needs of each organization. A model of culture based on Parsons' action theory is presented, comprising of four dimensions: adaptation; goal attainment; integration; and latency and pattern maintenance (the AGIL scheme). These dimensions are derived from the basic problems any social unit has to deal with in order to survive, and serve as a framework for classification of empirical data describing actions of individuals and collectives. A practical application of the AGIL model is demonstrated on data gathered from six middle management teams operating in an industrial enterprise. Attention is paid to the pivotal role of critical incidents in cultural assessment, and to the importance of linking the assessment with several different performance indicators. Artificial intelligence (neural networks) is engaged to model the relations between cultural variables and performance indicators in the six participating teams. Issues of validity are addressed, as well as the suitability of neural networks for classification of fuzzy data sets and complex data sets obtained from small groups (i.e. ill-defined data sets). Finally, the role of artificial intelligence in model and theory forming is discussed and recommendations for further research are made.

# Chapter 4

# Developing Diagnostics for High Performance Organization Cultures

**Paul R. Sparrow**
*Sheffield University Management School, Sheffield, UK*

## INTRODUCTION

Why should we take a culture–performance perspective on assessment? From an assessment perspective the topics of organizational culture and organizational effectiveness are inextricably linked (De Witte and van Muijen, 1999). Effective performance is seen to follow from culture because the organization's culture provides (Ott, 1989):

- shared patterns of interpretations and perceptions that show employees how to act and think;
- an emotional sense of involvement and commitment to organizational values and moral codes, i.e. what to value and how to feel;
- defined and maintained boundaries allowing groups to identify and include members in problem solving;
- learned responses to problems and commonly held understandings for organizing actions;
- control systems, that in turn prescribe and prohibit certain behaviours.

In the next chapter Payne notes that shared individual perceptions result in climates that vary in intensity, consensus and pervasiveness. Sackmann (this section) uses the concept of cultural complexity to capture this perspective. Clearly, there is a need for more sophisticated HR strategies given the varying results across these three attributes.

However, the field of organizational culture has dominated management thinking about problems of adaptability, change and competitive success in large organizations (Kilmann, 1984; Pettigrew, 1979; Schein, 1985). Culture is presumed to create appropriate states of mind, i.e. *the mental, emotional and attitudinal states that precede effective employee performance*. Sackmann (this section) outlines the four types of knowledge that constitute the cognitive aspects of culture. If these states of mind are shared across enough people, then there is a positive culture or climate, and organizational performance may be expected to follow.

Although interest in high performance organization cultures can be traced back to the 1970s when researchers and consultants at Harvard, Stanford, MIT and McKinsey began to explore the positive and negative impacts that organization culture could have, 30 years later the organizational effectiveness and culture assessment fields are still driven by long lists of questions. There are no definitive answers or agreed tools or techniques as yet. De Witte and van Muijen (1999) remind us of a series of critical questions about assessment of cultures, by re-playing the issues initially raised by Cameron (1980). What domain of activity should the assessment focus on? Whose perspective, or which constituency's point of view will be evidenced? What level of analysis should be used? What time frame is appropriate? What type of data should be used? What referent is being employed? These questions highlight the diverse range of approaches that have been taken to the problem of cultural assessment.

# THE PROCESSES TO WHICH ASSESSMENTS ARE APPLIED

Despite an absence of definitive answers to the questions raised by De Witte and van Muijen (1999), they point out that requests to analyze and assess organizational culture and align it with strategic options continue to be directed at academic and consulting organizations. The attraction of the construct is that it represents a global concept to help understand complex organizational problems. Sparrow and Gaston (1996) note that the need to develop viable assessments of organizational culture and climate has increased because:

1. The 1990s witnessed a continuing revolution in the nature and shape of organizations, with the emergence of new organizational forms, concepts of business process, and basis of the employment relationship and psychological contract. For example, Ruigrok and Achtenhagen (1999) have examined the shift from economic organizational forms towards network organizational forms (also referred to as cellular, individualized or horizontal structures) in four innovative German-speaking companies and found that the role of organizational culture as a co-ordination mechanism increased in importance over the period 1992–1997. The same is true across European organizations (Ruigrok et al., 1999).
2. As organizations have become more flexible, and traditional boundaries of hierarchy, function and geography are eroding, the boundaries that matter most are in the minds and perceptions of managers and the workforce.
3. Co-ordination of organizational behaviour is seen increasingly to rely on the

management of psycho-social boundaries and perceptions, or "soft-wired" aspects of strategic change, such as the way individuals pattern authority, tasks, politics, identity, manager–subordinate relationships and subordinate–peer perceptions (Sparrow, 1994).

Attempting to analyze cultural values and measure "gaps" between the existing and future desired state of affairs (the culture or climate as espoused versus the culture as experienced) has proven to be an attractive tool for a range of organization development, process consulting and culture change initiatives. The main processes or applications to which assessment has been directed include:

1. *Assessing the depth of impact or progress of culture change programmes* (such as customer service or total quality management processes). Organizations examine changes in climate (or the dimensions most closely related to the phenomenon under study) to take a "snapshot" of progress at different time-points in order to understand the depth of a change initiative (across different horizontal functions or vertical job levels).
2. *Providing a tool to link the design of reward and benefit systems* to facets of the organizational culture by assessing the extent to which various control systems send out consistent behavioural messages. Analyses of current and desired behaviours, styles and values (as reflected in a climate survey) are used to assist and inform the design of reward and benefit systems.
3. *Providing goals for team building* after major change events (e.g. mergers and acquisitions) where an assessment of differing climates between units may serve as a powerful basis for organization development interventions.
4. *Helping top teams articulate strategic and structural changes* in more actionable behavioural and value terms where organizations have found it difficult to articulate and convey strategic change in a meaningful way to their workforce. Climate surveys may help top teams express how the strategy or structure will work or may reveal such different "process" assumptions between members of a top team when talking about the same outcomes.
5. *Establishing cultural imperatives for technological changes* and new work system designs. Large amounts of money spent on change programmes around customer service, empowerment or quality can be wasted when the people engaged in the design of information systems, or implementation of business process re-engineering do not incorporate these assumptions into the technological or work process. Climate surveys can identify the intended behaviours, values and styles of a new system and produce a series of "cultural imperatives" around which system designers must operate.
6. *Identifying future management competencies* in a more strategic fashion. Increasingly management competency is seen to reside in the possession of specific attitudes and mindsets that allow managers to confront and understand their organization and the changing business environment. Identifying such competencies becomes a values-driven methodology with climate surveys used to help define what some of these values and behaviours might be.

In tackling such applications, academics and practitioners look at the assessment problem from a different perspective (De Witte and van Muijen, 1999). As noted by Sackmann (this section), researchers have tried to understand culture, and so attempt to "*measure to know*". Consulting firms need to know whether culture can be managed, and so "*measure to change*".

## THE MAIN ASSESSMENT INSTRUMENTS

Some of the documented academic instruments include Jones and Jones' Organizational Norms Opinionnaire (Alexander, 1978), the Harrison (1975) Organization Ideology Instrument, the FOCUS Questionnaire (van Muijen et al., 1996), the Organizational Culture Profile (O'Reilly et al., 1991), the Organizational Culture Indicator (Lawthom et al., 1997), the Organizational Climate Questionnaire – Form B (Litwin and Stringer, 1968), the Competing Values Framework (Quinn, 1988), and the Business and Organizational Climate Index (Payne and Pheysey, 1971; Payne et al., 1992). Several management consultancies, in their search for pragmatic ways of capturing the "perceptual reflection" of effective performance at the organizational level, have also introduced instruments that assess dimensions of climate or culture. For example, Saville and Holdsworth introduced the Corporate Culture Questionnaire (CCQ) and Organizational Effectiveness Profile, PA Consulting Group use the Organization Values and Styles Questionnaire (OVSQ), Human Synergistics use the Organization Culture Inventory and KPMG have been developing a high performance culture instrument. Smaller consulting companies tend to market specialized instruments. For example Austin Knight offer the Organizational Culture Index, whilst Braxton Associates (part of Deloitte Touche Tohmatsu International) developed Culture Print, which looks at Commitment to Quality, Customer Orientation, Innovation, Level of Bureaucracy, Cost Consciousness, Risk Propensity and Teamwork.

## ASSESSMENTS OF CULTURE OR CLIMATE?

The type of evidence that such instruments are assessing becomes clear when the distinctions drawn in the culture versus climate debate are considered. Cultural assessments tend to examine *group understandings* (often called "interpretive schema") that represent ways of perceiving, thinking or feeling in relation to a group's problems. Culture is therefore an organizational construct, which may be decomposed down to individual or personal implications. These implications are seen in the norms, beliefs and justifying ideologies that are based on explicit *system-sanctioned behaviours*. Such sanctioned behaviours are assumed to be appropriate, and beneficial, to all members of the system. The level of analysis in cultural assessments is therefore always that of *collective groups*. Attempts to measure culture also focus on deep elements of analysis, such as the *shared meanings, assumptions and values*. These are considered to underlie the more observable organizational policies. Attempting to measure culture is difficult in a standardized instrument, as it requires the researcher or consultant to tap *subconscious*, but taken-for-granted, learned responses. Culture researchers are more likely to focus on qualitative analysis, with data "discovered" rather than "measured" and use made of interviews, case studies and observation. Payne (1991) notes that if culture is implicit in the beliefs, values, norms and premises which underpin behaviour, then climate is more explicit and measures the distinctive patterns or regularities of behaviour and the material artefacts these produce.

Climate researchers have focused on more quantitative forms of measurement. Organizational climate is a related, but separate phenomenon to culture (Ott, 1989; Reichers and Schneider, 1990). Climate represents a synthesis of *perceptions* about a relatively stable set of value orientations of the organization as a whole, which influences the behaviour of the organizational members with respect to organizational effectiveness (De Witte and De Cock, 1988). The perceptions that climate instruments tap are principally derived from the formal and informal organizational policies, the practices and procedures that evidence such policies, the goals these policies are intended to serve, and the perceived means of attainment. Climate instruments therefore measure the *average* of how people perceive the organizational environment. They focus on formal and informal organizational policies, practices and procedures and tend to capture differences in human resource management (HRM) or organization design frameworks (including variables such as leadership, performance management and decision making) that have a mediating effect on output measures such as performance and satisfaction. Climate survey data then tap facets of organization and management style, espoused values and permitted behaviours. This is intended to provide a picture of obvious, explicit, self-reported and observable facets of culture. As such they do not evidence either surface level artefacts (such as language, myths, stories, sagas and legends) or underlying assumptions and rationales.

However, both culture and climate assessments describe ways in which individuals make sense of their organization and provide the context for organizational behaviour, allowing researchers, practitioners or consultants to describe, explain or even predict why some behaviours are more effective than others for a particular organization. Both concepts act as root metaphors or frames of reference for organizational analysis and focus on the importance of learned meanings through processes of learning and group interaction. Most of the recognized standardized instruments in the field assess the behavioural and value-driven facets of culture that may be *generalized across all organizations*, i.e. *psychological schema*, that are based on personal values. They tap *individual* or personal constructs, which may in the interests of organizational analysis be aggregated across organizations in order to reveal *conscious* and *shared perceptions* of the organization's standards and expectations for behaviour.

# TECHNICAL AND PSYCHOMETRIC PROTOCOLS FOR THE ASSESSMENT OF CLIMATE OR CULTURE

The first area of debate about assessment tools and techniques concerns standard psychometric protocols. Deep issues of validity go to the heart of most inventory-style data collection and there is no indisputable test of validity for culture or climate instruments. Within this first debate, there have in turn been two issues that have dominated discussion. What rules should be used to determine whether there is a collective climate? What are the most appropriate statistical protocols for assessment instruments to follow?

The aggregation issue revolves around the rules that should be used to determine whether there is a collective climate. Researchers agree that consensus among individual perceptions of the work setting must be demonstrated and tend to use the mean score to represent aspects of climate. Suggested criteria are that two-thirds of respondents should agree (Pace and Stern, 1958), or that there is a 90% level of agreement (Guion, 1973). The mathematical procedures that best represent underlying agreement and the validity of different forms of aggregation have been encapsulated in the debate between Jackofsky and Slocum (1988, 1990) and Payne (1990). A combination of inter-rater reliability with cluster analysis is used by Jackofsky and Slocum (1988, 1990) to identify climate dimensions, whilst Payne (1990) argues that a necessary precursor to any agglomerative methodology is the ability to explain membership in terms of some socio-psychological identity or structured collectivity.

What statistical measures are most appropriate for assessment? Climate researchers note that analysis of mean differences between organizations can obscure high levels of random variation on a dimension scale between and within organizations that may be due to other factors (Padmore et al., 1994). In an analysis of 56 organizational samples using BOCI, 35 complied with a strict set of rules to assess the level of internal consensus. Decisions have to be made about an acceptable level of agreement across climate scales (a criterion of $r = 0.70$ or above has been established as the accepted norm for agreement on intra-class correlations). Organizations typically use climate survey data to establish "culture-gaps", either between their own units or between their organization and others, at the level of climate scales. The level of agreement across individuals on their scores for separate climate scales therefore is an important issue. Rousseau (1990) has discussed the issue of consensual validity. Within-organization variation has to be less than between-organization variance, and within-unit variance has to be less than between-unit variance.

The choice of statistical measure is also important. Intra-class correlations control for the "elevation" effect. The consensus that is assessed is the *similarity of profile* across the different climate scales within a sample, *not the similarity of raw scores*. One individual may score a scale four whilst another scores it three. This does not affect consensus as long as both have placed the scale in the same relative position of importance. An organizational profile is deemed to display consensus if the sample of individuals within it rate the different climate scales in a sufficiently similar pattern, placing them in the same order of importance. Given that one individual's ranking of four on an item may represent the equivalent psychological perception of another individual's ranking of three, designing out systematic elevations such as this is a sensible procedure. It is essentially meaningless but would be treated as random variance if an alternative measure such as within-group inter-rater agreement ($r_{wg}$) was used.

There are, however, situations when a reliance on traditional psychometric criteria for the development of a culture or climate index does not make sense (Sparrow and Gaston, 1996). For example, inter-rater agreement across a scale does not necessarily indicate that a climate instrument is a useful instrument for comparing differences between organizational units. There are, and always will be, inherent problems in using raw data from any climate survey. They are not directly comparable since they reflect internal perceptions and judgements. One man's whole-hearted acceptance is another man's passing agreement. Systematic elevation effects may simply reflect individual response set or may truly reflect more negative or positive perceptions. Even where inter-rater reliability is demonstrated (by whatever mathematical technique) it is always in part a function of the sensitivity of the climate instrument. Extremely sensitive climate instruments would be expected to detect subtle sub-climates but in so doing will necessarily reduce inter-rater reliability. Conversely, high consensus across a random sample may simply reflect the fact that an insensitive set of questions has been asked. Everyone agrees or disagrees with the items because they are so obvious as to have no discriminative utility. Overall levels of inter-rater reliability of any climate survey database or levels of variation on scales within and across chosen units of analysis (in this case organizations) only provide an indication of the validity of climate surveys.

# PRACTICAL ASSESSMENT ISSUES

A number of practical assessment issues have been noted by Walker et al. (1996). They compared results from the administration of a qualitative and quantitative technique in the same organization. In practice there was considerable convergence between the findings of the qualitative and quantitative assessment methods. They were not interchangeable, and each had their particular strengths and weaknesses. The broad negative and positive perceptions of the organization were clearly reflected in both forms of assessment. The question was asked whether culture and climate instruments in fact just represent glorified attitude surveys? When expert raters categorized the statements generated by both the qualitative and quantitative methods it was clear that only surface level and more accessible elements of culture were being assessed.

The glorified attitude survey charge creates problems for the field of cultural assessment. Surface level assessments may be subject to broad perceptual framing. One of the issues noted by Walker et al. (1996) was that many of the quantitative scales adopted in instruments are themselves values-laden. For example, the Corporate Culture Questionnaire published by Saville and Holdsworth under the performance domain assesses dimensions such as concern for quality, customer orientation, and encouragement of creativity. The worry is that assessments might just pick up high level values-based judgements being made by employees rather than valid measurements on independent scales. Sparrow and Gaston (1996) examined whether this process could still result in the assessment of useful organizational attributes. They noted that in typical culture-gap analyses values-laden scale labels do indeed seem to create positive or negative response sets, such that organizations may be rated as all bad or all good by particularly disgruntled employees. However, organizational culture and climate instruments do still seem to possess a hidden benefit. This is the ability to assess, detect and reflect higher order perceptions (what Sparrow and Gaston called "climate maps") in which the ratees responses across all scales act as *overall metaphors* that describe the experience of living and working in the organization – rather than a collection of true scale measurements. Culture and climate inventories appear to reveal distinctive patterns of response which can be used to classify organizations. For example, cluster analysis of data from the BOCI revealed eight generic climate maps, reflecting three negative, one neutral and four positive variations of climate (Sparrow and Gaston, 1996). These were labelled as follows: endangered species; cope with the present but ignore the future; don't think it, don't say it and don't try it; social conscience; flexibility of thought and action; the future is quality, but you do it our way; isolated boffins; and have we really got a culture? The use of metaphors to aid the interpretation and classification of the revealed taxonomy supported the view that the climate and culture constructs captured in this study had much in common. Consequently, studies must be judged by their inclusiveness of data capture through multiple methods and the success with which they articulate "rich" and qualitative data in a meaningful form.

## DOMAIN RELEVANCE OF ASSESSMENT INSTRUMENTS?

The inclusiveness of capture issue raises a second major debate about assessment instruments. This concerns their domain relevance. A recent analysis of the domains used in several of the questionnaires listed above by DeWulf et al. (1999) found that nine primary domains or dimensions were being assessed, i.e. hierarchical relations, peer relations, relations between sub-groups, selection, socialization, reward, relations with clients, relations with competitors, and job design. The choice of these dimensions seemed to be implicit in the items rather than being driven by any coherent model of domain relevance. Most assessment items tended to be formulated at a general level so that they could not easily be attributed to these domains. The balance of items over these domains was also quite unequal. Hierarchical relations, rewards, job design and relations between sub-groups featured in relative order of the proportion of items dedicated to them. Given the sorts of applications to which assessments have been directed, noted above by Sparrow and Gaston (1996), i.e. design of reward systems, identification of competencies, and evaluation of organization designs, it is not surprising that the items noted by DeWulf et al. (1999) dominate quantitative assessment tools.

## DOES EMERGING EVIDENCE ON HIGH PERFORMANCE ORGANIZATIONAL CULTURES SUGGEST MORE APPROPRIATE ASSESSMENT DOMAINS?

The problem of a limited range in the assessment of perceptual domains noted above by Walker et al. (1996) suggests that we may still be developing inefficient assessment instruments. One way of tackling the domain issue is to focus assessments on those facets of culture that are associated with tangible benefits to organization, such as the delivery of high performance. We need to develop instruments that assess a more

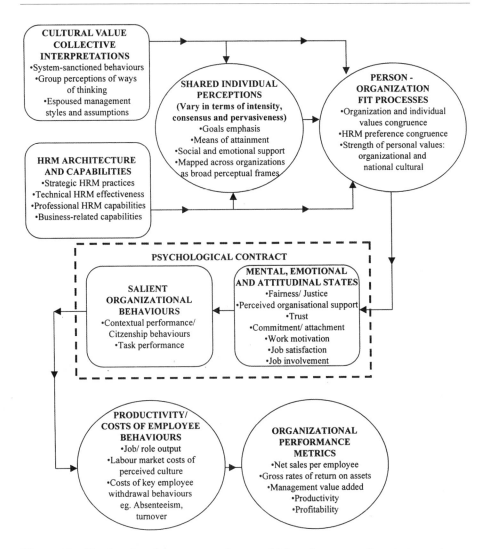

**Figure 4.1** The domains of assessment relevant to high performance culture instruments.

complete range of the causal factors that form part of the link between cultural values and organizational effectiveness, and have a clearer theoretical view as to why such domains should form important elements of assessment.

Until recently, however, the usefulness of the construct of culture has not been evidenced in the ultimate financial performance of organizations. Assessments have concentrated on yielding understanding about the organization as a human system (Schneider, 1990), not on prediction of outcomes. There is a difference between domains that are predictive of performance and domains that are useful for facilitating understanding. In the context of high performance, many of the scales useful for the broad agenda of understanding organizations prove to be redundant when applied to a narrower predictive situation.

In order to build a picture of the relevant domains, the following sections summarize some of the recent literatures that have a bearing on the culture–performance linkage process. The most relevant work concerns analyses of:

1. links between organizational values and performance;
2. links between organizational representations of culture, such as human resource management policies and practices, and organizational performance;
3. factors that are seen to cause important facets of the psychological contract and related domains such as commitment, satisfaction, justice, and organizational support.

# CAPTURING THE CULTURE/CLIMATE–ORGANIZATIONAL PERFORMANCE LINK

Focusing assessment instruments on performance-relevant domains requires an assessment of all those elements that are felt in some way to be causally related to organizational performance. However, an effective performance culture *is hard to emulate* because it is embedded in a complex set of links that operate all the way from the level of organizational culture through to eventual organizational performance. The creation of a generic set of values, perceptions and behaviours does not automatically lead to superior financial performance. The link may be destroyed at several important points. The design of cultural assessments must be guided by a model of the linkage process. Researchers must demonstrate that they understand how each of the links actually works, for two reasons:

1. It will help to establish the inherent validity of the diagnostic instrument.
2. By analyzing research that has examined the most important performance links, researchers can identify the most important items or artefacts to consider as evidence of a performance culture and also identify the questions to ask of an organization's culture.

The causal relationship, as best we know it, is shown in Figure 4.1. The elements in boxes represent the main domains or areas of assessment that should form part of a high performance diagnostic. The elements in circles are reflective of the processes that link these domains of assessment to each other. The model is based on research on the climate–performance link (Kopelman et al., 1990) and more recent work from the psychological contract literature (Guest, 1998) and the person–organization values fit literature (Vandenberghe and Peiró, 1999). These literatures are revealing important domains that lie at the heart of the culture–performance linkage process. The assessment of these domains should form a core of items in any instrument. In particular, the following sections argue that the shared individual perceptions of the HRM architecture and capabilities of the organization, and shared perceptions of the relevant mental, emotional and attitudinal states and salient organizational behaviours associated with the psychological contract, should form central assessment domains.

# THE CULTURAL VALUES–PERFORMANCE LINK

As argued in the section on culture versus climate assessments, any high performance diagnostic will necessarily tap and assess *perceptions* of the organizations' culture and climate. Values represent one of two fundamental starting points in the culture–climate–performance link. As a reflection of collective interpretations, cultural value assessments have to tap ways of perceiving, thinking and feeling (group understandings of appropriate problem solving), the norms, beliefs and justifying ideologies (the system-sanctioned behaviours), and the espoused management style and assumptions (the shared meanings). Which cultural values have been shown most clearly to be associated with superior organizational performance?

Kotter and Heskett (1992) draw attention to the original hypothesis that emerged from the attention given to the link between organizational culture and performance in the 1980s and early 1990s. This assumed that, regardless of the type of culture (which could be unique and suited to purpose), it was the *strength of culture* that was most predictive of performance. To the extent that all managers share relatively consistent values, then performance follows because of increased goal alignment, a stronger sense of motivation and intrinsic reward implicit in the "successful" cultures, and implicit controlling and sanctioning of appropriate behaviours without the need for expensive and stifling bureaucracy and co-ordination structures (Deal and Kennedy, 1982; Hofstede, 1980; Peters and Waterman, 1982; Schein, 1985).

This argument seemed to gather uncritical support from many senior managers at the time. Until recently, evidence for the influence of culture upon organizational productivity has been limited. However, the task of linking culture and climate to organizational performance has become more feasible due to the increasing weight of evidence that suggests there is a clearly identifiable high performance culture and climate. Organizations may therefore once again seek broad metaphors and methodologies to capture the phenomenon of change, adaptation and high performance. Two recent UK studies lend some support to the possibility of developing assessments for high performance organizational cultures. A 10 year longitudinal research programme by the Institute of Work Psychology at the University of Sheffield and the Centre for Economic Performance at the London School of Economics has examined the market environment, organizational characteristics and managerial practices that are empirically related to company financial performance of over 100 UK manufacturing companies (Patterson et al., 1998). Over half the companies participated in employee attitude and organizational culture surveys. These explore perceptions of organizational functioning in areas such as innovation, training, concern for employee welfare, performance pressure and formalization, and also measure some of the outcomes (job satisfaction and organizational commitment) that are assumed to facilitate the link to organizational performance. Given that the instrument measures "the aggregate of employees' perceptions of aspects of the organization" it strictly is measuring climate, not culture. It measures perceptions about the climate in terms of dimensions such as quality of communication, support for innovation, level of supervisory support, vision (the extent to which organizational members can clearly articulate the way forward), performance feedback (linking behaviour with goal setting and feedback) and reviewing objectives (the ability of the organization to review and change processes and procedures). It also includes items on manufacturing practices felt to be relevant to tapping manufacturing cultures, such as quality, a pressure to produce, and flexibility. An important guide to the work is the Competing Values Model by Quinn (1988), which emphasizes four sets of organizational values, each associated with effectiveness. The factor structure of these four quadrants has not yet been checked, but the validity of the constituent scales is apparently high. Some important findings have been reported based on an analysis of the link between employee ratings of organizational culture in 36 firms and their financial performance. Cultural factors accounted for some 10% of the variation in profitability between the two periods measured during the study. The results were even more striking in relation to change in productivity. When the results are examined in terms of predicting change in organizational performance, individual employee attitudes (commitment and job satisfaction) accounted for only 5% of the variation between companies. However, some 29% of the variation between companies in the change in productivity over a 3 or 4 year period could be explained by the measures of culture (Patterson et al., 1998). A very significant proportion of the change in productivity could be predicted by those cultural variables associated with rational goal and human relations values. However, it is important to note that out of 17 cultural scales, only *eight* were significantly related to performance. These were: Concern for employee welfare; Autonomy; Emphasis on training; Supervisory support; Vision; Emphasis on quality; Pressure to produce; and Performance feedback. Recent survey work by Guest (1998) for the Institute of Personnel and Development has also identified elements associated with high performance organizational climates. Analyzing data from 1997, they found that the most statistically important antecedents to an effective psychological contract were a culture or climate of high involvement, the operation of a large number of "high performance" HRM policies and practices (outlined later in this report), and the existence of flexible, autonomous job designs.

# THE HRM POLICY/PRACTICE–PERFORMANCE LINK

If cultural values have a strong impact on shared individual perceptions, then so too do the formal policies and practices. In particular, HRM policies and practices (which as noted above have formed a central topic in many climate survey assessment items) are linked to organizational performance by their ability to increase employee skills and abilities, promote positive attitudes and increase motivation, and provide employees with expanded responsibilities so that they can make full use of these skills and abilities (Patterson et al., 1998). The recent "black box" stream of research into the link between HRM policies and practices and organizational performance carries some useful messages for the design of high performance assessment instruments. The HRM policies, practices and philosophy help create an effective organizational culture at three levels of analysis (Becker and Gerhart, 1996):

- system characteristics and architecture, from which employees create their perceptions about the important guiding principles behind actual policies;
- policy alternatives that employees perceive are fitted (or not) with the organizational strategy, thereby reflecting a sense of coherence and alignment – this perception reinforces relevant behaviours that are seen to be linked with competitive success;
- the actual practices, which are perceived to reflect (or not) the best operations.

Assessment of perceptions of HRM policies and practices therefore has to tease out the underlying guiding principles and the sense of coherence and alignment with strategy. This assessment can be focused on those aspects of HRM policy and practice that are the most predictive of organizational performance. But what are they? An example of important system characteristics is seen in the research of Pfeffer (1994). He identified 16 characteristics that are associated with effective performance, each of which could form the basis of questionnaire items intended to elicit the perceived guiding principles of the organization: financial incentives for excellent performance; work organization practices that motivate effort and capture the benefits of competencies (know-how and skill); rigorous selection and selectivity in recruiting; higher than average wages; employee share ownership plans; extensive information sharing; decentralization of decision making and empowerment; work organization based on self-managed teams; high investment in training and skills development; having people do multiple jobs and job rotation; elimination of status symbols; more compressed distribution of salaries across and within levels; promotion from within; a long-term perspective; measurement of HR practices and policy implementation; and a coherent view of the employment relationship (psychological contract).

Another example of this kind of work is seen in the research of Huselid et al. (1997). They examined the relationship between organizational performance, the perceived quality of HRM in the organization, and the perceived capabilities of HRM staff in 293 US organizations. This work demonstrated a number of important findings:

1. Perceived effectiveness in strategic areas of HRM *was significantly related to financial measures of organizational performance*. Between 12 and 29% of variance in financial measures of performance was predicted by measures of perceived HRM effectiveness.
2. There are a number of areas of HRM in which the organization may be technically proficient, but which bear no relationship to organizational performance. These include things such as benefits and services, compensation, recruitment and training, safety and health, employee education and training, retirement strategies, employee/industrial relations, social responsibility programs, equal opportunities for females/minorities, management of labour costs, selection testing, performance appraisal, HR information systems, and assessment of employee attitudes. Whilst these areas are "nice to have", perceived effectiveness in these areas bore no relationship to financial measures of organizational performance.
3. There is considerable practical utility of having an effective HRM system architec-

ture. A one standard deviation increase in overall HRM effectiveness created a +5.2% increase in sales per employee, amounting to an increase in sales of $44 380 per employee.

The nine strategic areas of HRM that were associated with superior financial performance could serve as example policies or philosophies to be tapped in assessment items. The areas were: teamwork; employee participation and empowerment; workforce planning – flexibility and deployment; workforce productivity and quality of output; management and executive development; succession and development planning for managers; advance issue identification/strategic studies; employee and manager communications; and work/family programmes. The study by the Institute of Work Psychology (Patterson et al., 1998) also examined the link between "high performance work practices" and organizational performance and found two underlying "systems" of practices: acquisition and development of employee skills, i.e. selection, induction, training and use of appraisal; and job design, i.e. skill flexibility, job responsibility, job variety and use of formal teams. Scores across these two HRM systems were significant predictors of both change in profitability and change in productivity in the firms studied (19 and 18%, respectively).

Organizations then have *cultural values* and important *philosophies, policies and practices* that both send signals to employees about what behaviour is valued, and create the "architecture" through which effective behaviour is managed. Perceptions of these values and philosophies are learned over time. In terms of anticipated causal linkages, such specifications of both corporate values and effective HRM architecture are subsequently reflected in a number of important facets of the organizational climate. Historically the important shared individual perceptions have focused on the emphasis on achieving goals, provision of the means to do so and reward for doing so, support for the appropriate employee tasks, and a sense of social and emotional support of the employee's psychological contract (Kopelman et al., 1990). Any culture diagnostic must therefore be influenced by research into these three primary determinants of effective performance at the individual level.

## PERSON–ORGANIZATION FIT PERCEPTIONS

However, for the culture–climate–performance link to be effective, a series of important linkages must follow. It was noted in the introduction to this chapter that an effective culture and climate has to create *the mental, emotional and attitudinal states that precede effective employee performance*. The literature on perceptions of person–organization (P-O) fit provides the bridge through which shared individual perceptions of the climate are linked to the mental, emotional and attitudinal states associated with an effective culture. P-O fit processes need to feature in the assessments of culture. P-O fit is seen as the congruence between patterns of organizational values and patterns of what an individual values in the organization (Chatman, 1991). There is evidence to link perceptions of P-O fit to different forms of effectiveness. Congruence between individual and corporate values correlates significantly with job outcomes such as individual productivity, job satisfaction and commitment (O'Reilly et al., 1991). P-O fit across value orientations also contributes unique variance to job satisfaction, job involvement, organizational commitment, turnover intention and optimism about the organization's future (Harris and Mossholder, 1996). In a study of value profiles using the OCP, Vandenberghe (1999) found that recruits whose value profile is close to that of their employing organization were more likely to stay with it during the early employment period. Person–culture fit was linked to turnover versus staying decisions across the sample of Belgian health care organizations. However, the role of P-O fit in cultural assessments can be overstated. Vandenberghe and Peiró (1999) found that organizational values and individual value preferences were more predictive of outcomes such as commitment than was P-O value fit, which had a marginal impact. A study on the impact of cultural value orientations and P-O fit measures of HR preference and value fit in Kenyan employees on levels of job involvement similarly found that actual values were more predictive than values fit (Nyambegera et al., in press). Nonetheless, both actual values and P-O fit measures play a role in predicting appropriate mental, emotional and attitudinal states.

# THE ASSESSMENT OF MENTAL, EMOTIONAL AND ATTITUDINAL STATES AND SALIENT ORGANIZATIONAL BEHAVIOURS

There are a series of mental, emotional and attitudinal processes through which salient organizational behaviours linked to an effective culture have been shown to influence performance. The most important of the mental, emotional and attitudinal states are trust and an effective psychological contract, perceived level of organizational support, fairness and justice, work motivation, job satisfaction and job involvement. Organizational culture is clearly incorporated in people's psychological contracts (De Witte and van Muijen, 1999), which once developed is relatively stable. Hence, people are attracted to specific organizational cultures. Culture here acts as a stabilizer of individual behaviour. Once these mental, emotional and attitudinal states are established in a positive direction, *then*employees begin to exhibit a series of salient organizational behaviours, i.e. the behaviours that actually generate effective performance.

The moment a link is made between organizational culture and the psychological contract then the problem of maintaining a clear boundary between assessments of culture and climate and assessments of other psychological outcomes emerges. Few would argue that climate instruments should tap shared perceptions of constructs such as trust, fairness, involvement, commitment, and citizenship behaviours. Indeed, many organizations are using changes in work system design and business process to modify employee's work orientations and responsibilities and therefore the extent to which these sorts of mental, emotional and attitudinal states are seen as discretionary, or an inherent part of the job and organizational life (Coyle-Shapiro, 1999). Their assessment could be argued for on pragmatic grounds, let alone theoretical grounds of explaining the culture–performance link. However, when these base constructs are considered, the whole field is riddled with arguments about what should form separate domains of assessment, and what are the causal linkages between these domains. If psychologists cannot agree how to measure trust, commitment, citizenship and so forth, then measuring the shared perceptions of such constructs is even harder. However, some guidance can be given in these areas. It is not suggested that cultural assessments should include all the mental, emotional and attitudinal states that are related to performance outcomes, but shared individual perceptions of the most pertinent causal elements should surely be incorporated.

Of these elements the level of organization citizenship behaviours (OCBs) – also referred to as contextual performance – has emerged recently as an important linking mechanism. It has been linked to the level of cultural values fit and therefore represents a domain that high performance culture diagnostics should tap. OCBs became important as a possible explanation for the satisfaction–performance relationship. Contextual performance plays an important part in linking individual task performance to the broader organizational and social demands (Borman and Motovidlo, 1993, 1997). Perceptions of the OCB climate can therefore tap an important aspect of culture. It is rarely job specific, and tends to be shared across several jobs in an organization. It shapes the individual environment, is linked to organizational effectiveness, and is in turn a product of organizational culture (Allen and Rush, 1998). The recipients of OCBs may also be interpersonal or organizational. A distinction can also be made between OCBs that are seen as part of the job and accepted role requirement, or as a personal choice and therefore part of a reciprocal social exchange (Coyle-Shapiro, 1999). In fact, the job satisfaction–OCB link may in fact be due to the underpinning notion of fairness or justice, given that job satisfaction is a judgement about met and unmet expectations. Justice has been seen as a direct precursor of OCBs (Konovsky and Pugh, 1994), as has the level of perceived organizational support (Wayne et al., 1997) and commitment (as a form of emotional attachment) (Meyer and Allen, 1997; Pond et al., 1997).

The need to incorporate elements from this domain can also be seen because values – an important element of culture – are also an important determinant of contextual performance. For example, in a study of over 200 manufacturing employees, Goodman and Svyantek (1999) measured the impact that both perceived and ideal culture (as measured by the CCQ and Organizational Climate Questionnaire) had on contextual performance. The perceived culture (what the individual valued) accounted for a significant amount of performance, and the ideal culture accounted for a significant proportion of additional variance. Warmth, competence, reward, risk, standards, identity, customer and decision making accounted for the majority of the variance in performance. In line with the person–organization literature in general, P-O fit discrepancies accounted for from 2 to 6% of the variance in total contextual performance and task performance was also linked to P-O fit. In fact research has linked organizational value systems to a number of psychological outcomes associated with effectiveness. For example, a 6 year longitudinal study of organizational value systems showed that cultures emphasizing interpersonal relationships were more likely to produce lower staff turnover rates than other cultures (Sheridan, 1992), satisfaction-orientated norms are positively related to role clarity, personal satisfaction with the organization and intention to stay, whilst security-orientated norms are negatively related to these outcomes (Rousseau, 1990).

Finally, in a recent examination of some of the complex causation issues across these constructs, Coyle-Shapiro and Kessler (in press) drew attention to the role of perceived organizational support (a general perception by the employee of the extent to which the organization values their general contribution and well-being and an important element of many assessments of climate) and the subsequent fulfilment of obligations. Two questions were asked. Does perceived organizational support mediate the impact that the fulfilment of obligations and promises has on important psychological outcomes? Does the psychological contract account for useful additional variance in outcome behaviours? Survey data from 703 managers and 6953 employees of a British public sector local authority found that high levels of perceived breach of contract (89% felt that their employer had fallen short of valued transactional obligations and 81% felt it had fallen short of valued relational obligations) and psychological contract fulfilment did indeed account for unique and additional variance in explaining levels of commitment and organizational citizenship behaviour (OCBs).

## CONCLUSIONS

It has been argued that the assessment of high performance cultures requires a more balanced range of evidence. More attention should be given to items that tap the most predictive cultural values and the collective interpretations of system-sanctioned behaviours, ways of thinking and espoused management style that they generate. We can also direct assessment towards the appropriate aspects of the HRM architecture and capabilities, and the perception of relevant behaviours that can be seen from the guiding principles behind the systems architecture and policy alternatives. The person–organization fit perspective has also highlighted several important elements of the psychological contract that should be assessed at the shared individual perception level. These assessments should provide better insight into the mental, emotional and attitudinal states of fairness/justice, perceived organizational support, trust, motivation, satisfaction and involvement that result from assessments of person–organization fit, as well as the salient organization behaviours of commitment/attachment and contextual performance/organization citizenship behaviours.

The review of the evidence suggests that the development of a diagnostic for high performance organization cultures and climates is both a technically possible and scientifically defensible proposition. There is increasing confidence in the concept of high performance cultures. However, the assessment technologies that we have adopted have tended to be rather narrow in focus, both in terms of the limited domains of organizational attributes and individual sense making that they capture, and the limited range of methodologies employed. That said, it is important to appreciate that the search for high performance cultures is about prediction, whereas most assessment techniques are concerned with facilitating understanding. It inevitably represents a reductionist approach, seeking assessment instruments that can tap the most accessible sources of measurement and prediction. The advantage of such an approach, however, is that the search for relevant domains concentrates the mind and frees it from the often imponderable set of questions that most discussions of culture and climate tend to raise.

Moreover, a fair amount is now known about the organizational culture and climate dimensions that distinguish between organizations, based on the research in the late 1980s and early 1990s.

The pursuit of high performance culture diagnostics of course side-steps the agenda raised by those who seek assessments that broaden understanding, rather than just improve prediction. Subsequent chapters engage the arguments about quantitative versus qualitative forms of assessment, along with the need to assess and not just to predict. Indeed, MacKenzie Davey and Symon (this section) point out that the subjective qualitative nature of organization culture stands in stark contrast with the more unitary functionalist cultures deemed relevant for organizational performance. Culture is seen as a process, not an attribute, and therefore not amenable to diagnostic categorization. Payne (this section) also notes that shared individual perceptions result in climates that vary in intensity, consensus and pervasiveness. Sackmann (this section) uses the concept of cultural complexity to capture this perspective. Clearly, there is a need for more sophisticated HR strategies given the varying results across these three attributes. High performance cultures imply a change from fragmented to integrated or intense dimensions. Indeed, Payne has highlighted the different focuses of personnel management needed to create intensity, consensus and pervasiveness. He gives us a process perspective on cultural change, positioning assessment techniques merely as a tool to track and position any organizational unit at a point in time and space.

This chapter has used a culture–performance process perspective to highlight ways in which assessment instruments could be designed to tap into more appropriate domains. However, in taking the more functionalist and positivist perspective of high performance culture research, it is important to stress that this form of assessment need not be limited to quantitative methodologies. Qualitative tools and techniques can sit just as easily in a consultant's toolkit, even if they are harder to market and sell. The quantitative tools that fit most easily into a high performance perspective are those that examine organizational level attributes such as structure and function. Incorporating evidence from more qualitatively assessed processes of individual level sense making of cultures is not something that has featured strongly in the practitioner world. Yet this incorporation and capture of the linking processes (that flow from hard organizational artefact, through immediate perceptual processes and attitudinal responses, into deeper mental paradigms and individual cognitive schema, and then judgements and evaluation-linked outcome behaviours) must surely be a useful way of designing cultural assessment processes with better predictive validity? There must be room for culture and climate diagnostics, informed by richer – and in some instances more qualitative – investigation, that tap the most relevant individual sense making processes.

One last point to make about our methods of cultural assessment, driven by the debates initiated in the preceding chapters, is that we should perhaps question the design and development processes that lie behind the current stock of assessment tools. By starting with an assumption that cultures must be all about collective constructs, and then attempting to develop instruments that be given to individuals in order to capture this collectivity, are we really designing out much of the real representation of cultures? There has been a theoretical shift in culture research that has broadened our conceptualization of organizational effectiveness. We have moved away from a concentration on the assessment of the most accessible outcomes of culture – the collective values, attitudes, perceptions and behaviours of people – as a primary source of assessment evidence. Instead we seem to be moving towards a greater emphasis on eliciting the logics and pervasive influence that broad organizational attributes have on individual sense making. In the modern complex, ambiguous and uncertain world in which we live there seem no longer to be single truths (or in cultural terms implicit effective problem solving strategies), but rather multiple realities, multiple perspectives and economies of truth. Concentrating cultural assessments only on collectively shared sources of evidence, and then inferring culture, seems to be a reverse way of tackling the problem. These days, it might make more sense to get a valid assessment of individual realities as the primary source of data and assessment, and then use data interpretation strategies to reconstruct any collectivities that remain.

Finally, it is always valuable to look at other fields of enquiry and to see if the ideas and problems being experienced in one area provide some guidance for another. If we look at the range of work being conducted on organizational effectiveness – of which culture and climate research is one subset – some ways of improving assessment methodologies can be considered. For example, qualitative methods such as repertory grid and critical incidents have not featured much in published studies of high performance cultures and organizational effectiveness, and yet they have been at the heart of behavioural event investigation approaches to the assessment and specification of individual competencies associated with organizational effectiveness. They have also been one of the ways in which the influences of organizational culture on requisite employee behaviour have been captured. Competency assessment techniques have long attempted to interpret the types of behaviour appropriate for specific types of organizational performance by capturing processes of organizational learning and individual sense making. In competency analysis methodologies, assessment techniques have to capture the categorization constructs that represent the construct of "effectiveness" that are both generated by, and make sense to, individuals (Boam and Sparrow, 1992). These are then converted into statements about shared beliefs and assumptions of the organization, or indeed used to challenge such assumptions. Critical incident technique methods can be made relevant to the assessment of cultural effectiveness through their elicitation of inappropriate behaviours, hidden agendas, implicit psychological contracts, and effective problem solutions. The performance criterion adopted to allow respondents to elicit incidents can be manipulated to generate events and stories representative of the organizational culture. Organizations and consultancies have managed the tensions and vagueness than can be created by such data by triangulating bottom-up individually generated data with top-down approaches to creating a picture of effectiveness, such as functional or business process analysis, corporate values questionnaires, and expert team judgements. When we focus on the culture and climate dimension of effectiveness we need not allow the ease and simplicity of collecting data using perception-based quantitative scales (with the concomitant statistical hurdles associated with creating appropriate measurement) to dominate the design of assessment tools and techniques.

# REFERENCES

Alexander, M. (1978) Organizational Norms Opinionnaire. In J.W. Pfeiffer and J.E. Jones (Eds), The 1978 Annual Handbook for Group Facilitators. La Jolla, CA: University Associates.

Allen, T.D. & Rush, M.C. (1998) The effects of organizational citizenship behaviour on performance judgements: a field study and laboratory experiment. Journal of Applied Psychology, 83, 247–260.

Becker, B. and Gerhart, B. (1996) The impact of HRM on organizational performance: progress and prospects. Academy of Management Journal, 39(4): 779–803.

Boam, R. and Sparrow, P.R. (1992) Designing and Achieving Organizational Competency. London: McGraw-Hill.

Borman, W.C. and Motovidlo, S.J. (1993) Expanding the criterion domain to include elements of contextual performance. In N. Schmitt, W.C. Borman et al. (Eds), Personnel Selection in Organizations. San Francisco, CA: Jossey-Bass.

Borman, W.C. and Motovidlo, S.J. (1997) Task performance and contextual performance: the meaning for personnel selection research. Human Performance, 10: 99–109.

Cameron, K. (1980) Critical questions in assessing organizational effectiveness. Organizational Dynamics, 8(3): 66–80.

Chatman, J.A. (1991) Matching people and organizations: selection and socialization in public accounting firms. Administrative Science Quarterly, 36: 459–484.

Coyle-Shapiro, J.A.-M. (1999) TQM and organizational change: a longitudinal study of the impact of a TQM intervention on work attitudes. In W.A. Pasmore and R.W. Woodman (Eds), Research on Organizational Change and Development, Vol. 12. Greenwich, CT: JAI Press.

Coyle-Shapiro, J.A.-M. and Kessler, I. (in press) Consequences of the psychological contract for the employment relationship: a large scale survey. The Journal of Management Studies.

Deal, T. and Kennedy, A. (1982) Corporate Cultures. Reading, MA: Addison-Wesley.

De Witte, K. and De Cock, G. (1988) Strategic human resources management and organizational culture. Working paper, Centrum voor Organisetie en Personeelspsychologie, Katholieke Universiteit, Leuven.

De Witte, K. and van Muijen, J.J. (1999) Organizational culture: critical questions for researchers and practitioners. European Journal of Work and Organizational Psychology, 8(4): 583–595.

DeWulf, A., Poortinga, Y., Fontaine, J., De Witte, K. and Swinnen, M. (1999) Facetten van organisatiecultuur. Een systematische analyse van het concept, geconfronteerd met vragenlijsitems. Unpublished licentiate dissertation, Faculty of Psychology and Pedagogical Sciences, Leuven, Catholic University of Leuven, Belgium.

Goodman, S.A. and Svyantek, D.J. (1999) Person-organization fit and contextual performance: do shared values matter? Journal of Vocational Behaviour, 55: 254–275.

Guest, D.E. (1998) Is the psychological contract worth taking seriously? Journal of Organizational Behaviour, 19(Special Issue): 649–664.

Guion, R.M. (1973) A note on organizational climate. Organizational Behaviour and Human Performance, 9: 120–125.

Harris, S.G. and Mossholder, K.W. (1996) The affective implications of perceived congruence with culture dimensions during organizational transformation. Journal of Management, 22: 527–547.

Harrison, R. (1975) Diagnosing organization ideology. In J.E. Jones and J.W. Pfeiffer (Eds), The 1975 Annual Handbook for Group Facilitators. La Jolla, CA: University Associates.

Hofstede, G. (1980) Culture's Consequences. Beverly Hills, CA: Sage.

Huselid, M., Jackson, S. and Schuler, R.S. (1997) Technical and strategic HRM effectiveness as determinants of firm performance. Academy of Management Journal, 49(1): 171–188.

Jackofsky, E.F. and Slocum, J.L. (1988) A longitudinal study of climates. Journal of Organizational Behaviour, 9: 319–334.

Jackofsky, E.F. and Slocum, J.L. (1990) Rejoinder to Payne's comment on 'A longitudinal study of climates'. Journal of Organizational Behaviour, 11: 81–83.

Kilmann, R.H. (1984) Beyond the Quick Fix. San Francisco, CA, Jossey-Bass.

Konovsky, M.A. and Pugh, S.D. (1994) Citizenship and social exchange. Academy of Management Journal, 37: 656–669.

Kopelman, R., Brief, A. and Guzzo, R. (1990) The role of climate and culture in productivity. In B. Schneider (Ed), Organizational Climate and Culture. San Francisco, CA: Jossey-Bass.

Kotter, J. and Heskett, J.L. (1992) Corporate Culture and Performance. New York: Free Press.

Lawthom, R., Patterson, M., West, M.A. and Maitliss, S. (1997) Development of the Organizational Culture Measure – a New Measure of Organizational Culture. Sheffield: Institute of Work Psychology, University of Sheffield.

Litwin, G. and Stringer, R. (1968) Motivation and Organizational Climate. Boston, MA: Harvard University.

Meyer, J.P. and Allen, N.J. (1997) Commitment in the Workplace: Theory, Research and Application. Thousand Oaks, CA: Sage.

Nyambegera, S., Daniels, K. and Sparrow, P.R. (in press) Why fit doesn't always matter: the impact of HRM and cultural fit on job involvement of Kenyan employees. Applied Psychology: an International Review.

O'Reilly, C., Chatman, J. and Caldwell, D.F. (1991) People and organizational culture: a profile comparison approach to assessing person-organization fit. Academy of Management Journal, 34: 487–516.

Ott, S. (1989) The Organizational Culture Perspective. Pacific Grove, CA: Brooks/Cole.

Pace, C.R. and Stern, G.C. (1958) An approach to the measurement of the psychological characteristics of college environments. Journal of Educational Psychology, 49: 269–277.

Padmore, J., Gaston, K. and Payne, R. (1994) A pragmatic approach to the problem of aggregation in organizational climate research. Unpublished departmental paper, University of Sheffield Management School, Sheffield.

Patterson, M., West, M.A., Lawthom, R. and Nickell, S. (1998) Impact of people management practices on business performance. Issues in People Management Report No. 22. London: Institute of Personnel and Development.

Payne, R.L. (1990) Madness in our method: a comment on Jackofsky and Slocum's paper 'A longitudinal study of climates'. Journal of Organizational Behaviour, 11: 77–80.

Payne, R.L. (1991) Taking stock of corporate culture. Personnel Management, 23(7): 26–29.

Payne, R.L. and Pheysey, D. (1971) G.C. Stern's organizational climate index: a reconceptualization and application to business organizations. Organizational Behaviour and Human Performance, 6: 77–98.

Payne, R.L., Brown, A.D. and Gaston, K.C. (1992) Reliability and validity of an updated version of the Business Organization Climate Index (BOCI): a research note. Manchester Business School Working paper no. 227, Manchester University, Manchester.

Peters, T. and Waterman, R. (1982) In Search of Excellence. New York: Harper Row.

Pettigrew, A.M. (1979) On studying organizational cultures. Administrative Science Quarterly, 24(4): 570–581.

Pfeffer, J. (1994) Competitive Advantage Through People. Boston, MA: Harvard Business Press.

Pond, S.B., Nacoste, R.W., Mohr, M.F. and Rodriguez, C.M. (1997) The measurement of organizational citizenship behaviour: are we assuming too much? Journal of Applied Social Psychology, 27: 1527–1544.

Quinn, R. (1988) Beyond Rational Management: Mastering the Paradoxes and Competing Demands of High Performance. San Francisco, CA: Jossey-Bass.

Reichers, A.E. and Schneider, B. (1990) Climate and culture: an evolution of constructs. In B. Schneider (Ed), Organizational Climate and Culture. Oxford: Jossey-Bass.

Rousseau, D.M. (1990) Assessing organizational culture: the case for multiple methods. In B. Schneider (Ed), Organizational Climate and Culture. San Francisco, CA: Jossey-Bass.

Ruigrok, W. and Achtenhagen, L. (1999) Organizational culture and the transformation towards new forms of organizing. European Journal of Work and Organizational Psychology, 8(4): 521–536.

Ruigrok, W., Pettigrew, A., Peck, S. and Whittington, R. (1999) Corporate restructuring and new forms of organising: evidence from Europe. Management International Review, 39(2): 41–64.

Schein, E.H. (1985) Organizational Culture and Leadership. San Francisco, CA: Jossey-Bass.

Schneider, B. (Ed) (1990) Organizational Climate and Culture. Oxford: Jossey-Bass.

Sheridan, J.E. (1992) Organizational culture and employee retention. Academy of Management Journal, 35: 1036–1056.

Sparrow, P.R. (1994) The psychology of strategic management: emerging themes of diversity and managerial cognition. In C. Cooper and I. Robertson (Eds), International Review of Industrial and Organizational Psychology, Vol. 9. Chichester: Wiley.

Sparrow, P.R. and Gaston, K. (1996) Generic climate maps: a strategic application of climate survey data? Journal of Organizational Behaviour, 17(6): 631–651.

Vandenberghe, C. (1999) Organizational culture, person-culture fit, and turnover: a replication in the health care industry. Journal of Organizational Behaviour, 20: 175–184.

Vandenberghe, C. and Peiró, J.M. (1999) Organizational and individual values: their main and combined effects on work attitudes and perceptions. European Journal of Work and Organizational Psychology, 8(4): 569–581.

van Muijen, J.J., Koopman, P.L. and De-Witte, K. (1996) FOCUS op Organisatiecultuur. Schoonhoven: Academic Service.

Walker, H., Symon, G. and Davies, B. (1996) Assessing organizational culture: a comparison of methods. International Journal of Selection and Assessment, 4(2): 96–105.

Wayne, S.J., Shore, L.M. and Liden, R.C. (1997) Perceived organizational support and leader-member exchange: a social exchange perspective. Academy of Management Journal, 40: 82–111.

# Chapter 5

# A Three Dimensional Framework for Analyzing and Assessing Culture/Climate and its Relevance to Cultural Change

**Roy L. Payne**
*Curtin University of Technology, School of Psychology,*
*Perth, Australia*

## INTRODUCTION: THE NEED TO CAPTURE THE INTEGRATION, DIFFERENTIATION AND PSYCHOLOGICAL INTENSITY OF CULTURES

In attempting to answer the question, "Organizational culture and organizational climate – how close can they get?" (Payne, 1999), I developed a three dimensional framework for describing cultures. This framework appears in Figure 5.1. The framework was developed to help deal with the issue of the strength of the culture, because in most writings on culture it is implicit that the culture is a strong culture, but it is obvious enough that cultures also vary in strength. Indeed, when managers or organizational theorists relate culture to organizational performance it is explicit that the link to performance is based on a strong and distinctive culture. Kotter and Heskett (1992) have shown a link between the strength of culture and organizational performance. They measured the strength of the culture by asking managers to:

> Please rate firms competing in your industry (5 point scale) on the degree to which you feel their managers have been influenced in their decision-making by a strong culture.

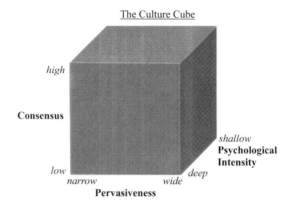

**Figure 5.1**  The culture cube.

1. To what extent have managers in competing firms commonly spoken of company name, "style" or way of doing things.
2. To what extent have managers in competing firms made the firms values known through a creed or credo and made a serious attempt to encourage managers to follow them.
3. To what extent have the firms been managed according to long-standing policies and practices other than those of just the incumbent CEO.


The ratings of the firms on strength of culture were then related to Return on Average Investment, and Net Income Growth for the years 1977–1988. There were moderately strong relationships for both performance indicators.

Denison (1990) measured strength of climate in 11 insurance companies and found that assets growth and premiums growth were both moderately strongly correlated with strength of climate for the next 3 years but the correlations weakened considerably thereafter.

One of the key assumptions about cultural strength is the idea that most of the people in the organization have absorbed the culture and behave in accordance with its beliefs and values. Thus, one of the dimensions in the model is concerned with the strength of consensus. This assumption of high consensus is labelled by Martin (1995) as, the Integration Perspective. In this perspective, if there is not high consensus, then there is no culture. In anthropological descriptions of cultures it is implicit that most of the people would see the culture the way the anthropologist has described it, because it is the people who have given the anthropologist the description through their words, behaviours and artefacts. In studies of organizational cultures through the use of climate questionnaires consensus has been measured by using statistical methods to assess the degree of agreement amongst individuals in the way they perceive the organizational climate. This has not been done so much to measure the strength of consensus itself but more to see if there is enough agreement to justify using the mean score on a climate scale as an accurate description of the climate. One of the earliest measures of climate in schools and colleges was developed by Pace and Stern (1958) who only attributed a quality to the organization if more than 66% of the population/ sample endorsed the existence of the quality. Guion (1973) argued that 90% endorsement would be more appropriate. The problem with doing this is that organizations then vary in the number of qualities attributed to them which makes comparative studies more difficult. Consequently the mean score became the preferred statistic. There have been debates about which measure of consensus is the most appropriate and what is an acceptable level of agreement to define consensus but studies still appear in the literature which ignore the level even when it is lower than recommended (Payne, 1997). In a study of perceived climate in 332 educational colleges Zammuto and Krakower (1991) found that only 25% of them had a high enough level of consensus to reach the recommended level of agreement. This study was only assessing climate as perceived by senior people, where one would have expected that it would be easier to obtain consensus.

The difficulty of obtaining high levels of consensus in large, complex organizations led to an interest in searching for clusters of people within the organization that did agree on what the climate is like. These studies used cluster analysis to identify such groups of people and some studies have been able to find them (Gonzalez-Roma et al., 1999; Jackofsky and Slocum, 1988) and others have not (Patterson et al., 1996). I have argued that even if such clusters are identified they can only be treated as psycho-socially meaningful if they have some other identifiable reason to be treated as such. Examples of such psycho-social meaning include being in the same department, or level of the organization, or all belonging to some identifiable clique (Payne, 1990). Again, some studies have found meaningful clusters, such as in the first phase of the Jackofsky and Slocum study where there was a strong departmental identity, and in the Gonzalez-Roma et al. study where there was a hierarchical level clustering effect, but no effect by department, shift, job location or organizational tenure. The existence of such clusters of people with common views of the climate suggests the existence of subcultures in the organization and Martin (1995) argues that this is such a common finding in organizations that it justifies a view of culture in its own right. She calls this the Differentiated Perspective.

Such a perspective assumes that people from different functions (finance, marketing, R&D, production, sales, etc.) will develop different sets of values and norms because they are trying to do different things, they face different environmental conditions, and they have different educational/professional backgrounds which shape the cultures they create. The differences by level within some of these will lead to subcultures within the functions themselves. Large production departments often contain people with very different levels of education and skill associated with differences in socio-economic status which themselves lead to differing sets of values and norms of behaviour. This implies, of course, that there are degrees of differentiation. Nobody has systematically compared organizational cultures/climates on such a dimension as far as I know, though the Aston group's measures of specialization and decentralization have been used to measure structural differentiation (Pugh et al., 1968).

The Differentiation Perspective still assumes that within the subcultures there is a level of integration. Some organizational culture theorists (March and Olsen, 1976;

Starbuck, 1983; Weick, 1969) have argued that a high level of integration is a rare event, because individuals are largely pursuing their own agendas, that change within the organization and its environment is continually disrupting relationships, and that these ambiguous conditions create anarchical relationships that prevent the formation of integrated subgroups. This view of organizational cultures is called the Fragmented Perspective (Martin, 1995). The main point of this chapter is to illustrate why the degree of cultural integration, and consensus in particular, is a major dimension of the culture cube and to raise the question – what does variation in integration imply for the management of cultural change? Before tackling this, however, it is necessary to describe the other two dimensions of the culture cube.

The horizontal dimension in the cube (Figure 5.1) is named Pervasiveness to indicate the range of behaviours and beliefs that the culture imposes on its members. Some organizations attempt to influence a wide range of these. Priests in the Catholic Church have to conform to standards of dress, interpersonal relations (celibacy), rituals, beliefs and norms of behaviour which relate to virtually everything they do. Military and paramilitary organizations control more of these than do business organizations, but some business organizations impose standards of dress and behaviour more tightly than do others (Apple Computers versus IBM in the 1970s). Tribal cultures control a greater range of behaviours and beliefs than do large democratic cultures. Whilst this is obvious enough it is not an aspect of culture that has been systematically studied in organizational culture research. The cube indicates that a culture will be stronger where its influence on members of the culture is pervasive.

The final dimension of the culture cube is labelled Psychological Intensity. This is conceived as a dimension ranging from attitudes, through behaviour, through values to what Schein (1985) calls "taken-for-granted assumptions" or unconscious beliefs. Where people are operating on the basis of the taken-for-granted assumptions then it follows that their values, behaviours and attitudes will be consistent with the taken-for-granted assumptions. Again, religious organizations and cults are examples of organizational cultures that create this level of intensity in their members. Weaker cultures strive to influence attitudes and behaviours and often succeed in doing both, though the link between attitudes and behaviour is by no means perfect (Ajzen and Fishbein, 1980). It becomes harder to influence values but organizations clearly strive to do this and often succeed. The link between values and behaviour is usually stronger than the attitude–behaviour link. Many organizations will be happy to have people behave according to their requirements and not worry too much if people do not also espouse congruent values, though organizational leaders will probably require them to at least express *attitudes* to customers which are consistent with the organization's expressed values. Many employees conform behaviourally without accepting the values or attitudes of the organization qua organization.

In terms of the culture cube the Integrated Perspective on culture would clearly place such organizations in the top right part of the cube. Most people agree (high consensus) with the values and assumptions that the organizational culture promotes (strong psychological intensity) and the beliefs and behaviours cover a relatively wide range of areas of conduct (wide pervasiveness). An organization representing the Differentiated Perspective would be located in the central area of the cube. There would be less

**Table 5.1** Cultural types and cultural change processes[a]

| | Integrated paradigm | Differentiated paradigm | Fragmented paradigm |
|---|---|---|---|
| Degree of consistency | High consistency | Consistency and inconsistency | Lack of consistency/ clarity: irreconcilable inconsistencies |
| Degree of consensus | Organization-wide | Within, not between, subcultures | Issue-specific consensus and much confusion |
| Reaction to ambiguity | Denial | Channelling | Acceptance |
| Nature of change process | Revolutionary | Incremental | Continual |
| Scope of change | Organization-wide | Localized and loosely coupled | Issue-specific change among individuals |
| Source of change | Often leader-centred | Internal and external | Individual adjustments |
| Implications for managing change | If superficial then controllable. If deep then difficult | Predictable and unpredictable sources and consequences | Relatively uncontrollable due to being continual |

[a] Based on Meyerson and Martin (1987).

consensus because different parts of the organization would be pursuing different goals and under different sets of assumptions. This would mean that there is a lower level of pervasiveness as each part manages its own more limited boundaries. Within each subculture the intensity might still be quite deep, but in relating to other parts of the organization the focus would be more on behaviours than values so the psychological intensity overall would be lower. Cultures consistent with the Fragmented Perspective would probably be quite pervasive in the range of beliefs and behaviours they produce as individuals pursue their own ends rather than those of the collective. There would be low consensus, however, and relatively weak psychological intensity with a concern for current behaviours and attitudes rather than long-term values. The exception would be the deeply held assumption that "ambiguity rules". It is worth a note of caution in discussing the Fragmented culture. The examples of such cultures quoted by Meyerson and Martin (1987) are of organizations such as classrooms, R&D laboratories and innovative industries. Whilst one can accept that ambiguity may exist around the tasks of such groups none of them appear to be wildly different in other areas of behaviour such as in the way they treat people, the way they dress and talk, the rewards they get from their employment, etc. Just how fragmented such organizations are seems questionable. Within the cube framework this can be explained as applying to a rather limited range of beliefs and behaviours (low pervasiveness). The broader society in which the organizations are located influences a much wider range of beliefs and behaviours and there is a reasonably strong consensus about those. This consensus enables the society to function, and also gives people the scope to be individualistic within a prescribed area of activity.

# CULTURE PARADIGMS AND CULTURE CHANGE

Meyerson and Martin (1987) have already asked questions about change processes in these three different organizational cultures. Table 5.1 summarizes their conjectures and is based on two of their tables that have been slightly modified.

As can be seen from Table 5.1, Meyerson and Martin (1987) propose that to change an Integrated culture there must be a revolution that is organization-wide and usually led by a cultural champion or leader. The revolution must be strong enough to change a culture that is psychologically intense and widely held by the members of the organization. The new culture must be powerful enough and attractive enough to also function at that level of intensity. As Schon (1971) observed, many cultures are characterized by "dynamic conservatism" and strive like mad to stay the way they are. Cultural change on this scale is difficult to achieve. Failure may leave the organization in a state more like that of the Differentiation Perspective. As Table 5.1 shows change for Differentiated cultures is more incremental, more patchy in its occurrence, and open to the influence of outside forces as well as forces from within. Change here is less "managed" than "coped with" as each part of the organization strives to preserve its influence and integrity. Subsections collaborate with other sections to protect themselves rather than ensure the success of the total enterprise, but the collaboration is usually effective enough to ensure survival. In the Fragmented culture both the internal and external environments are so high on ambiguity that continuous adjustment is the norm. Change is so common that it is hard to observe it because there is so little stability to provide the contrast that would enable one to see change. The sources of change are issue-specific and largely driven by individuals and small groups of temporary collaborators. Change is not managed or coped with, it is a way of being.

Having described and contrasted these three "paradigms" the authors themselves make a sort of paradigm shift by using them as a way of seeing the world rather than classifying it. Any organization, they claim, should be seen from each of the three perspectives, for if one views cultures from only one perspective, then one becomes blind to other things that are happening within it: "...It is crucially important, for full understanding, to view any one organizational setting from all three paradigmatic viewpoints. This three paradigm perspective draws attention to those aspects of cultural change that are, and more importantly perhaps, are not amenable to managerial control." (Meyerson and Martin, 1987, p. 643).

If this is the case then it becomes relevant to search for tools/procedures that help the researcher/change agent/manager to look for the presence of these three sorts of cultural phenomena. Meyerson and Martin (1987) themselves highlight the difficulty of three paradigm vision. In a very insightful article called "The Three Faces of Eden", Edmonson (1996) explicates the difficulties of analyzing organizations by contrasting the approaches of Schein (1985), Argyris (1982) and Senge (1990). She shows how their different conceptual frameworks produce different diagnoses for the organization and hence different change strategies. Certainly, the in-depth approaches of all three are useful tools for analyzing complex cultures and helping the people in them to change the cultures they have created, but whether trying to integrate them would provide a clearer picture of a culture and how to change it is yet to be demonstrated.

Another major tool for diagnosis has been the survey or climate questionnaire. In Payne (1999), I argued that the three dimensional culture cube can be used to guide the design of survey instruments in such a way as to expose the degree to which the organization is exhibiting each of the three paradigm perspectives described by Martin (1995). The questionnaire was called the Culture Intensity Questionnaire, though it offers a structure rather than a questionnaire per se. The psychological intensity dimension was operationalized as presented in below:

> The cultural intensity questionnaire: the questionnaire is designed to describe your organization's culture with an emphasis on measuring how strong it is. This is achieved by getting you to describe how many people hold certain views, for example, and by assessing how intensely the culture is felt by considering whether it is primarily held as an attitude, largely expressed as behaviour, or is rooted in deeply held values/beliefs. Your initial reactions to the questions may well be your most accurate, so if in doubt be guided by those thoughts. The questions all have the same format. For each aspect of culture you are asked to indicate how many people would (a) publicly express a positive attitude towards it, (b) behave that way (whatever their attitude), (c) have it as a deeply held value (whether they behave that way or not), (d) have it as such a fundamental belief that it is "taken-for-granted" without them necessarily expressing their awareness of it.

**Example**: With respect to: "Giving a fair day's work for a fair day' pay"

| | | | | |
|---|---|---|---|---|
| (a) *People would express a positive attitude to it* | All/most people 4 | Many 3 | Some 2 | Few/none 1 |
| (b) *People behave in line with it* | All/most people 4 | Many 3 | Some 2 | Few/none 1 |
| (c) *People value it deeply* | All/most people 4 | Many 3 | Some 2 | Few/none 1 |
| (d) *It is so fundamental here, it's just taken for granted by* | All/most people 4 | Many 3 | Some 2 | Few/none 1 |

> Sometimes all the answers will be the same, but often there will be inconsistencies between attitudes, behaviours and values or beliefs. A culture is strong when most people adopt it and there is consistency of values, beliefs and behaviours.

The pervasiveness dimension can be operationalized through defining the content of the culture, i.e. the norms of behaviour, values and taken-for-granted assumptions that are important in describing the culture. These are best generated from the members of the culture themselves and they may be obtained by interviews, observation, and/or participation in the culture. Documents might also provide important sources of information about what concerns the people in the organization. Existing questionnaire instruments may be a source of important dimensions. Hofstede's work on values produced a list of five dimensions that seem to have had relevance to a wide range of national cultures (Hofstede, 1980, 1991). They concerned the distribution of power, the way to deal with ambiguity/uncertainty, masculinity–femininity, individualism versus collectivism and whether the culture was concerned with retaining traditional ways of organizing society or whether it promoted the notion that social order should be based on negotiation rather than obligation. A straightforward list of things to consider would be:

- What goals does the culture have?
- Who has power and what rewards and sanctions go with it?
- When should things be done?
- Where should they occur?
- How should people do them?
- Why should things be done the way they are?

The greater the range of behaviours, values and beliefs that are controlled by the culture the more pervasive it is. Pervasiveness has not been a major concern in the past because most comparative approaches to culture assume that the dimensions they measure can in theory be applied to any culture. Hofstede's dimensions are good examples, but some aspects of culture may not be relevant to some other culture, or they may be relevant to so few of the people that they are not an important consideration. In another culture they may be central, e.g. witchcraft or animism or science. Many modern organizations may not have science as an important element of their culture even if they use its products on a daily basis. Anthropological approaches to culture are much more likely to reveal the pervasiveness of the culture. In designing a questionnaire based on the cube it is desirable to include common aspects of culture as well as ones that are perhaps idiosyncratic to the particular organization.

As the cube indicates the degree of consensus is also a most important determinant of the strength of a culture. In climate questionnaire studies consensus has been measured by statistical coefficients which vary from zero to one and measure the degree to which the members of the organization/department/team agree on any particular question or set of questions that form a scale. The higher the coefficient the stronger the consensus. Those who adopt the Integration Perspective on culture have set guidelines for indicating whether the consensus is strong enough to justify attributing the quality to the cultural entity. For a commonly used statistic, the within-group correlation $r_{wg}$, the cut-off point has been 0.7. In applying the bootstrap technique to climate data, Padmore and Payne (1995) found that this is too low a bound, but this no longer matters. The proposition here is that such coefficients can be used to measure the degree of consensus. Thus, in looking for evidence of Integration in an organization one could test how strong it is throughout the organization. One could test how strong it was for different aspects of the culture and even in a well-integrated culture it may be acceptable that for some elements of culture there is not high consensus. It could even be the case that creating low consensus on some topic is actually important to the organization, e.g. the importance of religion or political persuasion in a business organization, or in many, but not all schools.

In looking for evidence of the degree of Differentiation in an organization it would be possible to examine degrees of consensus by department, by organizational level, by level within departments, etc. Again, content would be relevant, for there may be consensus about some aspects of the culture (we ought to make a profit) but not others (how one goes about doing it). An organization would be more differentiated if it had consensus within a range of subgroups and the content of the culture also differed within the groups. These are the conditions that Meyerson and Martin (1987) describe as localized and loosely coupled. The variation in the coefficients of consensus across the groups and the dimensions would give an idea of the degree of differentiation in an organization.

In the Fragmented organization there should be only low levels of consensus throughout the organization and on many aspects of culture, though this would presumably not apply to Hofstede's dimension of ambiguity/uncertainty where there should be strong consensus about accepting it and promoting its virtues. As I have already indicated I suspect that there will still be moderate consensus about some fundamental aspects of the society's culture, or people would not get along with each other well enough even to deal with the ambiguity surrounding key tasks. That is, they would agree about such necessities as dress, communication manners, etc. A measure which taps a wide range of dimensions would help reveal these minimum cultural areas and the minimum levels of consensus required to enable the Fragmented culture to function within its own definition of functioning.

Even within the Fragmented Perspective it is expected that there will be some measure of consensus at any one point in time. Temporary allegiances are commonplace. Over time, however, the regular use of such a questionnaire should reveal changes in the patterns of consensus and those areas of the culture where consensus exists (or does not). The use of the index of agreement and the ability to compare levels of consensus through methods such as cluster analysis will help reveal the effects of the ongoing change that is believed to characterize the Fragmented culture.

## USING ASSESSMENT TO TRACK MULTI-DIMENSIONAL CULTURAL CHANGE

The previous section has aimed to show how a questionnaire can be designed to measure the three dimensions of the cube and how to use the data from it to indicate the strength of consensus in different parts of an organization and the domains in which the consensus exists. Through such analyses one can more accurately describe organizations as having Integrated, Differentiated of Fragmented cultures. Such information could be used to investigate the consequences of such different cultures for the people in them and for the organization qua organization. Used over time such information could throw further light on changes in the culture and the forces that brought about the change.

This raises the question – what do we mean by culture change? Deal and Kennedy (1982) define it as, "...real changes in the behaviour of people throughout the organization. In a technical sense we mean people in the organization with new role-model heroes, telling different stories to one another, spending their time differently on a day-to-day basis, asking different questions and carrying out different work rituals." (p.

158). The Trice and Beyer (1993) definition is, "We will reserve the term *culture change* to refer to planned, more encompassing, and more substantial kinds of changes than those which arise spontaneously within cultures or as part of conscious efforts to keep an existing culture vital." (p. 395). A few pages later Trice and Beyer describe three kinds of culture change. They are:

1. *Revolutionary and comprehensive* which is characterized by being pervasive, of high magnitude, of varying degrees of innovativeness, though radical new cultural forms are relatively rare, and the length of time it takes varies.
2. *Subunit or subculture* which is much less pervasive, usually moderate in magnitude, variable in its innovativeness, and in the time it takes to bring the change about.
3. *Cumulative comprehensive reshaping*: this has wide, pervasive effects, though its magnitude is usually moderate, as is the degree of innovativeness involved, and it takes places over long time periods.

The first two of these bear close similarity to the Integrated and the Differentiated paradigms described by Meyerson and Martin (1987). The change in type 1 is clearly from one integrated culture to another, which is why it is revolutionary. The second is from one form of differentiation to another with the change moderate in terms of its pervasiveness, intensity, and consensus in the terms of the culture cube framework. The third type of change is not the same as change in the Fragmented paradigm. According to Meyerson and Martin (1987), change in a Fragmented culture is relatively continuous and has localized effects rather than pervasive ones, and it is much less deliberate (no reshaping is implied).

This difference suggests a potential limitation. The problem is that the Meyerson and Martin (1987) framework looks at change *within* each of the three paradigms and in the Fragmented paradigm it implies that change is continuous but never major. The framework does not consider whether it is possible for a Fragmented culture to become Differentiated or Integrated. It is worth noting that if it is unlikely for a Fragmented culture to change in this way, then it is almost certainly the case that it would be because the members of the culture all think the same about the prominence of uncertainty, and the value of living with it. Paradoxically, this would turn it into an Integrated culture (but low on pervasiveness). Equally the framework does not consider how an Integrated culture could change into anything other than another Integrated culture, and the same applies to the Differentiated culture. In reading about actual changes to organizational cultures, however, it is clear that movements in all directions occur: from integrated to differentiated, from differentiated to fragmented, from fragmented to differentiated and from fragmented to integrated, etc.

An advantage of considering cultural change within the framework of the cube is that it can avoid such typological thinking. The cube offers the possibility of moving from one space to another. The three dimensions raise questions about which direction and how far to go in any particular direction. Organizations can be conceived as becoming less integrated, more differentiated and more fragmented, etc. rather than being one or the other. The theoretical advantages of thinking dimensionally, or in terms of general variables rather than categorical variables, are described by Hage (1972) as:

1. General variables, by being applicable to all cultures and historical epochs, allow us the possibility of finding a universal law.
2. General variables make classification more subtle.
3. Although it is harder to demonstrate, general variables make thinking much easier.

And to misquote Lewin (1951), "There is nothing so practical as a good theoretical framework."

# CHANGE AND THE THREE DIMENSIONS

Since changes in these ⟨??⟩ are dependent on changes in the three dimensions of the cube it follows that it is necessary to consider what needs to be done to move organizations along each of the three dimensions. The framework outlined in Figure 5.2 was originally designed to describe the main processes involved in the development of cultures over time (Payne, 1991). The framework proposes that cultures pass through the phases of conception, conversion, and consolidation and that they either collapse or change to some degree or other. At each of these stages the cultural processes involve leadership communication and control. These require different activities at the different stages of cultural development. The figure provides examples of these for a general approach to developing a culture. A useful way of thinking about movements along the three dimensions of the culture cube is to apply the same framework to each dimension.

## Psychological Intensity

This dimension is concerned with whether the organizational leaders are concerned with obtaining the behaviours they want from people through influencing their attitudes and behaviour or through influencing their fundamental beliefs about what should be done and how it should be achieved. At this deeper level of intensity it is assumed the correct behaviours follow automatically and volitionally. The content of Figure 5.2 was designed with the assumption labelled here as the Integration paradigm. That is, that a strong culture involved deep psychological intensity. It shows the processes that dominate at different stages of the development of a culture. By the time consolidation is reached the leadership and communication processes have established control of beliefs and behaviours through the manipulation and control of symbols, through the systematic generation of normative expectations, and finally by systems and procedures (rules) that are fully internalized by the members of the culture. This strength is a potential long-term weakness that potentially threatens to lead to collapse unless change itself is a core value of the culture, and environmental turbulence might force change even in a change-oriented culture.

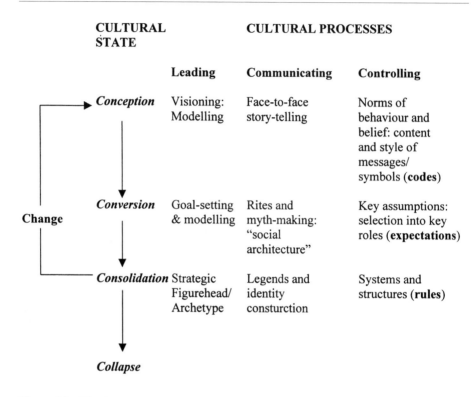

**CULTURAL STATE**

**CULTURAL PROCESSES**

| | Leading | Communicating | Controlling |
|---|---|---|---|
| *Conception* | Visioning: Modelling | Face-to-face story-telling | Norms of behaviour and belief: content and style of messages/symbols (**codes**) |
| *Conversion* | Goal-setting & modelling | Rites and myth-making: "social architecture" | Key assumptions: selection into key roles (**expectations**) |
| *Consolidation* | Strategic Figurehead/Archetype | Legends and identity consturction | Systems and structures (**rules**) |

**Change**

**Collapse**

**Figure 5.2**   The development of cultures.

What if the organizational designers are content to operate through attitudes and behaviours alone? The leaders' aims for the organization would need to be clearly articulated and the behaviours they see as achieving the aims clearly expressed. The leaders would need to provide excellent role models of the behaviours and communicate them by demonstration and example. Formal and informal reward systems would focus on conformity with behaviours that achieve the organization's goals. There would be little concern with shaping values and beliefs as long as goals are being adequately achieved. Rites and symbols would be designed to recognize those who conformed – employee of the month, success charts, etc. would be the trappings of organizations operating at this cultural level. An unusual example I encountered in a medium size manufacturing organization was WHIFFO awards where the letters stood for "Willing Helper in Fight For Organization". Personnel selection would focus on instrumentality rather than the search for people who wanted a deeper career commitment. Reward systems would be tailored to suit the instrumental needs of such a workforce through such systems as flexitime. The rate of progress through the stages of conception, conversion and consolidation should be much more rapid than in a culture that is trying to work at a deeper level of psychological intensity. This should also make it easier to change attitudes and norms once the authority of the senior people to establish them has been legitimated. Organizations offering relatively simple, routine jobs with low career potential create cultures with these properties because they suit the conditions that face them. According to Rousseau (1998) the psychological contract is transactional.

## Pervasiveness

In theory pervasiveness is independent of psychological intensity though in practice it is likely that an organization that wishes to create a deep level of intensity is likely to aim to influence a wider range of beliefs and behaviours than one happy to just influence behaviours and attitudes. Large, government-funded schools on the other hand may strive to influence a relatively wide range of behaviours at school without aiming to offer a well-developed, universal credo. In this way they differ from some elite private schools. Japanese business organizations have a more pervasive influence on their employees' lives and work cultures than do Western business organizations (Lincoln, 1990). Professional organizations generally influence a greater range of beliefs and behaviours than do non-professional organizations both directly and indirectly through the controls of the professional bodies to which their employees are affiliated. With regard to Figure 5.2 as a framework for considering the processes through which high pervasiveness may be achieved, it is apparent that, at conception, the vision must clearly articulate the range of behaviours and beliefs that are to be encompassed. The stories and face-to-face encounters must cover the range in a compelling fashion. The variety of parables in the Christian gospels is paradigmatic. At conversion stages of the process the goals set must involve the range of behaviours and beliefs and the leaders must role-model the same range. The "social architecture" must include myths, stories, symbols and artefacts suitable to the same range. Processes of selection must ensure that recruits desire to accept such a wide influence and to role-model them as well as possible. Apostles and acolytes are the prime targets in the conversion phase. At consolidation the systems and structures must be designed to continually reinforce the importance of founders and promote the legends that they have created. The rules will by now have developed to cover a wide range of contingencies along with the sanctions and rewards that are associated with compliance and contravention. Generally speaking, cultures focussing on a narrow range of behaviours/beliefs will need to expend much less effort, but the processes involved are much the same and might be very intense for the areas of beliefs and behaviours the cultural shapers have selected. Some sports teams and direct selling organizations are examples of such cultures. The degree of pervasiveness then is very much determined by the conception of the culture right at the start of its development, though experience may well lead to a narrowing as leaders realize how difficult it is to influence wide areas of people's lives. Such over-ambitiousness may well have been the ultimate downfall of many an aspiring demagogue or turnaround manager.

## Consensus

The problems facing those aspiring to have a highly pervasive culture are not dissimilar to those facing people who strive for high consensus. As indicated already, the strongest cultures are those which achieve both as well as deep intensity. Again, Figure 5.2 outlines the processes that are likely to lead to high consensus. At conception it is vitally important that the vision and goals of the culture are clear, as well as what people have to do to succeed in the culture and the rewards and consequences that will flow from successful participation. To reach everybody, communication processes become central. They must be regular, probably multi-media to attract the attention of diverse groups, and involve people in the messages they convey through participation in activities such as ceremonies and rites de passage. Deviations from what is expected must be dealt with early and in ways that encourage others to support the punishment of deviants. In the stages of conversion and consolidation the same basic processes occur but they become much more tightly controlled, and systematized through the development of both face-to-face contact and sets of regulations and systems which reinforce the norms/values that are central to the organization. The "Organization Man" should be easy to describe, easy to mimic and well-supported by the organization's communications and public relations departments.

In writing about managing and maintaining cultures Trice and Beyer (1993) offer eight prescriptive aphorisms (p. 392). They are:

1. Don't assume continuity, work for it.
2. Respect the past, but adapt to the present.
3. Adapt existing ideologies to current challenges and crises.
4. Locate and reduce cultural disparities.
5. Manage the politics and subcultural relations.
6. Encourage the use of cultural forms (rites, myths, etc.).
7. Emphasize continuity in socialization.
8. Encourage and develop maintenance leadership.

These are offered to establish an Integrated culture, of course, but high consensus is central to such a conception of culture. The above can also be seen as expressions of the processes that need to occur if high consensus is required, even in organizations where there is low pervasiveness, and low psychological intensity. Maintaining systems that spread the "words", that are on the lookout for threats from within, that are sensitive to external forces for change, and that are flexible to circumstances is vital to sustaining high consensus.

## CONCLUSION

The aim of this chapter has been to offer a framework that can be used to encompass the widely differing views of organizational culture that seem established in the organizational literature. It has attempted to show how thinking in three dimensions can encompass the three major conceptions of climate but free one from the limitations of thinking in typologies. It has demonstrated that one of the limitations of typological thinking has been to consider change *within* a paradigm but not *between* paradigms. This process, it is argued, is easier to accomplish if one thinks about change within each of the three dimensions of the framework simultaneously. The framework of the Cultural Intensity Questionnaire is offered as one way of empirically describing and monitoring culture and culture change.

# REFERENCES

Ajzen, I. and Fishbein, M. (1980) Understanding Attitudes and Predicting Social Behaviour. Englewood Cliffs, NJ: Prentice-Hall.

Argyris, C. (1982) Reasoning, Learning and Action: Individual and Organizational. San Francisco, CA: Jossey-Bass.

Deal, T.E. and Kennedy, A.A. (1982) Corporate Cultures: the Rites and Rituals of Corporate Life. Reading, MA: Addison-Wesley.

Denison, D. (1990) Corporate Cultures and Effectiveness. New York: Wiley.

Edmonson, A. (1996) Three faces of Eden: the persistence of competing theories and multiple diagnoses in organizational intervention research. Human Relations, 49(5): 571–595.

Gonzalez-Roma, V., Peiro, J.M., Lloret, S. and Zornoza, A. (1999) The validity of collective climates. Journal of Occupational and Organizational Psychology, 72(1): 25–40.

Guion, R.M. (1973) A note on organizational climate. Organizational Behavior and Human Performance, 9: 120–125.

Hage, J. (1972) Techniques and Problems of Theory Construction in Sociology. New York: Wiley.

Hofstede, G. (1980) Culture's Consequences: International Differences in Work-Related Values. Beverley Hills, CA: Sage.

Hofstede, G. (1991) Cultures and Organizations: Software of the Mind. London: McGraw-Hill.

Jackovsky, E.F. and Slocum Jr., J.W. (1988) A longitudinal study of climate. Journal of Organizational Behaviour, 9: 319–334.

Kotter, J.P. and Heskett, J.L. (1992) Corporate Culture and Performance. New York: Free Press.

Lewin, K. (1951) Field Theory in Social Science. New York: Harper.

March, J.G. and Olsen, J.P. (1976) Ambiguity and Choice in Organizations. Bergen: Universiteitsvorlaget.

Martin, J. (1995) Organizational culture. In N. Nicholson (Ed), Encyclopedic Dictionary of Organizational Behaviour, pp. 376–382. Oxford: Blackwell.

Meyerson, D. and Martin, J. (1987) Cultural change: an integration of three different views. Journal of Management Studies, 24(6): 623–643.

Pace, C.R. and Stern, G.G. (1958) An approach to the measurement of psychological characteristics of college environments. Journal of Educational Psychology, 49: 269–277.

Padmore, J. and Payne, R.L. (1995) A pragmatic approach to the problem of aggregation in organizational climate research: part 2. Discussion paper, Sheffield University Management School, Sheffield.

Patterson, M., Payne, R.L. and West, M. (1996) Collective climates: a test of their socio-psychological significance. Academy of Management Journal, 39(6): 1675–1691.

Payne, R.L. (1990) Madness in our method: a comment on Jackofsky and Slocum's paper, 'A longitudinal study of climates'. Journal of Organizational Behavior, 11: 77–80.

Payne, R. (1991) Taking stock of corporate culture. Personnel Management, July: 26–29.

Payne, R.L. (1997) Never mind structure – what about climate? In T. Clark (Ed), Advancement in Organizational Behavior: Essays in Honour of D.S. Pugh, pp. 89–104. Aldershot: Ashgate.

Payne, R.L. (1999) Culture and climate: how close can they get? In N.M. Ashkenazy and C.M. Wilderom (Eds), International Handbook of Organizational Culture and Climate. Beverley Hills, CA: Sage.

Pugh, D.S., Hickson, D.J., Hinings, S.R. and Turner, C. (1968) Dimensions of organization structure. Administrative Science Quarterly, 13: 65–105.

Rousseau, D.M. (1998) The Psychological Contract Inventory. Pittsburgh, PA: Carnegie-Mellon University.

Schein, E. (1985) Organizational Culture and Leadership. San Francisco, CA: Jossey-Bass.

Schon, D.A. (1971) Beyond the Stable State: Public and Private Learning in a Changing Society. London: Temple Smith.

Senge, P. (1990) The Fifth Discipline: the Art and Practice of the Learning Organization. New York: Doubleday.

Starbuck, W.H. (1983) Organizations as action generators. American Sociological Review, 48(1): 91–103.

Trice, H.M. and Beyer, J.M. (1993) The Cultures of Work Organizations. Englewood-Cliffs, NJ: Prentice-Hall.

Weick, K. (1969) The Social Psychology of Organizing. Reading, MA: Addison-Wesley.

Zammuto, R.F. and Krakower, J.Y. (1991) Quantitative and qualitative studies of organizational culture. Research in Organizational Change and Development, 5: 84–114.

# Chapter 6

# Recent Approaches to the Qualitative Analysis of Organizational Culture

**Kate Mackenzie Davey**
*and*
**Gillian Symon**

*Department of Organizational Psychology,
University of London, London, UK*

## INTRODUCTION

The concept of culture encapsulates, perhaps more clearly than any other, current debates within organization studies. Research and practice in the area of organizational culture stretches from the evangelical writings of Tom Peters, to the reflexive deconstructions of Calas and Smircich. The concept has been transformed from its anthropological roots to a site of confusion and ambiguity. In the next chapter, Sackmann outlines ways to unravel some of this complexity. However, organizational culture has become a:

Catch all idea ... stimulating, productive, yet fuzzy. (Van Maanen, 1987, p. 3)

Meyerson (1991, p. 256) claims that when the term was first applied to organizations:

...culture was the code word for the subjective side of organizational life... its study represented an ontological rebellion against the dominant functionalist or 'scientific' paradigm.

This would clearly signal the appropriateness of qualitative approaches to examining and analyzing culture. However, functionalist approaches to organizational culture evolved, emphasizing the importance of strong unitary cultures integrated throughout the organization (Peters and Waterman, 1982). Indeed, Schein (1992, p. 248) has argued that "if things are ambiguous, then by definition, that group does not have a culture". Such approaches are associated with attempts to "manage" culture, in particular to change culture in the belief that certain organizational cultures produce certain valued organizational performance outcomes (such as increased productivity).

Functionalist accounts may present the danger of nominalizing what was originally seen as a dynamic concept and viewing it as something an organization "has" rather than something an organization "is". Smircich (1983) argues, from a symbolic interactionist (anthropological) perspective, that culture studies should be concerned not with what an organization does and how it can perform more effectively, but with how organization is accomplished and what it means to be organized (Smircich, 1983, p. 353). Culture is seen as a process of organizing and not as an attribute of organizations. Generally, studies of culture aim to describe the context of the organization as experienced by those working within it. Functionalists will attempt to measure aspects of this context, classify it, link it to organizational efficiency and change it. By contrast, symbolic interactionists will attempt to discover what being part of an organization means to people and the processes by which it is understood and enacted. This implies that the methodological approach to the study of culture will depend on the perspective adopted by the researcher, with functionalists attempting to extract specific, generalizable cultural dimensions that can then be evaluated and quantified through survey methods, while symbolic interactionists adopt more descriptive, idiographic "qualitative" methods. This chapter seeks to review the latter type of analysis and, in doing so, explores to what extent the dichotomy between quantitative and qualitative methods is reflected in current fieldwork. We first consider what might constitute a general "qualitative" approach to cultural analysis.

## QUALITATIVE APPROACHES TO CULTURAL ANALYSIS

At first glance, distinguishing qualitative approaches to assessing organizational culture may seem obvious: qualitative approaches are the opposite of survey-type assessments, eschewing the quantification of phenomena. Indeed, this seems to be the dichotomy underlying the distinction made by Denison (1996) between climate and culture research. While he describes various dimensions on which the two kinds of studies may be distinguished, the use of qualitative methods is firmly associated with culture research, while climate research involves comparative surveys. However, Denison does not really define what is meant by the umbrella terms "qualitative methods" and "quantitative methods", seeing the distinction as unproblematic. In fact, this distinction has given rise to much discussion (e.g. Henwood, 1996; Symon and Cassell, 1998). Symon and Cassell (1998) conclude that the distinction between qualitative and quantitative methods is a "red herring" because either approach can be informed by different underlying epistemologies. A method that does not involve the quantification of phenomena may be guided by a positivist understanding of what constitutes warrantable knowledge (e.g. that it be objective, independently verifiable and generalizable) as much as by, for example, a social constructionist understanding (e.g. that knowledge is created through social interaction). Such different underlying epistemologies may be reflected in how researchers understand what is meant by the term "organizational culture", how this can be assessed and how the data can be interpreted and used.

This lack of a simple dichotomy may explain why Denison goes on to conclude that the distinction between culture and climate research has now become muddied. This may not in fact be the substantive change that Denison claims (as he suggests, driven by a need to publish culture research in more prestigious journals) but may simply reflect the fact that the methodological distinction has never been that clear-cut. This does not, however, lead us to the same conclusion as Denison, that data are simply "benign" (Denison, 1996, p. 646). Data may exist "out there" ready for collection from some perspectives (e.g. within a positivist paradigm), but from others they are created in the process of conducting research.

Where does this debate leave us? It is not for us to lay claim to a particular definition of "qualitative" and identify this as "correct" (Cassell and Symon, 1998). Consequently, we have taken a more eclectic view and reviewed studies that *the authors themselves* identify as "qualitative". Under the general heading of "qualitative", however, we will see many different perspectives on what constitutes culture, the objectives of assessing culture, and what can be concluded from these assessments. The distinctions between different approaches taken by different researchers in this area may arise from their definition of the term organizational culture, their purpose in investigating the phenomenon and their epistemological perspective.

# EXAMPLES OF "QUALITATIVE" APPROACHES TO CULTURAL ANALYSIS

We have already discussed the problems with labelling specific approaches to collecting and analyzing data as peculiarly qualitative. In this section, therefore, we can only aim to review those methods that claim to attempt to probe organizational values and beliefs idiographically or in more depth than traditional survey instruments.

In presenting this review, we need to adopt some sort of sense making framework. Any category system has problems: some methods may not fit easily into just one particular category; researchers may use the same method in very different ways; the dimensions of the framework may be debatable and so on. However, in our analysis, we have come to the conclusion that the "qualitative" methods that have been applied to the analysis of organizational culture specifically can be broken down into two main areas: those that adopt methods from the psychological disciplines and those that adopt methods from sociological/anthropological perspectives. This has some similarity with the latter two of the Mohan (1993) categorization of systemic, cognitive and symbolic approaches. The systemic frame emphasizes quantitative measures and examines organization structure and function. The cognitive frame examines individual sense making through cognitive maps and constructs. The symbolic frame emphasizes understanding through studying metaphors and stories in organizations.

In each section, we describe more specifically our definitions of these two broad areas. Within each area, we then focus on a number of specific methods, identified by their users as "qualitative", and discuss their relevance and contribution to the study of organizational culture. It is not the purpose of this chapter to describe in detail how to use specific methods – interested readers are referred to the relevant literature for further information.

# PSYCHOLOGICAL APPROACHES

As suggested by Mohan's framework, qualitative approaches from a psychological perspective may focus on "individual sense making". These are methods that seek to gather data from individual employees and then build these up into an overall picture of an organizational culture (perhaps including some group differences). All the methods outlined below have been developed for use in other sub-disciplines of psychology (social, clinical, educational) and adapted to investigate organizational culture. Studies of this sort are still very much in their infancy and examples of the application of the method in this area are often restricted to only one published study.

## Repertory Grid

The method of Repertory Grid analysis is based on Kelly's Personal Construct Theory. Originally mainly used in clinical and educational settings to investigate socio-cognitive constructs relevant to specific individuals, it has become popular amongst organizational researchers and practitioners for investigating a range of occupational behaviours (e.g. Jankowicz, 1990). Thus, its original clinical use for working with particular individuals has been expanded to allow for the comparison and generalization of constructs amongst a particular population (Stewart and Stewart, 1981).

Repertory (Rep) Grid analysis has been envisaged as relevant to the study of organizational culture because it is hypothesized as allowing access to perhaps subconscious beliefs and values – the method encouraging a deeper contemplation of these by individuals than, for example, a straightforward interview. Thus, it is expected to tap "deeper" levels of culture, i.e. fundamental assumptions, such as conceptualized by Rousseau (1990) and Schein (1990). In a comparative study of different qualitative methods for analyzing culture, Locatelli and West (1992) concluded that Rep Grid did allow better access to fundamental assumptions than the discussion group (although they found the Twenty Statements Test, see below, to be of overall greater utility). In addition, the underlying assumption of Personal Construct Theory, that "a person's thought processes are psychologically channelled by the ways in which events are anticipated" (Gammack and Stephens, 1994, p. 76), seems to fit well with the notion of culture providing a sense making framework for the interpretation of organizational events.

Rep Grid is viewed as a "qualitative" method because it allows individuals within the culture to define their own constructs, rather than these being imposed by the researcher in a survey, thus achieving some contextual relevance. In contrast to in-depth interviews, Rep Grids are sometimes preferred because, in structuring the conversation between analyst and respondent, they allow for a more "systematic" investigation: objectively valid and reproducible (Gammack and Stephens, 1994). It is notable, however, that in studies by both Langan-Fox and Tan (1997) and Locatelli and West (1992), it is assumed that the culture constructs generated "would need to be given back to members of the department in questionnaire form in order to build a picture of the department" (Locatelli and West, 1992, p. 9). Indeed, Langan-Fox and Tan argue that the strength of the Rep Grid technique is that it offers the benefits of both qualitative and quantitative approaches. Some of the descriptions of the Rep Grid method, e.g. as objective, reproducible, etc., seem to fit better with the concerns of a more positivist epistemology than those of the interpretivist or constructionist epistemology one might associate with "qualitative" approaches. These observations illustrate our doubts, outlined earlier, concerning the drawing of hard and fast distinctions between qualitative and quantitative approaches.

As indicated above, researchers who have used the technique themselves recognize the problem of extracting constructs from individuals and then attempting to build up a picture of a set of shared beliefs and assumptions that may define the culture of an organization. This is normally tackled by categorizing the constructs across individuals through a method such as content analysis. It is possible some nuances of meaning are lost in the process. More seriously, this assumes that consensus and generalization are the objects of the analysis, denying conflict and ambiguity in our conceptualization of culture. Other potential difficulties with the method as a way of "accessing" culture may include the selection of meaningful elements for eliciting constructs. Locatelli and West (1992) used different kinds of organizational events; Langan-Fox and Tan (1997) used different individuals seen to encapsulate the different cultures described before and after an organizational change intervention. Different kinds of elements may have very different implications for the kinds of constructs generated and will reflect underlying assumptions of the researcher or practitioner as to what constitutes culture and how it may be tapped.

The utility of any method in the analysis of organizational culture is not an objective evaluation, depending very much on the definitions and purposes adopted by the researcher or practitioner. As yet, few attempts have been made to apply Rep Grid to cultural analysis. The study by Langan-Fox and Tan (1997) applies Rep Grid to investigating the culture of a specific organization for a specific purpose. In their case they wished to perform a "culture audit" that would indicate whether a recent culture change programme had been successful, specifically whether the "new" culture was now seen to be shared by organizational managers. In these objectives, we can see an underlying functionalist paradigm. It is assumed that culture can be managed and changed through specific interventions and in a direction desired by senior organizational members, and it is believed that managers need to have a shared perception of culture in order to transmit this to staff. This is very much an instrumental perspective that advocates a unitarist view of culture. Comparing this to earlier distinctions, we see that methods claimed to be qualitative may just as well be used within a functionalist paradigm as within a symbolic interactionist paradigm, and that the categorization of systemic and cognitive by Mohan (1993) may not be absolute.

Other assumptions that may underlie the use of Rep Grids to analyze organizational culture include the belief that culture can be depicted as a snapshot in time. Gammack and Stephens (1994) argue that Kelly originally used the method with patients over a period of time to build up a picture of their personal constructs. This does not appear to be how the method is used in studies of culture. Using the Grids with a range of organizational members at one point in time suggests a view of culture as static and ahistorical. In addition, the focus on constructs, individual short statements that may be descriptions of people and events rather than the organization itself, gives a rather fragmented picture of culture.

## Twenty Statements Test

The Twenty Statements Test (TST) was originally designed to investigate concepts of self, with the assumption that identity is a form of internalized, negotiated social categorization and that individual action is influenced by such categorizations (Rees and Nicholson, 1994). For example, "I am a woman" is an internalization of a socially constructed label that then may affect the person's social behaviour. Respondents are asked to complete 20 statements beginning with the prompt "I am...", these statements then being categorized in terms of a system devised by McPartland (1965). Where the method has been adapted to investigate organizational culture, the prompt has been "This organization is..." or "This department is..." (depending on the level of analysis) and previously existing systems for analyzing culture (e.g. Rousseau, 1990) have been applied to the resultant data sets (Locatelli and West, 1992; Walker et al., 1996).

Why might this method be suitable for investigating organizational culture? If one were to view organizational culture as analogous to its identity, then this application would seem appropriate. However, these two terms may not be synonymous: organizational identity would seem to imply something of an external image, such as might be perceived by clients or investors. Locatelli and West (1992), the first to attempt to apply this method to the study of culture, suggest that some definitions of culture imply a negotiated social categorization process in much the same way as outlined for identity in the assumptions behind TST and that therefore "may also be viewed as a social object from a symbolic interactionist perspective..." (p. 3).

Similar to the Rep Grid, TST is identified as qualitative because the respondents generate their own concepts. In addition, it is suggested that the TST, as it is completed by the individuals themselves, may encourage respondents to make more confidential statements (Locatelli and West, 1992), the implication being that more in-depth analyses can be achieved. In contrast to Rep Grids, however, the method itself is less complex to administer, while retaining the supposedly attractive quality of structuring the data collection process, and, it is claimed, is more "transparent" to the respondent (Rees and Nicholson, 1994, p. 53). In addition, the TST may tolerate the generation of contradictory statements about the culture, thus allowing for differentiation and ambiguity in cultural descriptions to emerge (Walker et al., 1996).

Again, like the Rep Grid, statements generated by individuals are clustered in thematic groups – a process that may validated by specific tests of inter-rater reliability. Claims may be made about "dominant cultural themes" on the basis of this process

(Walker et al., 1996) that are certainly questionable from some epistemological perspectives. These concerns for content analysis, quantification and validation again hint at more positivist concerns in the analysis of data generally. They may also suggest a more functionalist outlook on the analysis of culture.

Both the studies by Locatelli and West (1992) and Walker et al. (1996) were specifically designed to evaluate the TST as a method for assessing organizational culture, so in both cases were applied in organizations as tools for a culture "audit". In both cases, the method was seen as efficient and effective in comparison with other methods and to some extent as going beneath the surface manifestations of culture to the underlying beliefs and values, if not the underlying assumptions (Rousseau, 1990). However, Walker et al. are rather more temperate in their praise of the method, emphasizing the need to discuss resultant categories with respondents to check attributed meanings and concluding that the TST is useful for identifying further areas for exploration with organizational members (perhaps in interviews) rather than as a final statement of the nature of the existing culture. The method is also open to some of the other criticisms aimed at the Rep Grid.

## Critical Incidents

Critical Incidents Technique (CIT), a structured form of interviewing, was originally derived to identify effective and ineffective job performance (Chell, 1998). However, McClelland (1976) also used CIT to examine trust in organizations, and more recently it has been applied to determine how new recruits come to understand the behavioural norms of their organizational culture (Gundry and Rousseau, 1994), i.e. how they become socialized into the organization.

CIT has been viewed as appropriate for cultural analysis because the critical events described in the interview are specifically those that "generate insight into the organization and [the individual's] role in it" (Gundry and Rousseau, 1994). Such events are seen as conveying information concerning behavioural norms (one of the more "surface" manifestations of culture in the analysis by Rousseau (1990)), the interpretation of which (as behaviours in which to engage or avoid) leads to the individual's adoption of particular behaviours and therefore social assimilation into the organization. Perhaps in a similar fashion to stories (see following section), such incidents may be interpreted as conveying information as to, for example, in/appropriate behaviour, hidden agendas and implicit psychological contracts. Gundry and Rousseau argue that because new recruits may be exposed to similar events and because organizations may seek to manage the impressions they convey, common interpretations may be made by individuals, leading to agreement concerning behavioural norms (i.e. a "common" culture).

Chell (1998) argues that CIT can be regarded as a qualitative method because it allows the researcher to "get closer to the subject" (p. 55). The data are ecologically valid, context "rich" and allow clarification of their meaning to the individual (Chell, 1998; Gundry and Rousseau, 1994). Much like the Rep Grid, Chell (1998) favours the CIT over the interview as it is more focussed. Like all the methods reviewed in this section, common themes can be identified in the individual's interpretation of the events (through content analysis) to allow for the identification of behavioural patterns, or as Gundry and Rousseau (1994) put it, an "indigenous typology" (p. 1072).

Indeed, this is what Gundry and Rousseau (1994) seek to achieve in their application of CIT to the analysis of newcomer socialization. Gundry and Rousseau acknowledge the problem of extrapolating from individual level measurement to a group or organizational level construct but argue that "individual perceptions of behavioral norms [are the] key building blocks of culture" (p. 1074). New recruits were asked to describe five incidents in a questionnaire, which had revealed important insights on the organization to them. These incidents were categorized using grounded theory methodology to come up with 62 types of incidents (checked through inter-rater reliability). The frequency of different types of incidents was compared across organizations, the researchers concluding that particular existing cultural norms in organizations were associated with the adoption of particular socialization tactics by managers.

The CIT has the advantage of grounding the cultural analysis very much in specific events that have actually occurred in the organization. What is more, at least at the start of the analysis, the interpretation of these events is that of the individual employees. However, in common with most of the techniques in this section, events and interpretations are then grouped together in categories seen to represent the organizational culture as a whole. Individual perceptions of behavioural norms as the "building blocks" of culture reflect an underlying assumption of the researchers as to the nature of culture. Some researchers may disagree with this characterization given the original definition of culture as a collective concept. Furthermore, like the TST, the assumption that the increased frequency of certain categories indicates an objective picture of what that organization is "really like" may be unwarranted. Again this is a rather fragmented approach to take to cultural analysis.

## Attribution Analysis

The application of attribution theory to cultural analysis has been a very recent advance (Silvester et al., 1999). Stemming from a socio-cognitive perspective on individual action, attribution analysis is concerned with investigating cognitive biases in the attribution of causality (e.g. the tendency to assume that individual behaviour results from aspects of their personality rather than situational constraints). Again the theory has been "scaled up" to investigate group processes of sense making – as a potential definition of organizational culture:

> ...the dynamic product of a process of collective 'sense making' where individuals communicate and agree common explanations for work-related events in an effort to understand, predict and control their environment. (Silvester et al., 1999, p. 4)

Attribution analysis is a data analysis strategy rather than a data collection strategy. Data are usually collected through individual interview transcripts and then analyzed for the use of particular attributions, e.g. whether the cause of an event is seen to be stable over time or to be amenable to change (Silvester, 1998). Like the other methods already reviewed, its "qualitative" nature is due to the fact that constructs are not imposed on the respondent as they would be in a questionnaire. However, unlike the other methods, freely elicited comments are not then grouped according to emergent themes but analyzed according to an existing coding framework derived from more general attribution theory. Again, the method is assumed to be able to access a more in-depth account of culture.

In the one study so far to apply this strategy to cultural analysis, the research focused on assessing similarities and differences in group attributions for the success or failure of a culture change programme (Silvester et al., 1999). Thus, the method did not appear to be used to assess culture itself. To this extent, the utility of the method for cultural analysis specifically must be viewed as yet to be explored. Indeed, given the definition above, one might have hoped the method would be used to access this "dynamic" process in a more dynamic fashion. In the published paper, there is very little consideration even of what was actually said in the interviews, the emphasis very much being on counting the different kinds of attributions that were made and comparing this across groups. So here again, categorization, quantification and concerns over the reliabilities of ratings turn what might have been an interesting in-depth analysis of organizational processes into something more superficial.

## Discourse Analysis

Within social psychology, the last decade has seen a growing focus on language and conversation in the social construction of reality (Parker, 1992; Potter and Wetherell, 1987; Shotter, 1993). Eschewing the search for an "objective truth" by the application of scientific methods, it is proposed that versions of reality are instead created through our social interactions, particularly through language. Thus, this work is drawing on very different underlying assumptions about the nature of reality (ontology) and how knowledge is created (epistemology) than the studies so far described. This perspective has found its methodological expression in discourse analysis (Potter and Wetherell, 1987). Written works or conversation or interview transcripts are analyzed to discover what versions of reality are created to fulfil what kinds of purposes. In relation to organizational culture, the method of discourse analysis, therefore, does not fit well within a functionalist paradigm. Instead, the implication is that organizational culture may be constructed and re-constructed everyday in the conversations of employees. Such a method has been labelled "qualitative" because it focuses on the free expression of complex ideas by individuals (Gamble and Gibson, 1999).

Discourse analysis has so far found little application in the area of organizational analysis in general, less still as a method of cultural analysis specifically. A very recent study by Gamble and Gibson (1999), however, has used discourse analysis to investigate the effect of national cultural values on the process of executive decision making, specifically financial controllers' explanations for their involvement (or otherwise) in the development of budgetary control processes in the Hong Kong hotel trade. Gamble and Gibson appear to define culture as "implicit values" which, they argue, are therefore not easily articulated or even fully conscious. Again we see here the desire to use "qualitative methods" to go beyond surface descriptions of organizational life. They did not ask their interview respondents directly about cultural influences on decision making, preferring instead to ask about their personal involvement in the financial decision making process and then analyze the resultant transcripts to identify words or short phrases that pertained to cultural influences on explanations for involvement or non-involvement. From their analysis, they were able to draw conclusions about the differences between the Chinese approach to decision making (reflecting a focus on co-operation and avoiding conflict) and Western approaches.

Despite their claim to be using discourse analysis, the analysis presented in the paper does not seem to concur with the tenets of this approach. For example, there is a concern that specific organizations might "distort the data" and that utterances should be "consistent" (p. 229). In discourse analysis, contradictions and variability are seen as unavoidable; indeed their analysis can be valuable in exposing particular functions of the discourse produced in specific contexts (Potter and Wetherell, 1987). The objective of the Gamble and Gibson (1999) study is clearly to categorize and find generalizable themes that might reflect some underlying reality, much as the other studies described in this section, rather than the constructionist perspective usually adopted by discourse analysts. Gamble and Gibson may have adopted the analysis strategy without the underlying epistemology. Consequently, we have yet to assess the utility of discourse analysis for cultural analysis.

## Lessons to be Drawn from Psychological Approaches

The studies described above indicate that researchers working within a psychological perspective are beginning to take seriously the call for the adoption of qualitative techniques in the analysis of organizational culture (Jermier et al., 1991). However, the spread of studies is still very limited. In particular, in many cases only one or two research groups have adopted specific techniques; thus, we are very far from building up an in-depth picture over several studies of the utility or effectiveness of specific methods.

The techniques are explicitly defined as qualitative because categories are not imposed by the researcher (although such categories are then derived from these data entirely by the researcher, defined as "emergent") and the data are viewed as ecologically valid (although they are then subjected to testing of the generalizability of the categories derived, often through questionnaires and statistical analysis). Most of the studies conducted have tended to apply their qualitative methods from within a positivist epistemology, and often a functionalist perspective on culture, leading to a rather restrictive view of the use of qualitative methods for cultural analysis. In parti-cular, from the review above, we see a common concern to derive generalizable themes from the "rich data" generated (often testing these themes in quantifiable question-naires). Thus, some of the supposed benefits of qualitative methods are lost. The view of culture is often a unitarist one, but some scope may be made for a limited amount of differentiation (e.g. group differences). Ambiguity, however, seems actively discour-aged, despite the fact that qualitative methods may lend themselves to this analytical concern.

The use of these methods so far also seems to bear out the concerns of Hollway (1991, p. 145) as to the distortion of the cultural concept:

Although the idea of culture suggests a theoretical shift of target to a domain outside the individual... 'culture' has been quickly reduced to concepts such as attitudes and values which themselves are contained within a social psychological set of assumptions.

The problem of building up a picture of an holistic organizational culture (which may be more than the sum of its parts) that may be differentially constructed at different times in different contexts from the responses of specific individuals at one point in time are rarely explicitly acknowledged in these studies. Indeed, they all share the assumption that culture is to be found in the values, beliefs and behaviours of individuals, rather than, for example, through social interactions. While this is one possible definition of culture it denies other possibilities and to this extent such studies must remain, at best, very partial accounts. Whether these kinds of methods could be used to explore a more dynamic and socially constructed concept of culture remains to be seen.

# ANTHROPOLOGICAL APPROACHES

The notion of organizational culture originally emerged from anthropological studies (Denison, 1996). In contrast to the novelty of the psychological studies we examined earlier, many of the classic studies of organizational culture are based in the ethnographic approach of anthropology. However, there are barriers to a straightforward description of ethnographic analyses of organizational culture. First, since culture is a fundamental concept in anthropology it is often used as a means of investigating some more specific aspect of an organization (e.g. gender: Alvesson, 1998; management: Watson, 1994; emotion: Van Maanen and Kunda, 1989). Secondly, as Denison and others point out, ethnographic studies do not sit easily within the requirements for publication in academic journals. They tend to be long and detailed, highly specific and do not fit within the scientific model requiring replicable and generalizable knowledge. Finally, the requirements for "good" ethnography are contested with differing emphases on reflexivity, reliability and political sensitivity. These issues leave many authors struggling with an uneasy mix of methodologies and ontologies.

Rather than the clear divisions in the last section, the methods discussed here overlap. This section will first examine broad ethnographic studies concentrating on work in the field and the collection of data from multiple sources. This will then be contrasted to specific studies of stories and history to examine culture.

## Ethnography

These studies are based in an involvement in the day to day activities that characterize the organization: observation of rites, rituals and artefacts and studies of language use, social interaction and stories and myths. The methods emphasize the importance of complete immersion in the field. Researchers may be outside observers, internal participants or somewhere in between. Some studies argue for one researcher to be in the organization and one to remain outside to maintain objectivity in analysis (Alvesson, 1998). The methods for gathering data include observation of social interactions occurring spontaneously, participation in formal events, interviews, and collection of written documents, videotapes and other artefacts. The stress is on living among the data in order to learn the rules of organizational life. Interaction with organization members should be for a frequency and duration sufficient to understand how and why they construct their social world as it is and to be able to explain it to others.

Ethnography rejects the aim of prediction for one of understanding. Ethnography concentrates on notions of meaning and is based in the social construction of knowledge. Rosen (1991, p. 6) considers that understanding culture implies "a perspective exploring how the shared meaning system of the members of any particular organization is created and recreated in relationship to the social processes of organization". This emphasis on processes of social construction requires long-term observation and participation in the day to day life of the organization. A drawback of this approach is that, generally, the richness of the data and the amount of detail covered mean that such studies are more likely to be published in book form than in journal articles.

The Witmer (1997) account of Alcoholics Anonymous (A.A.) is unusual in that it is an article using an ethnographic approach to culture that is scrupulous in its description of theory, method and analysis. She argues that "As A.A. members accept themselves and each other, they create and are created by an organizational culture of sobriety" (p. 325). She uses structuration theory (Giddens, 1984) as an approach to examining the communicative elements of organizational culture. Witmer's approach is interesting in following the argument of Martin (1992) for a multiperspective approach combining integration, differentiation and fragmentation views of culture. Her approach is both social constructionist interpretivist and realist. She draws on the Jick (1983) notion of within method triangulation to explore the validity of her findings.

Witmer collects a huge amount of data from a wide variety of sources over a year. She attends meetings and social events as a participant observer; she collects 60 "self stories" (Denzin, 1989), transcribes tapes made from meetings and available for sale, examines formal histories and informal weekly newsletters and carries out formal and informal interviews. Her analysis uses NUD*IST to code transcripts and she describes the ongoing and iterative process of data gathering and analysis in some detail.

She discusses the ways in which A.A. functions to help alcoholics through its communication practices. This is through the routines practised in social interaction. For example, all members have to recite the formula "I am Clifton and I am an alcoholic" before they are acknowledged by the group, "Hi, Clifton". The group concentrates on narratives of the horrors of previous drinking lives and the pleasures of a current sober life. There are routines associated with the privilege of being a member of the group. History, like many corporate histories, emphasizes the role of the group founder "Big Al" (p. 336) and the organizational founders (Bill W and Doctor Bob, p. 337). Witmer suggests that the culture of the organization becomes internalized as tacit knowledge that members apply to all their social interactions. "Members recursively recreate the A.A. organizational structures in order to function in sobriety. A.A. members' frequent interactions with one another away from the temporal meetings, coupled with organizationally imposed time limitations, allow the recovering alcoholic to re-enact the structures of signification, legitimation, and domination that both constrain and recreate the alcoholic self." (p. 344). Her study enables her to look both at the intensity with which the group she studies adopts the A.A. culture and also the ways in which culture may be conflicted, fragmented and differ between groups. She considers, for example, individual differences in definitions and the role of masculine domination.

Witmer addresses culture as a process open to change. Unlike the psychological studies, she concentrates on the interaction between individuals and culture rather than accessing culture through categorizing individual perceptions. She argues that structuration avoids the problems of the micro-macro level by focusing on the interaction between agents and the institution rather than looking at agents within an organizational culture. She also discusses the extent to which these mechanisms may be specific to the local culture. However, a peculiar quality of this study is the use of the absent author and the complete lack of any personal presence of reflexivity in the study. While adopting a theoretical position in interpretivism this study maintains the conventions of an objectivist and positivist account. It is concerned with the achievement of individual change through membership of an organizational culture.

In contrast to this, Rachel (1996) emphasizes the messiness of ethnography and her own role "as a subject of the practices and discourses of the various communities that constituted my study" (p. 113). She describes ethnography as a craft emphasizing the time to learn and to practice and the cost of such studies and is deliberately explicit about her role and subjective experience of "doing ethnography". These differences are part of the continuing debate about the role of reflexivity in research.

## Story Analysis

The study of stories, which could be one aspect of ethnography, may be dealt with separately. Stories told within organizations articulate organizational frames of reference (Shrivastava and Schneider, 1984). The dramatization of organizational events conveys important cultural meanings (Trice and Beyer, 1993, p. 79). Hansen and Kahnweiler (1993) argue that stories are derived from shared norms and values and so act as "cultural codes". Stories are seen therefore as both expressing and imposing meanings in organizations.

Stories are quite specifically defined. Hansen and Kahnweiler say that "Stories differ from gossip and other forms of corporate communication in that they possess a setting, a cast of characters, and a plot that resolves some sort of crisis" (p. 1393). Martin (1992) suggests that they also contain a moral that may both reflect and guide the belief systems of the story teller. The stories may be those published corporate glossies (Martin et al., 1983), emerge in informal discussions at work (Boje, 1991) or be elicited by questionnaire (Stevenson and Bartunek, 1996). The two studies examined here used elicited stories.

Hahnsen and Kahnweiler emphasize the role of their examination of stories from human resource development (HR) professionals and corporate executives drawn from a range of different organizations in order to identify differences between *occupational* cultures. "Subjects" were asked "to tell a story about any event portraying any cast of characters that could have occurred in their organization in the last 6 months" (p. 1397). Additionally they used semi-structured interviews, field observations and "visualizing". This last method included selecting a series of pictures and using them to illustrate a story.

They examine their stories for a series of psychological issues: sense of ego, conflict, impression of others, decision making and aberrant behaviour. The assumption is that the culture will be reflected in or produced by individual psychological variables. Like the psychological studies mentioned above they do not address social interaction directly. They explicitly state that their planned use of qualitative research has allowed them access to their participants' views and a flexibility that they could not achieve through experimental research. This contrast with the positivist experimental method appears to be an apology for a qualitative approach. It allows participants to generate data but these data then have to be rigorously categorized. They have taken some pains to ensure reliability (multiple coders and multiple data collection methods) and internal validity (acceptance by participants). They point out that external validity is irrelevant, as they are not attempting to predict or generalize. However, they do appear to consider that their interpretations can be applied to HR generally.

Stevenson and Bartunek (1996, p. 86) also identify stories "as a means of determining the understanding(s), or culture(s), present within a particular organization or organizational group". Their measure of culture in their investigation of power, interaction, position and agreement in a US school used stories. As part of a questionnaire they asked: *If you were telling a story or anecdote that captures the essence of what its like to work at this school, what would you say?* The stories were then content analyzed and categorized into five types of predicament. They draw on grounded theory in treating these categories as emergent from the data.

This study attempts to empirically investigate Martin's three approaches to culture. Rather than seeing these as three viewpoints of an investigator, they use an empirical approach to identify which is "true". They appear to be treating culture as a stable variable situated within individuals, very much as the psychological approaches have done. The study is working with specifically elicited stories in an artificial format rather than emergent, lived social processes. It is divorcing the individual story from its natural social context. We have no way of knowing whether these stories would ever be told to newcomers or how far they are shared in social interaction. Categorizing stories in this way reduces the richness of the data and obscures the function of stories, losing any of the ambivalence and contradictions that might be explored through discourse analysis.

Hansen and Kahnweiler (1993, p. 1391) are explicit in their approach to "a research methodology which utilizes story telling as a vehicle for understanding, explaining and comparing corporate cultures". They go on to claim that "this ethnographic technique can be used systematically to examine and to correlate the expectations for interpersonal relations found in organizational subcultures" (p. 1392). Both studies of analysis through stories described here are clearly using ethnographic methodology for functionalist ends. For them, "Storytelling, in sum, represents a largely untapped vehicle for the orderly study of corporate life" (p. 1392), which seems a long way from the messier qualitative studies described by Kunda (1992) and Van Maanen (1987). Indeed it may be questioned how far these reflect the "thick description" which is allegedly a characteristic of qualitative research.

## Analysis of Organizational History

One approach to analyzing culture is to study the ways in which it has emerged over time. Deal and Kennedy (1982) and Peters and Waterman (1982) celebrate the success of an organization's founder and Schein (1992) concentrates on an analysis of the psychodynamics of early leaders. Accounts by organization members are treated as uncontested by these writers. For example, the history of IBM is drawn entirely from a book written by the founder's son. Even Pettigrew (1979), whose approach to culture is more complex and sophisticated, uses documentary sources in ways that tend to privilege the importance of entrepreneurial founders. This tendency to see the organization's culture as a reflection of the founder's beliefs and values reinforces a unitary view of culture.

Business histories have traditionally been produced as the result of a commission and have tended not to encourage critical investigation. As a result, both historians and organizational scholars have treated them with considerable scepticism. However, there are exceptions. Whipp and Clark (1986) produced a critical history of innovation at Rover using interviews and citation from company documents including Director's minutes, Boje (1995) used written narratives and audio and video-tapes to examine multiple variations of the Disney stories, and Church (1996) argued that Nuffield left "a culture which inhibited corporate adaptability" (p. 582). Critical historical analysis of organizations is, therefore, possible.

Rowlinson and Procter (1999) scorn warnings that official publications cannot be treated as serious data because they are purely a public relations exercise. They argue that most organization's archives, far from being carefully groomed, are completely chaotic. In fact, historians and ethnographers face the same problem of locating and defining sources and constructing a story. Old style commissioned business histories can be treated as primary cultural artefacts in the same way as interview transcripts (Silverman, 1993).

Historical narratives must be subject to verification. To achieve this historians provide "copious footnotes referring to traceable sources". Ethnography, on the other hand, calls for verisimilitude or the look of truth. Case studies often disguise the identity of the organizations they study, which is necessary to preserve the confidentiality of their informants (Martin, 1992; Watson, 1994). Rowlinson and Procter claim that while historians tend to be inveterate empiricists obsessed with setting the record straight, there are exceptions like Schama (1989) who clearly accepts the fictional element in history.

The concept of organizational culture and its various subjective elements can be linked to the treatment by Hobsbawm (1983, pp. 1–2) of "invented tradition" which presents a form of historical unity and continuity constructed in retrospect. An example of the reflexive use of historical data to examine culture is given by Rowlinson and Hassard (1993) in their "History of the Histories of Cadbury". Here they use the notion of invented tradition to demonstrate the way in which significance was retrospectively attached to the founders' Quaker beliefs.

However, organizational culture approaches imply that history alone is not enough. Pettigrew uses documents to reinforce stories from interviews. Peters and Waterman

(1982) split history from myth, arguing that a good anecdote is more persuasive than historical fact. Similarly, Schein (1992) argues that cultures simplify and reinterpret the events of history to fit into themes that make cultural sense. Thus, culture researchers tend to emphasize the use of history to reinforce current stories rather than as an end in itself. Van Maanen (1987, p. 72) argues that "it is possible to analyze groups from an ahistorical perspective". Organizational culture is revealed through the traces that can be uncovered in the present. Ethnographers emphasize "remembered history" over that studied by historians (Alvesson and Berg, 1992).

Rowlinson and Procter (1999) argue that while there are a number of reasons why studies of organizational culture and business history have not proved compatible, there is a strong case for developing this area. Limitations so far have been based in the different theoretical and practical background, treatment of data and approach to analysis of the two areas. First, business histories have tended to be atheoretical. They were usually commissioned hagiographies emphasizing founder-centred corporate culture and emphasizing unity and continuity over time. Secondly, anthropological tools favoured by ethnographers have emphasized the spoken word above the written records favoured by historians. Finally, the influence of post-structuralism on culture studies undermines history's emphasis on uncovering "the facts" in favour of acknowledging the subjectivity of accounts.

## Lessons to be Drawn from Anthropological Approaches

The recent empirical papers described here do not appear representative of the anti-positivist stance claimed for ethnography. None could be accused of messiness and most show a scrupulous attention to issues of reliability and neglect or downplay any ambiguity or contradiction. Theoretical or review papers, in contrast, espouse a more critical approach to evidence. They emphasize the importance of reflexivity and sensitivity to issues of power and politics. However, concern with issues of voice, of acknowledging who is speaking and who has the privilege of being heard, is largely absent from the papers we have examined. They generally follow the traditions of scholarly reporting in presenting an orderly account from an invisible author.

It would appear that aspects of qualitative methods are being adopted within the mainstream without regard for the fundamental epistemological and political issues raised. However, it is not clear how far this reflects the original aims and orientations of the researchers and how far this is an artefact resulting from the cultural norms of academic writing. Studies in the field, generate a huge amount of data. Any account will have to be rigorously edited to fit within the space restraints of journals.

Surprisingly, then, it seems that recent qualitative analyses of culture derived from anthropology are subject to some of the same limitations as those identified in the psychological work. The work we examined on stories especially categorized qualitative data and so lost some of the thick description idealized in culture research. Ethnographic studies tend to concentrate on specific artefacts rather than offering a general view of culture.

# FUTURE DEVELOPMENTS

Ethnographers are increasingly concerned with the craft of writing about culture as much as the craft of researching it. One argument is that post-modernism has made us more tolerant of the source of different forms of evidence but more critical and reflective in our analysis of this evidence (Calas and Smircich, 1999). So, while the distinction between those approaches that are heavily dependent on statistical analysis and those that are not may weaken, the distinction between those who attempt a totalizing metanarrative and those who reflect on the implications of their own little stories will become greater. Analyses will be expected to examine the relation between power and knowledge and to be ambivalent about the ways in which knowledge is represented. Writers will be expected to adopt a clear and explicit ethical posture and reflect on whose interests their reports will serve. At first glance this would appear to be consistent with Denison's optimistic view.

> Data, one must conclude, are actually rather benign. It is our interpretations that bring meaning to them, label the phenomenon, and conceptualise the link between research and action. The capacity to tolerate (and encourage) multi-faceted interpretations of eclectic forms of evidence may in fact be a requisite level of complexity for understanding the extraordinarily complex topic of organizational culture. (Denison, 1996, p. 646)

However, as we mentioned earlier, there is an implicit realist assumption that data exist and just have to be collected. The social constructionist view of data as negotiated and interactively constructed demonstrates the argument for reflexivity in accounts. Post-modernism challenges an objective stance on knowledge, arguing that we are all subjectively positioned. Our particular standpoint will not only influence our interpretation but, more fundamentally, will have an impact on what we see as data. The solution is not the positivist approach of making the author invisible but the reflexive position of openness.

So far it would seem that while Calas and Smircich (1999) present a well supported case for the future of organizational research, it is not the only possibility. One suggestion may be that while we have become more tolerant of different and qualitative approaches to *evidence* we are reluctant to move away from positivist models of *analysis* and *reporting*. Qualitative data are being added to a realist and functionalist analysis of organizations. It is a source of data for triangulation that may help overcome some of the limitations of purely quantitative analysis.

# CONCLUSION

The qualitative analysis of organizational culture has used methods derived from psychology and anthropology. While theoretical analysis suggests a number of clear dichotomies between quantitative and qualitative, functionalist and interpretivist, the empirical data do not neatly fit these categories. The research reported is qualitative in the sense that it uses open-ended data elicited from participants. However, it does not consistently conform to the other characteristics associated with qualitative research.

Data are often categorized for analysis, reducing the richness and complexity, and are often elicited from individuals in artificial circumstances (interview or survey) rather than observed naturally in the field. Understandings of culture tend to identify common themes from individual accounts rather than interactive constructions observed socially and the picture presented is static rather than processual. It seems that while qualitative analysis is ideally suited to exploring the concept of culture the opportunities presented have yet to be fully exploited.

# REFERENCES

Alvesson, M. (1998) Gender relations and identity at work: a case study of masculinities and feminities in an advertising agency. Human Relations, 51: 969–1005.

Alvesson, M. and Berg, P.O. (1992) Corporate Culture and Organizational Symbolism. Berlin: Walter de Gruyter.

Boje, D.M. (1991) The storytelling organization: a study of story performance in an office supply firm. Administrative Science Quarterly, 36: 106–126.

Boje, D.M. (1995) Stories of the storytelling organization: a postmodern analysis of Disney as "Tamara-land". Academy of Management Journal, 38: 997–1035.

Calas, M.B. and Smircich, L. (1999) Past postmodernism? Reflections and tentative directions. Academy of Management Review, 24: 649–671.

Cassell, C. and Symon, G. (1998) Quiet revolutions and radical transformations. Organization Studies, 19: 1039–1043.

Chell, E. (1998) Critical incident technique. In G. Symon and C. Cassell (Eds), Qualitative Methods and Analysis in Organizational Research. London: Sage.

Church, R.A. (1996) Deconstructing Nuffield: the evolution of managerial culture in the British motor industry. Economic History Review, 159: 561–583.

Deal, T. and Kennedy, A. (1982) Corporate Cultures: the Rites and Rituals of Corporate Life. Reading, MA: Addison-Wesley.

Denison, D.R. (1996) What is the difference between organizational culture and organizational climate? A native's point of view on a decade of paradigm wars. Academy of Management Review, 21: 619–654.

Denzin, N.K. (1989) Interpretive Interactionsim, Vol. 16. Applied Social Research Methods Series. Newbury Park, CA: Sage.

Gamble, P. and Gibson, D. (1999) Executive values and decision-making: the relationship of culture and information flows. Journal of Management Studies, 36: 217–240.

Gammack, J. and Stephens, R. (1994) Repertory grid in constructive interaction. In C. Cassell and G. Symon (Eds), Qualitative Methods in Organizational Research. London: Sage.

Giddens, A. (1984) The Constitution of Society: Outline of the Theory of Structuration. Berkeley, CA: University of California Press.

Gundry, L. and Rousseau, D. (1994) Critical incidents in communicating culture to newcomers: the meaning is the message. Human Relations, 47: 1063–1087.

Hansen, C.D. and Kahnweiler, W.M. (1993) Storytelling: an instrument for understanding the dynamics of corporate relationships. Human Relations, 46: 1391–1409.

Henwood, K. (1996) Qualitative inquiry: perspectives, methods and psychology. In J. Richardson (Ed), Handbook of Qualitative Research Methods for Psychology and the Social Sciences. Leicester: BPS Books.

Hobsbawm, E. (1983) Introduction: inventing traditions in The invention of tradition. E. Hobsbawn and T. Ranger (Eds), Cambridge: Cambridge University Press.

Hollway, W. (1991) Work Psychology and Organizational Behaviour. London: Sage.

Jankowicz, A. (1990) Applications of personal construct theory in business practice. In G. Neimeyer and R. Neimeyer (Eds), Advances in Personal Construct Psychology, Vol. I. New York: JAI Press.

Jermier, J., Slocum, J., Fry, L. and Gaines, J. (1991) Organizational subcultures in a soft bureaucracy: resistance behind the myth and facade of an official culture. Organization Science, 2: 170–194.

Jick, T. (1983) Mixing qualitative and quantitative methods: triangulation in action. In J. Van Maanen (Ed), Qualitative Methodology, pp. 135–148. Beverly Hills, CA: Sage.

Kunda, G. (1992) Engineering Culture. Philadelphia, PA: Temple University Press.

Langan-Fox, J. and Tan, P. (1997) Images of a culture in transition: personal constructs of organizational stability and change. Journal of Occupational and Organizational Psychology, 70: 273–294.

Locatelli, V. and West, M. (1992) On elephants and blind researchers: methods for accessing culture in organization. Discussion paper no. 95, ESRC Centre for Economic Performance.

Martin, J. (1992) Cultures in Organizations: Three Perspectives. Oxford: Oxford University Press.

Martin, J., Feldman, M.S., Hatch, M.J. and Sitkin, S.B. (1983) The uniqueness paradox in organizational stories. Administrative Science Quarterly, 28: 438–453.

McClelland, D. (1976) A Guide to Job Competency Assessment. Boston, MA: McBer.

McPartland, T. (1965) Manual for the Twenty Statements Problem (Revised). Kansas City, MO: Department of Research, Greater Kansas City Mental Health Foundation.

Meyerson, D. (1991) Acknowledging and uncovering ambiguities. In P. Frost, L. Moore, M. Louis, C. Lundberg and J. Martin (Eds), Reframing Organizational Culture. Beverly Hills, CA: Sage.

Mohan, M.L. (1993) Organizational Communication and Cultural Vision: Approaches for Analysis. Albany, NY: SUNY Press.

Parker, I. (1992) Discourse Dynamics. London: Routledge.

Peters, T.J. and Waterman, R.H. (1982) In Search of Excellence. London: Harper and Row.

Pettigrew, A.M. (1979) On studying organizational cultures. Administrative Science Quarterly, 25: 570–581.

Potter, J. and Wetherell, M. (1987) Discourse and Social Psychology. London: Sage.

Rachel, J. (1996) Ethnography: practical implementation. In J.T.E. Richardson (Ed), Handbook of Qualitative Research Methods for Psychology and the Social Sciences. Leicester: BPS Books.

Rees, A. and Nicholson, N. (1994) The Twenty Statements Test. In C. Cassell and G. Symon (Eds), Qualitative Methods in Organizational Research. London: Sage.

Rosen, M. (1991) Coming to terms with the field: understanding and doing organizational ethnography. Journal of Management Studies, 28: 1–24.

Rousseau, D. (1990) Assessing organizational culture: the case for multiple measures. In B. Schneider (Ed), Frontiers in Industrial and Organizational Psychology, Vol. III. San Francisco, CA: Jossey-Bass.

Rowlinson, M. and Hassard, J. (1993) The invention of corporate culture: a history of the histories of Cadbury. Human Relations, 46: 299–326.

Rowlinson, M. and Procter, S. (1999) Organizational culture and business history. Organization Studies, 20: 369–396.

Schama, S. (1989) Citizens: a Chronicle of the French Revolution. London: Penguin.

Schein, E. (1990) Organizational culture. American Psychologist, 45: 109–119.

Schein, E. (1992) Organizational Culture and Leadership, 2nd Edn. San Francisco, CA: Jossey-Bass.

Shotter, J. (1993) Conversational Realities. London: Sage.

Shrivastava, P. and Schneider, S. (1984) Organizational frames of reference. Human Relations, 37: 795–809.

Silverman, D. (1993) Interpreting Qualitative Data. London: Sage.

Silvester, J. (1998) Attributional coding. In G. Symon and C. Cassell (Eds), Qualitative Methods and Analysis in Organizational Research. London: Sage.

Silvester, J., Anderson, N. and Patterson, F. (1999) Organizational culture change: an inter-group attributional analysis. Journal of Occupational and Organizational Psychology, 72: 1–23.

Smircich, L. (1983) Concepts of culture and organizational analysis. Administrative Science Quarterly, 28: 339–358.

Stevenson, W.B. and Bartunek, J.M. (1996) Power, interaction and the generation of cultural agreement in organizations. Human Relations, 49: 75–103.

Stewart, V. and Stewart, A. (1981) Business Applications of Repertory Grid. London: McGraw-Hill.

Symon, G. and Cassell, C. (1998) Reflections on the use of qualitative methods. In G. Symon and C. Cassell (Eds), Qualitative Methods and Data Analysis in Organizational Research. London: Sage.

Trice, H. and Beyer, J. (1993) The Cultures of Work Organizations. Englewood Cliffs, NJ: Prentice Hall.

Van Maanen, J. (1987) Tales of the Field: on Writing Ethnography. Chicago, IL: University of Chicago Press.

Van Maanen, J. and Kunda, G. (1989) "Real feelings": emotional expression and organizational culture. Research in Organizational Behavior, 11: 43–103.

Walker, H., Symon, G. and Davies, B. (1996) Assessing organizational culture: a comparison of methods. International Journal of Selection and Assessment, 4: 96–105.

Watson, T.J. (1994) In Search of Management. London: Routledge.

Whipp, R. and Clark, P. (1986) Innovation and the Auto Industry. London: Pinter.

Witmer, D.F. (1997) Communication and recovery: structuration as an ontological approach to organizational culture. Communication Monographs, 64: 324–349.

# Chapter 7

# Cultural Complexity in Organizations: the Value and Limitations of Qualitative Methodology and Approaches

**Sonja Sackmann**
*Institüt für Personal- und Organisationsforschung,
Universität BW München, Munich, Germany*

## INTRODUCTION

The concept of culture applied to organizations has received much attention in the management literature since the early 1980s with differing interests. While organizational theorists were predominantly interested in a better understanding of organizational life, practitioners wanted to know how to manage and control this additional organizational variable or use it as another tool to better manage organizations. The increasing interest in shareholder value has, in addition, raised the question of to what extent culture or different kinds of cultures may contribute to the performance of a firm and how (see Part II, Chapter 4).

All these kinds of interests require first an understanding of what culture applied to organizations *actually is* before it can be researched, assessed and managed, and before its contribution to performance can be determined. Such an understanding refers to both the concept as well as to its specific realization within a concrete organization. Depending on the conceptualization of culture, different kinds of operationalizations of its core components and different kinds of assessment methods may be more or less appropriate for investigation.

During the past 20 years, the concept of culture in organizational settings has been increasingly refined and differentiated. Early works in the organization theory and management literature assumed one culture to one organization, considered organizational boundaries also to be the natural boundaries of organizational culture and emphasized homogenous cultures.[1] More recent work differentiates between cultural integration, cultural differentiation and cultural fragmentation (Martin, 1992). Others look at culture as something that may be composed of multiple cultures (Phillips and Sackmann, 1992) and that may encompass integrated, differentiated or fragmented aspects simultaneously. Payne (Part II, Chapter 5) notes that shared individual perceptions result in climates that vary in intensity, consensus and pervasiveness. Such perspectives lead to what I have called "cultural complexity" in organizations (Sackmann, 1997).

This chapter will start from the cultural complexity perspective and address research and assessment issues (the word assessor is used instead of researcher, but the messages are the same for people in both roles) related to cultural complexity in organizational settings. Based on the notion that the "what" that is going to be assessed influences the "how" it should be assessed, the concept of culture and cultural complexity will be explored with the respective implications for research. Given the conceptualization of cultural complexity, emphasis will be placed on qualitative research issues, exploring their contributions as well as their limitations. In a concluding section, future research issues are discussed.

## WHAT DOES "CULTURAL COMPLEXITY" MEAN? CRITICAL IMPLICATIONS FOR ITS ASSESSMENT

The concept of cultural complexity is based on a specific understanding of *culture* and *its characteristics* (namely complexity) within the context of organizations. Both are explicated in this section since they have immediate implications for its study and assessment. As in the field of anthropology in which the concept of culture is rooted, different meanings and understandings are associated with the concept of culture (Sackmann, 1989). Based on a cognitive perspective (Sackmann, 1991a), the essence of culture can be defined as:

> a cultural knowledge base *commonly-held* by a *group* of people. This cultural knowledge base is *typical* for the group. It serves as guides to acceptable perception, thought, feeling, and behaviour, and it may become manifest in the group's values, norms, behaviours and artifacts. The cultural knowledge base is *tacit*, *acquired*, and *passed on* to new members of the group.

This definition has several implications for the study of culture of which the most important will now be discussed.[2] Each definitional element in turn will be examined.

---

[1] For a more detailed discussion see, for example, Sackmann (1991a).
[2] For a more detailed discussion of these implication see Phillips and Sackmann (1992).

# Cultural Knowledge Base

If a cultural knowledge base (Sackmann, 1991a) is considered the essence or the core of culture, research efforts need to focus on this cultural knowledge base.[3] Cultural knowledge is, unfortunately, nothing material but something that people hold in their minds. The cultural knowledge base consists in part of invisible, unspoken, taken-for-granted premises, that are not directly observable. Instead, they need to be inferred. Inferences about this cultural knowledge can be made from manifestations such as verbal and non-verbal behaviours as well as artefacts. Examples of culturally relevant verbal behaviours are specific jargon (Martin et al., 1985), humour (Vinton, 1983), the way people address each other or the language that is in use within the specific organization setting. Examples of culturally relevant non-verbal behaviours are rites, rituals, or ceremonies (e.g. Trice et al., 1969). Artifacts are, for example, buildings, the use of space, pictures, furniture, technology, products, etc. All manifestations belong to the cultural network (Sackmann, 1983). An understanding of these cultural manifestations requires, however, an exploration of the underlying meanings which members of a specific cultural setting attribute to them.[4] Such an exploration implies a deep probing into the specific cultural setting, into its culture core of sense making, meaning creation and meaning attribution. It requires an appreciation and an understanding from within the research setting rather than from the outside by a researcher who plays the role of an "onlooker" (Evered and Louis, 1981). Exclusive reliance on cultural manifestations for understanding a given culture context can be misleading since those manifestations may be relics of the past having lost their original meaning (Sackmann, 1991b). To achieve an understanding of the sense making and interpretation mechanisms of a cultural setting, assessors, therefore, need to probe into its cultural knowledge base. Cultural manifestations can be used for purposes of validation.

Furthermore, the cultural knowledge base implies that the essence of culture is not only composed of one specific kind of cultural knowledge but instead of an interconnected system of knowledge. This implies that assessors need to acknowledge the existence of a cultural knowledge structure that is interconnected even if they focus in their research just on certain aspects which are of topical interest to them. It also means that assessors need to critically question their choice and resist the urge to only focus on those aspects of cultural knowledge which are easily discernible. Examples from past research show that the latter point is a critical one. While organizational culture was mostly defined in a holistic way, being composed of basic values, norms, and beliefs, some research efforts were, however, focussed on single cultural components such as values (e.g. Peters and Waterman, 1982), norms (Allen, 1984; Kilmann and Saxton, 1983), or basic assumptions (e.g. Schein, 1985). For this reason, Sackmann (1985, 1991a,b) has operationalized the culture core in terms of cultural knowledge being composed of four different kinds of knowledge:

---

[3] The cultural knowledge base is a specific operationalization of cognitive constructs such as basic assumptions and beliefs. Research efforts which focus on cognitive concepts such as basic beliefs (Sapienza, 1985), the collective programming of the human mind (Hofstede, 1980), or basic assumptions (Phillips, 1990; Schein, 1985) are included.

[4] For a more detailed discussion of this issue see Sackmann (1991b).

- *Axiomatic knowledge*[5] is composed of the basic axioms or assumptions set by the group members. Axiomatic knowledge refers to the "why" of things and cannot be further reduced or explained. The central axioms or basic assumptions of a group may refer to the kind of people that are believed to fit best with the group, the kind of structural arrangements that are believed to be the best for the group to pursue its goals and to attract the desired people, as well as axioms about the ultimate purpose of the group, and about its strategy.
- *Directory knowledge*[6] refers to the "how" things are done in a group. What are the typical ways of approaching and solving a problem? How are decisions typically being made? What are the best ways to recruit and socialize people into the organization? How is daily work accomplished? How do members interact with each other and with members from other groups, etc?
- *Recipe knowledge*[7] refers to prescriptions. Recipe knowledge represents lessons learnt in past experiences. It contains recipes of success and recipes of failure and contains, hence, strong recommendations of what to do and what not to do in terms of what works and what does not work – always, however, on the basis of past experience.
- *Dictionary knowledge* refers to the "what" – what is addressed in an organization, what is not, what is considered an issue, what is a non-issue. Dictionary knowledge serves organizational members as a dictionary that contains the labels relevant in a given organization and their specific meaning and interpretation within that cultural context.

These four types of cultural knowledge are collective cognitive representations of different facets of organizational reality within a given group. They delineate the collective meaning structure underlying the group members' perceptions, thoughts, feelings and actions. This conceptualization enables organizational researchers to assess the complexity of the cultural context of a firm in differentiated ways. This conception allows the assessment of potentially existing and forming subcultures and various degrees of integration, differentiation, and/or fragmentation within a cultural knowledge base as well as between the four different kinds of cultural knowledge. Based on my research, one may, for example, hypothesize that the amount of recipe knowledge is positively correlated with the performance of a firm – the more recipe knowledge available without correlates in directory knowledge, the more likely it is that the performance level of the organization is low.

---

[5] Axiomatic knowledge is similar to basic assumptions (Phillips, 1990; Schein, 1985). In regard to content, axiomatic knowledge is, however, not restricted to the five assumptions that go back to the work of Kroeber and Kluckhohn (1952).

[6] Directory knowledge refers to the knowledge or cognitive constructions in regard to practices. My research has shown that organizational members may not be aware of the axiomatic knowledge; their practices which are grounded in directory knowledge may nevertheless represent operationalizations of the existing axiomatic knowledge base. Hofstede et al. (1990) even argue that practices are most important in revealing culture at the organizational level.

[7] Recipe knowledge is in its nature closely related to norms.

## Commonly-Held

*Commonly-held* by a group implies that culture is a collective phenomenon rooted in a group rather than being based on individual perceptions (although shared) as is the case with organizational climate. This implies for assessors that data collected from individuals such as interview or observational data need to be critically examined to see if they represent only individual perceptions and opinions or if they represent cultural knowledge pertaining to a group of people and are, hence, rooted in a collectivity. Statements about culture and cultural differences can therefore be based only on an analysis of aggregated data. The common practice of using "key" informants is therefore insufficient in uncovering the cultural knowledge base of a group. Not only may the ideas of a key informant represent an idiosyncratic view, in addition his or her basic beliefs may belong to a subculture unrecognized by the researcher, which leads us to the next problem. Sparrow (Part II, Chapter 4) outlines some of the statistical conventions for establishing consensus with climate data.

## By a Group

Cultural knowledge commonly-held *by a group* is a further specification of the collectivity to which this knowledge base applies. In the early 1980s, cultural boundaries as such were frequently not questioned and assumed to be identical with organizational or national boundaries. The larger an organization, the more likely it is, however, that it is composed of subgroups. For assessment purposes, these subgroups can be either predefined on the basis of existing theory or their emergence may be the very focus of research (e.g. Sackmann, 1985, 1992).

Assessors have, therefore, focussed on identifying commonalities in assumptions as the precursor to drawing boundaries around the cultural group. Boundaries are drawn around anticipated or hypothesized groups, and then cultural commonalities are surfaced to support maintaining or adjusting those boundaries of shared understandings and interpretations (Gregory, 1983; Grinyer and Spender, 1979; Martin et al., 1985; Phillips 1990; Sackmann, 1985; Van Maanen and Barley, 1984). Consequently, unanticipated groupings as well as emerging ones can be identified.

Organizations as cultural settings may be composed of subcultures that overlap, that are superimposed upon, or are nested within any single organization (Louis, 1983), and group membership may be temporary and shifting, leading to groupings which may change membership depending on the issue at hand. Depending upon the size and characteristics of the focal group, data need to be collected from the full group membership or from a stratified or random sample of all members (e.g. Phillips, 1990, pp. 74–104). The size of the hypothesized or emerging group(s) may make cultural investigation methodologies cumbersome and therefore may need some modification in terms of a "mid-range" methodology (Sackmann, 1985, pp. 55–83, 1991b).

## *Typical* for the Group

Culture – the commonly-held knowledge base – which is typical for a group distinguishes one group from an other. It defines who are "we" and who are "they" in regard to a specific issue. Only through performing comparisons and contrasts with other groupings at the same as well as different levels of analyses can assessors decide what is typical for one group and hence different for another. The "typical" shared understandings which have been used to characterize a group as "unique" may also belong to a larger cultural context in which the group under investigation is embedded and which was not investigated in the course of the study (e.g. Martin et al., 1983). Assessors need to recognize

> ...that the specific site in question is [only] *potentially* a site of distinctive culture; that the presence of cultural phenomena in or at the site, as well as the determination of specific aspects of culture distinctive to the site, are matters to examine rather than to assume. (Louis, 1983, p. 78)

Potential cultural influences may stem from a variety of cultures located at different levels and/or cross-cutting these various levels as indicated in Figure 7.1.

Assessors must attend in their research efforts to the existence of a multiplicity of cultural groupings that may be layered upon, cross-cutting, and/or located within the focal group and that may influence the group's cultural knowledge base. At the organizational level, subcultures may exist due to different functions, different hierarchical levels and/or different time spent within the organization. These subgroups may act independent of each other, they may complement each other, or they may be in conflict with each other. In addition, each one of these subcultures may be confronted with

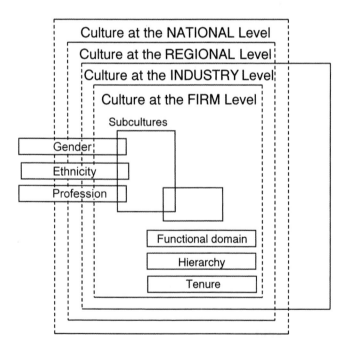

**Figure 7.1** The different levels of culture that influence culture at the firm level.

issues of gender, ethnicity, religion and/or profession. Furthermore, the cultural context of the organization is influenced by the industry to which it belongs, and by the region as well as by the nation in which it is located.

When designing, carrying through and reporting about the research project, assessors need to be aware of the possible existence of these multiple cultural influences that may shape the cultural knowledge base of the group under investigation. In addition, each organizational member may be a carrier of multiple cultures thus challenging the researcher in regard to the salience of a specific culture membership at any given moment. This notion leads to the problem of cultural dynamics existing within the organization – the interplay of not only different subgroup cultures but also the inter-play of multiple identities within each subgroup member (e.g. Hernes, 1997) and their shifting identities (Dahler-Larsen, 1997) as different issues become salient. All these factors contribute to cultural complexity.

## Tacit

Cultural knowledge, especially axiomatic knowledge, is *tacit* not only in the sense that it is unspoken, but more importantly in the sense that the knowledge holders are no longer consciously aware of it. Once learned and practised over some time, cultural knowledge and its implications for practise become routine and they are routinely applied. The knowledge holders hold and apply their knowledge automatically without conscious reflection. This tacit quality of cultural knowledge makes it difficult to surface. Assessors, therefore, should use probing data collection methods, as well as additional data and feedback from the research setting to challenge the inferences they are making from observations and verbal accounts as they proceed to identify the cultural knowledge base.

## Acquired and Passed on

The notion that cultural knowledge is *acquired* and *passed on* has implications regard-ing the selection of data sources. To be considered a member of a group with a distinctive cultural knowledge base requires a socialization process which takes time. Long-term members may be good representatives of a particular culture. They may, however, no longer be able to articulate the cultural specifics since they are so much a "product" of the specific subculture(s) and apply the cultural guidelines for perceiving, thinking, feeling and acting unconsciously in their daily routines. Members who are relatively new to a group may not yet have learned the entire base of cultural knowledge important to that group. Being relatively new, they tend to have something that I like to call a "tourist perspective". They may be able to pinpoint some of the group's typical cultural knowledge because they are still able to make comparison to their prior experiences from other organizational settings. Although it is preferable to have long-term group members as informants, newer group members may, therefore, provide interesting insight about the inferences being made. For these reasons, a cross-section of informants in regard to tenure in a group may be advisable.

## Complexity

At the organizational level, the various subcultures and their specific dynamic interplay may result in cultural *complexity* – a cultural context that may be integrated or homogenous as well as differentiated or heterogeneous, or even fragmented as Sackmann (1997) states:

> The concept of cultural complexity (…) encompasses both ideas: simultaneously existing multiple cultures[8] that may contribute to a homogeneous, differentiated, and/or fragmented cultural context. Hence, the cultural complexity perspective suggests that culture in organizational settings is much more complex, pluralistic, diverse, contradictory, or inherently paradoxical than previously assumed, conceptualized, or acknowledged. (p. 2)

> …The resulting picture of cultural life in organizational settings may thus be full of contrasts and contradictions, showing aspects of harmony next to differentiation with or without dissent and a multiplicity of cultural identities that may be in a constant flux depending on the issues at hand. (p. 4)

In addition, in our modern world individuals contribute to this cultural complexity since they are considered simultaneous carriers of several cultural identities. Individuals are assumed to belong to various cultural groupings at any given time. Depending on the issue at hand, different cultural identities may become salient. Hence, existing group boundaries may shift rather quickly and swiftly. Dahler-Larsen (1997) showed in his study that depending on the issues at stake, Danish flight attendants from SAS identified themselves either as members of SAS or shifted their most important identity to being Danish. When, how, and to what extent these identity shifts may occur and how they influence, for example, performance are empirical questions yet to be answered. In an increasingly multi-cultural work context, these questions will need to be addressed in future research. How can such a complex cultural context with its inherent dynamics be researched?

# QUALITATIVE RESEARCH METHODOLOGIES – A SINE QUA NON FOR RESEARCHING CULTURAL COMPLEXITY?

Given the above conceptualization of culture with its characteristics in terms of cultural complexity and the resulting implications for research, no single method is able to reveal the cultural complexity of an organization nor is one research project able to capture the cultural complexity of a given organization in total. Assessors need, therefore, to be consciously aware of the choices that they need to make in each phase of the research project – choices of inclusion that are at the same time choices of exclusion.

---

[8] See Figure 7.1 for potential subcultures.

Among organization theorists, the primary focus of culture research was and still is – especially in regard to cultural complexity – to gain a better understanding of organizational life, that is, description. To that end, specific cultural settings are researched in depth – primarily with qualitative research methods on the basis of an inductive research approach. Only on the basis of such a grounded theoretical knowledge can actions be recommended to managers, and may behaviours be explained or even in probabilistic terms be predicted.

The nature of the assessment question(s), that is, the purpose of the assessment as well as the availability and the quality of theoretical knowledge in that area, determines which assessment paradigm(s) may be the most appropriate one(s) for the investigation. The first major choice concerns, therefore, the *focus* of the assessment and the central questions to be answered, that is, *the specific cultural issues under investigation.*

- Do I want to investigate differences at the national (e.g. Hofstede, 1980), geographical (e.g. Weiss and Delbecq, 1987), industry (e.g. Grinyer and Spender, 1979; Phillips, 1990), organizational (e.g. Schein, 1985), or suborganizational (e.g. Van Maanen and Barley, 1984) level?
- Or do I want to learn more about the potential existence and formation of subcultures in a given organization (e.g. Sackmann, 1991a, 1992)?
- Do I want to get an understanding of the critical cultural issues within an organization and their dynamics (e.g. Sackmann, 1991a; Schumacher, 1997; Ybema, 1997)?
- Or do I want to focus on a pre-selected issue of, for example, socialization processes, decision making processes (e.g. Burrus, 1997), or the death of an organization (e.g. Eberle, 1997)?
- In addition to gaining an insider's understanding of certain cultural issues, do I also want to be able to explain certain cultural phenomena (e.g. Koene et al., 1997)?
- Do I want to give recommendations for actions to managers (e.g. Globokar, 1997)?
- Or do I even want to make predictions about cultural issues in certain contexts?

The next set of critical choices concerns the *research methodology and assessment methods*. If the aim of the primary research is to gain a better understanding of cultural complexity in a given organization from an insider's point of view, the methodology of choice for investigating cultural complexity is based on naturalistic inquiry starting with an inductive approach. An inductive approach is advisable if little theoretical knowledge exists about the phenomenon in question (Van Maanen, 1979). In such a case, the aim is to develop a sound theoretical basis grounded in organizational life rather than developed purely from a researcher's desk. The result of such an inductive, grounded research approach (Glaser and Strauss, 1967) may lead to propositions or even hypotheses for further investigation in which deductive, quantitative approaches may be employed.

An inductive as compared to a deductive approach implies that the rescarcher gets immersed into the research setting without introducing his or her preconceptions about culture, cultural complexity and the research issues at hand. S/he attempts to bracket his or her own assumptions (e.g. Schütz, 1947) and tries to gain first a thorough descriptive understanding of the sense making and meaning creating mechanisms from the inside before making judgements and/or evaluating observations (see Table 7.1). This process

**Table 7.1**  A comparison of an inductive and deductive research approach

| Inductive approach (emic research) | Deductive approach (etic research) |
| --- | --- |
| Investigation from an insider's perspective to capture the insider's understandings and interpretations of the research setting (rich descriptions) | Investigation from an outsider's perspective with an exclusive focus on issues related to the research question (no concern about rich descriptions) |
| Relevant concepts and dimensions emerge from the research site – own assumptions and theoretical knowledge are bracketed | Concepts are pre-selected from relevant theory and introduced to the research setting from the outside |
| Researcher as participant within the research site interacting with the members | Researcher is an onlooker from the outside – no interaction, possibly only transaction |
| Constant comparisons can be made as research efforts progress | Once the research question, research design and methods are developed and data collection has started, no changes can be made |
| Research is grounded in a specific time, place and social reality | Research is rather independent of the specific time, place and social reality |
| Idiosyncratic, in-depth case descriptions | Results can be generalized to the population from which the sample was drawn |
| Purpose to generate theory of little explored phenomena | Purpose to test propositions derived from existing theories |

of bracketing one's own preconceptions while gaining an insider's understanding yet keeping enough distance to avoid the danger of becoming an insider presents quite a challenge in in-depth qualitative research.

Such an inductive approach with the purpose of gaining an in-depth understanding is rooted within the paradigms of constructivism, interpretivism, and radical theory applying methodologies of ethnography, ethnomethodology, phenomenology, hermeneutics, and/or dialectis. All these paradigms and the respective methodologies are rooted in the tradition of *Verstehen*.[9] Constructivism is based on the assumption that social reality is not objectively given; instead, social reality is actively constructed and reconstructed by people acting and interacting in social settings (e.g. Berger and Luckmann, 1966). Interpretivism which is closely related claims that the understanding of the meaning of social settings needs to be derived from the various perspectives of their actors. The generation of such an understanding is its very purpose as compared to scientific explanations sought in natural science research.[10] Radical theory basically asserts that a thorough understanding of social reality can only be gained through dialectical, hermeneutic approaches.

---

[9] Verstehen means to gain a basic understanding of a given setting from the perspective of insiders. This approach has received increasing attention in the social sciences as a reaction to the shortcomings of positivism and the scientific method where a set of hypotheses is deducted from existing theories and investigated using the appropriate methods within the natural science tradition. In a nutshell, "radical" social scientists complained that the scientific method produced explanations of issues at various significance levels with, however, little relevance to "real" social life as perceived by actors.

[10] For a more detailed discussion of constructivist and interpretivist approaches see Schwandt (1994).

Combinations of constructivism, interpretivism, and radical theory are therefore *the* paradigms of choice to conduct research with the aim of gaining an insider's perspective of the cultural context. Within these paradigms, qualitative research methodologies and data collection methods are predominantly applied. As Denzin and Lincoln (1994, p. 100) explain:

> Constructivism (…) adopts a relativist (relativism) ontology, a transactional epistemology and a hermeneutic, dialectical methodology. The inquiry aims of this paradigm are oriented to the production or reconstructed understandings, wherein the traditional positivist criteria or internal and external validity are replaced by the terms *trustworthiness* and *authenticity*.[11]

In the next steps of developing a research design and deciding about sampling, data collection and data analysis methods, thoughtful assessment and research efforts apply not only a combination of data collection and data analysis methods, they are also able to combine different research paradigms and create inventive research designs to take into account the specifics of the concept of culture and its complexity within organizational settings.

To summarize, a thoughtful study of cultural complexity needs to take into consideration the following critical issues in its various research phases and assessment activities:

| | |
|---|---|
| cultural knowledge base | issues of *paradigm(s), theory, design and data collection*: what kinds of cultural knowledge to decipher and how to decipher them? |
| commonly-held | issues of *design and sampling*: which aspects of the knowledge base are commonly-held and which are individually-held? Comparisons between individuals and between groups to determine relevant group. |
| by a group | issues of *design and sampling*: which group(s) at which level(s) of analysis? Pre-selection of a group on theoretical grounds versus emerging groupings in regard to a specific issue? |
| *typical* for the group | issues of *design, data-collection and data-analysis*. |
| tacit | issues of *data collection and data analysis*: how to elicit the critical but tacit cultural knowledge? |
| acquired and passed on | issues of *sampling*: who has what kind of knowledge and in which ways is it systematically biased? |
| complexity | issues of *design, sampling, data collection and data analysis* to capture the multiplicity of subcultures and their dynamic interplay at the organizational, group as well as the individual level including potential contradictions and paradoxes. |

These issues need to be considered in each step of the research process. Table 7.2

---

[11] See also Guba and Lincoln (1994).

**Table 7.2**   Researching cultural complexity: critical choices

| | |
|---|---|
| Paradigm | Constructivism, interpretivism, radical theory |
| Methodology | Hermeneutics, dialectical approach, ethnography, ethnomethodology |
| Design | Inductive – single case research at the outset with a possible move toward deductive approach applying, for example, the method of successive comparisons |
| Sampling | Selecting a representative sample of members of the group(s) relevant to the cultural issue(s) under investigation or for the study of emerging groups/cultural issues |
| Data collection | Creative combination of different methods with an issue focus and a triangulation approach to capture the tacit phenomenon and the issue(s) under investigation as well as for reasons of research quality (see below) |
| Data analysis | Adequate approaches for the chosen data collection methods |
| Interpretation | Critical questioning of personal biases and probing for alternative interpretations (re-interpretation, critical discussions with other assessors – dialectical approach) |
| Research quality | Explicit discussion of the choices made in each phase of the research process, triangulation methods |

These issues need to be considered in each step of the research process. Table 7.2 contains an overview of the critical choices and how issues of cultural complexity can be addressed.

Within the research tradition of *Verstehen* and the paradigms of constructivism, interpretivism, and/or radical theory researchers have creatively tailored methodologies, design and sampling issues as well as data collection methods to their specific research interests and the organizational setting(s) under investigation. Thus, the shortcomings of earlier research efforts as criticized by Schein (1985, pp. 113–114) have been overcome:...Many of the methods advocated by corporate culture analysts (Kilmann, 1983; Pettigrew, 1979; Schwartz and Davis, 1981; Silverzweig and Allen, 1976; Tichy, 1975) seem to assume that if one just asks the 'right' questions initially, one can decipher the culture.

Resulting research designs of a more differentiated stream of research are mostly variations of an in-depth case analysis. Approaches are, for example, detailed ethnographies (Koot, 1997; Schumacher, 1997; Sharpe, 1997), specifically tailored combinations of ethnographic and quasi-ethnographic methods such as participant observation (Burrus, 1997; Gregory, 1983; Sapienza, 1985), in-depth interviews (e.g. De Vries, 1997; Phillips, 1990, 1994; Sackmann, 1991a,b; Schein, 1985; Vinton, 1983; Ybema, 1997), group discussions (Schein, 1985), the use of a focus group (McGovern and Hope-Hailey, 1997), assumptional analysis (Kilmann, 1983), a combination of cause maps and social network analysis (Nelson and Mathews, 1991), action research (Globokar, 1997), historical analysis/analysis of secondary data (Eberle, 1997), cognitive mapping methods such as causal mapping (Axelrod, 1976; Narayanan and Fahey, 1990), the repertory grid technique (Reger, 1990), argument mapping (Fletcher and Huff, 1990), narrative semiotics (Fiol,

1990), or projective techniques such as a critical incidence technique and the drawing of a given cultural context as perceived by the people concerned (Sackmann, 1990).

In their effort to condense, analyze, systemize, and report the collected data, researchers have applied a priori developed frameworks with their respective categories and theoretically derived dimensions or used existing typologies (Handy, 1978; Pümpin, 1984; Sackmann et al., 1992). Others have employed the categories and dimensions of empirically derived frameworks (e.g. Hofstede et al., 1990; Phillips, 1990; Schein, 1985). Another approach is to let the relevant categories and/or dimensions of a given culture emerge from the research, and to use these in the organization and presentation of the findings (e.g. Burrus, 1997; Eberle, 1997; Kleinberg, 1989; Laurila, 1997; Sackmann, 1991b, 1992; Sharpe, 1997; Van Maanen 1979; Ybema, 1997).

The methods employed in data analysis need to fit the chosen data collection methods and the research questions. They tend to be some form of theoretical content analysis such as theme analysis, semiotics, or, for example, the critical interpretation of developed drawings from different perspectives. Issues of internal validity that deal with the question of "How do I know that I really have captured an understanding of cultural complexity in the given setting?" can, for example, be tackled by re-interpretations of the collected data by other assessors, dialectical discussions with other assessors, as well as feeding the results back to the people from which data were collected and discussing with them their appropriateness. Mental tests can be performed to see if one has captured the insider's perspective. As each interview progressed, Sackmann (1991b) asked questions and started to answer them mentally to herself as a check to see to what extent she had grasped the interviewee's understanding and interpretation.

In the interpretation phase of the collected data, assessors need to critically question themselves in relation to whether they interpret the data from the insider's perspective or if they transcend to the research community and their own theoretical perspectives and, hence, translate the findings to the other community. One of the major criticisms often voiced in regard to anthropological research is not knowing if the reported findings are characteristic of the research setting or rather a representation of the assessors' personal biases and a reflection of their professional training. Several approaches may be used as counter measures in the interpretation phase such as re-interpretation of the data at a later stage (Sackmann, 1991b), interpretation of the data by other assessors who may come from the same or from a different discipline and a comparison of the results of both analyses.

As mentioned above in the citation by Denzin and Lincoln (1994), the traditional measures of validity and reliability cannot be applied in qualitative research in their original meaning to ensure research quality. Triangulation is an important tool to ensure quality in qualitative research. Janesick (1994) differentiates five kinds of triangulation methods on the basis of the work of Denzin (1989):

- data triangulation: the use of a variety of data sources;
- investigator triangulation: the use of several different assessors or evaluators;

**Table 7.3**  The strengths and limitations of qualitative research approaches in regard to cultural complexity

| Strengths | Limitations |
| --- | --- |
| Rich, detailed, and meaningful descriptions of the cultural setting under investigation to develop grounded theory | Difficult to compare findings from the case study with other case studies |
| Insights about the dynamics of cultural complexity (e.g. contradictions, paradoxes, shifting group boundaries related to different issues, etc.) | Generalizations beyond the researched setting are not possible |
| | Recommendations for actions apply only to the specific case |
| Interactive – assessors get immediate feedback if their questions or research methods may not be adequate for the setting under investigation | No explanations or predictions can be made about the researched phenomena |
| Adaptive/flexible – all methods, research activities and research questions can be adjusted as research efforts progress to respond to new insights | Performance issues are rarely an issue Remaining doubt: has the researcher really captured the essence of the research setting or do the findings and interpretations reflect predominantly the researcher's personal and professional biases? |
| Insights gained from the research lead to propositions/hypotheses grounded in organizational life | Costly in terms of time needed for data collection and data analysis |

- methodological triangulation: the use of multiple methods to study a single problem;
- interdisciplinary triangulation: to approach a problem from different disciplines.

In general, a critical quality measure of qualitative research is "Nachvollziehbarkeit" – helping the readers understand how one has achieved the results, enabling them to critically evaluate the appropriateness of the results and their interpretations, and enabling other assessors to potentially repeat the study.[12] To this end, assessors need to report and discuss the choices explicitly made in each phase of the research project. Examples of creative research approaches to investigate different aspects of cultural complexity are, for example, Sackmann (1991a), Sharpe (1997) or Ybema (1997).

---

[12] Assessors need, however, to be aware that this kind of investigation is bounded to the space and time in which it happened. Even if one repeats the study in the same setting with the same research approach, results may vary if the time is not identical.

# STRENGTHS AND LIMITATIONS OF QUALITATIVE RESEARCH METHODOLOGIES

The very strength of qualitative research methodologies also represents also their short-comings. Both will be discussed in this section. They are summarized in Table 7.3. Given that the primary purpose of qualitative research approaches is to gain a rich and detailed understanding of the cultural complexity from the insider's perspective, qualitative research approaches clearly have their strengths in developing grounded theory in regard to the issues under investigation. In the case of cultural complexity such an approach is valuable since little knowledge exists, for example, about the dynamics of multiple cultural memberships, shifting identities in regard to these memberships and about the impact these multiple memberships have on the individuals, the respective groups, and the cultural context at the organizational level and their impact on performance issues. Little is also known about the "messiness" of cultural contexts, about inherent contradictions and paradoxes.

Another strength of qualitative approaches is their adaptability and flexibility. As research efforts progress and new knowledge is generated both about the research setting as well as about the issues under investigation, these insights can be used to adjust sampling techniques, data collection methods as well as research questions. The resulting propositions or hypotheses to be investigated in future research are grounded in organizational life as compared to hypotheses that have derived from the desk of a researcher.

The results gained from qualitative research are, however, bound to the specific case under investigation. Direct comparisons cannot be made with results gained from other case studies unless these studies were designed for comparison. In addition, the results cannot be generalized to other settings. Because of the focus on understanding, explanations of behaviour remain at a descriptive level, and predictions are not the focus of this kind of research. Links to performance are, therefore, rarely explored. In times of increasing competition, managers being pressed to produce results and the enhanced sensitivity toward shareholder value, practitioners have increasingly high expectations of receiving help from organization theorists. This help is not only sought when problems have occurred and assessors may be called in the role of a consultant (e.g. Globokar, 1997). Instead, proactive answers are expected that help guide managerial decision making. This implies that practitioners will increasingly approach assessors for information regarding the effects of certain organizational designs and their related cultural context. There will be increasingly more questions about performance issues. The proposition by Barney (1986) that culture may be the very source of sustained competitive advantage will need to be followed up and specified through empirical research. The question is whether researchers want to leave this area to the field of consultancy or if they are also prepared in addition to theory building to make recommendations for practitioners. If the answer is yes, deductive, quantitative approaches have to complement existing efforts.

A critical issue of qualitative research is validity. Do the reported findings really capture the essence of the research setting? To what extent do they reflect systematic biases of the researcher and his or her professional training? Another limitation refers to cost. The time necessary to spend in the research setting, and the time needed to condense, systemize and analyze qualitative data is rather extensive. A detailed understanding of a specific cultural setting can only be gained over a certain period of time. Ethnographies vary, for example, between (rarely) a few months and several years. Furthermore, the extensive amount of data need to be, in the case of interviews, transcribed and the transcripts require some form of condensation. The more data, the more difficult and time consuming these research activities will be. If the suggested method of investigator and interdisciplinary triangulation is applied, additional financial resources may be needed.

In summary, the primary focus of inductive research approaches applying qualitative methodologies and methods is to gain a better understanding of organizational life – in our case from the perspective of cultural complexity. Such efforts yield rich data about a specific case, and they help develop grounded theory. As a result, propositions or hypotheses may emerge that need to be investigated in future research. Unfortunately, the gained insights cannot be extended to other organizational settings – they are bounded and limited to the single case.

# FURTHER AVENUES TO EXPLORE

There are basically three avenues into which future research on cultural complexity will hopefully develop. The first one is an increasing number of research projects that combine inductive and deductive, and quantitative and qualitative research methodologies. The second one is the development of a growing taxonomy of case studies on cultural complexity comparing and contrasting the various cases. The third approach will be to conduct increasingly more research with a deductive methodology once more knowledge about cultural complexity has been generated with qualitative as well as combined research approaches.

## Combination of Inductive and Deductive Research Methodologies

In terms of methodology, a stream of more recent studies has moved away from purely qualitative approaches combining different kinds of methodologies as well as data collection and analysis methods. Examples are the studies of Laurila (1997), Sackmann (1991b, 1992), and Ybema, 1997. In his longitudinal study, Laurila combined oral history, different kinds of interviews, documentary, and survey data with several cross-checks over time to assess the constellation of subcultures at the management level using the incidence or issue of a technological change as a trigger to get to the core of culture.

Sackmann (1991b) developed a "mid-range" methodology to cope with the problems of assessing the cultural knowledge base within an organization from an insider's view *and* being able to generate hypotheses about the emergence and formation of subcultures. These hypotheses were then tested in a subsequent phase of the research project. The design of successive comparisons (Diesing, 1971) allowed the research project to move from an inductive approach in the beginning of the research project to an increasingly deductive approach toward the end of the research project.

Ybema conducted an in-depth study of an amusement park combining data collected from document analysis, participant observations, (in-depth) interviews, question-naires, feedback sessions, and a standardized survey questionnaire to investigate the kinds of subcultures with their characteristics, their interactions, and their paradoxes and how the members cope with these cultural paradoxes.

All three studies provide rich insights into the specific cultural settings under inves-tigation. These insights were gained through combined qualitative and quantitative approaches. They go beyond the descriptions of, for example, ethnographies. They represent, however, single cases with results that cannot be generalized to other cases – "only" leading to propositions or hypotheses that may be tested in future research.

## Developing a Growing Taxonomy

The insights gained from single case assessment may become even more powerful by systematically comparing and contrasting the results with findings gained from other case studies. The result would be an increasingly growing taxonomy in regard to issues of cultural complexity in organizational settings. Such a compilation is, however, cumbersome with little rewards in terms of originality. Nevertheless, I consider such a taxonomy to be a next step in systemizing and combining existing single case research, and eventually building upon each other's work. A further step would be to deliberately build upon each other's work in designing and conducting qualitative research.

## Deductive Research on the Basis of Generated Knowledge

The third direction for future assessment methods is an even stronger combination of qualitative and quantitative methodologies and methods. The more grounded theory that is developed about cultural complexity, the more easy and/or likely it will be for researchers to deduce interesting, relevant and challenging hypotheses for empirical investigation applying deductive methodologies and quantitative methods. Such approaches will allow us to investigate impacts of certain cultural issues, for example, on performance. Larger scale studies of cross-cultural studies comparing issues of cultural complexity across different organizations will help shed light on more general aspects. An interesting study leading in this direction was conducted by Koene et al. (1997). The researchers tried

> to bridge the gap between the one-sided comparative quantitative focus on cultural diversity as an independent variable (influencing organizational perfor-mance and determining the level of analysis at which the variable has to be understood) and the qualitative in-depth focus on the issue of diversity and its antecedents. (pp. 274–275)

This study was part of a quantitative empirical research project investigating the impact of organizational culture and leadership on organizational performance in supermarket stores. A questionnaire was developed combining different leadership scales and items to measure three aspects of organizational climate. This questionnaire was answered by 1229 employees located in 50 different stores of the same retail chain in The Netherlands. In the data analysis, within-group agreement and between-group variation were assessed as well as the impact of organizational structure, demography, and communication climate on the level of cultural agreement in the firm.

Such a stream of theoretically well-grounded deductive, quantitative research could address issues of cross-cultural interactions at various levels of analysis. When and under what circumstances do certain cultural groupings become important and why? How do cultural groupings interact with each other in regard to differing issues? How do individuals manage cultural complexity and multiple memberships across settings? How do these factors influence individual, group and organizational performance?

This kind of research could also address issues of cultural fit more systematically. That is, depending on the nation, region, and industry in which a firm operates, studies could investigate the characteristics of the most appropriate cultural context. At the moment, all practitioners seem to strive toward more flexibility, more adaptability and toward more self-organization within the context of a learning organization. Similar to innovation (Burns and Stalker, 1961), not all contexts may, however, require the same level of flexibility, adaptability and/or self-organization.

To conclude, the field of culture and cultural complexity has still many white spots left for serious researchers. Inductive research approaches applying qualitative methodologies are a sine qua non to grasp the core of culture and cultural complexity from the insider's perspective. As the knowledge base about cultural complexity grows with increasingly more thoughtful studies being conducted, innovative research methodologies can be developed to combine qualitative and quantitative methods and to start answering questions about various kinds of effects of different kinds of cultural issues.

# REFERENCES

Allen, R.F. (1984) A systematic norm based methodology for bringing about change. Paper presented at the conference Managing Corporate Cultures, Pittsburgh, PA.

Axelrod, R. (1976) Structure of Decision. Princeton, NJ: Princeton University Press.

Barney, J.B. (1986) Organizational culture: can it be a sustained source of competitive advantage? Academy of Management Review, 11(3): 656–665.

Berger, P.L. and Luckmann, T. (1966) The Social Construction of Reality. New York: Penguin Press.

Burns, T. and Stalker, G.M. (1961) Mechanistic and organic systems. The Management of Innovation, pp. 119–125. London: Tavistock.

Burrus, K. (1997) National culture and gender diversity within one of the universal Swiss banks: an experiential description of a professional woman officer and president of the women managers' association. In S.A. Sackmann (Ed), Cultural Complexity in Organizations. Inherent Contrasts and Contradictions, pp. 209–227. Thousand Oaks, CA: Sage.

Dahler-Larsen, P. (1997) Organizational identity as a "crowded category": a case of multiple and quickly-shifting "we" typifications. In S.A. Sackmann (Ed), Cultural Complexity in Organizations. Inherent Contrasts and Contradictions, pp. 367–389. Thousand Oaks, CA: Sage.

Denzin, N.K. (1989) The Research Act: a Theoretical Interdiction to Sociological Methods, 3rd Edn. New York: McGraw-Hill.

Denzin, N.K. and Lincoln, Y.S. (Eds) (1994) Handbook of Qualitative Research. Thousand Oaks, CA: Sage.

De Vries, S. (1997) Ethnic diversity in organizations: a Dutch experience. In S.A. Sackmann (Ed), Cultural Complexity in Organizations. Inherent Contrasts and Contradictions, pp. 297–314. Thousand Oaks, CA: Sage.

Diesing, P. (1971) Patterns of Discovery in the Sciences. Chicago, IL: Aldine-Atherton.

Eberle, T.S. (1997) Cultural contrasts in a democratic nonprofit organization: the case of a Swiss reading society. In S.A. Sackmann (Ed), Cultural Complexity in Organizations. Inherent Contrasts and Contradictions, pp. 133–159. Thousand Oaks, CA: Sage.

Evered, R. and Louis, M.R. (1981) Alternative perspectives of the organizational sciences: "inquiries from the inside" and "inquiries from the outside". Academy of Management Review, 6(3): 385–389.

Fiol, M.C. (1990) Narrative semiotics: theory, procedures and illustration. In A.S. Huff (Ed), Mapping Strategic Thought. New York: Wiley.

Fletcher, K.E. and Huff, A.S. (1990) Argument mapping. In A.S. Huff (Ed), Mapping Strategic Thought. New York: Wiley.

Glaser, B.G. and Strauss, A.L. (1967) The Discovery of Grounded Theory: an Ethnomethodological Approach. Chicago, IL: Aldine.

Globokar, T. (1997) Eastern Europe meets West: an empirical study on French management in a Slovenian plant. In S.A. Sackmann (Ed), Cultural Complexity in Organizations. Inherent Contrasts and Contradictions, pp. 72–86. Thousand Oaks, CA: Sage.

Gregory, K. (1983) Native-view paradigms: multiple cultures and culture conflicts in organizations. Administrative Science Quarterly, 28: 359–376.

Grinyer, P.H. and Spender, J.C. (1979) Recipes, crises, and adaptation in mature businesses. International Studies of Management and Organization, IX(3): 113–133.

Guba, E.G. and Lincoln, Y.S. (1994) Competing paradigms in qualitative research. In N.K. Denzin and Y.S. Lincoln (Eds), Handbook of Qualitative Research, pp. 105–117. Thousand Oaks, CA: Sage.

Handy, C.B. (1978) Zur Entwicklung der Organisationskultur durch Management Development Methoden [Developing organizational culture through management development]. Zeitschrift für Organisation, 7: 404–410.

Hernes, H. (1997) Cross-cutting identifications in organizations. In S.A. Sackmann (Ed), Cultural Complexity in Organizations. Inherent Contrasts and Contradictions, pp. 343–366. Thousand Oaks, CA: Sage.

Hofstede, G. (1980) Culture's Consequences. International Differences in Work-Related Values. Beverly Hills, CA: Sage.

Hofstede, G., Neuijen, B., Ohayv, D.D. and Sanders, G. (1990) Measuring organizational cultures: a qualitative and quantitative study across twenty cases. Administrative Science Quarterly, 35(2): 286–316.

Janesick, V.J. (1994) The dance of qualitative research design. Metaphor, methodology, and meaning. In: N.K. Denzin and Y.S. Lincoln (Eds), Handbook of Qualitative Research, pp. 209–219. Thousand Oaks, CA: Sage.

Kilmann, R.H. (1983) A dialectical approach to formulating and testing social science theories: assumptional analysis. Human Relations, 36(1): 1–22.

Kilmann, R.H. and Saxton, M.J. (1983) Kilmann-Saxton Culture-Gap Survey. Pittsburgh, PA: Organization Design Consultants Incorporated.

Kleinberg, J. (1989) Cultural clash between managers: America's Japanese firms. In S.B. Prasad (Ed), Advances in International Comparative Management, Vol. 4, pp. 221–244. Greenwich, CT: JAI Press.

Koene, B.A., Christophe, A., Boone, J.J. and Soeters, J.L. (1997) Organizational factors influencing homogeneity and heterogeneity of organizational cultures. In S.A. Sackmann (Ed), Cultural Complexity in Organizations. Inherent Contrasts and Contradictions, pp. 273–293. Thousand Oaks, CA: Sage.

Koot, W.C.J. (1997) Strategic utilization of ethnicity in contemporary organizations. In S.A. Sackmann (Ed), Cultural Complexity in Organizations. Inherent Contrasts and Contradictions, pp. 315–339. Thousand Oaks, CA: Sage.

Kroeber, A.L. and Kluckhohn, C.K. (1952) Culture: a critical review of concepts and definitions. Harvard University Peabody Museum of Archeology and Ethnology Papers, Vol. 47.

Laurila, J. (1997) Discontinuous technological change as a trigger for temporary reconciliation of managerial subcultures: a case study of a Finnish paper industry company. In S.A. Sackmann (Ed), Cultural Complexity in Organizations. Inherent Contrasts and Contradictions, pp. 252–272. Thousand Oaks, CA: Sage.

Louis, M.R. (1983) Organizations as culture-bearing milieux. In L.R. Pondy, P.J. Frost, G. Morgan and T.C. Dandridge (Eds), Organizational Symbolism, pp. 39–54. Greenwich, CT: JAI Press.

Martin, J. (1992) Cultures in Organizations: Three Perspectives. New York: Oxford University Press.

Martin, J., Feldman, M.S., Hatch, M.J. and Sitkin, S.B. (1983) The uniqueness paradox in organizational stories. Administrative Science Quarterly, 28: 438–453.

Martin, J., Sitkin, S.B. and Boehm, M. (1985) Founders and the elusiveness of a cultural legacy. In P.J. Frost, L.F. Moore, M.R. Louis, C.C. Lundberg and J. Martin (Eds), Organizational Culture, pp. 99–124. Beverly Hills, CA: Sage.

McGovern, P. and Hope-Hailey, V. (1997) Inside Hewlett-Packard: corporate culture and bureaucratic control. In S.A. Sackmann (Ed), Cultural Complexity in Organizations. Inherent Contrasts and Contradictions, pp. 187–205. Thousand Oaks, CA: Sage.

Narayanan, V.K. and Fahey, L. (1990) Evolution of revealed causal maps during decline: a case study of Admiral. In A.S. Huff (Ed), Mapping Strategic Thought, pp. 109–133. New York: Wiley.

Nelson, R.E. and Mathews, K.M. (1991) Cause maps and social network analysis in organizational diagnosis. Journal of Applied Behavioral Sciences, 27(3): 379–397.

Peters, T.J. and Waterman Jr., R.J. (1982) In Search of Excellence: Lessons from America's Best-Run Companies. New York: Harper and Row.

Pettigrew, A.M. (1979) On studying organizational cultures. Administrative Science Quarterly, 24: 570–581.

Phillips, M.E. (1990) Industry as a cultural grouping. Doctoral dissertation, Graduate School of Management, University of California, Los Angeles, CA. Dissertation Abstracts International, 5102-A. (University Microfilms No. 9017663)

Phillips, M.E. (1994) Industry and mindsets: exploring the cultures of two maero-organizational settings. Organization Science, 5(3): 384–402.

Phillips, M.E. and Sackmann, S.A. (1992) Mapping the cultural terrain in organizational settings: current boundaries and future directions for empirical research. The John E. Anderson Graduate School of Management at UCLA, Working paper series, Center for International Business Education and Research (CIBER), No. 92-05.

Pümpin, C. (1984) Unternehmenskultur, Unternehmensstrategie und Unternehmenserfolg [Corporate culture, corporate strategy and corporate performance]. Paper presented at the ATAG conference Die Bedeutung der Unternehmenskultur für den künftigen Erfolg Ihres Unternehmens [The importance of corporate culture for the future success of your firm], Zurich.

Reger, R.K. (1990) The repertory grid technique for eliciting the content and structure of cognitive constructive systems. In A.S. Huff (Ed), Mapping Strategic Thought, pp. 71–88. New York: Wiley.

Sackmann, S.A. (1983) Organisationskultur: die unsichtbare Einflussgrösse (Organizational culture: the invisible influence). Gruppendynamik, 14: 393–406.

Sackmann, S.A. (1985) Cultural knowledge in organizations: the link between strategy and organizational process. Doctoral dissertation, Graduate School of Management, University of California, Los Angeles, CA. (University Microfilms No. DA85255878)

Sackmann, S.A. (1989) The framers of culture: the conceptual views of anthropology, organization theory, and management. Paper presented at the Academy of Management Annual Meeting, Washington, DC.

Sackmann, S.A. (1990) Diagnose von Sozialen Systemen (Diagnosis of social systems). In G. Fatzer and K. Eck (Eds), Supervision und Beratung (Supervision and Consultation), pp. 341–361. Edition Humanistische Psychologie.

Sackmann, S.A. (1991a) Cultural Knowledge in Organizations: Exploring the Collective Mind. Newbury Park, CA: Sage.

Sackmann, S.A. (1991b) Uncovering culture in organizations. Journal of Applied Behavioral Sciences, 27(3): 295–317.

Sackmann, S.A. (1992) Culture and subcultures: an analysis of organizational knowledge. Administrative Science Quarterly, 37: 140–161.

Sackmann, S.A. (1997) Cultural Complexity in Organizations. Inherent Contrasts and Contradictions (Hrsg.). Newbury Park, CA: Sage.

Sackmann, S.A., Phillips, M.E. and Goodman, R. (1992) Exploring the complex cultural milieu of project teams. PM-Network, VI(8): 20–26.

Sapienza, A.M. (1985) Believing is seeing: how organizational culture influences the decisions top managers make. In R. Kilmann, M. Saxton, R. Serpa and Associates (Eds), Getting Control of the Corporate Culture. San Francisco, CA: Jossey-Bass.

Schein, E.H. (1985) Organizational Culture and Leadership. San Francisco, CA: Jossey-Bass.

Schumacher, T. (1997) West coast Camelot: the rise and fall of an organizational culture. In S.A. Sackmann (Ed), Cultural Complexity in Organizations. Inherent Contrasts and Contradictions, pp. 107–132. Thousand Oaks, CA: Sage.

Schütz, A. (1947) Some leading concepts of phenomenology. Social Research, 12: 77–97.

Schwandt, T.A. (1994) Constructivist, interpretivist approaches to human inquiry. In N.K. Denzin and Y.S. Lincoln (Eds), Handbook of Qualitative Research, pp. 118–137. Thousand Oaks, CA: Sage.

Schwartz, H. and Davis, S. (1981) Matching corporate culture and business strategy. Organizational Dynamics, 10(1): 30–48.

Sharpe, D.R. (1997) Managerial control strategies and subcultural processes: on the shop floor in a Japanese manufacturing organization in the United Kingdom. In S.A. Sackmann (Ed), Cultural Complexity in Organizations. Inherent Contrasts and Contradictions, pp. 118–251. Thousand Oaks, CA: Sage.

Silverzweig, S. and Allen, R.F. (1976) Changing the corporate culture. Sloan Management Review, 17(3): 33–50.

Tichy, M. (1975) How different types of change agents diagnose organizations. Human Relations, 28(9): 771–779.

Trice, H.M., Belasco, J.E. and Allutto, J.A. (1969) The role of ceremonials in organization behaviour. Industrial and Labor Relations Review, 23(1): 40–51.

Van Maanen, J. (1979) Reclaiming qualitative methods for organizational research. Administrative Science Quarterly, 24: 52–526.

Van Maanen, J. and Barley, S. (1984) Occupational communities: culture and control in organizations. In B.M. Staw and L.L. Cummings (Eds), Research in Organizational Behaviour, Vol. 6, pp. 287–365. Greenwich, CT: JAI Press.

Vinton, K. (1983) Humor in the work-place: its more than telling jokes. Paper presented at the Western of Management, Santa Barbara, CA.

Weiss, J. and Delbecq, A. (1987) High-technology cultures and management: Silicon Valley and Route 128. Group and Organization Studies, 12(1): 39–54.

Ybema, S.B. (1997) Telling tales: contrasts and commonalities within the organization of an amusement park – confronting and combining different perspectives. In S.A. Sackmann (Ed), Cultural Complexity in Organizations. Inherent Contrasts and Contradictions, pp. 160–186. Thousand Oaks, CA: Sage.

# Chapter 8

# Assessment of Cultures: a Way to Problem Solving or a Way to Problematic Solutions?

**Iva Smit**

*E&E Consultants, Netterden, The Netherlands*

## INTRODUCTION

Organizational cultures are widely recognized for their considerable influence on the well-being of industrial as well as non-industrial enterprises and their employees. While many studies stress the relation between organizational culture and performance, very few studies systematically explore this relation. This is not surprising because it is difficult to measure cultures with scientific accuracy, and instruments that objectively measure performance are rare and limited.

While the outcomes of organizational actions are tangible, or at least reasonably observable, the underlying cultural patterns work on unconscious, taken-for-granted levels and tend to be vague, ambiguous, and complex. The elusiveness of cultural patterns is reflected in the research methods designed to assess them. To start with, there are more than 160 different definitions of culture (Leys, 1990). Many researchers and practitioners develop their own terminology and define a set of cultural dimensions fitting their specific work perspective, which complicates the comparison of different methods and limits their use. Most of the existing assessment methods are oriented on the *description* of cultures and have no provision for linking cultural patterns with functioning results. Instruments that *analyze* the link between behavior and its outcomes are typically designed for individuals, not for organizational units.

Neither the descriptive nor the analytical instruments provide sufficient information for the design of tailored interventions, the former because they do not indicate how various cultural patterns actually affect the outcomes and what can be done to improve the situation, and the latter because they typically concentrate on a narrow range of functioning aspects isolated from the overall cultural pattern, which can lead to one-sided interventions (e.g. teams improving their productivity but getting burned up in the process). Additional complications stem from the causal relation between cultural patterns and functioning outcomes, which is not one-directional but circular, with cultural patterns and outcomes mutually influencing each other. Thus, while culture may be defined as the way in which a group of people solves problems, the ways of understanding cultures can be quite problematic.

In this chapter, various instruments and techniques will be presented and combined into a method that enables us to systematically assess organizational cultures and their impact on organizational health, that is, on the ability of an organization to survive and prosper in its environment. The purpose of the method is to:

1. describe and distinguish cultures of various organizations or organizational units;
2. produce information and guidance for the design of interventions tailored to the particular needs of each organization.

The method is based on a model of culture derived from the action theory of Parsons (the AGIL model), and on artificial intelligence data processing techniques. The AGIL model was selected because it has a solid theoretical base, can be easily applied in practice, and is compatible with a number of currently used cultural and organizational models. The AI techniques are particularly powerful when used for an in-depth analysis of small units (teams). For that reason, this chapter is written from a team perspective. However, the method is applicable to organizations of any size. An application of the method will be demonstrated on a cultural assessment of six teams operating in an industrial enterprise.

## CULTURE AND COPING

To survive, to sustain life, human beings interact in a variety of ways with each other and with their environment, and in this process produce and reproduce different cultures (Godelier, 1986). Culture can be described as a shared common resource of a group of people, a pattern of assumptions, beliefs, and other responses learned while coping with problems of survival (Carrithers, 1992; Schein, 1985). In the words of Trompenaars (1993, p. 6):

... Culture is the way in which a group of people solves problems.

Culture provides an integrated perspective and meaning to situations, it guides group members in their actions, in their understanding and interpretation of the world around them, it directs their attention and value orientation, and influences how they will cope with new or unexpected situations. It also gives the group a historical perspective and a view of its identity because by dealing with its particular predicaments each group develops its own problem solving style and a unique set of characteristics (Schein, 1985; Shweder, 1991; Trompenaars, 1993).

The powerful influence of culture on human behavior led a number of cultural theoreticians (e.g. Malinowski, 1944) to the conclusion that culture is an imposing, deterministic force, and that people do things because of their culture. Carrithers stressed that such a view is incomplete because humans first and foremost relate to each other, not to the abstraction of culture: "People do things with, to, and in respect of each other, using means that we can describe, if we wish to, as cultural" (Carrithers, 1992, p. 34). Cultures develop through relationships: through relationships we invent new ways of thinking and acting; through relationships we learn how to speak, how to understand symbols, how to deal with problems in proven and acceptable ways; through relationships we acquire our basic beliefs and assumptions about life and survival and become members of our respective cultures (Carrithers, 1992).

Such an interactive learning process has tremendous advantages because it enables large amounts of people to use the skills and knowledge developed by their predecessors without having to reinvent the wheel all over again. Moreover, by providing a common language and conceptual categories, culture reduces ambiguity and anxiety (Parsons, 1977b; Schein, 1985). The pattern of governing assumptions and implicit premises offers proven solutions to recurring problems, which, being applied repeatedly, drop out of consciousness and are used in an "automatic" manner (Schein, 1985). The automatic application of problem solutions provides for an efficient performance of regular activities. On the other hand, it can lead to reduced effectiveness and even to stress because by implicitly promoting a certain set of solutions and filtering out others, a deeply ingrained pattern of assumptions and beliefs could limit creativity and the ability to cope with new situations. When we define culture as the way in which a group of people solves problems, and stress as a state arising from the perception of not being able to deal with a given problem (e.g. Cox and Ferguson, 1991), we can conclude that a group – or a team – collectively experiencing difficulties or stress in some areas of its operations did not develop adequate culture in these areas.

To strengthen such inadequate cultural domains, we need to know where they are located, how do they actually affect the team's functioning, and what are the possible remedies. In addition, we also need to know what is the team's "natural" problem solving style, so that the intervention fits with the team's existing repertoire, and, if possible, uses it to effectuate the enhancement (Smit, 1997). As simple as it sounds, this is not an easy task because cultural patterns are typically vague, ambiguous, complex, and strongly interrelated (Schein, 1985). Or, as Hackman (1990, p. 8) put it, they come "in complex tangles that often are as hard to straighten out as a backlash on a fishing reel". In the following sections, techniques will be presented that help us to untangle such patterns.


# THE AGIL MODEL

The AGIL model originates from Talcott Parsons' theory of action. Parsons devoted a significant part of his working life to the study of action, and his action theory is closely associated with culture. In Parsons' view, cultural assumptions both constitute the guiding pattern of social action and are formulated and reformulated in action in the effort of human beings to resolve the never ending stream of existential problems. Hence, action is "the stuff" out of which personalities, social systems, and cultures are built (Parsons, 1951, 1977b).

The AGIL model evolved over several decades, during which Parsons used it for the analysis of development and functioning of individuals, teams, and societal systems (e.g. Parsons, 1937, 1951, 1960, 1971, 1977a,b, 1978). The first version of the model emerged from a work on categorization of role structures in social systems (Parsons and Shils, 1951). The model was then merged with the results of functioning analysis conducted by Robert F. Bales (1950). Bales, who researched interaction processes among members of small goal-oriented teams, found that teams are in their functioning continuously confronted with four basic problems pertaining to:

1. adaptation to external situations;
2. instrumental issues concerning satisfaction of needs and desires of the team members;
3. integration of the members within the team;
4. expressive issues (Parsons et al., 1953).

Parsons combined the conclusions of Bales with his own classification of actions and defined a four-dimensional action space, where the dimensions represent the four basic problems and are called *A*daptation, *G*oal attainment, *I*ntegration, and *L*atency and pattern maintenance.

The four action dimensions are interrelated, and are all considered equally essential for satisfactory functioning. However, the L-dimension has a governing role over the AGI-dimensions (Parsons 1960, 1977b), and so represents the deepest cultural levels (Schein, 1985; Trompenaars, 1993). The dimensions are not discrete, but cover the action space continuously and share elements on their boundaries (Parsons, 1977b).

Parsons gave a dynamic twist to his action theory by proposing that an action system dealing with a situation goes through a cycle of phases. A phase may be regarded as a state of the system in a given time interval, when it is mainly active in only one dimension, since preponderance of all dimensions cannot be achieved at one point in time. Each phase is characterized by a given combination of pattern variables connected with the activity appropriate to that phase. Parsons discerned the following pattern variable pairs: neutrality–affectivity, specificity–diffuseness, universalism–particularism, and performance–quality (sometimes called achievement–ascription). He also considered a fifth pair, self-orientation (individualism)–collectivism, which is now frequently used in cultural studies, but concluded that this pair represents a deeper, more stable property of a system rather than a cyclically changing action pattern (Parsons et al., 1953).

Recently, several researchers and practitioners, for instance Hampden-Turner (1994) and Trompenaars (1993), used the pattern variable pairs to investigate cultural differences between various countries. However, assessment based on the pattern variable pairs gives us an indication of the general orientation of preferred problem solutions in a given culture, but it does not tell us how effective the solutions are. Moreover, considering practical interventions, the variables represent perhaps a fundamental, but a limited value set. Another consideration is that the pattern variable pairs reportedly reflect cultural differences at national levels, but may not necessarily lead to meaningful results at organizational levels (Smit, 1997). To conclude, rather than focusing on the four pairs of pattern variables, the presented method is based on the four AGIL dimensions, which are described in more detail in Table 8.1.

To express the dynamic character of the AGIL dimensions, it is practical to combine Parsons' rather static descriptions with the modal verbs *can*, *will*, *must*, and *may* (Table 8.1). The verbs are helpful for delineation of actions in a cultural context (Schabracq et al., 1996), for elucidation of the dynamics of the stress process (Schabracq and Winnubst, 1995), and also for design of tailored interventions, as Hakkenberg (1992) demonstrated in her study on problem solving and strategy development sessions in various groups.

Because the AGIL dimensions are functionally dependent on each other, it is important that regardless of their principal tasks, teams develop adequate solutions for all four basic problems. Although teams may go through phases characterized by a temporary dominance of one dimension, if a team systematically neglects one or more of the basic problems, it is likely to jeopardize its tasks and the well-being of its members.

Not only problems, but also solutions can be classified with the AGIL categories. Classification of actions into predetermined categories, however, is not the primary function of the model in this application. The model is not the end point but the starting point of the cultural assessments, where it serves as a theoretical base supporting a systematic exploration of cultural patterns.

**Table 8.1**   The AGIL cultural model

| Cultural dimension | About what the team: | Assumptions concerning (derived from Parsons, 1977a,b): |
| --- | --- | --- |
| Adaptation | Can | Challenge, skills, resources, exploration of new possibilities, risk and uncertainty, the ability to deal with new or trying situations, the ability to apply knowledge to manipulate one's environment |
| Goal attainment | Will | Organization of power, responsibility, control (in relation to satisfaction of needs and desires), leadership and other organizational roles, competence |
| Integration | Must | Normalization and coordination of action so that specialized contributions complement one another; justice, regulation, norms, rules, feedback, communication, binding, membership, solidarity, influence |
| Latency and pattern maintenance | May | Values and beliefs providing a sense of direction and meaning, conception of the desirable, knowledge, experience, commitment, motivation, expression of emotions, symbols, code, and language |

# COMPARISON WITH OTHER MODELS

In this section, the AGIL model will be briefly compared with several cultural and organizational models (see Table 8.2). The comparison is by no means meant as an exhaustive review of cultural models, but as an attempt to indicate the position of the AGIL model in the "cultural space". A detailed version of this comparison is in Smit (1997); for those interested in a comprehensive review, a very informative analysis of numerous cultural frameworks is presented in Erez and Early (1993).

The British cultural anthropologist *Malinowski* (1944) viewed culture as a man-made environment, perpetuated and sustained by human action. He described culture in terms of four imperatives and responses (*economics, political organization, social control*, and *education*). Parsons seemed to be strongly inspired by Malinowski, as the early versions of the AGIL dimensions show a remarkable fit with the imperatives and responses.

*Hofstede* (1980) is one of the pioneers who introduced the concept of cultures to the corporate world. He studied national cultures of 40 independent nations and empirically determined four dimensions in which cultures differ. Each participating country was ranked for its position on the four dimensions, and the results were compiled into cultural maps of the world.

Hofstede (1994) suggested that organizational cultures should not be measured along the same dimensions as national cultures because cultural differences reside at the national level in values and at the organizational level in practices. Hofstede's six organizational dimensions are spread over the AGIL space unevenly, with a strong emphasis on integration.

*Hampden-Turner* (1994), *Hampden-Turner and Trompenaars* (1993) and *Trompenaars* (1993) also investigated differences between national cultures. Their research was based on Parsons' pattern variables universalism–particularism, achievement–ascription, neutrality–affectivity, and specificity–diffuseness, to which they added individualism–collectivism, and attitudes concerning time and one's environment. They measured the preference of the participants for one or the other side of the pattern variable orientations, but concluded that the opposing poles are more complementary than opposing. Hampden-Turner (1994) perceived the issue as essentially circular, and proposed that synergy is the best way to deal with the dilemmas of opposing value orientations. In this sense, he goes a step further than Parsons, who also described a cyclical connection of the opposing value orientations, but remained in a sequential mode of operation. In Parsons' view, the value orientations indicate "dilemmas of choice in situations where it was not possible for action 'to go in all directions at once'" (Parsons et al., 1953, p. 66).

*Schein* (1985) concentrated on the diagnosis of organizational cultures. He used five dimensions, with which he covered very much the same cultural space as Parsons, but divided the space somewhat differently, with some dimensions stretching over two AGIL dimensions.

The *7S-model* resulted from the research by Pascale and Athos (1981) concerning the success of Japanese enterprises. The model comprises seven interrelated parameters, which should be in balance. Each parameter is equally important, but *shared values*

**Table 8.2** Comparison of AGIL with several cultural and organizational models

| | Adaptation | Goal attainment | Integration | Latency |
|---|---|---|---|---|
| Malinowski | Economics | Political organization | Social control | Education |
| Hofstede (national) | Uncertainty avoidance | Power distance | Individualism–collectivism | Masculinity–femininity |
| Hofstede (organizational) | Process versus goal orientation | Normative versus pragmatic orientation | Employee versus job; parochial versus professional orientation; open versus closed; loose versus tight control (norms) | – |
| Schein | The nature of human activity Organization's relationship to its environment | The nature of human relationships to its environment | – | Nature of reality and truth Nature of human nature |
| 7S-model | ???? Skills | Strategy Structure | Staff Systems | Shared values Style |
| Laungani | Materialism–spiritualism | Free will–determinism | Individualism–communalism | Cognitivism–emotionalism |
| Von Oech | Explorer | Warrior | Judge | Artist |

reside in a central position. The overall setup of the model and the individual parameters are comparable to the AGIL model. As is shown in Table 8.2, the parameters can be traced almost two times around the AGIL scheme, once on a higher, more philosophical level, and the second time on a lower, instrumental or operational level. From the AGIL point of view, one parameter representing the adaptation dimension on the higher level is missing. This parameter reflects how an organization deals with risk and challenge; it is the *spirit*, or the *stamina* with which the organization approaches the unknown, the unpredictable, the ambiguous (Smit, 1997).

The focus of the research by *Laungani* (1992) is the bearing of different value-orientations on health models and on the problems of dealing with health issues across various cultures. His model comprises four value dimensions, where the two concepts underlying each core value are to be understood as extending along a continuum. Values and behaviors can be represented at any point along the continuum and may, over time, change in either direction.

*Von Oech* (1990) does not directly concentrate on cultures, but on interventions that challenge fixed assumption patterns. He asserted that in order to survive in a society, one has to follow all kinds of rules. So from a practical point of view, it makes sense to comply with rules. But this can become a mental lock because we tend to follow rules even when they became obsolete as the context in which they were valid changes. To become more creative, and to get a fresh view on the deep assumptions we have about ourselves and our environment, Von Oech (1992) developed a method that challenges our customary ways of thinking in the four action dimensions which he calls *Explorer*, *Warrior*, *Judge*, and *Artist*.

## MEASURING CULTURES: DILEMMAS OF ACTION AND CULTURAL MAPS

Cultural patterns operate on more or less unconscious levels and therefore they are not easy to identify and it can take a considerable amount of time to unravel them (Schein, 1985). However, the underlying beliefs and assumptions, which are "invisible" during tranquil periods, become apparent in critical situations (e.g. Meyer, 1982; Parsons, 1951). It is not always possible or practical to observe teams when they deal with crises, but various critical situations can be simulated by dilemmas presented to team members via questionnaires or interviews. Dilemmas – situations involving a choice between alternatives that are both to a certain degree unsatisfactory – confront us with views incongruent with our basic rules and beliefs. Being obliged to respond to such incongruent views challenges our perception of reality and incites us to take a stand on the particular issue by explicating our own, culturally determined beliefs (Smit and Schabracq, 1997). The selection of a questionnaire or an interview depends on the design and goals of the cultural assessment. However, to ensure meaningful interventions, the dilemmas should evenly cover the AGIL area, and should be relevant for the target teams.

In the application of the presented method an interview comprising five dilemmas and several open questions was used. The interview took approximately 30 min per person. The participants were asked to describe how their *team* responds to the presented problems and to elucidate in their own words the reasons for that particular choice of actions. So each interviewee actually became an informant reporting about his or her own team. The obtained information was compiled into a cultural map, where each dilemma and question had a set of possible responses (cultural elements) generated from the responses of all participants. Based on the elements activated by its members, each team had a unique profile, which delineated the team's coping repertoire (Smit and Schabracq, 1997).

Compared with the more traditional survey approach, this method asks a relatively small number of questions, but produces a wider range of responses, which are not known in advance. Consequently, the resulting cultural map does not obtain a small number of widely generalized elements, but a relatively large number of minimum content elements (Shweder, 1991), where each participant may score on more than one element per response. Again, to collect, code and prepare the data set manually for further processing can be very time consuming. When possible, a far better solution is to conduct the interview in a so-called group facilitation room, sometimes also called group decision room, electronic boardroom, etc. (DeTombe, 1994). The room comprises a file server and a set of connected (personal) computers, which can be used to interview all team members simultaneously, while preserving the anonymity of their answers. Besides time saving, the use of the facilitation room can also improve data quality because the participants can get collectively involved in clustering the responses to categories with a shared meaning. Furthermore, the resulting cultural maps are immediately in an electronic form and ready to be analyzed, which prevents errors in preparing the data base manually.

## TEAM HEALTH

As with culture, health can be defined in various ways. In many definitions, health and disease, or dysfunction, are entangled in circular reasoning, each being defined in relation to the other (Meyer, 1996). Practical applications of such definitions are culturally dependent, for health is perceived in terms of desirable functioning and disease represents a deviation from a norm, which may vary from one culture to another (Laungani, 1992; Meyer, 1996). From a different perspective, Vaillant (1977), rather than describing health as functioning without problems, suggested that health is the condition that enables functioning *despite* problems.

The focus of this section is on team health, that is, on the capacity of a team to exist in its environment and to find a fit between its cultural assumptions and the external realities while obtaining and assessing information, categorizing and predicting environmental events, responding to the environment, and measuring the outcomes (Antonovsky, 1991; Parsons, 1960; Schein, 1985). The mastery with which a team assesses the demands of its environment and translates them into action is reflected in its *effectiveness*.

Hackman (1990) proposed a three-dimensional concept of team effectiveness. The first dimension refers to the extent to which a team meets or exceeds the performance standards related to its productive output (in terms of quality, quantity, and timeliness). The second dimension is concerned with the development of a team as a whole, that is, with the degree to which the process of working in the team enhances the ability of its members to work together on a longer term basis. This dimension is very important from the cultural perspective because it implies relationships, and relationships are essential for cultural development. The third dimension addresses the growth and well-being of individual team members. The effectiveness of a given team depends on the team's results in all three dimensions. A failure to meet the effectiveness criterion in one dimension can start self-fueling spiral developments, which jeopardize effectiveness in the remaining dimensions and ultimately can result in disintegration of the team.

When measuring team effectiveness, it is imperative that the measure – further referred to as *coping signature* – is multidimensional. Unfortunately, the majority of effectiveness measures used in practice only represent various versions of Hackman's first dimension (quality, quantity, profitability, etc.). This can lead to lopsided interventions, which perhaps boost performance in the short term, but hamper long-term development. Moreover, effectiveness measures tend to reflect what is considered good and desirable in an organization, and as such influence what people perceive as meaningful and how they prioritize problems. Consequently, any cultural intervention has a far better chance to succeed when it is accompanied with fitting and meaningful effectiveness measurements.

## DATA PROCESSING: NEURAL NETWORKS

Neural networks (NNs) are artificial intelligence systems that are well-suited to performing tasks which are usually difficult to handle with traditional computers (Klimasauskas et al., 1989; Lippman, 1987; Medsker and Liebowitz, 1994). The design of NNs was inspired by the neuronal morphology of the human central nervous system. Just as the human brain is composed of neurons, which play a very important role in information processing and decision making, artificial neural networks are composed of densely interconnected processing elements (PEs), in which computation takes place (Gupta, 1992). Comparably to neurons, PEs provide a mapping operation from a multidimensional input vector to a scalar neural output.

Unlike traditional expert systems that contain knowledge in the form of explicit rules, neural networks can be trained to perform tasks through a process of learning from examples. In this way, a neural network establishes a relation between inputs and outputs without any a priori knowledge of the rules governing the relation (Fontaine, 1993; Medsker and Liebowitz, 1994; Tan et al., 1996). Moreover, while traditional expert systems have difficulties with poorly defined situations and may fail abruptly upon receiving unexpected input, NNs are intrinsically fault tolerant and can handle information representing imprecise knowledge (Fontaine, 1993; Tan et al., 1996). Because NNs are data driven, i.e. the data processed by a network are not forced through predetermined fixed equations but the network configures itself in accordance with the general trends of the data (Klimasauskas et al., 1989), they are useful for formulation of hypotheses and for deduction of models describing previously unknown phenomena.

There is an ongoing discussion among computational specialists about the advantages and disadvantages of NNs and other learning systems in comparison with statistics. Cherkassky et al. (1994) argued that both statistical and NN methods are asymptotically "good", that is, they provide dependable estimates when the number of samples is very large. Yet, asymptotic performance is irrelevant in the real world, which usually provides us with meager and finite data. Consequently, no single method dominates all other methods for all possible data sets. Since the research goal is not to find the best method but to find a method that works best for a given data set, the selected method should conform to the properties of each particular set.

Data sets may be classified by their quality (completeness, sharpness) and by the complexity of the problem they describe. Statistics reportedly produce the best results on high quality data with partially known, somewhat complex causal rules, while qualitatively poor data with unknown, highly complex causal rules can be better analyzed by neural networks (in 't Veld et al., 1992).

Medsker and Liebowitz (1994, p. 192) recommended the use of NNs for problems where: standard technology is inadequate, ineffective, or too difficult to implement; qualitative or complex quantitative reasoning is required; many highly interdependent parameters are involved, so that a clear understanding of the analysis and solution of a problem is difficult; data are intrinsically noisy or error-prone; project development time is short, and the training time for the networks is reasonable.

According to both criteria, a typical – vague, ambiguous, fuzzy, noisy, highly complex and interrelated – cultural data set is a good candidate for NN analysis. NNs are specially recommendable for cultural assessment of smaller organizational units, where the number of measured cultural elements (independent variables) is too large in relation to the sample size, because sophisticated statistical analyses do not perform well on such under-defined data sets (Amick and Walberg, 1975).


# OPERATION OF NEURAL NETWORKS

There are two main phases in the operation of a neural network: learning (sometimes called training) and recall. *Learning* is the process in which a network adjusts itself in response to a given stimuli. *Recall* is the processing of a stimulus presented at the input of the network and creating a response at the output. A deeper description of the NN parameters and learning strategies is beyond the scope of this chapter and can be found for instance in Klimasauskas et al. (1989), Medsker and Liebowitz (1994), or Van Rijswijk (1995).

In the presented application a fast back-propagation network was used. Back-propagation is a powerful technique based on *supervised* learning, where the output generated by the NN is compared with the measured output, and the network gradually configures itself by backward processing of the output error until fitting (non-linear) input–output mapping is produced. A trained network is then a model of the input–

output transformation (Dasgupta et al., 1994). Accuracy of about 80% is acceptable for further use of the NN model by a human expert (Medsker and Liebowitz, 1994).

A successful *learning* process results in a *generalization power* of the network, that is, in the capacity to produce reasonable output for incomplete, noisy, or previously unseen inputs. The generalization capacity of a NN pertains only to the data set on which it was tested and is related to the internal validity of the NN model. It does not imply that the obtained results can be automatically generalized to other settings.

## CLASSIFICATION AND RECOGNITION OF CULTURAL PATTERNS

Having a reasonably accurate NN-based cultural model does not yet mean that we can *distinguish* teams from one another because we cannot say that a culture *has* or *has not* a certain set of values; we can merely say something about the relative strength of a particular value set in the culture (e.g. Benedict, 1935; Shweder, 1991). Furthermore, the "value strength" is not identical for all members of a culture. Laurent (1993) and Trompenaars (1993) expressed this in terms of a normal distribution. There is a large variation in each culture, but there are also typical tendencies by which cultures can be characterized. Therefore, it is not very meaningful to describe cultural membership in "black and white" terms, that is, with *crisp sets* (e.g. [0,1]). Such memberships can be better described with *fuzzy sets* that allow for description of concepts in which the boundary between having a property and not having a property is not sharp (Yager, 1990; Zadeh, 1965), so that different degrees of membership indicating the strength of adherence to the cultural properties can be indicated.

In this study, the trained NN calculated a coping signature from the interview responses of each participant. The distance of the NN calculated signature from the actual team signatures determined the participants' degree of team membership as recognized by the NN.

## IMPACT ANALYSIS AND DESIGN OF INTERVENTIONS

The trained NN is a model of the impact the cultural elements have on the health indicators constituting the team coping signatures. The knowledge of the NN is implicit, but it is possible to calculate the impact (direction and strength) of each input on each output. Because the cultural elements are in the model interconnected, the calculated impact strength is not absolute, but relative within the whole pattern (Van Rijswijk, 1995). The calculated impact is valid only in the indicator value range in which the model was tested, and should not be generalized to areas outside of this range.

Based on the impact calculation, we can identify patterns of cultural elements that have a significant positive or negative effect on the health indicators *in the NN model*. The actual team scores in the significant pattern give us an indication about the strengths and weaknesses of each team in relation to the health indicators.

In complex cases, we can "reverse" the NN operation and use the model to search for cultural patterns that are likely to produce desirable health indicators. Another AI method – genetic algorithms – can be employed to supervise the search (see for instance Medsker and Liebowitz, 1994; Van Mameren, 1998). Such a search typically results in several potential intervention scenarios, which can be further selected to fit with the problem solving style of the target team.

## PRACTICAL APPLICATION

A practical application of the AGIL method will be demonstrated by an assessment of six middle management teams operating in an industrial enterprise based in the Netherlands. Three teams operated in research (code names A, B1 and B2), and three operated in manufacturing (C1, C2 and D). The teams ranged in size from 12 to 31 members and there were 145 people in total, 61 of whom participated in the study. In all teams, the age of the participants was mixed and encompassed all age categories between 25 and 60 years. The members of teams B1, C1 and D were all men, while the remaining teams were composed of both men and women. All teams were stable units satisfying the Schein (1985) criterion for social units in which culture can be found (Smit, 1997).

The interview was focused on key operational issues, which were identified in cooperation with the upper managers associated with the participating teams. Each dilemma and question represented a probe into a specific functioning aspect in the AGIL space. The interview resulted in a cultural map with 352 elements. The team coping signatures comprised nine health indicators: timeliness, quality and quantity of production, existence strength (a rather rough measure gathered from various sources), and sick leave (total; short, medium, and long term; frequency). Sick leave was included because in the Netherlands a significant proportion of sick leave is attributed to work-related stress (Smit, 1997).

A fast back-propagation network was used to model the relation between the cultural elements (inputs) and the coping signatures (outputs). The NN converged to an accuracy level of 90% (recall values had a deviation of 10% from the actual values presented to the NN in learning). This means that the network was able to classify the cultural responses and quantify them with reasonable accuracy to a set of team health indicators (Smit et al., 1996). Based on the NN calculated coping signatures, 80% of the participants were correctly recognized as members of their own team, that is, the calculated degree of team membership was the highest for their actual team. This is a rather high recognition percentage, as the typical recognition in systems based on statistics is for similar tasks around 50%. However, such comparisons ought to be made carefully because the results are dependent on a number of (unequal) parameters (Dasgupta et al., 1994).

The trained NN calculated the impact (strength and direction) of every cultural element on every team health indicator. The impact matrix ($352 \times 9$) was thus reduced to significant relations, and can be post-processed to show

1. the impact of the most dominant elements in the cultural profile of a given team on all health indicators;
2. the strongest positive (desirable) and negative (undesirable) elements in each AGIL dimension;

3. team profiles on the elements with the strongest impact on a given health indicator. For instance, in Figure 8.1 are exhibited the elements with the strongest positive and negative impact on sick leave, and the percentage of A-team members who considered these elements to be active in their team (activation strengths). This information can be used to design an intervention targeted at a decrease in the A-team's sick leave. For instance, we can suggest to the team to turn their focus from element I12, which is related to high sick leave, and base their actions more on elements L5L5, L5G1, or other elements that are already present in the team's pattern, but are underdeveloped. We can also try to enrich the team's pattern by introducing new "positive" elements, in this case G4A4 and I1I6.

When designing the interventions, we have to use caution before pronouncing any cultural element either "good" or "bad". In fact, only very few elements in this study had a purely negative or positive impact on the health signature: most elements were positively connected with some indicators and negatively with others. By analyzing the impact of each cultural element on the diverse team health indicators, the NN assists us in the identification and balancing of "controversial" elements, which are very desirable for one or more indicators and very undesirable for others.

While investigating the results of the assessment from various perspectives, a pattern of elements steadily positively related to team health gradually emerged. Despite the small scale of this study, most of the concepts in this "healthy" pattern are congruent with the characteristics of salutogenic environments (Antonovsky, 1991), well-functioning teams (e.g. Hackman, 1976, 1990; Kets de Vries, 1995; Schein, 1985) or families (Skynner, 1987). For instance, the pattern, which is described in detail in Smit (1997) and Smit and Schabracq (1998), comprised elements valuing challenge, well-defined responsibility (boundaries), control over own work contribution, assumption pattern update via active feedback, knowledge transfer to new/young people, openness to different concepts and "and-and" (win-win) approach toward conflicts.

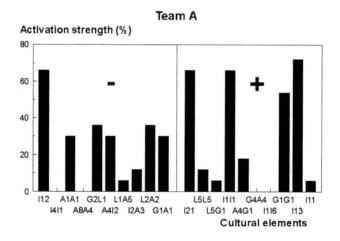

**Figure 8.1**   Significant elements: Sick Leave

Each team had its own approach and put emphasis on different elements of the "healthy" pattern; nonetheless, the teams that reported health problems completely missed several elements, while the very healthy teams scored relatively high in the whole pattern. The healthy teams also demonstrated a dynamic, continuously tested pattern integrity in the sense that their assumptions about what they *can*, *will*, *must* and *may* do while solving problems were congruent (Smit and Schabracq, 1998). Thus, we can conclude that team health does not depend on a single trait or behavior, but is sustained by a pattern of cultural elements.

# CONCLUSIONS AND FUTURE AREAS OF RESEARCH

The presented AGIL method combined with neural networks enables us to systematically describe and distinguish organizational cultures, to elucidate the relation of various cultural patterns to organizational health, and to apply this information to design interventions targeted at tailored enhancement of coping repertoires in organizational settings. The method can be applied on a large scale, producing more general results, or on a small scale, for instance for assessment of several teams operating in a specific field, where the results are likely to reflect beliefs and assumptions typical for that field. The obtained cultural profiles can also be used for assessment of one or more organizational units over a longer time period, and for comprehensive compatibility assessments of organizations that shall be merged, as well as for facilitation of the merge.

In future research, attention should be paid not only to the configuration of the cultural patterns, but also to the *frequency* with which the pattern elements are applied, for frequency measures can lead to a deeper understanding of the patterns' effectiveness (Vaillant, 1977). Further, the results of testing the AGIL method in several industrial teams indicated that cultural patterns of teams enjoying excellent health are characterized by integrity that was missing in the less healthy teams. Therefore, it would be valuable to investigate the effects of specific interventions on the process of integrity building in teams where this process is lacking or insufficient.

The back-propagation NN used in the applications successfully analyzed the fuzzy, difficult data set and established relations between cultural patterns and health indicators, without any previous knowledge of the rules guiding the relation. Yet, the supervised, back-propagation networks focus on inputs that have a strong impact on the output values and "neglect" the less powerful inputs. To identify patterns that are perhaps not directly related to the health indicator values, but are essential for functioning in a given organization, the supervised NN could be extended by an *unsupervised* network (e.g. a Kohonen network). The desirability of outputs is not indicated in an unsupervised NN, and the network organizes itself internally so that each processing element responds strongly to a different set of closely related input stimuli. Such input clusters often represent distinct – known or unknown – real world concepts. Unsupervised learning can thus be instrumental for formulation of new concepts or theories. The disadvantage of this approach is that the currently available technology lacks sufficient reliability (Van Rijswijk, 1995; Varfis and Versino, 1992). Some progress was recently made in this area (e.g. Brand, 1997), but a lot of research still needs to be done before the unsupervised techniques can be used for cultural assessment in practice.

Artificial intelligence techniques offer a number of advanced approaches for assessment of cultural maps and for the design of tailored interventions. However, we ought to keep in mind that a map is not the territory, and although a good map can considerably ease the problem solving journey, people, not the computer system, have to live with the actual solutions and their consequences. So not the methods and techniques, but human beings shall remain central in the process of building healthy organizational cultures.

# REFERENCES

Amick, D.J. and Walberg, H.J. (1975) Introductory Multivariate Analysis. Berkeley, CA: McCutchan.

Antonovsky, A. (1991) The structural sources of salutogenic strengths. In C.L. Cooper and R. Payne (Eds), Personality and Stress: Individual Differences in the Stress Process, pp. 67–104. Chichester: Wiley.

Bales, R.F. (1950) Interaction Analysis. Cambridge, MA: Addison-Wesley.

Benedict, R. (1935) Patterns of Culture. London: Routledge and Kegan.

Brand, S. (1997) Combinaties van Neurale Netwerken (Combinations of Neural Networks; in Dutch). Verslag. Rotterdam: Hogeschool Rotterdam.

Carrithers, M. (1992) Why Humans Have Cultures. Oxford: Oxford University Press.

Cherkassky, V., Friedman, J.H. and Wechsler, H. (1994) Preface to Proceedings of the NATO Advanced Study Institute from Statistics to Neural Networks, Theory and Pattern Recognition Application, held in Les Arcs, Bourg Saint Maurice, France. Berlin: Springer-Verlag.

Cox, T. and Ferguson, E. (1991) Individual differences, stress and coping. In C.L. Cooper and R. Payne (Eds), Personality and Stress: Individual Differences in the Stress Process, pp. 7–30. Chichester: Wiley.

Dasgupta, C.G., Dispensa, G.S. and Ghose, S. (1994) Comparing the predictive performance of a neural network model with some traditional models. International Journal of Forecasting, 10(94): 235–244.

DeTombe, D.J. (1994) Defining Complex Interdisciplinary Societal Problems. Amsterdam: Thesis Publishers.

Erez, M. and Early, P.C. (1993) Culture, Self-Identity, and Work. New York: Oxford University Press.

Fontaine, G.A.P. (1993) Machine Conditions Monitoring and Diagnosis Using Neural Networks. Graduation thesis. Delft: Delft University of Technology.

Godelier, M. (1986) The Mental and the Material. London: Verso.

Gupta, M.M. (1992) Virtual cognitive systems (VCS). Neural Network World, 6(92): 621–628.

Hackman, J.R. (1976) The design of self-managing work groups. Technical report no. 11, School of Organization and Management, Yale University.

Hackman, J.R. (1990) Groups That Work (and Those That Don't). San Francisco, CA: Jossey-Bass.

Hakkenberg, A. (1992) Keuzen en Logica in Onderzoek en Beleid (Choices and Logic in Research and Policy; in Dutch). Assen: Van Gorcum.

Hampden-Turner, C. (1994) Corporate Culture. London: Piatkus.

Hampden-Turner, C. and Trompenaars, A. (1993) The Seven Cultures of Capitalism. New York: Doubleday.

Hofstede, G. (1980) Motivation, leadership, and organization: do American theories apply abroad? Organizational Dynamics, Summer: 42–63.

Hofstede, G. (1994) Cultures and Organization Intercultural Cooperation and its Importance for Survival. London: Harper-Collins.

in 't Veld, L.J., Koppelaar, H. and Pellikaan, R. (1992) Neurale begrotingsmodellen (Neural budgeting models; in Dutch). Informatie, 34(6): 349–355.

Kets de Vries, M.F.R. (1995) Life and Death in the Executive Fast Lane. San Francisco, CA: Jossey-Bass.

Klimasauskas, C., Guiver, J. and Pelton, G. (1989) Neural Computing. Pittsburgh, PA: NeuralWare.

Laungani, P. (1992) Cultural variations in the understanding and treatment of psychiatric disorders: India and England. Counseling Psychology Quarterly, 5(3): 231–244.

Laurent, A. (1993) Managing across cultures. Lecture given at INSEAD, Fontainebleau, France.

Leys, M. (Ed) (1990) Perspectieven op Organisaties: Cultuur in Organisaties (Organizational Culture; in Dutch). Heerlen: Open Universiteit.

Lippman, R.P. (1987) An introduction to computing with neural nets. IEEE ASSP Magazine, April: 4–22.

Malinowski, B. (1944) A Scientific Theory of Culture. Chapel Hill, NC: University of Carolina Press.

Medsker, L. and Liebowitz, J. (1994) Design and Development of Expert Systems and Neural Networks. New York: Macmillan.

Meyer, A.D. (1982) Adapting to environmental jolts. Administrative Science Quarterly, 27: 515–537.

Meyer, F. (1996) Introduction to J. van Alphen and A. Aris (Eds), Oriental Medicine, pp. 11–15. Boston, MA: Shambhala.

Parsons, T. (1937; paperback edition 1968) The Structure of Social Action. Glencoe, IL: The Free Press.

Parsons, T. (1951) The Social System. Glencoe, IL: The Free Press.

Parsons, T. (1960) Structure and Process in Modern Societies. Glencoe, IL: The Free Press.

Parsons, T. (1971) The System of Modern Societies. Englewood Cliffs, NJ: Prentice-Hall.

Parsons, T. (1977a) Social Systems and the Evolution of Action Theory. Glencoe, IL: The Free Press.

Parsons, T. (1977b) The Evolution of Societies. Englewood Cliffs, NJ: Prentice-Hall.

Parsons, T. (1978) Action Theory and the Human Condition. New York: The Free Press.

Parsons, T. and Shils, E. (1951) Toward a General Theory of Action. Cambridge, MA: Harvard University Press.

Parsons, T., Bales, R.F. and Shils, E.A. (1953) Working Papers in the Theory of Action. Glencoe, IL: The Free Press.

Pascale, R.T. and Athos, A.G. (1981) The Art of Japanese Management. New York: Penguin.

Schabracq, M.J. and Winnubst, J.A.M. (1995) Werk en mentale belasting (Work and mental load). In M.J. Schabracq and J.A.M. Winnubst (Eds), Mentale Belasting in het Werk (Mental Load at Work; in Dutch), pp. 19–34. Utrecht: Lemma.

Schabracq, M.J., Cooper, C.L. and Winnubst, J.A.M. (1996) Work and health psychology: towards a theoretical framework. In M.J. Schabracq, J.A.M. Winnubst and C.L. Cooper (Eds), Handbook of Work and Health Psychology, pp. 3–29. Chichester: Wiley.

Schein, E.H. (1985) Organizational Culture and Leadership. San Francisco, CA: Jossey-Bass.

Shweder, R.A. (1991) Thinking through Cultures. Cambridge, MA: Harvard University Press.

Skynner R. (1987) Explorations with Families. New York: Routledge.

Smit, I. (1997) Patterns of Coping: a Study of Team Cultures and Health. PhD dissertation. Utrecht: Utrecht University.

Smit, I. and Schabracq, M.J. (1997) Stress, performance and organizational cultures. International Journal of Stress Management, 4(4) 275–289.

Smit, I. and Schabracq, M.J. (1998) Team cultures stress and health. Stress Medicine, 14(98): 13–19.

Smit, I., Van Rijswijk, J. and Frietman, E.E.E. (1996) A neural network model of organizational cultures. In L. Dekker, W. Smit and J.C. Zuidervaart (Eds), HPCN Challenges in Telecomp and Telecom: Parallel Simulation of Complex Systems and Large-Scale Applications, pp. 267–277. Amsterdam: Elsevier.

Tan, C.L., Quah, T.S. and Teh, H.H. (1996) An artificial neural network that models human decision making. Computer, March: 64–70.

Trompenaars, F. (1993) Riding the Waves of Culture. London: Nicholas Bealy.

Vaillant, G.E. (1977) Adaptation to Life. Boston, MA: Little, Brown.

Van Mameren, R. (1998) A Comparative Implementation of different AI Techniques for Pattern Classification within a Socio-Cultural Data Set. Graduation thesis. Delft: Delft University of Technology.

Van Rijswijk, J. (1995) Neural Netwerk Model van Organisatieculturen (Neural Network Model of Organizational Cultures; in Dutch). Verslag. Delft: Delft University of Technology.

Varfis, A. and Versino, C. (1992) Clustering of socio-economic data with Kohonen maps. Neural Network World, 6(92): 813–834.

von Oech, R. (1990) A Whack on the Side of the Head. New York: Warner Books.

von Oech, R. (1992) Creative Whack Pack. Stamford, CT: US Games System.

Yager, R.R. (1990) An introduction to fuzzy set theory. In Tutorials of the International Conference on Fuzzy Logic and Neural Networks, Iizuka, Japan.

Zadeh, L.A. (1965) Fuzzy sets. Information and Control, 8: 338–353.

# Section III

# Culture and its Implications for Individuals and Organizations

Jennifer A. Chatman

The four chapters in this section are eclectic. They draw from different disciplines (economics, sociology, group and social psychology), focus on a variety of outcomes such as internalization, enculturation, group performance, and innovation, and offer two innovative formal modeling approaches for assessing the influence of organizational culture on members. But, they share one important characteristic in that each chapter represents an interesting departure from prior conceptual and methodological approaches to understanding organizational culture.

J. Richard Harrison and Glenn R. Carroll explore how organizational demography and influence networks affect cultural transmission and member enculturation using a computer simulation. They begin by summarizing their innovative computer simulation research to date. Though, as they point out, computer simulation rarely constitutes the ultimate stopping point in a research program, it allows for valuable experimentation to characterize the mechanisms associated with a construct. Their simulation approach is particularly useful for identifying how these mechanisms, and the relationships among them, contribute to the dynamic evolution of culture. This process is extremely difficult to assess using most conventional research methods. They elaborate on their prior model of cultural transmission by considering the combined role of networks and demographic heterogeneity in affecting cultural variability within simulated organizations.

Benjamin E. Hermalin provides an elegant comparative analysis of the approaches to culture that economists have developed. He uses a game-theoretic approach focusing on coordination, or the convention-setting aspect of organizational culture, and repeated games in which repetition provides a substitute for contracting. Taken together, he views culture as a substitute for explicit communication, as an unspoken language giving directives to organizational members. He identifies the important contributions that economists can make to better understanding organizational culture. They can explore the consequences of various assumptions, such as formal versus social control, and various dynamic processes, such as the diffusion of culture, using formal logic and models. Economists are also well positioned to evaluate the costs and benefits derived from marketplace interactions so that they can identify ways for organizations to optimally influence their cultures.

Francis J. Flynn and Jennifer A. Chatman question the connection between strong corporate cultures and reduced innovation. They argue that this perceived connection stems from a misunderstanding of culture strength and content, two concepts that are clearly unique, but are often blurred. Culture strength reflects levels of conformity among organizational members, and culture content determines whether such conformity is demanded in a uniform manner. They present a set of propositions that consider the conditions under which organizations are likely to strike a balance between creativity and social control. This requires developing cultural norms that foster the divergence and uniqueness necessary for the creative process to occur, while maintaining the cohesion among members necessary to develop and implement creative ideas.

Finally, Elizabeth A. Mannix, Karen A. Jehn, and Sherry Thatcher extend organizational culture research by examining how it influences group behavior within organizations. They start by examining the circumstances under which team cultures form, and the consequences of such subcultures for organizations. They derive a compelling set of testable hypotheses and a model that allows for a window into the complex interplay between various levels of analysis within organizations. Their model has important implications for such cross-level issues as, for example, how group norms affect individuals, or how societal norms affect organizational culture.

The most important combined contribution of this section is that each chapter debunks a myth about studying culture: that economists are, somehow, not well-equipped to address such intangible phenomena as culture; that a phenomenon as complex as culture cannot usefully be reduced to a computer simulation; that small groups at all levels of organizations are not potent agents of cultural change; and that strong cultures necessarily stifle innovation. The chapters, therefore, open new doors, or doors that were prematurely shut, to gain insight into organizational culture.

# Chapter 9

# Modeling Organizational Culture: Demography and Influence Networks

**J. Richard Harrison**
*School of Management, University of Texas at Dallas,*
*Richardson, TX, USA*

*and*

**Glenn R. Carroll**
*Graduate School of Business, Stanford University,*
*Stanford, CA, USA*

## INTRODUCTION

Individuals acquire organizational culture through socialization and it is well understood how socialization occurs as a result of peer pressure and other influence tactics. But understanding the on-going processes by which members new to a formal organization become enculturated requires consideration of at least two additional factors.

First, the demographics of organizational membership determine not only who is around in the organization to exert influence but also the extent to which organizational culture is itself stable. It is obvious that organizational members come and go and that average tenure levels will affect the socialization of others. Equally important, however, is the structure of the tenure distribution. If the tenures of members overlap greatly, then culture is likely transmitted across time with ease. As tenure overlap diminishes, then a more intense transmission mechanism is likely needed. In the extreme case of no overlap in tenure, cultural regeneration depends on formal institutions or external actors or events.

Second, the structure of influence patterns within the organization affects the intensity of socialization pressures experienced by individuals. The location of an individual within an influence network, the characteristics of others in the network and the influence of each network member combine to produce socialization intensity. Over time, the system also possesses high feedback: one's participation alters the influence network and affects the characteristics of others.

Although both tenure distributions and influence networks affect individuals, these are fundamentally properties of the collectivity, not the individual. Both phenomena also lend themselves to explicit modeling, permitting their examination beyond the individual-level focus of much of the research on organizational culture (e.g. Chatman, 1991). The goal of this chapter is to discuss and develop issues related to incorporating demographic considerations and influence network considerations into models of organizational culture.

The analysis builds on and extends a previously established model of organizational culture and its transmission over time (Carroll and Harrison, 1998; Harrison and Carroll, 1991). As currently developed, the model is demographic in nature; we focus attention here on refining its representation of person-by-person influence patterns. Specifically, we investigate a variety of dynamic interaction principles imposed on the influence processes of members. These principles are drawn from theory and research about social cohesion, influence processes, and small group dynamics. They specify how the strength of influence might vary, including processes based on aggregate characteristics of all members as well as some based on the similarity of individuals. When allowed to operate over time, each set of principles generates a particular network influence structure within the organization. The substantive questions we address concern the extent to which variations in the structure of the network affect enculturation and other cultural processes within the organization.

We use computer simulations to examine the behavior of the model over time and under a range of conditions. The simulations allow us to vary the demographic conditions and the interaction principles of influence among organizational members and to examine the impact of the variations on organizational outcomes. In our investigations, we focus on several substantive issues of interest to organizational researchers. These issues include: random versus cohort-based influence (where social influence is a function of proximity in hiring dates), size of peer group, rate of turnover, and inequality of influence in the network. For outcomes, we explore the mean and variance of enculturation levels of organizations over time.

In this chapter, we first discuss the use of models and simulation methods to study organizational culture. We then review the Harrison–Carroll model of cultural transmission in organizations and its empirical implications. Previous investigation of the model using computer simulation techniques has shown that it generates empirical predictions broadly consistent with many known patterns of culture across different structural forms of organization (Harrison and Carroll, 1991). The model also has been used to explore the plausibility of assumptions commonly made by organizational demographers to explain estimated associations between length of service (tenure) distributions and organizational outcomes such as turnover, innovation and performance (Carroll and Harrison, 1998). It has also recently been translated to the macro level to address questions about cultural heterogeneity in age and size dependence in organizational mortality (Harrison and Carroll, 2001).

# ON MODELING CULTURE AND USING SIMULATION METHODS

Scientists now widely recognize computer simulation as a basic way of conducting scientific investigations (Axelrod, 1997; Waldrop, 1992). A simulation project begins with a model of the behavior of a system the researcher wishes to investigate. The model consists of a set of equations or transformation rules for the processes through which the system variables change over time. To simulate, the model must then be translated into computer code. The resulting program is run on the computer for multiple time periods to produce the outcomes of interest, which can be analyzed statistically or graphically.[1]

For basic organizational research, the model underlying a simulation represents a set of theoretical propositions. It should be evaluated as one would any theory, meaning that criteria of logical consistency, explanatory power, empirical import, elegance and parsimony all apply. By this reasoning, one errs in thinking of a computer simulation as a way to build highly complex models of reality. Like overly complex theory, a simulation with many variables and transformations really explains little. Similarly, simulation output or findings contribute little to the advancement of research without an understanding of the theoretical mechanisms producing them. In our view, a good simulation allows sufficient experimentation to characterize the mechanisms involved. Finally, simulation rarely constitutes the appropriate stopping point for any research program; it is perhaps better to consider it a rigorous starting point or stock-taking point, one from which the empirical world might be better interpreted or tested.

To avoid excessive complexity in computer simulation, social scientists develop simplified models of the phenomenon under investigation, ignoring many plausible influences in order to concentrate on the processes deemed to be the most crucial or of greatest interest. This strategy permits one to examine the consequences of the focal processes unencumbered by complicating influences (without denying their existence – and additional processes can always be incorporated in the model in subsequent studies). The simulation findings help in understanding the phenomenon studied to the extent that the focal processes play an important role in influencing it.

For example, in a simulation analysis reported below in this chapter, we examine the relationship of tenure distributions and cultural similarity to organizational influence networks. Influence networks may be affected by many social and psychological mechanisms, such as political processes, similarity-attraction processes, and social identification processes, but by confining our attention to the effects of tenure distributions and cultural similarity, we are able to isolate the relationships of interest for the purpose of the analysis. In a sense, this strategy is analogous to that of controlled

---

[1] Actually, the model could consist of a single process, although simulations are usually used to study systems in which multiple processes operate simultaneously.

laboratory experiments. Simulations obviously have some disadvantages relative to laboratory experiments, since the "actors" are artificial agents rather than human subjects. But they also have a number of advantages, including perfect control (unobserved heterogeneity and unwanted influences are eliminated), less restriction on sample size, the ability to manage greater complexity in experimental design, and the ability to track precisely the behavioral steps leading to the outcomes of interest (the computer's memory is not subject to the biases of subjects' recollections and other problems of reconstructing causes for human behavior).

Computer simulation can aid enormously in theory construction. Most importantly, it renders irrelevant the problem of analytic intractability inherent in much formal theory – mathematical relationships can be handled computationally using numerical methods. This feature allows theorists to make realistic assumptions rather than compromise with analytically convenient ones, as is common in deductive theory. Computer simulation also partially overcomes the empirical problem of data availability – a simulation produces its own data.[2]

Despite the pioneering work of James March and colleagues (Cohen et al., 1972; Cyert and March, 1963) and James Coleman (1964), the use of computer simulation in the social sciences has lagged behind the natural sciences. One reason for this may be accessibility – many social scientists may lack the training to evaluate and interpret simulation studies. Another possibility is that simulation is given short shrift in social science methodological training curricula. Many social scientists may also be averse to the level of abstraction involved in simulations (as well as in mathematical modeling in general). An objective of this chapter is to help overcome these obstacles – to demonstrate the utility of simulation analysis in studying social phenomena, and organizational culture in particular.

In contemporary organizational research, computer simulations help in studying the behavior of complex systems, or systems composed of multiple interdependent processes. In such systems, each of the individual processes may be simple and straightforward, and each may be well understood from previous research or at least well supported theoretically. But the outcomes of the interactions of the processes may be far from obvious, especially over time. Simulation enables the systematic examination of the simultaneous operation of these processes over time.

For example, the simulations described below for cultural transmission in organizations involve three basic processes. New members enter the organization (first process), current organizational members undergo socialization (second), and some members exit the organization (third). Although each of these three processes has been investigated thoroughly, research on organizational culture has focused on the socialization of current organizational members. New insights into organizational culture can likely be gained by studying an organizational system that includes entry and exit as well as

---

[2] The first well-known computer simulation involved the design of the atomic bomb in the Manhattan Project during World War II. The complex systems of equations used in the design process could not be solved analytically, and data were impractical – in addition to the unknown risks of attempting to set off atomic explosions, there was not enough fissionable material available at the time for even a single test. Over the decades following the war, simulation became an accepted and widely used approach in physics, biology, and other natural sciences.

socialization. Simulations makes it possible to do this, including understanding how the three basic processes interact to generate the behavior of the organizational system.

This kind of investigation does not square neatly with many social scientists' ideas about cumulative research programs. Many methods textbooks state that successful development of cumulative knowledge about a phenomenon proceeds linearly and sequentially down a path from less structured qualitative approaches to the highly structured approach of formal modeling. The textbook by Ragin (1994), for example, claims that qualitative research methods work best for developing new theoretical ideas and making interpretations of a theory or a phenomenon's significance; quantitative research is directed towards the "goals of identifying general patterns and making predictions".

By this view, organizational culture should be analyzed with a mixture of qualitative and quantitative methods, perhaps with a nod to the qualitative. There is little doubt that the phenomenon exists and that it exerts powerful effects, which vary across organizations. However, consensus has yet to emerge about which theories are most plausible and merit rigorous study. The qualitative camp of culture researchers wants to spend more time exploring the rich multidimensional character of organizational culture, presumably to advance novel theory or because of the problems of systematically assessing cultures whose content dimensions may vary across organizations. The quantitative camp insists on moving forward with systematic empirical research, presumably to sort out the many various theoretical ideas that have already been advanced. Consequently, discussions of organizational culture too often are consumed with debate about epistemology and measurement rather than about the phenomenon or the processes generating it.

Our view is that the presumed linear sequence of cumulative knowledge development from qualitative (and informal) to quantitative (and formal) may be debilitating. And, in the case of organizational culture, we think it could be downright counterproductive. Some phenomena (such as organizational culture) are inherently more difficult to measure and although we admire attempts to do so, we do not believe that theoretical progress needs to wait for breakthroughs in measurement technology. In particular, we see no reason why theoretical insights from qualitative and other observations might not be directly translated into formal models. Indeed, we believe that doing so potentially improves the theory in many ways and that formalization efforts may in turn help researchers better target their efforts.

We also believe that development of theories and models may generate new empirical strategies. This is not to say that modeling organizational culture will help in measuring culture directly – it may or may not.[3] Rather, establishing a formal model of organizational culture holds out the possibility of uncovering systematic connections between previously unconnected observables – a consequence of the logic of the model. In other words, tracing through and understanding the implied connections between variables may show an expected covariation between two or more observable variables that can be used as a hypothesis in systematic empirical research.

---

[3] Of course, to the extent that the model improves precision of the concept, then it should facilitate measurement.

# A MODEL OF CULTURAL TRANSMISSION IN ORGANIZATIONS[4]

Our model of cultural transmission in organizations is multilevel. The model represents processes occurring to individuals in an organization yet can be used to make comparisons in structural characteristics across organizations. The model shows high face validity in that it is capable of reproducing observed levels of cultural intensity in known organizational forms based on the demographic, recruitment, and socialization characteristics of these forms (Harrison and Carroll, 1991).

## Modeling Framework

Many attempts to model culture and related phenomena (such as beliefs, tastes, or knowledge) in simulations start with an objective representation of each individual on a set of specified attributes. Typically, the attributes are binary (or other highly limited integer) variables and the set is finite and unordered. For instance, March (1991) uses 30 variables that can each take on three values $(-1, 0, 1)$ to represent the dimensions of beliefs in a model of organizational knowledge. Carley (1991) uses up to 40 binary variables to represent the "facts" known by individuals in a group's culture. Epstein and Axtell (1996) use a string of 11 binary variables to represent the cultural attributes of individuals. And, Harrington (1998, 1999) uses a binary distinction among flexible and rigid agents to represent the behavioral rules in environments with hierarchical selection. From these data on objective representations, the cultural attachment of individuals is then assessed via criteria imposed by the researcher (e.g. those with similar scores are more culturally similar). Similarly, cultural intensity and homogeneity for the group or organization are evaluated with aggregate measures (e.g. a very homogeneous culture would be one where all individuals have similar scores on all or most of the dimensions).

The Harrison–Carroll model uses a different type of representation scheme for organizational culture. This model assumes that an individual's propensity to embrace the values and norms of a particular organizational culture can be meaningfully represented by a single measure indicating the degree to which an employee fits management's cultural ideal. Representing culture by a single variable does not imply that it is inherently unidimensional but, rather, that in a specific organizational context some overall managerial assessment about one's cultural predisposition and acceptance is possible, even though cultural content is usually found to be multidimensional in empirical work (Hofstede, 1980; Hofstede et al., 1990; O'Reilly et al., 1991). This representation focuses on cultural fitness rather than on the constellation of underlying cultural content dimensions that determine fitness.

This measure of cultural fit is referred to as the enculturation level. Enculturation can occur before an individual joins an organization (for example, in a professional school), and employees can be further enculturated through socialization (Chatman, 1991).

---

[4] This section adapts and updates parts of Harrison and Carroll (1991).

Although management groups will differ in the types of factors they use to assess the level of enculturation, they include knowledge, qualification, and willingness to embrace and comply with the culture, and may reflect such factors as work experience and education. For a given individual $i$, we denote his or her enculturation level by the variable $C_i$, which can take on values between 0 (no fit with management's cultural ideal) and 1 (a perfect fit).

The cultural transmission model is based on three mathematical functions and a set of embedded parameters. The functions give: (1) the number of persons hired in a period of time; (2) the process of change in the enculturation level of each person within the organization; and (3) the number of persons departing from the organization in a period of time. The parameters of the model control the growth rate of the organization, the recruitment rate to vacancies, the selectiveness of the recruitment process with respect to cultural criteria, the intensity of socialization, the natural decay rate of socialization, and the turnover rate. We discuss briefly each function in turn, using the relevant parameters as necessary.

## Hiring Function

Let the number of persons hired in a time period be denoted by NH($t$), and the number of vacancies by NV($t$). Organizational hiring can be modeled as

$$\text{NH}(t) = \sum_{j=1}^{\text{NV}(t-1)} H_j(t)$$

where

$$H_j(t) = \begin{cases} 1 \text{ if position } j \text{ is filled in period } t, \\ 0 \text{ otherwise} \end{cases}$$

and

$$\text{NV}(t-1) = \{\text{NV}(t-2) - \text{NH}(t-1) + \text{ND}(t-1) + \text{GR}[N(t-1)]\}$$

and GR is the organizational growth rate associated with stochastic changes in the number of positions, ND($t$) represents the number of persons departing the organization at time $t$, $N(t)$ is the number of members of the organization at time $t$, and a stochastic rate of recruitment to vacant positions (RR) is used to find values of $H_j(t)$.

Individual hiring can be conceived as drawing individuals from a pool of candidates. The pool has a distribution of values on the desired characteristics, and the distribution is known for the pool. Because cultural criteria are subtle and not readily observable in many instances, the choice of any particular individual is somewhat random. In fact, the characteristics of the pool are determined by the selectiveness of the hiring policies of the organization (Chatman, 1991). The candidate pool is more or less centered on the desired characteristics, and more or less noise is tolerated in the information used in the selection process.

Hiring on the basis of cultural criteria is simulated by randomly drawing values of $C_i$ from parameterized distributions. The parameters of the distribution are defined by the hiring policies of the organization. At each time period, therefore, $NH(t)$ persons are hired with a variety of fits with the management-desired culture of the organization.

## Socialization Function

Any individual's change over time with respect to socialization is a combination of the pulls from three sources: management, peers (fellow employees), and decay. The three forces likely vary in their relative strengths. The expected change in socialization is modeled as a function of the individual's distance from a target for each source (the maximum value of 1 for management; the group enculturation mean for peers; and the minimum of 0 for decay), multiplied by a parameter. The model also introduces an error term to allow for noise in the process. The Harrison and Carroll (1991) model posited the function for socialization-change intensity as

$$SI_i(t) = \frac{SMR[1 - C_i(t - 1)] + SNR[\overline{C} - C_i(t - 1)] + SDR[0 - C_i(t - 1)]}{SMR + SNR + SDR} + e$$

where $e$ is an error term and SMR, SNR and SDR are parameters representing the pulls toward ideal socialization (from management), mean socialization level (from peer pressure), and zero socialization (from decay), respectively. In effect, the denominator normalizes the function $SI_i(t)$ to ensure that an individual's $C_i$ score remains between 0 and 1. The error $e$ is constructed to be normally distributed with mean 0 and adjustable variance.

Individuals can be more or less susceptible to socialization, whatever its source. Susceptibility is greatest at the time of entry into the organization and then declines with tenure (Louis, 1980). Newcomers are unfamiliar with an organization's culture and, consequently, are more open to social influence as they adapt to their new environment. Over time, as they adjust their cultural orientations in response to organizational socialization, they gain familiarity with the culture and become increasingly resistant to further change. We simulate susceptibility to socialization forces with the following equation:

$$SU_i(t) = TA1 + \exp\{-TA2 - TA3[u_i(t - 1)]\}$$

where $u_i$ is individual $i$'s tenure with the organization. With the parameter values used here (TA1 = 0.02, TA2 = 0.60, TA3 = 0.30), susceptibility begins with a value less than unity and declines exponentially with tenure toward a non-zero asymptote. It is important for the value of the function to remain between 0 and 1 because it will be used below as a multiplier. In this specification, TA1 is associated with the asymptotic level of susceptibility, TA2 with the level of susceptibility at entry (tenure equals zero), and TA3 with the speed of the decline in susceptibility with increasing tenure from the entry level to the asymptotic level.

The socialization function is completed by taking an individual's prior enculturation level $C_i(t - 1)$ and adding to it the effect of socialization-change intensity $SI_i(t)$ multiplied by its influence $SU_i(t)$. That is,

$$C_i(t) = C_i(t - 1) + [SU_i(t)][SI_i(t)]$$

Distributional measures of the $C_i$ scores characterize the organizational culture at any particular point in time. In particular, dispersion measures such as the standard deviation of enculturation across all individuals indicate cultural heterogeneity.

## Turnover Function

Turnover might be connected to organizational culture for at least two reasons. First, individuals who do not accept the culture might be motivated to leave voluntarily (Chatman, 1991). Second, those who do not fit in and who fail to change might be forced to leave involuntarily. In both cases, the issue may be thought of as one of alienation (Wanous, 1980), related to the distance between an individual's embodiment of the culture, $C_i$, and the management ideal of 1. We formalized the alienation process with the term $AR[1 - C_i(t - 1)]^3$, where AR is a parameter allowing greater or less sensitivity to alienation as a cause of turnover. The value of this expression increases rapidly as $C_i$ approaches 0, but in general the effect of alienation on turnover in the model is much smaller than the effect of other (non-cultural) factors.

Allowing all other reasons for leaving an organization (Chatman and Jehn, 1994) to be captured in an adjustable base-turnover factor (associated with the parameter ER), the number of persons departing the organization in time period $t$ is then given by

$$ND(t) = \sum_{i=1}^{N(t-1)} D_i(t)$$

where

$$D_i(t) = \begin{cases} 1 & \text{individual } i \text{ leaves in period } t, \\ 0 & \text{otherwise} \end{cases}$$

The stochastic rate of departure for individual $i$, used to find $D_i(t)$, is

$$RD_i(t) = ER + AR[1 - C_i(t - 1)]^3$$

where both ER and AR are parameters of the rate.

# ANALYTICAL USES OF THE CULTURAL TRANSMISSION MODEL – FINDINGS AND IMPLICATIONS

We have conducted three sustained investigations using the model. The first is about variations in cultural transmission by organizational form, designed to explore how organizational characteristics affect the development and maintenance of an organization's culture. The second is about the relationship between organizational culture and demography, because the influence of organizational demography on organizational culture has been underemphasized in previous work. The third is about the role cultural heterogeneity plays in age and size dependence in organizational mortality; we believe that culture can affect organizational survival (an argument implied by theoretical work on age dependence) but has not been adequately addressed in organizational mortality studies. We briefly describe each investigation in turn.


## Findings on Organizational Form

In initial explorations with the model, we varied parameter settings for each of the following: recruitment selectivity; socialization intensity by source; turnover rate; and organizational growth rate. We organized these variations in clusters that correspond to commonly used stylized notions about organizational form. We studied the model's behavior for seven generic organizational forms: Japanese-style form (characterized by high recruitment selectivity, intensive socialization by management, long-term employment, and high growth); American manufacturing form (low recruitment selectivity, weak socialization by management, low turnover, and low growth); governmental–bureaucratic form (moderate recruitment selectivity, weak socialization by management, low turnover, and low growth); professional form (very high recruitment selectivity, weak socialization by management, moderate turnover, and low growth); entrepreneurial form (moderate recruitment selectivity, moderate socialization by management, moderate turnover, and very high growth); Z-type form (moderate recruitment selectivity, moderate socialization by management, low turnover, and high growth); and collectivist–democratic form (high recruitment selectivity, intensive socialization by coworkers, low turnover, and no growth). Our analysis consisted of assessing: (1) how long it took each form to reach an equilibrium or stable culture over time; (2) the mean level of enculturation at equilibrium; and (3) the heterogeneity in culture as indicated by dispersion in culture scores around the mean.

The findings gave substantial credibility to the simulation model: the simulated organizational forms behave in plausible ways consistent with expectations and common knowledge about the forms. For instance, the strongest cultures, as indicated by the mean level of enculturation, are found in the Japanese, professional and Z-type forms. The weakest culture is in the so-called American manufacturing form. Cultural heterogeneity, as given by dispersion around the equilibrium mean, is lowest for the professional and collectivist–democratic organizational forms, again conforming to expectations. Overall, this pattern of findings shows that the model can reproduce basic known differences in cultural intensity across organizational forms, providing some validation for the model.

The model also yielded three potentially important new insights into the cultural transmission process. First, rapid growth and high turnover often aid in establishing cultural stability. The effect of rapid growth is the result of higher susceptibility of new employees to socialization. Second, organizational culture becomes stronger as organizations decline in size. Culture intensifies in declining organizations because employees with low enculturation scores (and usually short tenure) are most likely to exit, in our model. Third, some organizational forms are inherently more unstable culturally, suggesting that they are also more conflict-prone because of demography.

## Findings on Culture and Demography

Internal organizational demographers study the influence of tenure or length of service (LOS) distributions on organizational outcomes, operating through intervening social processes that can be viewed macroscopically as organizational culture. Simply put, internal organizational demographers assume that demographic heterogeneity within an organization corresponds with cultural heterogeneity, which in turn affects outcomes such as turnover, innovation, and firm performance. In our second study with the model, we looked into this intervening process by examining the plausibility of the assumption about a positive relationship between heterogeneity in LOS and in culture (Carroll and Harrison, 1998).

In conducting these investigations, we adapted the model to resemble a top management team (TMT) because that is the social unit most empirical research on demography examines. Top management teams are social organizations in and of themselves, and they are thus subject to similar processes of entry, socialization, and exit. Enculturation was defined in terms of the preferences of the chief executive officer (CEO) or the board of directors. New team members were chosen from a candidate pool with a distribution of values on desired characteristics, although in this context candidates may be viewed as hired from the outside or selected from other parts of the organization. Peer socialization represents socialization by other team members, and size refers to the team rather than the entire organization. We modeled teams of two average sizes, five persons and 20, keeping the growth rate fixed at 0 to correspond to constant team size. Because the top management team constitutes a distinctive cultural milieu, the tenure terms in the socialization and turnover functions indicated tenure with the team.

Because the CEO is usually a member of the TMT, we fixed one position with this status, setting his or her initial enculturation score near 1 (ideal enculturation). After entry, the CEO is treated exactly like any other member of the team. The CEO is thus subject to all the forces in the model; in particular, socialization by other TMT members can, over time, lower the CEO's enculturation score. Using this interpretation makes the management pull factor in the socialization function ambiguous, so we set the parameter SMR to 0, leaving peer socialization as the primary influence on cultural change.

Our study consisted of simulating culture in many TMTs under various demographic conditions. The simulation output for each TMT gives a culture score for each individual at each point in time and a measure of cultural heterogeneity can be constructed for each team at each time period (for comparability we used the conventional measure used by organizational demographers – the coefficient of variation in tenure). Heterogeneity in LOS varies across time and across teams by demographic conditions. By pooling data across time or across TMTs, it is possible to estimate the strength of the association between cultural heterogeneity and LOS heterogeneity.

Our findings show that the assumption of positive correlation between heterogeneity in LOS and in culture holds for the model under a very wide range of conditions, a finding that supports the common demographic research framework. Among various conditions, we found the assumption to be most plausible in organizational contexts with both high recruitment selectivity and strong peer socialization.

The discipline imposed by our modeling efforts also led us to uncover a number of methodological and conceptual shortcomings of typical research practice that deserve attention if the program is to sharpen its contributions. In particular, the model developed here helped in the discovery of a "disruption effect" associated with entry and exit from the TMT, which strongly confounds the association between LOS heterogeneity and cultural heterogeneity, making interpretation of many studies highly problematic.[5] It made clear the built-in relationship between turnover and the LOS distribution, impugning studies using LOS variation as a predictor of turnover without adequate controls. It also highlighted the importance of a well-specified theoretical model for the construction of empirical measures.

To be sure, much of this might have been deduced from more specific considerations without the full model, but it had not been, despite a great deal of research activity on this topic. Accordingly, we cannot help but think that the model's structure provided an insightful perspective that allowed us to see these problems and that it imposed a discipline on our thinking that facilitated analysis. In some cases, the full model was necessary to understand the effects of complex interacting processes – for example, the disruption effect requires the simultaneous operation of entry, exit, and enculturation processes. In other cases, once effects are deduced from the model, it becomes apparent that these effects are at work in phenomena independent of the model (for example, the built-in turnover relationship).

Based on the insights and findings of the simulation analysis, we offered a number of specific recommendations for organizational demographers, including decomposing the theoretically central tenure-based measure of heterogeneity currently in wide usage – the coefficient of variation in tenure (and its cousins). The primary problem with this measure is that it combines the effects of too many hypothesized processes with potentially inconsistent effects. In its place, we proposed three theory-derived measures of heterogeneity: heterogeneity from socialization, heterogeneity from group cohesiveness, and heterogeneity from common historical experiences. We believe that decomposing effects of demographic heterogeneity based on these three processes will facilitate understanding. Each shows a simpler relationship between tenure and an underlying process than does the combined measure. Each also shows promise in empirical analysis based on the simulated data. As a result, we believe that all three measures merit consideration and exploration in empirical studies on organizational demography.

## Findings on Cultural Heterogeneity and Organizational Mortality

A major limitation of the cultural transmission model described above is the representation of organization growth, which is modeled using an unrealistic constant rate of growth (GR). The organizational size distribution implied by this specification does not even roughly correspond to observed size distributions of organizations. Given the

---

[5] Sørenson (2000) has subsequently demonstrated the possible impact of the disruption effect on empirical work in internal organizational demography. In a study of television station managers, he showed empirically that failure to control for entry and exit events in investigating LOS effects can generate spurious findings.

importance of size for many organizational characteristics, this limitation makes it difficult – if not impossible – to link the model of culture to other macro phenomena in plausible ways.

Harrison and Carroll (2001) developed a macro version of the model. The macro model addresses these limitations of the established model. It represents changes in organizational size as the result of combined arrival and departure processes. The macro model also: (1) allows for both organizational growth and decline within the same parameter settings; (2) introduces a new specification for stochastic variation in growth; and (3) generates simulated size distributions of organizations more closely resembling those observed in real industries.

The macro model facilitates extension to ecological concerns, including organizational mortality. It does so by allowing for incorporation of appropriate variables – organizational age, size, and cultural intensity – into the organizational growth–decline process. In Harrison and Carroll (2001), these extensions were accomplished by linking the rates at which new organizational members are added to and dropped from the organization to organizational culture. We envisioned organizational death as occurring when the size of the organization shrinks to zero members. We used this setup to investigate questions about the relationship between organizational culture and the probability of death. Specifically, we investigated the relationships between cultural heterogeneity and age and size dependence in mortality rates.

Stinchcombe (1965) anticipated the effect of culture on organizational mortality in his famous discussion of the liability of newness, where he observed that new organizations are typically peopled with strangers attempting to invent and learn new roles. Stinchcombe argued that socialization may be especially problematic under such conditions. A reasonable interpretation of his argument holds that cultural heterogeneity may be high in new organizations and this makes it difficult to develop goals and routines. Cultural heterogeneity would also likely increase turnover, making organization even more problematic. By these arguments, the heterogeneity of culture should affect the shape of organizational mortality rates. It would suggest that cultural variations might account in part for negative age dependence in organizational mortality.

But the story does not end there. While Stinchcombe's analysis of this particular issue is fine as far as it goes, it just does not go far enough, especially in terms of the employment dynamics of new firms. Notice that Stinchcombe's arguments are based on what is essentially a cohort analysis of the initial employees of a firm: they start out as strangers attempting to do new things and, with time, they become more familiar with themselves and their interdependent activities. The problem is that the employment base of a new firm typically changes quickly and sometimes even radically. The initial members often leave (at least some of them) and new members enter, perhaps in large numbers. Departures likely affect the established culture within the organization. And, new members require socialization and mutual adjustment by incumbent members. Given certain demographic inflows and outflows, the changing mix of persons in the organization implies that the exact same arguments advanced by Stinchcombe might generate a different form of age dependence in mortality. Given the complexity of the employment dynamics of new firms, this issue may have seemed too problematic at the time to Stinchcombe (1965) and hence he understandably concentrated on a simple scenario. Using a formal model and simulation techniques, however, makes neither the complexity of the employment dynamics of new firms nor the mixing of growth scenarios in an organizational population intractable. This is again a case where the various parts of the processes seem to be understood well enough to describe mathematically – the complexity arises from their interdependence in the system, especially as it unfolds over time.

Harrison and Carroll (2001) show that the macro model successfully generates the widely observed liabilities of newness and smallness in organizational mortality (see Carroll and Hannan, 2000, for a discussion of these liabilities). It also generates significant effects of cultural heterogeneity on organizational mortality. When examined together, the effects of size and cultural heterogeneity dominate and often eliminate any detectable effect of age. Thus, the simulation model generates age dependence in organizational mortality but this age dependence can be accounted for by the effects of small size and cultural heterogeneity.

The relationship between size and cultural heterogeneity is complex. For many simulated conditions, the data support a statistically significant interaction term between size and cultural heterogeneity. It seems that the combinations of (1) low growth and high selectivity and (2) high growth and low selectivity produce the interaction effect. For example, in the high growth, low selectivity and high alienation condition, the findings show that as organizations grow, mortality decreases with size for organizations that develop and maintain stronger (more homogeneous) cultures but not for organizations that have weaker (more heterogeneous) cultures. In general, Harrison and Carroll (2001) conclude that cultural heterogeneity mediates size and growth effects on organizational mortality, suggesting that Stinchcombe's arguments concerning the liability of newness imply a complex relationship between organizational size and culture that is not obvious from purely age-based considerations.

## NETWORKS OF INFLUENCE – EXTENSION OF THE MODEL

In the established model of cultural transmission detailed above, peer socialization occurs in a simple manner: the average enculturation of others in the organization exerts a pull on the individual that moves his/her score toward the average (the strength of the pull is given by the parameter SNR). Using the average of others' scores in this way implies that each peer has equal influence at every point in time. The communication network typically associated with such a structure is one where all individuals have equally strong ties to all other individuals (see Friedkin, 1998; Scott, 1991).

While using this simplified representation made sense in developing the model's general structure, it clearly leaves room for further development. After all, full and equal access (let alone influence) to all individuals in an organization rarely occurs, even in small organizations. Obviously, variations in the structure of influence have the potential to produce major differences in organizational cultural systems and their outcomes.

We initiate here an extension of the model in this direction. We work with the influence processes directly and do not deal with the communication patterns that produce them.[6] We first develop a general framework for modeling influence among individuals in a cultural system. We then describe how we envision influence processes changing over time.

## Modeling Framework

The established model sets an individual $i$'s enculturation score at time $t$, $C_{i,t}$, based on three factors: (1) his/her previous enculturation level; (2) the individual's susceptibility to socialization (a decreasing function of tenure); and (3) the intensity of socialization forces he/she faces (which combines pulls from management, peers and decay). Before incorporating explicit person-by-person influence considerations, we simplify this general structure. We drop the susceptibility factor entirely because the widely observed pattern of decreasing susceptibility is itself likely an outcome of person-by-person influence processes; in other words, over time the cultural influence network is likely to stabilize individuals' enculturation levels. We also disregard the socialization pulls from management and decay in order to better isolate effects from the influence network. These simplifications leave us with a model with the general form

$$C_{i,t+1} = f(C_{i,t}, G_{i,t})$$

where $G_{i,t}$ is another function giving the effects of the influence network structure at time $t$ between $i$ and all other members $j$.

We next describe the influence system. We start by defining the variable $S_{ji,t}$ as the influence that person $j$ exerts on person $i$ at time $t$. We fix $S_{ji,t}$ to be a continuous variable that ranges from 0 to 1 ($0 \leq S_{ji,t} \leq 1$). So, when $S_{ji,t} = 0$, person $j$ has no influence on $i$; when its value is 1, $j$ has maximum influence. Of course, the actual cultural change that $j$ might induce on $i$ likely depends not only the amount of influence he/she exerts but also on how culturally similar or dissimilar the two of them are. Let cultural similarity be given by the difference in their enculturation scores. Although absolute cultural similarity can be defined as the absolute value of this difference, we use here "directional" cultural similarity by retaining the sign of the difference. Then, the cultural effect of $j$ on $i$ can be given by the product of influence and similarity, $S_{ji,t}(C_{j,t} - C_{i,t})$. If $C_{j,t} > C_{i,t}$, then the effect of $j$ on $i$ is positive, tending to increase $C_{i,t}$; if $C_{j,t} < C_{i,t}$, then $j$ tends to decrease $C_{i,t}$.

With these elements in place, we can set the influence function $G_{i,t}$. This function lets individual $i$ be influenced by all other members $j$ in the organization or team. It does so by summing across their proportional contributions, determined by group size:

$$G_{i,t} = \sum_{j \neq i} S_{ji,t}(C_{j,t} - C_{i,t})/(n - 1)$$

---

[6] The relationship between influence and communication is important but not central to our current concerns. We believe that for socialization and other cultural processes, influence is primary. In a later extension, it may make sense to attempt to model the communication network as well.

where $n$ is the number of persons in the group or organization. Making the function for the enculturation score at time $t + 1$ a linear combination of $C_{i,t}$ and $G_{i,t}$, so that the new culture score for $i$ is given by the previous score plus an adjustment due to influence, yields

$$C_{i,t+1} = C_{i,t} + aG_{i,t}$$

where $a$ is simply a weighting parameter with values between 0 and 1 and is inversely associated with cultural inertia; that is, cultural change occurs more slowly for lower values of $a$.

## Dynamic Influence Process

Influence patterns clearly change over time in a group or organization. The source of this change may be exogenous but it may also be a function of cultural similarity and previous influence patterns – in other words, it might be endogenous. A novel aspect of the model we explore here is the manner in which such dynamic influences occur.

In our view, a good way to start modeling the dynamics of influence is to assume that change is relational. By this we mean that how much more or less influence a person has on another depends in large part on the cultural similarity of the two individuals involved. When two individuals are culturally similar, they likely interact more and have more influence on each other than on other, less similar individuals. The increased interaction likely causes them to recognize and appreciate their similarity even more fully, thus leading them subsequently to assign even greater significance to each other's opinions and behavior. In this dynamic influence process, other individuals who have lower cultural similarity have less influence on one another. These individuals likely get less interaction time and have less influence; even if there might be a limited common cultural basis, it often does not get recognized and appreciated. And, known differences likely get heightened and exacerbated with decreased interaction. So, individuals who are highly dissimilar relative to available others tend to have less and less influence on one another over time.

Overall, in a group or organizational setting, each individual experiences similarity-based influences, to a greater or lesser degree, from each other individual. This means that even though absolute cultural similarity (the difference in two individuals' encul-turation scores) may still matter, individuals nonetheless drift toward those closest to them culturally. Without hard evidence to determine the functional form for the relative influence dynamics, we make the simplifying assumption that the relative influence of each other person on an individual is related to the mean level of cultural similarity among those available as interaction partners. That is, we specify that when the cultural similarity between an individual and another person exceeds the mean level of simi-larity between that individual and all other persons in his/her network, then the influ-ence of that person will increase over time. Conversely, when the cultural similarity between an individual and another person falls below the mean level of similarity between that individual and all other available persons, then the influence of that person will decrease over time. In both cases, the exact magnitude of change in the other person's influence depends also on the absolute cultural similarity between the two individuals.

The model to generate these processes is given by the following. We first construct the mean cultural difference for all individuals $j$ associated with individual $i$:

$$D_{i,t} = \sum_{j \neq i} |C_{j,t} - C_{i,t}| / (n - 1)$$

where $n$ represents the number of persons in the group or organization. We next calculate the weighting for the change in influence of each person $j$ on $i$ as

$$W_{ji,t} = (1 - |C_{j,t} - C_{i,t}|)^4 - (1 - D_{i,t})^4$$

In the first term on the right-hand side of the equation, the absolute value of the difference is subtracted from 1 so that the highest weighting occurs when $C_{j,t} = C_{i,t}$; in the second term, the mean distance is also subtracted from 1 for comparability. Both terms are taken to the fourth power to increase the weighting for more similar individuals and to decrease it for less similar individuals, relative to the mean difference. Changes in influence over time are then given by

$$S_{ji,t+1} = S_{ji,t} + bW_{ji,t}(1 - S_{ji,t}) \text{ if } W_{ji,t} > 0$$

and

$$S_{ji,t+1} = S_{ji,t} + bW_{ji,t}S_{ji,t} \text{ if } W_{ji,t} < 0$$

where the weighting parameter $b$ varies from 0 to 1 and is inversely associated with inertia in the network's influence change process. The multiplier of $W_{ji,t}$ in the first equation, $(1 - S_{ji,t})$, causes influence to change in the direction of 1 (maximum influence) when $W_{ji,t} > 0$, and the multiplier of $W_{ji,t}$ in the second equation, $S_{ji,t}$, causes influence to decrease toward 0 (no influence) when $W_{ji,t} < 0$.

Figure 9.1 illustrates how the influence of individual $j$ on individual $i$ changes in this model from time $t$ to time $t + 1$ (shown as the vertical axis, labeled SDIFF) as a function of the cultural similarity of the two individuals (indicated by the cultural distance CDIFF the absolute value of the difference in the individuals' enculturation scores) for the case when $S_{ji,t} = 0.5$ and $D_{i,t} = 0.25$. Note that despite the smoothness of the curve, the direction in which influence moves depends on whether cultural similarity falls above or below the mean (that is, whether CDIFF is above or below 0.25). Note also that when individuals are more similar than the mean (CDIFF < 0.25), the increase in influence is greater than is the decrease in influence when they are less similar than the mean by the same amount. In other words, very similar individuals (relative to the mean cultural difference) experience stronger increases in influence on one another while very dissimilar individuals experience much weaker decreases in influence. We believe this asymmetry is sensible, since we expect that more similar individuals interact more intensively.

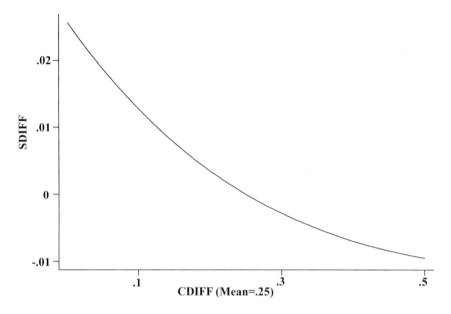

**Figure 9.1**   Influence change as a function of cultural similarity.

## Model Comparison

Most network-based models of influence rely on binary representations of influence or tie strengths among individuals in a group or organization. These models also typically contain fixed, or at least exogenous, influence processes. By contrast, the model advanced here represents influence with continuous variables and posits an endogenous process of influence change over time. Both of these features are highly attractive in our view because we think they reflect realistic assumptions about the processes involved in the formation and transmission of organizational culture.

It is worthwhile to note that a major reason we can depart from conventional paths and incorporate these features into the analysis is because of our use of simulation. Although other analysts commonly recognize the value of these approaches, they do not implement them because they are mathematically intractable or empirically overly demanding. Simulation methods allow us to overcome these otherwise formidable obstacles.

## FINDINGS ON DEMOGRAPHY AND NETWORK COMMUNICATION STRUCTURES

We report here simulation experiments with the extended model designed to examine the effects of variations in five factors on the cultural system of a formal organization. The first three factors can be characterized as primarily demographic in nature: turnover rates, hiring processes, and organizational size. The final two concern primarily the structure of influence processes: cohort-based influence and inequality in influence. The first four of these variations are controlled by specification in the simulation program; variations in inequality arise as a consequence of the processes modeled. In examining these factors, we focus on their effects on the mean enculturation level as well as the heterogeneity of culture among members of a team or organization. We now describe each set of issues and how they are treated in the simulation.

## Demographic Factors: Turnover, Hiring, and Size

Turnover, hiring, and organizational size are potentially important factors because such demographic conditions set the stage for the operation of influence in a cultural system. Although it is commonly thought that turnover undermines stability and thereby causes culture to deteriorate, two previous analyses show that this need not be the case. In a model of organizational learning, March (1991) demonstrated that limited turnover aids in learning by introducing new information to the organization. Similarly, Harrison and Carroll (1991) found that turnover allows a strong culture organization to flush itself of relatively unencultured members faster, thus raising levels of enculturation and propelling the system toward equilibrium (see also Krackhardt and Porter, 1985). In both cases, turnover assists in adaptation of the system over time. However, it is also clear that turnover can be detrimental to culture, as when whole generations of individuals depart, erasing the collective memory of the system.

How might these different views be reconciled? The effects of turnover may be nonlinear; they may also be confounded with size and hiring selectivity. Small organizations are much more impacted by multiple departures, which may comprise a substantial proportion of the organizational membership. But large organizations typically preclude intensive interaction among all members on a regular basis. Moreover, turnover effects are mediated by the characteristics of the replacement members. The issues are potentially very complex. So, we investigate these factors by designing simulation conditions that systematically produce variations in each.

We model turnover here using a slightly different specification than previously. Recall that in the established model (discussed above), individual-level turnover is given by the hazard rate for individual $i$ as

$$RD_i(t) = ER + AR[1 - C_i(t - 1)]^3$$

where both ER and AR are parameters, the first indicating a baseline rate of departure and the second associated with alienation (an individual's distance from the perfect culture score). We use here a modified formulation, one that bases alienation on cultural distance from the other members of the organization rather than from a perfect score. We do this by making alienation a function of the squared distance of an individual's enculturation score from the enculturation mean $\overline{C}$. This gives an individual hazard rate of

$$RD_i(t) = ER + AR[C_i - \overline{C}]^2$$

where the culture variables are again measured at $t - 1$ but the subscripts have been dropped for clarity.

The simulation experiments vary both the strength of the baseline turnover rate and the strength of the alienation effect, including a condition for no turnover. Appendix A provides the exact parameters used for each; in reporting our findings we simply refer to the levels as high, low, and no turnover.

The hiring policy variations address the cultural selectivity of the hiring process. Members of the labor pool from which new entrants are selected vary in their cultural fit with the organization because of prior socialization, and the organization may put more or less effort into selecting entrants with a good fit. The selectivity of the hiring process is simulated by assigning each new entrant $i$ an enculturation score $C_i$ given by

$$C_i = CM + (CS)(\varepsilon)$$

where CM is the mean enculturation level of new entrants, $\varepsilon$ is drawn from $N(0,1)$, the standard normal distribution, and CS is a multiplier to adjust the variance. We keep CS fixed at 0.15 and vary hiring selectivity by setting CM to either 0.3, 0.5, or 0.7 to represent low, intermediate, and high hiring selectivity.

We also vary organizational size. We do this simply by setting the number of persons in the organization at different fixed levels of 5, 15, or 25. Size does not vary over time: there is no growth mechanism in the model and when a person departs from the organization he/she is immediately replaced.

There is nothing compelling about the particular values we chose for parameter settings. We simply selected values to give a reasonable range of variation in the parameters to examine the model's behavior under a variety of conditions. Other settings could have served just as well. For example, larger sizes could have been used (although the differences in outcomes tend to diminish as size becomes very large); the size range we chose is realistic for small organizations and for top management teams. Of course, the parameter choices are constrained to some extent by feasibility considerations – for example, it would not be sensible to set the turnover rate so high that the entire organization's membership turns over in each time period.

## Structure of the Influence Network: Inequality and Cohort-Dependence

The two network structure variables we examine here both relate to larger debates about the structure of influence and its relationship to organizational demography and culture. Inequality in the influence network reflects in part the differences between network theorists Burt (1992) and Podolny and Baron (1997) about the optimal design of social networks. Burt (1992) argues forcefully and unconditionally for information-ally efficient networks, those with minimal redundancy in ties and information. Such networks are characterized by "structural holes" in his terminology; a network with large structural holes also usually possesses a high level of inequality. Podolny and Baron (1997) accept this assessment when it concerns social networks where the purpose is to find and identify reliable information (e.g. locating job opportunities). But they argue that for purposes of identity and normative sanctioning such a network is not effective. Instead, they suggest that a dense network with overlaps and redundancies creates clearer expectations, making the sense of attachment greater; violations of norms are also more likely to be caught and sanctioned within a dense network, leading to possible expulsion of chronic deviants. By this reasoning, the less hierarchical network may be better for producing solidarity and homogeneity in an organizational culture.

As specified now, the model already produces much variation in levels of inequality in the influence network. In the simulations, these variations appear spontaneously within each simulation condition. So, instead of developing new simulation conditions to examine the effects of inequality, we examine the issue within and across the variety of other simulation conditions. We do this by calculating two measures of influence network inequality for each simulated organization at each point in time. The first is an overall inequality measure; it is computed as the average, for the previous 24 month period, of the difference between the individual with the highest net influence (average influence on others less average influence of others on him/her) and the individual with the lowest net influence. The second is a measure based on the individual who has maximum influence on others. This measure is calculated as the average, for the previous 24 month period, of the ratio of the average influence on others of the individual with the greatest influence to the average influence on others for the full organization. In both cases, the higher the score, the greater the inequality in the influence network.[7]

Turning to the second network structure factor, cohort-based influence, takes us back to contemporary research on internal organizational demography. As mentioned above, this research examines the causes and consequences of organizational demography on a variety of organizational outcomes (Pfeffer, 1983). Much internal organizational demography investigates the effects of tenure or length of service (LOS) distributions on organizational outcomes, operating through intervening social processes that can be viewed macroscopically as organizational culture (Carroll and Harrison, 1998). Indeed, internal organizational demographers typically assume that demographic heterogeneity corresponds to cultural heterogeneity, which in turn affects outcomes such as turnover, innovation, and firm performance. A common way this is assumed to happen is through cohort-dependent processes of mutual influence: those individuals who enter the organization at similar times have shared socialization experiences, join and help develop common groups, and experience common historical events within the organization (Pfeffer, 1983).

In examining the effects of cohort-based influence, we compare simulated organiza-

---

[7] We chose to create new measures for network inequality rather than use standard network measures. Standard measures tend to assume binary values for network ties whereas our tie strengths are continuous in [0,1]; further, many standard measures require exogenous influences to make the calculation of the measures mathematically tractable, and our influence structure is completely endogenous. In the simulations reported here, the inequality of influence variable ranges from 0.32 to 0.52 and the maximum influence variable ranges from 1.12 to 1.40.

tions where there is no cohort basis of influence with those where such influence operates in a particular way. In modeling cohort-based influence, we focus on the entry process. We do this by setting the strength of both who influences a new entrant and whom he/she exerts influence upon as functions of recency of entry (or inversely, tenure) of incumbent organizational members. In other words, a person entering an organization with many long-tenured individuals will not be heavily influenced by them and will also not exert much influence upon them (Pfeffer, 1983). By contrast, a person entering an organization with many others who have recently entered will be greatly influenced by them and will also have an impact on them. In the more typical situation, a person entering an organization will find both short- and long-tenured individuals, and he/she will be more influenced by, and exert more influence on, those who entered more recently.

The cohort-based influence process is modeled by the manner in which the person-by-person influence scores $S_{ij}$ between incumbent members and new entrants are set at the time of entry of the new members. In the model without cohort-based influence, each new entrant $i$ is assigned a full set of influence scores $S_{ij}$ drawn randomly from a uniform distribution, U(0,1). The influence of each incumbent $j$ on the new entrant $i$ ($S_{ji}$) is also drawn from this distribution.

We believe that common historical experiences are important in cohort-based influence processes (Pfeffer, 1983). So, in modeling this condition we set influence to be a function of absolute similarity in tenure. More precisely, in setting the influence of an incumbent $j$ on the new entrant $i$ we use the following rules. We first draw a random uniform deviate and square it so that the average influence of incumbents on new entrants is less than in the non-cohort setup; we label this value as $\zeta_{ji}$. We next calculate a cohort-based influence score $\phi_{ji} = 1 - \alpha(u_j + \varepsilon)$, where $\alpha$ is simply a weighting factor (set to 0.01 in the simulations reported here), $u_j$ denotes the tenure of person $j$ and $\varepsilon$ is a disturbance drawn randomly from N(0,1), the standard normal distribution. We then finally set the influence of each incumbent $j$ on the new entrant $i$ to be the larger of the two. That is, $S_{ji} = \max(\zeta_{ji}, \phi_{ji})$.

We set the new entrant's influence on the incumbents in a similar way. That is, we start by drawing a random uniform deviate and squaring it; we label this value $\zeta_{ij}$. We next calculate a cohort-based influence score $\phi_{ij} = 1 - \beta(u_j + \varepsilon)$, where $\beta$ is a weighting factor (set to 0.02 in the simulations reported here rather than 0.01 as above, since the influence of new members on incumbents is likely to be less than the influence of incumbents on new entrants), $u_j$ denotes the tenure of person $j$ and $\varepsilon$ is a disturbance drawn randomly from the standard normal distribution N(0,1). We then set the influence of new entrant $i$ on each incumbent $j$ to be the larger of the two values. So, $S_{ij} = \max(\zeta_{ij}, \phi_{ji})$.

Finally, we allow new entrants $i$ and $k$ to influence each other by $S_{ik} = 1 - |0.05\varepsilon|$, with a minimum of 0, where $\varepsilon$ is a disturbance drawn randomly from a standard normal distribution N(0,1). In general, persons entering the organization at the same time will strongly influence one another under this process.

Taken together, these specifications define the condition that we call cohort-based influence.

## Simulation Experimental Design

Exploring the above factors together potentially gives us 54 basic simulation conditions. These come from the combinations of three variations in turnover (no turnover, low turnover, high turnover), three variations in hiring selectivity (0.3, 0.5, and 0.7), three variations in size (5, 15, and 25), and two variations in cohort-based influence (random and cohort-based). The variations in influence network inequality arise "naturally" as a result of the simulated influence process and thus are not built in directly as design conditions; instead these variations appear spontaneously within each of the 54 basic conditions.

We simulated each basic condition for 100 trials. Each of the trials represents a simulated organization; each is initiated at time 1 with initial $C$ and $S$ values drawn as random deviates from normal and uniform distributions, respectively (the seeds for generation vary across trials, of course). Each trial organization operates for 300 time periods (representing months) before it is stopped. We save the data from the entire history of the trials, not just the ending time. We report here analyses based on pooled periodic snapshots of the data. Specifically, we combine data from each trial taken at every 60 period time point (representing every 5 years); the outcome variables of interest at each time point are average values for the preceding 24 time periods. So, each trial contributes five observations to the dataset. The total number of observations in the file equals 27 000, resulting from five periodic observations of each of 100 trials for each of 54 conditions.

## Simulation Findings

In exploring the extended model, we focus on the mean enculturation level as well as the heterogeneity of culture among members of a team or organization. To give an overview, we report in Table 9.1 distributional information about the mean enculturation level across conditions. As the first row shows, the mean of the mean enculturation level across the 27 000 observations of simulated data is 0.500. The median of mean enculturation is almost identical, at 0.501. The similarity of these statistics should not be interpreted as a lack of variability across trials and conditions. As the minimum and maximum values show, the range of the mean across observations is high, going from a low of 0.141 to a high of 0.883. The standard deviation of mean enculturation across observations is 0.1306, indicating healthy variability.

The statistics about mean enculturation suggest a well-behaved, or at least symmetric, distribution across observations and simulation runs, as depicted in Figure 9.2 (which shows the mean enculturation score on the horizontal axis and the fraction or proportion of runs on the vertical axis labeled Fraction). It is also somewhat polymodal, with 0.500 representing an overall mode and two smaller peaks falling above and below. The two smaller peaks correspond to hiring selectivity settings of 0.3 and 0.7, respectively; the central peak is higher because selectivity does not come into play in the no turnover condition, and because the influence process tends to pull new hires entering with enculturation scores of 0.3 or 0.7 toward the center of the distribution under some conditions.

What accounts for the variation in mean enculturation levels? Table 9.1 also provides some simple breakdowns of distributional information by time period and by simulation condition. The means of the mean are remarkably stable across these breakdowns (with the exception of the effects of hiring selectivity). Variability in the mean level of enculturation apparently increases as a function of time and turnover – in both cases, the standard variation of mean enculturation drifts upward. Variability in mean enculturation also increases for more extreme selectivity values (0.3 or 0.7 rather than 0.5). Although the effects are less dramatic, it also appears that variability in mean enculturation decreases with cohort-based influence and with organizational or group size.

Because the means are so stable across conditions, it makes no sense to analyze mean enculturation with statistical methods predicting the mean, such as ANOVA (analysis of variance) and regression analysis. Instead, we conducted informal analyses of the distributions of mean enculturation by condition: we graphed $\overline{C_i}$ by condition and compared the shapes visually. (This is an exercise that is possible only because the simulation generates so much data.) The two strongest and most interesting breakdowns involved comparing distributions across, first, combinations of size and turnover and, second, variations in the inequality of influence. Figures 9.3 and 9.4 show these distributions, respectively (both figures display the mean enculturation score on the horizontal axes and the fraction or proportion of runs on the vertical axes labeled Fraction). In Figure 9.3, the mean of enculturation is graphed by nine categories of a

**Table 9.1** Distribution of mean enculturation level ($\overline{C_i}$) across simulation runs by condition

|                             | Mean  | Median | Minimum | Maximum | Standard deviation |
|-----------------------------|-------|--------|---------|---------|--------------------|
| All conditions ($N = 27\,000$) | 0.500 | 0.501  | 0.141   | 0.883   | 0.1306             |
| Period 1                    | 0.500 | 0.501  | 0.198   | 0.827   | 0.1087             |
| Period 2                    | 0.500 | 0.502  | 0.168   | 0.805   | 0.1300             |
| Period 3                    | 0.500 | 0.501  | 0.141   | 0.839   | 0.1354             |
| Period 4                    | 0.500 | 0.501  | 0.146   | 0.883   | 0.1374             |
| Period 5                    | 0.501 | 0.501  | 0.179   | 0.832   | 0.1395             |
| No turnover                 | 0.501 | 0.502  | 0.285   | 0.688   | 0.0497             |
| Low turnover                | 0.500 | 0.501  | 0.141   | 0.832   | 0.1504             |
| High turnover               | 0.500 | 0.500  | 0.162   | 0.883   | 0.1615             |
| Selectivity 0.3             | 0.377 | 0.337  | 0.141   | 0.677   | 0.0987             |
| Selectivity 0.5             | 0.500 | 0.500  | 0.313   | 0.677   | 0.0413             |
| Selectivity 0.7             | 0.623 | 0.662  | 0.320   | 0.883   | 0.0969             |
| No cohort                   | 0.500 | 0.501  | 0.141   | 0.839   | 0.1313             |
| Cohort                      | 0.500 | 0.502  | 0.159   | 0.883   | 0.1299             |
| Size 5                      | 0.499 | 0.502  | 0.141   | 0.883   | 0.1370             |
| Size 15                     | 0.501 | 0.502  | 0.211   | 0.773   | 0.1281             |
| Size 25                     | 0.501 | 0.501  | 0.232   | 0.768   | 0.1265             |

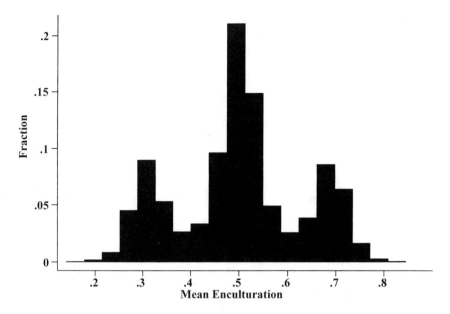

**Figure 9.2**  Distribution of mean enculturation across simulation runs.

cross-classification of size and turnover: sizeturn 1, 2 and 3 indicate those conditions where turnover is zero and size varies from 5 to 15 to 25, respectively; sizeturn 4, 5 and 6 set turnover to low and let size vary in the same order; sizeturn 7, 8 and 9 set turnover to high and let size vary in the same way. In Figure 9.4, mean enculturation is graphed by levels of inequality of influence. Here we broke the inequality score into five arbitrary categories: ineqcat 1 implies an inequality score between 0 and 0.2; ineqcat 2 between 0.2 and 0.4; ineqcat 3 between 0.4 and 0.6; ineqcat 4 between 0.6 and 0.8; and ineqcat 5 over 0.8.

Consistent with the standard deviations seen in Table 9.1, the turnover effect in Figure 9.3 seems to be dominant. The top three graphs (associated with zero turnover) show much tighter distributions (in part because there are no new entrants) than either of the lower sets (associated with low and high turnover). However, a size effect is still apparent: within each row (same turnover level), the distributions tighten as you move right (across increases in size). So, turnover and size appear to jointly affect the variance in mean enculturation. Higher turnover produces more variation in the mean; greater size produces less variation.[8]

Comparisons across levels of inequality in influence suggest that the effects of this variable on variation in mean enculturation are not as strong as those of size and turnover. The graphs in Figure 9.4 show that the distribution changes shape slightly as inequality of influence rises. It is most normally shaped when inequality of influence is greatest. It is also most dispersed for the three lower levels of inequality in influence

---

[8] We also looked at these distributions for the last observation period only and found the same patterns. So, the effects of size and turnover do not appear to be functions of simulation time.

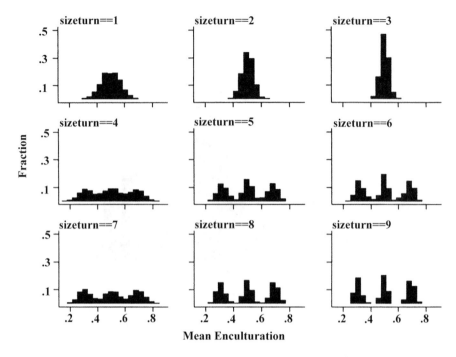

**Figure 9.3**   Distribution of mean enculturation by size and turnover conditions.

(compare the top row to the bottom one). So, even though the relationship looks complex, it also appears as though lower inequality in influence is associated with higher variation in the mean level of enculturation.

Table 9.2 provides distributional information about the variance in enculturation

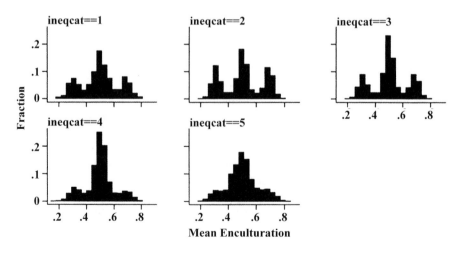

**Figure 9.4**   Distribution of mean enculturation by influence inequality categories.

**Table 9.2**   Distribution of variance in enculturation across simulation runs by condition

|  | Mean | Median | Minimum | Maximum | Standard deviation |
|---|---|---|---|---|---|
| All conditions ($N = 27\,000$) | 0.0045 | 0.0042 | 0 | 0.0376 | 0.0040 |
| Period 1 | 0.0057 | 0.0050 | 0.00002 | 0.0376 | 0.0039 |
| Period 2 | 0.0043 | 0.0041 | 0.0000005 | 0.0284 | 0.0039 |
| Period 3 | 0.0042 | 0.0040 | 0 | 0.0299 | 0.0039 |
| Period 4 | 0.0041 | 0.0039 | 0 | 0.0270 | 0.0039 |
| Period 5 | 0.0041 | 0.0039 | 0 | 0.0285 | 0.0040 |
| No turnover | 0.0005 | 0.0000 | 0 | 0.0103 | 0.0010 |
| Low turnover | 0.0053 | 0.0050 | 0.00002 | 0.0346 | 0.0030 |
| High turnover | 0.0075 | 0.0073 | 0.00009 | 0.0376 | 0.0033 |
| Selectivity 0.3 | 0.0046 | 0.0043 | 0 | 0.0337 | 0.0040 |
| Selectivity 0.5 | 0.0044 | 0.0040 | 0 | 0.0376 | 0.0039 |
| Selectivity 0.7 | 0.0045 | 0.0043 | 0 | 0.0346 | 0.0040 |
| No cohort | 0.0050 | 0.0048 | 0 | 0.0376 | 0.0044 |
| Cohort | 0.0039 | 0.0037 | 0 | 0.0346 | 0.0034 |
| Size 5 | 0.0039 | 0.0027 | 0 | 0.0376 | 0.0043 |
| Size 15 | 0.0047 | 0.0046 | 0 | 0.0270 | 0.0039 |
| Size 25 | 0.0049 | 0.0051 | 0 | 0.0192 | 0.0037 |

across simulation runs. Across all conditions and observations combined, the mean variance in enculturation is 0.0045. The median is slightly lower, at 0.0042. Again, we see variation across the observations, ranging in variance from 0 to 0.0376. The standard deviation of the variance is almost as high as the mean, with a value of 0.0040.

Figure 9.5 shows the distribution of the variance in enculturation across the 27 000 observations. The horizontal axis of the figure shows the variance in enculturation scores while the vertical axis labeled Fraction indicates the fraction or proportion of runs on the vertical axis. Obviously, the distribution is skewed, with a long right tail (not all of which can be seen in the plot). So, in conducting statistical analyses of variance in enculturation we work with a transformed variable, the natural logarithm of the variance in enculturation.

Table 9.3 reports the analysis of the natural log of the variance in enculturation. It shows regressions of the log enculturation variable on the relevant demographic and influence network variables. Model a is a baseline model incorporating only a set of dummy variables for the simulation time period of the observation (we omit the period 1 dummy, so effects are contrasts to the first period). It shows that as simulation time increases, the variance in enculturation declines. These time-period effects persist in all estimated models.

The other models in Table 9.3 include the demographic and influence network variables in the regression specification. Model b adds a set of dummies for the turnover

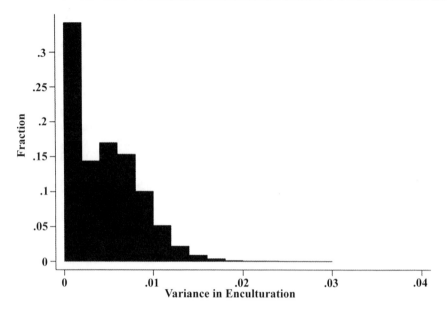

**Figure 9.5**  Distribution of variance enculturation.

level (the no turnover condition is omitted and provides the contrast), a dummy for
selectivity (the central setting, 0.5, contrasted with the more extreme settings of 0.3 and
0.7, which have symmetrical effects), the size value, and terms for the size–turnover
interaction implied by Figure 9.3. This model suggests that the variance in enculturation is significantly higher in the higher turnover conditions relative to the no turnover
condition, although the difference between these two higher turnover conditions is not
significant. The estimates also show that larger size increases cultural variability, but
that higher turnover mitigates this effect somewhat. Selectivity has no significant effect.

Model c includes the influence network variables separately with the time period
dummies. We use a dummy for the cohort-based influence condition (contrasted to the
random condition). For inequality of influence and maximum influence, we use actual
values since these variables are continuous. The estimates show that the cohort-based
influence network and influence inequality (overall and individual maximum) decrease
cultural variability significantly. Notice, however, the lower $R^2$ values, suggesting that
the influence network contributes less than demography.

Models d and e report specifications that include the demographic and influence
network variables together. Model d uses all 27 000 observations in estimation;
model e uses only the last observation (period 5) for each trial (5400 observations).
It is encouraging that the two sets of estimates basically agree with each other despite
some differences in coefficient values. Indeed, we find the estimates to be remarkably
stable: for the most part, these joint models show the same significant effects observed
earlier in the simpler models. The only exception is the cohort effect in model e, which
becomes insignificant for the final time period; additional analysis shows that the cohort
condition has its strongest effect on cultural variability in earlier time periods. Inter-

**Table 9.3**  Regression estimates of simulation conditions and other covariates on natural log of variance in enculturation

|  | Model a | Model b | Model c | Model d | Model e |
|---|---|---|---|---|---|
| Constant | −5.47*[a] | −10.3* | 14.5* | −10.2* | −16.7* |
| Period 2[b] | −0.910* | −0.910* | −0.530* | −0.912* |  |
| Period 3 | −1.64* | −1.64* | −1.16* | −1.65* |  |
| Period 4 | −2.29* | −2.29* | −1.79* | −2.30* |  |
| Period 5 | −2.80* | −2.80* | −2.28* | −2.81* |  |
| Low turnover[c] |  | 6.07* |  | 6.17* | 9.99* |
| High turnover |  | 6.59* |  | 6.68* | 10.6* |
| Selectivity[d] |  | −0.034 |  | −0.034 | 0.014 |
| Size |  | 0.087* |  | 0.090* | 0.095* |
| Cohort[e] |  |  | −1.12* | −0.082* | −0.009 |
| Inequality |  |  | −0.958* | −2.61* | −3.64* |
| Maximum influence |  |  | −15.1* | 0.835* | 1.97* |
| Size X (low turnover) |  | −0.062* |  | −0.071* | −0.078* |
| Size X (high turnover) |  | −0.068* |  | −0.077* | −0.082* |
| $R^2$ | 0.099 | 0.756 | 0.343 | 0.763 | 0.961 |
| N | 27 000 | 27 000 | 27 000 | 27 000 | 5400 |

[a] $*p < 0.001$.
[b] The omitted category for this variable is Period 1.
[c] The omitted category for this variable is No turnover.
[d] This variable is set to 1 for CM = 0.5 and 0 otherwise.
[e] The omitted category for this variable is No cohort-based influence.

estingly, the one effect that changes sign in the joint models is the maximum influence variable, which changes from a significant negative effect to a significant positive one. So, these findings suggest that inequality of influence generally dampens cultural variability but that when a single individual has undue influence, cultural variability increases.

# DISCUSSION AND CONCLUSION

Organizational culture is one of those enigmatic social phenomena that most analysts agree is important but few agree about how to study. Typically, the differences among scientists pivot on questions of measurement and interpretation. A widely held approach to social science suggests that theoretical progress ought to wait until these technical issues are resolved. Another less used approach suggests instead that formal theoretical activity might precede the development of widely accepted measurement tools. In pursuing this alternative approach in studying organizational culture, we rely heavily on computer simulations. In particular, we use simulations to comprehend the behavior of mathematical models where the component functions are simple and fairly easy to understand but where their joint operation, especially over time, is highly interactive and complex. This is a major reason for using computer simulations in social science, in our opinion.

Our simulation efforts with cultural transmission models have focused on four questions. In the first study (Harrison and Carroll, 1991), we showed that the model could reproduce the cultural stability observed in organizations and that it could account for widely observed variations in cultural intensity and heterogeneity across organization forms. In the second study (Carroll and Harrison, 1998), we demonstrated the plausibility and problems of widely used assumptions about the relationship between heterogeneity in an organization's length of service distribution and cultural heterogeneity. In the third study (Harrison and Carroll, 2001), we showed using a macro translation of the model that cultural heterogeneity can play a significant role in organizational mortality processes often linked to organizational aging and known as the liability of newness.

In the fourth study, initiated here, we extended the model to explore the consequences of demography and structural variations in the influence network. The extensions we incorporated into the model possess two attractive novel features: (1) continuous measures of network tie strength or influence; and (2) endogenous dynamic influence processes.

As reported here, the extended model shows remarkable stability. The mean of the mean enculturation level across conditions remains virtually constant. However, turnover rates and organizational size appear to jointly affect the variance in mean enculturation levels: higher turnover and greater size combine to reduce variation in the enculturation mean. It also appears as though lower inequality in influence is associated with higher variation in the mean level of enculturation.

Cultural variability within the organizations generated by the extended model does differ by demographic and influence network conditions. The findings show that as simulation time increases, the variance in enculturation within an organization declines. We also see that the variance in enculturation is significantly lower when influence is cohort-based, as is commonly assumed in current empirical research. By contrast, high turnover produces significantly higher cultural variability.

Perhaps the most intriguing findings concern the variables related to the distribution of influence within the organization. In general, we find that greater inequality of influence lowers cultural variability within the organization. However, the simulations also show that when a single individual has very high influence, cultural variability increases (after the overall structure of influence has been controlled). We regard this outcome as provocative and worthy of additional investigation.

Finally, we note that although some analysts may regard our focus here on demography and influence networks as issues of secondary importance to the study of organizational culture, this view may prove to be wrong. Both factors could play a major role in explaining cultural problems and processes. For instance, because of the many mergers taking place among highly visible companies, a problem of great interest among executives and researchers concerns how to integrate two pre-existing organizational cultures. Most discussion that we have heard on the topic focuses on describing the basic contents of the two cultures and then assessing their mutual compatibility. How can the collectivistic culture of company X be integrated with the individualistic culture of company Y? How can company A's entrepreneurial culture be preserved in the bureaucratic environment of company B? Will a merger between the German company J and the American company K work despite their deep cultural differences? Because certain demographic systems are much more fluid than others, the answers may very well depend less on the closeness or compatibility of the two cultures than on the demographics of the two organizations. Only empirical research can tell. But until these types of alternative explanations are developed and investigated, the study of organizational culture will stay mired in the quagmire of content analysis.

# ACKNOWLEDGEMENTS

We wish to thank the Institute of Industrial Relations, University of California at Berkeley for research support as well as the Applied Logic Laboratory, University of Amsterdam. We also appreciate helpful comments from Jenny Chatman.

# APPENDIX A. PARAMETER SETTINGS FOR VARIOUS SIMULATED CONDITIONS

| Variation in: | Parameter | Setting | | |
|---|---|---|---|---|
| | | No | Low | High |
| Turnover | ER | 0 | 0.02 | 0.04 |
| | AR | 0 | 0.40 | 0.40 |
| | | Low | Intermediate | High |
| Hiring selectivity | CM | 0.3 | 0.5 | 0.7 |
| Size | $n$ | 5 | 15 | 25 |
| Constant parameters: | | | | |
| Change in enculturation | $a = 0.05$ | | | |
| Change in influence | $b = 0.075$ | | | |
| Hiring variance | $CS = 0.15$ | | | |
| Cohort influence at entry | $\alpha = 0.01, \beta = 0.02$ | | | |

# REFERENCES

Axelrod, R. (1997) Advancing the art of simulation in the social sciences. In R. Conte, R. Hegselmann and P. Terna (Eds), Simulating Social Phenomena. Berlin: Springer.

Burt, R.S. (1992) Structural Holes. Cambridge, MA: Harvard University Press.

Carley, K. (1991) A theory of group stability. American Sociological Review, 56: 331–354.

Carroll, G.R. and Hannan, M.T. (2000) The Demography of Corporations and Industries. Princeton, NJ: Princeton University Press.

Carroll, G.R. and Harrison, J.R. (1998) Organizational demography and culture: insights from a formal model. Administrative Science Quarterly, 43: 637–667.

Chatman, J. (1991) Matching people and organizations: selection and socialization in public accounting firms. Administrative Science Quarterly, 36: 459–484.

Chatman, J. and Jehn, K. (1994) Assessing the relationship between industry characteristics and organizational culture: how different can you be? Academy of Management Journal, 37: 522–553.

Cohen, M.D., March J.G. and Olsen, J.P. (1972) A garbage can model of organizational decision making. Administrative Science Quarterly, 17: 1–25.

Coleman, J.S. (1964) Introduction to Mathematical Sociology. Glencoe, IL: The Free Press.

Cyert, R.M. and March, J.G. (1963) A Behavioral Theory of the Firm. Englewood Cliffs, NJ: Prentice-Hall.

Epstein, J. and Axtell, R. (1996) Growing Artificial Societies. Cambridge, MA: MIT Press.

Friedkin, N.E. (1998) A Structural Theory of Social Influence. Cambridge: Cambridge University Press.

Harrington Jr., J.E. (1998) The social selection of flexible and rigid agents. American Economic Review, 88: 63–82.

Harrington Jr., J.E. (1999) Rigidity of social systems. Journal of Political Economy, 107: 40–64.

Harrison, J.R. and Carroll, G.R. (1991) Keeping the faith: a model of cultural transmission in formal organizations. Administrative Science Quarterly, 36: 552–582.

Harrison, J.R. and Carroll, G.R. (2001) Modeling culture in organizations: formulation and extension to ecological concerns. In A. Lomi and E. Larsen (Eds), Dynamics of Organizational Societies: Information, Structuration and Computation, Cambridge, MA: MIT Press/AAAI Press.

Hofstede, G. (1980) Culture's Consequences. Beverly Hills, CA: Sage.

Hofstede, G., Neuijen, B., Ohayr, D.D. and Sanders, G. (1990) Measuring organizational cultures. A qualitative and quantitative study across twenty cases. Administrative Sciences Quarterly, 35: 286–316.

Krackhardt, D. and Porter, L.W. (1985) When friends leave: a structural analysis of the relationship between turnover and stayers' attitudes. Administrative Science Quarterly, 30: 242–261.

Louis, M.R. (1980) Surprise and sense making: what newcomers experience in entering unfamiliar organizational settings. Administrative Science Quarterly, 25: 226–251.

March, J.G. (1991) Exploration and exploitation in organizational learning. Organization Science, 2: 71–87.

O'Reilly, C.A., Chatman, J. and Caldwell, D. (1991) People and organizational culture: a profile comparison approach to assessing person-organization fit. Academy of Management Journal, 34: 487–516.

Pfeffer, J. (1983) Organizational demography. In L. Cummings and B. Staw (Eds), Research in Organizational Behavior, Vol. 5. Greenwich, CT: JAI Press.

Podolny, J.M. and Baron, J.N. (1997) Resources and relationships: social networks and mobility in the workplace. American Sociological Review, 62: 673–693.

Ragin, C. (1994) Constructing Social Research: the Unity and Diversity of Method. Newbury Park, CA: Pine Forge Press.

Scott, J. (1991) Social Network Analysis. London: Sage.

Sørenson, J. (2000) The longitudinal effects of grouptenure composition on turnover. American Sociological Review, 65: 298–310.

Stinchcombe, A. (1965) Social structure and organizations. In J.G. March (Ed), Handbook of Organizations. Chicago, IL: Rand McNally.

Waldrop, M.M. (1992) Complexity: the Emerging Science at the Edge of Order and Chaos. New York: Simon & Schuster.

Wanous, J.P. (1980) Organizational Entry. Reading, MA: Addison-Wesley.

# Chapter 10

# Economics and Corporate Culture

**Benjamin E. Hermalin**
*Haas School of Business, University of California,
Berkeley, CA, USA*

## INTRODUCTION

Most non-economists would question whether economists know anything about culture. Indeed, given some faculty meetings I have been through, I imagine they might go so far as to say economists are uncultured. Although the second sentiment probably does go too far, there is certainly merit to the first. In particular, with a few exceptions (notably Crémer, 1993; Hodgson, 1996; Kreps, 1990; Lazear, 1995), economists have ignored the issue of corporate culture in their studies of firms and other organizations.[1] There are many reasons for this lack of attention: culture is not relevant in most economic modeling; culture is not rational (or at least not obviously so) and, hence, does not fit well with the rational-agent methodology of neoclassical economics; and culture is difficult to define or measure, making it hard to use or control for in econometric analyses.

By writing this chapter, I am agreeing with the proposition that corporate culture is worthy of study by economists and is amenable to our methods. It is worthy because corporate culture is an important determinant of firms' capabilities and performance. Moreover, it both complements and substitutes for many of the other governance structures that economists have long studied. By amenable, I do not necessarily believe a complete *economic* theory of corporate culture is feasible. But even so, economics can contribute to a better understanding of corporate culture by shedding light on

---

[1] Although, as Crémer (1993) notes, at points, the discussion in the book by Arrow (1974) on organizations contains ideas that clearly foreshadow what would later be called corporate culture. Hodgson (1996) suggests that the "old" (before Coase (1937) and Williamson (1975)) institutional tradition in economics (e.g. the work of Thorstein Veblen) could also be seen as sympathetic to current notions of corporate culture.

specific facets of corporate culture that are less amenable to analysis by other social sciences.

This chapter begins by reviewing, synthesizing, and commenting on earlier work by economists on corporate culture, with particular attention given to Kreps' famous article. The second half of the chapter is spent discussing how certain insights from other economic analyses of organizations can complement our understanding of corporate culture.[2]

## KREPS (1990) RECONSIDERED

Kreps offers two reasons for economists to consider corporate culture. First, understanding culture – and organizations more generally – is necessary for understanding how firms implement strategy:

> The actual purpose of the firm *qua* organization is not considered [by textbook economics]. This is rather strange, for if one has an economic mind-set, one must believe that the firm itself performs some economic (efficiency-promoting) function. From there it is a short step to consider as part, perhaps the largest part, of successful strategy those actions designed to increase the firm's organizational efficiency. (From the Introduction.)

Kreps' second reason is his belief that economics have now developed the theoretical tools to study culture and he wants "to present the outlines of the theory that is developing", while encouraging his readers to develop it further.

## THE KREPS (1990) MODEL

Kreps' analysis of corporate culture is built from the following ingredients:

- *Formal* contracts are costly or defective in many situations. As Williamson (1975) and others have observed, formal contracting can be costly: there are bargaining costs, costs associated with monitoring the agreement, and costs associated with enforcing the agreement. In addition, formal contracts contingent on the appropriate variables can be infeasible: states or actions upon which the ideal contract would be contingent are not verifiable[3] or, somewhat equivalently, too difficult to specify in advance. That is, as economists would put it, only *incomplete* contracts could be feasible in many situations of interest.
- Firms are repeat players. Contracts are one way to induce cooperation from parties who would otherwise have incentives not to cooperate. Repeated games are another way: one player's deviation from cooperating today can be punished by other

---

[2] The reader interested in the more general topic of the economics of organization (with, however, little to no discussion of corporate culture) would do well to consider the surveys by Gibbons (1998, 1999) and MacLeod (1995). MacLeod's survey is the most technical of the three.

[3] Following the convention in economics, a variable is *verifiable* if its value can be learned by a judge or other outside party called upon to adjudicate a dispute.

players refusing to cooperate in the future. Provided the one player's future benefits from all cooperating in the future outweigh the gains today from his not cooperating, this punishment will deter non-cooperative behavior.[4] Critical to exploiting this benefit from repeated games is that one player, at least, be long-lived; that is, able to play in multiple periods. Firms satisfy this requirement and, typically, so do their senior officers.

- In many situations, inducing cooperation through repeated play is cheaper than inducing it contractually. For example, it would seem cheaper to have an oral agreement to cooperate that is enforced by repeated play than to have lawyers draw up a formal agreement that obtains the same result. In other situations, desirable outcomes can be supported in repeated games that cannot be supported contractually. In particular, it could well be that the variables upon which the ideal contract would be written are observable to the parties – they know whether each of them is cooperating and who defected if cooperation breaks down – but not verifiable. In this case, repeated play can achieve what formal contracting cannot.

- Multiple equilibria. Many games, including repeated ones, have multiple equilibria (i.e. stable outcomes). The players may need some means of coordinating on which equilibrium they are to play.

- Unforeseen contingencies. Not all contingencies can be foreseen.[5] In a world in which there are unforeseen contingencies, parties may need to trust each other to do the right thing should such a contingency arise. Unforeseen contingencies are often given as another reason for contractual incompleteness.[6]

The first three of these ingredients have a role to play in making sense of corporate culture in Kreps' model, but do not in themselves explain it. After all, there is a large body of economics that makes use of these ingredients to explain a wide variety of organizational phenomena, none of which could be described as culture.[7] It is the final

---

[4] Among economists, this benefit from repeated interaction is often cited as the "folk theorem". Among non-economists, it is often associated with Axelrod (1984), who found that the best strategy in a repeated prisoners' dilemma game was the "tit-for-tat" strategy that rewarded cooperation and punished non-cooperation.

[5] Despite superficial similarity, the notion of unforeseen contingencies is distinct from the idea that some contingencies are difficult to specify in advance: the latter idea refers to contingencies that the parties can foresee but have difficulty specifying, while the former refers to contingencies that they do not even foresee.

[6] This view, however, is not as straightforward as it might seem: as long as the parties to a contract recognize that there could be unforeseen contingencies, they can still write a "complete" contract in the sense that they can insert a "none-of-the-above clause" into the contract; that is, a clause of the form, "should some contingency not mentioned above occur, then we agree to do…". Hence, to have what Hermalin and Katz (1993b) call a *literally* incomplete contract requires assuming the parties are boundedly rational – they can not foresee that they might have failed to foresee certain contingencies. On the other hand, even if they are merely boundedly rational, a none-of-the-above clause might be problematic because it fails to makes distinctions among different unforeseen contingencies. For this reason, culture, which could make appropriate distinctions, could be necessary. See the introduction to Hermalin and Katz for a more in-depth discussion of these issues.

[7] Broadly, these come under the heading of *implicit contracting* (see Section 2 of Hart and Holmström, 1987 for a survey). There has also been a large literature – know as the *incomplete contracts literature* – that has explored just the first of Kreps' ingredients, parties' *in*ability to write ideal (i.e. complete) contracts (see Section 3 of Hart and Holmström, 1987, or Hart, 1995, for partial surveys).

**Figure 10.1**   Coordination games between junior and senior personnel.

two elements – multiple equilibria and unforeseen contingencies – that "introduce" culture. Although Kreps seems at times to suggest that both these elements are needed, a more careful reading of his work suggests that each is sufficient, sometimes in combination with the first three elements, to provide insights into culture.

## MULTIPLE EQUILIBRIA

To illustrate how multiple equilibria relate to culture in Kreps' model consider Figure 10.1a,[8] which illustrates a game to be played in some firm between a senior person and a junior person. Each player has a choice of two actions (strategies), A or B. There are, thus, four possible outcomes corresponding to the four possible pairings of actions. The payoffs to the players corresponding to these four outcomes are shown as the numbered pairs in the cells of the table in Figure 10.1a. The first number in each pair is the payoff to the senior person should that outcome occur and the second number is the payoff to the junior person. Hence, for example, if the senior person chose A and the junior person also chose A, then the senior person would get 3 and the junior person would get 2.

This game has two pure-strategy Nash equilibria: in one, each player takes action A; in the other, each player takes action B.[9] What standard game theory does not tell us, however, is which of these two equilibria we should expect to see played.[10] Culture, on the other hand, might. Suppose that it is understood, as a matter of culture, that juniors are to defer to seniors (readers at universities – particularly in Europe – can no doubt relate to this norm). Consequently, juniors and seniors expect that the A–A equilibrium will be played since it is the better equilibrium for the senior player. Put somewhat differently, absent culture, nothing allows us – and, thus, the players themselves – to predict which equilibrium will be played. Neither we, nor the players, can, therefore, know which equilibrium is to be played. For the players, this is something of a disaster, since nothing then prevents one player choosing A and the other B; that is, they risk getting nothing. A strong cultural norm of deferring to seniors, however, eliminates this risk. In other words, culture increases the predictability of others' actions.

---

[8] The game-theory *cognoscenti* will recognize this as the "battle of the sexes" game.

[9] Recall that an outcome is a Nash equilibrium if neither player would *unilaterally* wish to change his or her strategy given the strategy his or her opponent is to play. Hence, for instance, if both are to play A, then neither would unilaterally want to change to B because to do so would reduce his or her payoff from a positive amount (3 or 2) to 0. Likewise if both are to play B, a unilateral deviation would mean a reduction in payoff.

[10] As a technical matter, there is also a third Nash equilibrium in mixed strategies. There is, however, no need to explicitly consider this equilibrium in what follows.

Junior

|          |     | A        | B        |
|----------|-----|----------|----------|
| Senior   | A   | $S, j$   | $0, 0$   |
|          | B   | $0, 0$   | $s, J$   |

**Figure 10.2**   General coordination game between junior and senior personnel.

Observe that only one of Kreps' ingredients has been used, multiple equilibria. The other ingredients can be added in to yield a more flavorful story. For instance, instead of "leaving it open" as to which equilibrium is played, the players could contract in advance to play the A–A equilibrium. A contract could, for example, stipulate that a player who plays B must pay the other player 4. This transforms the game into the one in Figure 10.1b. This modified game has just a single equilibrium in which each player chooses A.[11] This contract, therefore, duplicates what the cultural norm achieves. If, however, this contract is costly to write or enforce, then it could be worse than relying on the cultural norm. Alternatively, the players' actions and payoffs could be unverifiable, which renders a contract such as this infeasible.[12] Unforeseen contingencies can also be tossed into the stew: consider Figure 10.2. Provided $S > s > 0$ and $J > j > 0$, this generalizes the game of Figure 10.1a. Imagine, now, that there are many such coordination games that junior and senior personnel will be called to play. What A will be and what B will be is not known *ex ante*, nor are the values of $S$, $s$, $J$, and $j$ known. A player may not even know in advance if he will be the junior or senior player. Moreover, we can readily imagine that the potential players cannot even foresee the details of all possible coordination games they may face; that is, the details could be unforeseen contingencies. In such a situation, contracting is probably infeasible: the cost of verifying every time the necessary details of the game – in particular is it a coordination game fitting the model of Figure 10.2 – could be prohibitive. Indeed, it is easy to imagine that the relevant variables are not verifiable at any cost. Yet, if there is a cultural norm in place of deferring to seniors, then the players are nevertheless assured of avoiding disastrous outcomes in which one plays A and the other plays B.

This discussion suggests that culture can avert disastrous outcomes. This is not the same, however, as saying that culture leads to optimal outcomes. For the game of Figure 10.1a, the cultural norm does lead to an optimal outcome: the A–A outcome in Figure 10.1a maximizes joint payoffs – 5 is the largest possible sum – so it is, therefore, Pareto efficient. For the more general game (Figure 10.2), the story is more complicated. If we assume that transfers between the players are not feasible, then the A–A outcome is still Pareto efficient – a move to any other outcome would make the senior player worse off. If, however, transfers are feasible and $S + j < s + J$,

---

[11] It is readily seen that A is a *dominant* strategy for each player: no matter what she expects her opponent to play, she does better to play A.

[12] Since this contract also requires one party to pay the other a penalty, it could also be infeasible as a matter of law – a court could refuse to enforce it in the case of an A–B or B–A outcome, citing the *penalty doctrine* or the law's abhorrence of forfeiture (e.g. see the Restatement (Second) of Contracts, Section 356 [St. Paul, MN: American Law Institute Publishers, 1981]).

**Figure 10.3**   Possible coordination games between junior and senior personnel.

then the players would be better off playing the B–B equilibrium: the junior player can make a transfer, $t$, to the senior player such that $s + t > S$ and $J - t > j$. Therefore, whenever $S + j < s + J$, the defer-to-seniors cultural norm does *not* lead to an optimal outcome (at least if transfers are feasible).

In a world in which transfers are feasible, one might imagine an extension of the defer-to-seniors norm that leads to optimality: both play A unless $S + j < s + J$. In that case, both play B and the junior player transfers

$$t^* = \frac{S + J - s - j}{2}$$

to the senior player (a little algebra reveals that $s + t^* > S$ and $J - t^* > j$).[13] Call this the extended-deference norm. The problem with this norm, unlike the basic defer-to-seniors norm, is that it is *no longer rational for one of the players to abide by it*. In particular, why, having played the B–B outcome, would the junior player make herself worse off by actually transferring $t^*$ to the senior player? She would do better to pocket the whole $J$.

This is where, *possibly*, repeated games can come to the rescue. It is also where we can make this more of a story about a *corporate* cultural norm. To make the discussion slightly more concrete, suppose that, with probability $p$, the game to be played is the "A-game" in Figure 10.3, while, with probability $1 - p$, its the "B-game". Assume $S > 2$. Observe that, in the A-game, the welfare-maximizing equilibrium is, thus, the A–A equilibrium, while, in the B-game, its the B–B equilibrium. Suppose that a given player lives two periods. In the first period of his life, he is a junior. In the second (last) period of his life, he is a senior.[14] Suppose the cultural norm is the extended-deference norm (here $t^* = 5$), but now suppose there is a punishment imposed on a junior who violates it. Specifically, when a norm-violating junior becomes a senior, the next generation junior plays B regardless of which game is realized. Moreover, this new junior makes no transfers to the senior. Provided a junior has either followed the extended-deference norm in playing against a norm-adhering senior or punished a norm-defying senior, he expects that the extended-deference norm will apply when *he is* a senior. Otherwise, he expects to be punished. Consider a junior playing against a norm-adhering senior. Clearly, there is no benefit to him from playing B in the A-game (he will get 0 instead of 1). There is also no benefit to him from playing A in the B-game

---

[13] Actually, any $t$ such that $S - s < t < J - j$ would do – I chose the mid-point simply to be concrete.

[14] Although distinct from Crémer (1986) in formulation and interpretation, it is worth pointing out that Crémer also explores an overlapping generations game in the context of an organization.

(he will get 0 instead of at least 5). The only question is whether he will transfer 5 in the B-game. Suppose he does not, then he gets 10 today. Next period, he anticipates that he will play against a B-playing junior (I will verify in a moment that this junior will want to play B). Hence, his best response is to play B as well, which yields him a payoff of 1 regardless of which game occurs. His total payoff from violating the norm is 11.[15] Now suppose he adheres to the norm when he is a junior in the B-game. Then, today, he gets 5. Next period, he anticipates that he will play against a norm-adhering junior (again, I will verify this in a moment). Hence, with probability $p$ he will get $S$ and with probability $1 - p$ he will get 6 ( $= 1 + t^*$). His total expected payoff is $5 + pS + 6(1 - p)$. This is greater than 11 if $S > 6$; that is, when $S > 6$, he will want to adhere to the norm. Note these calculations apply to any junior, so if he has adhered to the norm, he can expect the next generation's junior to do so as well. The only thing left to check is that a junior who faces a norm-defying senior will punish. Observe that if the senior believes she will be punished, she will rationally play B, so the junior gets 0 today if he plays A. He will also be punished tomorrow, which means he gets 1 tomorrow. His total for both periods if he *does not* punish when he should is 1. If, instead, he punishes (plays B) when he should, then his expected payoff today is $2p + 10(1 - p)$ and his expected payoff tomorrow is $pS + 6(1 - p)$ – a total of $(2 + S)p + 16(1 - p)$, which exceeds 1. Hence, he does better to punish when he is supposed to: he will, indeed, punish a norm-defying senior. Putting all this together, if $S > 6$, then the extended-deference norm can be supported as an equilibrium of a repeated game.

Some comments on this last analysis. First, repetition *will not* save the day if $S < 6$; that is, repetition will not always help (a point to which Kreps also alludes). Second, note that the above analysis depends critically on each generation's junior knowing precisely how the previous generation's junior behaved. This is where, arguably, the "corporate" comes into corporate culture – corporations are well-known as repositories of information (Crémer, 1993; Hodgson, 1996). Hence, for instance, this generation's junior may hear others in the corporation gossip about what a jerk such and such a senior was.[16] As Kreps points out, even if information about past deviations is not perfectly accurate (e.g. gossip is sometimes inaccurate or sometimes fails to inform), a benefit from repetition can still be had provided this information is reasonably accurate.

The analysis so far has illustrated the following: the need to choose among multiple equilibria can, in itself, provide a role for culture. The other ingredients are not necessary, although they certainly add some flavor to the analysis. At times Kreps himself hints that selecting among multiple equilibria is all that is needed to introduce culture into economic models (for example, when he discusses why American students will settle on particular equilibria in a game that calls upon them to divide a list of American cities – American culture, in particular a sense for the importance of the Mississippi river or the Mason-Dixon line as dividers, causes the players to settle on particular

---

[15] The technically sophisticated reader will have noticed that I have not discounted the second period payoff. Given the finite life of each player there is no need to do so; qualitatively similar results would hold if I introduced discounting.

[16] Indeed, a prominent phenomenon in any society is its eagerness to identify (*label*) its deviants (e.g. see Erikson, 1966, or, somewhat less on point, Goffman, 1963).

equilibria). At other times, however, he seems to suggest that the other ingredients are equally important. As I have tried to show here, that would be equivalent to confusing the beef with its seasonings.

Before concluding this section, it is worth pointing out that there is another literature in economics that appeals to culture to choose among multiple equilibria. Simple casual empiricism reveals that even within the same industry different firms behave differently. One explanation is that competition among these firms leads to asymmetric equilibria – it is not an equilibrium to behave identically. This is the approach I took in Hermalin (1994). Another approach, more relevant to the current discussion, is the one pursued by Morita (1998) and Okuno-Fujiwara (1994): they note, like many other observers, that American firms and Japanese firms exhibit different internal behaviors even when in the same industry. These authors develop models of firm organization that have multiple equilibria and argue that one equilibrium is consistent with the behavior of American firms and another is consistent with the behavior of Japanese firms. Related to the discussion here, they suggest that it is cultural differences between the US and Japan that has led the firms in these two countries to settle on different equilibria with respect to their organization. Admittedly, these authors are relying on *national* culture, which is not the same as *corporate* culture. On the other hand, certainly national, regional, or professional cultures must influence corporate culture.[17] That is, measured differences in the latter could be due, in part, to differences in the former. In addition, the organizational differences that national or regional cultural differences induce could appear to be the consequence of differences in corporate culture.

This discussion raises another issue: where does a corporate culture come from? Like any "input" used by the firm, corporate culture would seem subject to the make-or-buy decision. Does a firm essentially rely on the prevailing (i.e. national, regional, or professional) cultural norms or does it craft its own? Even without knowing how cultures are made, it seems reasonable to expect that crafting your own culture is costly and, therefore, not worth it for some organizations – they, instead, will "buy" the prevailing culture (i.e. relying on the societal or professional norms recruits bring with them rather than socializing them). Hence, although these organizations may be seen as having weak cultures – i.e. not distinct from the prevailing culture – their culture could still matter, particularly for interregional or international comparisons as suggested by the work of Morita (1998) and Okuno-Fujiwara (1994).[18]

# UNFORESEEN CONTINGENCIES

As interesting as multiple equilibria are to the theory Kreps sketches, much of what he

---

[17] See Hofstede et al. (1990) for evidence that national culture affects firms and Chatman and Jehn (1994) for evidence that industrial culture (characteristics) affects firms. Vandello and Cohen (1999) provide evidence on regional variations in culture norms across regions of the US.

[18] Related to this is the empirical work of Lin and Png (1998), who find evidence to support the hypothesis that the importance of kinship in Chinese culture facilitates the use of contracting – as opposed to direct ownership – as a means to resolve opportunistic behavior in direct investments in the People's Republic of China.

|              |              | Employee |             |
| ------------ | ------------ | -------- | ----------- |
|              |              | Trust    | Don't trust |
| Boss         | Treat fairly | 7, 5     | 2, 3        |
|              | Exploit      | 9, 0     | 4, 1        |

**Figure 10.4**   Game between boss and employee.

has to say works without any reference to multiple equilibria. To illustrate this, consider the game in Figure 10.4:[19] this is a game between a boss and an employee. The boss can treat the employee fairly or exploit him. The employee can play in a trusting way or in a not-trusting way. The latter strategy offers the employee some protection against exploitation, but is harmful to him if the boss plays fairly. Observe that *exploit* is a dominant strategy for the boss – against either strategy of the employee, her payoff is greater if she exploits than if she treats fairly. She can, therefore, be expected to exploit. The employee's best response to being exploited is *don't trust*. Hence, the equilibrium outcome is the bottom-right cell. Observe that this outcome is not optimal: both players would be better off in the top-left cell. Unhappily, as we have just seen, if the game in Figure 10.4 is played just once, then this better outcome is *un*attainable.

As discussed above, repeated games can come to the rescue. In particular, suppose that the game is repeated next period with probability $\beta$, $0 < \beta < 1$. Imagine, too, that this probability remains constant.[20] For the moment, imagine that both the boss and the employee live at least as long as the game is repeated. Consider the following strategies for the players: the boss treats the employee fairly every period, unless she has exploited him in the past, in which case she continues to exploit him in this and every future period, and the employee trusts the boss, unless she has ever exploited him in the past, in which case he plays *don't trust* in this and every future period. Note, in the first period, that these strategies call for the boss to treat fairly and for the employee to trust. Is this an equilibrium? Without going into all the details of the theory of repeated games (e.g. see Gibbons, 1992, Section 2.3, for an introduction to this theory), the answer is *yes* provided the expected payoff to the boss of treating fairly outweighs the gain today from exploiting a trusting employee, but having to play against an untrusting employee forever after; that is, provided

$$\sum_{\tau=0}^{\infty} \beta^{\tau} \times 7 \geq 9 + \sum_{\tau=0}^{\infty} \beta^{\tau} \times 4$$

A little algebra reveals that this condition holds if $\beta \geq 2/5$ (i.e. if the probability of a game next period is at least 40%). Intuitively, provided she has never exploited the employee, the boss perceives the future expected benefit of being fair as outweighing the benefit of exploiting the employee given the strategy she anticipates the employee is playing. Note that if it is credible the boss will treat fairly (i.e. if $\beta \geq 2/5$), then the

---

[19] This normal-form "trust" game is similar in spirit to the extensive-form "trust" game that Kreps introduces in his Figure 1.

[20] As Kreps reminds us, this is equivalent to imagining the game is infinitely repeated with certainty but there is financial discounting.

employee does better to trust than not to trust. Moreover, off the equilibrium path (i.e. if the boss has exploited), the employee does better not to trust given that he now anticipates the boss will always exploit him. In summary, we have seen that the fair treatment–trust outcome can be consistent with rational, self-interested play by both parties in a repeated game in which $\beta \geq 2/5$.

In this model, the employee need not be a long-lived player.[21] Since period by period he is simply playing his best response to what the boss is supposed to do given the history of the game, he could live only one period *provided each generation's employee knows the history of the game to that point*. The boss, on the other hand, must be long-lived. Although, similar to the junior–senior analysis of Figure 10.3 or the game considered by Kreps, she need not be infinitely lived – some overlapping generations story in which each generation's boss sells her stake in the firm to the next generation's boss is sufficient to make each generation's boss sufficiently concerned about the long run that cooperative play (i.e. the efficient outcome) can be sustained. For example, suppose at the end of each period, the boss can sell the firm to a new boss, the proceeds from which will fund the old boss's retirement. Suppose that each generation's employee expects his boss to treat him fairly if every boss in the firm's history has done so, but otherwise he expects to be exploited. The expected value, $V_F$, of a firm in which bosses treat their employees fairly is

$$V_F = \frac{7\beta}{1 - \beta}$$

Suppose that there is a fairly competitive market in which to sell the firm, so that the old boss gets $V_F - \varepsilon$ for it; where $\varepsilon \geq 0$, but not too large. On the other hand, the expected value of a firm in which a boss has exploited an employee, $V_E$, is only

$$V_E = \frac{4\beta}{1 - \beta}$$

Again suppose a boss selling such a firm gets $V_E - \varepsilon$. Consider a firm in which bosses have so far treated their employees fairly. This generation's boss will continue this tradition provided today's payoff from doing so plus the greater value of the firm exceeds the payoff from exploiting plus the lower firm value; that is, provided

$$7 + V_F - \varepsilon \geq 9 + V_E - \varepsilon$$

A little algebra reveals that this is equivalent to our original condition,

$$\sum_{\tau=0}^{\infty} \beta^\tau \times 7 \geq 9 + \sum_{\tau=0}^{\infty} \beta^\tau \times 4$$

Hence, as advertised, we will still observe the efficient outcome even with a one-period-lived employee and an overlapping-generation boss (assuming $\beta \geq 2/5$). This last point helps to make this a story about *corporate* culture: observe that the reputation for

---

[21] Again see Crémer (1986) for another example of a game among overlapping generations within an organization.

treating employees fairly resides with the firm, not an individual. Corporate reputations or traditions can, thus, sustain desirable outcomes.

Observe that "fair treatment" and "exploitation" are fairly amorphous concepts. Typically, whether a behavior is "fair" is specific to the situation. For instance, giving a bad office to a poorly performing employee could be seen as fair, but giving the same office to a good performer could be seen as unfair. *Ex ante*, it is difficult to foresee all the possible behaviors that could be judged fair or unfair and, likewise, to enumerate all the situations in which they are fair or unfair. Here is where unforeseen contingencies arise. What is fair and what is exploitation cannot be defined in advance, yet, under the rules of a given culture, *ex post* behavior can be judged fair or not. In many ways, the situation is like pornography in the US – material is legally obscene if it violates community standards and whether it, in fact, violates community standards is judged *ex post* under the criterion that people know obscene material when they see it.[22] Corporate culture thus enters into this model in two ways: one as reputation or tradition and two as the means of defining compliance with the reputation or tradition when future circumstances are difficult or impossible to define *ex ante*.

Of course, if "fair treatment" or "exploitation" cannot be defined in advance, but must be judged *ex post* according to the prevailing culture, one might also imagine that the payoffs are equally ill-defined. That is, the precise payoffs in the game shown in Figure 10.4 could be unforeseen.

Although the precise actions and payoffs could well be unforeseen, the *consequences* are not *necessarily* unforeseen. An example may help illustrate what I mean. A firm lures away a top manager from a rival. Before moving, he attempts to reach firm agreements on as much as he can with his new employer. But he knows that situations can arise, which he failed to anticipate, in which he would want his new employer to take an action that benefited him but was costly to his new employer. As a specific example, imagine he does not foresee that his current daycare arrangement will fall apart and that the best alternative daycare provider will require him to pick up his child half an hour earlier than before. This, in turn, means he must leave work half an hour early. Although he is willing to make up the work by arriving earlier in the morning or by working at home, such a schedule imposes a cost on the employer (e.g. because of difficulty in scheduling meetings). The employer can bear that cost or it can require he stay until 5, although this means a worse daycare arrangement for his child. Or the employer can use the employee's request as an excuse to hold up the employee and renegotiate aspects of the employment contract. Again we have the "trust" game of Figure 10.4: the employee can "trust" – go to a new firm knowing that he will be vulnerable – or "not trust" – stay put; likewise the employer can accommodate the employee – let him adjust his schedule without penalty – or "exploit" him – force him to stay until 5 or otherwise give something up. Whereas the employee could not anticipate that he would want to change his schedule (i.e. specific actions and payoffs), he could anticipate that he would be relying on his new employer to treat him fairly (i.e.

---

[22] To paraphrase the "I know it when I see it" standard for pornography set down by the US Supreme Court Justice Potter Stewart. Personally, the definition I have favored – which is not original to me – is pornographic material is material read with one hand.

that he would face games like that in Figure 10.4). Part of his decision process, then, in deciding to switch employers was assessing the reputation (or culture if you will) of his potential new employer: how would he do in games like the one in Figure 10.4?

The fact that the consequences are foreseeable and, at a general level, the type of actions (fair treatment or exploitation) as well, raises the question of why contracts are not used. Why can't the parties write a contract that says that the boss will treat the employee fairly? The obvious – but seriously incomplete – answer is that it would be difficult for a judge or other dispute adjudicator to determine whether treatment was fair or not. That is, a judge's assessment of how the employee was actually treated is subject to error. However, as Edlin and Hermalin (1999) and Hermalin and Katz (1991, 1993a) demonstrate, imprecise assessments do *not* preclude efficient contracting: as long as the judge's assessment is correlated with what the boss actually did, the parties can rely on this assessment as follows. They write a contract calling for the boss to treat the employee fairly and, after the boss has acted, they renegotiate the contract in anticipation of what might happen should they go to court. Under fairly general conditions (e.g. see Edlin and Hermalin, 1999), the parties can construct a contract that duplicates the outcome they would have enjoyed were the boss's action verifiable without error. That is, as a matter of contract theory, there is no need to rely on culture at all, the parties can instead rely on formal contracts.

Despite having contributed to all three of these papers, I do not, in fact, believe that contracting is generally a substitute for culture.[23] First, as a matter of law, some of these contracts might not actually be enforceable. Second, more importantly, the costs associated with negotiating, monitoring, and enforcing these contracts could make them a less desirable means of inducing fair treatment – reputation can be equally effective and cost less. This is where the fact that inducing cooperation through repeated interaction is cheaper than inducing it contractually comes into play.

To summarize, repeated play is a substitute for contracting.[24] Although not necessarily a perfect substitute, repeated play is typically a less costly way of inducing cooperative behavior (i.e. behavior that is not optimal in a one-shot situation). So far, culture has not entered in. Where culture enters in these models is to define the actions: culture determines which actions are considered fair treatment and which are considered exploitation. More generally, culture defines what constitutes cooperative play – actions that are to be rewarded by future cooperation – and non-cooperative play – actions that are to be punished by withholding future cooperation. In this sense, culture substitutes for the impossible task of specifying all contingencies in advance. An employee may not, for instance, know in advance that cooperative play means allowing him to change his schedule to meet his childcare needs – but the culture will specify it as such should that particular contingency arise.

---

[23] Although the idea is not wholly insane either: there are many lawsuits by employees alleging unfair treatment, i.e. alleging that the boss violated the (implicit) employment contract.

[24] Schmidt (1995), citing his own work with Monika Schnitzer, points out that the *possibility* of formal contracting could destroy the possibility of using reputation when the two are close substitutes. Reputation is more sustainable the greater the difference between the cooperative and the non-cooperative payoffs. If non-cooperation results in switching to contracts and contracting is a close substitute for cooperation, then this difference is small and, consequently, reputation could be *un*sustainable.

# A CRITICAL ASSESSMENT OF KREPS

The previous discussion was intended to show that Kreps' theory of corporate culture is really two theories. One is a theory of culture as a way of ensuring coordination in games like those in Figures 10.1a and 2.2. The other is a theory of culture as a way of categorizing future contingencies for the purposes of sustaining cooperative play.

The first view could be called the culture-as-convention view. From a welfare perspective, it does not matter in the game of Figure 10.1a whether both players play A or they both play B. What is important is that they coordinate. In that sense, the game is analogous to whether we drive on the right (as in the US) or on the left (as in the UK): it does not matter which we choose as long as we are coordinated.

A convention is, of course, only one way to ensure coordination. An alternative is to negotiate and reach some agreement.[25] For example, each morning we could all discuss and agree on which side of the road we were to drive that day. However, as is immediate from this far-fetched example, in many contexts the costs of communicating to establish the coordinated outcome are large and a convention would, therefore, yield considerable savings (this anticipates some of the ideas in Crémer, 1993). Alternatively, the coordinated outcome could be dictated by some authority (e.g. a national driving committee). But except for one-off decisions, such as on which side to drive, this again involves costs: the authority must be apprised that coordination is needed, must assess the situation, and must transmit its decision. A general convention – such as defer to seniors – would save on these costs.

As we have just seen, a general convention saves considerably on the costs associated with explicit coordination. On the other hand, it, itself, is not without costs. By their nature, cultural conventions depend on people being aware of them, correctly knowing how to apply them, and being willing to enforce them. Hence, particularly when the corporate culture is unique, considerable expense could be incurred in socializing new employees (related to an earlier discussion, this may favor "buying" the prevailing national, regional, or professional culture over "making" a culture). In addition, reliance on convention over communication increases the odds of misunderstanding: for instance, two people playing the game of Figure 10.1a could each believe he or she was senior and – since they are relying on the convention, not communication – each could choose the action associated with the coordination outcome best for him or her (i.e. one plays A and one plays B). Kreps is silent on this issue, but clearly understanding these tradeoffs between the benefits and cost of culture is important. Future research should be devoted to both modeling these tradeoffs, as well as measuring them through field research.

Another issue left unexplored by Kreps is where these coordinating conventions come from. Recent work by Young (1993, 1998) has taken an adaptive learning approach to the issue: players are not fully rational, but can adapt their play as a

---

[25] Given that an agreement is a Nash equilibrium (no one wants to unilaterally deviate from coordinating), an oral agreement is all that is necessary. For instance, if we all decided to drive on the right, then we do not really need a formal contract since no one would unilaterally want to deviate from the agreement (i.e. cause a head-on collision).

function of past experiences. As Young (1998, pp. 34–36) shows, if the proportion of past experiences of both players playing A in the Figure 10.1a game is high enough, then adaptive learning will converge to both players playing A in every period; i.e. a convention will have been established. Likewise, if the proportion of past experiences in which B was played is high enough, then a convention of B playing will be reached. On the other hand, it is possible that if the proportions of times A and B are played are just right, then players oscillate between A and B, there is no coordination, and a convention is not reached.[26] Of course, if the players find themselves oscillating – or more generally no convention emerges – then presumably the players will revert to communication and explicit coordinating activities to achieve coordination (or to set a convention if "A" and "B" can be sufficiently well defined in advance). In other words, to understand the use of a cultural convention *vis-à-vis* another solution may require some understanding of how conventions evolve or fail to evolve.

The second interpretation of culture offered by Kreps is that of culture as a way of categorizing future unforeseen contingencies for the purposes of sustaining cooperative play. Although Kreps' argument is clear, a proponent of formalism in economics might fault it on the grounds that there is too much "hand waving". In particular, there is no formalization of unforeseen contingencies. But Kreps is not to blame: there are no good formalizations of unforeseen contingencies in the economics literature (see Dekel et al., 1998, for a survey of the current state of modeling unforeseen contingencies).

Whether one can adequately formalize the culture-as-defining-cooperation interpretation is an open question. Certainly, partially adequate formalizations are possible, but even these require a certain amount of "hand waving" *vis-à-vis* the impact of unforeseen contingencies.[27] To the extent one is willing to put up with hand waving, progress is possible. To the extent one is unnerved by it, future economic research on this aspect of corporate culture is on hold until the profession develops acceptable models of unforeseen contingencies and, more generally, bounded rationality (see Rubinstein, 1998, for an overview of the current state of modeling bounded rationality in economics).

# OTHER ECONOMISTS ON CORPORATE CULTURE

As noted in the Introduction, Kreps is not the only economist to address the issue of

---

[26] Suppose each player treats the proportions of A and B played by his opponent as his opponent's mixed strategy and plays a best response to it. Suppose that Junior played B and Senior played A in the first round. In the next round, Junior would play A and Senior would play B. In the third round, Junior plays his best response to a mixed strategy of (1/2,1/2) and Senior does likewise. Hence, Junior plays B – which yields him an expected payoff of 1.5 versus an expected payoff of 1 were he to play A. Similar reasoning finds Senior playing A. In the fourth period, Junior plays his best response to (2/3,1/3) and Senior to (1/3,2/3) which causes them to flip back. And the process continues indefinitely (provided we assume the correct tie-breaking rule should a player be indifferent between A and B; e.g. if we assume that Junior plays B when indifferent and Senior plays A when indifferent).

[27] An earlier version of this chapter considered a more explicit formalization of these issues, but it too required some hand waving.

corporate culture. In this section of the chapter, I consider the work of three other economists.

## CRÉMER (1993)

Crémer (1993) ignores potential conflict among the actors within a firm. In his approach, all actors are perfectly honest and trustworthy. The tension in his approach arises from his assumption that these actors' capacity to process, receive, and transmit information is a scarce resource. Consequently, there is a payoff to economizing on communication and, therefore, a common stock of knowledge – what Crémer defines as culture – is valuable.[28] That is, as was implicit in Kreps (1990), culture substitutes for explicit communication. But Crémer's view of corporate culture is more nuanced than his explicit definition might suggest. In particular, he decomposes culture into three components (p. 362):

1. A common language or coding.
2. A shared knowledge of pertinent facts.
3. A shared knowledge of the norms of behavior.

The first two suggest insights not contained in Kreps.[29] Given the earlier discussion of the third component in reviewing Kreps, here I will, consequently, focus on the first two components.

The importance of these two components can be illustrated by a recent discussion I had with a non-economist. She wondered if a growing demand for organic produce would raise the price of organic produce. I replied that since organic farming seemed likely to be a competitive industry, there would be a short-run price increase, but, in the long run, there would not be a noticeable change in price. To an economist, this explanation is readily grasped.[30] But it took half an hour to explain my conclusions to this non-economist. As a non-economist, she did not know the "pertinent facts" (e.g. that while the short-run supply curve in a competitive industry is typically upward sloping, the long-run supply curve, which is determined by the minimum of long-run average cost, tends to be flat; that is, the long-run price will equal the minimum of long-run average cost).[31] Related to this, she had not mastered the "common language and

---

[28] Crémer's precise definition of corporate culture is "the part of the stock of knowledge that is shared by a substantial portion of the employees of the firm, but not by the general population from which they are drawn" (p. 354).

[29] Although Kreps' discussion of common ways of sorting American cities – mentioned previously – certainly relates to the shared knowledge of pertinent facts.

[30] Although an economist would understand my explanation, this does not, admittedly, mean he or she would agree with it. In particular, he or she might dispute whether organic farming is a competitive industry. In addition, he or she might point out that even if the farmers have no market power, there may be parties in the distribution channel (e.g. wholesalers or supermarkets) that do have market power, and, hence, a shift out in demand could lead to a price increase at the cash register.

[31] To be precise, the long-run supply curve is flat provided that entrants are as efficient as established firms. In the case of organic farming, this strikes me – admittedly on the basis of little information – as a reasonable approximation.

coding" (e.g. what a "competitive" industry is). The cost of our not having a common "economics" culture is the opportunity cost of the time I spent responding to her question.

We could have avoided this cost if I had helped her or encouraged her to acquire a knowledge of basic microeconomics. Given the infrequency with which she asks me economic questions, such an upfront investment would make little sense. Viewed in this light, to the extent that culture is an *ex ante* investment to lower later communication costs, it becomes something to which economics can speak directly.

As an example, suppose that an employee needs to know in which rectangular region a given state occurs (e.g. in which sales area she should concentrate). Suppose there is a commonly understood coordinate system for identifying points in the relevant space (e.g. longitude and latitude or kilometers north and east of a prominent landmark). Then to identify a region, two pairs of coordinates must be sent, identifying diagonally opposed vertices of the rectangle in question; that is, a total of four numbers must be sent.[32] Suppose it costs $c$ to send a number. Imagine there are four possible regions. An alternative to sending the four numbers that identify each region each time is to assign each of the four regions a single number ("name") and to first communicate to the employee the "code book" (i.e. region $i$ is defined by coordinates $(x_1^i, y_1^i)$ and $(x_2^i, y_2^i)$). This requires an initial investment of $20c$. But for each subsequent communication, there is a savings of $3c$ since, now, only one number (the region number) must be sent. Hence, provided the employer anticipates sending at least seven messages, it pays her to invest in this "culture".[33] Fewer than seven messages, and a culture does not pay.

In real firms, of course, the employee is not always given a cultural code book on day one. Rather, new employees are often given the information indirectly. That is, there is gradual cultural diffusion rather than immediate diffusion. This could be because indirect methods are cheaper. For example, there is "free" learning of pertinent knowledge and coding that occurs by listening to the conversation of experienced colleagues at lunch (although there is an opportunity cost to having an "uncultured" employee during this period of gradual diffusion). In many circumstances, it would actually be too difficult to identify *ex ante* all the pertinent knowledge and its coding. In addition, even if a "code book" could be written, it would often be the case that a new employee could not absorb it all at once.[34] Hence, there will often be no realistic alternative to gradual diffusion. But even if gradual diffusion makes sense, some rates of diffusion will make more sense than others. Viewed in this way, cultural diffusion becomes a dynamic programming problem, something with which economists are quite familiar.

---

[32] There are alternative means of communicating the region (e.g. sending the southwest coordinate plus the length and width), but these all require four numbers.

[33] To be precise, future savings should be discounted. Doing so would not, however, change the nature of the argument.

[34] Although strong-culture firms make a point of conveying as much of the "code book" explicitly in an initial period following an employee's hiring (e.g. see O'Reilly and Chatman, 1996). Further, with respect to employees' ability to absorb it "all at once", this would depend on a number of factors, including their cognitive ability, existing values at entry, the amount of information, etc.

That is, a possible direction for future research in the economics of corporate culture would be to theorize about optimal cultural diffusion rates.[35]

Folk wisdom holds that the Inuit language has many different words for snow to allow the Inuit to make fine distinctions among different kinds of snow. The explanation is that snow is important to the Inuit. Similarly, in a firm where distinctions over certain states are important, we might expect a rich "language" to develop to help make these distinctions. As a newcomer to such a firm, I might rationally infer from this that I should pay particular attention to these states. That is, learning the language teaches me what I should consider important. But recognizing this, a firm might rationally want to develop a rich language – even when distinctions are not important – because it wants its employees to take things more seriously (note this relaxes Crémer's assumption of honest actors). Hence, a firm that really believes these distinctions are important will over invest in its language to signal that it really does hold these distinctions important.

To be somewhat more concrete on this signaling idea, imagine that there are two types of firms, each of which must deal with states in some space $S$. Let $P$ be a partition of $S$ and let $n$ be the number of elements (subsets of $S$) in $P$. A language can be seen as giving names to the elements in $P$ and a richer language is one that corresponds to a finer partition (i.e. one with a higher value for $n$). Let $P_B$ be the partition associated with the "base" language, which has a vocabulary of $b$ words. Suppose this base language is sufficient for both types of firms. A firm can add $w$ words to the language (employ a finer partition than $P_B$) at a cost of $cw$. For one type of firm, distinguishing the states is not that important. In particular, an effort of $e$ by a worker on distinguishing states returns only $\ell e$. For the other type of firm, distinguishing the states is important. For this type, an effort of $e$ returns $he$, where $h > \ell$. Suppose to succeed in the first type of firm, a worker must expend at least $e_\ell$ effort, while he would need to expend at least $e_h$ at the second type, where $e_h > e_\ell$. Workers dislike effort, but want to succeed. Consequently, if workers could distinguish the types of firms, they would expend $e_h$ in the "$h$"-type firm and $e_\ell$ in the "$\ell$"-type firm. Finally, allowing $w$ to be a continuous variable,[36] there must exist a $\hat{w}$ such that

$$\ell e_h - c\hat{w} = \ell e_\ell$$

What we should, then, expect in equilibrium is that an $h$-type firm will add $\hat{w}$ words to its language to signal that it is an $h$-type firm: workers believe that a firm with fewer than $b + \hat{w}$ words is an $\ell$-type firm and expend only $e_\ell$ in effort, but one with $b + \hat{w}$ or more is an $h$-type firm and expend $e_h$ in effort. Given these beliefs, it is not rational for the $\ell$-type firm to add $\hat{w}$ words, since the cost just cancels the benefit (fooling workers into working harder). But it is rational for the $h$-type firm, since the above equation

---

[35] The model of Garicano (1999) is somewhat related to this research plan. He, however, focuses on a static model that, in essence, considers how knowledge should be allocated among a firm's personnel to balance the cost of education against the cost of communication. In this sense, his approach is similar in spirit to the *formal* model in Crémer (this formal model does not, however, do justice to the richness of the ideas Crémer offers verbally).

[36] The analysis when $w$ must be a whole number is similar, but slightly more complicated. Hence, for convenience, I will treat it as continuous (a real number).

implies

$$he_h - c\hat{w} > he_\ell$$

(recall $h > \ell$).[37] Observe that adding $\hat{w}$ words is overkill – by assumption $b$ words were sufficient. This point could be generalized: to the extent that aspects of the culture cause new employees to make inferences about what is expected of them, we can easily imagine that some firms are induced to adopt an overly strong culture due to signaling considerations. To the best of my knowledge, this idea has not been explored in the literature on corporate culture.[38]

The reference to "code books" also suggests that culture can *worsen* agency problems. From novels and movies, we are all aware of secret signals and gestures used (in fiction, at least) by criminals to communicate without drawing the attention of the law-abiding or the police. There is no reason a similar phenomenon can not arise within a firm. Specifically, if a common culture reduces the costs of communication and, hence, coordination, then a *sub*-culture could reduce the costs of communication and coordination for a sub-group within the firm (e.g. lower-level employees) that wishes to conspire against another group (e.g. management). This suggests that the collusion-among-agents problem considered by Tirole (1992) (among others) could be exacerbated by culture (or sub-culture). This negative aspect of culture within corporations has not, as far as I know, been explored within economics.

In summary, it would seem that there is much that "off-the-shelf" economic theory can contribute to the shared knowledge and language aspects of corporate culture. It can, for instance, aid in studying these as investment problems (static or dynamic), the signaling aspects of culture, and the agency consequences of culture.

## HODGSON (1996)

Hodgson (1996) rejects the methodology of both neo-classical economics (specifically contract theory) and the "new" institutional economics (e.g. Coase, 1937; Williamson, 1975). His primary criticism is that these approaches take the representative actor as unchanging in her preferences, attitudes, and modes of thinking as she moves from one situation to the next. Hodgson argues that a more appropriate assumption is that these aspects of her personality are shaped by her situations; that is, how she views a situation, thinks about it, and even what she wants to achieve in it evolve as she becomes immersed in the situation. It is not, as in standard economics, that only the actor is acting: the situation is, in essence, simultaneously acting on the actor. Note, too, that in Hodgson's view, the situation changes the actor not only by providing her information

---

[37] For more on signaling models in general, see, for example, Gibbons (1992), Section 4.2.

[38] There is work in organizational behavior that has similarities to this, namely work on the symbolic nature of language (e.g. see Pfeffer, 1981). This work points out that "managers in organizations send signals about what is important and valued through mechanisms such as what they spend time on, what they ask questions about, *and what they talk about*" (Pfeffer, 1997, p. 125, emphasis added). This literature does not explain, in terms of rational actors, why these mechanisms are effective, nor the extent to which they would be deployed in equilibrium.

Junior

|        |   | A | B |
|--------|---|---|---|
| Senior | A | 3, 2 | 0, −k |
|        | B | 0, 0 | 2, 3 − k |

**Figure 10.5**   Coordination game between "cultured" junior and senior.

and skills – concepts that can be found in many neo-classical models – but also, most critically, by causing her preferences themselves to change.[39]

Two quotes from Hodgson illustrate the consequences of this view for understanding corporate culture:

> Corporate culture is more than shared information: through shared practices and habits of thought, it provides the method, context, values, and language of learning, and the evolution of group and individual competences. (p. 255)

> [Institutions] play an essential role in providing a cognitive framework for interpreting sensedata (*sic*) and in providing intellectual habits or routines for transforming information into useful knowledge. A result of the framing or cognitive effects of institutions is to promote conformism, or emulation – to use Veblen's term. The availability of common cognitive tools, as well as perhaps a congenital or learned disposition for individuals to conform with other members of the same group, work together to mold and harmonize individual goals and preferences. Significant shifts in preferences and goals are involved, and such outcomes are an important part of the institutional self-reinforcing process. (p. 263)

In Hodgson's opinion, corporate culture serves to mold the individual actor's preferences, attitudes, and modes of thinking.

To illustrate this view, recall the game of Figure 10.1a. When a junior joins the firm, his preferences are as shown there. But as time passes, he "buys into" the prevailing corporate culture, with the consequence that he feels he ought to defer to seniors. For instance, not deferring causes him discomfort. Suppose that this discomfort costs the junior $k$ units of psychological well-being, then culture has transformed the Figure 10.1a game into the game shown in Figure 10.5. If the discomfort from violating the deference norm is great enough – specifically, if $k > 3$ – then A becomes a dominant strategy for the junior and the unique Nash equilibrium of the game is for both players to play A. Observe that this formulation of what culture does achieves the same outcome as Kreps', but it does so in a different way. In Kreps' formulation, the junior defers to the senior not because that is what he inherently wants, but because he expects that the senior will play A and he does better to coordinate than not to coordinate. It is possible, in fact, that he even resents this outcome, since he knows that he would do better under the alternative B–B equilibrium. In contrast, Hodgson presumes that culture causes the junior to inherently prefer to play A. That is, he has "bought into"

---

[39] As a general rule, economists prefer to model preferences as fixed and exogenous. For exceptions, see Benhabib and Day (1981) or Hermalin and Isen (1999).

the norm to such a degree that he prefers to play A irrespective of strategic considerations. In this formulation, there is no question of the junior resenting the outcome; he has been programmed to like it.

Some observations are in order. First, if $k \leq 3$, then B–B remains an equilibrium. In other words, if the norm is not strong enough, then the same coordination problem considered in the Kreps section re-emerges. In this case, it is not the change in the junior's preferences induced by the defer-to-seniors norm that achieves coordination, but rather the *mutual* expectation that juniors will defer under this norm. That is, even when norms change preferences, it could still be their impact on expectations that makes them valuable.

This raises the issue of how one could distinguish empirically between Hodgson's view and Kreps'. As we have seen, both could independently explain an observed defer-to-seniors norm. Moreover, even if an attitudinal survey revealed some internalization of the norm, that could still fail to be the explanation for the norm's effectiveness (e.g. when $k \leq 3$). Conversely, internalization could be what creates the expectation: suppose that the population of juniors is split evenly into those who have strongly internalized the norm ($k > 3$) and those who have weakly internalized the norm ($k \leq 3$). A senior who meets a junior at random will play A – her expected payoff from playing A is, at worst, 1.5 versus, at best, 1 from playing B. But understanding this about seniors, even weak norm-internalizers will want to play A. Internalization has created expectation.

One might imagine that the two views could be better distinguished in situations resembling the game of Figure 10.4: if we have fair treatment and trust with*out* repetition between the players, then this would seem to suggest that the boss, at least, has internalized some fairness norm. Unfortunately, the controlled experiment that would test this is difficult to observe: by their very nature, interactions within firms tend to be repeated. Moreover, even if the boss does not play repeatedly with a given employee, the fact that she plays repeatedly with a sequence of employees, each of whom is likely to have some knowledge of her past history, can be sufficient for a reputation to be established (i.e. as noted previously, a single long-lived player can be sufficient for reputation to be effective; see Section 9.2 of Fudenberg and Tirole, 1991). Finally, although Hodgson is somewhat vague on how norms become internalized, one must imagine that it is through long-term exposure to the prevailing culture, which creates obvious problems for distinguishing between a game-theoretic view and a norm-internalization view.

This argument is not meant to cast doubt on norm internalization. Most of us tip at restaurants, are courteous to strangers, and do not take things that do not belong to us (even when detection is impossible). Although all these phenomena can be explained in terms of game theory, in particular using the Kandori (1992) "contagion" model,[40]

---

[40] The basic idea in Kandori (1992) is that cooperative behavior (e.g. tipping, courteousness to strangers, not stealing, etc.) is an equilibrium in which people play cooperatively unless they encounter a non-cooperative person (e.g. a non-tipper, a rude person, discover they have been robbed, etc.), after which they too play non-cooperatively. Hence, even if I will never meet my current opponent again and have no fear that my non-cooperativeness will be directly revealed to others, I may wish to cooperate rather than triggering a collapse of the social norm: by serving as a non-cooperative "contagion", I start an epidemic of non-cooperation and, eventually, I will start finding myself playing against non-cooperative players, to my detriment.

such explanations typically operate at the edge (or over) of what is plausible game-theoretic reasoning. For some phenomena, Occam's Razor requires us to favor norm-internalization over game-theoretic explanations.

Moreover, there is no reason to necessarily view norm internalization and game theory as antagonistic explanations. In many ways, they could be complementary. As noted earlier, internalization can generate game-theoretic expectation. Conversely, game-theoretic expectation might generate internalization: constant exposure to the defer-to-seniors norm may ultimately lead a junior to believe he actually prefers to defer. That is, my casual empiricism suggests that humans often adapt to the situations in which they find themselves by convincing themselves that they are in a situation that they would have chosen.[41] This is, perhaps, because they wish to avoid believing they have made a bad choice or are poor decision makers (O'Reilly and Chatman, 1986).

This last discussion raises more fundamental questions. If norms are internalized, then the question becomes how? Why do people internalize norms? And what is the mechanism by which this occurs? Hodgson is relatively silent on these matters. The best he can offer is "a congenital or learned disposition for individuals to conform with other[s]". And even the second possibility, "a learned disposition", is not wholly satisfactory because one can ask why do individuals learn this? Why are they prone to learning conformism rather than non-conformism?

A genetic disposition to conformism seems a more promising hypothesis. There has been some work in economics arguing that certain human behavioral traits make sense from an evolutionary perspective (e.g. Frank, 1988), but, with the exception of the growing field of evolutionary game theory (e.g. Weibull, 1995),[42] this has largely been outside the economics mainstream. Certainly, though, one can tell an evolutionary tale to make sense of a tendency to conform. Consider social animals such as fish that swim in schools or zebras that roam in tight herds on the African Savannah. The advantage of being together (conforming) is that it protects the individuals from predators. Those individuals who were more prone to conform would, then, have a higher survival probability and, hence, more off-spring than those less likely to conform. That is, conformity would provide an evolutionary advantage. But this is not the end of the story: there needs to be some biological mechanism that steers these creatures towards conformity. Presumably, something akin to anxiety or fear strikes these creatures when they break away from the school or herd. Therefore, it was the tendency to anxiety from non-conformism that was the biological mechanism selected for.[43] Current humans and other hominoid species are social and it seems plausible, therefore, that these same

---

[41] The "Stockholm" phenomenon, whereby hostages begin to identify with their captors, could be seen as an extreme example of this tendency.

[42] Evolutionary game theory in economics, in turn, builds on earlier work by biologists (e.g. see Hofbauer and Sigmund, 1988; Maynard Smith, 1982) that applied game-theoretic ideas to explain evolutionary forces.

[43] Weidensaul (1999) provides some indirect evidence for such a mechanism: two differences between domesticated dogs and their wolf ancestors are (i) the former are less timid and (ii) they produce different levels of the hormone thyroxine. These two differences are arguably related: thyroxine affects the adrenal gland and the fear response is, in part, controlled by adrenaline. In the domestication process, creatures who were less timid around humans would be selected for; that is, creatures whose thyroxine levels produced lower adrenal responses would be selected for. As it turns out, many of the differences between dogs and wolves – in particular, dogs' pædomorphosis *vis-à-vis* wolves – are all directly or indirectly controlled by thyroxine.

biological mechanisms were selected for in the family *Hominoidea*. After all, breaking norms often induces a sense of unease or tension in people.[44] In short, like fish and zebras, we are programmed to follow the herd.[45]

Bernheim (1994) offers a model of conformity somewhat consistent with these ideas: people have inherent preference for status (perhaps because status once afforded a superior likelihood of reproductive success). People whose behavior indicates a propensity to obey norms achieve greater status than those whose behavior indicates a propensity to disobey norms. People, therefore, choose to conform. However, as in Kreps (1990), "conformity" in Bernheim's model has a strategic rather than intrinsic motivation – people do not gain intrinsic satisfaction from conforming; instead they dislike conforming per se, but prefer to be perceived as conformists rather than non-conformists. That is, unlike that for which Hodgson is arguing, norms are not internalized in Bernheim's model.

## LAZEAR (1995)

Lazear (1995) can be seen as an attempt to formalize the process by which culture comes to be internalized. Lazear takes an evolutionary approach: preferences are like a genetic endowment. At each moment, $t$, an individual in a firm meets ("mates") with another individual. This meeting causes each individual to produce an offspring: his or her $t + dt$ self, whose preferences ("genetic makeup") are a mixture of his or her former preferences and those of the individual he or she met (the "parents'" preferences). Through manipulation by top management, some preferences ("genetic endowments") are favored; that is, their carriers are more likely to survive to "mate". In essence, although without her precision, top management is like a horticulturist selecting for desired traits in flowers. Lazear's model could, therefore, be seen as one of *artificial* selection rather than *natural* selection.

For the most part, the close genetic analogy that Lazear pursues (down to each individual possessing two preference alleles, A and B – for three possible genetic endowments, AA, AB, and BB) is cute, but unnecessary. His ideas can be conveyed more straightforwardly – and arguably in a manner more consistent with actual behavior – as follows. Suppose that there are two possible preferences (beliefs, mind-sets, etc.), A and B. Of these, A is the preference that top management wishes to promote. Assume the organization has many individuals, of which $p(t)$ proportion hold preference A and $1 − p(t)$ hold preference B at time $t$. At each moment in time, individuals in the organization are randomly paired off (meet). Let $s \in (0,1)$ denote top management's promotional effort in encouraging the adoption of A. Suppose this works to cause $s$ proportion of Bs who meet As to come to hold preference A. Hence, of the $1 − p(t)$ of

---

[44] For more on the evolution of human behavior, see Goldsmith (1991).

[45] Within economics, there are also information-based models for herd behavior (e.g. see Banerjee, 1992; Bikhchandani et al., 1992; Scharfstein and Stein, 1990). In essence, these models show that an individual will follow the herd because he draws a statistical inference that what the popular behavior is must also be the behavior that others have found is personally most rewarding.

**Table 10.1**   Proportion of organization, $p(t)$, who are "As" (to five digits)

| $t =$ | $s = 0.1$ | $s = 0.2$ |
| --- | --- | --- |
| 1 | 0.52498 | 0.54938 |
| 5 | 0.2246 | 0.73106 |
| 10 | 0.73106 | 0.88080 |
| 15 | 0.81757 | 0.95257 |
| 50 | 0.99331 | 0.99995 |

the organization's population that hold preference B, $p(t)$ of them will meet an A, and a further $s$ of those will switch from B to A. Hence, at each instance in time, the proportion of As is increasing by $sp(t)[1 - p(t)]$; that is,[46]

$$\dot{p}(t) = sp(t)[1 - p(t)]$$

Note that the greater is $s$, the faster the proportion of As increases. If we imagine that the organization begins at time 0 equally divided between As and Bs, then this differential equation has the solution

$$p(t) = \frac{e^{st}}{1 + e^{st}}$$

where $e$ is the base of the natural logarithm (i.e. $e \approx 2.7183$). Table 10.1 gives some values for $p(t)$. Suppose that the organization's cost today of choosing $s$ is $C(s)$, an increasing and convex function. Suppose that the instantaneous benefit at time $t$ to the organization from having proportion $p$ prefer A is $V(p)$, where $V(\cdot)$ is increasing on the interval $(1/2,1)$. If $r$ is the interest rate, then the organization chooses $s$ to maximize

$$\int_0^\infty V[p(t)]e^{-rt}dt - C(s)$$

For example, suppose that A and B refer to strategies in the game in Figure 10.6. Let $V(p)$ be the expected average payoff to members of the organization; that is,

$$V(p) = 3p^2 + 2(1 - p)^2 = 5p^2 - 4p + 2 \tag{1}$$

If $C(s) = 20s^2$ and $r = 0.05$ (i.e. the interest rate is 5%), then numerical calculations reveal that the optimal $s$ is approximately 0.37. It can be readily shown that if the interest rate, $r$, *falls* or the payoff in the A–A cell of the Figure 10.6 game increases, then this value for $s$ will increase.

Note that in Lazear's formulation, as here, $s$ is an upfront investment. One could also conceive of continual effort to promote the A-culture. In this case, the firm chooses a sequence of investments, $s(t)$, to maximize

$$\int_0^\infty (V[p(t)] - \hat{C}[s(t)])e^{-rt}dt$$

---

[46] Recall that a dot over a function indicates its time derivative; e.g. $\dot{p}(t) = dp(t)/dt$.

Player 2

|          |     |  A  |  B  |
|----------|-----|-----|-----|
| Player 1 |  A  | 3,3 | 0,0 |
|          |  B  | 0,0 | 2,2 |

**Figure 10.6**   Another coordination game.

(where $\hat{C}(\cdot)$ is an increasing and convex function) subject to

$$\dot{p}(t) = s(t)p(t)[1 - p(t)]$$

Although the first-order conditions for this program are readily calculated, they are not particularly informative in and of themselves. Manipulating them, one can show that $\dot{s}(t) < 0$ *in a sufficiently old organization* (i.e. when $t$ is large); that is, beyond some time we can be sure that the organization devotes continually less resources to promoting its culture. In contrast, for *young* organizations, it is not clear whether investments in culture promotion are steadily decreasing or increasing in the period following its birth.

   Although we now have a formalization of the *consequences* of the internalization process, this is not the same as explaining the internalization process itself. Why do individuals switch from A to B? And what activities are represented by $s$? Lazear (1995, p. 108) suggests some answers:

- Suppose that when an A meets a B there is some probability, $\sigma_1$, that the A complains to management about the B. Suppose, too, that there is some probability, $\sigma_2$, that management acts on that complaint and replaces the B worker with an A worker (i.e. fires the former and hires the latter). Here $s = \sigma_1 \times \sigma_2$. By rewarding "snitches" or otherwise encouraging low tolerance of Bs, management can work to raise $\sigma_1$. By increasing its efforts to replace identified Bs with new workers it identifies as As, management can work to raise $\sigma_2$.
- Suppose that workers play the game in Figure 10.6. When a payoff of 0 is realized (i.e. when a B meets an A), the B worker says to himself, "Something went wrong here." With probability $s$, he then recalls the training seminar, the distributed literature, or a motivational speech telling him that this is an A organization. Realizing his mistake, he then switches to playing A. By enhancing the effectiveness of the training seminar, the salience of the literature, or the frequency of speeches, management can raise $s$.

Note that neither explanation really addresses internalization of preferences *à la* Hodgson (1996): under the first explanation, no one's preferences change – workers with "bad" preferences are simply replaced with workers with "good" preferences. This is a Stalinist rather than Maoist approach (i.e. execution over re-education). Under the second explanation, all workers want to do the "right" thing – i.e. their interests coincide – but they only realize that they are "misbehaving" when things go terribly wrong (e.g. they get 0), at which point they re-assess their behavior. Observe that this explanation is more consistent with the convention aspect of culture than with the norm aspect of culture.

This discussion raises a couple of important issues. First, are norms internalized? Or are people holding certain norms selected for? These questions indicate that cross-sectional studies (e.g. comparing the attitudes of individuals at "strong" and "weak" culture organizations) are likely to shed little light on internalization. Rather, empirical work would have to be based on panel data (i.e. a longitudinal aspect is necessary), with care being taken to handle attrition in a statistically appropriate way.[47]

The second issue is what is being internalized. Or, in a similar vein, what does it mean to internalize a norm. As an American, have I internalized driving on the right or is driving on the right – given that I know the convention – merely a manifestation of my desire to protect myself, my passengers, and my car? If the former, then an approach like Hodgson's or Lazear's is appropriate. If the latter, then it would seem preferable to stay with the more game-theoretic approach of Kreps (1990) or possibly Young (1993, 1998).

Even staying with the Lazear approach, observe that the two elements in Lazear's model, managerial effort to foster a culture, $s$, and "mating", are each, independently, sufficient to generate the type of dynamics that he considers. For instance, let $\sigma$ be the probability that a B worker is "caught" and replaced with an A worker. Then

$$\dot{p}(t) = \sigma[1 - p(t)]$$

Consequently,

$$p(t) = 1 - Ke^{-\sigma t}$$

where $K$ is a constant determined by the initial condition (e.g. if $p(0) = 1/2$, then $K = 1/2$). If the initial cost of setting up a monitoring system with $\sigma$ effectiveness is $\tilde{C}(\sigma)$, where $\tilde{C}(\cdot)$ is increasing and convex, then the optimal monitoring effectiveness, $\sigma^*$, is the solution to

$$\max_{\sigma} \int_0^\infty V[p(t)]e^{-rt}dt - \tilde{C}(\sigma)$$

Hence, if $V(\cdot)$ is given by Eq. (1), $\tilde{C}(s) = 20s^2$, $p(0) = 1/2$, and $r = 0.05$, then $\sigma^* \approx 0.35$. A further examination of the dynamics shows that the value of $p(t)$ under this dynamic and the one in Lazear is exceedingly similar for $t \geq 5$ and $\sigma$ or $s \geq 0.3$.

Alternatively, suppose that as a holder of a minority opinion or preference, a worker is inclined to change to the majority opinion or preference with probability $\phi(p)$, where $p > 1/2$ is the proportion holding the majority opinion. Assume that if $p > 1/2$, then $\phi(p) > 0$ and $\phi'(p) > 0$. This model attempts to capture the idea that people are prone to conform and that the pressure to conform is greater the more conformists with whom one comes in contact. Then

$$\dot{p}(t) = \phi[p(t)][1 - p(t)]$$

Suppose, for example, that $\phi(p) = \alpha p$ for $p > 1/2$ ($\alpha \in (0,1)$), then

---

[47] See Chatman (1991) for an empirical study along these lines. She followed new employees of large accounting firms over a 2.5-year period. Her findings suggest that there is both socialization (internalizing) and selection at work.

$$p(t) = \frac{e^{\alpha t}}{\kappa + e^{\alpha t}}$$

where $\kappa$ is a constant determined by the initial condition; that is,

$$p(0) = \frac{1}{1 + \kappa}$$

Hence, $\kappa = (1/p(0)) - 1$; thus,

$$p(t) = \frac{p(0)e^{\alpha t}}{1 - p(0) + p(0)e^{\alpha t}}$$

For instance, if $p(0) = 0.6$ and $\alpha = 0.2$, then $p(10) \approx 0.92$. In this example, we have $dp(t)/dp(0) > 0$ and $dp(t)/d\alpha > 0$ – the greater the initial proportion of the majority initially, the greater it is at any future point, and the more responsive the minority is to the majority, the greater is the majority at any future point. Note this model is similar to Lazear's, except here $p(0) > 1/2$ and $\alpha$ is exogenous. Of course, if management can influence $\alpha$, then we are back to Lazear's model (although the derivation is different).[48]

An alternative is that $\alpha$ (more generally, $\phi(p)$) is a function of the importance of having a single culture. Hence, for instance, when coordination is more important, then $\alpha$ could be larger. That is, the more important conforming is, the more rapidly we conform.

Although, as this section illustrates, there are many ways to formalize the dynamics by which culture might be propagated, we are still left with the problem of understanding the underlying process. Is it inter-personal contacts (i.e. "mating") that spreads culture? And, if so, what leads to one person's culture displacing another's? To what extent, if any, is management able to influence the spread of culture? Indeed, is management spreading culture or simply weeding out the non-believers? Lazear demonstrates that economics can help us understand the propagation and diffusion of culture within a firm;[49] however, as this discussion demonstrates, economics is unlikely to *explain* the underlying mechanics by which these processes operate – for these, economic modelers must rely on their sister social sciences or even the biological sciences.

## COMPLEMENTARY INSIGHTS FROM THE ECONOMICS OF ORGANIZATIONS

The discussion so far has concerned economists' writing on corporate culture per se. In this section, I turn to the question of how results from the economics of internal and industrial organization could be used to enhance our understanding of corporate culture.

---

[48] Note, too, that we can readily conceive of other functional forms for $\phi(\cdot)$. For instance, we might want $\lim_{p \downarrow 1/2} \phi(p) = 0$, in which case $\phi(p) = \alpha(p - 1/2)$ would be a better model.

[49] Bikhchandani et al. (1992) and Young (1993, 1998), among others, also illustrate the ability of economics to model propagation and diffusion of aspects of culture such as conventions and fads.

# THE INTERSECTION BETWEEN IO AND CORPORATE CULTURE

To build on the Lazear (1995) analogy between culture and genes, the criterion for judging the desirability of a given culture is the corresponding fitness of the firm. That is, a culture can be judged only by the competitive advantages it yields the firm. In turn, to appreciate competitive advantages requires some understanding of the firm's competitive situation, which brings us to the area of microeconomics known as industrial organization. This section explores some ways in which industrial organization can complement an understanding of the importance of corporate culture and the diffusion of strong cultures within an industry.

# A MODEL OF UNIVERSAL ADOPTION OR NON-ADOPTION

From earlier discussion in the previous two sections, a reasonable assumption would seem to be that a strong culture leads to a more efficient organization; that is, one with lower *marginal* costs. But, as considered above, there is an overhead or fixed cost associated with instilling and maintaining a strong culture.[50] To formalize this, let a "cultured" firm's cost of producing $x$ units be $F_c + m_c x^2$. Similarly, let the cost for an "uncultured" firm be $F_u + m_u x^2$. Consistent with earlier discussions, assume that

$$0 < m_c < m_u \text{ and } 0 < F_u < F_c$$

that is, the cultured firm has lower marginal costs, but higher fixed costs, than the uncultured firm.

Finally, suppose that this is a perfectly competitive industry. This means (e.g. see Mas-Colell et al., 1995, Section 10.F) that in long-run equilibrium the only type of firm that survives is the type with the lower minimum average cost. Average cost is $mx + F/x$, which achieves a minimum at $x = \sqrt{F/m}$. Substituting this value of $x$ into average cost yields

$$\text{AC}^{\text{min}} = 2\sqrt{mF}$$

If $\text{AC}_c^{\text{min}} < \text{AC}_u^{\text{min}}$, then only cultured firms will survive in long-run equilibrium. If the inequality is reversed, then only uncultured firms will survive. A little algebra reveals that the inequality – and hence an equilibrium with only cultured firms – will hold if

---

[50] In this and subsequent discussion, I am abstracting from the issue of *how* a firm instills and maintains a culture. I am simply assuming that (i) it can (at a cost) and (ii) efforts to instill and maintain a culture are always successful. The second of these is, admittedly, unrealistic, but the conclusions reached in the analyses that follow would be relatively unaffected if we were to assume stochastic success. The *difficulty* of the analysis would, however, increase. In addition, by "strong culture" I mean culture that is both strategically appropriate and firmly accepted by the people within a firm. In this sense, I am conflating the concepts of *cultural content* and *cultural strength*. See Flynn and Chatman (2000) in this Handbook for a further discussion of these concepts.

$$\frac{m_{\mathrm{u}} - m_{\mathrm{c}}}{m_{\mathrm{u}}} > \frac{F_{\mathrm{c}} - F_{\mathrm{u}}}{F_{\mathrm{c}}}$$

that is, if the proportional reduction in marginal costs from having a culture is greater than the proportional increase in fixed costs from having a culture. If the proportional reduction is less than the proportional increase, then only uncultured firms will exist in long-run equilibrium.

Some observations on this analysis. First, observe that

$$\sqrt{\frac{F_{\mathrm{c}}}{m_{\mathrm{c}}}} > \sqrt{\frac{F_{\mathrm{u}}}{m_{\mathrm{u}}}}$$

This means that, in a cultured-firm equilibrium, each firm produces more than in an uncultured-firm equilibrium *ceteris paribus*.[51] Hence, in a cultured-firm equilibrium there will be fewer firms than in an uncultured-firm equilibrium *ceteris paribus*. Consequently, controlling for total industry production, we should observe fewer firms in a competitive industry in which corporate culture seems prevalent than in one in which it seems less prevalent. Since output correlates strongly with other measures of size, such as employees, it should also be that firms tend to have more employees when culture is a prevalent phenomenon than when it is not, all else equal.

With respect to empirical work, this prediction could cause problems when testing the Lazear (1995) prediction that a corporate culture is easier to instill in a small firm and that, therefore, smaller firms will tend to exhibit stronger corporate cultures. That the cost of instilling culture could be less the smaller is the firm indeed seems plausible (more on this momentarily), but the validity of Lazear's "therefore" also depends on how the *benefits* of culture vary with size (a point he does not address). If, as here, benefits are assumed to increase with size (since the benefit of reducing marginal costs is greater the more that will be produced), then one must compare whether the increase in benefits outweighs the increase in costs.

To aid in understanding this point, suppose, as a change to what was previously assumed, that the cost of $x$ is

$$F + \frac{x^2}{s}$$

where $s$, an endogenous variable, is the expenditure per worker on instilling and maintaining culture. As before, expenditures on culture reduce the marginal cost of production. Suppose that the production technology is such that each worker produces $\gamma$ units. Hence, if $L$ is the number of workers, then $\gamma L$ units are produced and the firm's total cost is

$$F + sL + \frac{\gamma^2 L^2}{s}$$

when expressed in terms of its workforce (size). Note that the marginal cost of culture

---

[51] Recall that in the long-run equilibrium of a perfectly competitive industry with homogeneous firms, each firm operates at the minimum of its average cost curve (e.g. see Mas-Colell et al., 1995, Section 10.F).

increases with size, $L$. But the marginal benefit does as well:

$$\frac{d^2}{dLds}\left(-\frac{\gamma^2 L^2}{s}\right) = \frac{2\gamma^2 L}{s^2} > 0$$

For a given $L$, the firm chooses $s$ to minimize total cost; hence, the optimal $s$ is $\gamma\sqrt{L}$. This is an *increasing* function of $L$, meaning that larger firms will invest more *per worker* in culture than smaller firms.

This is not, however, a fully general conclusion. Suppose the cost of instilling and maintaining culture in a firm with $L$ employees were $sL^\alpha$. Then the firm would choose $s$ to minimize

$$sL^\alpha + \frac{\gamma^2 L^2}{s}$$

The solution is

$$s = \gamma L^{\frac{2-\alpha}{2}}$$

This function is increasing in $L$ for $\alpha < 2$ – as in the previous paragraph, larger firms invest more per worker in culture than smaller firms. If, however, $\alpha > 2$, then this conclusion is reversed: smaller firms would then invest more per worker. Finally, if $\alpha = 2$, then investment per worker is independent of size. This analysis, thus, validates the earlier point that how culture varies with size depends critically on how the benefits and costs of culture vary with size. And while the *costs* of culture can be largely studied by looking at the firm in isolation, the *benefits* of culture will typically require some understanding of the firm's competitive environment.

## AN ASYMMETRIC MODEL OF CULTURE ADOPTION

The competitive model lends itself to equilibria with homogeneous behavior.[52] On the other hand, observation suggests that many industries are characterized by heterogeneous behavior. If we presume some link between culture and behavior, then such observations suggest that we should observe *intra*-industry heterogeneity in culture. Industrial organization can help explain this heterogeneity.

Building on earlier work of mine (Hermalin, 1994), consider an industry with just two firms, Y and Z. The timing of the model is that, first, the firms decide whether to invest in instilling and maintaining a corporate culture or not. Let $I$ be the cost of such an investment if undertaken. As before, the benefit of a corporate culture is that it lowers marginal cost. Let $m_u$ be the marginal cost of a firm that lacks a strong culture and $m_c$ be the marginal cost of a firm that has a strong culture, where $m_c < m_u$. After establishing a culture or not, each firm observes the strength of its rival's corporate

---

[52] To be precise, if $m_c F_c = m_u F_u$, then a heterogeneous equilibrium would be possible. Alternatively, if $m_c F_c < m_u F_u$ but there was an exogenous *limit* on the number of cultured firms, then the marginal firm could be uncultured and the equilibrium would be heterogeneous. These possibilities likely arise too infrequently for them to serve as adequate general explanations of heterogeneous equilibria.

$$Z$$

| | | Adopt | Don't |
|---|---|---|---|
| Y | Adopt | $\frac{(a-m_c)^2}{9b} - I, \frac{(a-m_c)^2}{9b} - I$ | $\frac{(a+m_u-2m_c)^2}{9b} - I, \frac{(a+m_c-2m_u)^2}{9b}$ |
| | Don't | $\frac{(a+m_c-2m_u)^2}{9b}, \frac{(a+m_u-2m_c)^2}{9b} - I$ | $\frac{(a-m_u)^2}{9b}, \frac{(a-m_u)^2}{9b}$ |

**Figure 10.7**  Culture adoption game between firms Y and Z.

culture. Then the firms decide how much to produce. Let industry demand be such that $p = a - bX$, where $p$ is the market price, $X$ is total industry output, and $a$ and $b$ are fixed positive parameters. Assume competition between these two firms is Cournot competition (e.g. see Mas-Colell et al., 1995, Section 12.C).[53] Consequently, if Y's marginal cost is $m_Y$ and Z's is $m_Z$, then the firms' profits (gross of investments in culture) are

$$\pi_Y = \frac{(a + m_Z - 2m_Y)^2}{9b} \quad \text{and} \quad \pi_Z = \frac{(a + m_Y - 2m_Z)^2}{9b}$$

respectively. Consequently, the culture-adoption game is the one shown in Figure 10.7. Observe that

$$(a + \tilde{m} - 2m_c)^2 - (a + \tilde{m} - 2m_u)^2 = \int_{m_c}^{m_u} 4(a + \tilde{m} - 2m)dm$$

Consequently, since the integrand is increasing in $\tilde{m}$, it follows that

$$\frac{(a - m_c)^2}{9b} - \frac{(a + m_c - 2m_u)^2}{9b} < \frac{(a + m_u - 2m_c)^2}{9b} - \frac{(a - m_u)^2}{9b} \qquad (2)$$

In words, the lower is your rival's marginal cost, the smaller the gain from reducing your own marginal cost. Intuitively, the lower your rival's marginal cost, the greater your rival's output, and the greater your rival's output, the smaller will be your output in the Cournot equilibrium, which means marginal cost reduction is less valuable to you.

A consequence of Eq. (2) is that there exists an interval of $I$s such that

$$\frac{(a - m_c)^2}{9b} - I < \frac{(a + m_c - 2m_u)^2}{9b} \quad \text{and} \quad \frac{(a + m_u - 2m_c)^2}{9b} - I > \frac{(a - m_u)^2}{9b}$$

For an $I$ in that interval, the game in Figure 10.7 has only two pure-strategy Nash equilibria: in one, firm Y adopts or invests in a corporate culture, while firm Z does not, and in the other, firm Z adopts or invests, while firm Y does not. Observe that we have

---

[53] Under Cournot competition, firms simultaneously choose their output. The price they receive is $p = a - bX$. Note that each firm's output imposes a negative externality on the other firm by reducing the price that the second firm will receive.

heterogeneity in both equilibria: one firm has a strong culture, while the other does not.[54,55]

If the cost of having a culture is very low (lies below the interval), then there is a single Nash equilibrium in which both firms adopt a strong culture. Conversely, if the cost of having a culture is very high (lies above the interval), then there is a single Nash equilibrium in which neither firm adopts a strong culture.

Another comparative static is with respect to $a$: as demand shifts out ($a$ increases), then the value of establishing a strong culture increases. Consequently, we can expect three regions: for low enough $a$, neither firm has a strong culture; for intermediate values, the equilibrium is heterogeneous; finally, for high values, both firms have a strong culture. This, in turn, suggests some empirical tests of this theory: for instance, it should be that the prevalence of strong cultures is greater in industries with higher output per firm than in industries with less output per firm. That is, all else equal, we should see stronger cultures in larger firms.[56]

With further regard to empirical work, this model suggests a puzzle for determining the long-run impact of culture. This model indicates that the strength of a firm's culture is a function of the size it expects to attain in equilibrium. That is, somewhat loosely, size determines culture. This, in turn, creates some issues for interpreting correlations between culture and firm success: could a positive correlation be spurious? Many measures of success, such as profits and longevity, are positively correlated with size. Could, then, the competitive opportunities that lead to large size explain both the strength of culture and the apparent success of the firm?

It is worth noting that one could also generate heterogeneous equilibria through other models. For instance, it is sometimes suggested that a strong culture makes the firm more efficient in a specific environment, but less efficient in other environments, relative to a firm with less culture. If there is sufficient uncertainty over future environments, then, staying with Cournot competitors, one can find equilibria in which one firm will adopt a strong culture, while the other will not (even if the cost of establishing a culture is zero).[57]

Another model that could generate heterogeneity would be a product-differentiation model. Suppose that instead of affecting marginal cost, culture raised the quality of the product or service of a firm (e.g. customers value dealing with a "service-with-a-smile" culture more). Consider a duopoly. If both firms adopt a strong culture or if neither does, then what the firms produce or provide will be perceived by consumers as

---

[54] For an $I$ in this interval, there is also a third Nash equilibrium in mixed strategies. Since this equilibrium will also yield heterogeneity with positive probability, the prediction of heterogeneity can be said to hold for all of the game's equilibria.

[55] Some readers may worry that these heterogeneous equilibria are the consequence of assuming that culture is a discrete decision. By analogy with the analysis in Hermalin (1994), it can, however, be shown that these conclusions can also be reached in a model in which culture is chosen from a continuum of possible values.

[56] This conclusion is driven by the assumptions of the model: marginal benefit of culture is increasing in size, while marginal cost is not (the cost of culture is a fixed cost). This conclusion would be reversed if the model were such that the marginal cost of culture was increasing faster with size than the marginal benefit.

[57] It is a reasonably well-known fact that Cournot competitors would prefer that their marginal costs be uncorrelated. The one cite, however, I know for this result is Dana (1991).

homogeneous. In turn, this means that consumers will decide from which to buy solely on the basis of price, which leads to a form of competition known as Bertrand competition (e.g. see Mas-Colell et al., 1995, Section 12.C). In Bertrand competition, economic profits are driven to zero by the ferocity of the price competition. If, instead, the firms differentiate their product or service along some non-price line (e.g. culture), then price competition is less fierce and the firms can make positive profits.

## LESSONS

This section has concerned itself with the importance of tying industrial organization into a study of corporate culture. To the extent that corporate culture is a choice variable for the firm, the level or intensity of a firm's culture depends on both the costs and benefits of a strong corporate culture. Whereas the costs can be reasonably understood by looking at the firm only, the benefits depend significantly on the firm's competitive environment. This, in turn, requires an examination of that environment and an understanding of the firm's strategic responses to it.

The nature of the conclusions that one can reach about corporate culture depend critically on the firms' competitive environment. Does competition encourage more or less culture? How might the strength of culture vary with the size of the firm? How do we interpret correlations between strength of culture and other firm attributes, such as performance? Answering these questions requires linking culture to industrial organization.

## FAIRNESS AND RELATED MODELS

A reasonable characterization of most economic models is that the rational actor is motivated solely by her payoffs. In particular, she will like equally all allocation processes that yield the same payoffs to her and what these processes provide others is irrelevant to her. Over the years, a minority of economists have recognized the extremity of that assumption and analyzed the consequences of individual actors caring about the process by which they receive their payoffs or caring about what payoffs others get (e.g. consider Frank, 1998; Rabin, 1993; Varian, 1974; Veblen, 1899). The extent to which these non-material concerns matter is both a manifestation of culture and an avenue through which manipulation of culture can affect behavior.

To appreciate how this might affect the study of culture, consider the following game between two individuals, Y and Z. Suppose that Y has \$100 and she decides to send $\phi$ dollars of it to Z, where $0 \leq \phi \leq 100$. Suppose that if she sends $\phi$ dollars, Z actually receives $3\phi$ dollars. Z then decides how much, $\psi$, to send back to Y. The payoff to Y is $100 - \phi + \psi$ dollars and the payoff to Z is $3\phi - \psi$ dollars. Although this game is quite artificial, it reflects many situations in which one individual (here, Y) can gain if she trusts another (here, Z) who controls the returns from her investment (here, the process that turns $\phi$ dollars into $3\phi$ dollars) to adequately share the proceeds of her investment with her.

If this game is played once and the players are fully self-interested, then Z would never return any money to Y. Since Y is rational, she would anticipate this and not send any money in the first place. Hence, in equilibrium, no money is sent. This is clearly worse for both players than a feasible outcome in which Y sends the entire $100 and Z returns more than $100.

In contrast, suppose that the players' utility functions are

$$U_Y = \ln(w_Y) - \mu f(w_Y, w_Z)$$

$$U_Z = \ln(w_Z) - \mu f(w_Z, w_Y)$$

where $w_t$ is the final wealth of player t, $\mu$ is a positive constant, and, following Rabin, $f(\cdot)$ is a "fairness" function. Specifically, suppose that

$$f(w_1, w_2) = \begin{cases} \dfrac{w_1 - w_2}{100} & \text{if } w_1 > w_2 \\ 0 & \text{if } w_1 \leq w_2 \end{cases}$$

That is, a player suffers some remorse if his final wealth exceeds the other player's because of the "unfairness" of the allocation.

Consider Z's play. If $\phi \leq 25$, then his final wealth can never exceed Y's, he can not feel remorse, and so he will want to keep all of the $3\phi$ he receives. In this case, Y chooses her final wealth to maximize

$$\ln(w_Y) - \frac{\mu}{100}(w_Y - w_Z) = \ln(w_Y) - \frac{\mu}{100}(4w_Y - 300)$$

The solution to this program is $w_Y = \min\{25/\mu, 100\}$, provided $\mu \leq 1/3$ (this proviso is necessary because we are considering the case where $w_Y \geq 75$). If, instead, $\phi > 25$, then it will be Z who can not have the smaller final wealth. Z will choose $\psi$ to maximize

$$\ln(3\phi - \psi) - \frac{\mu}{100}(3\phi - \psi - [\psi + 100 - \phi]) = \ln(3\phi - \psi) - \frac{\mu}{100}(4\phi - 2\psi - 100)$$

The solution to this program is

$$\psi = \begin{cases} \max\left\{3\phi - \dfrac{50}{\mu}, 0\right\} & \text{if } \dfrac{100}{\mu} \geq 2\phi + 100 \\ 2\phi - 50 & \text{if otherwise} \end{cases}$$

Observe, first, that if Y sends more than $25, then Z will return some of it provided $\mu$ is large enough. Assume this is the case, then Y chooses $\phi$ to maximize

$$\ln\left(\max\left\{100 + 2\phi - \frac{50}{\mu}, 2\phi - 50\right\}\right)$$

The solution is $\phi = 100$, Y sends all her money. Putting it all together:

- If $\mu \geq 1/3$, Y sends $100 and Z returns $150. That is, surplus is maximized when $\mu \geq 1/3$.

- Define $\mu^* \approx 0.22696.$[58] If $\mu^* < \mu < 1/3$, then Y sends $100 and receives $300 - (50/\mu)$ dollars in return. Note she receives back more than $100 if $\mu > 1/4$ and receives less than $100 back if $\mu < 1/4$. Despite the inequity in the sharing, surplus is still maximized in the region $\mu^* < \mu < 1/3$.
- If $\mu \leq \mu^*$, then Y sends nothing. Surplus is *not* maximized in this region.

From an organizational perspective, a firm would like, therefore, to ensure that $\mu > \mu^*$. That is, it would like to instill a culture that makes its employees sufficiently sensitive to fairness that Y can "trust" Z. There are many practices that might fit this bill. Examples are activities that build camaraderie, such as company picnics, an inviting staff lounge, company sports teams in local recreation leagues, and so forth. Alternatively, the organization could try to screen for fair-minded individuals or sanction employees who behave unfairly.

Observe that the kind of cooperation that occurs when $\mu \geq 1/4$ could also be achieved through a repeated game of the sort considered by Kreps (1990). Even if $\mu = 0$, an equilibrium can arise in a repeated game in which Y sends a $100 each period and Z returns an amount greater than $100. This equilibrium is supported by Y's threat to discontinue sending money should Z ever fail to return a sufficient amount to Y. In this case, we would be hard pressed to tell whether culture was sustained by repeated interaction among wholly selfish players or the internalization of a fairness norm. We could tell (at least reject wholly selfish players), however, if $\mu^* < \mu < 1/4$ – in this case, we would observe Y sending more than she received back, behavior that would be impossible if the players were wholly selfish.[59]

In a related vein, Kandel and Lazear (1992) consider the question of norm enforcement. These authors distinguish between *guilt*, which is internal, and *shame*, which requires observation by others. For instance, if I tip when traveling by myself far from home, then my tipping could be driven by guilt – I would feel bad if I did not tip. In contrast, if I tip only when dining with others or only at restaurants I frequent often, then my tipping is probably driven by shame – I worry about the disapproval I would suffer from others.

The basic ideas in Kandel and Lazear's article can be captured using the following teams model (based on Holmström, 1982): two employees (team members), Y and Z, each choose a level of effort, $a_Y$ and $a_Z$, respectively, that stochastically determines the team's output. Specifically, output, $X$, is $\zeta \times (a_Y + a_Z)$, where $\zeta = 1$ with probability $q$ and equals 0 with probability $1 - q$ $(0 < q < 1)$. Suppose that any realized output is shared equally by the team members. The standard assumption in this type of modeling (e.g. see Holmström, 1982) is that each member's utility has a form similar to

$$U = \frac{1}{2}X - \frac{1}{2}a^2$$

That is, it is equal to some function of his share of the output minus some function of his effort that represents his disutility of effort. Expected utility maximization would, then,

---

[58] $\mu^*$ is the solution to the equation $\ln(300 - (50/\mu)) = \ln(100) - \mu$.

[59] See Rabin (1993, 1998) for surveys of experimental evidence that supports rejecting the wholly selfish model of players in games like this.

lead each employee to choose $a = (1/2)q$. This, however, does not maximize *social* surplus: each unit of effort returns only $(1/2)q$ in expected output to a worker; that is, he perceives his *private* marginal benefit of effort to be $(1/2)q$. However, his effort also benefits his team member. Adding that benefit in, we see that the *social* marginal benefit is $q$. Since this is larger than the private marginal benefit, we can conclude that each worker expends too little effort *vis-à-vis* the social optimum. Or, as an economist might put it, neither worker values the positive externality that his effort has on his co-worker and, hence, expends too little effort.

In contrast to this standard formulation, suppose, first, that employees feel guilty if they expend less than first-best effort (i.e. if $a < q$), since they feel guilty about the harm their laziness causes their co-workers. Specifically, suppose that a worker's utility is

$$\hat{U} = \frac{1}{2}X - g(a) - \frac{1}{2}a^2$$

where $g(\cdot)$ is the guilt function. For concreteness, suppose

$$g(a) = \begin{cases} G \times (q - a), & \text{if } a < q \\ 0 & \text{if } a \geq q \end{cases}$$

$(G > 0)$. The equilibrium expenditure of effort is, then,

$$a = \begin{cases} \frac{1}{2}q + G, & \text{if } G < \frac{1}{2}q \\ q & \text{if } G \geq \frac{1}{2}q \end{cases} \tag{3}$$

Observe that guilt leads to a greater expenditure of effort than when workers are not prone to feeling guilty. Moreover, the greater is $G$, up to $(1/2)q$, the more effort workers expend. As with fairness, there is, thus, an incentive for the firm to pursue activities that will make workers feel guilty if they slack off. In general, I imagine these activities would be similar to those that instill fairness (see above).

In contrast to guilt, let us now consider shame. Shame requires that a slacking worker's co-worker be able to detect that he has slacked. A co-worker has this ability only when $\zeta = 1$, since otherwise there is no output. When $\zeta = 1$, workers can determine each other's effort by subtracting their own effort from $X$. Suppose that a worker's shame is $g(a)$, where $g(\cdot)$ is the function defined in the previous paragraph. Then each worker's expected utility is

$$\tilde{U} = \frac{1}{2}X - qg(a) - \frac{1}{2}a^2$$

In equilibrium, each worker's expenditure of effort is

$$a = \begin{cases} \frac{1}{2}q + qG, & \text{if } G < \frac{1}{2} \\ q & \text{if } G \geq \frac{1}{2} \end{cases}$$

Comparing this to the equilibrium effort given by Eq. (3), we see that for any $G$, $G < 1/2$, the workers expend less effort when motivated by shame than when motivated by guilt. This accords with Kandel and Lazear's more general finding that guilt is a stronger motivator than shame. But even if workers are motivated by shame, there is still a benefit to the corporation of trying to raise the amount of shame, $G$, they feel when caught. If, as seems reasonable, the amount of shame one feels is increasing in the number of people aware of his misconduct, then one way to raise $G$ is by increasing the notoriety of those caught misbehaving.[60]

As with fairness, the behaviors attributable to guilt and shame can also be explained using a repeated-game framework. Each worker expends $q$ in effort each period unless, in a previous period, aggregate output was something other than 0 or $2q$. In that case, he expends just $(1/2)q$ in effort. A high-effort equilibrium exists provided[61]

$$\frac{1}{2}q^2 \frac{1}{1-\beta} \geq \sum_{\tau=0}^{\infty} \beta^\tau (1-q)^\tau \left( \frac{5}{8}q^2 + \frac{\beta}{1-\beta}\frac{3}{8}q^2 \right) = \frac{q^2}{1-(1-q)\beta}\left( \frac{5}{8} + \frac{\beta}{1-\beta}\frac{3}{8} \right)$$

where $\beta$ is again the probability of continuing the game (alternatively, the financial discount factor). Provided $q > 1/2$ and

$$\beta \geq \frac{1}{2(2q-1)}$$

repeated play will induce first-best effort from both workers even though they are not susceptible to guilt nor to shame.

Although these models demonstrate that fairness, guilt, and shame can be incorporated into economic analysis in a way that connects to corporate culture, there are a number of questions still left unanswered. Why do feelings about fairness, guilt, and shame affect human behavior? Why are, assuming they are, these feelings susceptible to manipulation (e.g. how does a company picnic make employees treat others more fairly)?

As might be expected, there has been little work in economics examining the origin of feelings such as fairness, guilt, or shame. To the extent these have found their way into economic models, it has typically been simply to assume they exist and, then, as above, consider their consequences. An exception to this is Frank (1987, 1988), which considers the evolutionary advantages provided by being subject to certain feelings, such as guilt. In particular, under appropriate assumptions,[62] a population with a conscience (being subject to guilt) can resist a small invasion of guilt-free "mutants"; moreover, a population that lacks a conscience is subject to being overrun by a small invasion of guilt-prone "mutants". That is, in the language of evolutionary game theory, an equilibrium in which people "choose" to have a conscience is evolutionary

---

[60] This could also be done indirectly by heavily publicizing the names of those who *behaved*, since co-workers can infer from this who did not behave.

[61] This expression takes into account that if a worker deviates, he does best to choose $a = (1/2)q$. Of course, his deviation might not be detected immediately because $\zeta$ could equal zero that period. This, too, is accounted for in the expression.

[62] See Frank (1989) and Harrington (1989) for a debate over just how reasonable these assumptions are.

stable (see Maynard Smith, 1982; Weibull, 1995, for more on evolutionary stability). Yet showing that "guilt" could be evolutionarily advantageous is not, ultimately, to explain *why* we are subject to guilt. At some point, the underlying biological mechanism by which guilt works and how this mechanism evolved must be identified and understood.

On the other hand, social science is not a sub-discipline of biology (despite what some biologists might think). As long as we have evidence that people are subject to guilt (or shame or a preference for fair outcomes), then nothing prevents us from incorporating this into our models. Similarly, if we have evidence that these feelings can be manipulated in ways suggested above, then we are again free to incorporate such manipulation into our models of corporate culture. But this not a license for loose modeling – before we can take seriously a model that posits that company picnics lead to employees treating each other more fairly, we need either evidence to support this or a better understanding of the bio-evolutionary mechanisms behind it.

# INFORMAL AUTHORITY: LEADING AND DELEGATION

Much of the economic modeling of organizations considers situations of formal authority. One party, often dubbed the *principal*, has some formal authority to coerce another party, often dubbed the *agent*. This authority could represent the right to order the agent about or it could be the ability to set the agent's incentives.[63] Recently, however, the economics literature has begun to explore issues of *in*formal authority. Here, I will discuss two strands of the literature and their links to corporate culture.

# LEADERSHIP

Leadership is an important topic in sociological and psychological studies of organization. It has, however, received considerably less attention from economists.

One notable exception is Rotemberg and Saloner (1993), which considers the consequences of the leader (boss) having empathy with those under her.[64] In many ways, the analysis in Rotemberg and Saloner is similar to the analysis of fairness and guilt considered in the previous section. For instance, in keeping with the spirit of Rotemberg and Saloner, the leader could be Z in the money-transfer game considered above. If the leader is empathic, then the underling, Y, will know that the leader will behave fairly, which means the underling can trust the leader to return a sufficient amount of money to him. Or, to tie this more closely to real firm behavior, the underling could make investments that payoff for him only if the leader later recognizes them by increasing the underling's wage.

Some recent work of mine (Hermalin, 1998, 1999) is another exception. Unlike Rotemberg and Saloner, I stay more within the mainstream of neo-classical economics

---

[63] Typically, this authority is not absolute: the agent is almost always assumed to have the right to quit (or at least not accept employment initially). Often he is assumed to enjoy limited-liability protection, thereby preventing the principal from fining him.

[64] Also consider Rotemberg and Saloner (1998).

by positing that all actors are motivated solely by their own interests. I begin with the observation that a person is a leader only if she has followers. Following is an inherently *voluntary* activity. Hence, the essential question becomes how does a leader induce others to follow her.[65] As an economist, I presume that followers follow because it is in their interest to do so. What could make it in their interest to follow? One answer is that they believe the leader has better information about what they should do than they have. Leadership is thus, in part, about transmitting information to followers. But this can not be all: a leader must also convince followers that she is transmitting the *correct* information; that is, she must convince her followers that she is not misleading them.

The formal model I consider is related to the teams model considered in the previous section. Loosely, imagine the same model (with wholly selfish workers), except, now, the two values $\zeta$ can take are 1/2 and 1. We can also imagine that the team has $N \geq 2$ members, in which case each team member gets $1/N$ of the output.[66] Observe that the greater a worker thinks $\zeta$ will be, the more effort he will expend. Now suppose one team member, the leader, learns what $\zeta$ will be. This knowledge is her private information. If she thought that the other workers would believe her announcement, she would have an obvious incentive to always claim that $\zeta = 1$, since then she induces the most effort from her fellow team members and she, recall, gets $\zeta/N$ of that additional effort from each fellow team member. Of course, her fellow team members are not naive, they understand this temptation, so they rationally disregard her claims. But this is inefficient, since effort should be conditioned on its true marginal return, $\zeta$. To overcome this, the leader must convincingly signal her information. Hermalin (1998) considers two methods of doing so. One, the leader can "sacrifice", that is, give an *ex ante* gift to her followers when it is the good state (i.e. $\zeta = 1$). Two, the leader can "lead by example". In leading by example, the leader chooses her effort first and publicly. Based on her effort choice, the followers are able to infer what $\zeta$ must be and condition their efforts accordingly.[67]

Both Rotemberg and Saloner's work and my own can be related to corporate culture. In the case of Rotemberg and Saloner, the obvious relationship is culture as a mechanism to induce or enhance empathy. In my work, there are a number of avenues to explore. First, suppose that $\zeta$ reflects the importance of adhering to a cultural norm and effort now means a worker's effort to abide by the norm. Leading by example, then, reflects the oft-given advice that a leader should "walk the talk". That is, followers infer the importance of adhering to the norm by observing the degree to which the

---

[65] In this sense, I can be seen as modeling what Max Weber (Gerth and Mills, 1946) refers to as "charismatic" leadership.

[66] In Hermalin (1998), I show that dividing output equally is the optimal arrangement in many contexts (but not all). Even when it is not, the arguments presented here continue to hold when the team uses the most efficient division.

[67] Hermalin (1998) considers only a one-shot model. Hermalin (1999) extends the analysis to a repeated game, where I show that leader sacrifice and leading by example could still be important. In a repeated setting, two more mechanisms for inducing the leader to be honest can emerge: (1) the leader can simply develop a reputation for honesty; and (2) the leader can be induced to be honest by the promise of tribute from her followers (see Hermalin, 1999, for details).

leader adheres. Somewhat along the same lines, workers – particularly those new to the organization – could be seeking to identify the organization's norms. They may naturally look to a single person, the leader, as a model of appropriate behavior. Here, again, it is critical that the leader "walk the talk". Conversely, it is often claimed that part of being a leader is inducing others to break with the past. Now the cost of following the leader could be the disutility caused by violating old norms. Followers' willingness to do so could be influenced by their inference of how much importance the leader places on this change. Again, leading by example or sacrifice could be critical.

Another aspect to leadership that I have considered, but not written on, would be to consider leadership in the context of labeling theory (Erikson, 1966). When explicitly defining norms is difficult, perhaps because they are complex or finely shaded, followers could infer the appropriate norms from observing who the leader rewards, and how much, and who she sanctions, and how severely. Given that followers are making such inferences, the leader could wish to reward or sanction in a strategic way; that is, with an eye towards influencing both what her followers infer and the speed with which they infer it.

# DELEGATION

Delegation of authority is a common feature in all large organizations. Although various economists have studied aspects of delegation for years (arguably going back at least to Berle and Means, 1932), I will here discuss only Baker et al. (1999).

Baker et al. essentially consider a repeated version of the authority model set forth in Aghion and Tirole (1997). Their key insight is that authority can rarely be fully relinquished: the person who has the right to grant authority to another typically retains the right to rescind that grant at her choosing. If this person exercises that right opportunistically, then the advantages of delegation could be eliminated.

Formally, imagine that a principal hires an agent. By expending effort, $a$, the agent discovers, with probability $qa$, a project that could be undertaken ($0 < q < 1$). Assume the effort choice is binary: either the agent expends effort, $a = 1$, or he does not, $a = 0$. With probability 1/2, the project yields the agent a private benefit of $B_b^A$ and with probability 1/2, the agent's private benefit is $B_g^A$. Independently, the project yields the principal a benefit of $B_b^P$ with probability 1/2 and a benefit of $B_g^P$ with probability 1/2. Independence means that the four possible combinations of benefits are all equally likely. Assume that if there is no project, the benefit to each party is 0. The "b" benefit is bad and the "g" benefit is good in the sense that

$$B_b < 0 < B_g$$

Initially only the agent knows if he has discovered a project and what the benefits are. Before, however, he can undertake a project, he must reveal the benefits to the principal. And although the principal has, in some sense, delegated to the agent the decision to proceed or not with a project, she could, at this point, rescind that authority and veto a project. Assume that the principal cares only about her benefit and the agent cares about benefit minus cost of effort, $C(a)$, where $C(1) = \bar{c}$ and $C(0) = 0$. To close the model, assume

$$B_b^P + B_g^A > 0$$

and

$$\frac{1}{2}qB_g^A > \bar{c} > \frac{1}{4}qB_g^A$$

The first of these means that it is surplus maximizing to undertake a project that has a bad benefit for the principal, but a good benefit for the agent; in other words, it is surplus maximizing to undertake any project that is good for the agent. The meaning of the second expression will become clear in a moment.

Observe that the agent will suppress any project that would give him $B_b^A$. The expected social value, then, of the agent expending effort, *assuming the principal acts to maximize social surplus*, is

$$\frac{1}{2}q\left(B_g^A + \frac{1}{2}B_g^P + \frac{1}{2}B_b^P\right) - \bar{c}$$

(recall that any project that is good for the agent should be pursued). By assumption, this quantity is positive, that is, the organization wants the agent to expend effort. However, in a one-shot game, there is no reason to expect that the principal will act to maximize *social* surplus rather than her own. This means she would veto (rescind authority) whenever the project would yield her $B_b^P$. Since, however, a project that is good for both parties occurs with only probability 1/4, the agent would *not* expend effort if he anticipated this behavior by the principal – recall

$$\bar{c} > \frac{1}{4}qB_g^A$$

Hence, the threat of opportunistic behavior by the principal results in a socially undesirable equilibrium in which the agent does not expend effort.[68]

If, however, the delegation game is repeated, then an equilibrium can exist in which the agent does expend effort each period: provided the principal has never rescinded authority (vetoed a project), the agent expends effort. If the principal previously rescinded authority, the agent expends no effort. For an appropriately large value of $\beta$, this can be shown to be an equilibrium.

How does this relate to corporate culture? Note, as pointed out in footnote 68, one can both conceive of contractual solutions and convincingly argue against the assumptions necessary to rule out such solutions. The only possible merit to the repeated-game solution by Baker et al. (1999) is that it is cheaper than using contracts. In essence, this returns us to the discussion on unforeseen contingencies in the Kreps section. That is, delegation could viewed as a specific application of the more general ideas in Kreps (1990). In particular, delegation could be supported by a culture of worker autonomy or

---

[68] The reader may question this result, noting that there could be contractual solutions. That is right, but following Baker et al. (1999), I am assuming such solutions are not feasible (benefits are observable, but not verifiable). Of course, this assumption could be criticized on the grounds raised by me and my co-authors in Edlin and Hermalin (1999) and Hermalin and Katz (1991, 1993a), but more on this later.

voice. Actions by superiors that are perceived to violate such autonomy are violations of the culture.

## LESSONS

I have intended the discussion in this section to illustrate that some recent work in the economics of organization may have a natural link with the study of corporate culture. I have also sketched out some ways in which this link could be explored or how an appreciation for corporate culture could aid in the interpretation of this work. It is, of course, beyond the scope of this chapter to consider the *entire* economics of organization, but if we did, I am confident that we would find many more potential links to and uses for notions of corporate culture.

## CONCLUSIONS

This chapter has sought to examine how economics has been, to date, integrated into the study of corporate culture and how it might be in the future.

For the most part, I have followed a game-theoretic approach to corporate culture. Following Kreps, I have focused on two kinds of games: coordination games and repeated games in which cooperation is not an equilibrium of the one-shot (stage) game. The focus on coordination games leads to an emphasis on the convention-setting aspect of corporate culture. Having and understanding conventions can prevent coordination failures and economize on other means of ensuring coordination. Repetition can sustain cooperation in games in which cooperation would otherwise be lacking. In many such games, contracting could easily substitute for repetition. As I argued above, culture, as a means of defining appropriate behavior, is what could make repetition the better option: explicitly defining appropriate behavior, particularly in a world with unforeseen contingencies, is difficult and costly. An implicit, culturally given set of definitions would, therefore, be economizing relative to formal contracts.

The analysis of both these kinds of games leads to a view of culture as ultimately being a substitute for explicit communication. That is, culture is an unspoken language giving directives to the members of an organization (a view echoed by Crémer, 1993). Under this view, it might be better to write that a member of the organization *understands* the culture, rather than he or she is *part of* the culture. In particular, one's behavior represents the rational acceptance, based on the preferences one brings to the organization, of the cultural directives. This stands in contrast to the view argued for by Hodgson (1996), Kandel and Lazear (1992), and Rabin (1993) that culture operates by changing one's preferences. In their view, culture is internalized.

Introspection suggests that much of culture must be internalized. My notions of female beauty are probably very similar to most other American males. Moreover, these notions are often at odds with the standard notions of different cultures (e.g. beauty as suggested by Rubens). Certainly among the thoughts I have when I see a beautiful woman is *not*, "Rationally, should I choose to obey the cultural directive to respond to this woman's beauty in the following ways…"

On the other hand, once we as economists begin fooling with preferences, we risk losing the rigor imposed by neo-classical modeling conventions. An old joke illustrates what is at issue:[69]

> A philosophy professor wishes to validate Aristotle's claim that people are driven by the desire to be happy. "Mr. Smith", he asks, "what do you want?" "To make a lot of money." "Why?" "To buy things." "Why?" "Because that makes me happy." "Yes, Mr. Smith is driven by a desire to be happy", exclaims the professor triumphantly. "Ms. Jones, what do you want?" "To be a doctor." "Why?" "To help people." "Why?" "Because I enjoy helping people." "Yes, Ms. Jones is driven by a desire to be happy! And what about you Mr. Brown?" "I want to be sad", replies Mr. Brown with a sly look in his eyes.

If we were allowed to take Mr. Brown's claim at face value, then most of the conclusions of neo-classical economics would be turned on their heads. It is by sticking to a narrow and consistent set of assumptions that we are able to tease out interesting, plausible, and testable conclusions. Or, as John Freeman (1999) writes,

> All theory oversimplifies reality. The question is not so much what is left out, but how much can be explained with the simplest account. Adding variables or complications to the functional form imposes a cost on the theorist. That cost is the difficulty of falsification. If one throws everything that seems to matter into a theory, accounting for *every* observation and *every* anecdote, then falsifiability is threatened. (p. 174, emphasis added)

Playing with preferences is, thus, a potentially dangerous activity. Like other things that are dangerous, but have important uses – fire comes to mind – caution is in order. In particular, to allow culture to shift individuals from being solely self-interested to partially group-interested is a risk. If we are not careful, we will simply assume our conclusions or have a model that is so flexible that it can never be falsified. This is not to suggest that Kandel and Lazear (1992) or Rabin (1993) have been reckless, just that one following a similar approach must (i) exercise the same caution that these authors did and (ii) have strong evidence from experiments, other social sciences, or even biology, to support their assumptions.

Ultimately, it is not economists' comparative advantage to try to resolve the "directive versus internalization" issue.[70] First, there may be no resolution: like light, which can be seen as both a wave and a particle, culture may best be understood from multiple perspectives. Second, were a resolution possible, it likely requires an understanding of psychology, particularly evolutionary psychology, that is beyond the standard training of most economists. What economists can do is to explore the consequences of these assumptions (e.g. as do Crémer, 1993; Kandel and Lazear, 1992; Kreps, 1990; Rabin, 1993). Alternatively, they can seek to model the diffusion of culture as Lazear (1995) does or, for instance, by extending leadership models (e.g. Hermalin, 1998; Rotemberg

---

[69] A version of this joke was originally told to me by the sociologist Marion Levy.

[70] For an additional economist's take on the issue of internalization, see Kreps (1997).

and Saloner, 1993) as I suggested above.[71] Finally, they can employ their insights on costs and benefits, particularly those benefits derived from marketplace interactions, to investigate how organizations might optimally influence their cultures.

The economics of corporate culture is far from settled. Like the western US after Lewis and Clark's expedition, this territory has only begun to be explored – to say nothing of developed.[72] I hope others will find this a fertile territory in which to work.

## ACKNOWLEDGEMENTS

The author thanks Jennifer Chatman, Jacques Crémer, David Kreps, and participants at the Berkeley Faculty Colloquium for comments on an earlier draft. The author also acknowledges the financial support provided by the Willis H. Booth Chair in Banking & Finance, Cornell's Johnson Graduate School of Management, and the NSF under grant SBR-9616675.

## REFERENCES

Aghion, P. and Tirole, J. (1997) Formal and real authority in organizations. Journal of Political Economy, 105(1): 1–29.

Arrow, K.J. (1974) The Limits of Organization. New York: W.W. Norton & Co.

Axelrod, R. (1984) The Evolution of Cooperation. New York: Basic Books.

Baker, G., Gibbons, R.S. and Murphy, K.J. (1999) Informal authority in organizations. Journal of Law, Economics, & Organization, 15(1): 56–73.

Banerjee, A.V. (1992) A simple model of herd behavior. Quarterly Journal of Economics, 108(3): 797–818.

Benhabib, J. and Day, R.H. (1981) Rational choice and erratic behaviour. Review of Economic Studies, 48(3): 459–471.

Berle, A.A. and Means, G.C. (1932) The Modern Corporation and Private Property. New York: Macmillan.

Bernheim, B.D. (1994) A theory of conformity. Journal of Political Economy, 102(5): 841–877.

Bikhchandani, S., Hirshleifer, D. and Welch, I. (1992) A theory of fads, fashion, custom, and cultural changes as informational cascades. Journal of Political Economy, 100(5): 992–1026.

Chatman, J.A. (1991) Matching people and organizations: selection and socialization in public accounting firms. Administrative Science Quarterly, 36(3): 459–484.

Chatman, J.A. and Jehn, K.A. (1994) Assessing the relationship between industry characteristics and organizational culture: how different can you be? Academy of Management Journal, 37(3): 522–553.

Coase, R. (1937) The nature of the firm. Economica, 4: 386–405.

Crémer, J. (1986) Cooperation in ongoing organizations. Quarterly Journal of Economics, 101(1): 33–50.

Crémer, J. (1993) Corporate culture and shared knowledge. Industrial and Corporate Change, 2(3): 351–386.

Dana, J. (1991) Differentiation and emulation in games of strategic choice under uncertainty. Working paper, Department of Economics, Dartmouth College, Hanover, NH.

Dekel, E., Lipman, B.L. and Rustichini, A. (1998) Recent developments in modeling unforeseen contingencies. European Economic Review, 42(3–5): 523–542.

---

[71] As noted earlier, the work of Bikhchandani et al. (1992) and Young (1993, 1998) represent yet further means for economists to study cultural diffusion.

[72] Given that there were indigenous peoples living in the West at the time of Lewis and Clark's expedition, this, admittedly, might not be the most "PC" simile. On the other hand, the notion of an invasion might have considerable resonance with other, non-economist, social scientists.

Edlin, A.S. and Hermalin, B.E. (1999) Renegotiation of agency contracts that are contingent on verifiable signals. Working paper, Walter A. Haas School of Business, University of California, Berkeley, CA.

Erikson, K.T. (1966) Wayward Puritans. New York: Wiley.

Frank, R.H. (1987) If homo economicus could choose his own utility function, would he want one with a conscience? American Economic Review, 77(4): 593–604.

Frank, R.H. (1988) Passions Within Reason. New York: W.W. Norton & Co.

Frank, R.H. (1989) If homo economicus could choose his own utility function, would he want one with a conscience?: reply. American Economic Review, 79(3): 594–596.

Frank, R.H. (1998) Luxury Fever. New York: The Free Press.

Freeman, J. (1999) Efficiency and rationality in organizations. Administrative Science Quarterly, 44(1): 163–175.

Fudenberg, D. and Tirole, J. (1991) Game Theory. Cambridge, MA: MIT Press.

Garicano, L. (1999) A theory of knowledge-based hierarchies: communication, organization and technological choice. Working paper, Graduate School of Business, University of Chicago, Chicago, IL.

Gerth, H.H. and Mills, C.W. (1946) From Max Weber: Essays in Sociology. New York: Oxford University Press.

Gibbons, R.S. (1992) Game Theory for Applied Economists. Princeton, NJ: Princeton University Press.

Gibbons, R.S. (1998) Game theory and garbage cans: an introduction to the economics of internal organization. In J.J. Halpern and R.N. Stern (Eds), Debating Rationality: Nonrational Elements of Organizational Decision Making. Ithaca, NY: ILR Press.

Gibbons, R.S. (1999) Taking Coase seriously. Administrative Science Quarterly, 44(1): 145–157.

Goffman, E. (1963) Stigma: Notes on the Management of Spoiled Identity. Englewood Cliffs, NJ: Prentice-Hall.

Goldsmith, T.H. (1991) The Biological Roots of Human Nature. Oxford: Oxford University Press.

Harrington, J.E. (1989) If homo economicus could choose his own utility function, would he want one with a conscience?: comment. American Economic Review, 79(3): 588–593.

Hart, O.D. (1995) Firms, Contracts, and Financial Structure. Oxford: Oxford University Press.

Hart, O.D. and Holmström, B. (1987) The theory of contracts. In T.F. Bewley (Ed), Advances in Economic Theory Fifth World Congress. Cambridge: Cambridge University Press.

Hermalin, B.E. (1994) Heterogeneity in organizational form: why otherwise identical firms choose different incentives for their managers. RAND Journal of Economics, 25(4): 518–537.

Hermalin, B.E. (1998) Toward an economic theory of leadership: leading by example. American Economic Review, 88(5): 1188–1206.

Hermalin, B.E. (1999) Leading for the long-term. Working paper, Walter A. Haas School of Business, University of California, Berkeley, CA.

Hermalin, B.E. and Isen, A.M. (1999) The effect of affect on economic and strategic decision making. Working paper, Walter A. Haas School of Business, University of California, Berkeley, CA.

Hermalin, B.E. and Katz, M.L. (1991) Moral hazard and verifiability: the effects of renegotiation in agency. Econometrica, 59: 1735–1753.

Hermalin, B.E. and Katz, M.L. (1993a) Defense procurement with unverifiable performance. In J. Leitzel and J. Tirole (Eds), Incentives in Procurement Contracting. Boulder, CO: Westview Press.

Hermalin, B.E. and Katz, M.L. (1993b) Judicial modification of contracts between sophisticated parties: a more complete view of incomplete contracts and their breach. Journal of Law, Economics, & Organization, 9(2): 230–255.

Hodgson, G.M. (1996) Corporate culture and the nature of the firm. In J. Groenewegen (Ed), Transaction Cost Economics and Beyond. Boston, MA: Kluwer Academic Press.

Hofbauer, J. and Sigmund, K. (1988) The Theory of Evolution and Dynamical Systems. Cambridge: Cambridge University Press.

Hofstede, G., Neuijen, B., Ohayv, D.D. and Sanders, G. (1990) Measuring organizational cultures: a qualitative and quantitative study across twenty cases. Administrative Science Quarterly, 35(2): 286–316.

Holmström, B. (1982) Moral hazard in teams. Bell Journal of Economics, 13(2): 324–340.

Kandel, E. and Lazear, E.P. (1992) Peer pressure and partnerships. Journal of Political Economy, 100(4): 801–817.

Kandori, M. (1992) Social norms and community enforcement. Review of Economic Studies, 59(1): 63–80.

Kreps, D.M. (1990) Corporate culture and economic theory. In J.E. Alt and K.A. Shepsle (Eds), Perspectives on Positive Political Economy. Cambridge: Cambridge University Press.

Kreps, D.M. (1997) Intrinsic motivation and extrinsic incentives. American Economic Review, 87(2): 359–364.

Lazear, E.P. (1995) Corporate culture and the diffusion of values. In H. Siebert (Ed), Trends in Business Organization. Tübingen: J.C.B. Mohr (Paul Siebeck).

Lin, C.-C.S. and Png, I. (1998) Kinship, control, and incentives. Working paper, Department of Economics, National Chengchi University, Taiwan.

MacLeod, W.B. (1995) Incentives in organizations: an overview of some of the evidence and theory. In H. Siebert (Ed), Trends in Business Organization. Tübingen: J.C.B. Mohr (Paul Siebeck).

Mas-Colell, A., Whinston, M.D. and Green, J.R. (1995) Microeconomic Theory. Oxford: Oxford University Press.

Maynard Smith, J. (1982) Evolution and the Theory of Games. Cambridge: Cambridge University Press.

Morita, H. (1998) Choice of technology and labor market consequences: explaining U.S.-Japanese differences in management style. Working paper, Department of Economics, Cornell University, Ithaca, NY.

Okuno-Fujiwara, M. (1994) The economic system of contemporary Japan: its structure and possibility of change. Japanese Economic Studies, 22: 76–98.

O'Reilly, C. and Chatman, J.A. (1986) Organizational commitment and psychological attachment: the effects of compliance, identification, and internalization on prosocial behavior. Journal of Applied Psychology, 71(3): 492–499.

O'Reilly, C. and Chatman, J.A. (1996) Culture as social control: corporations, cults, and commitment. In B.M. Staw and L.L. Cummings (Eds), Research in Organizational Behavior, Vol. 18. Greenwich, CT: JAI Press.

Pfeffer, J. (1981) Management as symbolic action: the creation and maintenance of organizational paradigms. In L.L. Cummings and B.M. Staw (Eds), Research in Organizational Behavior, Vol. 3. Greenwich, CT: JAI Press.

Pfeffer, J. (1997) New Directions for Organization Theory. Oxford: Oxford University Press.

Rabin, M. (1993) Incorporating fairness into game theory and economics. American Economic Review, 83(5): 1281–1302.

Rabin, M. (1998) Psychology and economics. Journal of Economic Literature, 36: 11–46.

Rotemberg, J.J. and Saloner, G. (1993) Leadership style and incentives. Management Science, 39(11): 1299–1318.

Rotemberg, J.J. and Saloner, G. (1998) Visionaries, managers, and strategic direction. Working paper, Stanford Graduate School of Business, Palo Alto, CA.

Rubinstein, A. (1998) Modeling Bounded Rationality. Cambridge, MA: MIT Press.

Scharfstein, D.S. and Stein, J.C. (1990) Herd behavior and investment. American Economic Review, 80(3): 465–479.

Schmidt, K.M. (1995) Comment on W. Bentley MacLeod, 'Incentives in organizations: an overview of some of the evidence and theory'. In H. Siebert (Ed), Trends in Business Organization. Tübingen: J.C.B. Mohr (Paul Siebeck).

Tirole, J. (1992) Collusion and the theory of organizations. In J.-J. Laffont (Ed), Advances in Economic Theory: 6th World Congress. Cambridge: Cambridge University Press.

Vandello, J.A. and Cohen, D. (1999) Patterns of individualism and collectivism across the United States. Journal of Personality and Social Psychology, 77(2): 279–292.

Varian, H.R. (1974) Equity, envy, and efficiency. Journal of Economic Theory, 9: 63–91.

Veblen, T. (1899) The Theory of the Leisure Class. New York: Macmillan.

Weibull, J.W. (1995) Evolutionary Game Theory. Cambridge, MA: MIT Press.

Weidensaul, S. (1999) Tracking America's first dogs. Smithsonian, 29(12): 44–57.

Williamson, O. (1975) Markets and Hierarchies: Analysis and Antitrust Implications. New York: The Free Press.

Young, H.P. (1993) The evolution of conventions. Econometrica, 61(1): 57–84.

Young, H.P. (1998) Individual Strategy and Social Structure. Princeton, NJ: Princeton University Press.

# Chapter 11

# Strong Cultures and Innovation: Oxymoron or Opportunity?

**Francis J. Flynn**
*Columbia Business School, Columbia University,
New York, USA*

*and*

**Jennifer A. Chatman**
*Haas School of Business, University of California,
Berkeley, CA, USA*

## INTRODUCTION

Organizational scholars and managers agree that innovation is a critical determinant of organizational survival and success due, in part, to a rapidly changing and increasingly competitive business environment. As Amabile (1997, p. 40) stated, "[i]nnovation is absolutely vital for long-term corporate success... [N]o firm that continues to deliver the same products and services in the same way can long survive. By contrast, firms that prepare for the future by implementing new ideas oriented toward this changing world are likely to thrive." Despite the growing number of studies focusing on innovation, however, our understanding of how organizations cultivate innovation remains limited (Tushman and O'Reilly, 1997).

Case studies of exemplary organizations reveal a set of dimensions associated with innovation success (e.g. Kanter et al., 1997; Robinson and Stern, 1997; Zell, 1997). For example, 3M has created well over 50,000 products (usually over 100 major new products a year) and consistently obtains 30% of its revenue from products developed within the past 4 years (Nicholson, 1998). This constant stream of product innovations has kept 3M in the upper echelon of Fortune 500 firms for several decades and made it one of "America's most admired corporations" (O'Reilly, 1997, p. 60). But, how are 3M consistently and successfully innovative? The people they employed over the years have changed, and many organizations have replicated specific aspects of their structure without ever achieving similar results.

One factor that may have contributed to 3M's sustained innovation success is their strong organizational culture. By emphasizing norms that support the generation and implementation of creative ideas, 3M's culture transcended specific management practices and allowed 3M to be consistently innovative over a long period. To promote creativity, 3M advanced a supportive "value system" that encouraged organizational members to develop original and useful products (Peters and Waterman, 1982). And, the cohesion found among 3M's product development teams was seen as instrumental to implementing these creative ideas as successful product launches. In contrast, the notion that a strong, cohesive culture could be an essential component of innovation in organizations is often viewed with skepticism among academics. Many believe that strong cultures induce uniformity (e.g. Nemeth and Staw, 1989); in their view, ambiguity is needed to promote the behavioral variation essential for creativity in organizations (e.g. Nemeth, 1997). This presents organizational researchers with an intriguing paradox: cultural strength purportedly limits individual creativity, yet creativity may be even better directed, in terms of producing and implementing more relevant and better ideas, in a strong culture that emphasizes particular innovation-enhancing norms.

At the heart of this apparent paradox lies a limited consideration of culture and its effects on creativity and innovation in organizations. In particular, the distinction between culture content and culture strength has been blurred, which, in turn, has clouded the relationship between organizational culture and innovation. Our goal in this chapter is to clarify the impact of culture, particularly in terms of its content and strength, on an organization's ability to innovate.

Focusing on the organization as the level of analysis, we begin our discussion by briefly reviewing and integrating notions of organizational innovation and culture. We find that past research supports a relationship between emphasizing norms that foster creativity and implementation and successful organizational innovation. We then attempt to resolve some of the conflicting evaluations of the culture–innovation relationship by distinguishing between the concepts of culture strength and content. We also examine the purported constraints that group cohesion imposes on the relationship between culture and innovation by pressuring group members to conform to particular norms. Further, we suggest ways that various content-specific norms, particularly those focusing on individualism or collectivism, may be better suited for different stages of the innovation process. Throughout our discussion, we present a set of propositions to help guide future research exploring the relationship between organizational culture and innovation. We conclude by arguing that the apparent paradox between strong organizational culture and innovation results from an overly simplistic view of conformity and culture strength and content.

# DEFINING INNOVATION

Enhancing the creative performance of employees is a critical task for organizations interested in promoting innovation (e.g. Amabile, 1988; Kanter, 1988; Shalley, 1995; Staw, 1990). "When employees perform creatively, they suggest novel and useful products, ideas, or procedures that provide an organization with raw material for subsequent development and implementation" (Oldham and Cummings, 1996, p. 607). However, creativity is not a sufficient condition for innovation. Instead, the term innovation typically refers to the successful implementation of creative ideas. Following Caldwell and O'Reilly (1995), we define innovation as the combination of two processes: (1) creativity, or the generation of new ideas; and (2) implementation, or the actual introduction of the change. For the purpose of our discussion, we assume that creativity and implementation are distinct, sequential stages in the innovation process, although we recognize that the two stages may overlap substantially.

# INNOVATION IN ORGANIZATIONS

Innovation research has focused on identifying the determinants of creative potential at the individual level (e.g. Amabile, 1996) or the structural correlates of innovation at the organizational level (e.g. Cummings, 1965; Kanter, 1988; Thompson, 1965). Less attention has been given to groups of individuals that are charged with developing innovations, yet groups are increasingly responsible for innovation in organizations (e.g. Ancona and Caldwell, 1998). Leavitt (1975) suggested that groups, not individuals, should be the building blocks of organizations partly because they hold greater creative potential, and Hackman (1987) argued that groups may yield more creative products because they benefit from diverse members' interactions. As such, any discussion of organizational innovation should recognize that much of the innovation process occurs within work team environments.

Past research has identified several determinants of group creativity, including leadership, longevity, cohesiveness, heterogeneity, structure, size, communication patterns and resource availability (e.g. King and Anderson, 1990; Payne, 1990). A critical, yet less obvious source of influence on innovation are group norms. West (1990) identified four norms that increased the quantity and quality of group innovations: (1) vision; (2) participative safety; (3) task orientation; and (4) support for innovation. Caldwell and O'Reilly (1995) identified a similar set of cultural norms that focused on (1) support for risk taking, (2) tolerance of mistakes, (3) teamwork, and (4) speed of action.

Cultural norms can be a powerful means of stimulating innovation by attaching social approval to activities that facilitate innovation. Past research has found that norms are central to characterizing how work is conducted at the organizational and group levels (e.g. Chatman and Barsade, 1995; Earley, 1993) and may influence group creativity (e.g. Chatman et al., 1998). Thus, successful innovation may depend on the unique cultural norms that groups develop and the extent to which the group's cultural orientation aligns with, and is supported by, the organization's overall orientation (Amabile et al., 1996). In contrast to creativity research, innovation research has rarely focused on the underlying psychological processes that cause people and groups to develop innovative products and processes. Exploring the link between organizational culture, as it is manifest in norms, and innovation may provide insight into these psychological processes.

## THE RELATIONSHIP BETWEEN CULTURE AND INNOVATION

Though researchers disagree about how to conceptualize and measure organizational culture, it can be understood as a "system of shared values (that define what is important) and norms that define appropriate attitudes and behaviors for organizational members (how to feel and behave)" (O'Reilly and Chatman, 1996, p. 166). As a system of social control, organizational culture can influence members' focus of attention, behavior, and commitment. Through members' clarity about organizational objectives and their willingness to work toward these objectives, culture influences the attainment of valued organizational goals by enhancing an organization's ability to execute its strategy (e.g. Tushman and O'Reilly, 1997). Two primary concerns become relevant using this conceptualization: (1) the extent to which members agree and care about values and norms (culture strength); and (2) the extent to which these norms and values differ across settings (culture content). Further, by conceptualizing culture in terms of observable norms and values that characterize a group or organization, researchers can develop quantitative measurement schemes that allow for the psychometric assessment of core attitudes and behaviors culled from self-reports or observations (e.g. Denison and Mishra, 1995; Enz, 1988; O'Reilly et al., 1991; Rousseau, 1990).

Although researchers and practitioners generally agree that culture influences organizational performance, surprisingly few studies have actually tested this relationship. Denison and Mishra (1995) showed evidence that certain aspects of organizational culture are linked to growth and profitability. Both Gordon and DiTomaso (1992) and Kotter and Heskett (1992) found that firms emphasizing adaptability and change in their cultures were more likely to perform well over time, though the specific reasons for this relationship are unclear. Sorensen (1999) recently reanalyzed the Kotter and Heskett (1992) data and found that organizations with strong cultures performed more consistently over time only when industry volatility was low. Organizational learning may explain this effect. Strong culture firms may be unable to engage in exploration learning, or to discover alternative routines, technologies, and purposes that would be necessary in a volatile industry (Sorensen, 1999, p. 10).

The observation by Sorensen (1999) suggests that, depending on certain conditions, the presence of a strong culture may hinder innovation, yet improve organizational performance in other ways. Many researchers would agree that strong cultures can be detrimental, claiming that strength of agreement, in any form, effectively stunts innovation. Nemeth and Staw (1989), for example, have argued that as cohesion among group (or organizational) members intensifies, groups tolerate less deviation. Purportedly, it is this deviation from group culture, which we conceptualize as agreed upon norms and values, that furnishes the potential for innovation in organizations (Nemeth,

1997). If people are free to express any ideas they wish without fear of reprisal from other members of their group, more creative solutions will be generated.

In support of this argument, Nemeth and Staw (1989) reviewed several studies of conformity in the face of ambiguity, most of which were drawn from the classic Asch (1955) and Milgram (1974) experiments. Here, the presence of strong norms served to enforce a dominant perspective among group members. In an environment where such strong norms are in place, dissenters who may provide alternative perspectives will refrain from voicing their opinions for fear of rejection or ostracism. Instead, according to Nemeth and Staw (1989), many will choose to adopt the dominant perspective or at least affirm it in the presence of their peers. This tendency may be exacerbated in organizations, where "one of the most significant psychological tendencies is a strain toward uniformity, a tendency for people to agree on some issue or to conform to some behavioral pattern" (Nemeth and Staw, 1989, p.175).

Although the above argument makes intuitive sense, it is not exactly clear whether and how agreement limits innovation in organizations. For example, what if the norm that members of an organization expect adherence to is divergent thinking? In an analysis of IDEO, a successful product design firm, Sutton and Hargadon (1996) described how having norms that encouraged people to express "wild ideas" during brainstorming sessions enhanced the innovation process. "Facilitators and participants discourage criticism, even negative facial expression, but often nod, smile, and say 'wow' and 'cool' in response to an idea" (Sutton and Hargadon, 1996, p. 694). Brainstorming norms were strongly enforced in that those who did not conform to the norm to "be outrageous" tended to occupy lower positions of status in the organization.

Like psychologists, organizational sociologists disagree about whether strong cultures may inhibit innovation in organizations. On the one hand, Burns and Stalker (1961) posited that organizations with strong, organic structures were better suited for innovation than were those with mechanistic structures. To accomplish their objectives, organic structures rely on informal sources of control, such as organizational culture, whereas mechanistic structures rely on rules, procedures, and rigidities of formal hierarchy. On the other hand, March (1991) developed a simulation model that compared the ability of strong and weak culture firms to facilitate "exploitation" and "exploration" forms of learning. Tests of this model showed that strong culture organizations learned less from their environments and engaged in less exploration activity. March (1991) attributed this diminished capacity for exploration learning to the rapid socialization rates and resistance to alternative perspectives that characterized strong culture firms.

Finally, some scholars have asserted that organizations with strong cultures may limit their potential for innovation through selection processes. The Schneider (1987) Attraction Selection Attrition (ASA) model suggests that job candidates are more likely to apply to and join firms that they believe hold similar values to their own. If a firm has an easily identifiable culture, which is to say a strong culture, then an efficient self-selection process will probably ensue, assuming that applicants possess some self-insight. Efficient self-selection among potential entrants will increase the level of employee homogeneity in strong culture firms that may subsequently limit their potential for creativity, and in turn, innovation (e.g. Hoffman, 1959). The claim that homogeneity engendered by the selection process limits creativity is dubious, however, because the selection process can also deliberately favor innovation. Firms that value creativity as part of their organizational culture will likely attract highly creative applicants, which, in turn, should enhance their innovative potential. But, rather than debate whether homogeneity caused by efficient selection processes is problematic, it would be more useful to examine whether cultural strength truly hinders organizational innovation. A reasonable first step in this direction would be to clarify our understanding of culture strength and content, two concepts that are closely linked but often misconstrued in innovation research.

## DISTINGUISHING BETWEEN CULTURE STRENGTH AND CULTURE CONTENT, OR CONFORMITY AND UNIFORMITY: A KEY TO THE ORGANIZATIONAL CULTURE–INNOVATION RELATIONSHIP

Are culture and innovation opposing forces in organizations? Answering this question depends, in part, on how culture strength is conceptualized. A strong culture can be understood as one in which cohesion exists about values and behavioral norms, and such norms are consistently and rigorously enforced by all members (e.g. O'Reilly and Chatman, 1996). Here, norms are viewed as legitimate, socially shared standards against which the appropriateness of behavior can be evaluated (Birenbaum and Sagarin, 1976). Cultural norms influence how members perceive and interact with one another, approach decisions, and solve problems. Although the mere existence of norms suggests that there is some *conformity* among organizational or group members, it does not necessarily suggest that there is also *uniformity* among these members. Conformity entails bringing different peoples' interests into agreement, correspondence, or harmony. Uniformity, on the other hand, implies that a group of people is not simply in harmony, but identical to one another in terms of interests, attitudes, and behaviors. This distinction may seem unnecessarily detailed, but it is more than just a semantic clarification.

Norm strength in a group or organization reflects the extent to which members conform to those norms, but not necessarily the extent to which members behave uniformly. Two examples may help illustrate this point. First, a group norm that induces conformity but not uniformity is the understanding that "we agree to disagree". Such a norm can be found in many organizations (e.g. Sutton and Hargadon, 1996; Wetlaufer, 2000) and can be quite effective in achieving efficiency gains in decision making. For example, some organizations use the nominal group technique, in which decision alternatives are ranked by the number of votes from group members, and all members agree to endorse whichever decision alternative receives the most votes (e.g. Henrich and Greene, 1991). Second, cultural values can be characterized by strong norms that foster conformity, but not uniformity. In particular, individualistic cultures tend to value the unique contributions made by each member and the pursuit of individual interests above group interests (Triandis, 1995). Yet, individualistic norms may be strongly enforced, just as collectivistic norms are, if norm strength is defined in terms of agreement and not content. In a recent study of group norms, Chatman and Flynn (2000) found that individualistic and collectivistic groups did not differ significantly in terms of norm strength, which was defined as the extent to which norms were "widely shared" and "strongly held" and measured at three separate times during each group's lifespan. Thus, norm strength and content are independent forces.

There is also confusion about the influence of culture content, which refers to the exact behaviors or attitudes that are valued in a particular culture, on innovation. Some scholars believe that the very presence of shared norms in organizations constrains innovation, regardless of their content (e.g. Nemeth and Staw, 1989). But, the content of norms and the behaviors they support vary widely in organizations. For example, some organizations may have strong norms emphasizing dress (e.g. Pratt and Rafaeli, 1997) whereas other norms may emphasize where people should sit in meetings (e.g. Puffer, 1999) or when they should arrive (e.g. Sutton and Hargadon, 1996). Likewise, some norms emphasize similar thinking among team members, whereas other norms may emphasize divergent thinking (e.g. Sutton and Hargadon, 1996). Members of innovative firms may share the expectation that they will become technical leaders in their industries – which helps to legitimize divergent activity and increase the firm's tolerance for failure (Kanter, 1988).

Perhaps one reason that the concepts of culture content and strength have been blurred is that organizations known to have strong cultures have been compared to controlling and manipulative cults (O'Reilly and Chatman, 1996). In cults, of course, there is no tolerance for non-conformity, only strict adherence to a single set of attitudes, behaviors, and beliefs – that are, unfortunately, frequently dysfunctional and deviant (e.g. Festinger et al., 1964; Galanter, 1989). Japanese firms have often been likened to cults because their employees tend to demonstrate an unusually high level of commitment, bordering on blind allegiance (Lincoln and Kalleberg, 1990). Strong cultures in Japanese firms are established and maintained through the use of company songs, rigorous training programs, exercise sessions, mottoes, uniforms, and sports competitions (Clark, 1979). Similar approaches have been adopted and highly publicized in some US firms, such as Mary Kay Cosmetics (Biggart, 1989), Southwest Airlines (Freiberg et al., 1998), and McDonalds (Kroc, 1977). Each of these organizations has a strong culture, yet the organizational values they emphasize, including unanimity and uniformity, differ from those emphasized by other organizations with equally strong cultures.

Although not as sensationalistic, many firms challenge the link between conformity and uniformity, or culture strength and content. At 3M, for example, organizational norms encourage, reward, and recognize innovative employees and treat their inevitable mistakes as learning experiences, instead of reason for punishment (Nicholson, 1998). Employees at Hewlett-Packard (HP) strongly agree about the norms of the firm, but the norms emphasize individual freedom and autonomy to accomplish work goals (Cole, 1999). To demonstrate its commitment to individual freedom, HP often provides informal rewards, such as the legendary "Medal of Defiance", to employees for instances of useful dissent. Thus, HP's organizational culture is considered strong because of the high level of agreement among employees about "how things are done around here", not because employees work in a synchronous, lock-step pattern of uniformity (Packard, 1995). The manner in which United Hospitals Inc. (UHI), a multi-health-care corporation in the Philadelphia area, developed its corporate culture demonstrates the potential balance between strong culture and differences of opinion. In employee orientations at UHI, time is devoted to discussing "constructive dissent" – the act of making a positive recommendation for change that could result in a negative reaction by a manager (Markowich and Farber, 1989).

Firms with strong cultures can still demonstrate a risk-taking attitude and a high tolerance for conflict. At Coca-Cola, evidence of risk-taking norms can be found in employee meetings, internal publications, and human resource practices (Allen, 1994). The corporate giant even celebrated the 10th anniversary of the launch of New Coke, a notorious failure. According to one executive, "We celebrated the failure because it led to fundamental learning and showed that its okay to fail" (Dutton, 1996, p. 45). At Honda, employees have found a way to harness the benefits of contention and dissent (Pascale, 1993). Takeo Fujisawa, one of Honda's co-founders, observed that when his Japanese employees engaged in a heated discussion, it created a particular "wai-ga-ya-wai-ga-ya" sound. Fujisawa liked the sound and helped institutionalize "Waigaya" discussion sessions, in which rank is irrelevant and dissent is welcomed. American employees at Honda's Marysville, Ohio plant have become accustomed to the Waigaya concept. When an employee or manager is holding back from expressing an opinion during a meeting, he can suggest having a Waigaya session.

At Disney, a company that develops at least two new products a week, from rides at their theme parks, to TV shows and movies, to CD-ROMs and Little Mermaid makeup kits, Michael Eisner encourages a culture based on supportive conflict (Wetlaufer, 2000, p. 116). This includes the use of a "gong show" in which people pitching new animation film ideas are subjected to the possibility of being "gonged" if their ideas are not considered viable. In addition, the animation department holds marathon development meetings designed to force creative ideas out and then edit them without status differences interfering.

In summary, a strong culture can be a powerful form of social control because it provides agreed-upon standards that members may use to assess the appropriateness of their own and others' actions or beliefs. But, it would be incorrect to assume that strong, cohesive organizational cultures induce identical or uniform patterns of thought and behavior among members. As the preceding examples suggest, cohesive organizational cultures can emphasize divergent thinking because *cohesion relates to the strength of group norms rather than their content*. In addition to the anecdotal examples provided above, we examine psychological research on cohesion and the implications for innovation to gain further insight into the relationship between culture and innovation.

# A CLOSER LOOK AT THE EFFECTS OF GROUP COHESION ON INNOVATION

## Cohesion and Creativity

Group cohesion has been defined as "the degree to which members of the group are attracted to each other" (Shaw, 1981, p. 213), "the resultant of all forces acting on all members to remain in the group" (Cartwright, 1968, p. 74), and "the total field of forces that act on members to remain in the group" (Festinger et al., 1950, p. 164). Thus, cohesion specifically focuses on members' interest in maintaining membership, or the attractiveness of a group to its members (Goodman et al., 1987). This appeal of maintaining group membership may result in a higher level of normative agreement among members.

Research on groups has identified several negative consequences stemming from group cohesion that may hinder creativity in organizations. Janis (1982) found that groupthink, which is a pattern of faulty decision making that occurs when like-minded people reinforce one another's tendencies to interpret events and information in similar ways, might be a consequence of group cohesion and homogeneity. Members of homogenous groups, which tend to be highly cohesive, often fail to provide sufficient criticism of other members' ideas and possible alternatives (e.g. Hogg and Hains, 1998). Further, they tend to share only common information with one another (e.g. Gruenfeld et al., 1996) and resist differentiating themselves in order to maintain their relationship with others in the group.

Adopting certain roles, such as a "devil's advocate", can reduce the likelihood of groupthink occurring, even in highly cohesive groups (Janis, 1982). A devil's advocate can be anyone in the group who is willing to argue against a cause or position in order to determine its validity. Research has found that groups using a devil's advocate approach produce higher quality decisions than do groups using a consensual approach (e.g. Schweiger et al., 1986). Having a devil's advocate does not suggest the presence of weak norms, but it may reflect conformity about the value of voicing dissent to improve the group's outcomes. The behavior produced emphasizes a lack of cohesion, in the form of disagreement about task content, as a tactic for enhancing the group product. Realistically then, groupthink only poses a significant threat to performance within groups that do not anticipate its effects and respond appropriately by designing approaches to increase task conflict.

The "risky shift" phenomenon, in which groups tend to make riskier decisions than do individuals, is another negative consequence of group cohesion (e.g. Moscovici and Lecuyer, 1972). Individuals often experience deindividuation in groups (Diener, 1980), and thus are less threatened by and feel less accountable for the negative outcomes of group decisions. Researchers have assumed that risky shifts negatively influence group decision making (Stoner, 1968). Interestingly, the willingness to take risks is considered a positive determinant of creativity (Amabile, 1988) and, in turn, innovation. As individuals, organizational members may be more risk averse due to the personal costs of taking risks and benefits of being critical of risky ideas (e.g. Amabile, 1983). But, in groups, otherwise risk averse individuals may be more willing to consider potentially worthwhile risks. Thus, the risky shift phenomenon may be useful, as long as rationality is not sacrificed in terms of the degree or type of risk adopted. Further research is needed to test the extent to which the risky shift effect inhibits or enhances innovation in groups and organizations.

Escalation of commitment, or the tendency to invest additional time, money, or effort into what are essentially bad decisions or losing courses of action (Staw, 1976) may also influence the link between culture and innovation. Researchers have speculated that escalation of commitment causes decision making groups to retain unsuccessful or outdated ideas rather than adopt new, innovative ideas (e.g. King and Anderson, 1990). Group cohesion may contribute to members' tendencies to escalate their commitment to outdated ideas or processes because, given their interest in maintaining membership in the group, they may be reluctant to raise opposing views and, instead, support continuing down a flawed path (e.g. Gruenfeld et al., 1996; Janis, 1982). As mentioned earlier, developing a bifurcated decision procedure, providing some support for failure, and having an individual who is not invested in the initial decision offer constructive criticism may diminish the potential for irrational group decision making (e.g. Bazerman et al., 1984; Staw and Ross, 1987). Thus, some of the potentially harmful effects of cohesion can be anticipated and addressed through group or organizational design.

Critics who question the potential benefit of a strong culture on innovation argue that cohesion limits organizational members' willingness to deviate from norms (e.g. Nemeth and Staw, 1989). For example, the classic study of group influence by Asch (1955) has been cited as a clear example of how conformity in the face of pressure from fellow group members can result in uniformity of opinion. In the original Asch experiments, subjects were asked to evaluate whether two lines differed in length, usually after hearing a number of incorrect evaluations offered by confederates. Subjects tended to agree with the confederates' preceding evaluations, even when it was obvious they were wrong.

There are two problems with using the Asch experiments as evidence of the negative effects of social cohesion on innovation. First, subjects in the Asch studies generally had no prior relationship with one another, and thus it is likely that they had no sense of group cohesion. If they were a cohesive group, the study's results might have been different. Although it may sound counterintuitive, group cohesion might actually *increase* group members' willingness to deviate from some norms because cohesion provides members with a comfortable level of psychological safety that allows them to engage in divergent thinking and risk-taking behavior (Nystrom, 1979). As Nystrom (1979, p. 45) explained, when cohesiveness is high, a person recognizes "that he is not alone responsible for possible failures, which is reassuring". Such a high level of trust among members is invaluable because members must be willing to share information, particularly divergent information, in order to achieve optimal group performance (Nemeth, 1992). Second, because no explicit norms were established in these experimental settings *ex ante*, subjects utilized their knowledge about existing norms of social interaction, which emphasize adherence to the majority perspective. However, organizations are unique social settings; as such, common social norms do not always apply within them (Spataro, 2000). Indeed, it is plausible that organizations may develop specific norms that run counter to societal norms (e.g. Galanter, 1989). Therefore, researcher cannot assume that group cohesion inhibits innovation without studying norms as they exist in real organizational groups.

The assumption that norms promoting social cohesion will, in turn, discourage creativity is troublesome. In truth, there are many norms associated with cohesiveness that are necessary to promote creativity. For example, a norm mandating that organizational members share information will not only increase interaction and cohesion, but also expose members to diverse perspectives (e.g. Nemeth, 1992). And, past research suggests that a norm to entertain any brainstorming idea, no matter how wild and outrageous, is necessary in fostering creativity and is more likely to be found in highly cohesive groups within organizations (e.g. Sutton and Hargadon, 1996).

Nemeth (1997) argued that with each incidence of dissent, which is a position or idea that differs from the dominant one, creativity would increase linearly. "One must feel free to 'deviate' from expectations, to question shared ways of viewing things, in order to evidence creativity" (Nemeth, 1997, p. 60). Of course, this may be true only if norms allow for such disagreements to emerge in a productive manner. We concur that dissenting opinion can be useful in generating creative ideas, but dissenting opinions are often discounted for a variety of reasons that are unrelated to the quality of the opinion. In particular, ideas emanating from dissent for the sake of dissent or due to political conflict are not likely to be acknowledged. Rather, norms that foster greater tolerance of intellectual debate are more likely to engender creative ideas (e.g. Sutton and Hargadon, 1996).

We suggest that certain strong norms can facilitate the generation and expression of creative ideas. Strong norms that reward information sharing, particularly unique pieces of information, and emphasize greater tolerance for intellectual debate should reduce inhibitions and encourage divergent thinking (e.g. Stasser and Stewart, 1992). Further, norms that require organizational members to build upon others' ideas rather than limit their attention to their own ideas are vital to creativity (Sutton and Hargadon, 1996). Without a combination of diverse perspectives, groups charged with generating creative ideas may adopt the best individual idea rather than utilize their combined potential (Chatman et al., 1998). Taken together, this suggests the following proposition:

**Proposition 1.** Members of organizations that strongly agree and care about norms that encourage the expression of creative ideas (e.g. brainstorming, uncensored idea generation) will generate more creative ideas than those who agree less and/or care less about such norms.

## Cohesion and Implementation

Our discussion thus far has focused on the creative component of innovation. To understand how organizational culture influences innovation, however, it is important to also consider how creative ideas are implemented, that is, whether a new idea becomes a reality (Caldwell and O'Reilly, 1995). Although many claim that innovation is hampered by social cohesion, few would disagree with the notion that cohesion is necessary to implement creative ideas. Keller (1986) found that cohesion among members of R&D teams, whose primary role is to identify and develop new products, predicted their performance. Further, cohesiveness and participation predicted the quality and number of innovations produced (Anderson and West, 1998). And, innovative organizations were characterized by teamwork, effective (e.g. frequent, clear) communication, and interdepartmental cooperation, factors akin to social cohesion (Pillinger and West, 1995).

Researchers have outlined at least three advantages of social cohesion and informal control yielded by strong cultures as opposed to the formal control provided by hierarchical structures (Ebers, 1995; Kunda, 1992; O'Reilly and Chatman, 1996): (1) clearer direction for employees under ambiguous circumstances; (2) decreased need for monitoring and surveillance due to increased internalization of organizational objectives; and (3) increased satisfaction and decreased reactance despite the reduced individual freedom imposed by social control. The first of these advantages, providing direction when employees are faced with uncertainty, may be particularly important to implement innovations. The implementation of a creative idea is, by definition, a novel experience, and therefore, the confidence to take action in the face of ambiguity is essential to success. Kanter (1988) described the implementation of an innovation as an ambiguous process requiring extraordinary commitment, conviction, and enthusiasm by "champions", who attempt to manage the disruptive pattern of the innovation process and guide members' efforts in the desired direction. But, the need for champions can be reduced if organizations have developed cohesive norms supporting the innovation process. Just as unproven firms benefit from associations with others (e.g. Podolny, 1993), developing a coalition of supporters for an unproven innovative idea may provide a signaling function that facilitates its implementation. In other words, even if the quality of the idea itself is not readily apparent, the strength of group consensus may be compelling to skeptics.

Although cohesion among organizational members is likely to be associated with higher levels of agreement, it is possible that such agreement is variegated, applying to some processes but not others. For example, members of a cohesive organization may agree about their general approach to performing tasks, but lack agreement about specific methods to adopt in specific situations. Cohesive organizations may be innovative if they possess a high level of *process agreement* (e.g. Jehn, 1995) in order to complete tasks successfully and efficiently, but not *intellectual agreement*, which refers to the similarity of ideas and opinions they contribute that may limit their potential for creative thinking. The willingness to yield to others during the implementation stage may be one outcome of social cohesion. Past research found that when members' mental images of how a task should be approached and completed concurred, task accomplishment proceeded with relatively little conflict and uncertainty (Bettenhausen and Murnighan, 1991, p. 21). Thus, social cohesion, here conceptualized in terms of shared norms, can facilitate implementation for the very reason that it, allegedly, inhibits creativity.

We suggest that certain strong norms can facilitate the implementation of creative ideas. In particular, emphasizing task-oriented norms that focus on members' cooperation may determine the success of the implementation process (Abbey and Dickson, 1983). Norms that encourage adherence to an organizationally universal plan of action and preset deadlines should be more efficient for organizations striving to use innovation as a competitive advantage. By emphasizing a uniform approach to the work process during the implementation stage, organizations will be better equipped to deliver creative ideas quickly, as we suggest in the following proposition:

**Proposition 2.**   Members of organizations that both agree and care more about the value of task-oriented norms (e.g. being decisive, meeting deadlines) will be more likely to implement creative ideas successfully than will members of organizations that agree and/or care less about task-oriented norms.

To summarize, past theory and research on innovation suggests an interesting paradox: strong cultural norms may limit individual creativity, yet organizations require cohesion to implement creative ideas. How can organizations reconcile this inherent conflict? We propose that this paradoxical relationship between cohesion and innovation can be resolved by recognizing that normative agreement does not necessarily stifle creativity. Rather, it is the content (what is regulated) of group norms that determine innovation success. In the next section, we focus on a specific dimension of cultural norms, individualism–collectivism, and explain how each end of the continuum may be linked to different stages of the innovation process.

# THE ROLE OF INDIVIDUALISTIC AND COLLECTIVISTIC NORMS IN THE INNOVATION PROCESS

In our discussion of the relationship between organizational culture and innovation, we have proposed two critical ideas about the nature of norms. First, though norms are a powerful means of social control, they do not necessarily restrict and constrain members' abilities to be creative, and indeed, we have suggested that agreement on certain norms may lead to more, rather than less, innovation. Second, norms are often misconstrued as rigid rules of behavior that apply inflexibly in all social situations. However, as socially constructed standards, norms, and behavior emanating from norms, can be adjusted according to the mandate of their adherents. This second point is most critical in reconciling the culture–innovation paradox. Because norms are socially shared standards, organizational members should be able to emphasize different norms depending on whether the immediate objective is to generate creative ideas or implement them.

Two implicit assumptions found in the literature on norms may weaken this argument. One assumption is that every group, or organization, promotes a single set of norms, which is applicable in all situations. But, realistically, different norms may emerge or diminish at different times during the duration of a project (e.g. Chatman and Flynn, 2000; Gersick, 1988; Jehn and Mannix, 1998). For example, norms supporting team meeting attendance or the full participation of all team members may not exist early on in a project's lifespan because the pressure to complete the task is minimal. However, as the task deadline approaches, norms for meeting attendance and full participation by members may change, such that members are expected to attend and participate in all team meetings and decisions. Similarly, different norms may exist during the creativity stage of innovation than during the implementation stage. For example, norms may encourage members to offer novel, even outrageous, alternatives during the creativity stage, but disapprove of these suggestions during the implementation stage (e.g. Caldwell and O'Reilly, 1995).

Another problematic assumption is that cultural norms simply emerge – they cannot be intentionally constructed. Indeed, norms can be constructed, although perhaps more easily among groups of neophytes than members who share tenure and familiarity (Levine and Moreland, 1990). In a laboratory study, Chatman and her colleagues (Chatman and Barsade, 1995; Chatman et al., 1998) manipulated whether teams held collectivistic or individualistic norms simply by changing a few words and hypothetical compensation schemes in the materials presented to subjects the night before an experiment. Participants' behaviors were significantly affected by these seemingly minor differences. At IDEO, Sutton and Hargadon (1996) reported that brainstorming norms were simply posted on the wall to indoctrinate newcomers and remind existing members about how they should behave in all brainstorming sessions.

Given that norms can be established easily and may change according to the mandate of their adherents, researchers should focus on identifying which norms may be more appropriate for each stage of the innovation process. Some norms would obviously foster creativity (e.g. rewarding creative thinking, willingness to take risks), but there are also more subtle and pervasive norms that may influence members' willingness to both express and implement creative ideas. In particular, the concept of individualism–collectivism, which refers to the conceptualization of the self as either independent or interdependent in relation to others, can be used to describe how members of organizations interact with one another (e.g. Chatman et al., 1998; Earley, 1989, 1993). We propose that the overarching cultural dimension of individualism–collectivism may infuse the norms found in organizations, which, in turn, set the context for innovation.

## Individualism and Collectivism

Individualism can be defined as a social pattern that consists of loosely linked individuals who view themselves as independent of collectives, are primarily motivated by their own preferences, needs, rights, and the contracts they have established with others, give priority to their personal goals over the goals of others, and emphasize rational analyses of the advantages and disadvantages of associating with others (Triandis, 1995). The concept of individualism could be misconstrued as weak culture, but, in our view, individualism is a particular dimension of culture in which the self is defined as independent and autonomous from collectives. It represents the content of a culture and not its strength. Organizations seeking innovation may find it desirable to emphasize individualistic norms because they encourage members to pursue individual aspirations and allow members to confront and challenge one another without fear of reprisal (Triandis, 1995).

This is not to suggest that the complementary concept of collectivism is unsuitable for organizations seeking innovation. Collectivism can be referred to as a social pattern consisting of closely linked individuals who see themselves as parts of a collective (e.g.

family, coworkers, tribe, nation), are primarily motivated by the norms of, and duties imposed by, the collective, are willing to give priority to the goals of the collective over their own personal goals, and emphasize their connectedness to members of the collective (Triandis, 1995). A collectivistic orientation may help foster innovation in organizations by focusing members' attention on superordinate goals. For example, organizations increasingly use cross-functional teams, in part, to enhance the potential for product and process innovation (Shapiro, 1992). These functionally diverse teams can be difficult to manage because members' interests and points of view vary. A collectivistic orientation, emphasizing innovation as a collective goal over varying individual goals, increases the likelihood that such diverse teams will produce innovative outcomes (Chatman et al., 1998).

Past discussions of organizational or group creativity have often overlooked the benefits of keeping members' attention focused on a common goal. Rather, researchers have concentrated on the fundamental importance of dissent in enhancing creativity (e.g. Nemeth, 1997). But, without a shared schema that orients members toward a common goal, dissent could eventually lead to unproductive chaos. Dissent, or divergent thinking, can still be emphasized in collectivistic organizational cultures, so long as it is viewed as being useful in achieving the superordinate goal of innovation. Even in strong, collectivistic cultures, dissenting ideas will not necessarily be viewed as defiant. Instead, members will tend to accept ideas that are consistent with their collective values and reject ideas that challenge those values. If the collective value is dissent for the sake of creativity, then dissent will be welcomed and encouraged.

Some critics may argue that an individualistic emphasis is more appropriate when the goal is innovation because it will encourage the individual motivation and autonomy necessary to be creative. However, an organization with an individualistic orientation may be less likely to capitalize on its potential synergy and members may be less willing to both discount their own ideas and endorse their peers' superior ideas. Conversely, members of organizations emphasizing collectivistic norms and cooperation (Wagner, 1995) will be more likely to support an idea selected by the majority of members and agree upon an approach to its implementation (Erez, 1992). Thus, we propose that emphasizing collectivism will be more likely to result in the generation and implementation of innovative ideas than will emphasizing individualism. However, we add one critical caveat – that, when emphasizing collectivism, the goal would need to shift from divergent thinking during the creativity stage to consensus thinking during the implementation stage. This suggests the following propositions:

**Proposition 3.**   Organizations emphasizing collectivistic norms and divergent thinking will perform better during the creativity stage (e.g. generating more ideas) of innovation than will organizations emphasizing only one or the other, or neither, or both at a low level.

**Proposition 4.**   Organizations emphasizing collectivistic norms and non-divergent thinking will perform better during the implementation stage (e.g. speed of getting the product or service out the door) of innovation than will organizations emphasizing only one or the other, or neither, or both at a low level.

## Vertical and Horizontal Varieties of Individualism–Collectivism

Researchers have suggested that individualism and collectivism exist in horizontal and vertical forms (e.g. Triandis, 1996). In some cultures, hierarchy is most important, and in-group authorities regulate the behavior of in-group members (Vertical). In other cultures, social behavior is more egalitarian; that is, each member is treated as an equal (Horizontal). The vertical and horizontal varieties of individualism and collectivism may also be germane to the process of innovation. We have already suggested that emphasizing collectivism will contribute to organizational innovation so long as norms emphasize divergent thinking during the creativity stage and non-divergent thinking during the implementation stage. But, the extent to which a collectivistic group or organization is able to engender divergent thinking during the creativity stage may depend on the strength of its egalitarian emphasis, that is, the extent to which the horizontal form of collectivism exists. If members believe they are among peers, they will be less likely to censor their opinions than if they were in the presence of members with hierarchical authority over them. For example, an Israeli kibbutz is considered a highly collectivistic group, but because of their egalitarian emphasis, members welcome and even encourage intellectual arguments. Conversely, a collectivistic group or organization may be better able to promote non-divergent thinking during the implementation stage if norms support an authoritarian (vertical) social structure, such that lower status members deferred to higher ranking leaders. This suggests the following proposition:

**Proposition 5.** Collectivistic organizations that emphasize the horizontal form of collectivism during the creativity stage and the vertical form during the implementation stage will produce more and higher quality innovations.

## Radical and Routine Innovation as an Organizational Goal

Organizational goals must also be considered when constructing norms to foster innovation. Organizations may have different objectives that depend on their unique combination of strategy, resources, and existing market conditions (Nord and Tucker, 1987). For example, different types of behavior are needed to successfully complete radical, compared to routine, innovations (Zaltman et al., 1973). Further, past research has found that a country's national culture influences the organizational cultures of home country firms (e.g. Hofstede, 1991; Hofstede et al., 1990). Debate exists about whether American companies, which tend to be more individualistic, are better suited to develop radical innovations and whether Japanese firms, which tend to be more collectivistic, are better suited to develop routine innovations (e.g. Botkin, 1986). Because collectivistic norms demand adherence to a uniform approach to the work process, such norms yield greater efficiency, an essential component of routine innovation (Chatman and Flynn, 2000). Conversely, an individualistic orientation may be more appropriate if the goal is radical innovation because these firms are more likely to engage in "exploration learning", which is required in radical innovation (March, 1991).

These arguments imply that collectivistic organizations may be better suited to develop routine innovations and individualistic organizations may be better suited to develop radical innovations. However, we propose that a collectivistic orientation is better suited to generate both radical and routine forms of innovation in organizations. Although organizations in collectivistic countries may choose to develop routine innovations as a competitive strategy, it is not necessarily the case that the same organizations would be incapable of developing radical innovations if that were their explicit goal. Granted, adherence to a common goal will facilitate the implementation process, which is of paramount importance in routine innovation. But, collectivism also promotes the smooth flow of communication, which increases the sharing of knowledge, ideas, and information that enhances radical innovation (Erez, 1992). Therefore, whether the desired product is radical or routine, if members focus on innovation *as an organizational goal*, then synergy will be enhanced without inhibiting creativity, suggesting the following proposition:

**Proposition 6.**   Organizations with a collectivistic orientation will be more likely to develop successful radical and routine innovations than will organizations with an individualistic orientation.

## Heterogeneity and Individualism–Collectivism

Nystrom (1979) attempted to resolve the culture–innovation paradox by suggesting that member composition be altered according to the current stage of the innovation process. Early on, loosely joined heterogeneous groups should be constructed to facilitate the creative process, but as the creative idea becomes more clearly formulated, groups should be more cohesive and homogenous in order to facilitate implementation. Although intuitively appealing, the problem with this suggestion is the coordination difficulties it presents. It is doubtful that such a structural transition could be achieved in practice because any given group, or organization, may be involved in the introduction of several innovations at the same time, all at different stages in the process (King and Anderson, 1990). And, specific technical suggestions may be too great for more than one work team to grasp. Finally, the "implementation team" may lose the benefits of members' commitment generated by having had input into the task early on (Kanter, 1988).

The role of heterogeneity in enhancing innovation is complex. Cognitive and experiential diversity may add to the perspectives generated within an organization and facilitate clarifying, organizing, and combining novel approaches to accomplishing work goals (Jehn et al., 1999; Thomas and Ely, 1996). However, heterogeneous work groups tend to be less socially integrated and experience more communication problems, more conflict, and higher turnover rates than do homogeneous groups (Jackson et al., 1991; O'Reilly et al., 1989; Zenger and Lawrence, 1989). Further, employees who are more different from their co-workers report feeling more uncomfortable and less attached to their employing organization (Tsui et al., 1992). Thus, highly diverse organizations may have a more difficult time implementing creative ideas.

Decreasing the salience of members' individual differences and increasing the extent to which their organizational identity is salient can increase members' commitment and contributions to work goals (e.g. Chatman et al., 1998). With a collectivistic orientation that emphasizes group membership over other salient categories (such as demography or functional background), groups can retain the benefits of increased heterogeneity in, for example, past experience, while still maintaining sufficient cohesion necessary for effective implementation (Chatman and Flynn, 2000). This suggests the following proposition:

**Proposition 7.** Organizations employing members who are more heterogeneous will produce significantly more and higher quality innovations when they emphasize collectivistic versus individualistic norms, while organizations employing members who are more homogeneous will produce similarly moderate innovation regardless of whether their culture emphasizes individualistic or collectivistic norms.

## Patterns of Interpersonal Conflict and Individualism–Collectivism

Research that demonstrates the advantages of a collectivistic orientation on work team behavior (e.g. Wagner, 1995) suggests that collectivistic groups suffer from conflict less than do individualistic groups (e.g. Chatman et al., 1998). But, all groups and organizations, even those that are collectivistic, develop clear patterns of interpersonal conflict. The usefulness of such conflict, particularly how it helps or hinders innovation, may depend on its form and timing. For example, Jehn and Mannix (1998) showed that groups performed more effectively when task conflict was moderately high during the middle of the project, and process and relationship conflict were relatively constant at moderate and low levels, respectively, throughout the entire project. Certain types of conflict may be more appropriate for specific stages of innovation. Teams with higher levels of task conflict will produce more creative products, but, as argued previously, task conflict will be less desirable during the implementation stage. Relationship and process conflict, which are detrimental to group performance (e.g. Jehn, 1997), may be less desirable in both the creativity and implementation stages of innovation.

We argue that more beneficial patterns of conflict will emerge when collectivistic norms are emphasized. In an organization characterized by a collectivistic culture, relationship conflict would likely be minimized throughout the innovation process because collectivism promotes harmonious relationships among team members whereas an individualistic culture does not (Triandis, 1995). Process conflict should also be minimized given that members of collectivistic cultures adopt a uniform approach to task accomplishment (Earley, 1994). And, if collectivistic organizations succeed in promoting divergent thinking during the creativity stage and non-divergent thinking during the implementation stage, then task conflict will occur when it can contribute most, during the creativity stage.

**Proposition 8.** Organizations emphasizing collectivistic norms that also emphasize divergent thinking during the creativity stage and non-divergent thinking during the implementation stage will experience more beneficial conflict (task conflict) during the creativity stage, and less detrimental conflict (process and relational) throughout the project's duration.

To better understand the relationship between organizational culture and innovation, we focused on distinguishing between culture content and culture strength, two concepts that are fundamental to the culture–innovation relationship. Our primary conclusion from this discussion is that organizational culture will be more likely to contribute to the innovation process when members strongly agree and care about norms that emphasize divergent thinking when creativity is desired and non-divergent thinking when implementation is the goal. A number of additional complexities influence this relationship, however, and should be considered in future research. In particular, organizations are made up of an array of norms (e.g. Chatman, 1991; O'Reilly et al., 1991). Thus, the entire profile of norms that characterizes an organization's culture must be considered, rather than simply examining the extent to which, for example, individualism or collectivism is emphasized. Second, researchers need to examine how formal incentives may reward innovation and behaviors leading to innovation, although it is not completely clear whether such incentives will enhance, by demonstrating the organization's commitment to innovation, or diminish member's intrinsic motivation to be creative (Amabile, 1996). Finally, various exogenous conditions, such as the pace and accessibility of external technological developments and the availability of capable employees in the labor pool, will affect the relationship between organizational culture and innovation.

## CONCLUSION

We have argued that the relationship between culture and innovation is more complex than described in past research, which has proposed that normative agreement hinders innovation, particularly its creative component (e.g. Nemeth and Staw, 1989). Rather, the impact of culture strength on innovation depends on the nature of agreement more than its mere existence. If members collectively exhibit a higher level of agreement about the manner in which creative ideas should be generated, such as developing a brainstorming process, rather than what creative ideas should look like, greater creativity may emerge (e.g. Sutton and Hargadon, 1996). Further, research suggests that cohesion, which is derived from normative agreement, should facilitate the implementation process (e.g. Anderson and West, 1998; Keller, 1986). Although some argue that organizations cannot maintain these two seemingly conflicting sets of norms, we suggest that organizational norms emerge from the situational demands at hand, not just from members' attributes (e.g. West and Anderson, 1996). Thus, when the nature of an organization's task changes, norms can change accordingly.

The extant innovation literature lacks an agreed upon theoretical model that explains the conditions under which innovation is most likely to occur. To date, most attempts to model the characteristics contributing to innovation have focused on one component of innovation or another, either creativity or implementation, rather than considering the complete innovation process. Future research might reconcile this problem by focusing on the role that organizational culture plays in the innovation process. While some research shows that strong norms, or higher levels of cohesiveness, may lead to less creativity, simple generalizations from these findings may be incorrect. Instead, agreement and intensity about certain configurations of norms may enhance, rather than hinder, both the creativity and implementation components of the innovation process. Specifically, promoting horizontal (egalitarian) collectivism during the creativity stage will encourage the divergent thinking necessary to engender creativity and promoting vertical (authoritarian) collectivism during the implementation stage will encourage the non-divergent thinking necessary to facilitate implementation. By focusing on the collective goal of innovation throughout the entire process, organizations may achieve this duality and capitalize on their creative potential, which is derived from member heterogeneity and interpersonal conflict.

Our objective in this chapter has been to increase the salience of the distinction between conformity and uniformity in order to clarify the relationship between organizational culture and innovation. We argued that strong organizational cultures increase conformity among members through various selection and socialization practices that have been described by organizational culture researchers (e.g. O'Reilly and Chatman, 1996). These practices increase group cohesion, and ultimately, members' willingness to conform to organizational norms. But, conformity of this sort is not necessarily a detriment to innovation because, we argue, it can be distinguished from the content of the cultural norms emphasized. That is, cultures can emphasize conformity, in the form of adherence to shared norms, without dictating that members' behavior be identical to one another, or uniform. Though it might be more difficult to establish creativity enhancing norms in cohesive groups, it is still unclear why, and to what extent, this is true. Given the potential advantages of cohesion in facilitating the implementation of innovation that we have outlined here, future research should explore ways in which cohesion *could* also engender creativity.

We, therefore, propose that the culture–innovation paradox is not a paradox at all. Instead, the paradox misnomer stems from a conceptual misunderstanding about culture strength and content, two concepts that are clearly unique, but are often blurred in the innovation literature. Organizations can strike a balance between creativity and social control by developing cultural norms that foster the divergence and uniqueness necessary for the creative process to occur and still maintain the cohesion among members necessary to develop and implement creative ideas. Adherence to such norms will likely reduce the political and ego-based conflict that might exist among members who fail to trust and cooperate with one another and will be less likely to result in uniform attitudes, ideas, and behavior. Members may be highly committed to and intensely value non-conformity such that they encourage the contribution of divergent ideas and challenges to existing routines. Thus, the presence of strong organizational norms, depending on their orientation, may promote the attitudes and behaviors that are critical to organizational innovation.

# REFERENCES

Abbey, A. and Dickson, J.W. (1983) R&D work climate and innovation in semiconductors. Academy of Management Journal, 26(2): 362–368.

Agrell, A. and Gustafson, R. (1994) The Team Climate Inventory (TCI) and group innovation: a psychometric test on a Swedish sample of work groups. Journal of Occupational & Organizational Psychology, 67(2): 143–151.

Allen, F. (1994) Secret Formula: How Brilliant Marketing and Relentless Salesmanship Made Coca-Cola the Best-Known Product in the World. New York: HarperBusiness.

Amabile, T.M. (1983) The Social Psychology of Creativity. New York: Springer-Verlag.

Amabile, T.M. (1988) A model of creativity and innovation in organizations. In B. Staw and L. Cummings (Eds), Research in Organizational Behavior, pp. 123–167. Greenwich, CT: JAI Press.

Amabile, T.M. (1996) Creativity in Context: Update to "The Social Psychology of Creativity". Boulder, CO: Westview Press.

Amabile, T.M. (1997) Motivating creativity in organizations: on doing what you love and loving what you do. California Management Review, 40(1): 39–58.

Amabile, T.M., Conti, R., Coon, H., Lazenby, J., et al. (1996) Assessing the work environment for creativity. Academy of Management Journal, 39(5): 1154–1184.

Ancona, D. and Caldwell, D. (1998) Rethinking team composition from the outside in. In M. Neale, B. Mannix and D. Gruenfeld (Eds), Research on Groups and Teams, Vol. 1. Greenwich, CT: JAI Press.

Anderson, N.R. and West, M.A. (1998) Measuring climate for work group innovation: development and validation of the Team Climate Inventory. Journal of Organizational Behavior, 19(3): 235–258.

Asch, S. (1955) Opinions and social pressure. Scientific American, 193(5): 31–35.

Bazerman, M.H., Giuliano, T. and Appelman, A. (1984) Escalation of commitment in individual and group decision making. Organizational Behavior & Human Decision Processes, 33: 87–98.

Bettenhausen, K.L. and Murnighan, J.K. (1991) The development of an intragroup norm and the effects of interpersonal and structural challenges. Administrative Science Quarterly, 36: 20–35.

Biggart, N.W. (1989) Charismatic Capitalism: Direct Selling Organizations in America. Chicago, IL: University of Chicago Press.

Birenbaum, A. and Sagarin, E. (1976) Norms and Human Behavior. New York: Praeger.

Botkin, J. (1986) Transforming creativity into innovation: processes, prospects, and problems. In R. Kuhn (Ed), Frontiers in Creative and Innovative Management, pp. 25–40. Cambridge, MA: Ballinger.

Burns, T. and Stalker, G.M. (1961) The Management of Innovation. London: Tavistock.

Caldwell, D.F. and O'Reilly, C.A. (1995) Norms supporting innovation in groups: an exploratory analysis. Paper presented at the 54th Annual Meetings of the Academy of Management.

Cartwright, D. (1968) The nature of group cohesiveness. In D. Cartwright and A. Zander (Eds), Group Dynamics, 3rd Edn, pp. 91–109. New York: Harper & Row.

Chatman, J.A. (1991) Matching people and organizations: selection and socialization in public accounting firms. Administrative Science Quarterly, 36(3): 459–484.

Chatman, J.A. and Barsade, S. (1995) Personality, organizational culture, and cooperation: evidence from a business simulation. Administrative Science Quarterly, 40: 423–443.

Chatman, J.A. and Flynn, F.J. (2000) The influence of demographic composition on the emergence and consequences of cooperative norms in work teams. Academy of Management Journal, (in press).

Chatman, J.A., Polzer, J., Barsade, S. and Neale, M. (1998) Being different yet feeling similar: the influence of demographic composition and organizational culture on work processes and outcomes. Administrative Science Quarterly, 41: 423.

Clark, R. (1979) The Japanese Company. New Haven, CT: Yale University Press.

Cole, R.E. (1999) Managing Quality Fads: How American Business Learned to Play the Quality Game. New York: Oxford University Press.

Cummings, L.L. (1965) Organizational climates for creativity. Academy of Management Journal, 3: 220–227.

Denison, D.R. and Mishra, A.K. (1995) Toward a theory of organizational culture and effectiveness. Organization Science, 6(2): 204–223.

Diener, E. (1980) Deindividuation: the absence of self-awareness and self-regulation in group members. In P. Paulus (Ed), Psychology of Group Influence, pp. 209–242. Hillsdale, NJ: Erlbaum.

Dutton, G. (1996) Enhancing creativity. Management Review, 85(11): 44–46.

Earley, C.P. (1989) Social loafing and collectivism: a comparison of the United States and the People's Republic of China. Administrative Science Quarterly, 34: 565–581.

Earley, C.P. (1994) Self or group? Cultural effects of training on self-efficacy and performance. Administrative Science Quarterly, 39(1): 89–117.

Ebers, M. (1995) The framing of organizational cultures. Research in the Sociology of Organizations, Vol. 13, pp. 129–170. Greenwich, CT: JAI Press.

Enz, C. (1988) The role of value congruity in intraorganizational power. Administrative Science Quarterly, 33: 284–304.

Erez, M. (1992) Interpersonal communication systems in organisations, and their relationship to cultural values, productivity, and innovation: the case of Japanese Corporations. Applied Psychology: an International Review, 41(1): 43–64.

Festinger, L., Schachter, S. and Back, K. (1950) Social Pressures in Informal Groups. New York: Harper & Row.

Festinger, L., Riecken, H.W. and Schachter, S. (1964) When Prophecy Fails: a Social and Psychological Study of a Modern Group that Predicted the Destruction of the World. New York: Harper Torchbooks.

Freiberg, K., Freiberg, J. and Peters, T. (1998) Nuts!: Southwest Airlines' Crazy Recipe for Business and Personal Success. New York: Bantam Doubleday.

Galanter, M. (1989) Cults: Faith, Healing, and Coercion. New York: Oxford University Press.

Gersick, C.J.G. (1988) Time and transition in work teams: toward a new model of group development. Academy of Management Journal, 41: 9–41.

Goodman, P., Ravlin, E. and Schminke, M. (1987) Understanding groups in organizations. In L.L. Cummings and B. Staw (Eds), Research in Organizational Behavior, pp. 121–173. Greenwich, CT: JAI Press.

Gordon, G.G. and DiTomaso, N. (1992) Predicting corporate performance from organizational culture. Journal of Management Studies, 29(6): 783–798.

Gruenfeld, D.H., Mannix, E.A., Williams, K.Y. and Neale, M.A. (1996) Group composition and decision making: how member familiarity and information distribution affect process and performance. Organizational Behavior & Human Decision Processes, 67(1): 1–15.

Hackman, J.R. (1987) The design of work teams. In J. Lorsch (Ed), Handbook of Organizational Behavior, pp. 315–342. Englewood Cliffs, NJ: Prentice-Hall.

Henrich, T.R. and Greene, T.J. (1991) Using the nominal group technique to elicit roadblocks to an MRP II: implementation. Computers & Industrial Engineering, 21(1–4): 335–338.

Hoffman, L.R. (1959) Homogeneity of member personality and its effect on group problem-solving. Journal of Abnormal & Social Psychology, 58: 27–32.

Hofstede, G. (1991) Cultures and Organizations. New York: McGraw-Hill.

Hofstede, G., Neuijen, B., Ohayv, D. and Sanders, G. (1990) Measuring organizational cultures: a qualitative and quantitative study across twenty cases. Administrative Science Quarterly, 35(2): 286–316.

Hogg, M.A. and Hains, S.C. (1998) Friendship and group identification: a new look at the role of cohesiveness in groupthink. European Journal of Social Psychology, 28(3): 323–341.

Jackson, S., Brett, J., Sessa, V., Cooper, D., Julin, J. and Peyronnin, K. (1991) Some differences make a difference: individual dissimilarity and group heterogeneity as correlates of recruitment, promotions, and turnover. Journal of Applied Psychology, 76: 675–689.

Janis, I.L. (1982) Groupthink, 2nd Edn. Boston, MA: Houghton-Mifflin.

Jehn, K.A. (1995) A multimethod examination of the benefits and detriments of intragroup conflict. Administrative Science Quarterly, 40(2): 256–282.

Jehn, K.A. (1997) A qualitative analysis of conflict types and dimensions in organizational groups. Administrative Science Quarterly, 42(3): 530–557.

Jehn, K.A. and Mannix, E. (1998) The dynamic nature of conflict: a longitudinal study of intragroup conflict and group performance. Working paper, The Wharton School, University of Pennsylvania, Philadelphia, PA.

Jehn, K.A., Northcraft, G.B. and Neale, M.A. (1999) Why differences make a difference: a field study of diversity, conflict, and performance in workgroups. Administrative Science Quarterly, 44(4): 741–763.

Kanter, R.M. (1988) When a thousand flowers bloom: structural, collective, and social conditions for innovation in organization. In B. Staw and L. Cummings (Eds), Research in Organizational Behavior, Vol. 10, pp. 169–211. Greenwich, CT: JAI Press.

Kanter, R.M., Kao, J. and Wiersema, F. (1997) Innovation: Breakthrough Ideas at 3M, DuPont, GE, Pfizer, and Rubbermaid. New York: HarperBusiness.

Keller, R.T. (1986) Predictors of the performance of project groups in R&D organizations. Academy of Management Journal, 29(4): 715–726.

King, N. and Anderson, N. (1990) Innovation in working groups. In M. West and J. Farr (Eds), Innovation and Creativity at Work: Psychological and Organizational Strategies, pp. 81–100. Chichester: Wiley.

Kotter, J.P. and Heskett, J.L. (1992) Corporate Culture and Performance. New York: Free Press.

Kroc, R. (1977) Grinding it Out: the Making of McDonald's. Chicago, IL: H. Regnery.

Kunda, G. (1992) Engineering Culture: Control and Commitment in a High-Tech Corporation. Philadelphia, PA: Temple University Press.

Leavitt, H. (1975) Suppose we took groups seriously. In E. Cass and F. Zimmer (Eds), Man and Work in Society. New York: Van Nostrand Reinhold.

Levine, J.M. and Moreland, R.L. (1990) Progress in small group research. Annual Review of Psychology, 41: 585–634.

Lincoln, J.R. and Kalleberg, A.L. (1990) Culture, Control, and Commitment: a Study of Work Organization and Work Attitudes in the United States and Japan. New York: Cambridge University Press.

March, J.G. (1991) Exploration and exploitation in organizational learning. Organization Science, 3: 71–87.

Markowich, M.M. and Farber, J.A. (1989) If your employees were the customers. Personnel Administrator, 34(9): 70–73, 101.

Milgram, S. (1974) Obedience to Authority; an Experimental View, 1st Edn. New York: Harper & Row.

Moscovici, S. and Lecuyer, R. (1972) Studies in group decision: social space, patterns of communication and group consensus. European Journal of Social Psychology, 2(3): 221–244.

Nemeth, C.J. (1992) Minority dissent as a stimulant to group performance. In S. Worchel, W. Wood and J. Simpson (Eds), Group Process and Productivity. London: Sage.

Nemeth, C.J. (1997) Managing innovation: when less is more. California Management Review, 40(1): 59–74.

Nemeth, C.J. and Staw, B.M. (1989) The tradeoffs of social control and innovation in groups and organizations. In L. Berkowitz (Ed), Advances in Experimental Social Psychology, pp. 175–210. San Diego, CA: Academic Press.

Nicholson, G.C. (1998) Keeping innovation alive. Research-Technology Management, 41(3): 34–40.

Nord, W.R. and Tucker, S. (1987) Implementing Routine and Radical Innovations. Lexington, MA: Lexington Books.

Nystrom, H. (1979) Creativity and Innovation. New York: Wiley.

Oldham, G.R. and Cummings, A. (1996) Employee creativity: personal and contextual factors at work. Academy of Management Journal, 39(3): 607–634.

O'Reilly, B. (1997) The secrets of America's most admired corporations: new ideas, new products. Fortune, 135(4): 60–64.

O'Reilly, C.A. and Chatman, J.A. (1996) Culture as social control: corporations, cults, and commitment. In B. Staw and L. Cummings (Eds), Research in Organizational Behavior, Vol. 18, pp. 157–200. Greenwich, CT: JAI Press.

O'Reilly, C.A., Caldwell, D.F. and Barnett, W.P. (1989) Work group demography, social integration, and turnover. Administrative Science Quarterly, 34: 21–37.

O'Reilly, C.A., Chatman, J.A. and Caldwell, D.F. (1991) People and organizational culture: a profile comparison approach to assessing person-organization fit. Academy of Management Journal, 34(3): 487–516.

Packard, D. (1995) The HP Way: How Bill Hewlett and I Built Our Company. New York: HarperBusiness.

Pascale, R.T. (1993) The benefit of a clash of opinions. Personnel Management, 25(10): 38–41.

Payne, R.L. (1990) The effectiveness of research teams. In M. West and J. Farr (Eds), Innovation and Creativity at Work: Psychological and Organizational Strategies, pp. 101–122. Chichester: Wiley.

Peters, T.J. and Waterman Jr., R.H. (1982) In Search of Excellence: Lessons From America's Best-Run Companies, 1st Edn. New York: Harper & Row.

Pillinger, T. and West, M.A. (1995) Innovation in UK Manufacturing: Findings From a Survey Within Small and Medium Sized Manufacturing Companies. Sheffield: Institute of Work Psychology, University of Sheffield.

Podolny, J. (1993) A status-based model of market competition. American Journal of Sociology, 98: 829–872.

Pratt, M.G. and Rafaeli, A. (1997) Organizational dress as a symbol of multilayered social identities. Academy of Management Journal, 40(4): 862–898.

Puffer, S.M. (1999) CompUSA's CEO James Halpin on technology, rewards, and commitment. Academy of Management Executive, 13(2): 29–36.

Robinson, A.G. and Stern, S. (1997) Corporate Creativity: How Innovation and Improvement Actually Happen. San Francisco, CA: Berrett-Koehler.

Rousseau, D.M. (1990) Normative beliefs in fund-raising organizations: linking culture to organizational performance and individual responses. Group & Organization Studies, 15(4): 448–460.

Schneider, B. (1987) The people make the place. Personnel Psychology, 40(3): 437–453.

Schweiger, D.M., Sandberg, W.R. and Ragen, J.W. (1986) Group approaches for improving strategic decision making: a comparative analysis of dialectical inquiry, devil's advocacy, and consensus. Academy of Management Journal, 29: 51–71.

Shalley, C.E. (1995) Effects of coaction, expected evaluation, and goal setting on creativity and productivity. Academy of Management Journal, 38(2): 483–503.

Shapiro, B. (1992) Functional integration: getting all the troops to work together. In J. Gabarro (Ed), Managing People and Organizations. Boston, MA: Harvard Business School Press.

Shaw, M.E. (1981) Group Dynamics: the Psychology of Small Group Behavior, 3rd Edn. New York: McGraw-Hill.

Sorensen, J. (1999) The strength of corporate culture and the reliability of firm performance. Working paper, University of Chicago, Graduate School of Business, Chicago, IL.

Spataro, S. (2000) Not all differences are the same: the role of status in predicting reactions to demographic diversity in organizations. Dissertation, University of California, Berkeley, CA.

Stasser, G. and Stewart, D. (1992) Discovery of hidden profiles by decision-making groups: solving a problem versus making a judgment. Journal of Personality and Social Psychology, 63: 426–434.

Staw, B.M. (1976) Knee-deep in the Big Muddy: a study of escalating commitment to a chosen course of action. Organizational Behavior & Human Decision Processes, 16(1): 27–44.

Staw, B.M. (1990) An evolutionary approach to creativity and innovation. In M. West and J. Farr (Eds), Innovation and Creativity at Work: Psychological and Organizational Strategies, pp. 287–308. Chichester: Wiley.

Staw, B.M. and Ross, J. (1987) Behavior in escalation situations: antecedents, prototypes, and solutions. In L. Cummings and B. Staw (Eds), Research in Organizational Behavior, Vol. 9, pp. 39–78. Greenwich, CT: JAI Press.

Stoner, J.A.F. (1968) Risky and cautious shifts in group decisions: the influence of widely held values. Journal of Experimental Social Psychology, 4: 442–459.

Sutton, R.I. and Hargadon, A. (1996) Brainstorming groups in context: effectiveness in a product design firm. Administrative Science Quarterly, 41(4): 685–718.

Thomas, D.A. and Ely, R.J. (1996) Making differences matter: a new paradigm for managing diversity. Harvard Business Review, 74: 79–90.

Thompson, V.A. (1965) Bureaucracy and innovation. Administrative Science Quarterly, 1: 1–20.

Triandis, H.C. (1995) Individualism and Collectivism. Boulder, CO: Westview Press.

Triandis, H.C. (1996) The psychological measurement of cultural syndromes. American Psychologist, 51: 407–415.

Tsui, A.S., Egan, T.D. and O'Reilly, C. (1992) Being different: relational demography and organizational attachment. Administrative Science Quarterly, 37: 549–579.

Tushman, M. and O'Reilly, C.A. (1997) Winning Through Innovation: a Practical Guide to Leading Organizational Change and Renewal. Boston, MA: Harvard Business School Press.

Wagner, J.A. (1995) Studies of individualism-collectivism: effects on cooperation in-groups. Academy of Management Journal, 38: 152–172.

West, M.A. (1990) The social psychology of innovation in groups. In M. West and J. Farr (Eds), Innovation and Creativity at Work: Psychological and Organizational Strategies, pp. 309–333. Chichester: Wiley.

West, M.A. and Anderson, N.R. (1996) Innovation in top management teams. Journal of Applied Psychology, 81(6): 680–693.

Wetlaufer, S. (2000) Common sense and conflict: an interview with Disney's Michael Eisner. Harvard Business Review, 78(1): 114–124.

Zaltman, G., Duncan, R. and Holbeck, J. (1973) Innovations and Organizations. New York: Wiley.

Zell, D. (1997) Changing by Design: Organizational Innovation at Hewlett-Packard. Ithaca, NY: ILR Press.

Zenger, T.R. and Lawrence, B.S. (1989) Organizational demography: the differential effects of age and tenure distributions on technical communication. Academy of Management Journal, 32: 353–376.

# Chapter 12

# Does Culture Always Flow Downstream? Linking Group Consensus and Organizational Culture

**Elizabeth A. Mannix**
*Johnson Graduate School of Management,*
*Cornell University, Ithaca, NY, USA*

**Sherry Thatcher**
*Eller College of Business and Public Administration,*
*University of Arizona, Tucson, AZ, USA*

*and*

**Karen A. Jehn**
*The Wharton School, University of Pennsylvania,*
*Philadelphia, PA, USA*

## INTRODUCTION

Corporate culture has been defined and studied in a multitude of ways by scholars in fields ranging from anthropology, sociology, and psychology to strategy and economics. We adopt the view which defines culture as "... the pattern of beliefs and expectations shared by the organization's members" (Schwartz and Davis, 1981). Such beliefs and expectations result in norms that shape the behavior of individuals and groups. Norms are, in turn, driven by values, which provide the underlying rationale for these expectations (Cialdini et al., 1991; Enz, 1988; Katz and Kahn, 1978). While culture must be a system of *shared* beliefs, firms vary on the degree to which they have a "strong culture" – defined as the degree to which the value system is widely dispersed (crystallization) and strongly held (intensity) within the organization (Jackson, 1966; Katz and Kahn, 1978).

From the functional perspective, culture is viewed primarily as a means of social control – a means by which behavior and even beliefs are shaped and determined (O'Reilly and Chatman, 1996). As a result, culture can provide value to the organization through several mechanisms. Because organizations provide strong situations, culture can promote dedication and commitment from firm members (O'Reilly and Chatman, 1996). In addition, when organizational culture is congruent with corporate strategy, the behavior of firm members naturally promotes organizational goals, enhancing firm effectiveness (Nadler and Tushman, 1988; O'Reilly, 1989). Indeed, research has shown that this result is enhanced when the culture is strongly held throughout the organization (Kotter and Heskett, 1992). Of course, a strong organizational culture can also have detrimental effects such as hindering innovation and breeding myopia (Flynn and Chatman, this volume). Creating an atmosphere where people are pressured to work overtime or to give up vacation time is also a possible result of a strong culture.

A natural extension of the work on organizational culture is to understand culture's relevance to work teams. Many individuals find themselves spending more and more of their time working within groups or teams (Boyett and Conn, 1991; Katzenbach and Smith, 1993). Following the reasoning presented above, teams that have values and beliefs consistent with the organizational culture will enhance firm effectiveness. However, because of the intensity under which many teams work, and the amount of time spent together as a group, teams provide the opportunity for subcultures specific to the group to emerge (Sackmann, 1992). As such, it is important to examine the circumstances under which team cultures form, and their consequences for the organization.

In this paper we begin a discussion of organizational team culture by addressing the following questions. How do such teams come to a consensus on work values and behavior? What factors, both internal and external to the team, make this consensus more or less difficult? How is this consensus shaped by organizational culture and conversely, how might group value consensus influence the organizational culture? We then discuss the consequences of team value consensus and group norms on the types and levels of conflict, attitudes and behaviors, and team performance. We conclude with exploratory thoughts on teams as a catalyst for organizational culture change.

# TEAMS IN ORGANIZATIONS

In response to growing demands for efficiency and flexibility, organizations are using teams to do much of the work traditionally accomplished by individuals (Boyett and Conn, 1991; Katzenbach and Smith, 1993). Teams are used in organizations for a variety of purposes, and range from loosely constructed aggregates to highly interdependent work groups. In this paper we focus on the latter – complex task-performing teams that work together interdependently to produce a product or service, and have the authority to determine their own work strategies and manage their internal processes.

In order for teams to perform effectively there are functions that they must fulfill (Wageman and Mannix, 1998). We break these functions into two domains – task and relational. The study of task functions has included developing task strategies and task-related values (Liang et al., 1995; Wageman, 1995), setting team goals (Crowne and Rosse, 1995; Mitchell and Silver, 1990; Weingart, 1992), arriving at decision rules (Guzzo, 1982; Miller, 1989; Stasser et al., 1989), role differentiation and the division of labor (Jackson and Schuler, 1985; Moreland and Levine, 1992; Turner and Colomy, 1988). Relational functions include both internally directed and externally directed behaviors. On the internal side there are behaviors such as managing team boundaries and interpersonal relationships (Hackman, 1983, 1990; Goins and Mannix, 1999; Moreland, 1987), arriving at group values and norms of behavior (Argote, 1989; Bettenhausen and Murnighan, 1985; O'Reilly and Caldwell, 1985), and managing conflict (Ancona et al., 1991; Bazerman et al., 1988; Gladstein, 1984; Jehn, 1995). External behaviors include boundary-spanning and creating liaisons with external parties (Alderfer and Smith, 1982; Ancona, 1987, 1990; Katz and Tushman, 1981; Tushman, 1977), follow-through on information/links to clients (Hackman, 1990), accessing external information or resources (Pfeffer, 1986; Pfeffer and Salancik, 1978), as well as the implementation, recommendation, and review of final team output (Nadler and Tushman, 1988).

Although we do not claim that all of the above functional behaviors are essential to all teams at all times, we do argue that each of these functions is useful for the group in achieving a multi-faceted, high level of effectiveness. Following Hackman (1990) we define team effectiveness as the degree to which (1) the team's output meets the standards of quality of the people who receive or review that output, (2) the process enhances the team's ability to work together interdependently and effectively in the future, and (3) the group experience contributes to the personal well-being or satisfaction of the team members.

# CULTURE AND ORGANIZATIONAL TEAMS

As defined above, culture forms part of the informal organization that consists of beliefs and expectations about behavior – in other words, norms. Norms are informal rules that groups adopt to regulate group members' behavior; they are among the least visible and most powerful forms of social control over human action (Hackman, 1976; Sherif, 1936). While there has been a great deal of research on norms, most of it has focused on examining the impact norms have on other social phenomena (cf. Feldman, 1984). There has been relatively limited attention to how norms actually form, and who or what is responsible for the norms we see operating in teams.

The classic research on norm formation comes from Sherif (1936) and his work on the autokinetic effect. Sherif argued that his results demonstrated the basic psychological processes involved in the establishment of social norms; experience is organized around or modified by collectively produced frames of reference. Feldman (1984) has presented a task-oriented alternative to this concept of emergent norms. He proposes that norms form in one of four ways: explicit statements by supervisors or co-workers, that is, by fiat; critical events in the group's history; primacy, that is, based on early behavior patterns that set up group expectations; and/or, carry-over behaviors from past situations. Norms generated by fiat are similar to rules, in which a powerful individual explicitly expresses values, norms or prescribed behaviors. The remaining three forms might be categorized as variations of collectively emergent norms.

In a relatively recent study of how norms are developed, Bettenhausen and Murnighan (1985) examined the formation of norms using a multi-round negotiation exercise played over several weeks. They found that group norms regarding resource allocation emerged from the interaction between each group member's definition of the situation and the scripts or schemas that group members used to frame the situation. When group members had similar scripts, the group's interaction proceeded smoothly – each interaction confirmed the meaning that group members had attached to the action. When the scripts were not similar, however, conflict resulted which was not always easy to resolve. At times, group members made overt persuasion attempts to pull the group toward their interpretation through challenges to the implied norm.

Bettenhausen and Murnighan's finding is convergent with Levine and Moreland's model of group formation and development (Levine and Moreland, 1991; Moreland, 1987; Moreland and Levine, 1992). According to their model, group membership begins with an investigation phase which works at two levels: the individual looks for a group that can satisfy his or her personal needs, and the group looks for individuals that can satisfy its goals. If commitment between the group and the individual becomes strong enough, perhaps if the fit between underlying values is congruent enough, then a transition occurs; the individual enters the group and the socialization phase of group membership. During socialization the individual works to change the group to make it more satisfying, which may involve attempts to change norms and even values. At the same time, the group works to change the individual to increase his or her value as a member. When these mutual change attempts succeed, feelings of commitment are strengthened and a transition to role acceptance occurs, allowing the group to move to a subsequent maintenance phase. Otherwise, we might expect the individual to exit, or the group to experience serious difficulty (Moreland et al., 1996).

Thus, newly formed groups may or may not start with a high level of agreement, or consensus, on important work-related values. Of course, we must also consider that organizational teams are embedded within organizations. As a result of recruiting procedures and subsequent socialization, organization members are likely to be more similar in their values and expectations than if they had been drawn at random (Chatman, 1989; Schneider, 1987). Indeed, there is some evidence that individuals may reconstruct their individually held values to be consistent with their actions (Chatman et al., 1986). As such, if the organization requires individuals to perform counter-normative behaviors, organization members may eventually alter their values to be consistent with those behaviors. These forces may increase the similarity among organization members, thus reducing the potential level of value and norm diversity within work groups. This is one way that organizational culture influences team norms.

On the other hand, there is also evidence that different functional units may perform more effectively with different types of cultures (Tushman and O'Reilly, 1996). As such, cross-functional teams may find that the level of value and norm "congruence" is quite low at first. In developing norms that are unique to their team, these teams may find that their team culture is significantly different from the culture of the organization. The team may then be able to influence change in the organizational culture.

Thus, organizational teams present opportunities for conflict as well as conformity over work-related values and normative behavior, and for reinforcing as well as challenging the organizational culture. In order to understand the development of team culture, we must examine those factors that may influence group value consensus. We explore these relationships further through an examination of group composition.

# WORK GROUP COMPOSITION, DIVERSITY AND CULTURE

Heterogeneous groups are believed to be more creative and effective than more homogeneous groups (Jackson, 1992). As such, teams are often created to be cross- or multi-functional in nature. The concurrent engineering model, for example, prescribes this approach for the creation of multi-functional product development teams, requiring that a representative from every functional specialty in the development and manufacturing process be present on the design team from the start (e.g. Syan and Menon, 1994). Despite the differences in backgrounds, experience, skills or beliefs which might be represented within these work groups, in order to coordinate their efforts and function as a team, they must develop a group-based value system and accompanying set of expected and acceptable behaviors (Enz, 1988; Feldman, 1984; Schein, 1985).

Thus, the first place to start in exploring the relationship between group composition and team culture is to specify the types and consequences of potential heterogeneity within the team. Recently, Jehn et al. (1997, 1999) delineated three categories of diversity: social category diversity, informational diversity, and value diversity.

Social category diversity refers to mainly visible demographic characteristics such as age, sex, and race (Tsui et al., 1992). While visible characteristics often are not relevant to completing the given task, they do shape people's perceptions and behaviors through mechanisms of categorization and prejudice (Pelled, 1996). Empirical evidence indicates that people report being more committed, satisfied, and likely to remain in groups and organizations that are demographically homogeneous rather than heterogeneous (O'Reilly et al., 1989; Tsui et al., 1992; Verkuyten et al., 1993). Demographic dissimilarity among team members is further associated with poor communication, lower integration, increased conflict, and negative affective relations in the group (Bantel and Jackson, 1989; Jackson et al., 1991; Jehn et al., 1999; Tsui and O'Reilly, 1989; Zenger and Lawrence, 1989). McGrath et al. (1996) propose that these difficulties may be due to real underlying differences, to perceptions that create social distance and self-fulfilling prophecies, or to inequalities in status and opportunity within organizations and society at large.

Informational diversity includes underlying attributes of individuals such as work experience, education, and functional background that provide the individual with a skill set that influences how an individual perceives and approaches problems. Pfeffer (1983) suggested that diversity on work tenure would lead to more conflict and negative behavior. However, the information/decision making perspective suggests that such diversity will have positive implications on work group outcomes since the group will have access to a wider array of views, skills, and information (Gruenfeld et al., 1996; Jackson, 1992). In this vein, many theorists argue that knowledge or skill diversity can enhance group performance by enhancing the group's creative problem solving ability (Nemeth, 1986), primarily through cognitive conflict (Damon, 1991; Jehn, 1995; Levine et al., 1993). Further evidence from organizational settings supports this view. Educational diversity in top management teams was found to be positively related to a firm's return on investment and growth in sales (Smith et al., 1994). Similarly, Hambrick et al. (1996) found that top management teams that were diverse in terms of education, functional background, and company tenure exhibited a greater propensity for strategic action than homogeneous teams. Although diverse teams were slower decision makers, the overall net effect on firm performance measured as market share and firm profitability was positive.

Considerations of functional background, on the other hand, have given more equivocal results. Bantel and Jackson (1989) found that diversity among top management teams in a banking environment increased administrative innovations, but that this had no effect on technical innovations. Korn et al. (1992) found that functional diversity increased performance (measured as increases in ROA) in the furniture industry, but not in the software industry. The complex nature of functional heterogeneity is further illustrated in a study by Ancona and Caldwell (1992). They found that as functional diversity increased, team members communicated more often with outsiders, and that this helped them develop more innovative products. Yet, despite this potentially positive behavior, diversity had an overall negative effect on team performance. One reason for this may be that team diversity made it harder for team members to work well together on the non-creative implementation aspects of their task. For example, diverse teams were more likely to overspend their budgets and miss important deadlines (Ancona and Caldwell, 1992). Other negative effects for diversity have been found, such as the tendency for diverse teams to take longer to make decisions than more homogeneous teams (cf. Milliken and Martins, 1996). Thus, in circumstances where speed is associated with performance (such as in the software industry), the coordination problems experienced by heterogeneous teams may also impede performance (Eisenhardt, 1989; Korn et al., 1992; Smith et al., 1994).

Thus, knowledge, skill, and ability-based diversity can have both advantages and disadvantages for teams. Such diversity can enhance the generation of a variety of perspectives in a group, increasing the probability of innovation and creative decision making. Nonetheless, such diversity can also have negative effects on a team, though these effects may lie outside of the strictly functional domain. This difficulty occurs because people with different social category and informational diversity characteristics tend to have different experiences and views as to what is important in groups and the best way for groups to work together (Jehn et al., 1997). However, because these factors vary in how obvious they are to assess by other group members, and in how much impact that they may have on the group's critical tasks, they may emerge or remain latent (Feldman, 1984).

Lastly, and perhaps of most importance for our purposes, is value diversity. Value diversity occurs when members of a work group differ in terms of what they think the group's real task, goal, target, or mission should be. When group members have a high level of value consensus, members will tend to agree on norms regarding work, in turn promoting harmony and coordination (Jehn and Mannix, in press; Nemeth and Staw, 1989). By contrast, when low value consensus exists, members' core values and beliefs about their everyday work are challenged, causing friction and emotional upset (Bar-Tal, 1989; Schein, 1986). Differing values may cause group members to perceive situations and priorities differently, impeding the coordinated flow of work (Ravlin and Meglino, 1987). In addition, value differences between a leader and the rest of the group can be a continuous source of tension for the team (Gray et al., 1985).

Several factors may increase or reduce value diversity within a team. First, in newly formed groups, if a group is diverse on social category and informational diversity characteristics, consensus on work values may be difficult to reach. This is true even when teams explicitly seek a heterogeneous composition. In addition, the past experiences of the individual members are also likely to affect value consensus. As Feldman (1984) suggested, previous experiences in other groups will influence individual expectations. These different past experiences may have formed the basis of varied "normative scripts" which are likely to be played out in the new group context (Bettenhausen and Murnighan, 1985; Taylor and Crocker, 1981).

For teams in which some members have worked together before, we must consider the past relationships of group members. Groups in which members have had previous interactions are likely to possess more knowledge about one another's skills, perspectives and interpersonal styles (Harrison et al., 1998; Wittenbaum and Stasser, 1996). Interpersonal knowledge possessed by acquainted group members can also reduce conformity, and the suppression of alternative perspectives and judgments (Asch, 1952; Nemeth, 1986; Schachter and Singer, 1962). Gruenfeld et al. (1996) found that teams composed of individuals with preexisting relationship ties (familiars) were better able to pool unique information, arriving at the correct solution to a complex problem, than were groups of strangers. Shah and Jehn (1993) made a similar finding that task groups composed of friends exhibited greater task and emotional conflict while working on a complex decision task than did groups of strangers. Because the task required critical inquiry and analysis of assumptions, the conflict gave groups of friends a performance advantage. Thus, previous interaction may allow the surfacing of differences – including conflicts over work values. Such groups may not begin with value consensus, but may develop it over time.

Finally, it is important to consider the effects of the overall organizational culture on team values and norms. Organizations have the potential to provide strong situations, which is especially true when the organizational culture is intensely held and well crystallized throughout its membership (Davis-Blake and Pfeffer, 1989). As such, organization members are likely to comply with firm objectives for a variety of psychological reasons – informational salience, self-categorization and social identity processes, and the mechanisms of similarity/attraction (O'Reilly and Chatman,

1996). Thus, members of an organization are likely to hold similar work values, increasing the chances that team cultures will mirror the organizational culture. However, this is less likely to be true for organizations with a weak or poorly disseminated culture – for example, highly decentralized firms, or firms that have recently undergone mergers or other "shocks" that create uncertainty. It should also be less true when firm members are newcomers (Chatman, 1989), or individuals with certain personality characteristics who are less susceptible to influence (Jones, 1986).

We propose that when group members have consensus on work values, they will tend to agree on norms regarding work, creating a strong and crystallized culture in the group. By contrast, when value consensus is low, it will be more difficult for the group to develop a shared set of norms (group culture).

**Proposition 1.**   When group members have consensus on work values, they will develop a strong culture.

The general proposition above sets the foundation for our model of group value consensus and group culture. Value consensus (the inverse of value diversity) may be reached by initial visible similarity among group members, but it may also be engendered by the past experiences of group members, preexisting relationships, and the strength of the organizational culture in which the group is embedded (see Figure 12.1). Value consensus, in turn, influences a number of critical group process variables, such as conflict, that ultimately affects performance.

## GROUP PROCESS VARIABLES

There are several factors we could focus on to understand the impact of value diversity on group process and performance – internal issues such as setting team goals and arriving at decision rules, or external behaviors such as boundary-spanning. To some extent, however, the enactment of each of these functions relies on the team's ability to manage conflict (Wageman and Mannix, 1998). A group composed of individuals who are capable of handling conflict productively should be better equipped to enact task-relevant strategies and goals (Bar-Tal, 1989; Jehn, 1994; Jehn and Mannix, in press; Schein, 1986). On the other hand, when internal relations break down, the result can be

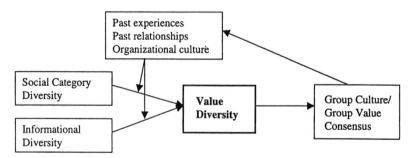

**Figure 12.1**   Relationships between group diversity and group culture.

motivation losses such as withdrawal or free riding (Maier, 1967; Steiner, 1972), or opinion conformity (Janis, 1982). Conflict, and its resolution, are fundamental to group functioning (Jehn and Mannix, in press). As such, in the following section we focus on the relationship between group value consensus and intragroup conflict.

There has been a debate in organizational research regarding whether agreement or disagreement within groups is advantageous (Eisenhardt and Zbaracki, 1992). One key to unlocking this complex relationship lies in the differentiation of conflict as either relationship or task-related (Cosier and Rose, 1977; Guetzkow and Gyr, 1954; Jehn, 1995; Pinkley, 1990; Wall and Nolan, 1986). Relationship conflict, also called affective conflict, is an awareness of interpersonal incompatibilities. Relationship conflicts frequently reported are about social events, gossip, clothing preferences, political views and hobbies (Jehn, 1997). This type of conflict often includes personality differences, animosity, and annoyance between individuals. Studies show that relationship conflict is detrimental to individual and group performance, member satisfaction, and the likelihood the group will work together in the future (Jehn, 1995; Jehn and Mannix, in press; Shah and Jehn, 1993). When group members have interpersonal problems or feel friction with one another, they may be distracted from the task, work less cooperatively and produce suboptimal products (Argyris, 1962; Kelley, 1979; Roseman et al., 1994; Staw et al., 1981).

Task, or cognitive, conflict is an awareness of differences in viewpoints and opinions pertaining to the group's task. Examples are disagreements among group members' ideas and opinions about the task being performed, such as disagreement regarding an organization's current hiring strategies or determining the information to include in an annual report. In contrast to relationship conflict, moderate levels of task conflict have been shown to be beneficial to group performance in various decision making and group tasks. Teams performing complex cognitive tasks benefit from differences of opinion about the work being done (Bourgeois, 1985; Eisenhardt and Schoonhoven, 1990; Jehn, 1995; Jehn and Mannix, in press; Shah and Jehn, 1993). Task conflict improves decision quality, as groups drop old patterns of interaction and adopt new perspectives; the synthesis that emerges from the conflict is generally superior to the individual perspectives themselves (Schweiger and Sandberg, 1989; Schwenk, 1990).

Finally, there are many group-related activities, some having to do with the actual task and others having to do with the process of doing the task or delegating resources and duties. Process conflicts are about logistical and delegation issues such as how task accomplishment should proceed in the work unit, who is responsible for what, and how things should be delegated (Jehn, 1997). Jehn (1997) delineates between task and process conflict based on findings of an ethnographic study of work groups. For example, when members of an R&D group disagree about data interpretation and the meaning of the results, they are experiencing task conflict. On the other hand, if they argue about who is responsible for writing up the final report and who will make the presentation, they are having a process conflict. Of the three conflict types, process conflict is the least examined. In one study, process conflict was associated with a lower level of group morale, as well as decreased productivity (Shah and Jehn, 1993). The logic proposed is that when a group argues about who does what, members are dissatisfied with the uncertainty caused by the process conflict and feel a greater desire to leave the group. In addition, Jehn (1997) notes that process conflicts interfere with task content quality and often misdirect focus to irrelevant discussions of member ability.

## Group Value Consensus and Conflict

We propose that the strength and crystallization of group culture is likely to affect the level and types of conflict within the group, which will in turn affect group performance. First, because group consensus on work values is likely to promote harmony among group members (Nemeth and Staw, 1989), increase attraction, and decrease tension (Schneider, 1983) in groups with stronger cultures, relationship conflict will be reduced (Jehn, 1994).

**Proposition 2.**   Group value consensus will decrease the potential for relationship conflict within the team and increase performance.

The same is not necessarily true, however, for task conflict. We propose that value consensus will provide an atmosphere in which task-related conflicts are more easily expressed. In other words, in such groups norms will develop which encourage task-focused conflict. To support this argument we draw a theoretical parallel between group value consensus and the positive relationships or attraction that is likely to result among group members. As classic social psychological theory has indicated, individuals are attracted to and form friendships with others who are similar to themselves on several dimensions – but most notably, attitudes and values (Newcomb, 1956). Thus, it may be proposed that groups that begin their interaction with high value consensus will be more likely to develop positive relationships and attitudes towards one another. Theorists have suggested, and research has demonstrated, that such positive relations are likely to result in a beneficial level of task conflict (Valley et al., 1995). As we described earlier, Shah and Jehn (1993) found that groups composed of friends exhibited greater task conflict while working on a decision task than groups of strangers, resulting in higher performance. Similarly, in a longitudinal study of continuing work groups, those with stable membership, who knew each other better, experienced constructive task conflict more frequently than groups for which membership was characterized by instability and change (Arrow and McGrath, 1993).

**Proposition 3.**   Group value consensus will increase the potential for task conflict within the team and will increase performance.

A third type of conflict known as process conflict is also influenced by group value consensus. Although less research has investigated process conflict and its antecedents, recent work suggests that groups with members of diverse educational majors (informational diversity) have more problems defining how to proceed than groups in which members have similar educational backgrounds (Jehn et al., 1997). We propose that differences in informational diversity can lead to value differences, making it more difficult for the team to make decisions about how duties and resources should be allocated. For instance, someone with work experience in accounting may value detail

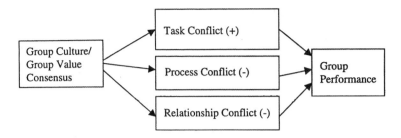

**Figure 12.2** Group value consensus, conflict, and performance.

much more than someone with a background in creative writing. The value differences will most likely influence the level of process conflict within the work group. We therefore propose that group value consensus, whether it is based on social category or information similarities, will decrease process conflict (Figure 12.2).

**Proposition 4.** Group value consensus will decrease the potential for process conflict within the team and increase performance.

## Group Attitudes and Behavior

Other group process variables that will be influenced by group value consensus are trust, respect, and competitiveness within the group. In groups with a high level of value consensus, members are more likely to trust and respect one another and feel that they are working toward a cooperative rather than competitive goal (Jehn and Shah, 1997). Thus, it may be proposed that groups that begin their interaction with high value consensus will be more likely to develop positive relationships and attitudes towards one another.

In a study of longitudinal conflict, Jehn and Mannix (in press) found that group value consensus decreased competition among team members and was the sole predictor of all three types of conflict. The results also showed that respect and trust were critical for building an environment of constructive conflict. We suggest that a primary source of trust-building and respect derives from common values regarding work (Figure 12.3).

**Proposition 5.** Group value consensus has the potential to increase trust and respect, and to decrease competitiveness among team members, increasing performance.

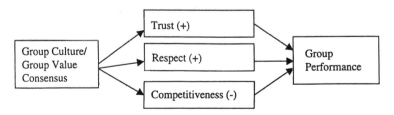

**Figure 12.3** Group value consensus, group process, and performance.

# SUMMARY AND DISCUSSION

Focusing on work groups and teams embedded within organizations, we discussed the determinants of group culture – particularly the emergence of group values and norms. We included both internal factors, such as group composition, as well as external influences, such as organizational culture. In addition, we explored the implications of the presence or absence of group value consensus and shared norms for group process (i.e. conflict) and performance.

In considering the effects of a strong (or weak) group culture on group process, we focused on the implications for conflict within the group, as well as group processes and attitudes such as trust, respect, and competition. We proposed that the strength and crystallization of group culture is likely to affect the level and types of conflict within the group, which will in turn affect group performance. Because group consensus on work values and norms is likely to promote harmony among group members, increase attraction, and decrease tension in groups with stronger cultures, relationship conflict will be reduced. We further proposed that value consensus is likely to decrease process conflict and increase task conflict, resulting in increased group performance.

In our discussion, we suggest that norms are a crucial component of establishing group value consensus. We did not discuss the types of norms that might be included in value consensus. One type of norm that is critical in ensuring group value consensus is a conflict openness norm. Norms within the group affect the degree to which individuals with value diversity will accept and engage in task conflict. Discussions about conflict are often avoided within groups (Brett, 1984; Tjosvold, 1991); however, recent research has suggested that open discussions about task-related conflict can be helpful within groups. Jehn (1995) found that open communication norms around task-related differences increased performance. When a group fosters norms that task differences are accepted, the discussions are well-managed and produce positive results (Jehn, 1997). For example, a group with open communication norms in the Jehn (1997) study investigated various alternatives and subsequently excelled at their tasks. A deeper exploration of the types of norms that foster group value consensus is critical in understanding team functioning.

As a final thought, we speculate on the strong situation that is created by teams. Given latitude by the organization, many teams are now almost entirely self-managing. These teams often have the authority to determine their work strategies and manage their internal processes (Wageman and Mannix, 1998). Given such freedom, teams have more opportunity to develop their own unique cultures, which have the potential to reinforce the overall firm culture, but also to deviate from the values and norms set by the organization, ultimately influencing the organizational culture (see Figure 12.4).

In the first instance, organizations can use teams to deliver the corporate culture. Given the intensity with which many teams work, and the level of interdependence between team members, these settings provide opportunities for the loyal "old-guard" to instruct newcomers in the expected and acceptable set of behaviors. Eventually, as we discussed earlier, newcomers are likely to adopt the team norms, and even values, as their own or they eventually exit from the situation. However, team norms that are reflective of organizational culture can have negative implications resulting in situa-

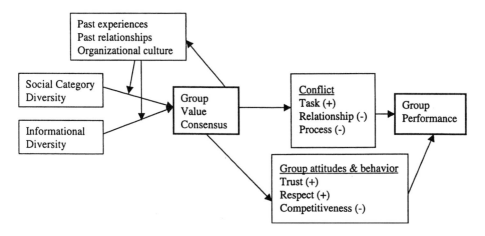

**Figure 12.4**  Model of group value consensus and performance.

tions reminiscent of groupthink (Janis, 1982). Strong organizational cultures may also inhibit creativity (Flynn and Chatman, this volume), breed myopia or influence people to be workaholics. Thus, group norms that mirror organizational culture may have positive or negative effects for the individual, the team, or the organization overall.

The second option, the development of divergent subcultures within teams, is also a possibility. In some instances, these subcultures may benefit both the group and the organization – for example, allowing R&D teams to value innovation and longer time frames, while sales teams value aggressiveness and shorter turn-arounds. As such, subcultures might exist in harmony with the rest of the organization, especially if their behaviors are congruent with the strategic goals of the organizations (Nadler and Tushman, 1988). On the other hand, given a weak organizational culture, environmental uncertainty, or recent changes in the organization such as down-sizing or mergers, strong teams may be able to effect changes in the organizational culture. Under what conditions teams serve to reinforce corporate culture, or they serve as catalysts for organizational change is, at this point, unknown. So, while this question carries with it a great deal of speculation, we believe that it offers the potential to move the study of organizational teams – and culture – in some fascinating directions.

# REFERENCES

Alderfer, C.P. and Smith, K.K. (1982) Studying intergroup relations embedded in organizations. Administrative Science Quarterly, 27: 35–65.

Ancona, D. (1987) Groups in organizations: extending laboratory models. In C. Hendrick (Ed), Group Processes and Intergroup Relations. Newbury Park, CA: Sage.

Ancona, D. (1990) Outward bound: strategies for team survival in an organization. Academy of Management Journal, 33: 334–365.

Ancona, D.G. and Caldwell, D.F. (1992) Bridging the boundary: external activity and performance in organizational teams. Administrative Science Quarterly, 37(4): 634–665.

Ancona, D., Friedman, R. and Kolb, D. (1991) The group and what happens on the way to "yes". Negotiation Journal, 7: 155–174.

Argote, L. (1989) Agreement about norms and work unit effectiveness: evidence from the field. Basic Applied Social Psychology, 10(2): 131–140.

Argyris, C. (1962) Interpersonal Competence and Organizational Effectiveness. Homewood, IL: Dorsey Press.

Arrow, H. and McGrath, J.E. (1993) Membership matters: how member change and continuity affect small group structure, process and performance. Small Group Research, 24(3): 334–361.

Asch, S.E. (1952) Social Psychology. Englewood Cliffs, NJ: Prentice-Hall.

Bantel, K.A. and Jackson, S.E. (1989) Top management and innovations in banking: does the composition of the top team make a difference? Strategic Management Journal, 10: 107–124.

Bar-Tal, D. (1989) Group Beliefs: a Conception for Analyzing Group Structure, Processes, and Behavior. New York: Springer-Verlag.

Bazerman, M.H., Mannix, E. and Thompson, L. (1988) Groups as mixed-motive negotiations. In E.J. Lawler and B. Markovsky (Eds), Advances in Group Processes: Theory and Research, Vol. 5. Greenwich, CT: JAI Press.

Bettenhausen, K. and Murnighan, J.K. (1985) The emergence of norms in competitive decision-making groups. Administrative Science Quarterly, 30: 350–372.

Bourgeois, L.J. (1985) Strategic goals, environmental uncertainty, and economic performance in volatile environments. Academy of Management Journal, 28: 548–573.

Boyett, J.H. and Conn, H.P. (1991) Workplace 2000: the Revolution Reshaping American Business. New York: Dutton.

Brett, J. (1984) Managing organizational conflict. Professional Psychology: Research and Practice, 15: 644–678.

Chatman, J. (1989) Improving interactional organizational research: a model of person-organization fit. Academy of Management Journal, 14: 333–349.

Chatman, J., Bell, N. and Staw, B. (1986) The managed thought: the role of self-justification and impression management in organizational settings. In D. Goia and H. Sims (Eds), The Thinking Organization: the Dynamics of Social Cognition, pp. 191–214. San Francisco, CA: Jossey-Bass.

Cialdini, R., Kallgren, C. and Reno, R. (1991) A focus theory of normative conduct: theoretical refinement and reevaluation of the role of norms in human behavior. Advances in Experimental Social Psychology, 24: 201–234.

Cosier, R. and Rose, G. (1977) Cognitive conflict and goal conflict effects on task performance. Organizational Behavior and Human Decision Processes, 19: 378–391.

Crowne, D. and Rosse, J. (1995) Yours, mine, and ours: facilitating group productivity through the integration of individual and group goals. Organizational Behavior and Human Decision Processes, 64: 138–150.

Damon, W. (1991) Problems of direction in socially shared cognition. In L.B. Resnick, J.M. Levine and S.D. Teasley (Eds), Perspectives on Socially Shared Cognition, pp. 384–397. Washington, DC: American Psychological Association.

Davis-Blake, A. and Pfeffer, J. (1989) Just a mirage: the search for dispositional effects in organizational research. Academy of Management Journal, 14: 385–400.

Eisenhardt, K.M. (1989) Making fast strategic decisions in high-velocity environments. Academy of Management Journal, 32(3): 543–576.

Eisenhardt, K. and Schoonhoven, C. (1990) Organizational growth: linking founding team, strategy, environment, and growth among U.S. semiconductor ventures 1978–1988. Administrative Science Quarterly, 35: 504–529.

Eisenhardt, K. and Zbaracki, M. (1992) Strategic decision making. Strategic Management Journal, 13: 17–37.

Enz, C. (1988) The role of value congruity on intraorganizational power. Administrative Science Quarterly, 33: 284–304.

Feldman, D. (1984) The development and enforcement of group norms. Academy of Management Review, 9: 47–53.

Gladstein, D. (1984) A model of task group effectiveness. Administrative Science Quarterly, 29: 499–517.

Goins, S. and Mannix, E. (1999) Self-selection and its impact on team diversity and performance. Performance Improvement Quarterly, 12(1):127–147.

Gray, B., Bougon, M.G. and Donnellon, A. (1985) Organizations as constructions and destructions of meaning. Journal of Management, 11: 83–98.

Gruenfeld, D., Mannix, E.A., Williams, K.Y. and Neale, M.A. (1996) Group composition and decision making: how member familiarity and information distribution affect process and performance. Organizational Behavior and Human Decision Processes, 67: 1–15.

Guetzkow, H. and Gyr, J. (1954) An analysis of conflict in decision making groups. Human Relations, 7: 367–381.

Guzzo, R. (Ed) (1982) Improving Group Decision Making in Organizations: Approaches from Theory and Research. New York: Academic Press.

Hackman, J.R. (1976) Group influences on individuals. In M. Dunnette (Ed), Handbook of Industrial and Organizational Psychology. Chicago, IL: Rand McNally.

Hackman, J.R. (1983) A normative model of work team effectiveness. Technical report #2, Group Effectiveness Research Project, School of Organization and Management, Yale.

Hackman, J.R. (Ed) (1990) Groups That Work (and Those That Don't): Creating Conditions for Effective Teamwork. San Francisco, CA: Jossey-Bass.

Hambrick, D., Cho, T. and Chen, M.-J. (1996) The influence of top management team heterogeneity on firms' competitive moves. Administrative Science Quarterly, 41: 659–684.

Harrison, D.A., Price, K.H. and Bell, M.P. (1998) Beyond relational demography: time and the effects of surface- and deep-level diversity on work group cohesion. Academy of Management Journal, 41(1): 96–107.

Jackson, J. (1966) A conceptual measurement model for norms and roles. Pacific Sociological Review, 9: 35–47.

Jackson, S. (1992) Team composition in organizations. In S. Worchel, W. Wood and J. Simpson (Eds), Group Process and Productivity, pp. 138–176. London: Sage.

Jackson, S. and Schuler, R. (1985) A meta-analysis and conceptual critique of research on role ambiguity and role conflict in work settings. Organizational Behavior, 36: 16–78.

Jackson, S., Brett, J., Sessa, V., Cooper, D., Julin, J. and Peyronnin, K. (1991) Some differences make a difference: individual dissimilarity and group heterogeneity as correlates of recruitment, promotions, and turnover. Journal of Applied Psychology, 76: 675–689.

Janis, I.L. (1982) Victims of Groupthink, 2nd Edn. Boston, MA: Houghton-Mifflin.

Jehn, K. (1994) Enhancing effectiveness: an investigation of advantages and disadvantages of value-based intragroup conflict. International Journal of Conflict Management, 5(3): 223–238.

Jehn, K. (1995) A multimethod examination of the benefits and detriments of intragroup conflict. Administrative Science Quarterly, 40: 256–282.

Jehn, K. (1997) A qualitative analysis of conflict types and dimensions in organizational groups. Administrative Science Quarterly, 42: 530–557.

Jehn, K. and Mannix, E.A. (in press) The dynamic nature of conflict: a longitudinal study of intragroup conflict and group performance. Academy of Management Journal.

Jehn, K. and Shah, P. (1997) Interpersonal relationships and task performance: an examination of mediating processes in friendship and acquaintance groups. Journal of Personality and Social Psychology, 72: 775–790.

Jehn, K., Chadwick, C. and Thatcher, S. (1997) To agree or not to agree: diversity, conflict, and group outcomes. International Journal of Conflict Management, 8(4): 287–306.

Jehn, K.A., Northcraft, G.B. and Neale, M.A. (1999) Why differences make a difference: a field study of diversity, conflict, and performance in workgroups. Administrative Science Quarterly, 44: 741–763.

Jones, G. (1986) Socialization tactics, self-efficacy, and newcomer's adjustments to organizations. Academy of Management Journal, 29: 262–279.

Katz, D. and Kahn, R. (1978) The Social Psychology of Organizations, 2nd Edn. New York: Wiley.

Katz, R. and Tushman, M. (1981) An investigation into the managerial roles and career paths of gatekeepers and project supervisors in a major R&D facility. Administrative Science Quarterly, 27: 103–110.

Katzenbach, J.R. and Smith, D.K. (1993) The Wisdom of Teams. Cambridge, MA: Harvard Business School Press.

Kelley, H.H. (1979) Personal Relationships. Hillsdale, NJ: Lawrence Erlbaum.

Korn, H.J., Milliken, F.J. and Lant, T.K. (1992) Top management team change and organizational performance. The influence of succession, composition, and context. Academy of Management Presentation, Las Vegas, NV.

Kotter, P. and Heskett, J. (1992) Corporate Culture and Performance. New York: Free Press.

Levine, J. and Moreland, R. (1991) Culture and socialization in work groups. In L. Resnick, J. Levine and S. Teasley (Eds), Perspectives on Socially Shared Cognition. Washington, DC: American Psychological Association.

Levine, J.M., Resnick, L.B. and Higgins, E.T. (1993) Social foundations of cognition. Annual Review of Psychology, 44: 585–612.

Liang, D.W., Moreland, R. and Argote, L. (1995) Group versus individual training and group performance: the mediating role of transactive memory. Personality and Social Psychology Bulletin, 21(4): 384–393.

Maier, N.R.F. (1967) Assets and liabilities in group problem-solving: the need for an integrative function. Psychological Review, 74: 239–249.

McGrath, J.E., Berdahl, J.L. and Arrow, H. (1996) Traits, expectations, culture, and clout: the dynamics of diversity in work groups. In S.E. Jackson and M.N. Ruderman (Eds), Diversity in Work Teams: Research Paradigms for a Changing Workplace. Washington, DC: American Psychological Association.

Miller, C. (1989) The social psychological effects of group decision rules. In P. Paulus (Ed), Psychology of Group Influence, 2nd Edn. Hillsdale, NJ: Erlbaum.

Milliken, F.J. and Martins, L.L. (1996) Searching for common threads: understanding the multiple effects of diversity in organizational groups. Academy of Management Review, 21(2): 402–433.

Mitchell, T.R. and Silver, W. (1990) Individual and group goals when workers are interdependent: effects on task strategies and performance. Journal of Applied Psychology, 75: 185–193.

Moreland, R. (1987) The formation of small groups. In C. Hendrick (Ed), Group Process, pp. 80–110. Newbury Park, CA: Sage.

Moreland, R. and Levine, J. (1992) Socialization in small groups: temporal changes in individual-group relations. In L. Berkowitz (Ed), Advances in Experimental Social Psychology, Vol. 15, pp. 137–192. New York: Academic Press.

Moreland, R., Levine, J. and Wingert, M. (1996) Creating the ideal group: composition effects at work. In E. Witte and J. Davis (Eds), Understanding Group Behavior: Small Group Processes and Interpersonal Relations, Vol. 2, pp. 11–35. Hillsdale, NJ: Erlbaum.

Nadler, D.A. and Tushman, M. (1988) Strategic Organizational Design: Concepts, Tools, and Processes. Glenview, IL: Scott Foresman.

Nemeth, C.J. (1986) Differential contributions of majority and minority influence. Psychological Review, 93: 23–32.

Nemeth, C.J. and Staw, B. (1989) The tradeoffs of social control in groups and organizations. Advances in Experimental Social Psychology, 22: 175–210.

Newcomb, T. (1956) The prediction of interpersonal attraction. American Psychologist, 11: 575–586.

O'Reilly, C. (1989) Corporations, culture and commitment: motivation and social control in organizations. California Management Review, 31: 9–25.

O'Reilly, C. and Caldwell, D. (1985) The impact of normative social influence and cohesiveness on task perceptions and attitudes: a social information processing approach. Journal of Occupational Psychology, 58: 193–206.

O'Reilly, C. and Chatman, J. (1996) Culture as social control: corporations, cults, and commitment. In B.M. Staw and L.L. Cummings (Eds), Research in Organizational Behavior, Vol. 18, pp. 157–200. Greenwich, CT: JAI Press.

O'Reilly, C., Caldwell, D. and Barnett, W. (1989) Work group demography, social integration and turnover. Administrative Science Quarterly, 34: 21–37.

Pelled, L. (1996) Demographic diversity, conflict and work group outcomes: an intervening process theory. Organization Science, 7(6): 615–631.

Pfeffer, J. (1983) Organizational demography. In L.L. Cummings and B.M. Staw (Eds), Research in Organizational Behavior, Vol. 5, pp. 299–357. Greenwich, CT: JAI Press.

Pfeffer, J. (1986) A resource dependence perspective on intercorporate relations. In M.S. Mizruchi and M. Schwartz (Eds), Structural Analysis of Business, pp. 117–132. New York: Academic Press.

Pfeffer, J. and Salancik, G. (1978) The External Control of Organizations: a Resource Dependence Perspective. New York: Harper and Row.

Pinkley, R. (1990) Dimensions of the conflict frame: disputant interpretations of conflict. Journal of Applied Psychology, 75: 117–128.

Ravlin, E.C. and Meglino, B.M. (1987) Effects of values on perception and decision making: a study of alternative work value measures. Journal of Applied Psychology, 72: 666–673.

Roseman, I., Wiest, C. and Swartz, T. (1994) Phenomenology, behaviors and goals differentiate emotions. Journal of Personality and Social Psychology, 67: 206–221.

Sackmann, S.A. (1992) Culture and subcultures: an analysis of organizational knowledge. Administrative Science Quarterly, 3: 140–161.

Schachter, S. and Singer, J. (1962) Cognitive, social and physiological determinants of emotional state. Psychological Review, 69: 379–399.

Schein, E.H. (1985) Organizational Culture and Leadership. San Francisco, CA: Jossey-Bass.

Schein, E.H. (1986) What you need to know about organizational culture. Training and Development Journal, 8(1): 30–33.

Schneider, B. (1983) An interactionist perspective on organizational effectiveness. In L.L. Cummings and B. Staw (Eds), Research in Organizational Behavior, pp. 1–31. Greenwich, CT: JAI Press.

Schneider, B. (1987) The people make the place. Personnel Psychology, 40: 437–453.

Schwartz, H. and Davis, S. (1981) Matching corporate culture and business strategy. Organizational Dynamics, 10(1): 30–48.

Schweiger, D. and Sandberg, W. (1989) The utilization of individual capabilities in group approaches to strategic decision making. Strategic Management Journal, 10: 31–43.

Schwenk, C. (1990) Conflict in organizational decision making: an exploratory study of its effects in for-profit and not-for-profit organizations. Management Science, 36: 436–448.

Shah, P.P. and Jehn, K.A. (1993) Do friends perform better than acquaintances: the interaction of friendship, conflict, and task. Group Decision and Negotiation, 2(2): 149–166.

Sherif, M. (1936) The Psychology of Social Norms. New York: Harper & Brothers.

Smith, K.G., Smith, K.A., Olian, J.D., Sims, H.P., O'Bannon, D.P. and Scully, J.A. (1994) Top management team demography and process: the role of social integration and communication. Administrative Science Quarterly, 39: 412–438.

Stasser, G., Kerr, N. and Davis, J. (1989) Influence processes and consensus models in decision-making groups. In P. Paulus (Ed), Psychology of Group Influence, 2nd Edn. Hillsdale, NJ: Erlbaum.

Staw, B.M., Sandelands, L. and Dutton, J. (1981) Threat-rigidity effects in organizational performance. Administrative Science Quarterly, 28: 582–600.

Steiner, I.D. (1972) Group Process and Productivity. New York: Academic Press.

Syan, C.S. and Menon, U. (Eds) (1994) Concurrent Engineering: Concepts, Implementation and Practice. London: Chapman & Hall.

Taylor, S. and Crocker, J. (1981) Schematic bases of social information processing. In E.T. Higgins, C.P. Herman and M. Zanna (Eds), The Ontario Symposium on Personality and Social Psychology, Vol. 1. Hillsdale, NJ: Erlbaum.

Tjosvold, D. (1991) The Conflict Positive Organization. Reading, MA: Addison-Wesley.

Tsui, A.S. and O'Reilly III, C.A. (1989) Beyond simple demographic effects: the importance of relational demography in superior-subordinate dyads. Academy of Management Journal, 32(2): 402–423.

Tsui, A., Egan, T. and O'Reilly, C. (1992) Being different: relational demography and organizational attachment. Administrative Science Quarterly, 37: 549–579.

Turner, R. and Colomy, P. (1988) Role differentiation: orienting principles. In E.J. Lawler and B. Markovsky (Eds), Social Psychology of Groups: a Reader. Greenwich, CT: JAI Press.

Tushman, M. (1977) Special boundary roles in the innovation process. Administrative Science Quarterly, 22: 587–605.

Tushman, M. and O'Reilly, C. (1996) The ambidextrous organization: managing evolutionary and revolutionary change. California Management Review, 8–30.

Valley, K.L., Neale, M.A. and Mannix, E.A. (1995) Friends, lovers, colleagues, strangers: the effects of relationships on the process and outcome of dyadic negotiations. Research on Negotiations in Organizations, 5: 65–93.

Verkuyten, M., de Jong, W. and Masson, C.N. (1993) Job satisfaction among ethnic minorities in the Netherlands. Applied Psychology: an International Review, 42: 171–189.

Wageman, R. (1995) Interdependence and group effectiveness. Administrative Science Quarterly, 40: 145–180.

Wageman, R. and Mannix, E. (1998) The uses and misuses of power in task-performing teams. In R. Kramer and M. Neale (Eds), Power and Influence in Organizations. Newbury Park, CA: Sage.

Wall, V. and Nolan, L. (1986) Perceptions of inequity, satisfaction, and conflict in task oriented groups. Human Relations, 39: 1033–1052.

Weingart, L.R. (1992) Impact of group goals, task component complexity, effort, and planning on group performance. Journal of Applied Psychology, 77: 33–54.

Wittenbaum, G.M. and Stasser, G. (1996) Management of information in small groups. In J.L. Nye and A.M. Brower (Eds), What's Social About Social Cognition? Social Cognition Research in Small Groups, pp. 3–28. Thousand Oaks, CA: Sage.

Zenger, T.R. and Lawrence, B.S. (1989) Organizational demography: the differential effects of age and tenure distributions on technical communication. Academy of Management Journal, 32: 353–376.

# Section IV

# Culture and Change

Chapter 13 addresses how culture change applies to a new form of organization called the "strategic enterprise". This kind of organization is responsive to highly competitive, rapidly changing environments. It combines features of a loosely structured holding company and a tightly controlled bureaucracy. It can focus across multiple businesses while leveraging shared resources and competencies. The chapter draws on the authors' extensive experience helping organizations transform their cultures. First, five lessons for successful cultural change are presented. These identify the action levers, leadership behaviors, and organizational outcomes that are essential for culture change. Then, the implications of these lessons for changing culture in the strategic enterprise are explored. This adds a new level of complexity to the change process. It requires creating distinct cultures for different business units while providing a limited yet essential set of shared values and beliefs for the overall enterprise.

Chapter 14 presents a social rules perspective on changing organization cultures. First, social rules theory is described and then organization culture is reformulated in terms of these concepts. Social rules link the cognitive-emotional elements of organization culture (e.g. values and assumptions) to observable organizational behaviors. Thus, members know their organization's culture through the rules they create, learn, and follow. Given this perspective, the chapter next explores possibilities for changing organization cultures through creating, modifying, and extinguishing social rules. This change process involves working with culture in three sequential yet overlapping stages: (1) surfacing information about social rules; (2) assessing the need to change social rules; and (3) implementing and institutionalizing social-rule changes if necessary. The chapter identifies specific roles for carrying out these change activities as well as techniques for working with culture. Finally, particular concomitants of success in cultural work are described.

Chapter 15 describes an approach to organizational culture developed by the author over the past decade. The framework is based on extensive research showing how organization culture affects organization performance. It is designed to be useful for executives who are trying to use culture as a point of leverage for organization change.

The chapter begins by discussing five important lessons about making organization culture relevant during the change process. Next, the culture framework that lies at the center of this approach is described along with an example of how it can be applied to diagnose an organization's culture. The framework is based on four cultural traits that have been shown to have a strong influence on organizational performance: involvement, consistency, adaptability, and mission. The chapter then presents an analysis of three organizations that are undergoing substantial change and are using this cultural approach to guide their change process. The final section of the chapter returns to a discussion of the lessons learned about how to conceptualize organizational culture in a way that makes it a key point of leverage for organization change.

# Chapter 13

# Culture Change in the Strategic Enterprise: Lessons from the Field

**David A. Nadler**

**Peter K. Thies**

*and*

**Mark B. Nadler**
*Mercer Delta Consulting, LLC, New York, NY, USA*

## INTRODUCTION

It should be apparent to all that we are witnessing a profound and, in some ways, unprecedented transformation in the essential nature of business organizations. With astounding speed, fundamental shifts in the business environment are driving corresponding changes in the way companies are designing their organizations in order to meet new strategic imperatives. Those changes, in turn, have massive implications for anyone engaged in the difficult work of transforming an organization's culture.

What we are seeing today is the emergence of what we describe as the "Strategic Enterprise". In contrast with both the loosely structured holding companies as well as the tightly organized, centrally controlled corporate monoliths of the past, the Strategic Enterprise represents a new organizational architecture created in response to the unique competitive challenges that have evolved in recent years. It is a complex organization, characterized by a variety of both tight and loose structural linkages between the corporate center and the various business units. The purpose of the Strategic Enterprise is to achieve both focus and leverage – to organize the discreet businesses loosely enough to allow a laser-like focus on activities requiring differentiated egies, such as new technologies or highly fractionated market segments, while leveraging the opportunities provided by core capabilities, pooled resources, and economies of scale. (For a more in-depth discussion of the Strategic Enterprise, see Nadler and Tushman, 1999.)

The single most critical issue driving these changes is time – more specifically, the demand for dramatically faster organizational speed in every facet of the enterprise. Not only product cycles, but also strategic life cycles, have been compressed to an incredible degree. As a result, organizations have to find ways to compete and innovate simultaneously in multiple market segments and in overlapping timeframes. In practical terms, that means successful companies have to create and nurture an array of businesses that compete with each other – and in some cases, even seek to make each other obsolete – in pursuit of enterprise-level strategic goals.

Working in this new and rapidly changing environment, we and our colleagues have gained some valuable lessons in recent years about how to engage in culture change that actually works. Many of the core principles that have formed the basis of our work over the years remain valid, but we have also concluded that some of the approaches that worked in the 1970s and 1980s are quickly losing their relevance in the age of the Strategic Enterprise.

Our purpose in this chapter is to present five important lessons, distilled from our work with more than 100 major organizations, that can help guide the successful transformation of organizational culture. After briefly summarizing those lessons, we will explore in further depth their implications for changing culture in the Strategic Enterprise. Those acquainted with our work will find much here that is familiar. Based upon our experience, certain principles and approaches have successfully withstood the test of time, but just as clearly, the new business environment imposes some new challenges for the successful transformation of culture.

# SUCCESSFUL CULTURE CHANGE: FIVE LESSONS

## Lesson 1: Culture Change, in and of Itself, is Rarely a Desirable Objective

Too many leaders make the mistake of thinking they can change behavior in an organization by changing its culture. In reality, it is usually the other way around: successful organizational change, driven by the need to change performance in ways that will help achieve strategic objectives, eventually results in fundamental cultural change. Nevertheless, we continue to see massive efforts grounded in the belief that culture change, in itself, is the ultimate goal rather than improving the organization's performance or the execution of its business strategy.

Historically, the notion of corporate culture has been shrouded in mystery and ambiguity. Because it has been hard to describe and harder to quantify, discussions of culture have taken on an almost mystical quality. Corporate campaigns aimed specifically and exclusively at culture change have often taken on an almost Orwellian tone, urging employees to adopt new values and behave in different ways. Internal communications campaigns have preached the message of culture change before any substantive changes actually occur. In those situations, the messages have rung hollow, planting the seeds of cynicism and disillusion that have so frequently surrounded corporate culture initiatives. The underlying belief has been that if you distributed enough posters, placards, and wallet cards, people would fundamentally change the way they performed their jobs. They did not.

By contrast, the actions that lead to real culture change are tangible, pervasive, directly connected to the organization's strategy, and fully integrated into the overall fabric of organizational life. Slogans, posters, and pep rallies in the absence of real change are not only pointless, they are actually counter-productive. They have high risk of exhausting resources and diluting the credibility of leaders to ask for "real change" when it is required.

## Lesson 2: Successful Culture Change Requires Concrete, Visible Actions Targeted at Those Specific Elements of the Organization That Provide the Levers For Change

Changing an organization's culture boils down to directing energy and effort toward changing four basic, identifiable aspects of organizational life: the behavior of institutional leaders; the execution of managerial practices; the organization's basic structure, systems, and formal processes; and actions taken with opinion leaders and other individuals who play key roles in both the formal and informal systems. This lesson is one of the enduring aspects of culture change. Our experience suggests that when culture change efforts explicitly target each of these four levers, the changes are more pervasive, long lasting, and clearly tied to improved organizational performance.

## Lesson 3: in the New Business Environment, Traditional, Programmatic Efforts at Culture Change Will Usually Prove Much Less Effective Than Efforts Designed to Change the Overall Organizational Context

To be sure, there have been situations in which large-scale, long-term culture change programs have worked; the Xerox Quality program and Corning Inc.'s "Growing Corning" are two notable examples. Programmatic efforts such as these explicitly identify the behavior, values, and underlying assumptions that form the basis of the desired culture. They often involve intensive individual and small-group interventions intended to challenge and change the basic beliefs of key leaders, followed by company-wide training and education programs. In most cases, these programmatic efforts include specific actions that are bundled and supported by an arsenal of communications initiatives.

Nevertheless, our experience shows that programmatic efforts at culture change rarely succeed because they require three essential ingredients: a direct connection to strategic imperatives; the zealous, personal leadership of the CEO; and an abundance of time – something on the scale of 5–7 years. You will sometimes find one of those ingredients and occasionally two, but it is rare to find all three. And as we mentioned earlier, speed is becoming a critical factor; we would be hard-pressed to find a major corporation today that can afford the luxury of spending 6 or 7 years to create major change the way Xerox, for instance, was able to back in the 1970s and 1980s. And despite their past success, senior leaders at Corning will tell you today that if fundamental behavioral change does not continue across the board and at an even faster rate than ever before, the competitive game will pass you by within a year or two.

We have come to believe that in most situations, the more effective alternative to programmatic efforts is to change the culture by changing the context for behavior. That requires changes in the organizational structure, reward systems, management processes, and individual actions of influential leaders. Over time, those changes are much more successful – and much faster – than programmatic efforts aimed specifically at changing people's values and beliefs.

## Lesson 4: the Emergence of the Strategic Enterprise Requires the Capability to Shape and Nurture a Variety of Dramatically Different Cultures, Held Together by the "Glue" of Enterprise-Wide Values

In most organizations, the goal has been to unify the enterprise through the development of a common culture. Subcultures, based on geography or professional discipline, for example, were acknowledged and tolerated. In the Strategic Enterprise, stark cultural differences must be encouraged. That is because the essential organizing principle of the Strategic Enterprise is "designed divergence" – the creation of multiple and widely varying business models suited to each business unit's particular strategy. Differing strategies and differing organization designs require differing cultures.

The most obvious example – though far from the only one – involves the Internet businesses that many companies are nurturing within the larger enterprise. It should be clear to all of us by now that in most instances, the cultural attributes required by Internet operations vary dramatically from those of mature, core businesses in terms of speed, risk taking, innovation, quality, decision making, compensation – the list goes on and on. It has become fashionable in some quarters to suggest that core businesses would be better off if they incorporated the e-business culture, but the fact is that the different businesses involve very different competitive challenges, customer requirements, and technological needs. No one size fits all.

At the same time, assuming a sound strategic case for maintaining a variety of radically different businesses under common ownership and management, senior leaders face the challenge of providing some basic values that provide coherence and identity – the "cultural glue", in essence – at the enterprise level. An example of cultural glue is the enterprise's approach to attracting, developing, and retaining talent. The values, philosophy, and approach to leveraging talent and developing leaders across diverse businesses can be used for competitive advantage if it is supported and implemented consistently.

What is required is the difficult balancing act of nurturing vastly different business unit cultures within the framework of consistent, strategy-based enterprise culture. Consequently, culture change has taken on a degree of complexity unknown in the past.

## Lesson 5: Without Question, the Most Critical Ingredient in Successful Culture Change Continues to be the Role of Senior Leaders

Our experience in working with evolving businesses in the past 3 or 4 years merely reinforces what we have learned over the past two decades: if your goal is to create the real changes that will result in fundamental culture change, there is no substitute for the active engagement of the CEO and the executive team. It is simply not enough for the top leaders to "sign off" on a program and then go through the motions while subordinates are left to carry the load. To the contrary, it is up to the top leaders to collectively assume the role of "chief architect" of the change process.

Indeed, the role of executive teams will only grow in importance with the emergence of the Strategic Enterprise. They will represent the only real point of connection between the disparate elements of the complex organization. The dual challenge we described in Lesson 4 will, in very real terms, become the executive team's challenge. Each team member will be responsible for nurturing the appropriate business unit subcultures while, at the same time, employing the full array of change techniques to inculcate the few essential values that give the enterprise a shared direction and identity. That responsibility cannot be delegated – only the most senior people can do it.

# IMPLICATIONS: CHANGING CULTURE IN THE STRATEGIC ENTERPRISE

Each of the lessons we have just introduced involves important implications for the design and leadership of culture change. Let us examine each in more detail.

## Implication #1: Move from Form to Function

Our first lesson is that culture change, in and of itself, is rarely a desirable objective. Let's face it: the term "culture change" carries a lot of baggage these days. While there might be rare cases in which the phrase actually inspires people to engage in profound change, the more typical responses among senior executives range from healthy skepticism to outright resistance. And those reactions seem mild when compared with what you encounter as you move out into the organization. In many Fortune 500 companies, top leaders have seen culture change efforts come and go without producing any noticeable change in either behavior or business performance. So they are understandably wary when the latest culture initiative lands on their desks.

Much of the skepticism is well deserved. Too often, culture change quickly degenerates from a strategy-driven change effort to mere "slideware". The emphasis on "cascading" the program – rolling it out to ever-expanding audiences – takes on a life of its own and begins to overwhelm the actual development and execution of real changes; for example, posters may indicate that customer service is a top priority and executives may appear on videos and commercials supporting this point. Yet there are no additional resources devoted to superior service, no metrics to measure customer satisfaction, insufficient technology to respond swiftly to customer concerns, and little authority given to employees with customer contact to make decisions on pricing, discounting, problem resolution, special orders, etc. So as more and more people are exposed to the communications aspect of the program without seeing any concrete results, the initiative takes on the look and feel of a "program du jour" and rapidly loses steam.

Yet, despite the widespread skepticism, the underlying interest in transforming culture is well founded. The increasing emphasis on the cultural aspects of organizational change is fueled by the continuing wave of mega-mergers, acquisitions, and spinoffs. These major restructurings make it more important than ever before to fundamentally change the ways in which companies are run and leaders do their jobs.

Furthermore, as the Strategic Enterprise and e-businesses emerge as new organizational forms, many of the same cultural issues exist in these companies as in traditional organizations. As we work with senior executives and discuss their view of the primary challenges facing their organizations, we keep hearing the same concerns:

- "Our strategy is great – we just can't execute."
- "We've reorganized, but nothing's changed."
- "We need to be more customer focused in order to compete."
- "The real problem is that everyone's accountable, yet no one's accountable."
- "What we really need is a changing of the guard."
- "Our biggest problem is that we can't seem to keep good people."
- "We're too slow and can't make decisions."
- "We're great at looking back and analyzing; we need to get better at looking forward and anticipating."

Our conclusion is that the purpose of culture change efforts remains relevant, important, and worthy of significant organizational effort. What is needed is a renewed emphasis on function to match the emphasis on form, focusing on the right issues, and attacking them in the right way. In today's strategic enterprises where speed is the order of the day, efforts that appear too big, too glossy, or lack visible punch are doomed to failure.

The imperative is to decide upon the specific actions to be taken and lay out the game plan for execution before announcing the effort to broad audiences. Ideally, the announcement of the plan for changing the culture would coincide with specific actions, such as major structural change. While the pressure to communicate intentions for culture change is always great at the beginning of the effort, we believe it is important to lead with function and follow with form.

In fact, experience suggests that companies are often better off if they avoid labeling their efforts as a "culture change". Many effective large-scale efforts to change "the way we do things around here" are not even conceived as culture change projects. Instead, they are integrated change efforts that have a new business direction or strategic thrust as their central theme. The Limited, Inc., for example, is focusing not on culture change itself but is executing an initiative entitled Building Leadership Brands. While there is no program called culture change, the net effect of the actions and decisions by Chairman Les Wexner and the senior team of The Limited, Inc. is a visible change in the culture of the company.

The imperative for those seeking to help corporations achieve fundamental culture change is to help key leaders stay focused on the desired results. Be willing to drop the term *culture change* and resist the temptation to package a series of change initiatives under one label or program name simply for communication purposes. Form follows function, and in the specific case of culture change, it is more important than ever to follow this rule.


## Implication #2: Concrete, Visible Actions Targeting Specific Aspects of Organizational Life Provide the Levers for True Culture Change

Those responsible for creating culture change face a massive array of options. Everyone has his or her own opinion about what works; bring a group together to brainstorm the possibilities and the recommendations will range all the way from symbolic acts such as removing the doors on executive's offices to more dramatic actions such as "firing everybody and re-hiring the ones you want". While many of the ideas might have merit in theory, pragmatism has to enter the conversation at some point. Every organization has finite resources and a limited capacity to absorb change. So the challenge is to carefully select a set of actions that are both "doable" and likely to have substantial impact. Of course, that is easier said than done.

The key to choosing the right approach to culture change is to keep in mind how organizations function. We tend to think about organizational performance in terms of a social systems model (see Figure 13.1) with an interrelated set of four components – the work, the people, the formal organization, and the informal organization, all of which interact to translate strategy into performance. Research and practice in the field of organizational behavior show that organizations are effective to the extent that they achieve fit among the primary elements (within the context of strategy).

As social systems, organizations are inherently resistant to change; they are actually designed to neutralize the impact of any attempts at change – for example, changing the structure alone will not fundamentally affect organizational behavior. In fact, the informal system will actually strengthen in response to the structural change; during times of change people rely on established relationships and informal processes in order to circumvent the new formal structure. The increasing strength of the informal system, if left untouched, can negate the impact of structural change if there is nothing else to support the change in direction, such as a change in reward systems and leader behavior. Consequently, the only way to create lasting culture change in a dynamic social system is to direct energy and effort toward changing four basic aspects of organizational life: the behavior of institutional leadership; the execution of managerial practices; the organization's basic structure, systems and formal processes; and the behavior of opinion leaders and other key individuals in the informal and formal system. Table 13.1 defines each of the four key change levers in more detail.

Practitioners and thought leaders agree. Herb Kelleher, the CEO of Southwest Airlines, is known for his ability to cultivate a highly effective culture. When asked

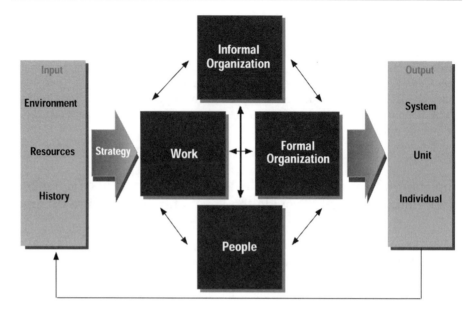

**Figure 13.1**  Congruence model of organizational effectiveness.

how he created and sustained the tight-knit, family culture at Southwest Airlines, he said, "There's no magic formula. Its like building a giant mosaic – it takes thousands of little pieces." (Lancaster, 1999).

Jim Collins, co-author of *Built to Last*, suggests that a relatively small set of powerful, symbolic "catalytic mechanisms" form the core of fundamental changes in the way businesses operate (Collins, 1999). These mechanisms are specific changes in policy, processes, or systems that turn objectives into performance.

Consider The New York Times Company, an organization undergoing a transformation in the way it is managed and operated. In the late 1990s, The Times Company certainly went through its share of management offsites and communications rollouts that helped set the stage for culture change. But ask managers to describe what is really changing, and they will describe very concrete actions taken by senior management – the inclusion of operating unit heads in policy deliberations, a more supportive and less antagonistic budgeting process, new initiatives to promote career development, and the departure of key executives who were uncomfortable with the more open, inclusive approach to management. Chairman Arthur O. Sulzberger Jr. and CEO Russell T. Lewis have gone out of their way to be visible and accessible to the people at operating units across the country, devoting valuable time and energy to dispelling the long-held notion that employees "out in the provinces" just did not matter to executives in New York. While Times Company leaders would be the first to tell you that their job is far from done, more and more of the organization is starting to see changes in the way the business is run that translate into a very tangible change in its culture.

**Table 13.1** Leverage points for culture change

| Lever | Definition | Objective |
|---|---|---|
| Organizational context | Structures, systems, and processes that drive organizational behavior, e.g. appraisal and reward systems, staffing and selection practices. | Implement changes in structure and systems that reinforce the desired behavior and results. |
| Institutional leadership | The action and behavior of the CEO, senior team, and senior line managers. | Increase leaders' ability to: articulate the new culture and expectations for each individual; model desired behavior; provide recognition of behavior consistent with business objectives; impose sanctions for undesirable behavior; perform symbolic acts to support the new business direction. |
| Individual behavior | The actions of individuals in the organization – particularly those of key opinion leaders. | Send signals about the desired change through the treatment of key employees. Whenever possible, publicly recognize and reward those who behave consistent with the desired direction. Impose visible sanctions on influential employees who resist required changes. |
| Management practices | The day-to-day actions of the individual managers – how they interact with each other, their subordinates, and their own management. | Give managers the tools to teach others about the desired change and sustain the new direction through their interactions with others. Directly promote behavior consistent with the new direction on the part of hundreds, even thousands, of people. |

## Implication #3: to Change Culture, Change the Context for Behavior

Our third lesson is that programmatic efforts at culture change are generally less effective than efforts geared toward changing the overall organizational context. Programmatic efforts, which attempt to modify people's values and beliefs, tend to be left unsupported by actions that actually change the environment in which behavior occurs.

We have all seen it and perhaps even experienced it ourselves: a small group of senior executives goes off to a high-impact offsite, and they come back excited and energized by all they have learned about their own behavior and how it affects other people. But unless these deep personal insights and heightened readiness for change are supported by a host of other changes involving the organization's structure, systems, and processes, the progress made by each individual will quickly dissipate. The result is the all too common "offsite syndrome" – the burst of post-offsite enthusiasm followed by a huge let-down when nothing happens back home to motivate or energize the 99.9% of the company who did not have the good fortune to attend the offsite.

Rather than developing a so-called "culture change program", we find it is much more effective to develop a set of integrated actions that affect behavior – resulting, over time, in a change in the culture. The four levers for change cited above provide a framework for identifying and creating these specific actions. These interventions, when employed in combination with one another, have succeeded in creating significant culture change. Table 13.2 summarizes these interventions.

The Limited, Inc., for example, has been working hard in recent years to fundamentally change many critical aspects of the way the company operates. Over the past 3 years, they have made changes to the portfolio of businesses, substantially changed the formal structure, redesigned core brand management and managerial processes, changed the compensation system for leaders, recruited outside talent at the highest levels of the company, and concentrated on how their senior leaders in both the businesses and the corporate center behave. From our vantage point, the result of these efforts is a fairly significant cultural change which has pulled on most of the key levers and has employed many of the interventions above. Both individual and organizational performance has significantly improved, yet there is no "program" called culture change.

Lucent Technologies has been working on significant culture change ever since its creation as part of the AT&T "trivestiture" in 1997. While Lucent has developed effective and far-reaching communications to describe the desired culture, the change is not happening because of clear communications alone. Right from the start, changes were made on multiple fronts to shape the desired culture:

- First, stretch goals were set for the organization and its key leaders.
- Then-CEO Henry Schacht and COO Rich McGinn worked extensively to align the executive team on the desired change.
- Tangible rewards and incentives were linked to the achievement of stretch goals.
- Schacht and McGinn aggressively modeled a collaborative approach to leadership and were both accessible and informal in their dealings with employees.
- External branding messages were closely linked to internal communications.
- Every Lucent employee received stock in the new company, ensuring that all employees were also shareholders.

As the Lucent example demonstrates, successful culture change efforts involve an integrated set of specific change initiatives tied together to support a new business strategy. Explicitly labeling these changes as "culture change" is not the issue; it is the actions that count.

**Table 13.2**   Targeted interventions for culture change

| Intervention | Actions | Intended outcomes |
| --- | --- | --- |
| Collaborative culture definition | Define dimensions and behaviors required for the new culture | Shared understanding and commitment to create the new culture |
| Measurement and gap analysis | Assess the gap between the current and desired cultures | Shared understanding of the priority gaps |
| Stakeholder analysis and engagement | Analyze key internal and external stakeholders to understand their position relative to the change | Commitment by key stakeholders to the proposed changes. Resistance to change kept to a healthy minimum |
| Senior leader behavior | Leader feedback process implemented with all senior managers | Senior managers model desired new behaviors |
| Structural change | Redesign of enterprise structure and/or senior leadership team | Alteration of reporting relationships and flow of information across and within groups |
| Management process redesign | Redesign of management structures, processes, and metrics | Develop new day-to-day processes that support and reinforce the required behaviors |
| Recognition and reward | Redesign of compensation and reward systems | Create a direct connection between new behaviors and personal outcomes (both monetary and non-monetary) |
| Formal feedback process | Development and implementation of explicit feedback processes | Desired new behaviors reinforced through ongoing, visible feedback process |
| Large group engagement | Working sessions of large groups to make progress on specific change initiatives | Concrete changes in the way people work together to accomplish business objectives |
| Educational interventions | Education and training programs which facilitate the rapid development of the desired new behaviors | Acquisition of desired new behaviors by management and employees throughout the business |
| Communications | Communications strategies integrated into a coherent message | Broad understanding of the need for and direction of change |
| In-depth individual interventions | Constructive coaching and actions taken with senior leaders | Senior managers "walk the talk" or leave the company |

## Implication #4: the Emergence of the Strategic Enterprise Renders Monolithic Approaches to Culture Change Obsolete

In the case of the Strategic Enterprise, culture change has taken on a degree of complexity unknown in the past; it requires the nurturing of vastly different business unit cultures within the framework of consistent, strategy-based enterprise culture. While traditional enterprise-wide change efforts "allow for" industry or business unit subcultures, culture change in the Strategic Enterprise should feature and leverage these subcultures. The implication for culture change is that each business requires the maximum ability to meet competitive challenges, customer requirements, and technological needs without destructive interference from the corporate center. The culture of the Strategic Enterprise should be built upon an explicit understanding of where there is value in protecting "states rights" within business units and where to encourage "federalism" to leverage skills, talents, and processes across the enterprise.

This involves a careful balance that few organizations think through with appropriate rigor. While there is a sound strategic argument for maintaining a variety of businesses with radically different cultures within a corporate framework of common ownership, the opportunities for true leverage across diverse businesses must be explored much more deeply and pursued much more selectively than in the past. At the heart of the issue is the general tendency of managers to overestimate the benefits of synergy across divisions, business units, and functions. As Goold and Campbell (1998) point out, there are several biases that lead managers to overestimate the potential for synergy. To be sure, there are opportunities for synergy within the Strategic Enterprise, but these should be examined carefully and tested before they are assumed to exist.

The Limited, Inc. has been thinking through this very carefully. Historically run as a collection of independent business, the company's previous culture was one of fiercely independent businesses with little guidance from "Inc." staff and minimal coordination across the company. While some of the businesses developed strong brands – Victoria's Secret, Abercrombie & Fitch, and Bath & Body Works come to mind – there was inconsistent performance among the various businesses and growing lack of brand differentiation.

One of the choices they have made very carefully is how the corporate center and the business should work together to achieve the company's objectives. Over the past 3 years, the company has focused on leveraging talent, experience, and key common processes across the businesses in order to strengthen their individual ability to establish competitive brands. While on the one hand the Limited, Inc. is developing strength in the corporate center, they have explicitly discussed the sources of leverage and selectively chosen areas for corporate intervention. This continues to be a complex transition, but the lesson is that achieving the right balance between federalism and states rights is one that requires careful attention and explicit discussion among senior leadership.

Another challenge for culture change in the Strategic Enterprise is how companies grow and manage Internet businesses within the larger enterprise. The speedier, entrepreneurial, and focused cultures of e-businesses hold many attractions, causing some leaders to believe that the traditional core businesses would be better off if they incorporated the e-commerce culture. Of course, the cultures of dot.com and e-business units are very different than mature core businesses in terms of speed, risk-taking, innovation, quality, and decision making. So we suggest that before leaping to the conclusion that the goal is to create a dot.com culture across the board, organizations should examine carefully and make explicit choices about where it pays to be big and where small is beautiful. The monolithic approach to culture change is not relevant when dealing with Strategic Enterprises.

The incubation of dot.com businesses within mature companies raises another important cultural issue. Let us consider the example of The New York Times Company again. In the summer of 1999, The Times Company consolidated its more than 50 websites in a new unit, Times Company Digital (TCD). The goal was to create a new, distinctive Internet portal that capitalizes upon the distinctive positioning afforded by The New York Times brand name and all it implies in terms of quality and credibility. Those attributes are inextricably linked with The Times Company's unique culture.

Here is the problem: as TCD adds new capabilities, it will bring in new people – both through individual hires and acquisitions. These new employees will not only come from outside The Times Company; most will not even speak the common language of journalism or the newspaper business. Unless The Times Company's unique values and beliefs are somehow inculcated in this new group – in a way that does not stifle the speed, entrepreneurial spirit, and risk-taking so essential to any e-business – TCD runs the risk of becoming indistinguishable from Yahoo, AOL, or any other Internet portal, and thus losing its source of competitive differentiation. That is the tricky balancing act we are talking about – allowing a unique subculture to flourish while providing the common values and beliefs that give the enterprise its distinct character.

A way of thinking about culture change in the Strategic Enterprise is to shift the focus from creating a one-culture company to creating an operating environment where diverse businesses with different models can coordinate where it pays to do so and be independent where focus is critical. This operating environment is not a one-size-fits-all culture, but rather, a core set of values, beliefs, and rules of engagement for how businesses should work together. Instead of dictating the look and feel of each business, the operating environment provides the means for capturing synergy and leverage where it makes sense. It creates shared expectations of behavior across the diverse businesses.

We are finding that creating a high-performance operating environment in the Strategic Enterprise is a matter of developing coherence and identity at the enterprise level to create the "glue" that holds related but distinct units together. Clearly the role of the corporate center is key to figuring this out. New models of the activist center are emerging which provide a framework for the role of the corporate center in the Strategic Enterprise (for more on this topic see Goold et al., 1994; Rheault and Trussler, 1996). An effective method of developing the glue is to explicitly define the role of the corporate center *vis-à-vis* the business units. Table 13.3 summarizes common roles of the corporate center, with company examples.

What we have learned is that a single, consistent culture is no longer relevant in the Strategic Enterprise. Instead, the focus is on developing glue at the center which holds

**Table 13.3**  Activist centre roles in the strategic enterprise

| Activist center role | Company example |
|---|---|
| Set strategic platform | Corning "deep dive" strategy development |
| Ensure quality talent at corporate and businesses | Xerox strategic selection Limited organization and performance review |
| Specialized services | Chase merger process Lucent acquisitions toolkit |
| Identify and capture efficiencies | BMS integrated customer strategies |
| Define core processes and specify execution "non-negotiables" | Limited, Inc. brand management process |

diverse units together. The key is to be clear about where value is gained from enter-prise-wide collaboration and to explicitly define the role of the center *vis-à-vis* the business.

## Implication #5: Its Still All About Leadership

Our lesson in this area: there is no substitute for the active engagement of the CEO and the executive team in culture change. Top leaders cannot simply review and approve the approach to culture change. They must be actively involved in building the approach and be ready, willing, and able to execute it. Limited, Inc. Chairman Les Wexner systematically obtains feedback from the businesses and the corporate centers regarding the transition. He then personally engages the senior leadership team in conversations on successes and lessons learned. This ongoing feedback and course-correction process improves the speed and reach of the change process.

There are two different yet critical roles for the executive team: chief architect of the approach and systems integrator during implementation (Thies and Wagner, 1998).

Carrying out the chief architect role requires the executive team to provide active leadership in three important ways: through defining the new operating environment; engaging the company's top leadership in the process; and developing a strategy for making the desired changes a reality. The systems integrator role involves choosing the key levers for change, selecting the appropriate interventions, providing the necessary resources, and monitoring progress (Table 13.4).

For example, the executive team of a major unit within a consumer product company created an "A-list" of eight change initiatives they would implement in order to achieve the desired results for the business. For each of the eight major initiatives, they developed action plans to drive progress in that area. Each executive team member was given responsibility for one or two of the "A-list" items. This became each executive team member's shared leadership role. The result of this team's work over time was a fundamental change in the business unit's culture, driven and led from the top by the executive team.

**Table 13.4** Roles for the executive team in culture change

| Executive team role | Role description |
|---|---|
| Change process architect | Identifying the need for change<br>Defining the new culture<br>Role modeling desired behaviors<br>Engaging leadership in the process<br>Diagnosing the current state |
| Systems integrator | Identifying leverage points<br>Chartering specific initiatives<br>Providing resources<br>Assessing progress |

# SUMMARY

Changing the culture of a large organization has never been easy, and it is not getting any easier.

The growing demand for organizational speed, coupled with the widespread cynicism spawned by decades of hollow culture change programs divorced from any real change, makes it highly unlikely that the traditional approach to sweeping cultural transformation will enjoy much success in the future. The key to effective change will be an understanding that changes in structures, processes, and systems, supported by appropriate leader behavior, should be targeted at producing specific changes in behavior directly related to performance and the achievement of strategic objectives. If those initiatives are successful, culture change will follow in due course.

The emergence of the new organizational model, the Strategic Enterprise, adds a new level of complexity to the already daunting challenge of culture change. Operating within one enterprise but focusing on different technologies, market segments, and distribution channels, business units will require their own, distinctive cultures. At the same time, in order to maintain cohesion and strategic focus, the company will have to provide a limited but essential set of shared values and beliefs that embraces all of its businesses within a single enterprise culture.

As a result, the role of senior leaders in culture change will become more important than ever before. Together, the CEO and the executive team will share the responsibility for designing and implementing the series of targeted initiatives that will transform and sustain cultures that support both the business unit and enterprise-wide strategic goals.

# REFERENCES

Collins, J. (1999) Turning goals into results: the power of catalytic mechanisms. *Harvard Business Review*, July–August.

Goold, M. and Campbell, A. (1998) Desperately seeking synergy. Harvard Business Review, September–October.

Goold, M., Campbell, A. and Alexander, M. (1994) Corporate-Level Strategy: Creating Value in the Multi-business. New York: Wiley.

Lancaster, H. (1999) Herb Kelleher has one main strategy: treat employees well. The Wall Street Journal, August 31st.

Nadler, D.A. and Tushman, M.I. (1999) The organization of the future: strategic imperatives and core competencies for the 21st century. Organizational Dynamics, Summer: 45–60.

Rheault, D. and Trussler, S. (1996) The corporate center: what is the right model? Directors & Boards, Winter.

Thies, P.K. and Wagner, D.B. (1998) Creating a high-performance operating environment. In D.A. Nadler and J.L. Spencer (Eds), Executive Teams. San Francisco, CA: Jossey-Bass.

# Chapter 14

# Working with Cultures in Organizations: a Social Rules Perspective

**Craig C. Lundberg**
*Cornell University, Ithaca, NY, USA*

## INTRODUCTION

The phenomena referred to as organization culture, after early charges of mysticism and faddism, has in recent years become both popular and legitimate, and has a growing literature as this handbook attests. Regardless of its evolving sophistication and contemporary stature as a field of study by scholars and as a source of inspiration for practitioners, organizational culture continues to be sidetracked by numerous, vigorously debated questions. Is culture something organizations are? Is organizational culture an independent or a dependent variable? For an organization, is there one culture, a set of subcultures, or both? Can organizational culture be known through objective assessment or only through interpretation or inference? Is each organizational culture unique or do they have features in common that permit comparative analysis? These sorts of questions and the discourses, debates, and schools of thought they engender serve as a double-edged sword for the field. On the one hand, they promote vitality and innovation by the advocates of one side or another, i.e. new studies, new methods, and new theories, as well as attracting scholars and practitioners. On the other hand, these sorts of questions and debated responses tend to stall synthesis, confuse and perplex interested parties, and stifle the translation of organizational culture knowledge into useful practice by organizational stewards and change agents.

Behind many if not most of the debated questions is a more fundamental, double-barreled one: is organizational culture amenable to change? And if so, can organizational culture change be managed? To date, responses have tended to be polarized. Yes, cultures are changeable and of course they can be managed (Turnstall, 1983), or no, cultures have a life of their own and this cannot be planned for or intervened with. The stance taken here is that such responses are overstated and gloss both the phenomena and our thinking about it. I will argue that some aspects of organizational cultures, sometimes, under some circumstances, can be intentionally modified. Explicating this stance becomes the focus of this chapter.

The significance of organizational culture, that is, why it has drawn the attention of scholars and practitioners alike, is probably because it raises to consciousness features of organizations and the behavior of their members heretofore relatively ignored. Cultures after all are essentially about meanings, deep, symbolic and otherwise, and meanings are always emotionally laden – two features largely taboo in organizational life. Cultures are also major sources of identity, provide nuanced behavioral guidance, reduce uncertainty, permit claims and justifications, and are much else of significance to persons joined together in pursuit of common goals. Even the ways of understanding organizational cultures have utility. We are counseled to look both close up at the details of cultural specifics as well as to stand back and see cultures as wholes, to alternate careful description and cautious interpretation, ways of knowing that are both insightful and have built-in correctives. In a relatively random, often ambiguous, and largely unknowable world, it can be argued that cultures are essential for collective activity and human health, development and survival. In a world of change – large and small, swift and slow, but ubiquitous and continuous – the influence of organizational cultures on change and the influence of change on cultures merit close attention.

The general process of changing organizational cultures strongly resembles both management and consultancy. Many would agree that managing, in its essence, is a process of defining goals, comparing these intentions and hopes for performance with what is actually occurring, and then acting to reconcile the two. Consultancy depends on a parallel process – diagnosis (the discovery of what is actually happening and what is desired and comparing these), action planning (designing how to move from the actual to the desired), implementation, and assessment. In management and consultancy, the crucial first step is to surface relevant information (e.g. Cummings and Worley, 1997; Greiner and Metzger, 1983; Schein, 1969), and so it is with cultural modification.

The general process of examining cultural systems is undertaken for many reasons. The main reason was just alluded to – it is part of a change agent's responsibilities, i.e. it is what she or he does (manager, consultant, or concerned organizational member). Yet there are also other reasons (Lundberg, 1993). Sometimes it is as simple as imitation or curiosity. Influential members hear about organizational culture work elsewhere and just want to know about their own culture. Sometimes culture surfacing is seen as an efficient socialization activity for newer members or to assist geographically or functionally dispersed members to become reacquainted with the central reality of the organization. Usually the activity of culture examination develops a greater cohesion among an organization's members – for itself or in anticipation of or as a basis for other executive actions such as management recruitment, long-range planning, or other planned renewal activities.

Regardless of the reasons for engaging in culture work, consequences are inevitable. As already mentioned, performing culture work, i.e. surfacing, etc., can enhance socialization and team development. Also, as members become more aware of their organization's culture, this awareness contributes to the body of information on which everyday decisions and actions are based. Such cultural awareness often leads to subtle as well as intentional self-correcting behaviors – reinforcing patterned behaviors seemingly congruent with the culture and altering those that are not. Culture work can and usually does prepare members for deliberate organizational diagnosis and redesign of formal structures, systems, and processes, i.e. knowing what is culturally feasible. Thus, when formal changes are proposed, e.g. goal setting and strategic/ tactical planning, culture work assesses if it is consistent with the culture. Sometimes, probably rarely, culture surfacing and assessment may mobilize the concern and energy that leads to a new vision for a desired culture and efforts to craft it.

To argue, as is the intent of this chapter, that some aspects of cultures, under some circumstances, are amenable to intentional management change suggests that we go beyond the contemporary culture debates as well as the piece-meal quality of the contemporary organizational change field and attempt to both see more and see differently via a frame-changing exercise. Specifically, this chapter offers two contributions to seeing more and seeing differently by changing the conceptual lens. One is to bring attention to and systematically begin to elaborate an emerging theoretical perspective on social behavior–social rules theory. The other contribution is to use social rules theory to reconceptualize organizational culture and organizational change which allows a deeper understanding of our title – working with cultures.

Our argument in favor of a social rules conception of organizational culture and change will proceed in two sections. The first is conceptual. Social rules theory is initially elaborated, hopefully finding a reasonable balance between presenting its essential ideas and being smothered by technical detail. Then, we show how social rules link concepts and activities as a way of thinking about organizational cultures. The second section is pragmatic. Here the title of this chapter – working with cultures – is discussed as the practice of surfacing, examining, and modifying as appropriate the social rules that make up and give meaning to organizational culture.

# TOWARD UNRAVELING ORGANIZATIONAL CULTURE AND CHANGE

The terms "organization" and "management" and even "change" have come to carry a heavy connotative freight; that is, each of these terms is presumed to be about prescriptive, logical, analytical intentions. "Everyone knows" that organizational success comes from first goal setting, and then formulating strategies and policies, designing structures and control systems, acquiring and allocating resources, and so on, and change almost always means planned change. Organization as designed, purposive, more or less formalized systems dominates managerial thinking, composing a paradigm of intentionality where there is the unquestioned presumption of logic (Weick, 1982) and a compelling climate of rationality (Staw, 1980). Any close observer of organizations "knows", however, that all sorts of activities, sentiments and outcomes exist beyond the intentional and that there is a rich shadow of understandings and explanations in addition to the patina of plans, designs, and formalizations of intentionality.

Some non-intentional aspects of organizations have of course drawn attention for several decades. In fact, there is now quite a history of efforts to counter balance rational, analytic, intentional thinking, e.g. human relations, the informal organization, organizational psychology, the social psychology of organizations, etc. These and other schools of thought have provided a strong legacy of useful ideas and models (and other values) as well as descriptive reality to be sure, but usually these have been viewed as auxiliary to, overlapping with, or paralleling the intentional formal system. An idea and a way of thinking, a symbolic meaning-centered paradigm, was needed that could be woven together with the intentional. This paradigm would allow us to reinterpret the observables brought to attention by the intentional as well as draw attention to additional significant phenomena. Organizational culture has come to sometimes serve this purpose.

## On Organizational Culture

While the concept of culture has been with us for quite a long time and has been enormously elaborated (e.g. Kroeber and Kluckhohn, 1963), the focus and the field known as organizational culture is of fairly recent origin (Schein, 1990), although the phenomena was emphasized by a few early writers on organizations (e.g. Jacques, 1951; Selznick, 1949). "Culture", organizationally conceived, pushes us into territory left insufficiently explored by ideas that came before it. Group norms for a while seemed sufficient to explain such phenomenon as why participants of off-site training reverted to their former behaviors and attitudes once they returned to their work setting. Organizational climate, although lending itself to measurement and association with many variables of importance, like norms, ultimately did not allow an explanation of the deeper casual aspects of how organizations function. By the 1960s, a growing emphasis on whole organizations began and concepts such as "system" were evoked to describe the patterns of norms, attitudes, and values organization-wide (e.g. Katz and Kahn, 1965; Likert, 1961). Needed, moreover, were explanations for variations in climate, norms, and organizational behavior, and levels of stability in group and organizational behavior (Hofstede, 1980; Kilmann, 1984; Ouchi, 1981; Schein, 1985).

While the phenomenon of organizational culture has always existed, its popularity is less than two decades old. However, the literature has grown swiftly. A succession of more carefully conceived and empirically based efforts has provided elaboration of what organizational culture is, how it may be studied, its relationship to strategy, structure, and management practices, as well as several cautions (e.g. Dyer, 1986; Frost et al., 1985, 1991; Kilmann et al., 1985; Martin, 1992; Wilkens, 1989). As with any growing field of study, however, the concept of organizational culture has come to have many definitions. While definitions abound, almost all of them contain one or more of several central ideas such as values (Barney, 1986; Gordon, 1985), shared meanings (Feldman, 1988; Louis, 1985), assumptions (Schein, 1990) and beliefs

(Lorsch, 1985; Schwartz and Davis, 1981). A distillation of the definitions and themes in the literature provides the following conceptual understandings of the phenomenon: there is at present a growing convergence that culture may be understood as a layered phenomenon, that it is composed of two or three interrelated levels of meanings from those relatively observable to those mostly invisible. Davis (1984) provided two, daily beliefs (about how things work) and guiding beliefs (about what is important to compete about and direct the business, and to manage and direct the organization). Schein (1985) specifies and labels three levels: artifacts and creations (technology, art, visible and audible behavior patterns), values, and basic assumptions. The three levels proposed by Dyer (1986) are artifacts, perspectives (socially shared roles and norms), and values and assumptions. The three levels proposed by Lundberg (1990) are a manifest level (symbolic artifacts, language, stories, ritualistic activities, and patterned conduct), a level of strategic beliefs, and a core level (values and assumptions).

Behind the many definitions, conceptual frameworks and points of view about organizational culture, several widespread understandings of the phenomena can be discerned:

- It is a shared, common frame of reference, i.e. it is largely taken for granted and is shared by some significant portion of members.
- It is acquired and governs, i.e. it is socially learned and transmitted by members and provides them with rules for their organizational behavior.
- It endures over time, i.e. it can be found in any fairly stable social unit of any size, as long as it has a reasonable history.
- It is symbolic, i.e. it is manifested in observables such as language, behavior, and things to which are attributed meanings.
- It is at its core typically invisible and determinant, i.e. it is ultimately comprised of a configuration of deeply buried values and assumptions.
- It is modifiable, but not easily so.

Four additional points require emphasis. The first is the fallacy of believing that there is just one organizational culture. While most organizations do have a more or less well-developed "umbrella" culture, it is also common that most organizational subsystems have cultures also, e.g. divisions or departments, major layers of the organization, as do the major occupations of the organization (Gregory, 1983; Louis, 1983; Trice, 1993; Wilkens and Patterson, 1985). And, there is always the question of congruence among subsystem cultures and between them and the umbrella culture. The second point to emphasize builds on the first. Organizational and subsystem cultures may vary considerably along a continuum of intraculture clarity and consensus. Some cultures, regardless of size, have meanings that are consistent and agreed upon, i.e. so-called "strong cultures". Other cultures may hold differentiated and multiple meanings. Meyerson and Martin (1987) go further by suggesting the following cultural alternatives: "integration" (where the meanings of the dominant coalition are shared organization-wide), "differentiation" (where meanings overlap, collide, or coexist across subsystems), and "fragmentation" (where meanings are usually multiple and more ambiguous across all units of analysis from person to organization). The point here is not to assume either an intra- or intersystem consensus of meaning. The third point to emphasize is that the examination of levels of meaning and the identification of meanings is quite difficult since such interpretive sense-making always reflects the cultural allegiances of those involved. Lastly, organizational culture research tends to appear in one or the other of two major pairs of perspectives, the functionalist and the interpretive (Smircich, 1983), and either the insider (emic) or outsider (etic) perspective (Louis, 1985; Pike, 1967) – each important and useful.

If we look closely at the many definitions, common themes, conceptual schemes, and perspectives for discovering organizational culture, we can notice that there are essentially just two components: observable patterned behavior such as norms, language, customs, etc., and inferred cognitive-emotional ideas such as assumptions, beliefs, and other shared meanings. We further notice that these two components vary by level of generality or scope, from the specific to the philosophical, and are linked. The ideas serve as frames which cue the observed activity, "A cue in a frame is what makes sense, not the cue alone or the frame alone" (Weick, 1995, p. 110). Meaning is therefore relational. Organizational culture is thus understood as an organized set of ideas that draws attention to the phenomenon of observable patterned behavior (activities and events) and gives them meaning. It is the nature of the relationship between culture ideas and their phenomenon that is crucial and it is here that social rules come into play.

## About Social Rules[1]

The contention here is that culture is linked to organization-specific observable beha-

---

[1] The perspective outlined by social rules theory has roots in several places. It draws on the rich theoretical traditions of Marx and Weber but is clearly distinct from them and goes beyond them in making use of contributions from organization theory, comparative institutional analysis, theories of social structuration, microsociology, linguistics, and ethnomethodology as well as the theoretical insights provided by a number of contemporary scholars who have developed rule and rule system ideas (e.g. Chomsky, 1965; Cicourel, 1974; Goffman, 1974; Harre, 1979; Lindblom, 1977; Twining and Miers, 1982). The perspective breaks from most prior social theorizing in two important ways. On the one hand, it is explicitly meso, that is, it fosters and actor-system syntheses. Reference here is to the two fundamentally different conceptions of man and society that underlie the vast majority of theories of social behavior. One stresses the human agent as the source of social regularities and the forces that structure social systems as well as the conditions of human activity. The other stresses a structure or system where either humans are not found or where humans enact roles and function in social structures or systems they cannot basically change. On the other hand, social rules theory embraces both static and dynamic dimensions. As such, social rules theory resembles the attempts at new syntheses by such theorists as Archer (1986), Bourdieu (1977), Crozier and Friedberg (1980), Giddens (1979) and March (1994) who have eschewed the conceptual restrictions that follow from assumptions of social systems as only purposive and functional. Burns and Flan (1987) have provided the most focused and detailed conception of social rules theory – but at the institutional level. The version of social rules theory presented below is philosophically consistent with the epistemology of Winch (1958) and builds upon the foundations provided by Burns and Flan. It extends the recent semi-micro applications of Lundberg (1998, 1999), and is consciously influenced by the theoretical work of March (1994) and Weick (1988). All conceptual edifices have one or more primitive statements or assumptions. Social rules theory is no exception. It requires that we accept the following: that human beings often act purposefully; that social activities take place in concrete transaction situations in which the actors involved have unequal resources and opportunities to realize their purposes and interests; that through their actions and interactions, social actors regulate and change their material, institutional, and cultural world; and that behavior is organized to a large extent on the basis of explicit and implicit, multiple systems of rules.

viors by means of social rules – that social rules on the one hand reflect the culture and on the other hand guide behaviors – and members thus "know" their culture through rules they have created, learned, and follow. Sets of social rules thus constitute shared cultural knowledge and shared ways of knowing. Organizational members will have membership in one or more cultures, i.e. the umbrella culture, the cultures of organizational subparts, occupational cultures, etc. Culture membership will vary in *centrality*, where centrality is a function of time spent, role or position occupied, and expertise in the activity of a cultural system. At a point in time, because of their centrality, persons will vary in their status and power, primarily reflecting their sophistication (knowledge and/or capability) about and their commitment to the set of rules that govern the cultural systems. *Rule sets* are made up of a set of related rules which govern the behavior of cultural system members with one another, with members of other systems, and with system relevant things and processes. Rules may be explicit and/or implicit and they specify, to a greater or lesser extent, who participates (and who is excluded), and who does what, where, when, and how in relation to others. Rules and rule sets do not account for the psychology of persons; they regulate behavior but do not determine it – constrained of course by the biological and physical as well as by socio-technical tools and structures.

Rule sets exist at four levels. At the institutional and societal level, there are *rule regimes* composed of meta-rules, which may be real or idealized, e.g. moral codes, constitutional laws, organizational principles, and so on. Rule regimes are essentially rules about rules and social system type, configuration and function. At the level of social systems, e.g. organizations and their subunits, there are *rule systems* for both long-term ongoing social systems and for shorter, time-bounded project systems, e.g. a task force. At the level of discreet events and activities, e.g. a task, a ceremony, or a job, there are *operation rules*. At the level of persons there are *personal rules* (individual rule sets commonly known as personality) which are individually inspired or motivated. Rule sets at all four levels are never in equilibrium because of changing personal rule knowledge and capability, personal motivation, and changes in encompassing rule sets as well as endogenous constraints. In general, higher-level rule sets have generative priority and tend to be less immutable than lower level rule sets.

The functions of rule sets are multiple, although not equal or balanced at any point in time: they differentiate intra- and intercultural system activities; they clarify communications among persons; they symbolically provide member and cultural system identity; they reduce uncertainty; they provide legitimization to the access and use of resources; and they enable members to make and justify claims. Rule and rule set compliance occurs because of perceived payoffs to cultural system members, the internalization of rules, sanctions in a cultural system, public opinion, and societal meta-rules that instruct persons to suspend serious questioning of rules and rule sets. Rules and rule sets are learned by culture system members through socialization and diffusion processes (though never perfectly), maintained in cultural systems via sanction and coercion processes (again rarely perfectly), and modified through persuasion, negotiation and conflict resolution processes. The existence of multiple agents with varying centrality and membership in multiple cultural systems allows for change. As human constructions, rules and rule sets structure the experience of persons, thereby giving meaning to experience. Persons, individually and collectively, acquire and have identities – conception of self-defined rules matching actions to situations – which define the essential nature of a person in a cultural system. Rules serve as prepackaged contracts, and, frequently, come to be assertions about what is good, moral, and true.

Rule sets are composed of four types of rules:

- *Descriptive rules* – non-time bound rules that specify nature and reality. Descriptive rules entail factual or descriptive formulations and refer to objects, states of the world, agents, events and developments. They categorize the world, making socially important distinctions as well as statements about patterns. Descriptive rules constitute scientific knowledge. Their generic form is: under circumstances (x,y,z...), then it is so that (proposition). A "proposition" is a probability statement of the relationship, associative or causative, between two or more ideas, i.e. constructs, concepts or variables, that has more or less empirical confirmation.
- *Situational rules* – rules that categorize situations by time, place, and/or social meaningfulness. While situational rules vary in their scope, they all provide presumably useful distinctions whereby the similarity of apparently dissimilar phenomena can be recognized and the differences among similar phenomena specified. Their generic form is: when propositions (r,s,t...) are salient, then specify (categories). "Categories" refer to configurations of objects, agents, activities, events, and states of the world which are socially distinguishable cognitively and linguistically.
- *Valuation rules* – rules concerned with what is or is not desirable, that is, those things pursued or avoided by persons in a sphere of activity. Their generic form is: under conditions (a,b,c...), assign positive/negative value to (categories).
- *Action rules* – rules which specify instructions about how to do something or how to respond to certain problems, circumstances, or situations. Action rules say how social decisions and activities should be organized or coordinated, that is, what to do, how to do it, when to do it, and with whom. Their generic form is: under situations (k,l,m...), then do/do not (action or procedure). Importantly, for every cultural system, there will be action rules that specify four action processes: (a) rule creation, (b) rule interpretation, (c) rule implementation, and (d) rule modification.

The evolving theory of social rules just described is grounded in a logic of appropriateness (March, 1994). Members of a cultural system are presumed to ask of themselves (explicitly but more commonly implicitly) three questions more or less constantly. What sort of situation is this? What is my identity in this situation? What rules apply? This questioning process is neither random, arbitrary, nor trivial; rather it is always serious and often emotionally complicated. Interestingly, the search for appropriate rules to follow is conditioned by the rule sets currently salient to a person. The reasoning process of the logic of appropriateness is one of using a rule set (of a cultural system) to clarify identities and situations and match rules to them. We emphasize that this process is in contrast to the common perspective on organizational behavior and management where action is based on an assessment of alternatives in terms of their consequences for preferences.

# A Reformulation of Organizational Culture

If rules and rule sets are understood as linking the cognitive-emotional elements of culture to observables of patterned organizational behavior, then we have laid the foundations for reconceiving organizational cultures as meaning-centered systems. A cultural system, equally applicable to organizations and their subparts, can now be described as having three levels of meaning, each of which has cognitive-emotional elements with a corresponding level of observable, patterned behavioral elements linked with a rule set as shown in Figure 14.1. The three levels of a cultural system are: core level, governance level, and operative level. At each of these levels, there are ideas (cognitive-emotional elements) that influence some corresponding activities and events (observable patterned behavior elements) by means of a rule set, without assuming this influence to be either fully determinant or perfect.

The first level of meaning for a cultural system, the core level, is composed of a set of more or less consistent values and assumptions, a rule regime, and a set of rectitudes. The values and assumptions serve as the axioms or precepts on which the vast majority of system thought and action is based (Drucker, 1994). Values are the collective sense of what should or should not be strived for, the real ideals and sins of the organization or subpart (Walter, 1984); assumptions are the shared premises upon which the organization or subpart (or more typically the dominant coalition) bases its world views, i.e. the essence of human nature, what constitutes truth, time and the relevant environment, whether certain classes of members deserve preferential treatment, etc. (Schein, 1985). A central value always has to do with change, e.g. whether change is desirable or not, feasible or not, easy or difficult to achieve, externally or internally initiated, and so on. Rectitudes are the symbolic observables that reflect the system's values and assumptions. Examples of rectitudes are logos, slogans, sages, vision and mission statements, long-range plans, stated objectives, and the like. Linking values and assumptions with rectitudes is a rule regime, a set of meta-rules concerned with rule system type, configuration and focus.

The second level of meaning for cultural systems, the governance level, is composed of a set of strategic beliefs, a rule system, and a set of activity/event recipes. This

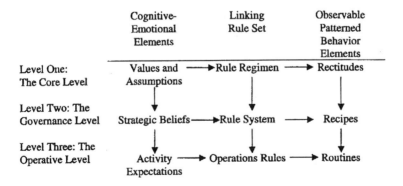

**Figure 14.1** Cultural systems as a three-tiered hierarchy of social rule linked cognitive-emotional-observable levels.

governance level of meanings guides the use of the expectations, rules, and routines at the operational level, i.e. when they should or should not be applied, by whom, when, where and how. Examples of recipes are both formal/intentional, e.g. stated strategies and policies, codes of conduct, formal structures, professional and occupational standards, macro technologies, etc., and informal, e.g. sagas, myths, customs and conventions.

There appear to be four general categories of governing strategic beliefs (after Lorsch, 1985): those that outline what the organization or subpart can become and do and what it won't attempt – matters of aspiration; those that contain convictions about what is necessary to do to satisfy stakeholders and other constituencies operationally; those relating to how the organization (or its subparts) can succeed in its context; and those relating to the appropriate ways of managing the organization (or subparts) that support the other categories. These strategic beliefs are also learned by organizational members and usually reflect the core level of meaning shared by the dominant coalition.

Level three, the operative level, includes activity expectations, operational rules, and corresponding behavioral routines. An activity expectation is a cognitive action–outcome relationship that specifies that action X will, with some probability, result in outcome Y. Whether consciously or unconsciously held, fictional or based on personal experience, causative action–outcome statements or expectations (Schultz, 1964) are the basis of both perception and interpretation. They predispose persons to perceive and experience specific organizational activities, events, and things in certain ways, to define what is and is not appropriate behavior, and so on (Isabella, 1992). Routines are person-centered, patterned, reoccurring behaviors about how to perform tasks, relate to others and socio-technical units, etc., both formally and informally. Examples of operational routines in organizations are SOPs, norms and rituals, position descriptions, instructions, micro-technologies, etc. Translating activity expectations into routines are operations rules, acquired by persons formally and informally through orientation and training, coaching, imitation, story-telling, and the like, and refined through first-hand and vicarious experience. Persons of course also bring some organizationally relevant operational expectations, rules and routines with them to the work arena.

In characterizing cultural systems as having three meaning levels, we need to highlight several features. One is the use of the phrase cultural system which may be applied to whole organizations, to formal and informal subparts of organizations, as well as to distinctive hierarchical organization levels, e.g. top, middle, and supervisory management, and occupational specialties, e.g. engineers, accountants. A second feature is that not only do cognitive-emotional elements influence observable elements through rules but the core level of meaning influences the governance level, and this level, in turn, influences the operative level – strongly in most cultural systems but not absolute. Third, we note the degree of correspondence among cognitive-emotional elements, rule sets, and observable elements for most cultural systems that have a reasonable history and a modicum of stability; this correspondence is probably quite high although seldom perfect. Lastly, we note that all but the largest cultural systems exist within more encompassing ones, e.g. the cultural system of a task force might be embraced by a departmental cultural system which is in turn found within the umbrella culture of the organization, which is within an industry culture, which is in a national culture.

All organizations in the modem world have three fundamental tasks: to manage their internal affairs, to adapt to their relevant environments, and to anticipate and prepare for their probable future (Lundberg, 1989). These tasks of internal adjustment, external alignment, and future anticipation differentiate the major types of organization change. Each is dealt with intentionally by managers through goals, plans, structures, control and communication systems and the like. The meanings attributed to these formalizations by organizational members are the product of both management's intentions and the cultural systems embedded in and encompassing the organization and its subparts. Organizational changes therefore are also cultural changes. Thus, organizational changes will be more or less consistent with the organization's cultural systems or even require changes (eventually) in those systems. It further follows that competencies for working with cultural systems are significant for organizational success and survival.

# WORKING WITH CULTURE

With a conceptualization of organizational culture systems via a social rules perspective in hand, we now turn to the discussion of how they might be influenced. Recalling that the focus of organizational culture systems change simply means that one or more rules or rule sets is modified, we will now explicate our earlier stance about managing cultural change – some things, sometimes, under some circumstances.

## Some Caveats/Reminders

Before delving into a pragmatic discussion of the what's, how's, and who's of where cultural systems change and the impact of cultural systems on other change efforts, it may be useful to reemphasize several points that condition the discussion that follows.

- Everything about organizations has symbolic significance. All things, places, relationships, structures, processes, events, goals, outcomes, behaviors, and so on – everything – has or can come to have meanings, and be rule-guided. Whether formal or informal, intentional or extra-intentional, everything organizational can be understood through the lens that cultural systems provide.
- Organizations are open systems. Thus, doing or not doing something to one aspect of an organization means there will be system-wide ramifications.
- Personal rule sets are seldom perfectly congruent with those of a cultural system, and the rule sets of one cultural system are seldom congruent with the rule sets of other systems. Thus, rule sets are rarely static.
- Everything symbolic is emotionally laden. Thus, the meanings in and about organizations and their cultural systems will generate feelings – positive or negative, strong or weak – on the part of their members.
- Changing meanings means changing social rules; to change social rules means following some social rules.

- The meaning of changes is in the minds of those persons affected, not those initiating them.

## The Possibilities for Cultural Change in Organizations

Conceiving of cultural systems as meaning-centered, where meaning resides in the social rules between a frame of cultural ideas and cued organization-specific patterned observables, provides a perspective on cultural system change different from both those who believe management can craft culture change as well as those who believe culture change cannot be influenced. If the reality for culture change is somewhere between these poles, we need to indicate the constraints and opportunities that outline the realistic possibilities.

- Since organizations are intentional, formal systems there is always the question of the degree of correspondence between them and the cultural systems associated with them. This question is usefully asked for the whole organization and the "umbrella" cultural system as well as for organizational subparts and their corresponding cultural systems. Operationally, this is a matter of comparing the consistency of the rule sets of each. Thus, one possibility for change is to increase or decrease the consistency between the formal organization's rules and the rule set of the corresponding cultural systems.
- Since cultural systems have three levels of meanings that are seldom perfectly congruent, another possibility for culture modification would be to alter this inter-level congruency by either increasing it or decreasing it by targeting changes in the rule sets of core or governance levels so that natural tendencies toward consistency would induce changes in other levels. Since organizations will almost always embrace two or more cultural systems, another change possibility is with regards to intersystem rule set consistency. Of special interest here are the rules of each cultural system with regards to intersystem linking. The number of cultural system linkages is of course a factor.
- Time affects cultural system change possibilities too. Generally speaking, the longer the time available to modify rule sets, the more evolution-like the change endeavor, and the shorter the time, the more planned change-like the change endeavor.
- Other factors influencing cultural system change have to do with the degree to which members are identified with the system, whether one or more members have central-ity in the system, and whether any members who are central also hold authoritative positions in the formal organization. Generally speaking, the more members that are highly identified with a cultural system, given some with centrality, the easier rule sets are to modify because of the viability of the four action rule processes. When a member is both central and has authority, rule set modification aligned with the formal organization is possible.

These change possibilities may occur singularly, in some sequence, or simultaneously. The alternatives bring time and rhythm into focus. Relatively little is known about these features of cultural system change. It seems likely, however, that there are parallels to organization change. It seems reasonable to posit that all cultural systems will exhibit continuous, incremental changes punctuated on occasion by more episodic, radical change (Watzlawick et al., 1974; Weick and Quinn, 1999). Changes in cultural systems occur when rules and/or rule sets change – either when one rule or more than one rule (in a rule set) is extinguished or created, or when rule sets become more or less consistent internally or between two or more rule sets, or when one or more rules are accentuated or suppressed in a rule set, or the diffusion or inculcation of rules, or because of changes in the personal rule systems of members, their identities or centrality. While cultural systems tend toward inertia, rules and rule sets are never quite static; they drift and pulsate continuously. As a minimum, members refine and improvise operations rules as they learn from their experience with routines. At the other extreme, members may have to modify rule systems or rule regimes in response to environmental changes, top management replacements, decrements in organizational performance, and the like (e.g. Huber and Glick, 1993).

Given the proclivity and the rhetoric of contemporary management toward hierarchical, centralized, and formalized organizations, it is no surprise that many managers seek to craft "strong" unitary organizational cultures, i.e. cultures that are consistent with one another, tightly linked with one another, and where cultural meanings are as close to organizational intentions as possible. Under these circumstances, cultures support management's intentions organization-wide. As natural and desirable as this may seem to managers, it may only be a reasonable aspiration in organizations under relatively simple and stable conditions. Under less than stable and/or simple configured externalities, the requisite organizational differentiations may be enhanced by cultural system variety. The possibilities for working with cultures become enacted realities through a process engaged in by agents using various culture change techniques. It is to this process we now turn.

## The Process of Working with Culture

The first change-oriented activity, *surfacing*, identifies the rules and agents of the focal rule set. Surfacing is information gathering – it begins by noting a desired or actual patterned behavior (i.e. a routine, recipe, or rectitude) and then inferring the rules that guide it. Surfacing involves noting the appropriateness and congruency among these rules/within the rule set, the degrees to which the agents are sophisticated about and committed to the rule set (their centrality), and whether there are action rules for the four rule processes.

Once rule and agent information has been acquired, the second activity is to *assess* it and as necessitated, to *modify* it. Assessment simply means judging the adequacy and appropriateness of the rule set/agent configuration. When inadequacies are discovered, attention turns to their modification by either reinterpreting or redesigning them. What are the sorts of inadequacies that might be discovered? Among the common ones are:

- Ambiguity. Whether they are inherently unclear or because members have incompletely learned them, ambiguous rules do not provide necessary behavioral guidance.

- Conflict. Two or more existing rules or rule sets may offer conflicting guidance to a member resulting in inconsistent behavior.
- Number. There may be too many or too few rules. Too many rules may reduce necessary member flexibility or creativity. Too few rules may leave some necessary patterned behavior unguided. Also the ratio of prescriptive/proscriptive rules can be inappropriate.
- Superstition. Rules that are inaccurate about cause and effect relationships may provide erroneous behavioral guidance.
- Identity. If members are not sufficiently identified with a rule set they may not be motivated to follow the rules.
- Centrality. If no member has centrality, i.e. expertise and power, action rule processes may not occur as needed.
- Linking. In part, a system's effectiveness and survival depends upon the adequacy of its rules by which it relates to other systems.
- Diffusion. Appropriate rules must be known by everyone in the cultural system to have coordinated behavior.

Assuming some desirable modification of one or more rules, the third change-focused activity involves the *implementation and institutionalization* of any redesigned/reinterpreted rules. Implementation may be as simple as acting in conformance with a new rule or rules and thus modeling the change. It is more usual, however, to also inform the other cultural system members of the change, especially those members who interpret and implement rules. Once known and first utilized, modified rules need to be repeatedly used, i.e. stabilized in practice. This institutionalization of modified rules is accomplished via inducements for rule conformity, i.e. how compliance pays off to members, and is influenced by members with centrality, e.g. appeals to reason, loyalty, fear, etc. It is important to reemphasize that the general process just outlined is almost always conditioned by the cultural systems' (or that system in which it is embedded) core values and assumptions and the strategic belief about change. Is change good or bad? Is change natural or not? Is change easy or difficult? Is change best initiated from inside or outside? Is it best managed from above or within? Is it most successful when done slowly or swiftly? Can it be done piece-meal or is it better to do it all at once? The answers to these questions will, exigencies aside, condition both the focus among possibilities and the general process of change endeavors.

## Roles for Culture Work

If cultures are entwined with organizations and the managing of internal operations, environmental adaptation, and appropriate anticipation of a probable future, it follows that members, perhaps especially management, need to be aware of culture, understand how it permeates organizational behavior, and know what they can and cannot do to modify it. If assisting organization members in their thinking and actions with regard to culture is so significant, what are the roles available for doing so? Working with culture occurs through three broad roles – here labeled cultural spokesperson, cultural diagnostician, and cultural facilitator.

The role of cultural *spokesperson* is essentially one of education and advocacy. The spokesperson actively assists organizational members, again especially managers, in several ways. One is to help members to appreciate and be sensitive to the symbolic importance and impact of organizationally specific events, persons, things and actions. Another way is to educate members on what culture is conceptually. This involves providing the ideas and how they are linked via social rules to patterned behaviors that enable members to think about their organizational experience in cultural terms. Part of this includes correcting the many fictions about organizational culture currently rampant in managerial folklore, e.g. that "strong" culture leads to excellence, that thinking about culture stereotypically such as "macho" is sufficient, that organizations have just one culture, that considering only the manifest, visible level of culture is sufficient, that cultures can be easily and quickly changed, etc. The cultural spokesperson also interprets the meaning of organizational objects, practices, and events. This ongoing articulation may, on occasion, go further by describing what the organization or its subparts mean in terms of strategic beliefs and core values and assumptions. Spokespersons also help colleagues understand how their culture fits with the industry, and relevant occupational, community, and regional or national cultures in which it is embedded. As new members join, cultural spokespersons are active in the acculturation process, i.e. going beyond showing which ropes to know and which to skip to providing the legacy of meanings behind them. All of the above, of course, are particularly useful when major organizational change occurs, e.g. mergers and acquisitions, sudden growth and down-sizing. Cultural spokespersons, in general, serve their colleagues as an ongoing cultural conscience, reminding them in a variety of ways that all aspects of organizational life are meaningful and this meaningfulness should not be ignored.

The role of cultural *diagnostician* involves assisting the organization and/or subpart in knowing its culture. This may take the form of assisting members to decide when it is useful to systematically identify their cultural system and, as needed, to provide technical assistance or appropriate methodologies. The diagnostician may also assist in training members in information gathering and analysis, guide the inquiry process, and even provide an independent check on aspects of the culture adduced. Diagnosticians are thus central in championing the culture-surfacing process. They also will gather, order, and interpret their own observations on the organization's cultural systems in an ongoing fashion, thus improving their counsel on the cultural significance or consequences of any managerial or change proposal. In general, the diagnostician role acts on the dual premises that knowing the organization from a cultural perspective reduces managerial and operational errors and that the occasional surfacing of cultural systems tends to enhance both organizational coherence and direction.

The role of cultural *facilitator* is to actively assist members to modify some aspect of their organization's cultural systems. There are several ways this role may be enacted. The facilitator, like the diagnostician, assists members in "processing" their culture, i.e. periodically bringing to awareness what the culture actually is. With this enhanced awareness, subsequent actions are more likely to be culturally congruent, members acculturated, etc. Another way the facilitator may work is to help management think through the cultural implications of their planning. Goals and plans always serve as organizational aspirations so they need to reflect any desired cultural shifts. Sometimes this means the facilitator is protective of key cultural elements and at other times promotes modification of social rules that shift desired new emphases of cultural systems. The facilitator may also actively provide counseling to members as their personal security is threatened by changes, legitimating and facilitating members grieving for lost cultural elements that are replaced during changes, and as cultural modification is typically a longer-term process, seeing that sufficient ongoing attention and energy continue to be invested in modification endeavors.

The roles for cultural work need to be performed by organizational members with centrality and sophistication in the focal cultural system, and these persons often can be helped by culturally knowledgeable and trusted outsiders such as consultants, staff personnel, or members of parallel units. These roles can of course all be performed by one person or by more than one person. The caveat for enacting all of these roles is the same as in everyday management – "first believe, then behave enthusiastically, consistently, and redundant with as much cultural sensitivity as possible" (Siehl and Martin, 1984).

## Techniques for Culture Work

Working with culture has thus far been portrayed as a general process of three general steps, undertaken for a variety of reasons, and enacted by means of three roles. The model behind the first stage of the general process, i.e. surfacing, utilizes a conceptual framework to focus on observable patterned behaviors resulting in information from which the social rules guiding those observables are inferred. But what information? Who gathers it and infers from it? How is information gathered and sense-making accomplished? The answers to these questions outline the array of techniques for culture surfacing, assessment and modification, and so forth.

Before describing culture work techniques, however, we should note the array of beliefs which ultimately condition their selection. Considerable variation exists about what constitutes an appropriate framework and hence information. At one extreme are those who rely on a simple, broad framework and the verbalizations of members. Davis (1984), for example, asks "as many people as possible, one at a time, if their company has a culture. My next question is, "Can you tell me about it?"" Most others utilize more complex frameworks and focus on concrete behaviors, because "managers cannot be asked what they believe but must be observed believing" (Sapienza, 1985, p. 69). Sathe (1985, p. 69) agrees: "The internalized beliefs and values that members of a community share cannot be measured easily or observed directly, nor can what people say about them be relied on when deciphering a culture. Other evidence, both historical and current, must be taken into account to infer what a culture is."

Information gathering, regardless of the framework used, is a matter of sampling. While large or small, samples will reflect the time and resources available. But sampling beliefs also dictate whether to sample situations and/or members, to do this randomly or selectively, and whether to sample under normal conditions (thus focusing on repetitive experiences) or "unusual" conditions (focusing on disruptions or contrast experiences, e.g. Louis, 1985). Similarly, when gathering information about whole cultural systems, there are those who believe in acquiring information which just provides a general understanding of the whole, and those who first focus on gathering information about certain cultural elements and then later aggregating them. Wilkens and Patterson (1985, p. 280) exemplify the former: "We suggest that a reasonable first step is to provides a means for key actors to talk about their views of what is unique and valuable about the company." Examples of what cultural elements are surfaced are symbols (Louis, 1983), myths and stories (Mitroff and Kilmann, 1976), legends (Wilkens and Martin, 1979) and rituals and ceremonies (Trice and Beyer, 1984).

While information of many types can be gathered, such information always reflects the conceptual frameworks brought to bear – and there are many, varying from the simple, e.g. the two categories of daily and guiding beliefs proposed by Davis (1984), to relatively complex, e.g. the levels-of-meaning frameworks noted previously. The actual gathering of information is, not surprisingly, accomplished via interviewing (ethnographically, open, and focused), observation, document examination, focus groups, delphi and nominal groups, and survey instruments. These methods, singly and in combination, provide the information from which cultural governing social rules are inferred. Surfacing information and rules at present takes two general approaches, each of which has several techniques.

One approach is termed a "cultural audit" (Lorsch, 1985; Schein, 1984), typically undertaken by or under the guidance of someone external. Even a minimal audit represents a considerable investment in time and energy. Most audits cyclically check both categorized information and inferred social rules until most members confirm their validity (e.g. Sarason, 1982). While this "iterative clinical" technique (Schein, 1985) is most common, sometimes it is augmented by or partially substituted by general survey instruments, e.g. the Kilmann (1984) culture gap survey, the Quinn and McGrath (1985) competing values survey, and the Enz (1986) values survey, or by an instrument generated after initial interviewing (e.g. Woods, 1989). Whatever the kind or amount of information gathered, assessment is helped when it is successively confirmed by the repeatedly refined interpretations and inferences of motivated and informed members.

The other approach for surfacing and assessing culture takes the form of one of three kinds of workshops. One begins with surfacing information about the focal cultural unit by an outsider with or without the assistance of qualified members. This information is fed back to all or a representative set of members and discussed until reasonable agreement is reached. Then, again assisted by the outsider, members infer the guiding social rules, assess their appropriateness, and make any modifications deemed useful. A second type of workshop, usually facilitated by an outsider, has a representative team of members surface manifest cultural elements, strategic beliefs, and core values and assumptions, and then go on to infer social rules, assess them, and so forth (e.g. Lundberg, 1990). The third type of workshop also involves organization members from the outset. Using some framework, the group generates cultural information, jointly interprets it and plans for further data collection – this cycle is repeated until a collaborative culture analysis exists (e.g. Marshall and McLean, 1988). Key to all forms of workshops is the motivation of the participants and uninterrupted time. These workshops, for maximum effectiveness, also need to be legitimated by the organization and attended by one or more members with both centrality and organization rank. The facilitator obviously needs a sensitivity to and skills about small group dynamics.

## Concomitants of Success

The success of culture work will hinge on a number of things. Some have already been discussed, i.e. the focus of modifying rules/rule sets within the available possibilities, the following of the process of rule/rule set surfacing and so on, through various culture change roles using available techniques. Two additional, critical factors that are requisite for cultural system change are authorization and the degree of compatibility with the prevailing umbrella cultural system.

One or more cultural spokespersons, with organizational authority, need to champion the activity, see that resources such as time and competent outsiders are available, and that outcomes are appropriately communicated. Where the encompassing cultural systems positively value change and/or openness, surfacing and other culture work tends to proceed easily. Pockets of resistance that are encountered can be overcome through counseling, training, positive public opinion and recognition, and rewards.

For cultural systems in organizations that are moribund, culture work is very difficult because it does not seem to hold the quick fixes commonly believed necessary for survival. This is ironic of course, since an inappropriate culture is usually behind failure, i.e. a cultural system that is too rigid, too inward-looking, or too past-oriented. Here severe efforts may be necessary, e.g. destroying the cultural system and reconstructing it with new people who hold more congenial personal rule systems. Between these extremes are numerous things that can, singularly but usually in combination, produce desired cultural changes. These, for example, include: replacing leaders of one cultural system with persons from another whose rule system is closer to the desired one; creating new emotionally charged rituals and ceremonies; creating new symbols and publicly reinterpreting the value of artifacts; exploding myths and discrediting sacred cows that preserve dysfunctional traditions; convincing or forcing members to adopt new behaviors more consistent with new beliefs and reinforcing these with rewards; bringing attention to desired things via measurement of them; simply articulating new values, assumptions and/or strategic beliefs and doing so repeatedly; initiating a culture surfacing workshop and/or audit; and consistently and dramatically modeling new values and beliefs.

# CONCLUDING COMMENTARY

This chapter has been based on the premise that cultural phenomena will increasingly become more important to understand and work with in organizations. Appreciating and deciphering cultural systems seems to be more and more vital for organizational renewal, enhancement, and change. Attention to the symbolic and to a meaning-infused organization not only serves members during times of relative stability but becomes imperative in times of organizational change, development, and transformation. In prior pages we have attempted to provide a sense of what organizational cultural systems are – as viewed through the lens of the emerging theoretical perspective of social rules – and how we might work with them. Since meanings guide behaviors, attention to meanings is paramount. Since meanings result from sense-making, then the surfacing, examining (and restating as needed) as well as the sharing of meanings is the process through which organizational change occurs. As organizational cultures become appreciated as not only the vehicle of organizational meaning and sense-making but also as a guidance system, members and managers alike will become ever more attentive to culture for promoting and protecting change. Thus, working with culture is the process in which the identification of shared social rules – about settings, about what is valued, and about action – can lead to the rule modifications which constitute changes in and by organizations. While we know quite a bit about what organizations and their members actually do, we know considerably less about why they do what they do, what they don't do, why what they do is effective, why forms of joint action persist, and what the longer-term effects of more or less coordinated actions are. The properties of social rules and rule sets, e.g. directing attention, providing justifications, defining identities, and generating and guiding action, among others, begin to relate to these concerns. The meaning-centered activities which constitute working with organizational cultures as advocated in this chapter, while promising in so many ways, are still being elaborated. Hence, we conclude with an invitation to practitioners and scholars alike to use and improve them.

# REFERENCES

Archer, M. (1986) The sociology of education. In N. Himmelstand (Ed), Sociology: the Aftermath of Crises. London: Sage.

Barney, J. (1986) Culture as a source of competitive advantage. Academy of Management Review, 11: 656–665.

Bourdieu, P. (1977) Outline of a Theory of Practice. Cambridge: Cambridge University Press.

Burns, T.R. and Flan, H. (1987) The Shaping of Social Organization: Social Rule System Theory with Applications. Beverly Hills, CA: Sage.

Chomsky, N. (1965) Aspects of the Theory of Syntax. Cambridge, MA: MIT Press.

Cicourel, A.V. (1974) Cognitive Sociology. New York: The Free Press.

Crozier, M. and Friedberg, E. (1980) Actors and Systems: the Politics of Collective Action. Chicago, IL: University of Chicago Press.

Cummings, T.G. and Worley, C.G. (1997) Organization Development and Change, 6th Edn. Cincinnati, OH: South-Western.

Davis, S.M. (1984) Managing Corporate Culture. Cambridge, MA: Ballinger.

Drucker, P.F. (1994) The theory of business. Harvard Business Review, September/October: 94–104.

Dyer Jr., W.G. (1986) Cultural Change in Family Firms. San Francisco, CA: Jossey-Bass.

Enz, C.A. (1986) Power and Shared Values in the Corporate Culture. Ann Arbor, MI: UMI Research Press.

Feldman, S.P. (1988) How organizational culture can affect innovation. Organizations Dynamics, Summer: 57–69.

Frost, P.J., Moore, L.F., Louis, M.R., Lundberg, C.C. and Martin, J. (Eds) (1985) Organizational Culture. Beverly Hills, CA: Sage.

Frost, P.J., Moore, L.F., Louis, M.R., Lundberg, C.C. and Martin, J. (Eds) (1991) Reframing Organizational Culture. Beverly Hills, CA: Sage.

Giddens, T. (1979) Central Problems in Social Theory: Action, Structure, and Contradiction in Social Analysis. Berkeley, CA: University of California Press.

Goffman, E. (1974) Frame Analysis: an Essay on the Organization of Experience. Cambridge, MA: Harvard University Press.

Gordon, G. (1985) The relationship of corporate culture to industry sector and corporate performance. In R. Kilmann, M.J. Sexton and R. Serpa (Eds), Gaining Control of the Corporate Culture. San Francisco, CA: Jossey-Bass.

Greiner, L.E. and Metzger, R.O. (1983) Consulting to Management. Englewood Cliffs, NJ: Prentice-Hall.

Gregory, K.L. (1983) Native view paradigms: multiple cultures and culture conflict in organizations. Administrative Science Quarterly, 28: 359–379.

Harre, R. (1979) Social Being. Oxford: Blackwell.

Hofstede, G. (1980) Culture's Consequences. Beverly Hills, CA: Sage.

Huber, G.P. and Glick, W.H. (Eds) (1993) Organizational Change and Redesign. New York: Oxford University Press.

Isabella, L.A. (1992) Managing the challenges of trigger events: the mind sets governing adaptation to change. Business Horizons, 35: 59–66.

Jacques, E. (1951) The Changing Culture of a Factory. London: Tavistock.

Katz, D. and Kahn, R.L. (1965) The Social Psychology of Organizations. New York: Wiley.

Kilmann, R.H. (1984) Beyond the Quick Fix: Managing Five Tracks to Organization Success. San Francisco, CA: Jossey-Bass.

Kilmann, R.H., Saxton, M.J. and Serpa, R. (1985) Gaining Control of the Corporate Culture. San Francisco, CA: Jossey-Bass.

Kroeber, A.L. and Kluckhohn, C. (1963) Culture: a Critical Review of Concepts and Definitions. New York: Random House.

Likert, R. (1961) New Patterns of Management. New York: McGraw-Hill.

Lindblom, C.E. (1977) Politics and Markets. New York: Basic Books.

Lorsch, J.W. (1985) Strategic myopia: culture as an invisible barrier to change. In R. Kilmann, M.J. Saxton and R. Serpa (Eds), Gaining Control of the Corporate Culture. San Francisco, CA: Jossey-Bass.

Louis, M.R. (1983) Organizations as culture-bearing milieux. In L. Pondy, P. Frost, G. Morgan and T. Dandridge (Eds), Organizational Symbolism. Greenwich, CT: JAI Press.

Louis, M.R. (1985) An investigator's guide to workplace culture. In P.J. Frost, L.F. Moore, M.R. Louis, C.C. Lundberg and J. Martin (Eds), Organizational Culture. Beverly Hills, CA: Sage.

Lundberg, C.C. (1989) On organizational learning: implications and opportunities for expanding organizational development. In R.W. Woodman and W.A. Pasmore (Eds), Research in Organization Change and Development, Vol. 3. Greenwich, CT: JAI Press.

Lundberg, C.C. (1990) Surfacing organizational culture. Journal of Managerial Psychology, 5: 19–26.

Lundberg, C.C. (1993) Knowing and surfacing organizational culture: a consultant's guide. In R.T. Golembiewski (Ed), Handbook of Organizational Consulting, pp. 535–547. New York: Marcel Dekker.

Lundberg, C.C. (1998) Leadership as creating and using social rules in a community of practice. In M.R. Rahim, R.T. Golembiewski and C.C. Lundberg (Eds), Current Topics in Management, Vol. 3, pp. 11–30. Greenwich, CT: JAI Press.

Lundberg, C.C. (1999) Organizational development as facilitating the surfacing and modification of social rules. In R.W. Woodman and W.A. Pasmore (Eds), Research in Organization Change and Development, Vol. 12, pp. 41–58. Greenwich, CT: JAI Press.

March, J.G. (1994) A Primer on Decision Making. New York: The Free Press.

Marshall, J. and McLean, A. (1988) Reflection in action: exploring organizational culture. In P. Reason (Ed), Inquiry in Action. Beverly Hills, CA: Sage.

Martin, J. (1992) Cultures in Organizations: Three Perspectives. New York: Oxford University Press.

Meyerson, D. and Martin, J. (1987) Culture change: an integration of three different views. Journal of Management Studies, 24: 623–647.

Mitroff, I.I. and Kilmann, R.H. (1976) On organization stories: an approach to the design and analysis of organizations through myths and stories. In R.H. Kilmann, L.R. Poudy and D.P. Selvin (Eds), The Management of Organizational Design: Strategies and Implementation. New York: American Elsevier.

Ouchi, W.G. (1981) Theory Z: How American Business Can Meet the Japanese Challenge. Reading, MA: Addison-Wesley.

Pike, K.L. (1967) Language in Relation to a Unified Theory of the Structure of Human Behavior. The Hague: Mouten.

Quinn, R.E. and McGrath, M.R. (1985) The transformation of organization cultures: a competing values perspective. In P.J. Frost, L.F. Moore, M.R. Louis, C.C. Lundberg and J. Martin (Eds), Organizational Culture. Beverly Hills, CA: Sage.

Sapienza, A.M. (1985) Believing is seeing: how culture influences the decisions of top managers. In R.H. Kilman, M.J. Sexton and R. Serpa (Eds), Gaining Control of the Corporate Culture. San Francisco, CA: Jossey-Bass.

Sathe, V. (1985) Managerial Action and Culture. Homewood, IL: Irwin.

Sarason, S.B. (1982) The Culture of the School and the Problem of Change. Boston, MA: Allyn and Bacon.

Schein, E.H. (1969) Process Consultation: its Role in Organization Development. Reading, MA: Addison-Wesley.

Schein, E.H. (1984) Coming to an awareness of organizational culture. Sloan Management Review, 25: 3–16.

Schein, E. (1985) Organizational Culture and Leadership. San Francisco, CA: Jossey-Bass.

Schein, E. (1990) Organizational culture. American Psychologist, 45: 109–119.

Schultz, A. (1964) The problem of rationality in the social world. In A. Broderson (Ed), Alfred Schultz: Collected Papers, Vol. 2. The Hague: Martines Nijhoff.

Schwartz, H. and Davis, S.M. (1981) Matching corporate culture and business strategy. Organizational Dynamics, Summer: 30–48.

Selznick, P. (1949) TVA and the Grass Roots. Berkeley, CA: University of California Press.

Siehl, C. and Martin, J. (1984) The management of culture: the need for consistency and redundancy among cultural components. Presented at the Annual Meeting of the Academy of Management, Boston, MA.

Smircich, L. (1983) Concepts of culture and organizational analysis. Administrative Science Quarterly, 28: 339–358.

Staw, B.M. (1980) Rationality and justification in organizational life. In B.M. Staw and L.L. Cummings (Eds), Research in Organizational Behavior, pp. 45–80. Greenwich, CT: JAI Press.

Trice, H.M. (1993) Occupational Subcultures in the Workplace. Ithaca, NY: ILR Press.

Trice, H.W. and Beyer, J.M. (1984) Studying organizational cultures through rites and ceremonials. Academy of Management Review, 9: 653–669.

Turnstall, W.B. (1983) Culture transition at AT&T. Sloan Management Review, 25: 1–12.

Twining, W. and Miers, D. (1982) How to do Things with Rules, 2nd Edn. London: Weidenfeld and Nicolson.

Walter, G. (1984) Organizational development and individual rights. Journal of Applied Behavioral Science, 20: 423–439.

Watzlawick, P., Weaklund, J. and Fisch, R. (1974) Change. New York: Norton.

Weick, K. (1982) The presumption of logic in executive thought and action. Prepared for the symposium Functioning of the Executive Mind, Case Western Reserve University.

Weick, K. (1988) Perspectives on action in organizations. In J. Lorsch (Ed), Handbook of Organizational Behavior. Englewood Cliffs, NJ: Prentice-Hall.

Weick, K.E. (1995) Sensemaking in Organizations. Thousand Oaks, CA: Sage.

Weick, K.E. and Quinn, R.E. (1999) Organizational change and development. Annual Review of Psychology, 50: 361–386.

Wilkens, A. (1989) Developing Corporate Culture. San Francisco, CA: Jossey-Bass.

Wilkens, A.L. and Martin, J. (1979) Organizational legends. Unpublished paper, Stanford University.

Wilkens, A.L. and Patterson, K.J. (1985) You can't get there from here: what makes culture change projects fail. In R. Kilmann, M.J. Saxton and R. Serpa (Eds), Gaining Control of the Corporate Culture. San Francisco, CA: Jossey-Bass.

Winch, P. (1958) The Idea of a Social Science and its Relation to Philosophy. London: Routledge and Kegan Paul.

Woods, R. (1989) Restaurant culture: congruence and culture in the restaurant industry. Unpublished dissertation, Cornell University.

# Chapter 15

# Organizational Culture: Can it be a Key Lever for Driving Organizational Change?

**Daniel Denison**
*IMD, International Institute for Management Development,*
*Lausanne, Switzerland*

## INTRODUCTION

The topic of organization culture often presents two contradictory images. The first view presents culture as "the glue that holds the organization together", and as a central part of the change process. This image has many precedents in the applied academic and popular management literature and presents a compelling case for culture being considered a central aspect of any organizational change. This perspective typically introduces culture as a wholistic concept to help managers conceptualize the organizational systems they have created, to understand the natural and social environments to which they are adapting, and to see the link between individual behaviour and organizational contexts (Kotter and Heskett, 1992; Hofstede, 1980a,b; Senge, 1990; Schein, 1992).

The second image of culture, however, is not nearly so optimistic. This viewpoint presents culture as much less central to the change process. As one manager put it, "culture is a word we use to explain what happened when we don't really know what happened". In this sense, culture is merely a "marginal" explanation for what has happened – one that we use when we don't know the real answer, or when we've already exhausted all the other important explanations (Abegglen and Stalk, 1985; Treacy and Weirsema, 1995).

To managers, this marginal perspective inevitably means that culture is something that is "nice to have", but clearly not a high priority. The academic literature on culture has often helped support this viewpoint by focusing on issues of epistemology over substance and by expressing insights in a form that is not always useful to managers who are searching for leverage during the change process (Denison, 1996; Brannen, 1999).

The approach described in this chapter has specifically tried to conceptualize organizational culture in a way that is useful for managers who are trying to create leverage during the change process. The chapter begins by discussing five important lessons about how to make the culture perspective relevant during the change process. Next, the focus turns to the culture framework that lies at the centre of this approach and presents a brief example of how the model can be applied to analyze an organization. This section is followed by an analysis of three organizations that have used this approach to guide their change process. The final section of the chapter returns to a discussion of the lessons learned about making organizational culture a key point of leverage during the change process.

# MAKING CULTURE RELEVANT TO THE CHANGE PROCESS: FIVE IMPORTANT LESSONS

This section outlines five lessons drawn from the author's experience in trying to use culture as a source of leverage for organization change. These lessons also help articulate the set of priorities that are reflected in the culture framework that follows.

## Taking the "Native's Point of View" Seriously

Much has been made in the academic literature on organizational culture of the importance of the "native's point of view" – that is, an understanding of the meaning of the situation from the insider's perspective. But while many academic writers have championed the native's point of view, we often seem to forget some of the most important characteristics of the "tribes" of managers that we study. As a group our "target audience" has little choice but to be highly instrumental, focusing nearly all of its energy on "producing results". In most cases, executives are highly time-constrained and outcome-oriented, and not very reflective. Thus, it is important to remember that they often do not have the time to understand the nuances of symbolic meaning that are most appealing to scholars.

It is ironic that a line of research that grew from a concern that organizational researchers should have more empathy for the people and the organizations that they study has not resulted in a body of knowledge that is more useful to the "natives". The scholarly body of knowledge on organizational culture primarily addresses the epistemological concerns of the researchers themselves over the "best way" to study cultures rather the original concerns of the "natives" (Van Maanen, 1988; Martin, 1992). As a result, many of the concepts that we have developed to understand organizations don't fit very well with the reality of the organizations. One is reminded of Kunda (1992) discussion in his book "Engineering Culture" of how cynical members of Digital

Equipment Company (DEC) began to describe their own organization using an analysis based on the academic jargon of the consultants and culture gurus who had worked with their organization.

The prime lesson seems clear: To provide leverage for organizational change, the insights of culture research much be presented in a form that makes sense to the members of the organization. The concepts and analytic strategies must be relevant to the narrow range of priorities of this "tribe", and must be present in a style and form that are as instrumental as it is. The rich and inspired scholarly literature may be very useful for generating insights, but it is often not so useful for expressing those insights in a way that leads to action.

## Creating a Systems Perspective

Many of the basic insights of the culture perspective have been about organizational systems. Beginning with the functionalist anthropology of the 1930s (Weber, 1930; Mead, 1934; Radcliffe-Brown, 1952), culture researchers have been concerned with the issues of internal integration and meaning, as well as external adaptation (Schein, 1992). Trying to explain the joint goals of meaning, integration, and adaptation has led to a focus on topics such as symbols, social structure, language, technology, and cosmology. Human beings create instrumental social systems that "work" – at least for a while – and also create a related system of symbolic meaning that reinforces functional relationships. The systems we create also have lots of inertia – they tend to remain stable until something causes both the symbolic meaning system and the adaptation system to change at the same time.

Contemporary work on organizational culture, however, has taken a more cognitive orientation (Geertz, 1973; Weick, 1979). This perspective focuses on the assumptions and beliefs held by organizational members and their expression through language and symbolic meaning. One interesting example of the influence of the cognitive perspective among culture researchers can be drawn from Schein's well-known model of the "levels" of organizational culture, presented in Figure 15.1.

Schein's approach "divides" culture into three levels. He argued that basic underlying assumptions lie at the root of culture, and are "unconscious, taken-for-granted beliefs, perceptions, thoughts, and feelings". Espoused values are derived from these basic underlying assumptions and are the "espoused justifications of strategies, goals, and philosophies". Finally, at the top level are "artifacts" which are defined as the "visible, yet hard to decipher organizational structures and processes".

Schein's model has influenced a generation of culture researchers to think in terms of distinct levels of culture and to believe that basic underlying assumptions are the foundation for values and artifacts. To be fair, this model does in some ways present a systems perspective on culture that allows us to understand a set of interrelated concepts. But Schein's model has also tended to lead researchers to take the idea of "levels of culture" a bit too seriously and often made it harder to see the linkage between levels. The perspective has tended to glorify basic assumptions as the true domain of culture without explaining their link to the more visible levels of culture.

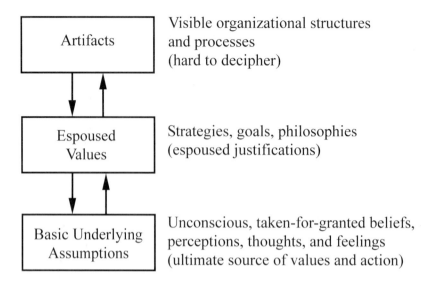

Artifacts — Visible organizational structures and processes (hard to decipher)

Espoused Values — Strategies, goals, philosophies (espoused justifications)

Basic Underlying Assumptions — Unconscious, taken-for-granted beliefs, perceptions, thoughts, and feelings (ultimate source of values and action)

**Figure 15.1**   Schein's model of culture.

This approach has also tended to emphasize the search for understanding at the cognitive level and to de-emphasize the more visible levels of culture.

Several important questions also go unanswered by Schein's model. To whom are these basic assumptions "unconscious"? Insiders? Outsiders? What happens to underlying assumptions once organizational members become aware of them? Presumably, researchers are aware of these assumptions, while organizational members are not. But what about the assumptions that organizational members are aware of but researchers are not?

Schein's emphasis on "espoused values" also tends to limit our ability to see the links across levels. The emphasis on espoused values begs the question of the role of "values-in-use" in linking basic core assumptions with the actions of organizational members and the more visible manifestations of culture. Finally, Schein's approach has also tended to trivialize those visible layers of culture, labelled as "artifacts", that are judged to be "hard to decipher". In fact, artifacts are quite easily deciphered by organizational members, who spend most of their time dealing with "artifacts". Changes in processes, strategies, structures, and technologies are quickly interpreted by organizational members and consume lots of their time and energy. Many executives react to the concept of "artifacts" quite negatively because it seems to leave an image of organizational members sifting through meaningless artifacts trying to make sense of their organizations and their work lives.

One of the most entertaining examples of the tight linkage between underlying assumptions, values, and artifacts comes from Michael Rosen's article "Breakfast at Spiro's" (Rosen, 1985). This article describes the annual holiday party at a successful American advertising agency. The garish display of wealth, the lavish bonuses, and an opulent setting all build to a climax as aspiring junior partners are awarded the ultimate gift – a fine silk French-made *Hermes* men's necktie! The Hermes tie reveals that style and panaché are as important as wealth and success – an important set of values that bind the firm together. The insights about the culture come not from the analytic distinction between the different levels, but in the realization that assumptions, values, and artifacts all fit together.

Thus, the more powerful approach to take when trying to create organizational change is one that links underlying assumptions with values, behaviour, and visible manifestations. The insights that come from the distinctions between levels are far less powerful than the recognition of patterns across levels. It is also important to display a keen knowledge and regard for the visible manifestations of the culture, in hopes that this will lead to a better understanding of the underlying values and assumptions that they represent. Reasoning from the visible manifestations back to the underlying assumptions creates far more leverage for organizational change than starting with the assumptions themselves.

## Providing a Comparative Benchmark, but Acknowledging Uniqueness

The organizational culture literature has often argued strongly for the uniqueness of organizations and has been less comfortable with a comparative approach to research and action (Martin, 1992; Denison, 1996). This aspect of the culture perspective can also be a barrier to creating leverage for organizational change. For most practising managers, the assertion that all organizations are unique undermines the importance of culture. If all organizations are unique then the best answer that we can hope for is "it depends". Customers and shareholders compare organizations and their products every day. Thus, in their endless quest for "delivering results", relatively few managers can see beyond a "best practice" perspective on organizational culture. Even if there are many aspects of organizational cultures that cannot be compared, when the objective is to use culture as a lever for change, it is important to begin by focusing on aspects of culture that can be compared.

As Schein's model helps to illustrate, it can be quite difficult to make generalizations about organizational culture when dealing at the level of basic underlying assumptions. The basic assumptions that an organization's members hold are often unique to the history and circumstances under which the organization developed. In addition, it also can be difficult to generalize about organizations when dealing with the visible manifestations of culture such as artifacts. As a matter of fact, many people wear Hermes ties, but the artifacts and symbols mean different things in different settings.

Many authors have argued persuasively, however, that organizations can be compared at the "values" level of analysis. For example, O'Reilly et al (1991) and his colleagues have used a values perspective to study the fit between individuals and organizations in public accounting firms. Perhaps the most interesting example of the power of using a comparative approach that focuses on values has been the cross-cultural work of Hofstede and of Trompenaars (Hofstede, 1980a,b; Hofstede et al, 1990; Trompenaars, 1994). Hofstede's work has focused on four well-known values of individualism, power distance, uncertainty avoidance and masculinity in his analysis of cross-cultural differences between organizations. His research links management and organizational practices with underlying values and assumptions and uses these dimensions to help understand similarities and differences in management practices around the world. His work has also focused on the importance of these same four traits for understanding differences among organizations (Hofstede et al, 1990). Trompenaars (1994) has also used values as a way to understand cross-cultural differences, by focusing on the way that members of different cultures resolve social dilemmas.

The approaches taken by Hofstede and Trompenaars are well accepted in the field of international business and have had a significant impact on practising managers. In contrast, the comparative approach has had far less acceptance among American culture researchers. Does anyone really believe that it is simpler to compare England and France than it is to compare Apple and IBM? The lesson here seems to be that a comparative approach to studying culture is not only viable, but that it is particularly valuable when the purpose is to motivate change.

## Focus on Performance Implications

As noted earlier, most executives are highly instrumental and are narrowly focused on delivering results. Academic concerns with epistemology and analytic insights often leave them cold. If executives address the topic of culture at all, it is usually to express frustration with the inability of their organization to implement change. They see the inertia of human behaviour as an obstacle to performance and efficiency. A much smaller proportion of leaders see culture as an important aspect of the capability of the human organization and as an expression of the knowledge that people have about their work.

Some managers, to be sure, do take a broader perspective on culture and its role in creating a motivating work environment. They may still be highly instrumental, but they are nonetheless clear that building a culture is one of the key means to the ends that they are trying to achieve. These executives are often quite reflective about their role as a leader, even as they are instrumental in their approach. Their intuitive belief that organizational culture makes a difference in business performance is supported by the brief literature that does link culture and performance (Denison, 1990; Denison and Mishra, 1995; Gordon and DiTomaso, 1992; Kotter and Heskett, 1992). But this perspective has not had much impact on the academic culture literature. Some academic authors have even argued that focusing culture research on organizational performance could have "socially pernicious" effects (Siehl and Martin, 1990), by presenting a way to conceptualize culture that is explicitly comparative and instrumental. But this research is quite helpful in convincing many leaders that understanding the culture of their organization and the importance that it has to their business is worth their time.

Using culture as a key lever for organizational change requires a persuasive way to frame the problem for managers. It must address their legitimate concerns about the instrumental value of culture change. Three approaches seem to help: (1) making managers aware of the evidence that links culture and performance; (2) helping them to understand the impacts, both positive and negative, that culture has on their own business; and (3) discussing culture using language that makes sense to managers and can be quickly linked to their own behaviour.

## Highlighting Symbols and Contradictions

Studying organizational culture focuses our attention on both meaning and survival. As the members of an organization hand down what they have learned to the next generation, they pass along a curious mix of "what is meaningful"? and "what has led to our survival"? As Schein and others have noted, cultures need to simultaneously fulfil the functions of internal integration and meaning as well as external adaptation. As our example of the "Hermes tie" shows, symbols convey meaning about both integration and adaptation, often at the same time. Getting to know the system of symbols in an organization can increase the leverage for change. Organizational change requires change in both the meaning system and the adaptation system, and these changes are always expressed in terms of the symbols and language of the organization. While these symbols may not be apparent to an outsider, members of an organization can translate the insights of an outsider into a system of symbols that has meaning in the local culture. This can also be a powerful source for change.

To create change, it is also important to focus on the internal contradictions and paradoxes that exist in any organization. All organizations face contradictory demands such as speed and quality, global and local focus, individual and team rewards, and integrating the old and new. The "culture" in fact, can often be most clearly understood as a system of meaning that explains the adaptation strategy that an organization has chosen as a response to a host of contradictory demands. In addition, different factions of the organization often compete with ideas and information to impose their point of view on others in the firm.

An example from a rapidly-growing. American computer company helps to illustrate. At its annual company Christmas party, the climax of an evening spent celebrating a year of spectacular growth came when hundreds of balloons were released. Inside each balloon was a new $100 bill. Whoever scrambled the hardest got the most money. The interesting part of the story is that the company, while dominated by America sales people who had driven the growth (and planned the Christmas party!), had nearly its entire source of competitive advantage generated by the R&D function, which is located outside America. In addition, one of the biggest sources of growth was European expansion. But, the scramble to pop the most balloons and get the most money was led by the same American sales people who were driving the growth. The message, that individual self-interest binds us together, is an attempt to resolve a basic contradiction between the interests of the individual and the interests of the team. But the message was perceived very differently by each of these groups and not equally shared by all.

Understanding paradox and contradiction is critical in creating change because change often implies finding new ways to reconcile old trade offs. Approaching the culture of an organization as a *logic* for the rich set of trade-offs that an organization has developed over time to help resolve the basic underlying contradictions helps in many ways. First, it helps to focus the discussion of the culture on an examination of the underlying contradictions and key trade-offs. Second, it helps to distinguish different sub-groups and sub-cultures and the sources of conflict on key organizational issues. Third, it helps to focus attention on how key underlying contradictions can be reconceptualized in the future.

These five lessons discussed here serve several purposes in this chapter. First, they are a statement of what the author has learned about using organizational culture as a point of leverage in creating change. As such, they build upon general prescriptions for creating change, such as "start at the top", or "build a business case", or "create small wins" (Kotter, 1996). But they are also a foundation for the development of the framework that is discussed in the rest of this chapter, as well as a set of lessons that was derived from applying this framework in a number of organizational change projects.

# A MODEL OF ORGANIZATIONAL CULTURE

This section presents a model of organizational culture that can be used for managing change (Denison, 1990; Denison and Mishra, 1995; Denison et al, 2000). Several characteristics differentiate this model from most others. First, it is rooted in research on how culture influences organizational performance, and is focused on those cultural traits that emerged from the research as having a key impact on business performance. In contrast to most frameworks that emphasize the uniqueness of organizational cultures, this model focuses on comparative generalizations about cultures at the values level. At the same time, the model acknowledges that there are many aspects of the deeper cultural levels of beliefs and assumptions that are difficult to generalize about across organizations.

## Understanding the Model

The model, as presented in Figure 15.2, is based on four cultural traits that have been shown to have a strong influence on organizational performance: involvement, consistency, adaptability, and mission. Each of these traits is measured with three component indexes, and each of those indexes is measured with five survey items. A complete listing of the items is included in the Appendix.

## *Involvement*

Effective organizations empower their people, build their organization around teams, and develop human capability at all levels. Members of the organization are committed

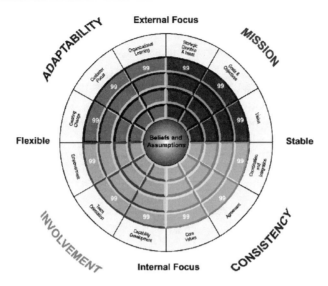

**Figure 15.2** Organizational culture model.

to their work, and feel that they *own* a piece of the organization. People at all levels feel that they have at least some input into decisions that will effect their work and feel that their work is directly connected to the goals of the organization. As an executive in one Korean company put it, "high involvement means *an engaged brain* – people apply their minds and hearts to the job and give all they've got". In the model, this trait is measured with three indexes:

**Empowerment.** Individuals have the authority, initiative, and ability to manage their own work. This creates a sense of ownership and responsibility toward the organization.

**Team Orientation.** Value is placed on working co-operatively toward common goals for which all employees feel mutually accountable. The organization relies on team effort to get work done.

**Capability Development.** The organization continually invests in the development of employee's skills in order to stay competitive and meet on-going business needs.

## Consistency

Research has shown that organizations are also effective because they are consistent and well integrated. People's behaviour is rooted in a set of core values, leaders and followers are skilled at reaching agreement (even when there are diverse points of view), and the organization's activities are well co-ordinated and integrated. Organizations with these traits have a strong and distinctive culture that significantly influences people's behaviour. In a 1990 case about Texas Commerce Bank and its legendary CEO, Ben Love, one of the senior loan officers put it clearly when he said: "I'm proud to walk in Ben Love's shadow". This type of consistency is a powerful source of stability and internal integration that results from a common mindset and a high degree of conformity. In the model, this trait is measured with three indexes:

**Core Values.** Members of the organization share a set of values that create a sense of identity and a clear set of expectations.

**Agreement.** Members of the organization are able to reach agreement on critical issues. This includes both the underlying level of agreement and the ability to reconcile differences when they occur.

**Coordination and Integration.** Different functions and units of the organization are able to work together well to achieve common goals. Organizational boundaries do not interfere with getting work done.

## Adaptability

But well-integrated organizations are often the most difficult to change. Internal integration and external adaptation can be at odds. Adaptable organizations are driven by their customers, take risks and learn from their mistakes, and have capability and experience at creating change. They are continuously improving the organization's ability to provide value for its customers. Organizations that are strong in adaptability usually experience sales growth and increased market share. When one CEO saw his organization's "bottom heavy" profile showing that involvement and consistency were high but adaptability was low, he immediately saw his organization's recent efforts to control cost in a different light. As he put it, "how can we expect to grow market share when we have our heads in the sand"? In the model, this trait is measured with three indexes:

**Creating Change.** The organization is able to create adaptive ways to meet changing needs. It is able to read the business environment, react quickly to current trends, and anticipate future changes.

**Customer Focus.** The organization understands and reacts to their customers and anticipates their future needs. It reflects the degree to which the organization is driven by a concern to satisfy its customers.

**Organizational Learning.** The organization receives, translates, and interprets signals from the environment into opportunities for encouraging innovation, gaining knowledge, and developing capabilities.

## Mission

Perhaps the most important cultural trait of all is a sense of mission. Organizations that don't know where they are going usually end up somewhere else. Successful organizations have a clear sense of purpose and direction that defines organizational goals and strategic objectives and expresses a vision of what the organization will look like in the future. The most troubled organizations are often those that have had to change their basic mission. As one future CEO of an electric utility said, "for 50 years, our mission was *to build bigger and better power plants*. Now I have to convince our people that their mission is *to provide consumers with safe and efficient options*". That's a big difference! When an organization's underlying mission changes, corresponding changes in strategy, structure, culture, and behaviour are also required. In this situation, strong leadership is required to define a vision for the future and build a culture that will support that vision. In the model, this trait is measured by three indexes:

**Strategic Direction and Intent.** Clear strategic intentions convey the organization's purpose and make it clear how everyone can contribute and "make their mark" on the industry.

**Goals and Objectives.** A clear set of goals and objectives can be linked to the mission, vision, and strategy, and provide everyone with a clear direction in their work.

**Vision.** The organization has a shared view of a desired future state. It embodies core values and captures the hearts and minds of the organization's people, while providing guidance and direction.

## Dynamic Contradictions

Like many contemporary models of leadership and organizational effectiveness, this model focuses on a set of tensions or contradictions that must be managed (Denison et al, 1995). Several contradictions are highlighted by the model – the trade-off between stability and flexibility and the trade-off between internal and external focus are the basic dimensions underlying the framework. In addition, the diagonal tensions in the model between internal consistency and external adaptation and between top-down mission and bottom-up involvement are also important.

Resolving these types of problems without making simple trade-offs is a real problems in most organizations. As the Vice Chairman of one large organization recently asked a group of managers, " Do we want higher product quality or lower cost? The answer is *yes*". It is easy to do one or the other, but difficult to do both. Organizations that are market focused and aggressive in pursuing every opportunity are often the same ones that have severe problems of internal integration. Organizations that are extremely well integrated and controlled usually have the hardest time focusing on the customer. Organization with a powerful top-down vision often find it difficult to focus on the empowerment and "bottom-up" dynamics needed to implement that vision. Effective organizations find a way to resolve these dynamic contradictions without relying on a simple trade-off. F. Scott Fitzgerald expressed the same concept when he said that "the test of a first rate mind is the ability to hold two contradictory ideas at the same time and still retain the capability to act" (Fitzgerald, 1945).

## Beliefs and Assumptions are at the Core

At the core of this model are underlying beliefs and assumptions. Although these "deeper" levels of organizational culture are difficult to measure, they provide the foundation from which behaviour and action spring. Beliefs and assumptions about the organization and its people, the customer, the marketplace and the industry, and the basic value propositions of the firm create a tightly knit logic that holds the organization together. But when organizations change or when they face new challenges from the competition, this core set of beliefs and assumptions, and the strategies, structures, and behaviours that are built on this foundation need to be reassessed. The organizational *system* and the culture that holds it together need to be examined more carefully.

None of the four cultural traits are unique to the model presented in this paper. The ideas came from executives interviewed during the research process and are widely reflected in the academic and popular management literature. They represent ideas about how to create an effective culture that have emerged during the research process. What *is* unique about the model is that it brings these concepts together, and presents them in a way that links managerial actions, cultural traits, and underlying assumptions into a framework based on research about what impacts organization performance. The model also forms the base for a diagnostic process that allows these traits to be measured and helps to paint a clear picture of the culture of an organization that suggests some clear links to action.

# PUTTING THE MODEL TO WORK: THREE CASE STUDIES

The best way to understand the model is to examine specific examples of how it has been used by organizations to understand and change their cultures. The first example, a one-hundred year old manufacturing firm, examines an overall profile of the organization's culture, whereas the second and third examples examine both the overall company profile and the profiles for different functional groups and levels of the organization.

## Manufacturing Company in Decline

This organization manufactures a durable goods product that is sold through a retail network that it does not control. The distribution network itself is consolidating and the company faces real "buyer power" for the first time. It has dominated its industry for years, but it now faces a new type of competition that seriously undercuts its products on price. Although business has been declining for the past five years, this past year was the first time that the senior executives did not receive their bonuses.

A cultural profile of the top management team is presented in Figure 15.3. The data for this profile came from a survey of the top 50 people in the organization (Denison and Neale, 1994). As noted above, each index is measured by five survey items, which are averaged to produce an index score. The results are presented in terms of quartile data, indicating that the organization's percentile score falls in the 1st, 2nd, 3rd, or 4th quartile in relationship to a database of nearly 500 organizations. This comparison, in effect, creates a benchmark between the target company and a sample of high and low performing firms.

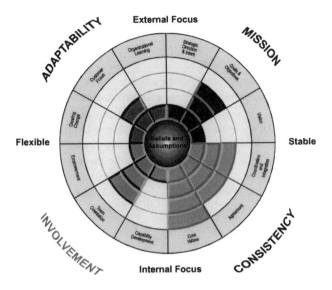

**Figure 15.3**   Profile of a 100-year-old manufacturing company.

Examination of the culture profile of the management team reveals some key organizational problems: All of the measures of adaptability are poor: learning and creating
change fall in the first quartile and customer focus falls in the second quartile. The only
strength in the area of mission is the operational focus on goals and objectives, indicating that there is little long-term vision or strategy. Involvement is also low, showing
strengths only in the area of team orientation. The only real strength that appears in this
profile is in the area of consistency, with the only top-quartile score being in core
values.

When the top management team looked at this profile, there was a long silence.
"What does this profile tell you about your organization"? the consultant asked. After
another long silence, one of them replied, "We're a team – going down together".
"Yeah, that's us", said another. The core values that held the group together were well
suited to the organization's past, but not necessarily to its future. The management team
also quickly linked other aspects of the profile to their situation – the emphasis on
operational issues in the mission area reflected the President's "mail room to board
room" career path and the relative neglect of longer-term strategic issues. When asked
about the team orientation data one of the managers chuckled and said, "well I guess
that all of those teams that we put in place aren't working very well yet". They had
created teams, but they had yet to change the way that work was actually done.

Looking at this culture profile brought together a number of different symptoms of
the organization's decline and linked them to the behaviour of the top management
team. Its tendency to ignore the customer and the competitive environment and reason
from the "inside-out" – taking the internal functioning of the organization as a given
and wondering why no one brought their products anymore – also came through

strongly in this analysis. The analysis also hit home with regard to the company's tendency to have short-term goals and objectives as their only real source of direction and to try to implement its strategy without a high level of involvement from the organization's members.

The analysis also made it quite clear that the behaviour of top management was at the centre of many of these problems. Since the research has shown that internally focused companies do not grow, the analysis also made the top managers more aware that they were unlikely to solve some of their most basic problems without a change in leadership behaviours. This analysis also made them aware of how few of the organization's leaders had the skill set that was needed to improve the situation. As a result, they began using the dimensions in the model as criteria in their leadership development process. Three years later, they have improved, changed the focus of their business, and continued to use the model and their data as a point of reference for their change process.

## Financial Services Firm: Creating Alignment Across Levels

The second example presents a more detailed case of a European financial services firm. One of the major issues in this organization was the degree of cultural alignment across levels – some of the business units showed major gaps between the top management team and the rest of the organization, while other business units showed close alignment. This is an important general issue in understanding and "managing " culture – the influence of a top management team on the culture of the organizational as a whole. Do the top leaders "create" the culture? Are there significant differences between different sub-groups in the organization? How should the inevitable differences between business units, functions, levels, regions, and different identity groups be reconciled with the concept of an "organizational" culture?

The traditional strength of this firm has been the capability of its analysts and professional staff. They have a high level of expertise and are recognized as the leaders in their sector of the industry. But as they attempt to compete in the increasingly global financial services industry, providing seamless delivery to global clients and cross-selling aggressively from one division to the other on the basis of the value proposition of the corporate brand, they often come up short. These changes in their competitive environment are forcing the organization to change from a classic professional bureaucracy (Mintzberg, 1979), like a law firm or a medical practice, to a service company that relies on a strong internal infrastructure to access all the organization's capabilities and deliver them to the customer.

The overall results for the entire organization, presented in Figure 15.4, are based on 365 responses across the entire management team. The results reflect many of the organization's key problems. Most of the low scores come in the areas of adaptability and consistency, reflecting the fact that the organization is primarily an internally-focused expertise-driven firm rather than an externally focused firm reacting to the marketplace, customers, and competitors. In addition, the problems in the area of consistency show why they often have problems in delivering co-ordinated response to their customers and achieving integration across different parts of the organization.

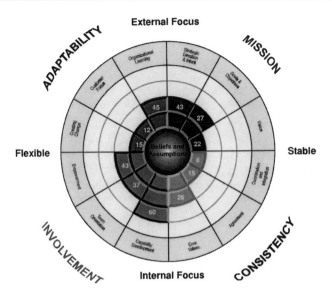

**Figure 15.4**  Company profile of financial services firm.

This combination of results was seen by many of the members of the organization as an illustration of the struggle they were having trying to understand the dynamics of the marketplace and translate that understanding into an internal system that could deliver their expertise to their customers.

Since this firm was also trying to address these problems by re-defining its vision and mission and communicating this throughout the organization, managers were also quite interested in the different perceptions of the culture across hierarchical levels. As they began to explore this, they quickly saw that some divisions had a large gap in perceptions between the top management team and the rest of the organization, while others had perceptions that were closely aligned.

The results for two of the divisions are presented in this chapter to illustrate some of the dynamics associated with cultural alignment across organizational levels. Figure 15.5 presents the results for the "core business", while Figure 15.6 presents the results for a recently acquired wholly-owned "subsidiary", which was acquired to help the company expand geographically.

The core business example in Figure 15.5 shows a substantial gap in nearly all areas between the leadership team and the rest of the organization. The leadership team's responses were much more positive and seemed to represent a detachment from the rest of the organization. This contrasts rather dramatically with the pattern of alignment in the subsidiary, presented in Figure 15.6, which shows both a positive profile and a high degree of cultural alignment across levels. In fact, in the subsidiary, some of results are more positive in the overall profile than they are for the top management group. Since it is the job of middle management to link the vision of the top leadership to the realities of the marketplace (Nonaka, 1988), these results raised a great deal of concern throughout the organization.

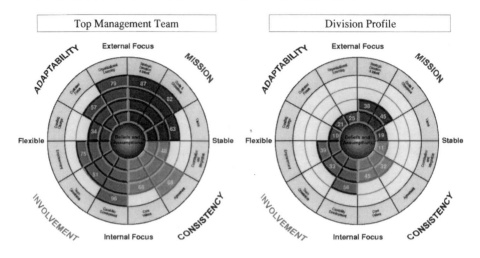

**Figure 15.5**  Financial services firm: core business.

Business units with a large cultural gap between the top leadership team and the rest of the organization faced a challenge from the executive board to address the problems and achieve better alignment across levels. They were encouraged to learn directly from the business units that had achieved better alignment and to apply the ideas that had worked in their own organizations. The lack of alignment was also considered by the top executives to be a key symptom of the their inability to penetrate their professional bureaucracy and "manage" it as an organization. This capability, in turn, was seen as a critical aspect of the transformation of the organization from a niche-based professional bureaucracy to a global financial services firm.

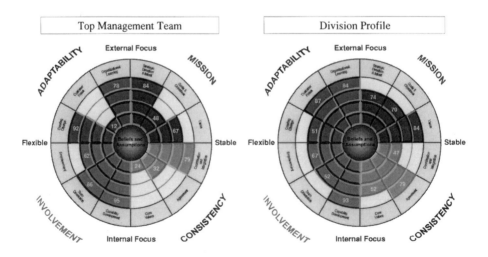

**Figure 15.6**  Financial services firm: wholly-owned subsidiary.

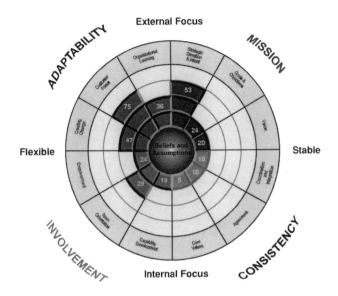

**Figure 15.7** Market-facing business unit.

## Speciality Metals Company: Creating a Market-Facing Business Unit

The third example presents the case of a European speciality metals company that created a market-facing business unit to serve the automotive industry. This reorganization changed the balance of power among the functions of the organization and required a substantial redefinition of the roles of all functional groups. Power shifted from the production end of the value chain to the sales and marketing end. But more importantly, the entire value chain now had to respond to the customer and the market-place. This case is presented in terms of several sets of profiles. The overall results are presented first followed by the results for several of the functional sub-groups.

As the overall results in Figure 15.7 show, reorganizing into a market-facing business unit did have a clear impact on the organizational profile. In contrast to the results for the entire corporation of which this automotive group was a part, most of the highest cultural scores came in terms of the adaptability and external focus. The problems, however, came in recreating the internal infrastructure needed to deliver. This example is based on responses of the 52 top managers and the results are presented in terms of percentile scores.

When the results are compared across the different functional management groups, an interesting pattern emerges. The management team, as shown in Figure 15.8, generally sees a stronger pattern in all areas and is particularly strong with respect to adaptability. Their results, however, still show the need for many improvements in the area of internal consistency. As one member of the organization said, "they get it!" – they understand the changes that the organization is trying to make.

The results for the sales and marketing team in Figure 15.9 show a different pattern. Nearly all of the areas of the model are strengths, except for coordination and integra-

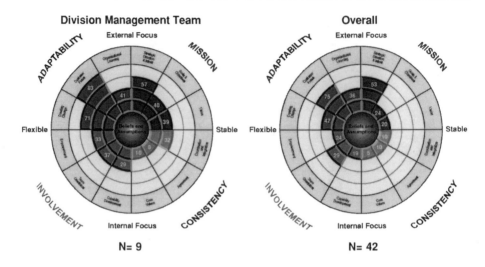

**Figure 15.8**  Division management team.

tion. The group's discussion of these results focused on the fact that marketing and sales people are very pleased with this reorganization, but from their perspective, still have a lot of trouble getting the organization to respond. Sales and marketing people see that the organization has changed its perspective, but still have a lot of explaining to do to their customers when their organization is unable to respond.

The least favourable perceptions of the organization's culture come from the operations function. Prior to the reorganization, production controlled most of the operation and held a great deal of power. In the past year since the re-organization, many things

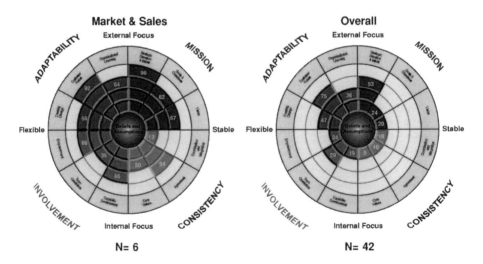

**Figure 15.9**  Marketing and sales.

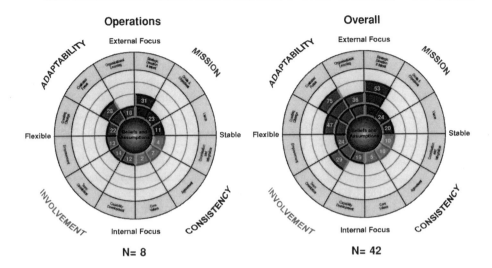

**Figure 15.10**   Operations.

have changed. Their "line of sight" to the customer has changed and they have yet to recreate a system that allows them to be responsive to the customer. Their results, presented in Figure 15.10, show that a lot of work remains if this organization is to reconstruct their internal infrastructure to be more responsive to the customer.

The results for the final group, the headquarters staff who are not a part of the top management team, are presented in Figure 15.11. These results also show a very different pattern from the other functions. They do perceive the increased importance of the customer, but otherwise, their scores are weak in all areas. It is particularly

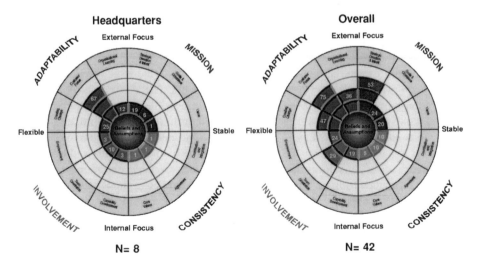

**Figure 15.11**   Headquarters staff.

interesting that all of the scores in the consistency area are at the 1st percentile, indicating that their scores are among the lowest ever recorded by any organization. But the results do make a lot of sense when taken in context – headquarters staff functions are typically internal service providers who focus on internal customers. Reorganizing into a market-facing business unit has radically changed the nature of the demand for their services and is causing them to totally redefine their role in the organization.

The overall pattern of results presented by this set of profiles helps to illustrate several important points about the culture of the organization. First, there is not one unitary view of the culture and in fact, competing views of the culture are at the heart of the change process. Second, this diverse set of profiles shows how impossible it is to present a unified view of the culture to customers or to other members of the organization. Third, and most important by far is that this analysis of the organization served as a stimulus and a reference point for an energetic, but constructive discussion of how the organization was adapting to the change process.

# USING CULTURE TO DRIVE THE CHANGE PROCESS: DISCUSSION AND CONCLUSIONS

This chapter has presented a framework for understanding organizational culture that has been developed as a means to apply the concept of culture to create leverage during the organizational change process. This approach departs from the typical treatment of organizational culture found in the academic literature in several important ways that are discussed in the beginning of this chapter. Highest priority is given to providing a framework that is useful to managers and executives and addresses the needs and concerns of the "natives", rather than the "anthropologists". This final section raises three points for discussion.

## Getting the Culture Issue on the Table

The approach presented in this chapter is an attempt to get the issue of organizational culture "on the table" as a key part of the change process. The approach is rooted in the observation that while organizational change is not possible without culture change, cultural issues are nonetheless frequently neglected during the change process. All too often, the good ideas that have been developed in the academic culture literature are not positioned in a way that allows the ideas to contribute to understanding and managing the change process. This limits the impact that the ideas can have, and further limits the learning that comes from an active involvement in the change process. As one well-known organizational theorist has noted, "When all is said and done, there is one main obstacle to an emergence on an anthropology of complex organizations: Access". (Czarniawska-Joerges, 1992). Using the ideas in this chapter to help frame culture issues can help to create the level of access necessary to influence the change process and allow for further learning in the future.

The link between underlying assumptions, values, meaning, behaviour, and action is inevitably a complex one. Those who understand the culture perspective tend to see these linkages quite clearly and thus have a lot to contribute during the change process. These skills are often rare among managers and executives. Many of them need a lot of help in bringing this perspective into action during the change process.

## Depth of Analysis

This chapter has presented a set of examples that has primarily focused on top management teams and has presented survey data from limited organizational samples. While it is important to recognize that leaders have great influence over the change process, the examples given here should not be taken to mean that the culture perspective is only appropriate at the management level. There are many examples that have used much larger samples and entailed a much greater depth of involvement and analysis than those that have been developed in this chapter. This chapter has presented multiple examples of how the culture perspective has influenced the change process, rather than giving greater depth of analysis on a single case. A similar point about depth of analysis can be made with respect to the use of qualitative and ethnographic insights in these projects. Each of the cases involved substantial time spent on site and the fieldnotes reveal insights from many different organizational settings – not just the Christmas parties! The cases presented in this chapter have been chosen to illustrate the application of the model, and have spent less time presenting the many qualitative insights that have been a part of these projects.

Depth of analysis is critically important in any organizational change process. The approach presented here, in practice, always relies heavily on the clinical insights that are a part of any successful organizational change process. Perceptive insiders and outsiders need to be involved in order to help translate the findings from a model-based analysis of the culture into practical recommendations for action. Depth of analysis is needed to support the insights from the survey data and bring them to life.

I was once in a meeting with a large consulting company that was considering using this model in a number of their organizational change projects. They asked me to meet with their "Research" committee so that they could ask me questions about the method, the measures, the applications, and so on. One of the members of the committee, who had recently received his Ph.D., joined the meeting by speaker phone. He kept asking me questions worthy of a doctoral defence – he asked about rigor, about the validity assessment, and about my assumptions regarding the use of qualitative data. His questions were annoying because they all assumed that the model and method were intended to be applied without any additional insight or knowledge about the organization. After a while, even the other members of the committee who were in the room seemed to be getting annoyed by his line of questioning. After completing his tour de force, he issued a summary critique: "Well then", he said, "I guess if you only had the survey results, then you wouldn't really know very much about the organization!" "finally", I said under my breath to the others seated at the table, "he got it!" Tools and frameworks are just that – they are designed to enhance and extend our capabilities, but they are never a substitute for real understanding of the situation at hand.

## Culture and Competence

It is also important to recognize that the cultural framework described in this chapter could perhaps have been presented as an "organizational effectiveness" framework or an "organizational change" model. In fact, one organization said to us, "we really like the framework, but our CEO won't let us use the word "culture". Can we call this thing something else"?

What makes this framework a "culture model"? How is it different from other approaches because it is a culture model? This framework is a culture model because it attempts to link strategies, systems, structures, and behaviours back to a common set of beliefs and assumptions. This approach is rooted in the belief that structures evolve from a set of beliefs and assumptions. During times of change, it is these assumptions and beliefs that need to be reconsidered, not just the structures and "best practices" that have evolved from them in the past. The traits and behaviours that are around the "outside" of the model are simply the outer layers of the onion – an understanding of the core beliefs and assumptions comes only as the layers are peeled away. These traits and behaviours can also serve as a "Trojan Horse" to lure a management team into a discussion of the deeper level of core beliefs and assumptions. They begin with data, benchmarks, and analysis, but they typically end with a more basic discussion of their beliefs and assumptions.

This focus on core beliefs and assumptions also makes the link between culture and competence much clearer. In settings as diverse as the transformation process in Eastern European firms (Kennedy, 1994), cutting edge corporate strategy (Prahalad and Hamel, 1990), and Japanese product development (Nonaka and Takeuchi, 1995), the message is clear – knowledge is often tacit and contextualized and usually comes embedded in a complex culture and a belief system. For example, a few years ago when Microsoft assumed that the computing world would remain centred around the PC, the knowledge and skills required for the internet seemed to be of secondary importance. As this assumption changed, "competence" was redefined. In pharmaceutical firms, a similar change came as the R&D process began to focus less on chemists developing compounds and more on bio-technologists searching for genetic solutions. Strategies, systems, structures, and behaviours are derived from these basic assumptions and the unique value of the culture perspective is the potential to link these levels together.

Creating a culture provides leverage by creating a "code" for an organizational system that influences behaviour over time. Culture is an important place to intervene when trying to create change that will last. Indeed, changes that are not reflected in an organization's culture will not last and will not be translated into action. There are many powerful concepts that have been developed to help understand cultures, but the challenge is to put those ideas into action. Hopefully, this chapter has describe one approach that can help executives and scholars to do so.

# ACKNOWLEDGEMENTS

The author wishes to thank IMD for the support that they have provided for this chapter. I also wish to thank the companies that I have used as anonymous examples and Professor Thomas G. Cummings for his comments and suggestions on earlier drafts of this chapter.

# APPENDIX A. ITEMS AND INDEXES IN THE ORGANIZATIONAL CULTURE SURVEY

| Trait | Index | Item |
| --- | --- | --- |
| Involvement | Empowerment | 1. Most employees are highly involved in their work.<br>2. Decisions are usually made at the level where the best information is available<br>3. Information is widely shared so that everyone can get the information he or she needs when it's needed<br>4. Everyone believes that he or she can have a positive impact<br>5. Business planning is ongoing and involves everyone in the process to some degree. |
| | Team orientation | 6. Cupertino across different parts of the organization is actively encouraged<br>7. People work like they are part of a team<br>8. Teamwork is used to get work done, rather than hierarchy<br>9. Teams are our primary building blocks<br>10. Work is organized so that each person can see the relationship between his or her job and the goals of the organization |
| | Capability development | 11. Authority is delegated so that people can act on their own<br>12. The "bench strength" (capability of people) is constantly improving<br>13. There is continuous investment in the skills of employees<br>14. The capabilities of people are viewed as an important source of competitive advantage<br>15. Problems often arise because we do not have the skills necessary to do the job. (Reversed Scale) |
| Consistency | Core values | 16. The leaders and managers "practice what they preach"<br>17. There is a characteristic management style and a distinct set of management practices |

*(continued)*

| Trait | Index | Item |
|-------|-------|------|
| | | 18. There is a clear and consistent set of values that governs the way we do business |
| | | 19. Ignoring core values will get you in trouble |
| | | 20. There is an ethical code that guides our behaviour and tells us right from wrong |
| | Agreement | 21. When disagreements occur, we work hard to achieve "win-win" solutions |
| | | 22. There is a "strong" culture |
| | | 23. It is easy to reach consensus, even on difficult issues |
| | | 24. We often have trouble reaching agreement on key issues. (Reversed Scale) |
| | | 25. There is a clear agreement about the right way and the wrong way to do things |
| | Coordination and integration | 26. Our approach to doing business is very consistent and predictable |
| | | 27. People from different parts of the organization share a common perspective |
| | | 28. It is easy to co-ordinate projects across different parts of the organization |
| | | 29. Working with someone from another part of this organization is like working with someone from a different organization. (Reversed Scale) |
| | | 30. There is good alignment of goals across levels |
| Adaptability | Creating change | 31. The way things are done is very flexible and easy to change |
| | | 32. We respond well to competitors and other changes in the business environment |
| | | 33. New and improved ways to do work are continually adopted |
| | | 34. Attempts to create change usually meet with resistance. (Reversed Scale) |
| | | 35. Different parts of the organization often co-operate to create change |
| | Customer focus | 36. Customer commenys and recommendations often lead to changes |
| | | 37. Customer input directly influences our decisions |
| | | 38. All members have a deep understanding of customer wants and needs |
| | | 39. The interests of the customer often get ignored in our decisions. (Reversed Scale) |
| | | 40. We encourage direct contact with customers by our people |
| | Organizational learning | 41. We view failure as an opportunity for learning and improvement |

(*continued*)

| Trait | Index | Item |
|-------|-------|------|
| | | 42. Innovation and risk taking are encouraged and rewarded |
| | | 43. Lots of things "fall between the cracks". (Reversed Scale) |
| | | 44. Learning is an important objective in our day-to-day work |
| | | 45. We make certain that the "right hand knows what the left hand is doing" |
| Mission | Strategic direction and intent | 46. There is a long-term purpose and direction |
| | | 47. Our strategy leads other organizations to change the way they compete in the industry |
| | | 48. There is a clear mission that gives meaning and direction to our work |
| | | 49. There is a clear strategy for the future |
| | | 50. Our strategic direction is unclear to me. (Reversed Scale) |
| | Goals and objectives | 51. There is widespread agreement about goals |
| | | 52. Leaders set goals that are ambitious, but realistic |
| | | 53. The leadership has "gone on record" about the objectives we are trying to meet |
| | | 54. We continuously track our progress against our stated goals |
| | | 55. People understand what needs to be done for us to succeed in the long run |
| | Vision | 57. Leaders have a long-term viewpoint |
| | | 58. Short-term thinking often compromises our long-term vision. (Reversed Scale) |
| | | 59. Our vision creates excitement and motivation for our employees |
| | | 60. We are able to meet short-term demands without compromising our long-term vision |

# REFERENCES

Abegglen, J. and Stalk, G. (1985) Kaisha, The Japanese Corporation. New York: Basic Books.

Brannen, M. (1999) Advancing the culture concept: a cross-field dialogue. Academy of International Business, Charleston, SC, November 20–23.

Czarniawska-Joerges, B. (1992) Exploring Complex Organizations: A Cultural Perspective. Beverly Hills, CA: Sage.

Denison, D. (1990) Corporate Culture and Organizational Effectiveness. New York: Wiley.

Denison, D. (1996) What IS the difference between organizational culture and organizational climate? A native's point of view on a decade of paradigm wars. Academy of Management Review, 21(3): 619–654.

Denison, D., Cho, H.J. and Young, J. (2000) Diagnosing organizational cultures: a model and method. Working paper, International Institute for Management Development.

Denison, D., Hooijberg, R. and Quinn, R. (1995) Paradox and performance: toward a theory of behavioral complexity in lanagerial leadership. Organization Science, 6(5): 524–540.

Denison, D. and Mishra, A. (1995) Toward a theory of organizational culture and effectiveness. Organizational Science, 6(2): 204–223.

Denison, D. and Neale, W. (1994) Denison Organizational Culture Survey. Ann Arbor, MI: Aviat.

Fitzgerald, F.S. (1945) The crack up. In E. Wilson (Ed), The Crack-up. New York: J. McLaughlin.

Geertz, C. (1973) The Interpretation of Cultures. New York: Basic Books.

Gordon, G. and DiTomaso, N. (1992) Predicting corporate performance from organizational culture. Journal of Management Studies, 29(6): 783–798.

Hofstede, G. (1980a) Culture's Consequences: International Differences in Work-Related Values. Beverly Hills, CA: Sage.

Hofstede, G. (1980b) Motivation, leadership, and organization: do American theories apply abroad? Organizational Dynamics, 9(1): 42–63.

Hofstede, G., Neuijen, B., Ohayv, D. and Sanders, G. (1990) Measuring organizational cultures: a qualitative and quantitative study across twenty cases. Administrative Science Quarterly, 35: 286–316.

Kennedy, M. (1994) Envisioning Eastern Europe: Postcommunist Cultural studies. Ann Arbor, MI: University of Michigan Press.

Kotter, J. (1996) Leading Change. Boston, MA: Harvard Business School Press.

Kotter, J. and Heskett, J. (1992) Corporate Culture and Performance. New York: Free Press.

Kunda, G. (1992) Engineering Culture. Philadelphia, PA: Temple University Press.

Martin, J. (1992) Cultures in Organizations: Three Perspectives. New York: Oxford University Press.

Mead, G.H. (1934) Mind, Self, and Society. Chicago, IL: University of Chicago Press.

Mintzberg, H. (1979) The Structuring of Organizations. Englewood Cliffs, NJ: Prentice–Hall.

Nonaka, I. (1988) Toward middle-up-down management: accelerating information creation. Sloan Management Review, 29(3): 9–18.

Nonaka, I. and Takeuchi, H. (1995) The Knowledge-Creating Company: How Japanese Companies Create the Dynamics of Innovation. New York: Oxford University Press.

O'Reilly, C., Chatman, J. and Caldwell, D. (1991) People and organizational culture: a profile comparison approach to assessing person-environment fit. Academy of Management Journal, 34: 487–516.

Prahalad, C.K. and Hamel, G. (1990) The core competence of the corporation. Harvard Business Review, 68: 79–91.

Radcliffe-Brown, A. (1952) Structure and Function in Primitive Society. London: Cohen.

Rosen, M. (1985) Breakfast at spiros: dramaturgy and dominance. Journal of Management, 11(2): 31–48.

Schein, E. (1992) Organizational Culture and Leadership. San Francisco, CA: Jossey–Bass.

Senge, P. (1990) The Fifth Discipline: The Art and Practice of the Learning Organization. New York: Doubleday.

Siehl, C. and Martin, J. (1990) Organizational culture: a key to financial performance? In B. Schneider (Ed), Organizational Climate and Culture. San Francisco, CA: Jossey–Bass.

Treacy, M. and Weirsema, F. (1995) The Discipline of Market Leaders: Choose Your Customers, Narrow Your Focus, Dominate Your Market. London: HarperCollins.

Trompenaars, F. (1994) Riding the Waves of Culture: Understanding Diversity in Global Business. New York: Irwin.

Van Maanen, J. (1988) Tales of the Field. Chicago, IL: University of Chicago Press.

Weber, M. (1930) The Protestant Ethic and the Spirit of Capitalism. New York: Scribners.

Weick, K. (1979) The Social Psychology of Organizing. New York: Random House.

# Section V

# Culture: the International Dimension

Nigel J. Holden

It has been pointed out that culture is one of two or three most complex words in the English language. Culture has certainly been a very problematical term in management and business studies. This is due in no small way to the fact that the prevailing concept of culture has been that which has been derived from anthropology. This particular view, which sees culture as a relatively stable, homogenous, internally consistent set of assumptions, values, and norms transmitted by socialization to the next generation, has been predominantly based on observations of pre-industrial societies – and in the service of imperial power, as Eagleton (2000) reminds us. This in itself should alert management scholars to the limitations of this essentialist view of culture especially as so few anthropologists actually study industrial or even so-called post-industrial societies.

Accordingly, as editor of this section of the Wiley Handbook, I have abstained from inviting a contribution explicitly on culture, which, however loosely or tightly defined, will always represent a vast canvas of themes, topics, ideas and perspectives. Being invited to commission seven chapters, I saw it as pointless to attempt reasonable coverage of what by general agreement might be termed core subjects. In the circumstances it made sense to request chapters on topics which might be said to combine contemporary relevance with a certain amount of lasting power, but from unusual perspectives.

This certainly applies to the contribution of Charles T. Tackney (Chapter 16), who throws unusual light on a topic about which one might have thought the last word had to all intents and purposes been said: Japanese management. Tackney argues that any theory of Japanese management that does not take account of the evolution of employment law in Japan is deficient. The crux of his argument concerns the role of life-time employment which far from being a cliché or social construct is "an institutionalized practice of post-war Japanese industrial relations", whose legal origins derive in part from the labour legislation of the Weimar Republic and in part from post-war American legislation. In this paradigm Japanese management is a product of foreign influences which, as Tackney suggests, may be a significant factor accounting for "the successful replication" of Japanese management practices in other countries. This chapter does not merely distance itself from the normal clutch of stereotypes about Japanese management. It also demonstrates how a "non-cultural" approach can be paradoxically and fruitfully applied to a phenomenon to elucidate aspects of its cultural embedding.

Stereotypes are the theme of Anna Zarkada-Fraser in Chapter 17. She begins by arguing that our need for identity is both counterbalanced and intensified by a need for a reference point to express "otherness". Stereotypes, whether useful crystallizations or blatant distortions, fulfil this function. Zarkada-Fraser then demonstrates how stereotyping influences the conduct of a range of international business operations including marketing, foreign direct investment and co-ordination of multinational corporations' activities. Stereotypes tend to be seen as pernicious, but Zarkada-Fraser argues that we live in an era of "total re-evaluation of space, time and our relationship with both" and we may no longer need "summary constructs to guide us in differentiating between groups and preserving homogeneity within groups".

In Chapter 18 Kate Gilbert examines management change in Central and East Europe, posing a challenging observation about these fraught processes. Are we talking more about a transition or more about a transformation? These terms have almost become casually synonymous, but Gilbert does well to keep the distinction clear. The term transition, she notes, implies "a teleological assumption that the destination of change is known and that the route is marked out". Transformation means "a process of destruction and disintegration". As the two processes are intertwined in reality, it means that the societies involved must decide what to abandon, what to retain, and what to modify. The choices are proving painful for the populations. One aspect of this contribution highlights the frequently poor reception of Western management know-how. Is its purpose to aid transition or bring about transformation? Gilbert suggests that deliverers of this know-how, whether educators or consultants, may have focused too much on economic and managerial change without understanding the social and cultural dimensions associated with them.

The international section of this handbook cannot avoid a contribution of that vexed term globalization, whose meanings cover everything from new-age consciousness to corporate neo-colonialism. In Chapter 19 Nigel J. Holden and Dorte Salskov-Iversen avoid the semantic quagmires and regard globalization as a sufficiently concrete feature of management discourse. They argue that knowledge and awareness of globalization shape and challenge managerial and organizational thinking with specific reference to communication processes and methods of co-ordination and control. They contrast the globalization discourse in two significant transnational corporations, one Danish and one Japanese, showing how the companies' respective discourse creates strikingly contrasting social constructions of globalization which in turn reflect markedly different forms of organizational governance.

Intercultural communication is the theme addressed by Marie-Thérèse Claes in Chapter 20. She points out, and this is often overlooked, that social rituals are translated not only into patterns of behaviour, but also into speech. It is language through which formality and informality, and directness and indirectness are conveyed, cued, and received; but the nature of these manifestations vary according from language to language, each with complex social codes and conventions and grammatical devices, and according to situations. In international business operations the differential use of language to control or accommodate can be a severe source of intercultural confusion resulting in possibly misleading impressions of a business partner's intention, integrity, and commitment. This chapter, with its sharp distinctions and references to several languages and cultural groups, is a salutary reminder to those who see the global economy as an increasingly monolingual entity based on the near universality of the English language in all principal endeavours of international life.

In Chapter 21 Gerhard Fink and Wolfgang Mayrhofer develop the notion of the organization as a problem-solving system from an intercultural perspective. In this view organizations generate resources internally and externally, and transform these into organizational capabilities which in turn are converted into core competencies for delivering benefits to customers and stakeholders. Under this scheme, firstly, organizational culture influences all internal processes of the organization, including those which create customer value; secondly, cultural and national diversity within the organization can become a resource for coping with a wide range of international management activities. Such a concept of the organizations requires knowledge and insights from several scientific disciplines: management, economics, psychology, and sociology not to mention anthropology, history, law and linguistics. Fink and Mayrhofer, noting the complexity of the modern business world, argue that the time has come for specialists in such fields to co-operate in developing conceptual tools to help managers leverage international resources more productively.

The contribution of Jan Ulijn and M. Weggeman, which forms Chapter 22, discusses the nature of innovation culture, arguing that in international work environments its characteristics are strongly influenced by the impact of national culture, corporate culture and professional culture in a given organization. Using a research design, making use of Hofstedian concepts of work-related values, the authors pose five questions about the influence of those factors on innovation culture with special reference to two key functions associated with product innovation: engineering and marketing. Making use of three metaphors, the fountain, the funnel, and the iceberg, they draw the conclusion that in innovation cultures in which Western and Oriental values come into play, there is a tendency for the former values to be associated with the need to create a successful product, whereas the latter values are important for promoting co-operation. The study demonstrates not only the complexities of the interplay of the different types of culture, but also, and not for the first time, the problems of the semantic overloading of the word culture.

# REFERENCE

Eagleton, T. (2000) The Idea of Culture. Oxford: Blackwell.

# Chapter 16

# The Modes of Social Relation in Japanese Management Practice

**Charles T. Tackney**
*Department of Intercultural Communication and Management,*
*Copenhagen Business School, Frederiksberg, Denmark*

## INTRODUCTION

The phrase "Japanese management" has achieved a rare significance in management and organisational culture research. Globally recognised, it is employed for a wide variety of purposes, often to compel or pursue strategic change within organisations. Despite this, "Japanese management" remains among the most obscure of expressions in management science. What, in fact, is "Japanese management"? How (if at all) does it differ from other approaches? Where did it come from? Is it uniquely Japanese? Why do some efforts to adapt it elsewhere fail, while others succeed? With the post-war miracle of Japanese economic development now a matter of history, does "Japanese management" have any enduring significance?

This chapter offers an answer to each of the preceding questions by framing our understanding of "Japanese management" in terms of the "web of rules" or "working rules" governing employment relations: a comparative/international industrial relations perspective (Dunlop, 1952, 1993). According to this perspective, national patterns of employment relations can be examined in light of the historical influence exerted upon them by workers, managers, government and each actor's representative agencies. The interdisciplinary openness of this approach enables us to define Japanese management with explicit reference to the central debate of post-war Japanese employment and management practice: the existence and nature of the lifetime employment system.

The lifetime employment system debate has long been, and continues to be, inescapably linked to Japanese management theory. Unfortunately, this linkage has often been extremely contentious; leading Japanese management theorists, including Masahiko Aoki and Kazuo Koike, assert that the lifetime employment system simply does not exist. They offer, instead, their own competing theories.

We now know, however, that case law in Japan has recognised lifetime employment as an institutionalised practice since the early 1960s. The industrial relations perspective presented in the following pages will define Japanese management, specifically its modes of social relation and modes of production, in terms of the culturally "thick" institution of lifetime employment and supporting institutions. With this awareness, we will then be able to explore what it is and, in light of this, evaluate the export potential of a properly defined Japanese management construct to other national settings.

## JAPANESE MANAGEMENT THEORY AND THE LIFETIME EMPLOYMENT SYSTEM DEBATE

Throughout the post-World War II decades, Japanese management practice has been defined in relation to enduring employment relations between Japanese managers and workers. Abegglen (1958a,b); Levine (1958) were among the earliest researchers to publish on the theme of post-war Japanese industrial organisation. Abegglen, through the simultaneous English and Japanese 1958 publication of *The Japanese Factory*: *Aspects of its Social Organization*, is credited with the remarkable achievement of introducing and popularising the term "lifetime employment" (shushin koyo) in both English and Japanese. He offered this term to account for observed tendencies of Japanese management to retain redundant staff. Levine, in turn, published the first systematic examination of Japan's industrial relations system: the "web of rules" or "working rules" governing employment relations in Japan. He, too, observed and reported long-term employment practices. Both scholars, to one degree or another, attributed long-term employment to residuals of feudal Japanese culture transferred, somehow, to the shop floor. Both implied that these inefficiencies were problems time and economic development would erase.

In 1985, Andrew Gordon published *The Evolution of Labor Relations in Japan*: *Heavy Industry, 1853–1955* (Gordon, 1985). In the Introduction to this text, he wrote, Abegglen "would not have written anything like *The Japanese Factory* had he gone to Japan a decade or more earlier, for not until the early 1950s did Japanese employment patterns come to resemble those since described by sociologists, economists, and anthropologists" (p. 1). This is a concise statement of the significance of Gordon's work; the evidence he reported constrains the institution of lifetime employment to the post-war era. He defined lifetime employment as a settlement worked out through the post-war struggles of Japanese management and labour (see also Gordon, 1998).

Abegglen, Levine, and Gordon are representative of a genre of scholars that recognise the critically important role played by institutions, institutional practices, and, for want of a more specific term, culture, in defining the working rules of Japanese industrial relations. These scholars see the lifetime employment system as an authentic research object that defines, and is defined by, Japanese management practices. Other researchers in this group include Cole, 1971b,c, 1972, 1979); Dore (1973,

1986, 1989); Shimada (1983, 1989, 1992a, 1992b), and Taira (1970; Taira and Levine, 1985). Throughout the post-war decades, these and other scholars sought to define the lifetime employment system, estimate workforce coverage, and even speculate on the potential for this system to serve as a model for economic development in other nations. This research stream, grounded in fieldwork and primary language sources, defined the initial theoretical parameters for Japanese management theory.

In the 1980s, Masahiko Aoki and Kazuo Koike, among others, introduced compelling theories of Japanese management (Aoki, 1986, 1987, 1988; Koike, 1983, 1987, 1988, 1991, 1995). This process of theory building derived from standard principles of social science and economic theory. Management scholars sought to minimise the role of culture and/or historical uniqueness in explaining Japanese management. A properly minimalist route, they felt, would permit development of valid and reliable models. Furthermore, such management models would hold promise for more effective assessment of what was rapidly becoming the nation's leading export in the 1980s: Japanese management itself.

Masahiko Aoki (1987) developed the theory of the "J-firm", or the corporative managerial model of the Japanese enterprise. This, he claimed, is a particular form of industrial organisation that developed and diffused throughout post-war Japan. This model differs from the collective bargaining model of the firm, prevalent in the US and UK, and the participatory management model that is common to Germany and the nations of Scandinavian. Kazuo Koike (1988) in turn, proposed that the comparatively unique dimensions of post-1945 Japanese management practices were due to the functional "white-collarisation" of Japan's blue-collar workers. A fundamental premise of white-collarisation is that the generalised skilling of Japanese workers was a requisite step in achieving the egalitarian features of post-1945 Japanese enterprises.

Both management theorists are careful to refrain from a complete negation of the role of Japanese history, culture and institutions in the development of the post-1945 working rules that govern Japanese industrial enterprises. Aoki, for example, recognised the significance of the post-war legal dissolution of Zaibatsu industrial arrangements. Subsequent public distribution of share ownership evolved into the now commonly recognised Keiretsu firm linkages. Aoki also recognised the importance of post-war industrial conflict in J-firm emergence. He thought that the Miike mining conflict of the early 1960s was instrumental in impressing upon Japanese management the very high value Japanese workers placed on job security. From this industrial conflict, Aoki argued, Japanese management began to design and deploy human resource polices that supported long-term employment.

By the early 1990s, Japanese management theory appeared to achieve "a life of its own" as a research area. Koike's theory is widely taught and highly influential within Japanese academic circles. It has been used to study the transfer of Japanese management practice to Southeast Asia (Koike and Inoki, 1990). Aoki's complex and carefully wrought game theory approach to Japanese management offered a comparatively elegant, self-validating system built upon minimal historical premises.

In addition, studies of various Japanese modes of production that had been developed during the "economic miracle" began to appear in press. These extolled a new era of productivity improvements and enhanced quality of working life for those employed in

Japanese-style management regimes (Womack et al., 1990; Elger and Smith, 1994; Kaplinsky and Posthuma, 1994).

# JAPANESE MANAGEMENT THEORY AND THE ASIAN CRISIS

For many reasons, the Asian crisis of the 1990s presents a life or death challenge to Japanese management theory. The period of Japan's post-war economic miracle is now history. Market and economic policy distortions associated with the "bubble economy" continue to prolong the slow pace of Japan's economic recovery from an unprecedented recession.

These issues alone have raised deeply troubled debate in Japan about the presumed managerial wisdom and flexibility of "Japan, Inc.". Overseas, the initial enthusiasm for Japanese management practice has faded (Graham, 1995). Instead, Japanese management is often characterised as an ultimate form of "management by stress". It has even been identified as an explicit threat to a nation's economic well-being, and this by a scholar fundamentally predisposed toward Japanese management practice (Milkman, 1991).

If Japanese management is so onerous, how do the Japanese themselves react to it? Consider, for example, an Economic Planning Agency (1994) analysis of average consecutive work years for men and women in several industrialised nations.

Table 16.1 indicates that average employment tenure in Japan paralleled that of Germany and France, but was more than 4 years higher than similar data for the United States. The 1994 Economic Planning Agency (EPA) report (1994: 298) then examined the Japanese employment system within the context of Japan's economic problems. The text suggests the underlying uncertainties that pervade Japanese management theory. The Agency wrote, "the prolonged economic recession and employment adjustments by companies are changing the basic conditions surrounding employment and

**Table 16.1** Consecutive years of work (male and female workers)[a]

| Nation | Consecutive years of work |
|---|---|
| Japan (1992) | 10.9 |
| Germany (1990) | 10.4 |
| France (1991) | 10.1 |
| Norway (1989) | 9.4 |
| UK (1991) | 7.9 |
| Canada (1991) | 7.8 |
| Australia (1991) | 6.8 |
| US (1991) | 6.7 |

[a] Source: Economic Planning Agency (1994: 298).

some worry that it is becoming difficult to maintain the Japanese employment system, which has supported the country's employment stability for so many years".

The EPA's sense of impending, inescapable change almost completely masks a singularly important piece of information in the data; Japan has the longest employment tenure of any of the industrialised nation(s) listed.

Thus, Japanese management theory remains in the doldrums. Nitta (1997: 267) tried to see if employment practices in Japan had changed "in the economic fluctuations that have occurred since the collapse of the bubble economy". He studied employment adjustment, unemployment, labour participation, working hours and white-collar employment. Why did he select these categories? Because, Nitta wrote, "it is hard to reach a common understanding of what precisely Japanese employment practices and labour relations were in the past... Defining even "life-time employment" is a rather complicated business" (Ibid.).

Nitta found that working hours were reduced, but little else. He concluded that the current employment adjustments have yet to reach the level of those following the oil shocks of the early 1970s.

Almost half a century of social science has passed since Abegglen and Levine first reported on lifetime/long-term employment practices in Japan. This employment pattern stubbornly persists in comparative studies of employment tenure. Are the theories of Aoki and Koike more valid than the ill-defined, culturally bound notion of lifetime employment?

The significance of this question is quite obvious to Aoki and Koike. Both scholars flatly deny the existence of any such institution. Aoki (1988: 51) wrote, "The term lifetime employment is nothing but a somewhat exaggerated idealisation of the relatively long job tenure at the J-firm, which the result of the incentive system". Underlying or complementing this incentive scheme is Aoki's reciprocal "gift exchange" construct. In this, workers offer firm-specific commitment and loyalty in exchange for long-term employment opportunities provided by management. Significantly, this presumes, "that management is reasonably farsighted" (Aoki, 1988: 176). Koike (1988: 266) is more critical of lifetime employment explanations for the Japan case. Not content to dismiss lifetime employment as a "myth," he has written that references to lifetime employment are based on "flimsy" research.

Unfortunately, neither scholar examined the influence of employment law on Japanese management theory.

# JAPANESE MANAGEMENT THEORY DEFINED BY THE LIFETIME EMPLOYMENT SYSTEM

## Lifetime Employment is a Legally Regulated Institutional Practice

Judicial recognition and regulation of "lifetime employment" as an institutionalised practice in the Japanese industrial relations system was first reported by Tackney (1995). The first case law reference to lifetime employment in Japanese history occurred in a 1961 Yokohama regional court decision ruled on the legality of dismissals. The dismissals were contested by a group of employees initially hired with the condition that their retirement age would be some years earlier than that of most other workers in the firm. The court first denied a claim made by those dismissed; "The 15 applicants assert that…they established a contract…similar to the lifetime employment labour contract of the regular employees. However, there is no evidence to compel the credibility of this claim" (Hanrei jijo, 1961: 12). Despite this rejection, the court went on to find that the mandatory retirement age of those dismissed was not the same as that of those hired under the "lifetime employment system" of the firm. And, in consequence, the court invalidated the dismissals.

Since 1961, more than 100 local, regional, and Supreme Court cases have contained explicit references to "lifetime employment". Most cases date after the oil shock era of the 1970s, which Nitta, as noted above, felt to be the highwater mark of economic restructuring in Japan to date. While stare decisis (the compelling role of legal precedent) does not obtain in Japan, these cases provide sufficient evidence to conclude that Japanese courts, since the 1960s, have recognised and, more importantly, regulated lifetime employment as a "crystallised custom" or institutionalised practice of Japanese employment jurisprudence (Kettler and Tackney, 1997).

The regulatory role of case law reference to lifetime employment is summarised in a 1987 regional court decision.

> For this dismissal case, [dismissals] "according to the inevitable circumstances of firm operations" (Labour Standards Law, Article 19: 1) should be made by management and labour on the basis of overall concrete conditions. However, the lifetime employment system is a principle of labour-management relations in our country. The premise is that the worker will have a continuing employment relation until retirement age. While the so-called rationalisation dismissal is wholly necessitated by the need to sustain operations on the side of management, the actual outcome is a destruction of the worker's pattern of life. Accordingly, the following conditions must exist before one can say that "inevitable circumstances of the operations" actually obtain… (Rodo hanrei, 1987: 45)

In this decision, the court invalidated 35 of 38 dismissals in a machine tools firm. The court further specified four conditions minimally obligatory for employers to engage in legally valid dismissals. First: dire financial circumstances of the firm. Second: documentation of concrete steps taken to avoid dismissals. Third: objective and clear dismissal standards. Fourth: the necessity and details of the personnel rationalisation must be sincerely explained to the workers and an effort must be made through adequate deliberations to obtain worker consent (Rodo hanrei, 1987: 45). The court stated, "If the preceding conditions do not exist, it cannot be said that the occasion is "according to inevitable circumstances of the operations" and dismissals when these conditions do not exist must be said to be invalid" (Rodo hanrei, 1987: 45).

Amidst the economic difficulties and restructuring of Japan's post-bubble economy, a 1997 Supreme Court decision stated that lifetime employment was "a given premise of our nation's labour circumstances" (Lex/DB case, 1997). Thus, lifetime employment is indeed real: an institutionalised practice of post-war Japanese industrial relations. As such, it is a legally compelling social institution far beyond the bi-lateral "gift exchange" envisioned by Aoki's "J-firm" construct. It remains a strong social model, reinforced by case law, in other employment circumstances throughout the country. In case law, even repeatedly renewed part-time employees are presumed to have a continuing employment relationship.

The appearance of lifetime employment in case law is clearly odds with the US New Deal origins of Japanese labour legislation and a Civil Code that permits labour contracts to be terminated by either party, given proper notice. A brief review of case law legal principles will explicate the modes of social relation that characterise the Japanese enterprise.

## Modes of Social Relation that Define the Japanese Management in the Enterprise

Two legal principles significantly influence the modes of social relation within the post-war Japanese enterprise. There is, first, the interrelated themes of just cause/abusive dismissal in employment relations. Second, social relations within the Japanese firm are further influenced by institutionalised employee participation in managerial prerogatives. Taken together, in light of the institutionalised practice of lifetime employment, these modes of social relation within the Japanese firm provide an important corrective to current models of Japanese management theory.

### *Just Cause/Abusive Dismissal Judicial Norms*

Post-1945 Japanese labour legislation is modelled on US labour law within a civil law legal system. Labour legislation and the Civil Code permit parties to cancel a contract, given proper notice. Despite this, case law citations on lifetime employment clearly invoke a widely recognised norm restricting the prerogative of Japanese managers to dismiss employees (Gould, 1984).

This norm, which is that of "just cause," is an adaptive appropriation of German labour law dating from the Weimar Republic (1919–1933), and it is grounded in the recognition that labour is subordinate, in significant respects, to the employer. It appears in Japanese case law because the earliest post-1945 interpretations of the nature of the employment contract came from a judiciary trained before World War II in European, particularly German, jurisprudence (Yanagawa et al., 1950).

Employer abuse of dismissal prerogative is a related, uniquely Japanese legal doctrine established very early in the post-1945 era (Kettler and Tackney, 1997). Ironically, it appears to have first been developed in response to the dismissal of Japanese workers employed at occupation military bases.

Simply put, Japanese legislation recognises "at will" contract termination, given notice, by either party. Japan's courts, however, from very early in the post-war era – indeed, more than a decade prior to the Miike mine strife – developed doctrine recognising the potential for employers to abuse the right to terminate contracts. This abuse of the dismissal prerogative is inherently associated with "just cause", which relates to the recognition of reciprocal societal obligations in contract, when a firm contemplates the dismissal of workers.


## Employment Participation in Managerial Prerogative

The working rules of Japanese industrial relations permit far greater potential for employee participation in Japanese management prerogatives than that which is possible in the United States. In addition, there is a greater potential responsiveness at the enterprise level to changes in market and society than is possible through the more rigid German model.

Management councils (keiei sanka kino/keiei kyogikai) were widely established by Japanese labour unions as part of the post-war democratisation process (Hazigawa, 1986, 1987, 1991). The first Central Labour Relations Commission (CLRC) saw these councils as a means to overcome a crisis in capital presented by "production control" actions, in which employees took over production of an enterprise (Kettler and Tackney, 1997). In response to a formal government request, the CLRC issued a directive in July 1946 that recommended the localisation of employee participation functions within collective bargaining agreements. This set of guidelines remains the last legal word on the matter to the present.

This novel step was a careful adaptation of German works council and co-determination schemes. By avoiding legislative recourse, the CLRC pre-empted conservative influences that might have exerted pressure on any such proposed legislation in the Japanese Parliament (Diet). This approach also insured closer linkages between market changes and the life of the industrial enterprise than could have been achieved through legislative control. Finally, localisation of participation structures within collective bargaining agreements prevented the establishment of a "ceiling" or "limit" on the extent to which employees could exercise their voice in the management of the firm.

Management councils, under various guises, remain a defining feature of Japanese management from a comparative perspective MOL, 1995). More than 80% of unionised firms in Japan have established consultation processes and procedures. More than 70% of all Japanese firms having 5000 or more employees maintain formal consultation structures. Councils are found in 68% of firms with 1000–4999 employees and in 62% of firms with 300–999 employees (Abegglen, 1958). Consultation topics determined by collective bargaining range from basic management strategies, to employee welfare and company finance. As noted earlier, the courts have established case law norms that oblige consultation between management and workers particularly in the event of planned redundancy dismissals (seiri kaiko). This consultation process is often conducted through the management council.

The function and strength of these consultation mechanisms vary. At times, consultation may amount to little more than a one-sided management presentation. It more often involves the solicitation of informal feedback and the formal inclusion of workers' views in company policy. In a small percentage of Japanese firms, management consultation operates according to consensus.

**Table 16.2**  Regular (seiki) employee participation rate by gender[a]

| Year | Combined (%) | Male (%) | Female (%) |
|------|--------------|----------|------------|
| 1984 | 84.8 | 92.4 | 71.1 |
| 1985 | 83.8 | 92.8 | 68.1 |
| 1986 | 83.5 | 92.7 | 67.9 |
| 1987 | 82.6 | 92.4 | 66.0 |
| 1988 | 81.9 | 92.0 | 65.1 |
| 1989 | 81.0 | 91.4 | 64.1 |
| 1990 | 80.0 | 91.3 | 62.1 |
| 1991 | 80.3 | 91.6 | 62.9 |
| 1992 | 79.6 | 91.1 | 61.9 |
| 1993 | 79.3 | 90.7 | 61.7 |
| 1994 | 79.8 | 91.6 | 61.8 |
| 1995 | 79.2 | 91.2 | 61.0 |
| 1996 | 78.5 | 90.7 | 60.4 |
| 1997 | 76.9 | 89.6 | 58.4 |

[a] Sources: Nihon Rodo Kenkyu Kiko (1998: S85).

## Continuity and the Contours of Change in Japanese Management

Despite pressures, the stable aspects of the lifetime employment system remain very much in evidence. Table 16.2 lists the percentage of the overall labour force employed as "regular employees" (seiki koyosha). A regular employee is defined as one employed on an indefinite term contract. The data in this table exclude those who are "directors" (yakuin) of firms.

The most recent data available from a February 1999 Labour Force Survey indicates some decline in the overall number of regular employees (fewer regular employees, August 1, 1999). This degree of decline is hardly suprising in light of the long-term economic difficulties confronting Japanese management. The relatively minor changes in overall labour force composition are, however, noteworthy. Regular male employees still constitute 88.9% of all working males. Regular female employees, in turn, constitute 54.8% of all working women. Japanese management, in Japan, remains firmly embedded within the modes of social relation described above: employee protection from abusive dismissal and participation in managerial prerogative.

The stability of workforce composition in Japan is then best understood from a comparative perspective. To this end, Abraham and Housemen (1989: 517) studied long-term employment elasticities by sex in the Japanese and US workforces. While they found employment elasticities higher for female Japanese workers than for their male counterparts, the elasticitiy of Japanese women was still "significantly less than those for either American men or American women". Stability in employment has long been, and continues to be, a key factor in Japanese management theory.

We can briefly review some recent developments that may impact the future of Japanese management practice.

# REVISION OF THE 1947 LABOUR STANDARDS ACT

The most notable legislative development in the late 1990s was the formal revision of the Labour Standards Act. This was passed by the Japanese Parliament (Diet) in 1998 and took effect in 1999[1]. This revision was the outcome of years of consultation and was subject to sustained opposition on the part of organised labour. The push for revision appears to have been motivated by a general rush toward "deregulation" in Japan, with changes occurring in several areas of employment regulation. Three-year term contracts have become possible for certain professional positions. Yet, the predominant regular employee status – indefinite contracts – remains normative.

This legislative revision explicitly impacts one mode of social relation proposed in this chapter as central to Japanese management theory. An amendment to Article 22 of the Act now obliges the employer to deliver without delay a certificate stating the reason for any worker being dismissed. Yamakawa (1998: 9) wrote, "if a reason for discharge is clarified, it will be easy for the courts to determine whether the discharge is based on a just cause".

As we have seen, case law norms defining the minimum conditions for possibly acceptable "just cause" dismissals are, in fact, very narrow. The new obligation now compels employers to specify the grounds for exercising their dismissal prerogative. Ironically, this appears to leave the employer open to more rapid accusations of abusive dismissal. In fact, the failure to provide a cause for the dismissal itself may be a potentially illegal action. This may lead the courts to invalidate dismissals by provisional dispositions[2]. Thus, the outcome of the amended legislation appears to invite further juridification, not deregulation, of employment law. And this, in turn, will create greater pressure upon management to avoid dismissals.

# EQUAL EMPLOYMENT OPPORTUNITY LAW

Evidence of women being treated differently in Japanese workplaces was previously noted in the comparative decline of women workers as a percentage of regular employees. This trend must be viewed against the countervailing increase in the labour participation rate by Japanese women. While comparatively more women are entering the workforce, they are likely to be employed on a casual, contract or part-time basis.

The Equal Employment Opportunity Law (Danjo koyo kikai kintoho) (1985) was intended to insure that workers are assessed on the basis of their ability, not their sex. The practical significance of this law remains in dispute (Sugeno, 1992; Sano, 1995). The law prohibits discriminatory treatment of women only in areas pertaining to training, health/welfare, retirement, resignation, and dismissal procedures. The following areas were considered obligatory for equal treatment: recruitment, employment, employment arrangements (location), and promotion. In the instance, "obligatory" meant that violations were not expressly prohibited by law. Chuma (1999: 146)

---

[1] See any of the three information annuals for a Japanese summary of this revision. See Yamakawa (1998) for a good English summary.

[2] For an explanation of the origins of provisional dispositions, see Kettler and Tackney (1997).

explained that a major reason for this distinction was "a lack of national consensus about changes induced or compelled by law in the personnel management methods of individual firms".

In 1997, recruitment and hiring were shifted from "obligatory" to "prohibited" by a Diet proposal. After passage of this revision, employer violations in these areas became expressly prohibited. Firms failing to provide evidence that they intended to improve illegal procedures faced public disclosure.

The effect of this revision, as with the initial legislation, will remain in dispute. The significance for Japanese management theory, however, is beyond refute; absent compelling legal obligation, Japanese managers display no greater effort to modify entrenched, even illegal, behaviour than their counterparts in other national settings. As Yoko Sano (1995: 63) wrote, "One reason why the employment opportunity law has not been extensively practised is, according to some opinion, because there are no penalties for violations".

## NEW LABOUR UNION ORGANISATIONAL FORMS

By 1993, the increased vulnerability of middle level management in Japan to "at will" dismissals led to the formation of a new union structure: the Tokyo Managers Union, and regional affiliates. Union members come from a wide range of firms and employment circumstances, often also having membership in an enterprise union in the firm from which they were dismissed. The union was formally recognised as a valid union structure by a Central Labour Relations Commission decision. The president of this independent union has published a variety of texts, among them, *I'll teach you "how to fight" with your company* (*Kaisha to no tatakaikata oshiemasu*) (Shitara, 1998). Originally founded with 14 members, Tokyo branch membership exceeded 700 by 1998. New branches have been formed in Osaka and Nagoya. In addition, a non-managerial class union affiliate, the Network Union, began in 1998. Focused on younger workers, membership in this affiliate is largely female. These union members struggle against redundancy dismissals through the courts, Japan's Labour Relations Commissions, and various media intensive routes.

## CONCLUSIONS

This chapter sought to answer several enduring questions regarding the nature and significance of Japanese management theory by focusing on the modes of social relations in the post-war Japanese enterprise. Japanese management is a culturally embedded management form featuring two modes of social relations: employment security through "just cause" and abusive dismissal principles and employee participation in managerial prerogative as specified in collective bargaining agreements.

Japanese management, which arose in relation to the institutionalised practice of lifetime employment, can be traced to adaptive legal appropriations from European, particularly Weimar era Germany, and US legal sources. The elements of job security and management participation go far beyond anything in evidence in the United States since the New Deal. These same characteristics offer flexibility in social form and adaptability to market changes not possible in the legislatively constrained German case.

An important lesson from explicating the modes of social relation in Japanese management concerns the remarkable potential for variation in form over the post-war decades. Employee participation in management is defined in firm-specific collective bargaining agreements: "Japanese management" is hardly monolithic. As David Kettler and I wrote in 1997, "Diversified by the distinctive histories of various firms, Japanese management practices are nevertheless everywhere shadowed by the institutional memory of the struggles that created them" (Kettler and Tackney, 1997).

The particular historical emergence of "Japanese management" in the post-war era is unique. The positive dimension of these developments need not remain a domestic possession. Japanese management, including the various modes of production that accompany it, can be successfully replicated elsewhere. Due care need be given to the functional appropriation of modes of social relation to the new national setting.

In principle, this replication could conceivably proceed on a firm-specific basis, presuming, as Masahiko Aoki does, a reasonably farsighted management team capable of commitment to employee job security and management participation. At the level of national practice, however, the evidence of post-war Japanese management itself argues strongly against the achievement of a critical mass of participatory firms absent judicial encouragement. The case law history of Japan makes quite clear that Japanese management practice emerged against the "better judgement" of substantial numbers of Japanese employers.

This exploration of the modes of social relation in post-war Japanese management practice offers a potent strategic tool for those involved in economic development in industrialising nations. It specifies the delicate balance achieved in post-war Japan in elicitation of remarkable levels of worker commitment with appropriate, timely participation and reward. This exploration also provides analytical categories for worker representatives in nations where management participation and employment security remain an unfulfilled dimension of working rules in a national industrial relations system.

# REFERENCES

Abegglen, J.C. (1958a) The Japanese Factory: Aspects of its Social Organization. Glencoe: Free Press.

Abegglen, J.C. (1958b) Nihon no keiei (Management in Japan). Tokyo: Diamond.

Abraham, K.G. and Houseman, S.N. (1989) Job security and work force adjustment: how different are U.S. and Japanese practices? Journal of the Japanese and International Economies, 3: 500–521.

Aoki, M. (1986) Horizontal vs. vertical information structure of the firm. The American Economic Review, 76: 971–983.

Aoki, M. (1987) The Japanese firm in transition. In K. Yamamura and Y. Yasuba (Eds), The Political Economy of Japan: Volume 1, The Domestic Transformation. Stanford, CT: Stanford University Press, 263–288.

Aoki, M. (1988) Information, Incentives and Bargaining in the Japanese Economy. Cambridge: Cambridge University Press.

Chuma, H. (1999) Rodo keizai (Labor Economics). Imidas. Tokyo: Suesha. pp. 139–148.

Cole, R.E. (1971a) Japanese Blue Collar. New Haven, CT: Yale University Press.

Cole, R.E. (1971b) Labor in Japan. In B.M. Richardson and T. Ueda (Eds), Business and Society in Japan, 29–62.

Cole, R.E. (1971c) The theory of institutionalization: permanent employment and tradition in Japan. Economic Development and Cultural Change, 20: 47–70.

Cole, R.E. (1972) Permanent employment in Japan: facts and fantasies. Industrial and Labor Relations Review, 26: 615–630.

Cole, R.E. (1979) Work, Mobility, and Participation. Berkeley, CA: University of California Press.

Dore, R. (1973) British Factory–Japanese Factory: The Origins of National Diversity in Industrial Relations. London: George Allen and Unwin.

Dore, R. (1986) Flexible Rigidities: Industrial Policy and Structural Adjustment in the Japanese Economy, 1970-80. Stanford, CT: Stanford University Press.

Dore, R., Bounine-Cabal, J. and Tapiola, K. (1989) Japan at Work: Markets, Management and Flexibility. Paris: Organization for Economic Co-operation and Development.

Dunlop, J.T. (1952) Industrial Relations Systems. New York: Henry Holt.

Dunlop, J.T. (1993) Industrial Relations Systems (revised edition). Boston: Harvard Business School Press.

Economic Planning Agency (1994) Economic Survey of Japan: 1993–1994 (English translation 1995). Tokyo: Printing Bureau, Ministry of Finance.

Elger, T., Smith, C. (1994) Global Japanization? The Transnational Transformation of the Labour Process. London: Routledge.

Gordon, A. (1985) The Evolution of Labor Relations in Japan. Heavy Industry, 1853–1955. Cambridge, MA: Harvard University.

Gordon, A. (1998) The Wages of Affluence: Labor and Management in Postwar Japan. Cambridge, MA: Harvard University Press.

Gould, W.B. (1984) Japan's Reshaping of American Labour Law. Cambridge, MA: MIT Press.

Graham, L. (1995) On the Line at Subaru-Isuzu: the Japanese Model and the American worker. Ithaca, NY: Cornell University Press.

Hagizawa, K. (1986) Procedures and structures of collective bargaining at the enterprise and plant levels in Japan. Comparative Labor Law, 7: 3: 277–308.

Hagizawa, K. (1987) Dantai kosho (Collective Bargaining). Tokyo: Nihon rodo kyokai.

Hagizawa, K. (1991) Dantai kosho (Collective Bargaining). Tokyo: Nihon rodo kenkyu kiko.

Hanrei jijo (Legal precedent times) (1961) 270: 11–26.

Kaplinsky, R. and Posthuma, A. (1994) Easternisation: the spread of Japanese management techniques to developing nations. Essex: Frank Cass.

Kettler, D. and Tackney, C. (1997) Light from a dead sun: the Japanese lifetime employment system and Weimar labour Law. Comparative Labour Law and Policy Journal, 19(1): 101–141.

Koike, K. (1983) Internal labor markets: workers in large firms. In T. Shirai, (Ed), Contemporary Industrial Relations in Japan. Madison, WI: University of Wisconsin Press, 29–62.

Koike, K. (1987) Human resource development. In K. Yamamura and Y. Yasuba (Eds), The Political Economy of Japan. Volume 1: The Domestic Transformation. Stanford: Stanford University Press, 289–330.

Koike, K. (1988) Understanding Industrial Relations in Modern Japan. London: Macmillan.

Koike, K. and Inoki, T. (1990) Skill Formation in Japan and Southeast Asia Tokyo: University of Tokyo Press.

Koike, K. (1991) Shigoto no keizaigaku (The Economics of Work). Tokyo: Toyo Keizai.

Koike, K. (1995) The Economics of Work in Japan. English Translation of Koike (1991). Tokyo: LTCB International Library Foundation.

Levine, S.B. (1958) Industrial Relations in Postwar Japan. Urbana, IL: University of Illinois Press.

Lex/DB case (1997) 28021615 (proprietary data base listing).

Milkman, R. (1991) Japan's California Factories: Labor Relations and Economic Globalization. Los Angeles, CA: Institute of Industrial Relations, University of California.

MOL (Ministry of Labour) (1995) Japan's Current Labour Management Communications (Nihon no Roshi Komunikeshion no Genjo). Ministry of Labour Policy Secretariat Survey Section. Tokyo: Ministry of Finance.

Nihon Rodo Kenkyu Kiko (Japan Institute of Labour) (1998). Rodo Hakusho (Labour White Paper). Tokyo: Nihon Rodo Kenkyu Kiko (Japan Institute of Labour).

Nitta, M. (1997) Employment relations after the collapse of the bubble economy. In B. Junji (Ed), The Political Economy of Japanese Society, Vol. 2: Internationalization and Domestic Issues. Oxford: Oxford University Press.

Rodo H. (1987) Ikegai Iron Works Case (Ikegai tekko jiken). Labour Law Precedent, 1–15; 506: 44–80.

Sano, Y. (1995) Human Resource Management in Japan Tokyo: Keio University Press.

Shimada, H. (1983) Japanese industrial relations – a new general model? A survey of English-language literature. In T. Shirai (Ed), Contemporary industrial relations in Japan. Madison, WI: University of Wisconsin Press. pp. 3–28.

Shimada, H. (1989) Japan's industrial culture and labor-management relations. In Japan Institute of Labor, Searching for a New System in Industrial Relations: Proceedings of the 30th Anniversary International Symposium. Tokyo: Japan Institute of Labor.

Shimada, H. (1992a). Japan's industrial culture and labor-management relations. In S. Kumon and H. Rosovsky (Eds), The Political Economy of Japan: Volume 3, Cultural and Social Dynamics. Stanford, CT: Stanford University Press, 267–291.

Shimada, H. (1992b) Structural change and industrial relations: Japan. In A. Gladstone, H. Wheeler, J. Rojot, F. Eyraud and R. Ben-Israel (Eds), Labour Relations in a Changing Environment. Berlin: Walter de Gruyter. pp. 233–241.

Shitara, K. (1998) Kaisha to no Tatakaikata Oshiemasu (I'll Teach you "How to Fight" your Company). Tokyo: Gendai Shorin.

Sugeno, K. (1992) Japanese Labour Law. Tokyo: University of Tokyo Press.

Tackney, C.T. (1995) Institutionalization of the Lifetime Employment System. Ph.D. dissertation. Ann Arbor: UMI. 9608158. Madison, WI: Industrial Relations Research Institute, University of Wisconsin.

Taira, K. (1970) Economic Development and the Labor Market in Japan. New York: Columbia University Press.

Taira, K. and Levine, S.B. (1985) Japan's industrial relations: a social compact emerges. In H. Juris, M. Thompson and W. Davis (Eds), Industrial Relations in a Decade of Economic Change. Madison, WI: Industrial Relations Research Association. pp. 247–300.

Fewer regular employees, longer periods of unemployment (August 1, 1999). Working conditions and the labor market. Vol. 38, No. 8. http://www.jil.go.jp.

Womack, J.P., Jones, D.T. and Roos, D. (1990) The Machine that Changed the World: the Story of Lean Production. New York: Harper.

Yamakawa, R. (1998) Special Topic: Overhaul after 50 years: The Amendment of the Labour Standards Law. Japan Labour Bulletin, 1 November, 5–12.

Yanagawa, M., Furuyama, H., Ogata, S., Takashima, R. and Saito, H. (1950) Hanrei rodo ho no kenkyu (Research in Labour Law Legal Precedent). Tokyo: Romu Gyosei Kenkyujo (Labour administration research institute).

# Chapter 17

# Stereotyping in International Business

**Anna Zarkada-Fraser**
*School of International Business, Griffith University, Brisbane,*
*Australia*

*Hang on to your prejudices, they are the only taste you have got*
Anatole Broyard, quoted in Shweder (1995: 75).

## INTRODUCTION

This chapter acknowledges and explores the nature and existence of stereotypes and stereotyping. It considers the effect of stereotyping within the context of international business and profit generation and contemplates in-depth issues associated with trade, direct foreign investment, internationalization and country of origin effects, as well as the commercial exploitation of stereotypes in wider contexts.

At the core of each individual human being and community is the need for identity. Literally meaning "same-ness", identity is a rarely defined and largely problematic construct (Bottomley, 1997). Within the given historical and socio-political context of our space and time we have some ability to construct, choose or challenge our personal and collective identities. To do that, however, we invariably require a reference point. In order to understand what constitutes "same" we need to identify that which is different; we need an "other" delineated in such a way as to limit the dissonance within the construct of what is "same" (Schaller and Gideon, 1999). The raising of boundaries and the definition of "other-ness" requires the processing of information that is not always readily available and even when it is available it appears to be too vast to process. Faced with a complex task, the human or the group mind – a distinction that has for long puzzled social psychologists but can be resolved by accepting that all beliefs, including social ones, exist in the minds of individuals (Stangor and Schaller, 1996) – resorts to an efficient solution. It employs selective processing of the most context-appropriate, salient points to create a "shorthand characterization of whole groups" (Klineberg, 1964: 33). If this process of abstracting and summarizing information was not employed, then we would end up with the map that the cartographers of the Empire drew in the classic Jorge Luis Borges tale: so detailed that it ended up exactly covering the whole territory. We abstract reality into maps, "pictures in our heads" (Lippman, 1922; Klineberg, 1964: 33) that serve as a set of cognitive tools for positioning ourselves, predicting or understanding the behaviour of "others" and guiding the way we relate to them. These pictures are stereotypes.

## A Traditional View of Stereotypes

Stereotypes maintain and propagate crystallized, shared views about the "characteristic qualities of ethnic, religious, gender, sexual orientation, age, political, interest, activity and occupational groups (…) and many others" (Mackie et al., 1996: 41). Simply put, stereotypes are the beliefs we hold about the personal attributes of people that belong to a group of which we are not a member (Klineberg, 1964; Ashmore and Del Boca, 1981; Biernat, 1995). The underlying assumption of almost all research into stereotypes (Oakes et al., 1994) is that they "constitute a very partial and inadequate way of representing the world" (Lippman, 1922: 72) through undiscriminatingly assimilating "varying types of experience into the same pattern of fallacious similarity" (Katz and Schanck, 1938: 89). Under the light of a typically modern epistemology, stereotypes have been described as inherently deficient (Lippman, 1922), "absurd and contradictory" (Katz and Schanck, 1938: 89) categorical knowledge structures that are simply wrong (Funder, 1995) because they lack the "sharpness of inclusion and exclusion of scientific concepts" (Katz and Schanck, 1938: 89). They are presented as if they were inductive generalizations of credible observations when really they are based on hearsay, anecdotes and unverifiable claims that "people say" or "it is generally believed" (Klineberg, 1964). As products of unsubstantiated beliefs, the attributes they convey are inferred rather than observed as well as context dependent (Taylor, 1981).

As a cognitive process, stereotyping has been described as quasi-pathological (Mace, 1943) and the product of authoritarian personalities with low tolerance for ambiguity, mental rigidity and narrow mindedness (Adorno et al., 1950). It is not surprising then, that as the result of such mental processes stereotypes have been described as "weapons (…) sharpened and strengthened by powerful emotions" (Klineberg, 1964: 151). The stereotyping process shapes our view of "others" in such a rigid way (Lippman, 1922) that it interferes with our ability to objectively approach our relations with them (Klineberg, 1964). Subsequently, the resulting mental images, and the emotions that they elicit, have a high level of susceptibility to manipulation for political gain (Klineberg, 1964). The sparks of collectively held negative stereotypes can be fanned into the flames of prejudice (Oakes et al., 1994) and thus provide justifications for "oppressive policy making" (Anderson, 1993: 76) or even violence in the quest for "ethno-national purity" (Bottomley, 1997: 43). As Gunew (1993: 47) succinctly put it, when people "come to the crossing of boundaries" they, "in the twinkling of an eye", fix the "other" "as though with full knowledge, into the stereotype".

## Current Views on Stereotypes

Since the 1940s, however, a number of studies have demonstrated that there can be a "kernel of truth" in stereotypes (Oakes et al., 1994). The traditional assumptions of inherent rigidity, irrationality and "badness" have been challenged by three important observations. First, that stereotypes are sensitive to international relations (Buchanan, 1951; Klineberg, 1964), so they are not rigid but dynamic and responsive to external events. Then, that they reflect intergroup relations (Sherrif, 1967) so they are not irrational but explicable when the context in which they emerged becomes known. And finally, that individual behaviour is determined by group membership (Asch, 1952) that could reflect stereotypes that the stereotyped group itself accepts, so they cannot be all, and always, bad. Although still unable to address individual differences, stereotypes can encapsulate important features of a group (Oakes et al., 1994) and can be understood as instances of the normal social cognition processes of categorizing (Allport, 1954; Tajfel, 1969).

Stereotypes are related to social reality in a powerful and dynamic way and do not exist in a social vacuum. They are common to all individuals (Tajfel, 1969), widely held (Klineberg, 1964; Oakes et al., 1994) and shared by group members through their socially mediated experience. The achieved consensus is simply a function of the ability of group membership to condition members to expect and actively seek to co-ordinate their perceptions and behaviour with the other group members (Haslam et al., 1999). Communication is at the heart of a variety of stereotyping phenomena. Previous research has demonstrated how shared stereotypes function as an efficient means of communicating about groups and how these very communications may perpetuate and reinforce existing stereotypes (for a review of the literature see Schaller and Gideon, 1999). As people are likely to present themselves to others in ways that they believe will gain them respect and acceptance they might, consciously or unconsciously, adopt an impression management strategy that perpetuates old imagery or influences the process of new stereotype formation. The contents of emerging stereotypes have been shown to be related to the specific contents of the interpersonal communications that produced them as well as to reflect the motives of individuals (Schaller and Gideon, 1999).

Moreover, recent research has demonstrated that stereotypes need not be seen as simply information reduction mechanisms. If that was the case, then it would be impossible to substantiate how such a "crude type of assessment" (Cooper and Kirk-caldy, 1995: 5) could become so pertinent in guiding human behaviour. Instead, stereotypes can be better understood as elaborations that help us make sense of not only the content, but also the structure of actions and interactions with other people (Oakes et al., 1994). They provide coherence and some semblance of predictability in complex situations (Taylor, 1981) and can facilitate efficient decision-making (Maheswaran, 1994). Efficiency, however, does not necessarily equal optimality in the decision making process. Neither does it guarantee the best possible outcome for all parties affected by the decision. It is from this potential discrepancy that problems can arise.

# EFFECTS OF STEREOTYPING ON INTERNATIONAL BUSINESS

Of all the possible stereotypes, the ones with most direct relevance to the conduct of business in an international environment are those concerned with differentiating between ethnic groups, commonly referred to as national stereotypes. Klineberg (1964) conveyed the effects of stereotypes on international relations in a few short and powerful statements. They "create barriers to international understanding" (p. 33), "lessen the likelihood of international cooperation" (p. 33) and result in such an emotional climate that, superseding logic, "constitutes a major barrier to the meeting of minds" (p. 152).

## Functions of Stereotypes in the Context of International Business

Stereotypes invariably involve some evaluation of the groups concerned. We usually ascribe positive epithets to our own group and negative ones to others. This process allows us to articulate our fears in a way that does not affect our self-image. We justify our emotions by quoting a negative stereotype so we can rationalize mistrust, hostility, even discrimination towards other groups. Moreover, we can easily discredit individuals or ideas that are unfamiliar to us without having to provide convincing arguments (Oakes et al., 1994; Vickerman, 1999). The particular images of the world embodied in stereotypes, being hypotheses that seek confirmation (Lippman, 1922), cause the individuals that hold them to seek evidence that sustains these images and reject facts that could change them. The self-reinforcing and emotional nature of stereotypes makes them difficult to dislodge (Vickerman, 1999), thus creating a vicious circle.

The labels that we use for groups including our own – what Chase (1938) called the "tyranny of words" – automatically create expectations of attributes and behaviour. We expect other people to be and behave in a way that confirms the stereotypes we hold for their group, so when they appear inconsistent with the stereotype we simply categorize them as the exceptions, rather than re-examine the stereotype. Similarly, we often adjust our own behaviour to fit expectations that others impose on us on the basis of our group membership. In both cases, the stereotypes reinforce our identity through difference (Schaller and Gideon, 1999). Finally, each stereotype provides a particular frame of reference. By utilizing a different frame of reference for the same behaviour we evaluate what is essentially the same as different – just like in the old saying: "I am firm, you are stubborn, he's pig-headed"! (Klineberg, 1964).

It can be naturally deduced from the preceding argument that national stereotyping affects people's willingness and ability to engage in business with individuals from other countries. What all Greeks have known since time immemorial "ὁμοιος ομοίω αεί πελάζει" – like always seeks like – social and educational psychology have systematically demonstrated: social and psychological dissimilarities can have a limiting effect on people's ability to communicate with one another (Triandis, 1960; Padget and Wolosin, 1980).

A function of the construct of identity is that a sense of one's place in relation to other people or groups is dependent on mutual identification of common objectives and based on shared understandings (Bottomley, 1997). Multiple shared understandings increase the probability of successful identification and reduce the need for explanations of what is essential information about the self, thus increasing the scope for efficient and mutually satisfying communication. The conduct of business is dependent on the creation of shared understandings, communication and the achievement of common objectives.

Three levels of analysis can be employed for demonstrating the specific areas of business activity that are particularly susceptible to negative interference from stereotypes: macro, firm and individual level. On a macro level, stereotypical schemas about other countries, as a whole, can influence trade and internationalization decisions. On a firm level, stereotypes can affect the relationship of multinationals with host countries and their people, relationships between national firms within multinationals and the fate of specific products in foreign markets. Finally, on an individual level they can have a profound impact on sales or other types of negotiations and on the future of expatriate managers and their staff. Some of the major empirical research findings on particular areas of international business activity are presented in the following sections.

## Trade, Foreign Direct Investment and Internationalization

Traditional international trade theories focus primarily on cost factors (Porter, 1990). This observation was confirmed in a recently published, most comprehensive review and critique of influential theories of international trade, foreign direct investment and firm internationalization (Morgan and Katsikeas, 1997). The role that national stereotypes play in the development of international trade and investment patterns around the world is largely unexplored territory. It has been suggested that a more realistic conceptualization of these patterns could be achieved by positioning cost factors on the supply side and the stereotypical country of origin effect on the demand side of a model (Lampert and Jaffe, 1997).

The incorporation of national stereotypes into international trade and investment theory can have interesting policy implications. Countries that wish to attract foreign investment, especially in the form of manufacturing facilities, or to develop new technology industries and increase their exporting potential could invest in public relations campaigns focused on countering the effect of negative stereotypes and creating a positive, investment-friendly image (Lampert and Jaffe, 1997). Correspondingly, if the policy objective is to increase consumption of domestically produced goods then the image of the home country should be upgraded and promoted to domestic consumers. This approach has been adopted by a number of governments in many countries, either in support of or as a surrogate to protectionist trade policies.

Despite the many controversies surrounding the predictor variables of international involvement decisions of the firm and their impact, there appears to be a general consensus on the systematic and sequential nature of the process. The focus is on the cognitive aspects of decision making and so the critical affective factors are largely ignored.

Managers are generally portrayed as having an allegiance to some particular form of capital for which they seek profitable outlets (Porter, 1986) by selecting an ethno-centric, polycentric or geocentric strategy on the basis of rationally constructed fore-casts. Recent qualitative research, however, has successfully challenged this approach by demonstrating that in making and articulating strategic choices, managers seek primarily to establish their own positions within organizational structures and are, thus, primarily "concerned with their own identity" (Cooper et al., 1998: 541).

In the classical theoretical framework, perceptions about the target country are treated as a cohort of factual information on political, economic and socio-demographic factors that is systematically collected and rationally assessed to establish a country's level of political risk (e.g. Young, Hamill, Wheeler and Davies, 1989; Czinkota and Ronkainen, 1995; Douglas and Craig, 1995: 73). A departure from this emotionally sterile conceptualization of managerial decision-making can be found in behavioural models that focus on the human dimension of relationships in international business.

A construct that is generally acknowledged as a contributing factor to internationa-lization decisions, especially as a determinant of market selection, is that of psychic distance (e.g. Dichtl et al., 1984; Johanson and Vahlne, 1990). It is related to nationality and experience in a complex and dynamic structure (Crick and Chaudhry, 1995; Shoham and Albaum, 1995).

Psychic distance has been described as the measure of international outlook as well as the sum of factors preventing the flow of information to and from the market (Stöttinger and Schlegelmilch, 1998). Within this construct, there is scope to incorpo-rate national stereotyping that has been found to be related to the degree of acceptance of "other-ness" and a person's degree of open-mindedness (Adorno et al., 1950) as well as act as information filters (Allport, 1954; Lee et al., 1995). Psychic distance expresses a degree of affinity or a perceived dissimilarity – something like the absolute difference between the beliefs about the "self" and the stereotypes that describe the "other".

At a more fundamental, personal level, the question is to what degree are stereotypes affecting the willingness to become involved in a business relationship with partners from other countries. "Relying on cultural stereotypes to predict the behaviour of foreign business partners is not a risk worth taking. But it's a gamble that business people undertake every day" (Fung, 1999: 10) It appears that preconceived ideas about the socio-economic traits of other countries can significantly affect business sellers' interest in firms from certain countries (Abdul-Malek, 1975). The results of empirical investigations of the dynamics of psychic distance are largely inconclusive (Stöttinger and Schlegelmilch, 1998). However, it is generally accepted that psychic distance contributes significantly to the development of the atmosphere surrounding relation-ships in international markets (Leonidou and Kaleka, 1998). It could be argued that stereotypes can create a negative atmosphere that precedes the relationship and poten-tially preclude it from ever developing.

## Co-ordination of Multinational Corporations' Activities

It has been noted that decisions about cross-border joint ventures, mergers or acquisi-tions are, at least partly, based on the cultural stereotypes decision-makers hold about the competence and character of managers in the target country (Cooper and Kirkcaldy, 1995). The psychic distance literature has, mostly indirectly, examined the problem in the context of a buyer in one country and a seller in another. Very little systematic research, however, has been carried out on the effect of the stereotypes that managers in multinational corporations hold about their counterparts in the same organization that are based in other countries. Moreover, little is known about the ways in which these stereotypes influence the strategy formulation process and the functional co-ordination among subsidiaries. One notable in-depth study that was recently published addresses these issues in great detail (Cooper et al., 1998) and demonstrates how the "seamless coordination" of a major consultancy firm was wishful thinking rather than widely espoused and successfully implemented strategy. Interestingly, the main findings of this study clearly concur with insights into stereotypes provided by sociology and psychology.

Stereotypes are employed in order to make sense of the manager's own world and position in it in two different ways: (a) to explain and illustrate how the "self" – as part of an "imagined community" (Anderson, 1991) tied to a place, family, language and history – is clearly different from the "other" and (b) in order to determine organiza-tional identity through country affiliation. The differentiation between in and out groups can provide a justification for the application of different frames of reference in eval-uating intra-firm dynamics and the automatic discrediting of alien ideas – the "not invented here" syndrome. The status and real or imagined historical role the managers' own country played in the creation of the international firm is related to intra-firm seniority of managers at the same nominal organizational rank (Cooper et al., 1998).

In articulating their strategic positions, managers are more likely to use terms that reflect their perceived national identity and what they see as typical characteristics of their race. The strategic choices of the other participants to the decision making process are also explained by pointing out deficiencies of their character which are not observed in the individuals but simply known through "national stereotypes, histories and char-acteristics" (Cooper et al., 1998: 541). Overall, evaluative terms, drawn from national stereotypes, are used more often than the language of capital to make points that "could have been made without reference to nationality" (Cooper et al., 1998: 543).

This tendency becomes more pronounced when conflict is described. In order to justify their position as superior to those of their counterparts in other countries, managers reiterate negative stereotypes instead of pointing out the merits of their own arguments. Regardless of where they come from or which of their counterparts they describe, they explain the conflict as a result of a simple fact: "we" are inter-nationally orientated, rational, proactive, and part of the collectivity but "they" are insular, isolated and reactive (Cooper et al., 1998).

Finally, Cooper et al. (1998) observe that problems caused by stereotypes are not confined to the relationship between subsidiaries but appear to form part of the global brain at the centre of the organization. Moreover, the realization that nationalism stands in the way of achieving really seamless co-ordination of the global firm does not stop managers from repeating the same mistakes in new locations and situations.

## Country of Origin Effects in Marketing Across National Borders

Country-of-origin (COO) or product country image (PCI) effects have attracted a lot of attention in the marketing literature. In the period 1965 to 1997 approximately 100 COO studies were carried out in 34 named, and 30 unnamed countries (reviewed in Al-Sulaiti and Baker, 1998). The attitudes of consumers towards a vast range of consumer and industrial products (from juice to fashion, playing cards to life insurance and heavy machinery to "simple goblet") manufactured in over 60 countries and regions were investigated using a multitude of methodologies. The most significant observations about the effect of national stereotypes on intended purchasing behaviour and perceptions are here summarized.

Stereotypes do exist and influence the product evaluation process (Reirson, 1966; Bannister and Saunders, 1978; White and Cundiff, 1978; Chassin and Jaffe, 1979; White, 1979; Hong and Wyer, 1989; Johanson et al., 1994; Lin and Sternquist, 1994; Diamantopoulos et al., 1995; Tse et al., 1996; Zhang, 1996). This applies to both consumers and industrial buyers (Papadopoulos and Heslop, 1993).

Attitudes towards the people of a nation are related to preconceived ideas about the country's products (Schooler, 1965) so a bias against the country of origin extends over to its products (Schooler and Wildt, 1968) and differentiates them from the ones produced in the subjects' country (Lillis and Narayana, 1974). Stereotypes about products are related to the economic, political and cultural characteristics of the country of origin (Crawford and Lamb, 1981; Han, 1990; Ahmed et al., 1994; Okechuku, 1994) and the perceived geographic or psychic distance (Bilkey and Nes, 1982; Samiee, 1994).

The way in which national stereotypes affect specific products, however, differs according to the product (Niffenegger et al., 1980; Hugstad and Durr, 1986). Moreover, stereotypes are strongly influenced by availability of the product in question (Nagashima, 1970) and familiarity (Nagashima, 1970; Khanna, 1986; Okechuku, 1994). When important information about the product is ambiguous or missing, or when the buyers have limited knowledge and ability to process complex technical data, then the stereotype is used as a surrogate variable to evaluate the product (Kaynak and Cavusgil, 1983; Johansson et al., 1985; Maheswaran, 1994). Branded products appear to be relatively immune from COO effects (Gaedeke, 1973).

The COO effect is related to socio-demographic (Greer, 1971; Anderson and Cunningham, 1972; Dornoff et al., 1974; Bailey and Pineres, 1997) and psychological characteristics (Anderson and Cunningham, 1972) of the respondents. Knowledge of a country of origin affects the perceptions of consumers (Darling and Kraft, 1977). Similarly, experienced exporters are more likely to hold favorable views of imported products than non-exporters (Abdul-Malek, 1975). A "halo construct" appears to be in operation in the sense that as familiarity with a country's products increases the stereotype becomes a "summary construct" that embodies beliefs about product attributes and affects consumers' attitudes to brands (Han, 1989). Finally, stereotypes, as well as the preference for domestic over imported goods (and vice versa) vary over time (Nagashima, 1977; Chao and Rajendran, 1993).

Summary reviews of the main issues examined in the literature have a tendency to mask the fact that the findings of the studies contradict as often as they confirm each other. One of the most important questions that still remain largely unresolved is the possibility of "blanket" stereotyping across all products and by extension people, the culture and the country as a whole. Some studies indicate that this is the case (Han and Terpstra, 1988; Leonidou et al, 1998) whilst others demonstrate that individuals hold a variety of stereotypes for the same country and they apply them selectively, in accordance with a set of other cues, including product category (Niffenegger et al., 1980; Hugstad and Durr, 1986; Hooley et al., 1988).

It is commonly assumed that the stereotype simply fills in missing information (Hong and Wyer, 1989; Leonidou et al., 1998) but little is known about the specific mechanisms for processing this piece of information. If country of origin is taken as a heuristic for product evaluation, then, in a manner similar to any other social stereotype (Bodenhausen and Lichtenstein, 1987), it would be expected to override all other information and to substitute all cues. This has not been sufficiently demonstrated in marketing studies. What has been shown, however, is that as a schema, the stereotype not only affects judgements about the product but information retention (Kochunny et al., 1993; Maheswaran, 1994), the interpretation of facts, the elaboration of attributes, the thought generation process and content as well as subsequent evaluations (Maheswaran, 1994).

Overall, the effects of the country-of-origin stereotypes appear to be similar to those observed in any other area of human behaviour. They are summaries of salient attributes that form mental images that affect behaviour. They are long lasting but not permanent; inflexible but not totally rigid. One would expect that they could be manipulated by careful positioning strategies and the creation of a brand, a product identity that lifts the individual item above the crowd of a nameless group of similar items. From the practitioners' perspective, the answer to the question what do you do when "fairly or unfairly, your product has been stereotyped-stamped and branded" seems to be simple enough: change the stereotype. This can be achieved through "a gradual process that must be sustained over a long period of time" (Ryan, 1999: 26). The disassociation of a product from a pervasive national stereotype involves the implementation of strategies such as educating consumers using aggressive and proactive public relations; identifying and targeting new market segments; aligning perceptions with reality through careful identification of the characteristics of existing customers, the product and its attributes and fostering long-term corporate partnerships with opinion leaders and communities.

# THE PROFITABLE BUSINESS OF NATIONAL STEREOTYPING

From Aristophanes to contemporary television sitcoms, stereotypes are the cornerstone of some of the most culturally influential and financially successful comedy because ridiculing the deficiencies of groups of "others" makes people feel good about themselves. Jokes have been acknowledged to be major carriers of stereotypes. A lot of what we know, or think we know, about other races comes from comedies and anecdotes. Not many people would blindly accept stereotypical information that they have acquired through an exaggerated caricature that is known to be intended to entertain. That is not to say that a satirical treatment of stereotypes is good, or always in good taste, but at least it comes with a big, and widely understood *caveat emptor*.

Stereotypes, however, can be socially harmful when they are presented in a realistic context, not as caricatures but as factual statements, alongside characters that the consumers of the cultural product can identify with. When in a film the "other" is seriously presented next to a realistic portrayal of the "self", then a misleading semblance of reality is created and the stereotypical information is likely to be accepted as fact. Still, however, the marketing function of the stereotype is similar to that of the comic representation: it attracts attention and tells people what they want to hear – that they are "good" and others are "bad". Some stereotypes seem to be preferred by consumers to other, and the successful ones are perpetrated, year after year, movie after movie.

If one is to believe Hollywood, there are only two types of Japanese people, the geisha in white face and peculiar behaviour patterns and the aggressive, cruel samurai, WWII army officer or businessman. Overall, the "Japanese are seldom if ever allowed to be ordinary people on screen" (Murakami, 1999: 54). The change of the uniform of the male characters reflects changes in international relations and political or economic imperatives whilst the unchanging female stereotype demonstrates the pervasiveness of Western male sexual fantasies. From a business perspective, the fact remains that it is the exoticism of the main characters, together with the postcard views of the snow capped Mt. Fuji that attract the movie goers. With the increased popularity of cable TV and video tapes, films that made the studios a lot of money a long time ago are still a cash generating product world-wide.

It is not just Asian stereotypes, however, that are the stock of successful cinema products. Italians are consistently presented as Mafiosi. As former Governor Mario M. Cuomo put it "if you have a large assembly of vowels in your name, the first thing some people wonder is if there's a criminal connection" (Haberman, 1999: 1). With the African–American stereotypes being labelled as clearly politically incorrect, an increase in the prominence of West Indians, stereotyped as Rastafarian coons and criminals has been observed (Vickerman, 1999). Hispanics seem to have a wider range of stereotypes attached to them: "the bandit, the half-breed harlot, the male buffoon, the female clown, the Latin lover, and the Dark (i.e. mysterious) lady" (Vickerman, 1999: 90) whilst for Australians there is but one – Crocodile Dundee.

Science fiction has remained relatively free of racial stereotyping (Staples, 1999). The ability to create purely imaginary creatures, however, has recently been used in order to reproduce many of the most pervasive national stereotypes in a way that borders on racism. The recently released blockbuster movie that is likely to generate unprecedented profits in merchandising, Star Wars Episode I: The Phantom Menace, uses costume, speech patterns and behaviour that imply the sinister Asian, the greedy and crooked Middle Easterner, the "anything for profit" hooked-nosed Jew and the intellectually inferior, confused Carribean–American (Leo, 1999).

Overall "ethnic characters are hot" (Seiler, 1999), as slurring "others" makes "us" feel superior and whatever makes people feel good about themselves is likely to be an attractive product to purchase and consume. And the history of cinema has provided ample proof of this observation.

It is not only the producers and directors of films that have identified the selling potential of both gross and subtle national stereotyping. The same imagery, perpetuating the same old views of certain nationalities, is also extensively used in advertising (Elliott, 1999). A number of corporations are happy to be identified with the stereotypes that are assigned to their nationality, if it promotes their products (Hiestand, 1997). Others use stereotypes of their targeted consumers (Anonymous, 1998; Garrett, 1998). In any case, consumers identify with stereotypes in a way that makes what is morally, socially or creatively weak potentially good from a sales point of view (Cebrzynski, 1998).

Gender stereotypes are widely recognized as socially constructed and of morally dubious standing nowadays. The same however is not true for ethnicity. Even if the concept of the socially constructed self is accepted as such, a concept, that does not necessarily mean that the acceptance makes any difference in the way daily life is experienced (Anderson, 1995). Nationalities (and ethnic groups within multicultural societies) that have organized and powerful political lobbies, or the ability to instigate collective action, have managed to force the media to, at least, attempt to provide some positive portrayals. Those that lack the necessary power structure to influence attitudes are still providing profitable raw material for the media, one of the most successful global business sectors.

Caution in blindly accepting stereotypes even when there is evidence that they do contain elements of truth is generally advised (Cooper and Kirkcaldy, 1995). This should apply to believing the stereotype to be true as well as purchasing and consuming products of the business of stereotyping. It would appear, however, that the caution is not generally heeded. The fact remains that as long as people are willing to buy the product, there is no way to force the media to abandon stereotypes without taking away the freedom of expression (Haberman, 1999). Unless, of course, the media themselves, or the manufacturers of products that are being advertised have a code of their own that excludes issues that are morally or socially unacceptable, and some already do (Wynter, 1998).

# AN ALTERNATIVE VIEW OF THE WORLD

The history of the development of research on stereotypes from the early 1920s to the present day bears a striking similarity to the successive phases of the image. The stereotype, being an image itself, develops from a reflection of basic reality, to masking and perverting basic reality, to masking the absence of reality, to finally bearing no relation to any reality whatever, thus becoming its own pure simulacrum (Baudrillard, 1983).

Havel (1995: 233) described a Bedouin wearing traditional robes over his jeans on his camel, with a transistor radio, without any desire for ridicule but also without "shedding an intellectual tear over the commercial expansion of the West that destroys alien cultures". Vegemite, an icon of Australian culinary taste, is produced by Kraft and soy sauce can be purchased in most Greek supermarkets. International trade has helped create a world where "the inside is out (...) and the outside is in (...)" (Shweder, 1995: 78). Nowadays, travel and globalization have provided us with means of transcending cultural tastes, preferences and sensibilities. We face parts of ourselves in the cultures that we visit and we adopt ideas and ways of doing things from the cultures that visit us, thus we are constantly faced with opportunities to be "astonished by the integrity and value of alien things" (Shweder, 1995: 48).

The "contact hypothesis" postulates that interracial contact promotes harmonious race relations (Yancey, 1999). For people involved in international business, direct contact with people outside the borders of their own country is an item on their daily agendas. Events in remote parts of the world can change their personal circumstances as quickly as those that take place in their immediate neighbourhood. And what is more important, their livelihoods and careers depend on their ability to transcend stereotypes and maintain successful interactions between the "self" and the "other". In a world that has suffered a lot of bloodshed and destruction caused by blindly believing stereotypes and sustaining prejudices, international business, and the people involved in it, can become an agent of change. They really have a vested interest in at least trying.

What we are faced with at turn of the 20th century is a total re-evaluation of space, time and our relationship with both, as well as our relationship with individuals and groups that would – in the clear-cut framework of modernity – be considered as alien. Could it be possible that the sharp distinctions between the "self" and the "other" are no longer relevant? Do we really still need summary constructs to guide us in differentiating between groups and preserving the homogeneity within groups? Is it possible that the unity that human beings naturally seek can no longer be found in "sameness" as opposed to "otherness"?

As Shweder (1995: 48) put it, unity can be found "in a universal multiplicity which makes each of us so variegated that "others" become fully accessible and imaginable to us through some aspect or other of our own complex self". This is not to suggest that some newfound humanism has already eliminated stereotypes. What I am simply suggesting, is that we have probably reached a point in our social development where we can understand and value each other by recognizing the power of our prejudices as a limit to nihilism and by simply accepting and celebrating our differences.

# REFERENCES

Abdul-Malek, T. (1975) Comparative profiles of foreign customers and intermediaries. European Journal of Marketing, 9 (3): 198–214.

Adorno, T.W., Frenkel-Brunswick, E., Levinson, D.J. and Sanford, R.N. (1950) The Authoritarian Personality. New York: Harper.

Ahmed, S.A., d'Astous, A. and El-adraoui, M. (1994) Country of origin effects on purchasing managers' product perceptions. Industrial Marketing Management, 23 (4): 323–332.

Allport, F.H. (1954) The Nature of Prejudice. Cambridge, MA: Addison Wesley.

Al-Sulaiti, K. and Baker, M.J. (1998) Country of origin effects: a literature review. Marketing Intelligence and Planning, 16 (3): 150–159.

Anderson, B. (1991) Imagined Communities: Reflections on the Origins and Spread of Nationalism. London: Verso.

Anderson, K.J. (1993) Otherness, culture and capital: "Chinatown's" transformation under Australian multi-culturalism. In G.L. Clark,, D. Forbes, and R. Francis (Eds), Multiculturalism, Difference and Postmodernism. Chesire: Longman.

Anderson, W.T. (1995) Epilogue: the end and beginning of enlightenment. In W.T. Anderson (Ed), The Truth about the Truth: De-confusing and Re-constructing the Postmodern World. New York: Jeremy Tarcher/Putnam.

Anderson, W.T and W.H. Cunningham (1972) Gauging foreign product promotion. Journal of Advertising Research, 12 (1): 29–34.

Anonymous (1998) Lowes places Andy Cole in a chip shop for latest Reebok ad. Campaign, August 28: 4.

Asch, S.E. (1952) Social Psychology. New York: Prentice Hall.

Ashmore, R.D. and Del Boca, F.K. (1981) Conceptual approaches to stereotypes and stereotyping. In D.L. Hamilton (Ed), Cognitive Processes in Stereotyping and Intergroup Behavior. Hillsdale, NJ: Erlbaum.

Bailey, W. and Pineres, S. (1997) Country of origin attitudes in Mexico: the malinchismo effect, Journal of International Consumer Marketing, 9 (3): 25–41.

Bannister, J.P and Saunders, J.A. (1978) UK consumers' attitudes towards imports: the measurement of national stereotype image. European Journal of Marketing, 12 (8): 562–570.

Baudrillard, J. (1983) Simulations (Simulacres et simulation). New York: Semiotext(e).

Biernat, M. (1995) The shifting standards model: implications of stereotype accuracy for social judgement. In Y.-T. Lee, L.J. Jussim, and C.R. McCauley (Eds), Stereotype Accuracy: Toward Appreciating Group Differences. Washington, DC: American Psychological Association.

Bilkey, W.J. and Nes, E. (1982) Country-of-origin effects on product evaluations. Journal of International Business Studies, 13 (1): 88-99.

Bodenhausen, G.V. and Lichtenstein, M. (1987) Social stereotypes and information-processing strategies: the impact of task complexity. Journal of Personality and Social Psychology, 52 (5): 871–880.

Bottomley, G. (1997) Identification: ethnicity, gender and culture. Journal of Intercultural Studies, 18: 41–48.

Buchanan, W. (1951) Stereotypes and tensions as revealed by the UNESCO International Poll. International Social Science Bulletin, 3: 515–528.

Cebrzynski, G. (1998) Stereotypical ads not necessarily bad, but at least get real. Nation's Restaurant News – the Weekly Newspaper of the Food Service Industry, 32: 14.

Chao, P. and Rajendran, K.N. (1993) Consumer profiles and perceptions: country-of-origin effects. International Marketing Review, 10 (2): 22–39.

Chase, S. (1938) The Tyranny of Words. New York: Harcourt.

Chassin, J. and Jaffe, E. (1979) Industrial buyer attitudes toward goods made in Eastern Europe. Columbia Journal of World Business, 14: 74–81.

Cooper, C.L. and Kirkcaldy, B.D. (1995) Executive stereotyping between cultures: the British vs. German Manager. Journal of Managerial Psychology, 10 (1): 3–6.

Cooper, D.J., Greenwood, R., Hinings, B. and Brown, J.L. (1998) Globalization and nationalism in a multinational accounting firm: the case of opening new markets in Eastern Europe. Accounting Organizations and Society, 23 (5/6): 531–548.

Crawford, J.C. and Lamb, C.W. (1981) Source preferences for imported products. Journal of Purchasing and Material Management, 17: 28–33.

Crick, D. and Chaudhry, S. (1995) Export practices of Asian SMEs some preliminary findings. Marketing Intelligence and Planning, 13 (11): 13–21.

Czinkota, M.R and Ronkainen, I.A. (1995) International Marketing. Fort Worth, TX: The Dryden Press, Harcourt, Brace College Publishers.

Darling, J.R. and Kraft, F.B. (1977) A comparative profile of products and associated marketing practices. European Journal of Marketing, 11 (7): 11–23.

Diamantopoulos, A., Schlegelmilch, B.B. and Preez, J.P. (1995) Lessons for Pan-European marketing? The role of consumer preferences in fine-tuning the product-market fit. International Marketing Review, 12 (2): 38–52.

Dichtl, E., Leibold, M., Köglmayr, H.G. and Müller, S. (1984) The export decision of small and medium-sized firms: a review. Management International Review, 24 (2): 49–60.

Dornoff, R., Tankersley, C. and White, G. (1974) Consumers' perceptions of imports. Akron Business and Economic Review, 5: 26–29.

Douglas, S.P. and Craig, C.S. (1995) Global Marketing Strategy. New York: McGraw-Hill.

Elliott, S. (1999) Marketing and the mob: a marriage of convenience now a Madison Avenue favorite. New York Times, May 26.

Funder, D.C. (1995) Stereotypes, base rates, and the fundamental attribution mistake: a content based approach to judgemental accuracy. In Y.-T. Lee, L.J. Jussim, and C.R. McCauley (Eds), Stereotype Accuracy: Toward Appreciating Group Differences. Washington, DC: American Psychological Association.

Fung, S. (1999) Risky business. Across the Board, 36 (7 July/August): 10–11.

Gaedeke, R. (1973) Consumer attitudes towards products made in developing countries. Journal of Retailing, 49: 13–24.

Garrett, J. (1998) Ikea has a dig at Englishness. Campaign, (September 25) 18.

Greer, T.V. (1971) British purchasing agents and European Economic Community: some empirical evidence on international industrial perceptions. Journal of Purchasing, 7: 56–63.

Gunew, S. (1993) Against multiculturalism: rhetorical images. In G.L. Clark, D. Forbes, and R. Francis (Eds), Multiculturalism, Difference and Postmodernism. Chesire: Longman.

Haberman, C. (1999) A stereotype Hollywood can't refuse. New York Times, (July 30, late Edn): 1.

Han, C.M. (1989) Country image: halo or summary construct? Journal of Marketing Research, 26 (May): 222–229.

Han, C.M. (1990) Testing the role of country image in consumer choice behaviour. European Journal of Marketing, 24 (6): 24–39.

Han, C.M. and Terpstra, V. (1988) Country-of-origin effects for uni-national and bi-national products. Journal of International Business Studies, 19 (2): 235–255.

Haslam, A.S., Oakes, P.J., Reynolds, K.J. and Turner, J.C. (1999) Social identity salience and the emergence of stereotype consensus. Personality and Social Psychology Bulletin, 25 (7 July): 809–818.

Havel, V. (1995) The search for meaning in a global civilization. In W.T. Anderson (Ed), The Truth about the Truth: De-confusing and Re-constructing the Postmodern World. New York: Jeremy Tarcher/Putnam.

Hiestand, M. (1997) Norwegians don't bat an eye over Nike ad. USA Today, (July 10): C10.

Hong, S. and Wyer, R.S. (1989) Effects of country-of-origin and product-attribute information processing perspective. Journal of Consumer Research, 16 (September): 175–187.

Hooley, G., Shipley, D. and Krieger, N. (1988) A method for modelling consumer perceptions of country of origin. International Marketing Review, 5 (3): 67–76.

Hugstad, P. and Durr, M. (1986) A study of country of manufacturer imact on consumer perceptions. In N. Malhotra and J. Hawes (Eds), Development in Marketing Science. Coral Gables: Academy of Marketing Science.

Johanson, J. and Vahlne, J.E. (1990) The mechanism of internationalisation. International Marketing Review, 7 (4): 11–24.

Johanson, J.K., Ronkainen, I.A. and Czinkota, M.R. (1994) Negative country-of-origin effects: the case of the New Russia. Journal of International Business Studies, 25 (1): 157–176.

Johansson, J.K., Douglas, S.P. and Nonaka, I. (1985) Assessing the impact of country of origin on product evaluations: a new methodological perspective. Journal of Marketing Research, 22: 388–396.

Katz, D. and Schanck, R.L. (1938) Social Psychology. New York: Wiley.

Kaynak, E. and Cavusgil, S.T. (1983) Consumer attitudes towards products of foreign origin: do they vary across product classes? International Journal of Advertising, 2: 147–157.

Khanna, S.R. (1986) Asian companies and the country stereotype paradox: an empirical study. Columbia Journal of World Business, (Summer): 29–38.

Klineberg, O. (1964) The Human Dimension in International Relations. New York: Holt, Rinehart and Winston.

Kochunny, C.M., Babakus, E., Berl, R. and Marks, W. (1993) Schematic representation of country image: its effect on product evaluations. Journal of International Consumer Marketing, 5 (1): 5–25.

Lampert, S.I. and Jaffe, E.D. (1997) A dynamic approach to country-of-origin effect. European Journal of Marketing, 32 (1/2): 61–78.

Lee, Y.-T., Jussim, L.J. and McCauley, C.R. (Eds.) (1995) Stereotype Accuracy: Toward Appreciating Group Differences. Washington, DC: American Psychological Association.

Leo, J. (1999) Fu Manchu on Naboo. U.S. News and World Report, (July 12): 14.

Leonidou, L.C., Hadjimarcou, J., Kaleka, A. and Stamenova, G.T. (1998) Bulgarian consumers' perceptions of products made in Asia-Pacific. International Marketing Review, 16 (2): 126–142.

Leonidou, L.C. and Kaleka, A.A. (1998) Behavioural aspects of international buyer-seller relationships: their association with export involvement. International Marketing Review, 15 (5): 373–397.

Lillis, C. and Narayana, C. (1974) Analysis of made in product images – an exploratory study. Journal of International Business Studies, 5 (Spring): 119–127.

Lin, L. and Sternquist, B. (1994) Taiwanese consumers' perceptions of product information cues: country of origin and store prestige. European Journal of Marketing, 28 (1): 5–18.

Lippman, W. (1922) Public Opinion. New York: Harcourt Brace.

Mace, C.A. (1943) National stereotypes. Sociological Review, 35: 29–36.

Mackie, D.M., Hamilton, D.L., Susskind, J. and Rosselli, F. (1996) Social psychological foundations of stereotype formation. In C.N. Macrae, C. Stangor and M. Hewstone (Eds), Stereotypes and Stereotyping. New York and London: The Guilford Press.

Maheswaran, D. (1994) Country of origin as a stereotype: effects of consumer expertise and attribute strength on product evaluations. Journal of Consumer Research, 21 (2 September): 354–365.

Morgan, R.E. and Katsikeas, C.S. (1997) Theories of international trade, foreign direct investment and firm internationalization: a critique. Management Decision, 35 (1): 68–78.

Murakami, Y. (1999) Hollywood's slanted view. Japan Quarterly, 46 (3 July/September): 54–62.

Nagashima, A. (1970) A comparison of Japanese and US attitudes towards foreign products. Journal of Marketing, 34: 68–74.

Nagashima, A. (1977) A comparative 'made in' survey among Japanese businessmen. Journal of Marketing, 41: 95–100.

Niffenegger, P., White, J. and Marmet, G. (1980) How British retail managers view French and American products. European Journal of Marketing, 14 (8): 493–498.

Oakes, P.J., Haslam, A. and Turner, J.C. (1994) Stereotyping and Social Reality. Oxford, UK and Cambridge, USA: Blackwell.

Okechuku, C. (1994) The importance of product country of origin: a conjoint analysis of the United States, Canada, Germany and The Netherlands. European Journal of Marketing, 28 (4): 5–19.

Padget, V.R. and Wolosin, R.J. (1980) Cognitive similarity in dyadic communication. Journal of Personality and Social Psychology, 39 (Winter): 654–659.

Papadopoulos, N. and Heslop, L. (Eds) (1993) Product Country Images, International Business Press, New York.

Porter, M. (Ed.) (1986) Competition in Global Industries, Harvard Business School Press, Boston, MA.

Porter, M. (1990) The Competitive Advantage of Nations. New York, NY: The Free Press.

Reirson, C. (1966) Are foreign products seen as national stereotypes? Journal of Retailing, 42 (Fall): 33–40.

Ryan, S. (1999) Overcoming negative stereotypes. Brandweek, (26 July): 26–29.

Samiee, S. (1994) Customer evaluation of products in global markets. Journal of International Business Studies, 25 (3): 579–604.

Schaller, M. and Gideon III, L.C. (1999) Influence of impression-management goals on the emerging contents of group stereotypes: support for a social-evolutionary process. Personality and Social Psychology Bulletin, 25 (7 July): 819–833.

Schooler, R.D. (1965) Product bias in the central American common market. Journal of Marketing Research, (November): 394–397.

Schooler, R.D. and Wildt, A.R. (1968) Elasticity of product bias. Journal of Marketing Research, 5: 78–81.

Seiler, A. (1999) Something to offend everyone: minority groups say hit films fill screens with stereotypes. USA Today, (June 28 Final Edn): 01D.

Sherrif, M. (1967) Group Conflict and Cooperation: Their Social Psychology. London: Routledge and Kegan Paul.

Shoham, A. and Albaum, G.S. (1995) Reducing the impact of barriers to exporting: a managerial perspective. Journal of International Marketing, 3 (4): 85–105.

Shweder, R. (1995) Santa Claus on the cross. In W.T. Anderson (Ed) The Truth about the Truth: De-confusing and Re-constructing the Postmodern World. New York: Jeremy Tarcher/Putnam.

Stangor, C. and Schaller, M. (1996) Stereotypes as individual and collective representations. In N.-C. Macrae, C. Stangor and M. Hewstone (Eds) Stereotypes and Stereotyping. New York and London: The Guilford Press.

Staples, B. (1999) Shuffling Through the Star Wars. New York Times, (June 20): 14.

Stöttinger, B. and Schlegelmilch, B.B. (1998) Explaining export development through psychic distance: enlightening or elusive? International Marketing Review, 15 (5): 357–372.

Tajfel, H. (1969) Cognitive aspects of prejudice. Journal of Social Issues, (25): 79–97.

Taylor, S.E. (1981) A categorization approach to stereotyping. In D.L. Hamilton (Ed), Cognitive Processes in Stereotyping and Intergroup Behaviour. Hillsdale, NJ: Erlbaum.

Triandis, H.C. (1960) Cognitive similarity and communication in a dyad. Human Relations, 13 (May): 175–183.

Tse, A., Kwan, C., Yee, C., Wah, K. and Ming, L. (1996) The impact of country of origin on the behaviour of Hong Kong consumers. Journal of International Marketing and Marketing Research, 21 (1): 29–44.

Vickerman, M. (1999) Representing West Indians in film: Ciphers, coons, and criminals. Western Journal of Black Studies, 23 (2): 83–96.

White, P.D. (1979) Attitudes of US purchasing managers toward industrial products manufactured in selected European nations. Journal of International Business Studies, 10: 81–90.

White, P.D. and Cundiff, E.W. (1978) Assessing the quality of industrial products. Journal of Marketing, 42 (January): 80–86.

Wynter, L.E. (1998) Business and race. Wall Street Journal, (April 1): B1.

Yancey, G. (1999) An examination of the effects of residential and church integration on racial attitudes of whites. Sociological Perspectives, 42 (2): 279–304.

Young, S., Hamill, J., Wheeler, C. and Davies, J.R. (1989) International Market Entry and Development. Englewood Cliffs, NJ: Prentice-Hall.

Zhang, Y. (1996) Chinese consumers' evaluation of foreign products: the influence of culture, product types and product presentation format. European Journal of Marketing, 30 (12): 50–68.

# Chapter 18

# Management Change in Central and Eastern Europe

**Kate Gilbert**

*Management Research Centre, Wolverhampton Business School, University of Wolverhampton, Telford, UK*

## INTRODUCTION

The 1990s witnessed the nations of Central and Eastern Europe (CEE) struggling to adjust to the collapse of one of the most audacious social experiments in history. Few people, either in East or West, could have foreseen how quickly the great edifice of communism would collapse, once the Berlin wall came down in 1989 and it became obvious that the Soviet Union lacked the will to fight to maintain its empire. The struggle of people and organizations to adapt, to build new market-oriented structures and processes, or to dig in, relying on old tried-and-tested strategies for survival in a hostile environment, has provided rich ground for research. In the sphere of business and management, organizational and managerial responses to the rapidly changing environment, and how they are conditioned by deeper factors of national culture, have been the subject of endless but disparate speculation and enquiry. This chapter draws together main threads of that enquiry, adopting a chronological framework – past, present and future – to enable some coherence in a dauntingly complex tangle of themes.

The first basic assumption of the chapter is that organizational cultures and behaviour, and to an extent managerial styles, are shaped and conditioned by wider societal cultures. In order to derive insights into the extent to which societal cultures in CEE converge or diverge, aspects of national cultures are located within a framework set by the multi-dimensional models of culture developed by Hofstede (1980, 1991) and Trompenaars (1993). Hofstede's model has found wide currency in CEE, even though his original Hermes studies gathered no data in the then Communist bloc. Trompenaars' work has the advantage of having been carried out in several of the region's countries, and gives some insights into the core values underlying management and organizational behaviour. In seeking to unravel the tangle of political, historical, social and situational threads which go to make up the fabric of culture in CEE, we enter a minefield of terminology. Focusing on the recent past, the term "Soviet-era" is used in preference to "Soviet", as that bald adjective refers to a regime, which was specific geographically and temporally. The term "communist" is similarly unsatisfactory as it denotes an ideology which was not universally ascribed to by the people of the countries concerned, and which still has other political manifestations elsewhere.

"Soviet-era" is thus used here as a generic term to denote activities, management practices or styles, or persons (e.g. the "Soviet-era manager") forged during the lifetime of the USSR's domination in CEE. In the case of Russia, Ukraine and Belarus, this covers the period from 1922 to 1991. In the case of other countries in the region, which were satellite states, it extended from the late 1940s to 1989. The intention is not to suggest that all countries were equally "Soviet", which would be to deny the distinct history of each nation (Jankowicz, 1994), nor to discount pockets of resistance in public, private, or organizational life (Soulsby, 1999), which would be an affront to countless nameless dissenters. Rather, the aim is to recognize and emphasize a certain shared experience of the command economy, and the existence of patterns of organization and management extending geographically across the region, and temporally into the post-Soviet age of transition. The catch-all term CEE is used to denote the European countries which were satellites of the USSR, *excluding* the Baltic states, which lie outside the region, and *including* Russia, although it is recognized that several of the republics of the Russian Federation lie beyond Europe.

The second basic assumption is that the sheer scale of the change in all dimensions of the business environment throughout the region has been so immense, that attempts to measure culture at a single point in time since 1989 is doomed to unreliability. In order to derive a baseline impression of how far changes have progressed, and how far they still have to progress, we examine the figure of the Soviet-era manager

For an overview of the contexts in which management change has taken place in CEE, we begin by grouping the region's nations into clusters according to their degree of progress in moving towards the market economy. A theme of the chapter is the tension between those transitional factors and experiences which the countries of CEE hold in common, and those giving each country a unique experience. The forces working to change the internal environments of CEE are examined. No survey of change in the region would be complete without a passing recognition of the role of the West in shaping (some would say distorting) the processes of change.

The final section turns to the future. As the peoples of CEE have grown accustomed to the whirlwind of change and started to analyze for themselves the processes that they are going through, a debate has emerged about the nature of the changes. Are they engaged in a transition or undergoing a transformation? Transition, with its connotations of travel, implies a (known) destination. It seems inconceivable that any of the countries would revert to the full-blown command economy, having relished the salty taste of the market. But is "western-style capitalism" the only destination on the line? For some it may be, notably those already negotiating entry to the European Union, but for others, such as the countries of the former Soviet Union, the destination may be elsewhere, or indeed, never reached.

# CULTURE AND MANAGEMENT

## Cultures Shared and Diverse

Some early Western analysis of management change in the countries of CEE tended to approach the topic as though the events of the second half of the twentieth century rendered the whole region culturally homogeneous. Yet writers emphasize that culture is deeply rooted in the soil of centuries-deep history, and conditioned by natural constants such as geography and climate (Schein, 1969; Hofstede, 1980; 1991; Trompenaars, 1993). For example, a Westerner wishing to grasp the dynamics and scale of societal change in Poland, tapping the source of core values on which management and organizational behaviour is based, must understand something of the history of Poland as a unique entity, and not only that more recent history of Poland, member of the Communist bloc. History might be shared, but how that history was experienced varied from country to country. "The problem is not the last 50 years, but the last 500" as Jankowicz (1994) put it. There are elements in each country's history and culture that make it distinctive and unique (Luthans et al., 1993); and any cultural changes, rather than simply wiping out the effect of the communist legacy, represent changes in whole social cultural *systems* whose roots stretch back down the centuries *and of which the communist years form a part*. These illuminate the reasons why the process of market-oriented transition has appeared smoother in Poland, Hungary and the Czech Republic than elsewhere. Aspects of management style in Poland and Russia may appear on a superficial level to be similar, but have very different roots and meanings for the actors involved. A tendency for Westerners to view the region from an external perspective, and therefore pay more attention to apparent similarities than subtle nuances of meaning, may be a major cause of the cultural insensitivities resented by these countries over the years.

## Applying Models of Culture to CEE

Reliable comparison of the organizational cultures of CEE is hampered by the absence of large-scale studies to operationalize and measure features of diversity and convergence. Researchers and writers both in CEE and the West have used the most well-known dimensional frameworks of culture, developed respectively by Geert Hofstede and Fons Trompenaars, to analyze and differentiate the national cultures of the CEE countries (Bollinger, 1994; Veiga et al., 1995; Naumov, 1996; Nasierowski and Mikula, 1998; Hofstede, 1993; Luthans et al., 1993; Trompenaars, 1993). These studies have tended to use standardized quantitative survey techniques in order to generate findings amenable to statistical analysis. Others have made important contributions to understanding cultural diversity in the region, by carrying out smaller-scale qualitative studies and/or writing from their deep personal experience and knowledge of the region (for example, Holden et al., 1998; Vlachoutsicos, 1998; Kostera, 1995, 1996; Janko-wicz, 1994; Simon and Davies, 1995; Puffer, 1994).

Hofstede's (1991) five-dimensional model of culture is probably the best-known and most widely-used (and abused) of its type. Based on factor analysis of a huge data set of attitudinal questionnaire responses from IBM employees around the world (Hofstede, 1980), it proposed that national cultures differ along four dimensions or indices; power distance, uncertainty avoidance, masculinity/femininity, and individualism/collecti-vism. Later, following work carried out in China and the Far East, Hofstede and Bond (1988) added a fifth dimension, Confucian dynamism, or short-term/long term time orientation. This seminal work has been hugely influential in encouraging emula-tors (Bollinger, 1994; Perlaki, 1994; Veiga et al., 1995; Naumov, 1996; Zaitsev, 1996; Nasierowski and Mikula, 1998), not least because the concepts underlying the dimen-sions are deceptively straightforward, and have compelling face validity. The original research which generated the model did not include any CEE countries except Yugo-slavia. This gap has provided opportunity for researchers and theorists to speculate and investigate using the model, with varying degrees of rigour, and varying results. Since 1991, Nasierowski and Mikula (1998) and Naumov (1996) have carried out studies in Poland and Russia, respectively, using Hofstede's dimensions, while Perlaki (1994), in a theoretical essay, ventured a generalized cultural typology for the whole of Eastern Europe. While limited by the fact that they did not replicate the original methodology precisely, these offer useful insights, particularly into the tensions between the cata-clysmic discontinuities of massive systemic change, and the fact that, while behaviours may change in response to changed circumstances, attitudes take longer, and the deeper level of core values may not change significantly at all (Schein, 1969). Cultures, almost by definition, value and make use of what has worked for a population in the past.

Hofstede's first dimension, power distance, is defined as "the degree of inequality among people which the population of a country considers as normal" (Hofstede, 1991). It can be summed up in his Orwellian borrowing "all societies are unequal, but some are more unequal than others". Power distance in CEE was postulated by Hofstede (1993) himself as being high: this was supported by Perlaki (1994) and Zaitsev (1996) and reinforced in numerous observations that Russian workers appear to prefer a fairly autocratic management style (Bollinger, 1994; Puffer, 1994; Puffer and McCarthy, 1995). Naumov (1996) study subsequently challenged this assumption, finding that his respondents scored very similar to Canada and the United States with relatively low power distance raising a number of thorny questions. To what extent is an *apparent* preference for an autocratic boss a reflection of the traditions of the communist era, a legacy that is now being shaken off? Can we expect power distance scores to decrease (as predicted by Veiga et al., 1995)? Or could there be the methodological problem that the instrument does not measure what it claims to measure? It is interesting to note that Poland, which has a more established democratic tradition than Russia, came out with a high power distance score on the study carried out by Nasierowski and Mikula (1998), congruent with studies by Yanouzas and Boukis (1993) and Perlaki (1994), who went so far as to state that differences between CEE cultures during the Soviet-era "can be *ascribed* to a relatively hard-line or rela-tively liberal political system in each country" (p. 300, my emphasis).

The second dimension, the individuality/collectivism continuum, relates to the extent to which members of a culture identify themselves as individuals rather than as members of a group. Several scholars and writers have noted the Slav tradition of relative cultural collectivism, with historical antecedents long before Marxism, such as the importance of village communities for survival in the harsh and threatening environment of the Great European Plain (Davies, 1996; Holden et al., 1998; Hosking, 1992; Hingley, 1978; Kelemen and Gardiner, 1999; Vlachoutsicos, 1998). Yet in the current maelstrom of change in the transition economies, the concept of collectivism presents problems. Of all the dimensions, it prompts the most vehement responses from people from CEE countries, some of whom dismiss collectivism as synonymous with communist ideology, others of whom use it as a sign of the region's cultural superiority to the materialism and personal greed of the West. Naumov (1996) result of an individualism score of 41 for Russia was lower than Hofstede's prediction at 50, although not much lower than the mean for the Mediterranean countries. Nasierowski and Mikula (1998) reported, on balance, a lower individualism score for their Polish respondents than for their Canadian comparators, although the Poles scored higher on valuing freedom – revealing perhaps a strongly situational factor at work. "Canadians take "freedom" and "challenge" for granted, whereas Poles believe that hard work is needed to achieve such a condition, and hence sacrifices should be made in terms of having less "personal time"" (Nasierowski and Mikula, 1998: 499).

The masculinity/femininity dimension is another source of ambiguity. "[M]asculinity pertains to societies in which social gender roles are clearly distinct...; femininity pertains to societies in which social gender roles overlap... (Hofstede, 1991: 82–83, emphasis in the original). Implications of masculinity for organizational life and cultures include a tendency towards large-scale organizational structures, an emphasis on formal and extrinsic goals and rewards, and high levels of internal competition. On the societal level, masculine cultures will tend to exhibit materialism, and an emphasis on economic growth over environmental conservation. Hofstede extrapolated from his original data on Yugoslavia that other countries from the communist bloc would score low in masculinity. Other writers have supported this notion by highlighting cultural traits evident in the pre-modern era, and showing how these have continued into the transition era. For example, even today, the mass of the population of Russia remains suspicious of businessmen. Yet it could equally be argued that they are so with apparent good reason, judging from contemporary scandals. While Zaitsev's study (1996) declared emphatically that "Russia is definitely a feminine country", Naumov's study found that Russians scored significantly higher on the masculinity index than Hofstede had predicted, and for Poland, Nasierowski and Mikula (1998) recorded levels slightly higher than Hofstede's original averages, but still significantly lower than Canada, the United States, and the UK. Perlaki (1994) on the other hand, equated femininity with modernity and thus postulated that Poland and the Czech Republic were becoming *more* feminine.

The fourth dimension of the model is uncertainty avoidance, representing the extent to which "members of a culture feel threatened by uncertain or unknown situations" (Hofstede, 1991: 113). It is open to misunderstanding, in that low UA may be interpreted as a willingness to take risks. Eastern Europeans, when introduced to the dimensions through lectures or translations, sometimes fix on the extreme levels of uncertainty with which they are having to cope as evidence that they "now" have low UA cultures. After all, uncertainty *cannot* be avoided. But the extent of stress across the region, evidenced by escalating rates of alcoholism, despair and suicide, falling levels of public health (UNDP 1999), and the urge to put one's faith in all manner of spiritualistic and New Age pseudo-religions, gives the lie to this perception. Uncertainty or the "great feared unknown" (Holden et al, 1998: 85) is alive and well and living in Eastern Europe, and people don't like it.

Based on questionnaire data from 15,000 managers in 47 countries, Trompenaars' (1993) study derived a seven-dimensional model of the differences between national cultures. Five dimensions pertain to relationships, and two to the orientation towards time and the environment. This study has the undoubted advantage of having included respondents from all the countries in the region with the exception of Ukraine and Belarus, thus allowing the possibility of making comparisons within the region. As well as the orientation to time (past, present and future) Trompenaars' framework shares a single dimension, individualism/collectivism, with Hofstede. Contrary to expectations, his results showed a surprising level of individualism in the respondents from CEE; those from Hungary, Czechoslovakia, Poland, Bulgaria, Romania and Russia all scoring in the top quartile for individualism. Given that other studies have tended to establish (or assume) an inherent and deep tendency towards collectivism, at least in Bulgaria, Romania and Russia, one has to speculate that there may be something unsafe about the validity of the questionnaire items, that the manager cohort surveyed is extremely untypical for the populations at large, or that situational factors operating at the time of the study skewed the results. Regarding individualism, it is not impossible that the questionnaire results could be interpreted either way. Trompenaars asked his respondents whether they preferred to make decisions alone or in a group, where everybody "has a say in the decisions that are made". Given that the respondents were managers, a marked preference for individual decision-making is empirical evidence of the tradition of one-man management, described in more detail below. Similarly, the response to a second item, whether responsibility for faults and mistakes should be borne by the individual or by the group, showed a strong preference to punish the miscreant as an individual. However, once we recognize the cultural tendency to work on the basis of "in-groups" which by definition have to isolate and eject deviants, the result could be interpreted to support collectivism, rather than individualism.

Other dimensions on the Trompenaars framework may help to resolve some of the ambiguities surrounding CEE cultures presented by the use of the Hofstede framework. For example, the neutral-affective dimension relates to the willingness to show emotion in the workplace and in public life, and the diffuse-specific dimension addresses the porosity of the boundaries between work life and personal life, and workplace and personal relationships. Several studies attest to the element of emotionality, positive and negative, in Eastern European business dealings, sometimes to the discomfiture of Western partners. Trompenaars' data showed a marked agreement among Czech, Hungarian and Russian respondents that companies should help employees with housing (a sign of diffusion of "private" concerns through organizational life). Only Polish managers demurred, with 71% disagreeing. This deep cultural preference helps to explain the reluctance of many CEE enterprises to shed their responsibilities for the welfare of workers and their families, in spite of economic imperatives to do so. These two dimensions illuminate the peculiar quality of organizational relationships in CEE, paradoxically humanistic and harsh, more satisfactorily than notions of masculinity versus femininity.

Regarding honesty and integrity, Puffer and McCarthy (1995) note traditional Russian culture's dual ethics system, with "deception in business dealings, but fealty in friendship". This would place Russia in the category of a particularist culture according to Trompenaars' (1993) typology of universalism versus particularism. Thus, stealing from the workplace was a heinous crime under Communist law, but people engaged in it almost routinely. *Blat,* the use of palm-greasing tactics to secure favours, such as a source of supply or a reduced production target in the plan, was customary. Where this became unethical was in the use of *blat* for personal gain, rather than for the benefit of the organization as a whole and its employees. The fifth dimension concerning the ways in which people relate to one another in a culture, ascription/ achievement, focuses on the ways in which a culture accords unequal status to its members. Here, the results obtained by Trompenaars are inconclusive on the CEE countries, except for a strong tendency towards ascription as compared with the UK and USA. This supports other studies which suggest that individually-based reward systems based on individual achievement targets may be less culturally acceptable in these countries (Walsh et al., 1993, although this trait may change as people are forced more and more onto their own resources for survival. This is one way in which the strength of a cultural trait might be skewed by the force of rapid change in the environment, i.e. tempering a trait that would tend to be stronger in more stable conditions. It is equally possible that the opposite might occur, for example, a short-term orientation to the future being exacerbated by the double pressure of strong uncertainty avoidance and high objective levels of uncertainty in the environment.

## Constraints on Cultural Theories

It is worth noting that Hofstede stresses that in his study, the dimensions accounted for just half of the differences between countries, the other half remaining specific to the particular countries. Clearly, dimensional cultural frameworks, while seductive, suffer from constraints and limitations due to the impossibility of carrying out systematic and reliable social research during the Communist period, and to the constant upheavals in the social, economic and political environments of the CEE countries since 1989. For the cross-cultural traveller, it is important to bear in mind always that cultural differences belong to whole populations: within any group interaction, individual differences will be more salient than cultural differences. And while there may be evident "fit" between characteristics of a national culture and organizational structures and systems "typical" of that culture, no claims to causality or determinism can be made.

Whichever dimensional framework we adopt, it is nevertheless clear that, while there are distinct and significant differences between countries, the region as a whole shares a cultural character which distinguishes it from the Southern European countries fringing the Mediterranean, and the post-industrial secular societies of North Western Europe.

The configuration of culture in the region resembles a patchwork quilt, in that each portion of the quilt may use prints of slightly different shade and detail, but overall, patterns emerge to repeat themselves. So when contrasting CEE with other geographical regions, the similarities are most salient (this is evident in Trompenaars' (1993) study); but when comparing Poland with Russia, Hungary with Bulgaria, and so on, the differences come into focus. As an example of this intra-regional distinctiveness, Jankowicz (1994) describes the roots of Polish managers' abiding "idiosyncratic stance towards authority", lying in the 15th century consolidation and ensuing endurance of the power of the nobility. Thus, Poles continue to address one another in aristocratic terms ("Pan" translating as "Lord"), and regard an autocratic style differently from the conventional Anglo-Saxon view: "the management style which [Westerners] call "autocratic" represents the responsible, paternal and hence ultimately protective stance without which the enterprise might easily fragment" (Jankowicz, 1994: 486).

# MANAGEMENT IN THE PAST

## The Soviet-era Manager

To unravel the dynamic tangle of management change in CEE, we must trace the thread of the legacy of Soviet-era management styles and practices. Who was the manager, what had shaped him (for it was almost invariably a male), and how did he respond to the events which unfolded after the breach of the Berlin wall?

Reporting on their experiences of training managers in CEE, Millman and Randlesome (1993) noted that a large proportion of senior managers were middle-aged. We can therefore assume that the majority received their scientific and professional education in the 1960s and 1970s, when scientific management principles were in the ascendant in the region, and that the career path described by Richman (1967) was typical of them and their contemporaries. As many as 90% of enterprise directors had an engineering background. On recruitment to an enterprise, a graduate engineer would be assigned to a period of 3 years work on the shop floor. Following that, promotion was generally straight up the line. Thus, managers in all industries and services were educated in the technology of their particular sector, but were almost totally ignorant of general management principles as they are understood in the West (Korotov et al., 1995), top managers often retaining the title "Chief Engineer" (Puffer, 1981; Hosking, 1992; Hibbert, 1991; Millman and Randlesome, 1993). Once in top management, they were generally content to stay at the head of the enterprise, as moving up into the ministerial apparatus held few rewards. Neither these directors nor the central planners saw management itself as a distinct area of knowledge, and the fact that they did not regard the skills of leadership as transferable from one industry to another led to a dearth of well-educated generalists at higher levels.

The stultifying effect of being in essence a state functionary charged with delivering the targets of the central plan is described by Richman (1967); Naylor (1988). Yet it would be an undue simplification to conclude that, as functionaries, enterprise directors were powerless or ineffectual. On the contrary, general directors of the major gas and oil enterprises liked to refer to themselves as "lions" or "tigers" (Holden et al., 1998).

The constraints of the command economy were such that the manager had to exercise considerable authority and occasional ingenuity to get the plan met; generating a management style described by Lawrence and Vlachoutsicos (1993) as "freedom to exercise authority while avoiding responsibility".

Although managers would spend relatively little time on formal human resource management processes (Lawrence and Vlachoutsicos, 1993), there was a strong tradition that the boss should be both accessible to his people, at whatever level in the organization, and should take an interest in their personal affairs (Komarov, 1991). At first sight this conflicts with the notion of high power distance. Paternalism labours under an apparent contradiction, as all this was to be accomplished with relatively little delegation of tasks or, in particular, decision-making responsibility (Puffer, 1993). Despite the apparent common touch of the boss there was little real democracy or fostering of participation in decision-making.

Patronage and influence were, and continue to be, key aspects of organizational culture, and illuminate the paternalistic nature of the leader's power. Paternalism does not necessarily imply any particular love or loyalty towards workers. On the contrary, May and Bormann (1993) noted managers' distrust and disdain for the workforce. Kublin (1990) observed that the Soviet-era manager had neither a carrot nor a stick. The tremendous pressures on him from above to fulfil the quarterly output targets, coupled with the limitations of the workforce, in a society which viewed individuals as expendable factors of production, led to an outwardly authoritarian and uncaring attitude, and internal anxiety and tension.

Differences between Western and Soviet-era conceptions of hierarchy are illustrated by the metaphor of the matrioshka, the traditional set of Russian nesting dolls in which each doll snugly holds another smaller one, down to the very tiniest (Vlachoutsicos, 1986; Vlachoutsicos and Lawrence, 1990; Lawrence and Vlachoutsicos, 1994). As well as being culturally apt, it neatly demonstrates how the Soviet-era system of task units differed from the commonly accepted Western model of hierarchy. In the Soviet-era system, *every* manager was responsible for *everything* in the hierarchy underneath him, and thus even the top man had to concern himself with fundamental operational issues. Lawrence and Vlachoutsicos (1994) emphasize the punishing long hours worked by the Soviet manager, and the time spent walking round the plant, discussing routine operational matters with line workers, which in a Western factory would be left to the foreman or junior managerial level. This tendency, coupled with the fear of the dire consequences of making mistakes (Vlachoutsicos, 1986; Manoukovsky, 1993), contributed to the dual system described by Vlachoutsicos (1986) as a combination of collective decision-making and one-man management (in Russian: *edinonachalie*). This sheds some light on the apparent paradox that, in the (Western) frameworks for conceptualizing culture, Eastern European cultures may appear at once both collectivist *and* (for the manager) individualistic. At the operational level, problems might be analyzed, options might be discussed, solutions might be put forward, by the team, but before any decision could be put into effect, however minor, it would have to go right up the line for ratification and legitimization, and then come back down again for implementation. Given that the stakes were so high, it is not surprising that Walsh et al.

(1993) in their experimental study of motivational approaches in a Russian factory found that a participatory style of management was generally unpopular.

## Systemic Crisis

Heads of enterprises were constantly fighting fires, metaphorically speaking. In the haphazard and often hostile environment of the Soviet-era industrial enterprise, accomplishing even the most routine tasks could take up reserves of energy and tenacity. It was commonplace for workers to stand idle for the first 2 months of a quarter, waiting for supplies to arrive or the crucial missing machine part to be installed, only to work at breakneck speed, night and day (known as "storming") to meet the targets, which had been set with no consideration for the problems of supply. A senior manager's powers of upward influence on the plan were crucial both to the success of his organization and to the satisfaction of the workforce (Aguilar et al., 1994). And, of course, his own fortunes rested on his ability to meet targets handed down from above (McCarthy, 1991). Puffer (1994) proposed that drive is a strong element of the Russian management arsenal, but that during the communist period its western concomitant, initiative, had been systematically stifled by the Communist Party. This was the case throughout CEE. While Party membership was not compulsory for managers, the further one went up the organizational hierarchy the more important good Party connections became (Vlachoutsicos and Lawrence, 1990; McCarthy, 1991; Orlov, 1991; Manoukovsky, 1993; Millman and Randlesome, 1993; Soulsby, 1999). For the relatively particularist cultures of Bulgaria and Russia (according to Trompenaars' framework) this would not create such tensions and internal problems as for the more universalist cultures of Poland and former Czechoslovakia.

Manoukovsky (1993) draws attention to the paradox of the plan at the top and crisis management at the bottom. Production shortfalls were a routine hazard of intermittent supplies and lack of investment in up-to-date capital equipment (Halborg and Adcock, 1993; Naylor, 1988; Louis et al., 1990; Filtzer, 1994). The top boss of every major organization had his fixer who spent his time on missions to do deals, often bartering, with other organizations (Hibbert, 1991; Holden et al., 1998). Managers were not willing to be open about this (Hibbert, 1991, which may go some way to explaining why the perception developed in the West that initiative was not a feature of Soviet management. This is not illogical: ingenuity and tenacity in securing supplies was needed but by the same token could not be openly valued (after all, central planning was supposed to work).

The extent of the waste, material and human, in the CEE economies was apparent as early as the mid-1950s (Richman, 1967; Hosking, 1992). The region in general, Russia in particular, is also noted for its vast natural resources but appalling waste, and destruction of the environment (Solzhenitsyn, 1991; Millman and Randlesome, 1993; Yergin and Gustafson, 1994; Pearson and Rondinelli, 1998). By the 1960s even Kosygin was exhorting the Central Committee of the Communist Party that something needed to be done about the waste endemic in the industrial system. Periodic and chronic labour shortages rendered this problem particularly acute. To speak of labour shortages in a situation of waste may seem paradoxical. However, the dynamic of industry dictated that enterprise managers should hoard labour in order to fulfil the plans at the close of each quarter, and so enterprise directors were in competition with one another to recruit and retain the best workers. Any enterprise that could offer better housing than the next was at a premium with the workforce, and labour turnover was a constant problem, except in one-enterprise towns. Newman and Nollen (1998) found that, as late as 1995, Czech managers still tended to fret about not "meeting the plan".

# MANAGEMENT IN TRANSITION

## Theatres of Change

### *Poland, Hungary, Czech Republic*

These countries, together with Slovakia, constitute the Visegrad group, named after their agreement in Visegrad in 1991 to adopt joint policies toward the European Union. Poland and Hungary, in particular, have generally been considered the "success stories" of the post-1989 era (Edwards, 1997; Blazyca, 1997), being further down the road to the market economy and contemplating the real prospect of admission to the European Union in 2005. Poland is feted as a "beacon for the rest of Europe" in the business press (Business Week, 28 June 1999: 58), even as her economy suffers the body blow of falling exports, caused by economic slowdowns in Italy, and the Russian financial collapse (Transition, August 1999). Culturally, these countries are distinctive, because they retained throughout the Communist period some vestiges of their former selves. Prior to World War II, all the countries in this cluster had an established tradition of looking west, rather than east, in economic and cultural terms (Davies, 1996). Due to its extensive industrialization in the 19th century, Czechoslovakia, for example, had been one of the most industrially-advanced countries of Europe before the Second World War (Newman and Nollen, 1998), on a par with Austria and Germany (although admittedly the centre of gravity of the economy had been the western areas around Prague). The trauma of the Soviet invasion of 1968 left a psychic scar on the Czech people and fuelled a national sense of destiny separate from the rest of the Soviet bloc. Borrowing Hofstede's (1991) metaphor for culture of "software of the mind", the Czech people under communism are a good example that this software is not readily re-programmable.

Each country has seen severe turbulence and systemic shocks, and for none has the course of progress to a market economy been smooth (Dangerfield, 1997; Edwards, 1997; Blazyca, 1997). In spite of promising forecasts, Poland's industrial development has been patchy since 1989. Her major private sector growth industries have been food and drink and construction (Blazyca, 1997). The electrical and mechanical engineering industries, which at 27.5% accounted for the largest proportion of Polish employment in 1993 (Blazyca, 1997), have experienced difficulties in responding to their exposure to the global marketplace. Here though, particularly in the automotive industry, there are stories of significant inward investment. Hungary had a tradition of small and medium enterprises which gave strong impetus to the rapid development of small-scale entrepreneurship after 1989 (Bogel and Huszty, 1999; Edwards, 1997). From the late 1960s onwards, Hungary had extended possibilities for companies to engage with market transactions, and had liberalized external trade to some extent, but the political regime remained largely unchanged (Child and Czegledy, 1996). While Hungary has had a disproportionate share of the region's foreign direct investment (FDI) since 1990 (Radice, 1995), there have been expressions of large-scale negative feelings about the influx of multinational companies, who are seen as threatening to Hungarian industry, for instance because of their ability to avoid import duties on finished products or components (Pearson and Rondinelli, 1998). In the Czech Republic, manufacturing industry remains the most important economical sector, although service industries contribute one-third of GDP (Dangerfield, 1997). The Czech Republic benefits from a relatively well-developed transport and service infrastructure, and its wealth of tourist attractions, both natural and architectural, offers considerable potential for foreign earnings.

## Slovakia, Bulgaria and Romania

Since the "Velvet Divorce" between the Czech Republic and Slovakia in 1993, Slovakia's pace of change has lagged behind that of its partners; a lag generally blamed on its relative dependence on former Soviet markets, its lack of shared borders with Western states, and the fact that Bratislava remains far less of a magnet for foreign income than its big sister Prague (Dangerfield, 1997). Add to this mix the corrupt government of ex-premier Vladimir Meciar (Frydman et al., 1996, who set back the pace of reform and put paid to Slovakia's hopes for an early entry to the European Union, and for our purposes Slovakia fits better with a group of "laggard" satellite states of the Soviet bloc, along with Bulgaria and Romania.

## Russia and the FSU

Despite the former dominance of Russia during the Soviet era, the 1990s has seen Russian organizations experience the most profound turbulence in its environment, the most catastrophic fall-off in production, and the least progress in the slow development of the institutions of a stable civil society, the foundation of a robust market economy. The economic crash of August 1998 was only one of a series of body blows to the fragile emerging market economy in Russia. Subsequent revelations of the extent of state, company and bank complicity in the exit and laundering of billions of dollars out of the country, dubbed the "iron triangle" (Transition, August 1999), compounded by evidence of Western collusion, have further shaken public confidence in business and the market. At the time of writing the world is witnessing a virtual meltdown of the Russian state, as Yeltsin, with almost medieval fervour, dismisses one government after another. As much as economic, the "bankruptcy of Yeltsin's Russia has been moral, ethical and political" (Moscow Times, 17 August 1999).

## The Drive to the Market

In the conditions of centralized planning and shortage in which the enterprise director had to lead, the traits and behaviours of the Soviet-era top manager were indeed functional and effective. And furthermore, to ensure that the organization could survive in the hurly-burly conditions of hyperinflation, boom-bust cycles and political turmoil characteristic of transition, strong-hand management (Manoukovsky, 1993) *continued* to present to many the most rational and credible option. Survival today is still, for most organizations, more important than long-term growth strategy. This may militate against the adoption of "modern" participative management techniques. In an emergency situation, an autocratic style of management may well seem more appropriate. If he starts to ask for advice, Manoukovsky (1993) warns, the image of the boss suffers, and worker confidence melts away.

Case studies of Western consultant interventions in management development indicate that CEE top managers, particularly those in heavy or extractive industries, often still view as positive the qualities seen by Western analysts as negative (Simon and Davies, 1995; Gilbert, 1998). An example is the difference in perceptions between a group of top oil and gas industry managers from Western Siberia, and a group of Tacis (EU) project consultants. What Westerners perceived as their main weaknesses (lacking in skills of marketing, pricing, cost accounting, planning, customer service), top managers saw as irrelevant to their role, which was to lead and command their organizations, and (formerly) to procure the necessary raw materials and components to meet the plan, making use of complex networking and negotiating skills (Gilbert, 1996). Those Westerners who were effective in that environment had the sensitivity to understand that their own effectiveness also was entirely dependent on a complex web of relationships. They fostered those relationships, and "learned to strike deals in a shadowy world of nods and winks where what counted was not formalized agreement but dependable complicity" (Wedel, 1998: 61).

Organizations may act in response to changes in the competitive environment, as described by Romanelli and Tushman (1994) but the experience of CEE suggests that as the scale and pace of environmental change increases, so environmental change shapes and conditions organizational change. Leaders may meet this challenge in one of three ways; proactively, either by embracing radical rather than incremental change (Newman and Nollen, 1998) or adopting a "punctuated equilibrium" approach alternating periods of rapid change with periods of respite (Romanelli and Tushman, 1994); or defensively by seeking to minimize internal changes and adopting a strategy of basic survival. The latter has been more characteristic of the Russian industrial manager, and Newman and Nollen (1998) give evidence that, even in the more benign environment of Czech Republic, true radical change has been comparatively rare. Of six enterprises which they studied in depth, only one had embraced a radical change strategy, discarding old core values. Three of the six were undergoing incremental changes in values relating to the relationship of the enterprise to its workers. No longer was continuing employment and a regular pay-packet seen as a right, and employment was now being seen more in terms of a contract contingent on performance. Still, in spite of needing far fewer employees than before the revolution, what downsizing had occurred tended to be very much at the behest of foreign strategic partners.

For CEE companies to compete effectively in the European market, they are forced to adopt the stringent quality procedures that have become the norm in the West. In CEE, where public shareholders rarely have enough power to influence decisions, and insider ownership often means top manager control of assets (Afanassieva, 1999), quality drives very much depend on managerial commitment. Usually, this comes down to one or two determined individual managers. This realization has a profound impact on managers, who are compelled to engage with a lengthy and tortuous process of assessment, investment and implementation. The drive for international accreditation such as ISO 9000 can only be led by someone with a high level of technical ability, who can command the unconditional respect of the workforce, and who is prepared to supervise all of the key stages personally, from documenting procedures to obtaining scarce capital for new equipment (Pearson and Rondinelli, 1998).

The picture regarding quality is by no means uniform, and can be paradoxical: it challenges the stereotype that all CEE products are technically inferior to their Western equivalents. Newman and Nollen (1998) cite the example of a Czech boiler making plant which had been manufacturing boilers to last at least 25 years and to withstand more adverse conditions than could reasonably be expected over the life of the product. They had been regarded as a "family silver" firm. Management strongly resisted cost pressures to get them to manufacture to a 15-year product lifespan, more standard to the market.

## The View from the Shop Floor

Employees share widespread perceptions that entrepreneurship is tainted by links with corruption and organized crime. In the early days of transition, when legislation and sources of finance were chaotic and inadequate to say the least, many managers were forced to work "at the margins of legality" (Bateman, 1997: 229) to survive. Ten years on, while the spectre of organized crime still dominates the common perception of business, especially in Russia, the average shop-floor worker continues to see entrepreneurial management as a threat. There are grounds for deep reservations about how far the rhetoric of management change has penetrated into the fabric of organizational life. As one manager in the study of Czech enterprises carried out by Soulsby and Clark (1996: 247) summed it up: "All the top managers have changed their views, but the workers still don't even know the words."

One of the paradoxes about "new" management ideas about team working and participation is that they may echo old thinking and ways of organizing the workforce. Exhortations to team working and increasing productivity may have an uncomfortable resonance with the rhetoric used by Party apparatchiks in the past, as one interviewee in a case study of a joint venture reflected: "some of the objectives and principles formulated in the mission statements and published in nice brochures and on plastic cards weirdly resemble the ill-famed slogans of the former regime" (Bogel and Huczsty, 1999: 364). On the other hand, Cosma and Duvel (1998), in a study of the development of total quality management (TQM) in the Bulgarian construction industry, suggest that, of the five key concepts of TQM (training, empowerment, partnering, teamwork and benchmarking), teamwork and partnering resonate with Eastern European companies *because* similar concepts were popular under communism, while other concepts, particularly empowerment, are difficult for managers (and presumably workers) to grasp. Effective change programmes therefore have to build on the foundation of existing knowledge and values, emphasizing aspects of the old ways of working which are robust and which strike a positive chord. The tradition of paternalism in leadership style endures in Russia. Access for the workers to their bosses still tends to be seen as a right. Managers remain: "ready to make exceptions for those who come to talk to them even if it is against established rules, and this is why most employees seek direct contact with the CEO. Furthermore, the image of a good manager in Russia is always associated with those who spend much of their time talking to people about their private questions, and requests." Manoukovsky (1993; 29). Puffer (1994), found that in some newer organizations younger managers did seem prepared to share power and adopt a more collegial style of decision-making than the Red Executives who clung to the principle of *edinonachalie*.

Nasierowski and Mikula (1998: 499) describe the outward signs of continuing high power distance in Poland vividly: "People make an effort to look powerful, which can be reflected in the high status of things…it should not come as a surprise that many Poles own cars whose price exceed their yearly salary. Large differences between wages and privileges are likely…. Managers do not see themselves as practical and systematic, yet they deny a need for support and tend to avoid consultations with subordinates before making decisions."

## The Role of the West

Early in the transition process, the assumption was that, with the shackles of the command economy removed, the former Comecon countries would undergo rapid restructuring of industry, reconstruction of the infrastructures of society, and be well on the way to functioning markets before the end of the century. The infamous 500-day Shatalin plan gave "a major priority to the management training of Soviet executives in Western business practices" (Hibbert, 1991). For a while, management education and training provided by Western experts, either in the West or in the East, appeared to offer a panacea across the region. For example, Csath (1989) in Hungary, Kozminski (1992, 1996) in Poland, Nicolescu (1992) in Romania, and Shekshnia (1991) in Russia, all made a strong positive case for management training on Western lines. Vikhanskii (1991) argued in contrast that it was of little use sending relatively small numbers of Eastern managers to the West for training when, in his country, "business schools are almost as easy to set up as shish-kebab stands at busy intersections" and, therefore, were at that time staffed by teachers who were at least as ignorant about business in the market economy as their students. Better, he argued, to train Eastern lecturers instead. A note of caution was expressed by Auerbach and Stone (1991). They were concerned about Western governments and managers' certainty about transferability of Western management techniques into the Eastern European, context. They based their scepticism on:

- the degree of variance in the speed and level of implementation in the West of new and presumed "better" approaches;
- the time it takes to transfer economic and managerial knowledge, experience and techniques, and the difficulties involved;
- the degree to which socialist (sic) approaches to management have become integrated in social and economic behaviour in the East.

Time has shown their caution to be well-founded, on all three counts. As with changes in organizations and management, so we see that there are differences in the ways that the countries of CEE have interacted with, and reacted to, Western organizations and programmes.

The Polish press coined the term "Marriott Brigade" for the army of Western short-term consultants who descended on the new Marriott Hotel in Warsaw, and used that as their base for their forays out to enterprises, via other international hotels (Wedel, 1998). They were glamorous, looked the part, and talked the talk, but left disillusion and scepticism in their wake. Hungarian managers complained of a succession of consultants arriving, engaging management in meetings for hours on end, taking away large quantities of information, finally producing a very short report with little new information or analysis. In the case of the CIS, the EU Tacis Interim Evaluation report (EC, 1997: 26) admits that, in the early years, "studies to understand how to transfer and what to transfer were the dominant forms of TA (technical assistance)". This led to an impression that consultants were often more concerned with demonstrating their own credentials to the donor agencies than in actually meeting the needs of the client organization (Gilbert, 1998). Wedel (1998) suggests that "the honeymoon was over" in Warsaw, Budapest and Prague as early as 1991, but that the Marriott Brigade simply moved east. (Indeed, there were signs in the literature of some disillusionment early on; see, for example, Kwiatowski and Sanders, 1993.)

Wedel (1998) bemoans the dismal failure of donors and consultants to recognize or *acknowledge* that privatization was not neutral or technical, but suffused with deep political significance. She observes that Western assistance could be perceived as helpful if and when consultants were seen by local officials and the public as advocates for the recipient nation. This was all too seldom the case. In Poland, Solidarity unionists set themselves against the activities of foreign consultants, for instance painting over the Ursus tractor factory entrance the message "A Foreign Elite Steals from Us while the Polish People are at the Bottom" (Wedel, 1998: 70).

In 1996, a step forward in mutual understanding between Russian top managers and Western consultants was made at a seminar organized by the Russian National Training Foundation, an opportunity for Westerners and Russians to explore their mutual perceptions (Holden et al, 1998; Vlachoutsicos et al, 1997). Regarding the attitude of top managers to consultants, it was felt that the consultancy business is distorted by foreign aid; it is regarded as "easy money" for consultants and beneficiaries alike, and so is not highly valued. Managers sometimes displayed contradictory attitudes, at once seeing consultants as arriving in the nick of time, like the Seventh Cavalry, to save the enterprise, and as agents of foreign powers, spying out the best takeover targets.

# MANAGEMENT OF THE FUTURE: TRANSITION OR TRANSFORMATION?

The term "transition" implies a teleological assumption that the destination of change is known and that the route is marked out. The anticipation of EU membership in the foreseeable future justifies the term "transition" for the Visegrad countries. "Transformation" demands a process of destruction and disintegration – perhaps more appropriate to the agonizing processes in the more Eastern countries of the region. Aspects of the management styles and practices of former and current eras, as outlined above, provide *prima facie* support for viewing the organizational cultures of CEE as being at once in flux and more resistant to change than some may have expected. Like a great river, culture has its currents and eddies. The extent of management change depends, not only on the country, but on which sector of the economy we look at, and on the choice of management or workforce perspective.

Industries slow to privatize and requiring major capital investment display management styles not far removed from the old days, except that attention to the vagaries of the Ministry plan has been replaced by attention to vagaries of the economy and fiscal system.

Everywhere change in heavy industry has tended to lag behind the development of light manufacturing and service industries, partly because of the vast amounts of capital investment needed to transform these industries, and to a large extent because they tend to be the last areas of the economy to be privatized, along with energy and extractive industries (Blazyca, 1997; Bateman, 1997; Newman and Nollen, 1998). One of the most striking features of the 1990s across the whole region has been how resistant to change, and how impervious to pressure, has been the dominant bureaucratic-administrative elite. Indeed, Bateman (1997: 228) maintains that "rent-seeking" through maintaining monopolistic market structures, has often been a sounder opportunity to make money than "competing through increased productivity, cost-minimization, attention to quality, and so on". "Crony capitalism" and the "kleptoklatura" are hard to shift, and Frydman et al (1996: 6) see this as a key issue for the near future:

"The post-communist transition thus requires, for economic as much as political reasons, that many of the old guard make room for the next generation of business leaders. It is that process that gets stymied by the managerial entrenchment resulting from nomenklatura privatization."

While everyone suffered to some extent in the economic crisis of August 1998, the embryonic, young professional middle class of Russia were particularly hit. These were not the wealthy new Russians, whose money had been made in ransacking the assets of old industries, but educated and highly-motivated employees of multinational companies and new local small and medium enterprises. In the space of 2 weeks, hundreds of thousands of twenty- or thirty-somethings, optimistic and affluent, lost their jobs and most of their savings as the banks shut up shop, and their Western expatriate colleagues packed up and left. It was a wake-up call to tell them the party was over and the real work was just beginning. Only time will tell what will happen to this new generation who carry within their number Russia's store of knowledge of finance, of marketing, and of Western styles of management. However, early indications are that the genie is out of the bottle, and change will continue. Some of these professionals have seen an opportunity in the slump in imports and have moved into small-scale manufacturing of consumer goods, with some success (Banerjee, 1999; Hoffman, 1999). In the service sector, mobile telecoms for example, small companies established and managed by young entrepreneurs are growing, dynamic, risk-taking, and aggressive in their marketing strategies. Managers display an informal style with employees, the rhetoric of teamwork is used. Yet, whether power distance appears to be diminishing, whether relationships between bosses and subordinates may *appear* less formal, there is little evidence that the locus of decision-making is becoming decentralized.

The term transformation implies a level of cultural transformation in core values – is there evidence that this is happening? Yes, among young managers and entrepreneurs who will form the vanguard of the new market-oriented enterprises. But they will have to challenge and combat a great deal of internalized and deeply entrenched traditional values. Small-scale research studies focusing on the attitudes and behaviours of managers should avoid the assumption that, because some individuals have changed their behaviour, the cultural values of workforces at large have also changed. Some of these values may have utility in the transition environment and be worth hanging on to, even protecting and nurturing: others may be subject to a dysfunctional de-coupling of values and behaviours, giving rise to psychological stress and inter-generational conflict. At the very least, ambiguities may be apparent in local organizational cultures, such as the need both for strong leadership and for decisions to receive the validating support of informal groupings, and such as the simultaneous weakness of individualism and rejection of collectivism, at least in the sense of the communist past (Nasierowski and Mikula, 1998). A similar ambiguity exists in attitudes towards time horizons; the objective fact of environmental change at breakneck speed does not imply low uncertainty avoidance, in Hofstede's (1991) terms, but in a high UA culture may give rise to high levels of social distress and ill-health, as the UN has observed in its report (UNDP, 1999).

The dimensions of Trompenaars' (1993) framework, in particular, resonate with impressions that CEE countries in general are more collectivist in nature, more diffuse in relationships, and more particularistic in application of norms than the US, Germany, and the UK. We cannot as yet draw any hard and fast conclusions about the way in which national cultures help or hinder the management change process in organizations in CEE. Certainly, there is need for future research, quantitative and qualitative, to map the contours of change in cultural characteristics of these countries over time. The jury remains out. Trompenaars himself reported at a meeting of the British Academy of Management in 1999 that follow-up surveys carried out in Russia through the 1990s show massive attitudinal swings, although Poland, Czech Republic and Hungary do appear to be stabilizing.

There would seem to be insufficient differences between these cultures, judging from the scanty data which we have so far, to explain the differentials in performance between, say Poland and Bulgaria, or Czech Republic and Russia. Naumov (1996) writes; "There is growing understanding of the business environments of the transitional economies, and how these business environments differ from one another. But we have no single definitive interpretation as yet on the true nature of the wider cultural contexts of the transitional economies, in which the business environment can be perceived as a subsystem". And yet we can see a compelling underlying logic at work. The countries of CEE are differentiated by the degree to which they have been able to attract, and retain, foreign investment, and the degree to which their own organizations have adapted to the developing marketplace. The demarcation lines in these clusters also correlate imperfectly, but noticeably, with apparent cultural tendencies, such as the higher levels of universalism in Poland and Czechoslovakia than those countries further East. But it would be a mistake to uncouple cultural variables from historical experience. The essential differential between these countries is as likely to be the fact that the Visegrad countries displayed key elements of modernity prior to falling under the Communist yoke. This marks them out from their less developed, and pre-modern, neighbours, and sets the course for transition. Grancelli (1995: 3) argues persuasively that the USSR displayed a phoney modernity, which disintegrated back into pre-modern chaos. "The new legislation on property rights is still ambiguous, contradictory, and subject to the interpretations of the local bureaucracy.... The support institutions are still rather primitive, and...management is more often than not engaged in survival practices which have little in common with the need to improve efficiency to reduce production and transaction costs". While culture is a key element in predicting whether change will be acceptable, recent history (the fate of the countries of CEE in the Second World War, their subsequent roles and fortunes in the Soviet era, their ability to attract foreign investment), is at least as significant in shaping management change in transition (Soulsby and Clark, 1996). These factors, coupled with the integrity of the new states and their institutions, will determine management optimism and confidence as much as underlying tendencies in national cultures. Culture may not set the direction or even the speed of change, but will be a major influence on the processes of adaptation and acceptance of change within the firm or organization.

# REFERENCES

Afanassieva, M. (1999) Managerial responses and enterprise adjustment: the case of the Russian defence industry. Proceedings of 5th Annual CREEB conference, on "The impact of Transformation on Individuals, Organizations and Society". Buckinghamshire Business School, Chalfont St Giles.

Aguilar, F.J., Loveman, G.W. and Vlachoutsikos, C.A. (1994) The Managerial Challenge in Central and Eastern Europe: as Viewed from within. Harvard Business School Working Paper 95-041. Cambridge, MA: Harvard Business School.

Auerbach, P. and Stone, M. (1991) Developing the new capitalism in Eastern Europe – How the West can Help. Long Range Planning, 24 (3): 58–65.

Banerjee, N. (1999) From Russia's Chaos, a New Breed of Entrepreneur. New York Times, July 20, p. 4.

Bateman, M. (1997) Business Cultures in Central and Eastern Europe. London: Butterworth Heinemann.

Blazyca, G. (1997) The business culture in Poland. In M. Bateman (Ed), Business Cultures in Central and Eastern Europe. London: Butterworth Heinemann, 60–87.

Bogel, G. and Huszty, A. (1999) Strategy making in Hungary. In Proceedings of 5th Annual CREEB Conference, on "The Impact of Transformation on Individuals, Organizations and Society", Buckinghamshire Business School, Chalfont St Giles, 358–365.

Bollinger, D. (1994) The four cornerstones and three pillars in the 'House of Russia' management system, Journal of Management Development, 13 (2): 49–54.

Business Week (1999) Poland: a beacon for the rest of Europe. Business Week, 28 June: 58.

Child, J. and Czegledy, A. (1996) Managerial learning in the transformation of Eastern Europe: some key issues. Organization Studies, 17 (2): 167–179.

Cosma, C. and Duvel, C. (1998) Total quality management in Eastern European construction: the paradigm shift. Total Quality Management, 9 (4–5): 38–40.

Csath, M. (1989) Management education for developing entrepreneurship in Hungary. In J. Davies, M. Easterby-Smith, S. Manns and M. Tanton (Eds), The Challenge to Western Management Development. London: Routledge, 137–151.

Dangerfield, M. (1997) The business culture in the Czech Republic. In M. Bateman (Ed), Business Cultures in Central and Eastern Europe. London: Butterworth Heinemann, 1–34.

Davies, N. (1996) Europe: a History. Oxford: Oxford University Press.

Edwards, V. (1997) The business culture in Hungary. In M. Bateman (Ed) (1997) Business Cultures in Central and Eastern Europe. London: Butterworth Heinemann, 35–59.

Filtzer, D. (1994) Soviet Workers and the Collapse of Perestroika. Cambridge: CUP.

Frydman, R., Murphy, K. and Rapaczynski, A. (1996) Capitalism with a comrade's face. Budapest: Central European University Press.

Gilbert, K. (1996) Management education and organisation development: the case of the Russian oil and gas industry. Journal of European Business Education, 6 (1): 14–31.

Gilbert, K. (1998) Consultancy fatigue: epidemiology, symptoms and prevention. Leadership and Organisation Development Journal, 19 (6): 340–346.

Grancelli, B. (1995) Organizational change: towards a new East-West comparison. Organization Studies Wntr, 16 (1): 1–25.

Halborg, A. and Adcock, D. (1993) Management education and perestroika. Journal of European Business Education, 3 (1): 21–35.

Hibbert, N. (1991) Management development; first principles. Argumenty i Fakty (Arguments and Facts), 2 (3): 7–8.

Hingley, R. (1978) The Russian Mind. London: Bodley Head.

Hoffman, D. (1999) Fall of ruble, it turns out, was a boon to Russia's industry. International Herald Tribune, August 17, 1999.

Hofstede, G. (1980). Culture's Consequences: International Differences in Work-related Values. Beverly Hills, CA: Sage Publications.

Hofstede, G. (1991) Cultures and Organizations: Software of the Mind. Maidenhead: McGraw-Hill.

Hofstede, G. (1993) Cultural constraints in management theories. Academy of Management Executive, 7 (1): 81–94.

Hofstede, G. and Bond, M.H. (1988) The Confucius connection: from cultural roots to economic growth. Organizational Dynamics, 16 (4): 4–21.

Holden, N.J., Cooper, C.L. and Carr, J. (1998) Dealing with the New Russia. Chichester: John Wiley.

Hosking, G. (1992) A History of the Soviet Union, 1917-1991. London: Fontana.

Jankowicz, A.D. (1994) The new journey to Jerusalem: mission and meaning in the managerial crusade to Eastern Europe. Organization Studies, 15 (4): 479–507.

Kelemen, M. and Gardiner, K. (1999) Paradoxes of managerial work: the case of Ghana and Romania. Proceedings of 5th Annual CREEB Conference, on "The impact of Transformation on Individuals, Organizations and Society". Buckinghamshire Business School, Chalfont St Giles, 278–297.

Komarov, E.I. (1991) The Woman Manager. Soviet Education, 33 (11): 56–81.

Korotov, K., Makeshin, A. and Stepanova, I. (1995) Is there any future for organizational development in the New Independent States? Organization Development Journal, 13 (3): 33–39.

Kostera, M. (1995) The modern crusade: the missionaries of management come to Eastern Europe. Management Learning, 26 (3): 331–352.

Kostera, M. (1996) The manager's new clothes: on identity transfer in post-1989 Poland. In M. Lee, H. Letiche, R. Crawshaw and M. Thomas. (Eds), Management Education in the New Europe. London: Thompson Business Press, 194–211.

Kozminski, A.K. (1992) Transition from planned to market economy: Hungary and Poland compared. Studies in Comparative Communism, 15 (4): 315–333.

Kozminski, A.K. (1996) Management education in the transitional economies of Central and Eastern Europe.

In M. Lee, H. Litiche, R. Crawshaw and M. Thomas (Eds), Management Education in the New Europe. London: Thompson Business Press, 163–179.

Kublin, M. (1990) The Soviet factory director: a window on Eastern Bloc Manufacturing. Industrial Management, March–April, 21-26.

Kwiatowski, S. and Sanders, P. (1993) Management development assistance for Poland: a playground for Western consultants. Journal of Management Development, 12 (1): 56–63.

Lawrence, P. and Vlachoutsicos, C. (1993) Joint ventures in Russia: put the locals in charge. Harvard Business Review, 71 (1): 44–54.

Lawrence, P. and Vlachoutsicos, C. (1994) Behind the Factory Walls: Decision-making in Soviet and Russian Enterprises. Boston, MA: Harvard Business School Press.

Louis, N., Mamut, A., Charkham, R. and Warren, A. (1990) Doing Business in the USSR. London: Kogan Page.

Luthans, F., Welsh, D.H.B. and Rosenkrantz, S.A. (1993) What do Russian Managers really do? An observational study with comparisons to US managers. Journal of International Business, 24 (1): 741–761.

Manoukovsky, A. (1993) Russian Management: How Far from the West? EFMD Forum, 93/2: 28–32.

May, R.C. and Bormann, C.J. (1993) Managerial Practices in the Former Soviet Union. Multinational Business Review, 1 (2): 67–73.

McCarthy, D.J. (1991) Developing a programme for Soviet managers. Journal of Management Development, 10 (5): 26–31.

Millman, T. and Randlesome, C. (1993) Developing top Russian managers. Management Education and Development, 24 (1): 83–92.

Nasierowski, W. and Mikula, B. (1998) Culture dimensions of Polish managers: Hofstede's indices. Organization Studies, 193): 495–509.

Naumov, A. (1996) Khofstedovo izmerenie Rossii. Upravleniya, 3: 70–103.

Naylor, T.H. (1988) The re-education of Soviet management. Across the Board, 25 (2): 28–37.

Newman, K.L. and S.D. Nollen (1998) Managing Radical Organizational Change. London: Sage.

Nicolescu, O. (1992) Management education in Romania. Journal of Management Development. 11 (5): 39–40.

Orlov, A. and Tkachenko, Iu. (1991) How to teach about the market economy. Soviet Education, 33 (11): 11–14.

Pearson, C.M. and Rondinelli, D.A. (1998) Crisis management in central European firms. Business Horizons, 41 (3): 50–60.

Perlaki, I. (1994) Organizational Development in Eastern Europe: learning to build culture-specific OD theories. The Journal of Applied Behavioral Science: 299–312.

Puffer, S. (1994) Understanding the bear: a portrait of Russian business leaders. Academy of Management Executive, 8 (1): 41–54.

Puffer, S.M. (1993) The booming business of management education in Russia. Journal of Management Development, 12 (5): 46–59.

Puffer, S.M. (1981) Inside a Soviet management institute. California Management Review, XXIV (1): 90–96.

Puffer, S.M. and McCarthy, D. (1995) Finding the common ground in Russian and American business ethics. California Management Review, 37 (2): 29–46.

Radice, H. (1995) Organizing markets in Central and Eastern Europe: competition, governance and the role of foreign capital. In E. Dittrich, G. Schmidt and R. Whitley (Eds), Industrial Transformation in Europe. London: Sage, 109–133.

Richman, B. (1967) Management Development and Education in the Soviet Union. Michigan: MSU.

Romanelli, E. and Tushman, M.L. (1994) Organizational transformation as punctuated equilibrium: an empirical test. Academy of Management Journal, 37: 1141–1166.

Schein, E.H. (1969) Process Consultation: its Role in Organisation Development. Reading, Mass: Addison-Wesley.

Shekshnia, S.V. (1991) The American MBA Program. Soviet Education, 33 (12): 84–92.

Simon, L. and Davies, G.F. (1995) Cultural, social and organisational transitions: the consequences for the Hungarian manager. Journal of Management Development, 14 (10): 14–31.

Solzhenitsyn, A. (1991) Rebuilding Russia: Reflections and Tentative Proposals. London: Harper Collins.

Soulsby, A. (1999) The impact of societal transformation on Czech managers: a study of post-communist careers. In Proceedings of 5th Annual CREEB Conference, on "The Impact of Transformation on Individuals, Organizations and Society". Buckinghamshire Business School: 97–116.

Soulsby, A. and Clark, E. (1996) The emergence of post-communist management in the Czech Republic. Organization Studies, 17 (2): 227–247.

Tacis (1997) Interim Evaluation Report. Brussels: European Commission.

Trompenaars, F. (1993) Riding the waves of culture: understanding cultural diversity in business. London: Nicolas Brealey Publishing.

United Nations Development Programme (1999) Human Development Report for Central and Eastern Europe and the CIS, 1999. New York: UNDP.

Veiga, J.F., Yanouzas, J.N. and Buchholtz, A.K. (1995) Emerging cultural values among Russian managers: what will tomorrow bring? Business Horizons, July–August: 20–27.

Vikhanskii, O.S. (1991) Let's train managers for the market economy. Soviet Education, 33 (11): 37–44.

Vlachoutsicos, C. and Lawrence, P. (1990) What we don't know about Soviet management. Harvard Business Review, 68 (6): 50–64.

Vlachoutsicos, C., Bogatova, E.B. and Holden, N.J. (1997) Grasping the Logic to Bridge the Gap: Increasing the Professional Effectiveness of Western Consultants and Management Educators in Russia. Workshop Report. Moscow: National Training Foundation.

Vlachoutsicos, C.A. (1986) Where the trouble stops in Soviet trade. Harvard Business Review, September–October, 82–86.

Vlachoutsicos, C. (1998) The dangers of ignoring Russian communitarianism. Transition, 9 (405): 13–14.

Walsh, D., Luthans, F. and Sommer, S.M. (1993) Managing Russian factory workers; the impact of US-based behavioral and participative techniques. Academy of Management Journal, 36 (1): 58–79.

Wedel, J.R. (1998) Collision and Collusion: the Strange Case of Western Aid to Eastern Europe 1989–1998. London: Macmillan.

Yanouzas, J.N. and Boukis, S.D. (1993) Transporting management training into Poland: some surprises and disappointments. Journal of Management Development, 12(1): 64–71.

Yergin, D. and Gustafson, T. (1994) Russia 2010 and What it Means for the World. London: Nicholas Brealey Publishing.

Zaitsev, A.K. (1996) How Russia was shaped. Paper Presented to the World Bank/NTF Workshop "Grasping the Logic to Bridge the Gap: Increasing the Effectiveness of Western Consultants and Management Educators in Russia. Moscow, 1–6 December.

# Chapter 19

# Managing Globalization: a Constructivist Perspective

**Nigel J. Holden**
*and*
**Dorte Salskov-Iversen**

*Department of Intercultural Communication and Management, Copenhagen Business School, Frederiksberg, Denmark*

*Knowledge shall be sought throughout the world*
19th century Japanese imperial slogan.

## INTRODUCTION

With that resounding slogan late 19th century Japan established its principle for emulating the great nations of the day – especially the France, Germany, Great Britain and the United States – in all compartments of national endeavour. Thus, it was that Japan became the first country in world history to acquire knowledge from far afield to modernize itself. Worldwide search for knowledge is no longer a Japanese, let a alone a state-driven, preoccupation: today, knowledge is being sought throughout the world, the main actors being internationally operating firms. This time the quest for knowledge implies a different kind of organizational set-up. In particular, notions of control/management based on power tied to the formal apparatus of the organization – in Foucault's terminology "sovereign power" – will not do. Modern managers need much more sophisticated government technologies to ensure a continuous flow of knowledge and its constant transformation in particular local settings into policies and strategies as well as globally competitive cutting-edge services and products.

This chapter is concerned with globalization and knowledge and how awareness of globalization and its relation to knowledge shapes and challenges managerial and organizational thinking, with specific reference to communication processes and methods of coordination and control. We will approach the discussion from a constructivist position, investigating the operation of discourses of globalization and knowledge on management and organizational patterns. It follows that we will be less concerned with the material effects of globalization and knowledge – though we do not doubt that both terms reflect the lived experience of people, organizations and nations. It is our contention that, in international business, a critical investigation of an organization's perception, appropriation and re-articulation of globalization, as evidenced in its discursive production, can offer valuable insights into the kind of logics and "sense" that inform, and eventually structure, its managerial and organizational response to global competition and the globalization of business organization.

The first section briefly spells out the constructivist stance adopted in this study and elaborates on the conceptual framework applied. The second and third sections investigate the rationalities underpinning prevailing discourses on globalization and knowledge. By way of illustration, the fourth section reports on how two specific organizations, in pharmaceuticals and electrical and electronic products respectively, conceptualize globalization and its consequences in their official discourse and how this influences their management ways.

# THE CONSTRUCTIVIST PERSPECTIVE: THE CONSTITUTIVE POWERS OF LANGUAGE

The emphasis on constructivism invariably brings the role of language, or discourse, to the fore when investigating social phenomena. The term discourse signals that language is viewed as a form of social practice, a mode of action, both socially shaped and socially shaping. If you are concerned with how meaning is generated, with how social identities, social relations and systems of knowledge and belief are being thrashed out in a particular social domain, language – or the discursive moment of the practice under scrutiny – is where you gain insights into the kind of representations upon which subjects act, and which they may reproduce, challenge or transform through myriads of discursive practices. As indicated above, this is not to say that there are not other facets of the social.

Globalization is very material and concrete when an American company removes its production to Thailand, electronically accesses expert knowledge across the globe on a 24-h basis, or introduces its business practices in a Danish subsidiary. These are not only social constructions. Such moments exist in a dialectical relationship with the discursive moment, which is unfolded here. The separation of discourse from material, tangible facets of the social is an analytical device, which enables us to establish a focus and a methodological framework, delimiting our exploration to the processes of ascribing meaning to things. Importantly, in this line of thinking, what counts as (common) sense is never fixed, but is constantly fought over and is thus inextricably bound up with notions of power.

While this approach is arguably more relevant in some contexts than in others, a number of interconnected developments in late capitalist society point to the increasing salience, most certainly also in organizational life, of discursive practices in the constitution and reproduction of power relations and social identities. Foucault's work on power/knowledge and the crystallization of this couplet in discourse is obviously essential here (McKinlay and Starkey, 1998). An order of discourse organizes knowledge, positions and places and defines what can be imagined and said in a given field of power, for instance a company, a political party, a family; and as such, it makes some actions more obvious, more natural, more taken for granted than others. In this view, the sustainability of a particular hegemonic project depends on its ability to label the world in a way that supports the interests it represents – not by sheer domination but by constructing alliances and granting concessions.

Amongst the wider social and cultural changes hinted at above, two features are of particular relevance for studies of organizational governance (Fairclough, 1995: 135). The first follows from the Foucauldian perspective and connects directly to the practice of modern management, or disciplinary power as opposed to sovereign power (Clegg, 1998: 29): to the extent that contemporary society can be understood as post-traditional in Giddens' sense of the word (Giddens, 1990: 45), relationships, identities and knowledge tend to be less fixed and more dependent on negotiations and dialogue. For management, this means that, increasingly, the exertion of power demands highly developed dialogical competences and control processes that rely on the self-surveillance of the employees and their emotional buy-in.

The second feature concerns the cultural consequences of consumerism and commodification, i.e. the general reconstruction of social life on a market basis. For organizations, being responsive to the ever-changing whims and desires of the sovereign consumer/customer, connects directly to one of the most influential globalization discourses, i.e. that which is concerned with change. Importantly, the culture of the customer also translates into what we might call "managing by customers" (Du Gay, 19998: 313), which subtly enables managers to withdraw from the "control" function. If employees buy in to the omnipotence of the customer, they will pursue excellence not because they are told so by their employer, but because they instinctively sympathize with the demands of the customers. These shifts create words and words create worlds "as part of an endless recursive cycle of social construction" (Oswick et al., 1999).

The next two sections offer a critical account of two closely related meta-discourses whose logics are informed by ideas about the wider social change outlined above and which contemporary organizations draw on when producing meaning. It should be stressed that quite often these meta-discourses are invoked very creatively and selectively by different organizations and do not necessarily descend upon local practices in a unidirectional way: invariably, local reinterpretations give rise to important modifications, or may even challenge what is taken for granted in the meta discourse.

However, by way of definition, to justify the term "meta", or an "order", such discourses, even if they are contested, must be seen to dominate the representation of a particular domain – otherwise they will not be sufficiently articulate to function as interpretative schemes for those who inhabit the domain in question. It is beyond the scope of this chapter to support the empirical evidence of the hegemonic nature of the discourses of globalization and knowledge with statistical material. We have relied on other sources for the establishment of this *fact*.

## GLOBALIZATION

Management and organizational theories, notes Stewart Clegg (Clegg and Clarke, 1999a: 2), "constitute grand narratives that exploit fashionable myths associated with signs of success, such as 'competitiveness', 'excellence, and quality'"; we could add knowledge and responsiveness, but the list is very long. The overarching narrative – the meta discourse – currently framing theories in the field, however, is that of globalization. As a signifier of the changing external context of business this discourse is fairly recent. By the mid-1980s, management textbooks began to include references to "globalization" (Mills and Hatfield, 1999: 53) as standard fare in their representation of the world in which businesses operate, while the first wave of truly popularizing literature on globalization began to come out in the late 1980s and early 1990s, examples include Ohmae (1990) and Thurow (1992).

Paul Hirst and Grahame Thompson represent a reaction against the school of thought that can be referred to as the hyperglobalist thesis (Held et al., 1999: 3), which, premised on an economic logic and often of a neoliberal leaning, heralds a new global age. In their much quoted work from 1996 (Hirst and Thompson, 1996b: 1). Hirst and Thompson dismiss the notion of globalization on empirical grounds and deplore its ubiquity in academia as well as amongst practitioners, across the political spectrum: it is a "fashionable concept in the social sciences, a core dictum in the prescriptions of management gurus, and a catch-phrase for journalists and politicians of every stripe" (Hirst and Thompson, 1996a,b: 1). We disagree with Hirst and Thompson's debunking the idea of globalization, though it is explicitly beyond the scope of this article to discuss how globalization should *rightly* be conceptualized.

Suffice it to say that we sympathize with critiques of positions that claim that nothing has really changed and that the old, international world system is intact (Amin, 1997: 125) and that we share views of globalization, such as Amin's, which see it as multi-levelness, hybridity and interdependence. This line of thinking also sits well with David Held et al.'s (1999: 16) definition of globalization as "a process (or set of processes) which embodies a transformation in the spatial organization of social relations and transactions – assessed in terms of their extensity, intensity, velocity and impact – generating transcontinental or interregional flows and networks of activity, interaction, and the exercise of power".

It follows that globalization cannot be viewed as a singular condition, nor does it reflect a simple linear developmental logic, which is exactly what Hirst and Thompson suggest when they reject the globalization thesis. In this study, we will nevertheless go along with Hirst and Thompson's observation about the *pervasiveness* of the idea of globalization, with special emphasis on its representation in the managerial and orga-nizational thinking. In the words of Du Gay, "regardless of whether the dominant 'globalization' hypothesis is overstated or indeed just plain wrong, an awful lot of things are being done in its name" (Du Gay, 1999: 79).

Across very different conceptualizations, globalization is almost always taken to have far-reaching consequences for organizational life in every organizational domain, whether public or private. A central theme in the globalization discourse, which forms the ideational backcloth to so many aspects of organizational life, is its dislocatory effects – the corollary is a state of massive uncertainty, which, in turn, can only be countered if we accept the inevitability and universality of change. In an interesting study of what they term "the tyranny of transformation", John Clarke and Janet Newman identify a number of narrative structures which can be found in very different types of texts and communications and which very effectively naturalize the changes which they endorse (Clarke and Newman, 1997: 34). Not seldom are such changes justified "in and through narratives which place them in globalized contexts of change". Clarke and Newman's imaginative phrase "a cascading imperative of change" (op. cit.: 46) captures the way notions about globalization, or perhaps more specifically, notions about the global economy, are invoked to legitimize change in a top-down fashion at all levels of society, whether at the global, national, organizational or individual level. The change envisioned can of course vary quite considerably but there is a striking similarity in the direction of change that the new global environment seems to suggest in organizational governance across social domains: it entails a move – which is construed as a natural consequence of global processes – away from an ineffective, bureaucratic, and unresponsive mindset towards one of efficiency, entrepreneuralism and responsiveness.

One of the most conspicuous changes that can be seen to flow from this understanding of globalization is the crucial role allocated to the idea of enterprise as a rationality of organizational governance. The surge of "enterprise" – or even the enterprise culture (Fairclough, 1992: 206) is of course closely related to the general reconstruction of social life on a market basis noted in section one. As a rationality of governance, it implies "the generalization of an 'enterprise form' to all forms of conduct – to the conduct of organizations hitherto being non-economic, to the conduct of government, and to the conduct of individuals themselves" (Graham Burchell, quoted in Du Gay, 1998: 300). The discursive dimension to this development can be observed in the way discourses associated with enterprise have come to colonize social domains and institutions which have not hitherto been associated with entrepreneurship and its perceived qualities as understood by proponents of enterprise culture: initiative, risk-taking, self-reliance and personal responsibility (Fairclough, 1995: 112; Du Gay, 1998: 299).

For commercial organizations, the enterprise culture should not come as a surprise. However, what is becoming increasingly clear is the way that the logic of entrepreneurship is seen to hold true for the individuals that inhabit these organizations, not only for collective economic units in the shape of private sector businesses and companies. In Du Gay's phrase, what we are currently witnessing is a process of "enterprising up nations, organizations and individuals", all in the name of globalization (Du Gay, 1999: 78). And as entrepreneurship necessitates a certain amount of autonomy and empowerment on the part of the entrepreneur, it has consequences for management, which will have to consider different modes of control in order to ensure corporate identification and commitment. In this vein, the volatility and ever growing demands of the global economy require individuals to assume responsibility for their own lives, also their working lives, where they are set free in order to pursue the goals of whatever business they belong to more innovatively and creatively than rigid rules can prescribe, in order to be more in tune with the customers out there and the perpetually shifting environment. What is needed is a management technique which harnesses the autonomous aspirations of the employee-turned-entrepreneur and reconciles them "with the collective entrepreneurialism of the corporate culture" (Rose, 1989: 117).

One result is that new demands can be conceived of, not as something imposed by management, but something which goes with being an integral part of the global economy, the customer culture. In such a set-up, management is about offering employees means of strategic self-manipulation "which reproduce a concept of freedom, though one actualized in the accomplishment of corporate control through self-control" (Deedtz, 1998: 168) – indeed cultural management.

It is against this background that management scholars and business commentators are advocating the conviction that survival in the modern globalized (or at least globalizing) economy (see e.g. Dicken, 1999) – sometimes referred to as the New Economy – as well as firms' ultimate source of competitive advantage lies in knowledge. Knowledge in this sense does not refer to formal knowledge but embraces "tacit and often highly subjective insights, intuitions, and hunches of individual employees and making those insights available for testing and use by the company as a whole" (Nonaka, 1998: 24). The perceived centrality of knowledge makes organizations ask how to "build the capability to learn from many environments to which they are exposed and to appropriate the benefits of such learning through their global operations in transnational innovations" (Clegg and Clarke, 1999b).

The purpose of this knowledge is that it abets innovation, not in a purely technical sense, but in the sense of being mentally prepared to respond and change, proactively, on a continuous basis. Thus, the notion of knowledge becomes a discourse in its own right. Though subsumed within the globalization discourse, its underlying rationality provides organizations with a specific lens and, consequently, with a particular set of techniques of intervention, or management. We will explore the notion of knowledge in some more detail below.

# KNOWLEDGE AND THE LEARNING ORGANIZATION

A learning organization has been defined as one which is "skilled at creating, acquiring, and transferring knowledge, and at modifying its behaviour to reflect new knowledge and insights" (Garvin, 1998: 51). In practice this means acquiring and exploiting knowledge from any source, for knowledge is "the one sure source of lasting competitive advantage" (Nonaka, 1998: 22) In this scenario the learning organization also becomes the knowledge-creating organization.

As Burgoyne (1998: 359) points outs, the concept of the learning organization was a product of what he calls the "excellence" movement of the 1980s, but many of the organizations of the 1980s which were held up as "excellent" failed to maintain this status in the 1990s. According to Burgoyne (1998: 359), "failure of adaptation or learning has been the obvious explanation". This supports Hodgson's (1998: 544–545) conviction that transforming an organization into a learning, knowledge-creating entity can be "painful", as there is no clearly established way.

The worldwide acquisition and exploitation of knowledge create, and are created by, conditions which Barham and Heimer (1998: 137) in their study of the industrial giant ABB describe as "global connectivity". This is not just a reference to the exploitation of new information and communications technology; this is also "a frame of mind that encourages people to take independent action yet feel part of responsible to a bigger whole from which they derive important competitive benefits and to which, in return, they must add value" (Barham and Heimer, 1998: 148). In their influential study of the transnational corporation, Harvard scholars Ghoshal and Bartlett (1998: 3) have pointed out that there must be a "a new management mentality" in global operating organizations as they reach out for "global efficiency, national responsiveness, and world-wide leveraging of innovations and learning, whilst creating 'a new management mentality'".

The processes and practices that are seen to intensify the patterns of global inter-connectedness are multiplying. One of the latest developments is the revolution forged by e-commerce, which is creating "new rules of engagement" (Economist, 1999a: 44). These new rules of engagement are being created by radical shifts in the business environment, asset definition, nature of change, and production (Sun-Netscape Alliance, 1999).

The shifts associated with these four factors are represented in Table 19.1.

The organizational implications of this transition are considerable and lend themselves to a very different kind of rationality which involves the re-imagining, among other things, of how people go about their work: how they think of themselves and their relations to the organization and its environment.

As a recent survey in the Economist (1999a: 44) noted:

'Is e-business the biggest thing since the industrial revolution, or is the Internet just another useful tool for speeding up business communications, a bit like a telephone? .... The big unknowable is how a completely networked world will change the way people work with each other. In the past, the rules of business were simple: beat the competition into submission, squeeze your suppliers and keep your customers in ignorance the better to gouge them. At least everybody knew where they stood. The new technology makes an unprecedented degree of

**Table 19.1**

| Factor | Shift from | Shift to |
|---|---|---|
| Business environment | Local/physical | Global/virtual |
| Asset definition | Tangible and "old" intangibles (i.e. "services") | "New" intangibles (i.e. knowledge, experience) |
| Nature of change | Periodic | Continuous |
| Production | Mass Production → mass customization | Mass personalization |

collaboration possible, but nobody can predict how far that will reach outside the boundaries of individual firms, and how people will adapt to rapidly shifting business alliances and federations. Nor is it clear how companies will respond to ever more demanding customers with perfect market information'.

This is an illustration of globalization as massive unpredictability. Again, even if there is no agreed way of understanding the phenomenon of e-commerce and the future it might generate, its organizational impact is fairly distinct. It fuels a strongly felt need for new ways of managing people and relating to the external environment, be it suppliers, customers, or competitors. Managers will become facilitators rather than mere doers and collaborative relations will replace cut-throat competition and short-term profit maximizing behaviour. In the words of Crainer (1999: 24), "from being functional specialists, managers are becoming sophisticated generalists, able to manage a potpourri of projects, people, resources, and issues". It is also clear that the future of work will be intimately bound up with interlinked processes of learning and knowledge-processing. According to management thinker Peter Drucker (quoted in: Crainer, 1998: 9).

> 'The single greatest challenge facing managers in the developed countries is to raise the productivity of knowledge and service workers. This challenge, which will dominate the management agenda for the next several decades. will ultimately determine the competitive performance of companies. Even more importantly, it will determine the very fabric of society and the quality of life in every industrialized nation'.

In the globalized economy Drucker's challenge means raising the productivity of knowledge and service workers who will be in multicultural teams and networked globally with arrays of stakeholders. This is only possible if such workers know how to learn for and *on behalf of* their organizations. Indeed the very future of management may lie in facilitating this kind of learning, and the cross-cultural implications of that are not yet understood in theory or practice.

The implications of this emphasis is that in their daily operations organizations must therefore learn to manage diversity, change and density of linkages in order to convert themselves into network organizations with the key, knowledge-mediating competence, namely "global connectivity" (Barham and Heimer, 1998). The key challenge, according to Japanese management guru Ikujiro Nonaka (1998) is to find "common cognitive ground among employees". Zahra (1999) uses the word "cognitive" in a slightly different context by stressing that the changes taking shape under the logic of globalization "will reshape the frontier of the cognitive maps of industries, companies, and managers".

Thus, it has been argued that "*with rare exceptions,* a firm's productivity will lie more in its collective intellect – that is, in its collective capacity to gain and use knowledge – rather than in its hard assets such as land, plant and equipment" (Ireland and Hitt, 1998). The idea of the collective intellect poses new challenges to managers: how can one create an intelligent organization, how can one ensure that the flows of knowledge which exist in and between and originates in people are somehow ploughed back into an organization, which in order to facilitate innovation, tends to have relaxed controls, highly decentralized structures, empowerment of workers. In short, "how do we determine that newly encouraged 'intelligence' gets exercised in line with managerial objectives?" (Clegg and Clarke, 1999a: 185).

MIT's Peter Senge, has argued that "the entire global business community is learning to learn together, becoming a learning community" (Senge, 1990: 4). He adds: "Whereas once many industries were dominated by a single, undisputed leader – one IBM, one Kodak, one Proctor & Gamble, one Xerox – today industries, especially in manufacturing, have dozens of excellent companies. American and European corporations are pulled forward by the example of the Japanese; the Japanese, in turn, are pulled by the Koreans and Europeans. Dramatic improvements take place in corporations in Italy, Australia, Singapore – and quickly become influential around the world" (Senge, 1990: 4).

Since that was written, Japan, which in the 1980s was "at the cutting edge of management and technology" (Dower, 1986: 316) and whose companies around the same time were "held up as exemplars of integrated global strategies" (Westney, 1999: 15), has languished in economic and political doldrums. Korea has seen its political economy being shaken at the foundations, where as European firms appear to have a mania for mergers and acquisitions. This is not to undermine Senge's point, for he appears to be fundamentally correct: despite changing national and organizational fortunes, the drive to be a more efficient operator at the global or at least international level through exploitation of knowledge acquired *anywhere* is now central to managers' thinking. In this sense managers fulfil – indeed enact – Senge's vision of a learning organization in which its members "are continually enhancing their capability to create their future" (Senge, quoted in: Hodgson, 1999).

It is tempting to envisage the emergence of new organizations – essentially Goshal's and Bartlett's transnational corporations – whose broad commitment to creating knowledge-based companies is both vouchsafing, and predicated upon, a unitary management discourse. Or to put that another way: the current writing on organizational learning and knowledge acquisition for global operations is premised on the existence of such a discourse. If that is the case, then the world is an easier place in which organizations can "provide a shared context where individuals can interact with each other and engage in the constant dialogue on which effective reflection depends" (Nonaka, 1998: 44). If that is not the case, then the requirement that organizations become "adept at translating new knowledge into new ways of behaving" (Garvin, 1998: 52) takes on awkward nuances in a world business where "there is a growing tendency for tariff and technological advantages to wear off, which automatically shifts competition towards cultural advantages and disadvantages" (Hofstede, 1994: 239). But either way the creation of knowledge-based organizations appears to be paving the way for a significant reconstitution of the way in which rules, roles and even emotions govern organizational life.

# GLOBALIZATION, KNOWLEDGE AND COMPANY DISCOURSE

Above, globalization was presented as a multifaceted term, subject to various inter-pretations. In so far as globalization refers to the recognition of the emergence of the global economy, it might be thought that the term would mean more or less the same thing to internationally operating companies. That is to say, we might expect such firms to use the term in company discourse to refer to more or less the same concept of Globalization. They don't. "globalization" is rarely spelt out at length and explained as to its roots, present manifestations and future implications. Its articulation tends to be constructed along a number of narrative structures which reduce globalization to a condition which invariably means change, whether presented as the harbinger of a brave new world of borderless trade (Higgins, 1999, quoted in Mills and Hatfield, 1999: 54), of uncertainty and turbulence, of dangers and threats, a survival-of-the-fittest game, or as a natural, organic development.

With this narrative closure in place, firms latch on to the globalization discourse to harness different organizational projects for change and develop distinctive discourses for their naturalization. In order to substantiate that claim, we examine the discourse associated with globalization in two internationally prominent companies. The first is Novo Nordisk, the Denmark-based pharmaceutical and health-care multinational; the second is Matsushita, the Japanese electrical and consumer electronics giant (note 1).

# NOVO NORDISK

Novo Nordisk is an international bio-industrial and pharmaceutical company with headquarters in Denmark (see Notes). The company is the result of a merger in 1989 of two Danish firms: Novo Industri and Nordisk Gentofte. Today the company has production facilities in eight countries and affiliates and offices in 61 countries world-wide. At the end of 1998 Novo Nordisk employed nearly 15,000 people, about a third of whom work outside Denmark. The companies health-care business accounts for 75% of total sales, the remaining 25% being contributed by sales of enzymes. Novo Nordisk is a world leader in diabetes care and the world's leading producer of industrial enzymes.

Novo Nordisk, whilst a big company by Danish standards, is a small specialist concern in comparison with the major pharmaceutical and health-care MNCs. As such it is vulnerable in a global industry in which the biggest players make a pastime of trying to take over and merge, but not often succeeding. Fear of take-over combined with the need to become global decided the Novo Nordisk's top management to intro-duce a new philosophy for running the company. Among other things this new philo-sophy would attempt to make the company more nimble by shifting the focus from top-heavy centralized processes controlled by top management in Copenhagen to local business processes controlled by local management. This in turn would help to close a sharply felt communication gap between top management and the rest of the company in and outside Denmark. The philosophy was termed the Novo Nordisk Way of Management, which was introduced in 1997, consisting of four components: Vision

21 (the company's mission statement), the co-called "fundamentals" or the ten funda-mental rules for management, the company's global policy, and its quality system.

By enforcing the Novo Nordisk Way of Management the company aims, in the words of its CEO Mads Ølivsen, to be "one of the companies setting the standards globally for social responsibility and reporting". That ambition requires, among other things, "a systematic dialogue with key stakeholders". As far its internal stakeholders, i.e. its own employees worldwide are concerned, the top management created a novel system for ensuring that the local business processes are developed through the contin-uous implementation of the Novo Nordisk Way of Management, one of whose aims is to encourage the sharing of value-adding practices throughout the entire organization. The system combines FACIT, an Intranet database to promote the exchange of knowl-edge across the company, and a group of carefully selected managers, called facilita-tors, whose task is to:

- make a review of compliance with the Novo Nordisk Way of Management at any unit worldwide;
- promote localization;
- stimulate the sharing of best practice;
- foster empowerment.

The rest of this section is devoted to the facilitator concept; its relevance for this chapter is that, as we shall see, the facilitators' role in transferring knowledge about the Novo Nordisk Way of Management, across functions and subcultures (also when these reflect different national cultures) in the company.

When the company decided to support the facilitator concept, the next step involved appointing a 14-strong team for an experimental period of 3 years. The positions, advertised through the company internally, were eventually filled by managers with more than 200 years of experience of the company among them. Their professional backgrounds ranged from general management, regional management, production, plant management, logistics, R&D, etc. All were highly committed to the company and each brought to the appointment a strong personal desire to add value to the company in a way which their previous positions precluded. The original 14 facilitators included six Danes, two Americans, one German, one Japanese, one Malaysian, one Spaniard, one German, and one South African. There was a permanent office for the facilitators at the Novo Nordisk headquarters north of Copenhagen.

The facilitators were formally constituted in October 1996. The brief was to work in groups of two and undertake a "facilitation" at any Novo Nordisk unit in any country which invited them to make a review (the word "audit", with its overtones of censor-iousness, is largely avoided). Units might be a marketing and sales department, an R&D facility, a legal department, production workers (at the head-office in Copenhagen cleaning staff took part in a facilitation).

In simple terms a facilitation required the facilitator duo to brief themselves on the unit in question, conduct the actual interview with staff, and then discuss with the unit manager findings on the degree of compliance or non-compliance with the Novo Nordisk Way of Management. Ideally there would be agreement between the facil-itators and the local management on the way forward. The reports filed by the facilitators are read by the top manager at headquarters who is their controller. These reports do *not* go to any other senior manager. This is done as a signal to a unit that a facilitation is not meant to be an intimidatory experience.

When the concept was first put into action, the facilitators were initially seen as "top management spies". This adversity helped to bond them together as a somewhat unusually constituted management team, but eventually their professionalism made converts and their expertise is now in constant demand throughout the company (the originally envisaged 40 days international travel has now reached 150). The experiment has been judged a success and will continue.

This is not the place to discuss the many interesting aspects of the facilitator concept from the more conventional management points of view. The task here is to comment on the facilitators as perpetrators and occasionally modifiers of the company management discourse. First we must note that the facilitators already knew "the company language", including specialist registers to do with science, law, medicine and business practice. As facilitators they had to familiarize themselves with the language of company policy, and they had to adapt this language to suit the function of facilitation.

The resulting language of facilitation had to fulfil certain requirements: it had to preserve the integrity of core values and precepts; it had to have appeal to every portion of the company across every function, across every departmental border – to sales-people in Beijing, to clinicians to Baltimore, to floor cleaners in Copenhagen. It had to be used therefore by facilitators as a medium of persuasion, and diplomatic intervention and occasional coercion. Their use of it, furthermore, had to be such that key messages were conveyed in and relayed from languages like Japanese, Chinese and Russian. Furthermore this language grew not by design, not just as the result of interactions with units, but as a facet of the experience-sharing process in which the facilitators partici-pated both in their operational duos and in their six monthly review meetings. It had become a language of self-education and mutual empowerment for the facilitators, while a key medium for reducing social distance and professional detachment of the company's top management from the lesser ranks throughout the entire Novo Nordisk organization.

The facilitator experience testifies to the importance of language as a field of social action, and the centrality of dialogical capacities when constructing managed subjects in a way which backgrounds management's role in stipulating new standards and shifting objectives. The facilitator concept encourages employees to take independent action at the local level, whilst feeling part of and being responsible to a bigger whole. In other words, employees can think of themselves as enjoying a degree of autonomy, and in the process, they internalize the control and surveillance that used to be exercised by the traditional management role. In Foucault's words, employees are developing technologies of the self. It is quite evident how the Novo discourse appeals to the entrepreneurial self of its employees, who are encouraged to engage themselves proac-tively in the enterprise, assuming co-responsibility for its future. The disciplinary regime that follows from this kind of understanding depends for its success on a radical reconstitution of the identities and relationships that can be observed in traditional organizational life.

The facilitator experience is also illustrative of how the sense of autonomy and freedom on which the knowledge worker's entrepreneurial self is premised invariably produces contested meanings. This requires a disciplinary regime which can handle ambiguity, identify compromise, and negotiate a degree of intersubjectivity across different positions in the organization.

# MATSUSHITA ELECTRIC

The Matsushita Electric Industrial Company of Japan (MEI), the major supplier of electrical and consumer electronics products under the principal brand-names of Panasonic and Technics, was ranked the world's 27th corporation in the Fortune Global Five Hundred of 1999 (Fortune, 1999). MEI's business is divided into four main product groups: consumer electronic and electric appliances, information and communication equipment, electrical and electronic components, and video and audio equipment. The company, which in 1998 had revenues totalling $60 billion, employs some 265,000 people, of whom 147,000 are non-Japanese employees working for the company in 218 overseas subsidiaries in 40 countries (Panasonic, 2000a). MEI is famed for the power – indeed the sacrosanctity – of its corporate culture, which is indelibly associated with the name of the company's founder, Konosuke Matsushita (1894–1989), one of the greatest industrialists of the 20th century (Pascale and Athos, 1983; Kotter, 1997).

The company that bears his name was founded in 1918 with a mere ¥100 investment. Fifty years later he would be revered in Japan as "the god of management" and even after his death in 1989 company thinking, decision-making and even organizational structures firmly bear his imprint (Ghoshal and Bartlett, 1998; Kotter, 1997; Matsushita, 1995). KM, as he is known in the company today, was an entrepreneur, marketer, inventor, organizational designer, and, in particular, a management philosopher, who was literally decades ahead of his time. KM's business philosophy, which is elaborated by the early 1930s and is even unusual by Japanese standards, has been well summarized by Ghoshal and Bartlett (1998: 47):

> 'The business philosophy, which has become institutionalized through "cultural and spiritual" training programmes and forms the basis of the morning assembly ritual held in facilities worldwide, defines the fundamental goals of the company and describes how they are to be achieved. The philosophy proposes that "the purpose of an enterprise is to contribute to society by supplying goods of high quality at low prices in ample quantity," and that "profit comes in compensation for contribution to society". It is encapsulated in the Seven Spirits of Matsushita: service through industry, fairness, harmony and cooperation, struggle for progress, courtesy and humility, adjustment and assimilation, and gratitude. Within Matsushita these values are regarded as more than platitudes. Managers refer to them constantly and use them to help make even the most basic operating decisions"

In the immediate post-war years the company struggled to survive, but as of the early 1950s, when its fortunes had been largely restored, its internationalization began in earnest. Wherever MEI executives did business in the world, the KM philosophy was used as the basis for interactions with employees, customers, and suppliers. In 1983 the company and its founder were the subject of Pascale and Athos's influential book *The art of Japanese management,* where we find this paean:

> 'Matsushita has become a great corporation that makes more than money, and is likely to go on doing so, for it has become an organizational system that meets the needs of society, its customers, its executives, and its employees, and it is "programmed" to adapt as may be necessary to changes that may come' (ibid: 28).

Since that was written, observers of MEI (e.g. Economist, 1999b; Ghoshal and Bartlett, 1988, 1998; Hoover, 1991; Kotter, 1997) have remarked on its general inability to innovate and break away from what Ghoshal and Bartlett (1998; 48, 364) call "the saga around the life and philosophy of Konosuke Matsushita" and his "profound and lasting influence on (the company's) administrative legacy".

The company has had – in theory at least – no problem in adapting its philosophy to suit the needs of an international company employing tens of thousands of employees worldwide. As the text of the current company web-site states: "his (KM's) conviction that a company remains indebted to society continues to be the foundation on which are policies are built. Directed by these policies, we are determined to improve the lives of people in the societies in which we do business, whilst providing the highest quality Panasonic products at reasonable prices to our customers" (Panasonic, 2000b).

According to Yoshihobu Nakamura (1998), a senior HRM executive based at the company headquarters in Osaka, the philosophy "is considered paramount in conducting business" and "constitutes the basis of business administration and underlies all decision-making processes". As for globalization, the basic objective of the company is to "aspire toward global coexistence" and "bring prosperity to the world and realize social progress and happiness by endlessly developing business which is satisfactory to people and society".

The philosophy of globalization has the following six tenets:

1. "We will operate our business in such a way that we are welcomed by the host country and we will carry out our business activities honoring local customs.
2. We will promote business in accordance with the host country's policies. Also we will make continuous efforts to have the host country understand the management philosophy of our company.
3. We will manufacture products and provide services that are competitive in international markets in terms of quality, performance, and cost, so that we can provide customers with added value.
4. We will promote global transfer and exchange of technology under a worldwide research and development system.
5. We will practice autonomous and responsible management, build up a strong management structure and generate our own capital for the expansion of our business.
6. We will manage our overseas companies with local employees and develop the skills of local employees for their advancement".

This philosophy and therefore the discourse of globalization derive directly from the company's philosophy fashioned in the 1930s. A casual glance at the key injunctions suggests that they should be easily adaptable to the era of globalization. But scrutiny of the wording makes it clear that the tenets reflect the age of 1970s and 1980s-style *internationalization*, when Japan was engrossed in nation-building through economic achievement, rather than the world view that underpins the new global economy of the 1990s and beyond.

MEI's emphasis on host countries both predicates and perpetuates a clear-cut distinction between Japanese/non-Japanese employees within the company itself. Thus, the requirement that the host country must "understand the management philosophy of our company" is rich in subtextual connotations. Experts on Japanese culture will detect the implicit assumption that any other country *will have* difficulty understanding the company philosophy because that philosophy is Japanese and must perforce remain impenetrable to non-Japanese employees and customers. Thus, the Matsushita philosophy is grounded in a world view which might be termed *ethnocentric globalism*, which differs radically from the conceptualization of globalization that dominates contemporary (American/Western) management and organizational discourse.

These comments about the company discourse are reinforced through the findings of a research project into the globalization of MEI conducted by Holden during 1998 and 1999. Both Japanese and non-Japanese managers served as informants. Research interviews with Japanese managers in Japan, the USA, Denmark, and the UK reveal no awareness of incompatibility between the basic company objectives and the philosophy of globalization. This is hardly surprising in the sense that these managers have been virtually indoctrinated with the Matsushita philosophy since their very first day as employees of the company (Holden, 1990). As for non-Japanese employees of the company, interviews conducted with managers in the USA, Germany, Spain, Austria and UK revealed a less clear-cut picture.

An American manager bluntly described the company philosophy as "Mickey Mouse".

Another suggested that the company deliberately wanted to retain a Japanese mystique over business operations. A third US manager, with several years experience of the company, expressed it thus: "the message from Osaka (the company headquarters) is: 'you don't understand our way of doing business'". A European manager declared that there was "too much looking down from the top" and that the company culture was not suited to people who were now urgently needed: change agents.

The lack of innovation in company practices and organizational structures to suit the globalized economy was a frustration among non-Japanese managers. "We are too divisional", said a European manager. On three continents there was, to quote one non-Japanese manager, "tunnel vision about globalization": a serious indicator that the discourse of globalization is unequally diffused and unequally understood within the company subsidiaries. As for localization, one European informant said that the company had been discussing this for 10 years, but there was always mistrust of non-Japanese managers. As evidence of that, of 58 MEI operations in Europe only eight have European managing directors. This suggests that either the company *fears* to implement point six of its philosophy of globalization or that European managers are held to be incapable of "running the show" in Europe.

These frustrations confirm that in the countries in which the interviews were conducted non-Japanese executives have to cope with the so-called "rice-paper ceiling": the amalgam of cultural and organizational issues that are not official but which may constitute a barrier to their advancement (see Kopp, 1999: 108). This issue and implications for the nature – and analysis – of Japanese management outside Japan has been the subject of an enormous literature starting in the 1980s (for a general overview see: Beechler and Bird, 1999; Jackson, 1993: 190; Kopp, 1999: 107; Trevor, Schendel and Wipert, 1986: 1, 249; White and Trevor, 1983: 123). It also has considerable significance as an influence on the character of the company discourse of globalization.

First of all, as noted, the globalization discourse derives from a business philosophy formulated some 70 years ago, and is therefore an emanation of the Japanese side of the rice-paper ceiling. This discourse, first fashioned in the Japanese language, is predominantly, if not exclusively, a kind of creed for Japanese members of the company, which they will digest uncritically because the thinking behind stems from the vision of the legendary KM. But for many non-Japanese managers in Europe and the USA, the same discourse, admittedly in translation, is evidently a source of confusion about the way in which the company is planning – or not planning – its future.

# CONCLUSIONS

This chapter set out to discuss how globalization may be managed. To that end, we have investigated the prevailing rationality of organizational governance with a specific view to how two prominent companies in their respective industries draw on the globalization discourse in their management ways. We started our investigation from the premise that globalization is a meta-discourse, an order of discourse, which across different understandings of what globalization really is and across social domains accomplishes certain narrative closures with implications for organizational life.

It was argued that, despite the diversity, the narrative forms which structure the currently dominant discourse of globalization all "carry the imperative of change" (Clarke and Newman, 1997: 40). Thus, in a very general way, globalization is understood to produce massive uncertainty. Firstly, for organizations and managers, this legitimizes demands for continuous change, which employees can then construe as inevitable, natural, not in any way to be challenged. Hence, in a subtle way, this causes managers to be removed from the power equation. Secondly, if change is a precondition, then knowledge, innovation and responsiveness are the answers. Traditional management techniques are not well geared to oversee and direct employee behaviour in a volatile, dynamic environment. Change management requires culture management and significantly alters the identities and relations of managers and employees. Especially in organizations that rely on individual and collective forms of capital there is evidence of how sophisticated communicative processes instil a sense of mission and direction into employees, cultivating "technologies of the self".

In the first case study, we saw how Novo can be seen to enact these concerns in its organizational discourse. Novo's reading and articulation of globalization and its relation to knowledge effectively frame its conspicuous reconstitution of the way in which rules, roles and emotions govern organizational life, as evidenced by the facilitator notion which, after a shaky start, constitutes a move away from traditional control practices towards more autonomy and self-management. Stanley Deetz has put it very concisely: "cultural and other forms of disciplinary control in these contexts become operant only to the extent that they are either internalized or reproduced in daily discourse and activities as a form of self-control" (Deetz, 1998: 156).

The case of Matsushita presents scholars of the discourse of globalization with a non-Western dimension which is deeply embedded in the general Japanese value system, but also snared in the highly conservative corporate culture of one of the world's biggest companies. Not for the first time a Japanese company awkwardly upstages Western thinking about a phenomenon which in its Japanese manifestation must be understood against the specific socio-cultural background of Japan. Anything to do with the Japanese language as a generator of "cult and myth" (Miller, 1982: 5), as a cradle of discourse, *and* with the transfer of Japanese thoughts into other cultural realms – all that will challenge, even disconcert Western observers without prior knowledge. Hence, in the case of the Matsushita corporation we encounter a discourse of globalization which is decidedly sui generis.

Indeed we are reminded of how contested the notion of globalization is. If viewed as an order of discourse or meta-discourse, the dominant reading accounted for in the above invariably exists in an oppositional or contradictory relationship to other conceptualizations of globalization. Thus, the discourse of globalization within the Matsushita corporation is not a unitary system equally embracing all employees. Rather it is a complex fusion of sacred, inviolate shibboleths for the Japanese employees to make them psychologically dependent on the company (Economist, 1999b), and of locally received variants which, whilst facilitating localization to some degree, reflect and produce differing degrees of comprehension, mystification, and even disregard. This suggests that the company has in large measure failed to make "host countries" understand the management philosophy in the USA, Europe and Australia.

A more disturbing conclusion is that the management philosophy and the derived philosophy of globalization do not represent a sufficiently robust platform for creating within the company a shared global mindset which adapts the message to suit business conditions. Rather they appear to be devices for *interpreting* business conditions to suit the message. Thus, the discourse of globalization within the Matsushita corporation seems to be far more preoccupied with inculcating behavioural and attitudinal conformity to the enduring universalistic, but geopolitically outdated vision of the company founder than with creating a fully ideational framework for representing the increasingly integrated world economy at the beginning of the 21st century.

The brief gaze into these two cases of course does not do justice to the material and the insights that can be derived from this kind of data, but we argue that discourse is an extremely relevant site for exploring the operations of the shifting rationality underpinning contemporary organizational governance. Furthermore, if we accept that "globalization", whether real or imagined, is thought of as a fundamental condition for businesses and organizations, then managing its conceptualization and ensuring the translation of its logics into the organizational design are becoming a central concern for business leaders.

## NOTES

The background material on Novo Nordisk is taken from the company's home page (http://www.novo.dk); the description of the facilitators is based on interviews conducted from September to December 1998 by N.J. Holden, M. Morsing and M. Planthinn of Copenhagen Business School. The information on the facilitators will form a case study for publication in the following book: Holden, N.J. (2001) cross-cultural management: a knowledge management perspective. London: Financial Times/Prentice Hall. The material on the Matsushita corporation and the cited informants' statements will be used in another research-based case study for the same publication.

## REFERENCES

Amin, A. (1997) Placing globalization. In Theory, Culture and Society. London: Age. Vol. 14 (2), 123–137.
Barham, K. and Heimer, C. (1998) ABB – The Dancing Giant. London: Financial Times/Pitman Publishing.
Barham, K. and Heimer, C. (1999) Identifying and developing international management competence. In S. Crainer (Ed), Financial Times Handbook of Management. London: Financial Times Management, pp. 685–697.
Beechler, S. and Bird, A. (Eds) (1999) Japanese Multinationals Abroad: Individual and Organizational Learning. New York: Oxford University Press.
Burgoyne, J. (1998) Learning organization. In The Concise Blackwell Encyclopedia of Management. C.L. Cooper and C. Argyris (Eds), Oxford: Blackwell.
Clarke, J. and Newman, J. (1997) The Managerial State. London: Sage Publications.
Clegg, S. (1998) Foucault, power and organizations. In A. McKinlay and K. Starkey (Eds), Foucault, Management and Organization Theory. London: Sage Publications.
Clegg. S. and Clarke, T. (1999a) Intelligent organizations? In S. Clegg, E. Ibarra-Colado and L. Bueno-Rodriquez (Eds), Global Management. Universal Theories and Local Realities. London: Sage Publications.
Clegg, S. and Clarke, T. (1999b) The organizational impact of globalization. A lecture delivered at Copenhagen Business School and based on Clegg, S. and Clarke, T. (1998). Changing Paradigms: The Transformation of Management Knowledge in the 21st Century. London: Harper Collins.
Clegg. S., Ibarra-Colado, E. and L. Bueno-Rodriquez (Eds) (1999c). Global Management. Universal Theories and Local Realities. London: Sage Publications.
Crainer, S. (1996) Key Management Ideas: Thinkers that Changed the Management World. London: Financial Times Management.
Crainer, S. (Ed) (1999) Financial Times Book of Management. London: Financial Times/Pitman Publishing.
Dicken, P. (1999) Global Shift: Transforming the World Economy. London: Paul Chapman.
Dower, J. (1986) War Without Mercy: Race and Power in the Pacific War. London: Faber and Faber.
Deetz, S. (1998) Discussing formulations, strategized subordination and selfsurveillance. In A. McKinlay and K. Starkey (Eds), Foucault, Management and Organization Theory. London: Sage Publications.
Drucker, P. (1998) The Coming of the New Organisation. Boston, MA: Harvard Business School Publishing, pp. 1–19. (First published in Harvard Business Review, January–February 1988).
Drucker, P. (1996) In Crainer, op. cit.
Du Gay, P. (Ed) (1998) Production of Culture, Cultures of Production. London: Sage.

Du Gay, P. In the name of 'Globalization': enterprising up nations, organizations and individuals. In P. Leisnik (Ed) Globalization and Labour Relations. Cheltenham: Edward Elgar Publishing Limited.

Economist (1999a) Survey: Business and the Internet, 26 June.

Economist (1999b) Putting the Bounce Back into Matsushita, 22 May: 67–68.

Fairclough, N. (1992) Discourse and Social Change. Cambridge: Polity Press.

Fairclough, N. (1995) Critical Discourse Analysis: The Critical Study of Language. London: Longman.

Fortune (1999) The Fortune Global 500: the World's Largest Corporations, 2 August.

Garvin, D.A. (1998) Building a learning organisation. In: Harvard Business Review on Knowledge Management. Boston, MA: Harvard Business School Publishing, pp. 47–80. (First published in Harvard Business Review, July–August 1993).

Ghoshal, S. and Bartlett, C.A. (1988) Matsushita Electric Industrial (MEI) in 1987. Harvard Business School: Case Study 9-388-144. Boston, MA: Harvard Business School Publishing Division.

Ghoshal, S. and Bartlett, C.A. (1998) Managing Across Borders: the Transnational Solution. London: Random House Business Books.

Giddens, A. (1990) The Consequences of Modernity. Cambridge: Polity Press.

Held, D., McGrew. A., Goldblatt, D. and Perraton, J. (1999) Global Transformations. Politics, Economics and Culture. Cambridge: Polity Press.

Higgins, J.M. (1999) The management challenge. New York: MacMillan. Quoted in Mills, J.M and Hatfield, J. (1999) From imperialism to globalization: internationalization and the management text. In S.R. Clegg, E. Ibarra-Colado, and L. Bueno-Rodriquez (Eds), Global Management: Universal Theories and Local Realities. London: Sage Publications, 37–67.

Hirst, P. and Thompson, G. (1996a) Globalization: ten frequently asked questions and some surprising answers. Soundings, 4.

Hirst, P. and Thompson, G. (1996b) Globalization in Question: the International Economy and the Possibilities of Governance. Oxford: Polity Press.

Hodgson, P. (1999) The learning organisation. In S. Crainer (Ed), Financial Times Handbook of Management. London: Financial Times Management, 538–547.

Hofstede, G. (1994) Cultures and Organisations: Intercultural Cooperation and its Importance for Survival. London: HarperCollins Business.

Holden, N.J. (1990) Preparing the ground for organisation learning: graduate training programmes in major Japanese corporations. Management Education and Development. Vol. 21 (3), 241–261.

Hoover, D. (1991) Matsushita Electric Industrial Co. IMD Case Study GM 468. Lausanne: Institute for Management Development.

Ireland, R.D. and Hitt, M.A. (1998) Achieving and maintaining strategic competitiveness in the 21st century: the role of strategic leadership. Academy of Management Executive, 13 (1): 43–57.

Jackson, T. (1993) Turning Japanese: the Fight for Industrial Control of the New Europe. London: HarperCollins.

Kopp, R. (1999) The rice-paper ceiling in Japanese companies: why it exists and persists. In S. Beechler and A. Bird, op. cit.

Kotter, J. (1997) Matsushita Leadership: Lessons from the 20th Century's Most Remarkable Entrepreneur. New York: Free Press.

Matsushita, M. (1995) The mind of management: Fifty years with Konosuke Matsushita. Toykyo: PHP Institute.

McKinlay, A. and Starkey, K. (Eds), (1998) Foucault, Management and Organization Theory. London: Sage Publications.

Miller, R.A. (1982) Japan's Modern Myth: The Language and Beyond. New York: Weatherhill.

Mills, A.J. and Hatfield, J. (1999) From imperialism to globalization: internationalization and the management text. In S. Clegg, E. Ibarra-Colado and L. Bueno-Rodriquez (Eds) Global Management. Universal Theories and Local Realities. London: Sage Publications.

Nakamura, Y. (1998) International human resources development by Matsushita Electric Industrial Co., Ltd. Asian Regional Conference on Industrial Relations. (No further particulars; manuscript supplied by Nakamura).

Nonaka, I. (1998) The knowledge-creating company. In Harvard Business Review on Knowledge Management. Boston, MA: Harvard Business School Publishing. pp. 21–45. (First published in Harvard Business Review, November–December 1991).

Ohmae, K. (1990) The Borderless World. New York: Collins.

Oswick, C., Keenoy, T. and Grant, D. (1999) Call for Papers, The Management Centre, University of London: King's College.

Panasonic (2000a) Information Supplied by Mr Yaoki Takahashi, Personnel Department, Panasonic (UK) Ltd.

Panasonic (2000b) http.//www.panasonic.com/host/company/profile/global.html.

Pascale, R.T. and Athos, A.G. (1983) The Art of Japanese Management. Harmondsworth, UK: Penguin Books.

Rose, N. (1989) Governing the Soul: The Shaping of the Private Self. London: Routledge.

Senge, P. (1990) The Fifth Discipline: the Art and Practice of the Learning Organization. New York: Doubleday.

Sun-Netscape Alliance (1999) Understanding the Net Economy Revolution. http://www.iplanet.com/center/nerev.html.

Thurow, L. (1992) Head to Head, London: Nicholas Brealey Publishing.

Trevor, M., Schendel, J. and Wilpert, B. (1986) The Japanese Management System: Generalists and Specialists in Japanese Companies Abroad. London: Frances Pinter.

Westney, D.E. (1999) Changing perspectives on the organization of Japanese multinationals abroad. In: Beechler, S.L. and Bird, A. (Eds), Japanese Multinationals Abroad: Individual and Organizational Learning. New York: Oxford University Press, 11–29.

White, M. and Trevor, M. (1983) Under Japanese Management. London: Heinemann.

Zahra, S.A. (1999) The changing rules of global competitiveness in the 21st century. Academy of Management Executive. Vol. 13 (1), 36–42.

# Chapter 20

# Direct/Indirect and Formal/ Informal Communication: A Reassessment

**Marie-Thérèse Claes**
*Institut Catholique des Hautes Etudes Commerciales,*
*Université Catholique de Louvain, Brussels, Belgium*

## INTRODUCTION

Directness and indirectness are sometimes given as causes of intercultural misunderstandings and confusions. These concepts are often linked to explicit and implicit communication styles, and to formality and informality. In business interactions, rituals and social rules are translated into patterns of behaviour and speech. In intercultural business communication, it is important to distinguish the degree and nature of formality and to separate formality from directness and indirectness. In this chapter, I want to explore the meanings and uses of direct or indirect speech, of formality and informality across cultures.

When, in 1959, Hall published *The Silent Language*, establishing the now famous distinction between high-context cultures and low-context cultures, his findings were based on personal observations and anecdotes. According to Leeds-Hurwitz and Winkin (1989), with his book, Hall founded the discipline of intercultural communication, and many a researcher has referred to it in order to explain the current interest in intercultural communication (Condon, 1981: 255). An important aspect of Hall's scientific approach is his ambition to address "men of action", which means that his approach is fore and foremost a pragmatic approach. Working at the US Foreign Service Institute, training diplomats, Hall quickly found that the teachings of an anthropologist had to have a "practical" value: his trainees did not want to talk about the concept of culture, they wanted to know how to use it. He then decided to concentrate on the "microcultural analysis" of culture: the tone of voice, gestures, time and space as aspects of culture (Hall, 1956). Hall insists on the unsuspected dimensions of interaction: "If this book has a message it is that we must learn to understand the "out-of-awareness" aspects of communication. We must never assume that we are fully aware of what we communicate to someone else." (Hall, 1981: 29 [1959]). Or, as Erich Fromm states on the cover of the 1981 edition of The Silent Language: "The Silent Language shows how cultural factors influence the individual behind his back, without his knowledge".

Hall opposes these unsuspected aspects of culture, or "informal culture" to "formal culture", traditional elements of culture, and to "technical culture", explicit knowledge based on science and technique. As an anthropologist, Hall is looking for "structured distinctions that transcend individual differences, and are finely integrated in the social matrix in which they appear." (Hall, 1963: 1006). He believes this observation is not exclusive to anthropologists, and that whoever is leaving for a foreign culture can be made attentive to the mechanisms of interaction, and hence can be made to understand the possible consequences of their behaviour on others. Others do not necessarily interpret our behaviour as we do, or as we would expect them to. According to Hall, a minimum of information about a culture is necessary in order to master interactional situations in that culture. Once a person has to live in the culture, they will continue learning on their own.

Hall follows the trend which had been established at the Foreign Service Institute by Trager (Hall and Trager, 1954), who states that linguistics must be extended beyond words, and uses the term "metalinguistics" for the "non-verbal" domain: the meaning of an uttering is the product of a combination of language with other non linguistic cultural dimensions. Hall's goal was to enlarge the anthropological notion of culture in order to include communication. He was inspired by anthropological sources such as Franz Boas, for whom communication is at the heart of culture, and by American linguists such as Edward Sapir, Leonard Bloomfield and Benjamin Lee Whorf (Hall, 1966). The anthropology he develops, he first calls "the anthropology of manners" (Hall, 1955), which aims at constructing a "frame of reference" that would help us to observe better, and to discover the significant differences of manners, or interaction styles.

## CONTEXT AND COMMUNICATION

The non-verbal, non-linguistic cultural dimensions that produce meaning, can be called the "context" in which verbal communication takes place. Hall then makes a distinction between high-context cultures and low-context cultures, according to the idea that "Context is the information that surrounds an event; it is inextricably bound up with the meaning of that event." (Hall and Hall, 1990: 6). According to Hall, "a high-context communication or message is one in which most of the information is already in the person, while very little is in the coded, explicit, transmitted part of the message. A low-context communication is just the opposite; i.e. the mass of the information is vested in the explicit code" (Hall, 1976, quoted in Hall and Hall, 1990: 6). This definition has led many researchers to believe that the explicit code is language. One should not forget, however, that language is one of the many possible codes, and other codes can be as explicit or implicit as language can be. There are many other codes, such as for example dress, greetings, gestures, sitting arrangements, eye contact, touching, that may convey different meanings within the same culture, but that may also be different in other cultures. Someone who doesn't know a particular code, cannot understand the message expressed in that code. A non-French speaking Belgian needs to know that a kiss is an everyday way of saying hello, even to strangers, and does not imply anything else. Schein (1999: 21) states that one realises that the important parts of culture are essentially invisible, that culture can be thought of as the "shared mental models" that the members of an organisation hold and take for granted. This is also called the "silent code" (Seeley and Seelye-James, 1994). This code can be learned, if one learns to understand the importance of the context on the interpretation of the code. In Agar's words (1994: 96): "Meaning is back, not just dictionary meaning, but meanings that stretch into the fundamental premises of identity. Language is reconnected to the situations of its use. Words and sentences are still around, but now they sit in the context of the discourse that contains them".

Since the publication of The Silent Language, the concept of context has become unavoidable in any reference to intercultural communication, although Hall did no define it precisely (Usunier, 1996). Components of the context of communication are the elements that surround the interaction: location, people, channel, time, and so on. This context will influence the interaction without people being necessarily aware. In fact, people are mostly unaware of the factors that influence their interaction. The concept has led to different interpretations and even confusion between implicit and explicit communication, direct and indirect communication, formal and informal communication, silence and speech.

The following wants to examine all these concepts, and re-examine the relationship that exists between them.

Following Hall's description of high and low-context (Hall and Hall, 1990), one could contrast high-context and low-context as far as information is concerned (Table 20.1).

From low-context to high-context, cultures can be classified as follows (Hall, 1976; Kohls, 1978), (Table 20.2).

## CONTEXT AND MEANING

From Table 20.1, it appears that context is linked to background information. A message takes on a particular meaning which is determined in function of other elements that make up its context (Corraze, 1992). The context plays a role in the interpretation: either it dominates, or it adds information. The meaning of the message depends on other stimuli, which at the same instant affect the receiver as well as the sender. Meaning is culturally-specific, socially determined (Greer and Stephens, 1998), and understanding or confusion may often be attributed to context sensitivity. Usunier

**Table 20.1**   High and low-context and information

| High-context | Low-context |
|---|---|
| Most of the information is already in the person, little is in coded, explicit, transmitted part of the message | The mass of the information is vested in the explicit code |
| Information flows freely from all sides: form and function of the organisation is centred on gathering, processing, disseminating information | Compartmentalise their personal relationships, their work, many aspects of day-to-day life; hence they need detailed background information |
| Irritation when LC people insist on giving them information they don't need | At a loss when HC people do not provide enough information |
| Want to make their own synthesis, want to see everything | Accept someone else's synthesis, bottom-line |

(1992: 114) has the following definition of context: "Le contexte recouvre l'ensemble des mécanismes d'interprétation, d'origine culturelle, qui permettent l'explication d'un message" (Context covers the whole of interpretive mechanisms, of cultural origin, that allow to explain a message). Smith (1965) rightly differentiates the message from its meaning. Context refers to events in the external environment as well as in the internal environment. Smith includes the "historical context", by which he means the genetic programme, and the "immediate context". Context is then a variable signal modulating the meaning of a set of invariable signals. This variable signal can be called "paralanguage", and includes the modalities of the voice, other vocal sounds such as yawning, laughing, shouting, coughing etc., which supply information on the affective state of the sender. Paralanguage can also include gestures such as nodding, indicating that the speaker should go on, or so called "emblems" (Ekman and Friesen, 1972), gestures that can be translated by words, and can replace words when vocal communication is impossible. Gestures and emblems vary greatly across cultures (Ekman and Friesen,

**Table 20.2**   Low-context and high-context cultures

| Low-context | Swiss German |
|---|---|
| | German |
| | Scandinavian |
| | United States |
| | French |
| | English |
| | Italian |
| | Spanish |
| | Greek |
| | Arab |
| | Chinese |
| High-context | Japanese |

1971). Birdwhistell (1971) claims that it was possible to recognise which language the former mayor of New York, La Guardia, was speaking, with the sound of the tape being cut. La Guardia spoke three languages: English, Italian, and Yiddish. We could say that he was also "multilingual" in his paralanguage or body language.

Obviously, non-verbal communication and verbal communication are not substitutes for each other, but correspond to different demands. Body language and gestures are not redundant, their suppression perturbs verbal communication. Indeed, the quality of the communication is greatly improved by the non verbal system: "We speak with our vocal organ, but we converse with our whole body" (Abercrombie, quoted in Argyle, 1975). Non-verbal communication makes hesitation on the receiver's side difficult, improbable, it doesn't allow for other information to impose itself, it is restraining, compelling (Corraze, 1992). This body language is socially acquired early in life, and maintained through habit. Its display rules are imposed by culture.

# LEVELS OF CONTEXT

One could distinguish context at three levels: the immediate context, the social context, and the cultural context.

At the level of "immediate context", Bateson (1973) speaks of "metacommunication", a communication concerning another communication: the content of the message has to be dissociated from the meaning that the sender is giving it through another signal which is exterior to it and exists at a different level. One can for instance emit a verbal message while associating it to a non-verbal communication which indicates the signal should not be taken seriously, like a wink or a smile. This immediate context gives the meaning, and allows the receiver to understand the verbal message in this particular instance.

On a social level, context is the background information that someone has, and that is common with other people. This is what Stalnaker (1974 [1991]: 472) termed "common ground": "Communication, whether linguistic or not, normally takes place against a background of beliefs or assumptions which are shared by the speaker and his audience, and which are recognised by them to be shared [...]. The more common ground we can take for granted, the more efficient our communication will be. And unless we could reasonably treat *some* facts in this way, we probably could not communicate at all". The concept of shared beliefs and assumptions has also been called "mutual knowledge" (Smith, 1982; Gibbs, 1987), "shared assumptions" (Sperber and Wilson, 1986), "scripts" (Schank and Abelson, 1977). One could also say that context is a shared code: if people have a common experience, a common background, they don't need to explain, half a word will be enough to make oneself understood. Hall (1976, quoted in Hall and Hall, 1990: 6) states that "Twins who have grown up together can and do communicate more economically (HC) than two lawyers in a courtroom during a trial (LC), a mathematician programming a computer, two politicians drafting legislation, two administrators writing a regulation.". From this, it appears that for Hall a communication can be high-context (HC) if people know each other well, like the twins, whereas when these people talk to someone they don't know, or in low-context

(LC) situations like a courtroom, they need "contexting", they have to use more words to make themselves understood, to create the context. The context is a shared code, and if the code is not shared, communication has to be low-context, or explicit. The more the code is shared or common, the less need for many words or explanations, the more what needs to be communicated is implicit, the more people know what is appropriate at what circumstances and with whom. "The greater the amount of knowledge and experience two communities share, the less important it is for them to express directly what they wish to say or write. Conversely, the less these communicators share, the more necessary it is for them to convey their meaning through words and gestures – that is, the less they can assume to be understood." (Victor, 1992: 138). Intimates, like family members or close friends, share a lot of common ground or codes, but according to Jucker and Smith (1996), even they must constantly negotiate and renegotiate their common ground, and they must often resort to explicit negotiation strategies to do so. Lane et al (1997: 50) identify the communication model as having and applying knowledge of a cultural "map", and the two subprocesses in finding commonalities are establishing a common reality and agreeing on common rules.

The "cultural context" are the rules of communicative messages that dominate in a culture. They include facial expressions, eye contact, posture, gestures, and the use of space.

Control of facial expressions is learned at an early stage: Harris et al (quoted in Feldman, 1982) estimate that in a Dutch population, 50 percent of the six year old subjects and 70 percent of the fifteen year old subjects are unable to manifest their anger or their fright. Face, with its wide variation of expressions, is also the non-verbal communication zone that we control best, it is the best "non-verbal lier" (Ekman, 1971). How much can or cannot be displayed is culture bound (Corraze, 1992). Cultural differences are important in the length of eye contact: it is strictly fixed, and it is noticeable when one moves from a Latin culture to anglophone cultures with their "civil inattention" (Goffman, 1963). Watson (1970) found relevant differences between the Arabs, the South-Americans and the South-Europeans on the one hand, with a longer exchange of looks than the Asians, the Indians and the North-Americans on the other hand. For the first group, looking away is impolite, whereas in the second group a "long stare" is experienced as aggressive or embarrassing.

Among the thousand possible postures that the human body can use without discomfort, cultures choose certain postures (Hewes, 1957). Obviously, the environment and its level of ethnicity impose or encourage certain postures rather than others. In an interesting observation, Jourard (1966) found that during one hour in a café in San Juan (Porto Rico), the frequency of cutaneous messages (touching) was 180, while the score was 110 in Paris, 2 in aineville (Florida), and 0 in London. Japanese people tend to communicate little about themselves to others, it is limited to the "public self", and extremely restricted in cutaneous signals (Barnlund, 1975).

As seen before, gestures are culturally ritualised. Morris et al (1979) have analysed cultural meanings of gestures. Underestimating this formalisation, or "conventionalism" risks to mislead us (Corraze, 1992).

Hall (1966) created the term "proxemics" to qualify anything that touches on the organisation and use of space. According to Sommer (1969), personal space refers to a

**Table 20.3** Small distance and large distance cultures

| | |
|---|---|
| Small distance | Arabs |
| | Indians-Pakistanis |
| | South-Europeans |
| | South-Americans |
| | Asians |
| Large distance | North-Europeans |

zone with invisible limits that surrounds the body, and which an intruder is not allowed to enter. This zone is also called "territory". Watson (1970), comparing distances during a conversation, found that distances increase (Table 20.3).

The differences are significant between the group of the first three cultures, the group of the next two cultures, and the last group.

# CONTEXT AND CODES

Similarly to Hall's conceptualisation of high and low-context communication, Bernstein (1964) distinguishes "restricted codes" and "elaborated codes". Restricted codes are shortened words, phrases and sentences, which rely heavily on hidden, implicit, contextual cues such as non-verbal behaviour, social context, and the nature of interpersonal relationships. They are a form of "shorthand" communication which does not rely on verbal elaboration or explication (Ferraro, 1998). Elaborated codes emphasise elaborate verbal amplification, and place little importance on non-verbal or other contextual cues. According to Ferraro (1998) relatively restricted or elaborated codes can be found in any speech community, although one or the other mode is likely to predominate.

Low-context cultures seem to rely on elaborated verbal codes, and demonstrate a positive attitude towards words. They have a tradition of rhetoric, and attach importance on the delivery of the verbal message. "A primary function of speech of this tradition is to express one's ideas and thoughts as clearly, logically, and persuasively as possible, so the speaker can be fully recognised for his or her individuality in influencing others." (Gudykunst and Kim, 1984: 140). In the US for instance, "effective verbal communication is expected to be explicit, direct, unambiguous" (Ferraro, 1998: 51). The degree of explicitness is often linked to the line of thought (Galtung, 19; Ulijn, 1994; Binon and Claes, 1996; Bennett et al, 1998): the germanic line of thought is said to be linear, focused, without digression, monochronic, handling one thing at a time, hence explicit; the romance or Latin line of thought is said to allow for digressions, to be polychronic, discussing several things at the same time, hence implicit.

In high-context cultures, verbal messages, although important, are only a part of the total communication context. "Words are inseparably interrelated to social relationships, politics, and morality. More wholistic approach to communication, its purpose is not to enhance the speaker's individuality through the articulation of words but rather to

**Table 20.4**  Communication patterns in high and low-context cultures

| High-context cultures | Low-context cultures |
| --- | --- |
| Rely on<br>  Restricted codes<br>  contextual cues | Rely on<br>  Elaborated verbal messages |
| Communication patterns<br>  Inexact<br>  Implicit<br>  Indirect<br>  Ambiguous | Communication patterns<br>  Precise<br>  Explicit<br>  Straightforward |

promote harmony and social integration. In such societies one is expected to be sensitive to subtle contextual cues and not to assume that critical information will always be verbalised." (Ferraro, 1998: 53). Speech patterns are more ambiguous, inexact (see Table 20.4).

According to Cannon (1991), the key lies in recognizing that communication starts with the receiver of the message, not the transmitter. Preparing a message includes an analysis of the ways it which it will be interpreted, and the task of those wishing to manage communication more effectively lies in structuring and organising these signals to achieve their desired end.

# CONTEXT AND CULTURAL DIMENSIONS

The distinction between high-context and low-context has been linked to many other concepts, such as: silence, trust, face and politeness, formality, individualism, power distance, uncertainty avoidance, but also to values such as truth, integrity, sincerity. These concepts are examined briefly in the next section.

## Silence

Silence is mostly associated with high-context cultures, because they are linked to the concept of "restricted code", which implies that they rely on non-verbal behaviour. Silence is then valued as a means of communication, and can have meaning. It is not unusual to leave sentence unfinished or to tolerate periods of silence. In Japanese, there is a verb meaning "to understand with the belly", which implies that an educated adult should be able to understand without words being spoken. According to Suzuki (1978: 168), Japan is "a society in which the common practice is to try to guess others' feelings and wishes before they are verbally expressed. This also explains why the Japanese themselves call their culture *sasshi no bunka*, lit., "guessing culture" and *omoiyari no bunka*, lit., "consideration culture"".

**Table 20.5**  Verbal communication in high and low-context cultures

|  | High-context | Low-context |
|---|---|---|
| Reliance on words to communicate | Low | High |
| Reliance on non-verbal communication | High | Low |
| View of silence | Respected, communicative | Anxiety-producing, non-communicative |
| Attention to detail | Low | High |
| Attention to intention | High | Low |
| Communication approach | Indirect, inferential | Direct, explicit |
| Literalness | Low, interpretive | High, non-interpretive |

According to Victor (1992), there is a variation in the reliance on verbal communication between extreme high and low-context cultures, which is summarised in Table 20.5.

To my mind, a distinction should be made however, between context and code. One can have a high-context culture with a restricted code, a high-context culture with an elaborated code, as well as a low-context culture with a restricted code and a low-context culture with an elaborated code. This means that silence can be valued in high-context restricted code cultures, but also in low-context restricted code cultures. High-context cultures are not necessarily cultures where verbal messages are sparse: in Arab cultures, communication is very verbal, and the Arabic language is filled with forms of "verbal exaggeration", with metaphors, proverbs and cultural idioms. In his study comparing the Arabic and North American style, Prothro (1955) concluded that "an assertive statement" in North American eyes would be weak and equivocating in the Arab cultures, where linguistic overassertion or "verbal overkill" are the rule: "statements which seem to Arabs to be mere statements of fact will seem to Americans to be extreme or even violent assertions. Statement which Arabs view as showing firmness and strength on a negative or positive issue may sound to North Americans as "exaggerated" (1970: 711, quoted in Gudykunst and Ting-Toomey, 1988: 105–106). Similarly, and according to Holden (2000: 123), the western businessperson needs to address the Russian "grandiloquence". Just as in high-context cultures with a restricted code, the meaning is not explicit in high-context cultures with an elaborated code: one has to interpret what is said or not said, according to the reigning code. Examples of combinations of context and code can be found in Table 20.6.

## Verbal Styles

Gudykunst and Ting-Toomey's (1988) classification into four stylistic modes of interaction allows for a fine distinction between direct and indirect style, elaborate and succinct style, personal and contextual style, instrumental and affective style. The direct-indirect style refers to the extent speakers reveal their intentions through explicit

**Table 20.6**   Context and code

|                  | High-context | Low-context |
|------------------|--------------|-------------|
| Restricted code  | Japanese     | Finnish     |
| Elaborated code  | Arabic       | German      |

verbal communication. The dimension elaborate versus succinct style encompasses three verbal stylistic variations: elaborate style, exacting style, and succinct style. This dimension deals with the quantity of talk: the elaborate style refers to the use of rich, expressive language in everyday conversation, the exacting style means that one's contribution in language interaction ought to be neither more nor less information than is required, and the succinct style includes the use of understatements, pauses, and silences in everyday conversation. The Arab and Middle Eastern communication patterns reflect an elaborate style; the use of an exacting style is characteristic of many Northern European and the US cultures, while succinct verbal communication style will be found in many Asian cultures.

Verbal personal style is individual-centred language (importance of personhood, hence use of personal pronouns for symmetrical power relationships), while verbal contextual style is role-centred language (importance of role relationships, hence use of formality for asymmetrical power relationships). The instrumental verbal style is sender-oriented language usage (goal-oriented verbal communication; digital), and the affective verbal style is receiver-oriented verbal usage (process-oriented, analogical, with expressive non-verbal behaviour). These different verbal styles are described in Tables 20.7–20.10.

"Verbal interactions styles reflect and embody the affective, moral, and aesthetic patterns of a culture" (Gudykunst and Ting-Toomey, 1988: 100): the authors use Hofstede's (1980) dimensions and Hall's (1976, 1983) low- and high-context schema to explain linguistic variations across cultures.

Even if there are differences between elaborated and succinct verbal styles (Japanese and Arab for example), there seems to be a clear distinction between Northern European or North-American styles and Asian, Japanese or Arabic styles, and this distinction concerns not only directness versus indirectness, but also individualistic versus collectivist cultures. According to Gudykunst and Ting-Toomey (1988: 89), "individualistic cultures focus on the 'I' identity and collectivist cultures focus on

**Table 20.7**   Direct and indirect styles

| Direct         | Indirect           |
|----------------|--------------------|
| USA            | Japan, China, Korea |
|                | Arab world         |
| Individualism  | Collectivism       |
| Low-context    | High-context       |

**Table 20.8**   Elaborated, exacting, and succinct styles

| Elaborated style | Exacting style | Succinct style |
|---|---|---|
| Arabic | Northern Europe | Japan |
| Middle Eastern | USA | Asian cultures |
| High-context | Low-context | High-context |
| Moderate uncertainty avoidance | Low to moderate uncertainty avoidance | High uncertainty avoidance |

the 'we' identity". The characteristics that are emphasised in both cultures are summarised in Table 20.11.

Gudykunst and Ting-Toomey add that "While meanings in low-context cultures are displayed overtly through direct communication forms, meanings in high-context cultures are embedded implicitly at different levels of the sociocultural context". Individualism versus collectivism seems to be an important determinant in the use of "context", and we will see later how this cultural dimensions plays a role in verbal style and face-negotiation. Other cultural dimensions such as uncertainty avoidance or power distance have also been linked to the verbal styles, as can be seen in the summary by Francesco and Gold (1998: 58), Table 20.12.

Uncertainty avoidance is an indication for elaborated or succinct verbal style. This would mean that there are two different verbal reactions to approach uncertain an novel situations: either understatements and silence, or elaborate word choice and exaggerated speech, or "flight or fight". As both styles can be found in high-context cultures, this reinforces my earlier statement that a distinction needs to be made between context and code.

Power distance is an indication for personal or contextual style. It is clear from Hofstede's research that a high score on power distance will usually be found in collective cultures, and a low score on power distance is typical for individualistic cultures; Interesting exceptions are Latin cultures in Europe such as France or Belgium, which combine individualism with a high power distance. If the power distance is large, the style of address is more easily predicted, because it is linked to the social status, and the status and title of a person will be known to a wide range of people. Formality, as we

**Table 20.9**   Personal and contextual styles

| Personal style | Contextual style |
|---|---|
| Northern Europe | Far East |
| USA | Southeast Asia |
|  | Africa |
| Low-context | High-context |
| Individualism | Collectivism |
| Low power distance | High power distance |
| Informal codes of interaction | Formal codes of interaction |

**Table 20.10**   Instrumental and affective styles

| Instrumental style | Affective style |
| --- | --- |
| North America | Asia |
| North Europe | Arab |
|  | Latin America |
| Verbal | Non-verbal expressiveness |
|  | Intuitive sense |
| Digital level | Analogical level |
| Low-context | High-context |
| Individualism | Collectivism |
| Self-face maintenance | Mutual-face maintenance |

will see, is more common with members of a high power distance cultures, hence of collective cultures, while members of an individualistic and low power distance culture often use a more personal and informal style. In this latter case, the style of address is determined by a complex interrelationship of factors such as the correct degree of formality, and appropriateness within the social and situational context. (Mead, 1994).

Mead (1994: 181) links power distance to ambiguity: "Where power distances are large, subordinates are weary of asking for clarification of ambiguous utterances lest this involve the superior in loss of face (by implying that he/she communicated inadequately the first time) and so work to make sure that they interpret correctly. They observe his/her behaviour, and predict appropriate responses in part on the basis of past experience. In turn the considerate superior tries to avoid ambiguity and unpredictability. But where power distances are small, a failure to make a correct interpretation:

costs less in terms of face;
can be easily repaired by asking for clarification."

## Social and Cultural Values

The link between context and social or cultural values can be examined from the insiders' point of view or from the outsiders' perspective. As usual in cultural char-

**Table 20.11**   Individualistic and collectivist cultures

| Individualistic (ex.: United States) | Collectivistic (ex.: Japanese culture) |
| --- | --- |
| Low-context | High-context |
| Individual value orientations | Group value orientations |
| Line logic | Spiral logic |
| Direct verbal interactions | Indirect verbal interactions |
| Individualistic non-verbal styles | Contextual non-verbal styles |
| Intentions are displayed clearly, and have direct correspondence with verbal and non-verbal patterns | Intentions and meanings are situated within the larger shared knowledge of the cultural context |

**Table 20.12** Major characteristics of the four verbal styles

| Verbal Style | Variation | Major characteristics | Cultures where found |
|---|---|---|---|
| Direct versus indirect | Direct | Message is more explicit | Individualistic, low-context |
| | Indirect | Message is more implicit | Collective, high-context |
| Elaborate versus succinct | Elaborate | Quantity of talk is relatively high | Moderate uncertainty avoidance, high-context |
| | Exacting | Quantity of talk is moderate | Low uncertainty avoidance, low-context |
| | Succinct | Quantity of talk is relatively low | High uncertainty avoidance, high-context |
| Personal versus contextual | Personal | Focus is on speaker, "personhood" | Low power distance, individualistic, low-context |
| | Contextual | Focus is on role of speaker, role relationships | High power distance, collective, high-context |
| Instrumental versus affective | Instrumental | Language is goal oriented, sender focused | Individualistic, low-context |
| | Affective | Language is process oriented, receiver focused | Collective, high-context |

**Table 20.13** High and low-context as valued by themselves

| High-context seen by themselves | Low-context seen by themselves |
| --- | --- |
| Polite: avoid embarrassment | Truth, honesty |
| Cautious | Frankness |
| Respectful | Sincerity |
| Supportive | Openness |
| Integrity = say what promotes harmony, what you're expected to say | Integrity: say what you think |

acteristics, our own ways are considered best, and we find fault with different approaches to life: all the others are crazy, as Asterix would say. Bringing together observations from authors such as Linowes (1997), Gudykunst and Ting-Toomey (1988), Ferraro (1998), Holden (1999), Salo-Lee (1999), one could collect observations about self and others in two tables, and they would not be exhaustive (Table 20.13).

The cultural variations that are linked to high and low-context cultures can be summarised in Table 20.14 (see also Table 20.15).

## Honesty, Integrity, Trust

As we can see, the ideas of honesty, integrity, trust are linked to the communication style: what makes us believe and trust what some people say, whereas we don't always know why we trust or distrust somebody? In his book "The Trust Effect", Reynolds (1997) identifies four practices: competence, openness, reliability and equity. Openness here means "tell them the score, give feedback", and the author uses expressions such as: *tell them what you think of them, straight talking, giving honest feedback*. It is clear that Western cultures believe that being sincere and honest means saying what you

**Table 20.14** High and low-context cultures as seen by each other

| High-context seen by low-context | Low-context seen by high-context |
| --- | --- |
| Tricky | Rude |
| Deceptive | Course |
| Of questionable integrity | Noisy |
| Questionable | Disruptive |
| Secretive | Insensitive |
| Unwilling to trust | Slow on the up-take |
| Arrogant | Lack observational skill to read between the lines |
| Inscrutable | |
| Conceited | Naive, lack of realism |
| Hide their feelings | Lack of self-control |
| Indirectness is a waste of time | Airing views that are better left unsaid |

**Table 20.15** High-context, low-context and cultural variations

| High-context | Low-context |
|---|---|
| Close **interpersonal relationships:** depend on stored or understood information | Relies on transmitted messages: information can be explicitly provided |
| Communication in loops | Straight line |
| Leisurely approach and indirect manner, emphasis broad objectives | Focus on specific details |
| Evaluate source of statement as much as its content (who) | Evaluate content (what) |
| Flexibility to meet changing situations | |
| Need someone to count on | Need correct information |
| | Faith in **legal codes and contracts:** Emphasis on written word |
| Individual interpretation governs interpersonal behaviour | Law is adhered to, respected, governs interpersonal behaviour |
| Personal promises binding: gentleman's agreement: stress on *who* | Personal promises not binding |
| Written word not binding | Written word binding |
| | Contract is binding: stress on *what* |
| Reliance on **non-verbal communication** | Reliance on words to communicate |
| Silence is respected, communicative | Silence is anxiety-producing: non-communicative |
| Listen to the pauses between words and gestures | Listen to the words between pauses |
| Attention to intention | Attention to detail |
| Indirect, inferential approach | Direct, explicit approach |
| Low literalness, interpretative | High literalness, non-interpretative |
| Ambiguity | Certainty |
| Central and peripheral information | Words vary little in their meaning: rude |
| Knowledge assumed | |
| Correlation with high **uncertainty avoidance:** uncomfortable with a stranger | Greater tolerance for ambiguous communication |
| Importance of **face-saving:** Politeness strategy, indirect plan | Confrontation strategy: direct plan |
| Directness = uncivil, inconsiderate, offensive | Directness = honest, inoffensive |
| Indirectness = civil, considerate, honest | Indirectness = dishonest, offensive |
| Verbal disclosure = loss of face | High amount of verbal self-disclosure |
| Vagueness tolerated: no straight answer | Vagueness not tolerated |
| Public shame | Personal guilt |

think. They place a great deal of power in words, whereas many Asian cultures show a certain mistrust of words, or at least have been aware of the limitation of words alone. Saying what you think usually implies saying it in a direct and explicit way, which is valued in some cultures as being honest and open. In Dutch, the expression *met de deur in huis vallen*, literally *to fall with the door into the house,* means to bring bad news without introduction, and is qualified by Vuysje and Van der Lans (1999: 83) as follows: "In the eyes of foreigners (Mediterranean or Asian cultures) this gives evidence of a nearly enigmatic clumsiness" (my translation). In Asian cultures, people are more prudent in what they choose to say and how they will say it: the high frequency of words such as *perhaps, maybe* is striking. Some things are better left unsaid, because airing them might create confrontation or loss of face. The desire to avoid embarrassment often takes precedence over the truth. There are many different ways of saying "no", and "yes" does not necessarily mean that the response is affirmative, but negative verbal messages will be avoided or suppressed. This cautious approach is linked to the concept of politeness.

## Politeness

Politeness may be interpreted in as many ways as there are cultures: what is considered to be polite, what counts as politeness is very different. All groups have social rules about politeness, and the presumed lack of politeness can easily lead to intercultural misunderstanding. Interruptions for example, are considered to be impolite for North Americans, Germans or Dutch people (Anglo German cultures), whereas Latin cultures enjoy interrupting and overlapping in their speech, because that shows interest in what is being said. The digressive way of a Latin-style presentation is seen as ill-prepared and rude by Anglo Germans, and the direct and linear style of these Anglo-Germans is considered to be rude and steering by Latin cultures (Bennett et al, 1998). Eye contact with a superior can be seen as polite or as a lack of respect. Politeness has to do also with the choice of formality or familiarity in the form of address. Changes in register answer subtle, implicit or explicit social rules, often as least partly unconscious.

Hall links context to formality: he speaks of "the high-context, familiar form of address", and "the low-context, formal form of address" (Hall and Hall, 1990: 7). A shift in the level of context is communication: a shift up indicates a warming of the relationship, a shift down communicates coolness and displeasure. According to Hall, first-naming in the United-States is an artificial attempt at high-contexting, and this "familiarity" tends to offend Europeans. On the other hand, in Japan, "The day starts with the use of honorifics, formal forms of address attached to each name. If things are going well, the honorifics are dropped as the day progresses", and "In the United States, the boss might communicate annoyance to an assistant when he shifts from the high-context, familiar form of address to the low-context, formal form of address" (Hall and Hall, 1990: 7), which implies that Japanese HC communication, as well as LC North-American communication, can be formal or informal. In other words, formality and informality exist in both LC and HC cultures. Formality would be used when people do not know each other well enough, or when someone wants to create distance by refusing to use the common implicit code.

Formality could then be seen as another code, distinct from context, but using context (the implicit common code) as a means of communication. Politeness and formality are expressed through language, but one should distinguish between linguistic meaning and social meaning or shared expectations.

In their famous book on politeness, Brown and Levinson (1978) refer to certain acts in human interaction, such as requests, criticisms and complaints as "face threatening acts" (FTA). According to the authors, people have "positive face" – they want to be appreciated and approved of – and "negative face" – they do not want to be impeded in their actions. Moreover, it is generally in everyone's interests that face should be protected. Strategies in interaction range from:

1. Bald on record (without redressive action): *Shut the window!*
2. Positive politeness: Shut the window, darling.
3. Negative politeness (using conventional indirectness): *I wonder if you'd mind shutting the window.*
4. Off record (using non-conventional indirectness, e.g. a hint): *Its cold in here.*
5. Don't do the FTA.

In strategies 1 and 5, politeness is irrelevant. The second and the third categories involve redressive action, and the fourth category uses an ambiguous utterance, the interpretation of which is left to the addressee. In a study on requests, Vázquez Orta (1995) compared the language used in Spanish and in English, and found that both languages differ in their preference for the use of specific substrategies. Requests can be realised linguistically with imperatives, interrogatives, and declaratives. Imperatives are used more directly in Spanish: *Pass me the salt*, in English one would have to add *please*. Interrogatives in English use modals: *Could you tell me the time?*, in Spanish they don't: *Me das fuego?* (You give me a light?). Declaratives include statements: *I want to check the possibility,*or hints: *Its cold in here*, in both languages. Does this mean that English is more polite? The author concludes that in Spanish the preference for hearer-oriented requests (use of "you") combines with a low incidence of downgrading (no use of "please"), while in English the reverse trend is apparent: less hearer-oriented (use of "I") and more downgrading (use of "please"). This would mean that England is a negative politeness society, while Spain is a positive politeness society. Although in Table 20.2 Spain is ranked as more high-context than England, Spanish requests seem to be more impositive, and English requests were found to use more indirectness. However, positive politeness is linked to the hearer's desire to be liked and appreciated, while negative face is liked to the hearer's desire for autonomy and freedom of action, which matches Ting-Toomey's (1988) theory about face and individualism-collectivism: "Individualist cultures are concerned with the authenticity of self-presentation style. Collective cultures are concerned with the adaptability of self-presentation image; this suggests that individualistic cultures are concerned with self-face maintenance and collective cultures are concerned with self-face and other-face maintenance. Further, individualistic cultures value autonomy, choices, and negative-face need, while collective cultures value interdependence, reciprocal obligations, and positive-face need." (Gudykunst and Ting-Toomey, 1988: 89–90).

Hence, the cultural dimension of collectivism versus individualism seems to determine whether communication will be high-context and indirect or low-context and direct. Communication will have to preserve the group harmony fore and foremost in the former case, while it aims at expression of the "authentic and true" self in the latter case. However, this cultural dimension can not be the only determinant, as we have seen that English culture for instance is very individualistic, and fairly implicit at the same time.

The degree of directness and formality can be explained by Hofstede's cultural dimensions, but only partially. Uncertainty avoidance is not necessarily linked to formality/informality, as we can see in Spain, where informality is frequent although the uncertainty avoidance index is higher than in Germany, where formality is greatly appreciated. Ambiguity seems to be not so much a problem of power distance, but of "implicit intelligence". Most cultures are collectivist, and probably implicit, but not necessarily formal; Collectivism probably has more to do with ritualised forms of communication, than with formality in the western sense of the word.

## CONCLUSION AND IMPLICATIONS FOR MANAGEMENT

Direct or indirect communication, formality or informality are not opposite categories, they can co-exist in any culture, depending on the setting, the interaction partner, the intent or the content, the language itself; in other words, depending on the context of communication. Being direct or indirect, formal or informal, can be used as a communication technique, and the choice is in itself a way of communicating intentions or relationships: so much is "formal pretense, social deception, obligation, mutual self-interest" (Holden, 1999). Formalisation, ritualisation, and conventionalism can be used voluntarily or involuntarily, they have different roles in different situations, and they can be used deliberately, as a technique in negotiations (Weiss and Stripp, 1985).

In communication, so much can be left unsaid if both partners share the same knowledge about the situation or conventions. On the other hand, it is obvious that in some cultures, where the strong group identification creates strong shared background knowledge and conventions, preservation of group harmony is valued more than outspokenness. In these cultures, meanings are hidden behind silences or behind words, and have to be looked for intentionally. In Ferraro's words (1998: 52), this high-context communication is a "more wholistic approach to communication, its purpose in many Eastern cultures is not to enhance the speaker's individuality through the articulation of words but rather to promote harmony and social integration".

Politeness is important: it means respecting the implicit rules, it is a set of strategies assuming the intelligence of the communication partner, hence there is no need to expose his face. Consequently, directness is often perceived as a form of impoliteness, because it attacks the person as well as the content. There are two forms of politeness, formality and face-saving: formality is peripheral (use of titles, of "please"), and face-saving is central. What counts as politeness is different, hence the importance of appropriateness in different situations (Gallois and Callan, 1997): communication register and style change according to explicit or implicit social rules, to protocol, to status. As stated in Berry et al (1992: 43): "Social behaviour takes place in a social and cultural context that varies widely from place to place". The difficulty is of course not knowing how the elements of a social system are organised or structured by each cultural group.

Effective communication assumes that the communication partner knows certain rules and structures of communication. The rules imply:

that the other is socially competent: he knows the world, the environment, the references;

that the other knows how communication is structured, and is able to make a distinction between central and peripheral;

that the other can infer messages, read between the lines;

that messages are encoded in different ways, not just in language, so one must accept and learn the other codes.

What is most important is mutual perception: how things are perceived by the other. The same communication style, or choice of words and register, can be perceived as being polite or impolite in different circumstances, but also in different cultures. Politeness is not universal, but culture specific. Effective intercultural communication requires "isomorphic attributions" (Triandis, 1975), that is that participants in an interaction have to give the same interpretation to behaviour. What is required, apart from "inside knowledge" (Gallois and Callan, 1997), is "empathy" (Bolten, 1995), "decentering" (Lane et al, 1997), "observational skills" (Ferraro, 1998), and the willingness to negotiate and renegotiate the common ground.

If globalisation is the emergence of a global interactive network of organisations with their "multiplicity of separate, overlapping, superimposed, or nested cultures" (Sackmann et al, 1997), it implies new structures where distinctions between nation-state values and practices may become less important, but where relationship management knows and uses new approaches or strategies. The new routines created by communication technologies may appear to be reducing the distinctions, yet the failure rate of cross-border mergers and acquisitions increasingly stresses the need for negotiation of "common ground".

# REFERENCES

Agar, M. (1994) Language Shock. Understanding the Culture of Conversation. New York: William Morrow and Co.

Argyle, M. (1975) Bodily communication. Methuen and Co. Ltd.

Barnlund, B.C. (1975) Communicative style in two cultures: Japan and the United States. In G. Zivin (Ed), The Development of Expressive Behaviour, pp. 427–456. New York: Academic Press.

Bateson, G. (1973) Steps to an Ecology of Mind. Paladin.

Bennett, J., Claes M.-T., Forsberg, J., Flynn N., Obenaus W. and Smith T. (1998) Doing Effective Presentations in an Intercultural Setting. Vienna: Ueberreuter.

Bernstein, B. (1964) Elaborated and restricted codes. Their social origins and some consequences. In J.J. Gumperz and D. Hymes (Eds), The Ethnography of Communication. American Anthropologist, 66 (6), Part II: 55–69.

Berry, J.W., Poortinga, Y.H., Segall, M.H. and Dase, P.R. (1992) Cross-cultural Psychology. Research and Applications. Cambridge, MA: Cambridge University press.

Birdwhistell, R.L. (1971) Kinesics and Context. Allen Lane: Penguin Press.

Bolten, J. (1995) L'apprentissage interactif et interculturel des langues étrangères. In U. Rau (Ed), La Communication Interculturelle. Un Concept Indispensable pour un Management Efficace, pp. 133–156. Montréal: Goethe Institut.

Brown, P. and Levinson, S.C. (1978) Politeness. Some universals in language use. Studies in Interactional Sociolinguistics, Vol. 4. Cambridge, MA: Cambridge University Press.

Brunner, J. (1998) Buckeye glass company in China. In A.M. Francesco and B.A. Gold (Eds), International Organisational Behavior. Readings, Cases and Skills, pp. 448–463. Upper Saddle River, NJ: Prentice Hall.

Cannon, T. (1991) Enterprise: Creation, Development and Growth. Oxford: Butterworth-Heinemann.

Carroll, R. (1988) Cultural Misunderstandings: The French-American Experience. Chicago, IL: University of Chicago Press.

Condon, J. (1981) Values and ethics in communication across cultures: some notes on the North American case. Communication, 6: 255–265.

Corraze, J. (1992) Les communications non-verbales. Collection Le Psychologue. Paris: Presses Universitaires de France.

Ekman, P. (1979) About brows: emotional and conversational signals. In Von Cranach (Ed), Human Ethology, pp. 169–249. Cambridge, MA: Cambridge University Press.

Ekman, P. and Friesen, W.V. (1971) Constant across cultures in the face and emotion. Journal of Personal and Social Psychology, 17: 124–129.

Ekman, P. and Friesen, W.V. (1972) Handmovements. Journal of Communication, 22: 353–374.

R.S. Feldman (Ed) (1982) Development of Non-Verbal Behavior in Children. Berlin: Springer Verlag.

Ferraro, G.P. (1998) The Cultural Dimension of International Business. Upper Saddle River, NJ: Prentice Hall.

Fisher, G. (1980) International Negotiation. A Cross-Cultural Perspective. Yarmouth, ME: Intercultural Press.

Francesco, A.M. and Gold, B.A. (1998) International Organisational Behavior. Readings, Cases and Skills. Upper Saddle River, NJ: Prentice Hall.

Gallois, C. and Callan, V. (1997) Communication and Culture. A Guide for Practice. Chichester: Wiley.

Gesteland, R. (1999) Cross-Cultural Business Bahavior. Marketing, Negotiating and Managing Across Cultures. Copenhagen: Copenhagen Business School Press.

Gibbs, R.W., Jr. (1987) Mutual knowledge and the psychology of conversational inference. Journal of Pragmatics, 11: 561–588.

Goffman, E. (1963) Behavior in Public Places. New York: The Free Press.

Greer, C.R. and Stephens, G.K. (1998) Employee relations issues for US Companies in Mexico. In A.M. Francesco and B.A. Gold (Eds), International Organisational Behavior. Readings, Cases and Skills, pp. 363–383. Upper Saddle River, NJ: Prentice Hall.

Gudykunst, W.B. (1983) Uncertainty reduction and predictability of behaviour in low and high-context cultures: an exploratory study. Communication Quarterly, 31/1: 49–55.

Gudykunst, W.B. and Ting-Toomey, S. (1988) Culture and Interpersonal Communication. Newbury Park, CA: Sage Publications.

Gudykunst, W.B. and Kim, Y.Y. (1984) Communicating With Strangers. An Approach to Intercultural Communication. Reading, MA: Addison–Wesley.

Hall, E.T. and Hall, M.R. (1990) Understanding Cultural Differences: Germans, French and Americans. Yarmouth, ME: Intercultural Press.

Hall, E.T. (1955) The anthropology of manners. Scientific American, 192: 25–30.

Hall, E.T. (1956) Orientation and training in government for work overseas. Human Organization, 15: 4–10.

Hall, E.T. (1959) The Silent Language. New York: Doubleday, 1981.

Hall, E.T. (1963) A system for the notation of proxemic behavoir. American Anthropologist, 65 (5): 1003–1026.

Hall, E.T. (1966) The Hidden Dimension. New York: Doubleday.

Hall, E.T. (1976) Beyond Culture. New York: Doubleday.

Hall, E.T. (1983) The Dance of Life: The Other Dimension of Time. New York: Doubleday.

Hall, E.T. and Trager, G.L. (1954) Culture and communications: a model and an analysis. Explorations, 3.

Hewes, G.W. (1957) The anthropology of posture. Scientific American, 196: 123–132.

Hinds, J. (1990) Inductive, deductive, quasi-inductive: expository writing in Japanese, Chinese and Thai. In Connor and Johns (Eds), Coherence in Writing, pp. 87–110. Alexandria, VA: Teachers of English to speakers of other languages.

Hofstede, G. (1984) Culture's Consequences: International Differences in Work-Related Values. Beverly-Hills, CA: Sage.

Hofstede, G. (1980) Cultures and Organizations: Software of the Mind. Beverly Hills, CA: Sage.

Holden, N. (1999) Formality/informality and directness/indirectness: some cross-cultural confusions. Paper presented at the workshop on formality/informality and directness/indirectness in management contexts. Copenhagen.

Holden, N. (2000) Coping with Russia as a bad fit. In R. Crane (Ed), European Business Cultures, pp. 111–127. Harlow: Pearson Education.

Jourard, S.M. (1966) An exploratory study of body-accessibility. British Journal of Social and Clinical Psychology, 5: 221–231.

Jucker, A.H. and Smith, S.W. (1996) Explicit and implicit ways of enhancing common ground in conversations. Pragmatics, 6 (1): 1–18.

Kohls, L.R. (1978) Basic concepts and models of intercultural communication. In M. Prosser (Ed), USIA Intercultural Communication Course, 1977 Proceedings. Washington DC: US Information Agency.

Lane, H.W., Distefano, J.J. and Maznevski, M.L. (1997) International Management Behaviour. Cambridge, MA: Blackwell.

Leeds-Hurwitz, W. and Winkin, Y. (1989) Eléments pour une histoire sociale de la communication interculturelle américaine: la mission du Foreign Service Institute. Les Cahiers Internationaux de Psychologie Sociale, 2–3: 23–41.

Linowes, R.G. (1997) The Japanese manager's traumatic entry into the US: understanding the American-Japanese cultural divide. In H.W. Lane, J.J. Distefano and M.L. Maznevski (Eds), International Management Behaviour. Cambridge, MA: pp. 91–106.

Matsumoto, M. (1988) The Unspoken Way: Harage – Silence in Japanese Business and Society. Tokyo: Kodansha International.

Mead, R. (1994) International Management: Cross Cultural Dimensions. Cambridge, MA: Blackwell.

Morris, D., Collett, P., Marsh, P. and O'Shaugnessy, M. (1979) Gestures, Their Origins and Distribution. Jonathan Cape.

Pinxten, R. (1994) Culturen Sterven Langzaam. Over Interculturele Communicatie. Antwerpen Baarn: Hadewych.

Prothro, E.T. (1955) Arab-American differences in the judgement of written messages. Journal of Social Psychology, 42: 3–11.

Reynolds, L. (1997) The Trust Effect. London: Nicholas Brealey.

Sackmann, S.A., Phillips, M.E., Kleinberg, M.J. and Boyacigiller, N.A. (1997) Single and multiple cultures in international cross-cultural management research. In S.A. Sackmann (Ed), Cultural Complexities in Organizations: Inherent Contrasts and Contradictions, pp. 14–48. Thousand Oaks, CA: Sage.

Said, E.W. 1995 (1978) Orientalism. Western Conceptions of the Orient. London: Penguin.

Salo-Lee, L. (1999) The myths of directness and indirectness. Paper presented at the Workshop on formality/informality and directness/indirectness in management contexts. Copenhagen.

Schank, R.C. and Abelson, R.P. (1977) Scripts, Plans, Goals and Understanding. An Inquiry Into Human Knowledge Structures. Hillsdale, NJ: Lawrence Erlbaum.

Schein, E.H. (1999) The Corporate Culture. Survival Guide. San Francisco, CA: Jossey-Bass.

Searle, J. (1979) Expression and Meaning. Studies in the Theory of Speech Acts. Cambridge, MA: Cambridge University Press.

Seelye, N.H. and Seelye-James, A. (1994) Culture Clash. Managing in a Multicultural World. Lincolnwood, IL: NTC Business Books.

Sinclair, J. (1980) Discourse in relation to language structure and semiotics. In S. Greenbaum, G. Leech and J. Svartvik (Eds), Studies in English Linguistics for Randolph Quirk, pp. 110–124. London: Longman.

Smith, N. (Ed) (1982) Mutual Knowledge. New York: Academic Press.

Smith, W.J. (1965) Message, meaning and context in ethology. Ameican Nature, 980: 405–409.

Sommer, R. (1969) Personal Space. Englewood cliffs, NJ: Prentice-Hall.

Sperber, D. and Wilson, D. (1986) Relevance, Communication and Cognition. Oxford: Basil Blackwell.

Stalnaker, R.C. (1974) Pragmatic presuppositions. In M.K. Munitz and P.K. Unger (Eds), Semantics and Philosophy. New York: New York University Press. Reprinted in S. Davis (Ed) (1991) Pragmatics. A Reader, pp. 471–482. Oxford: Oxford University press.

Suzuki, T. (1978) Words in Context. A Japanese Perspective on Language and Culture. Okyo: Kodansha International, revised paperback edition, 1984.

Thomas, J. (1998) Contexting Koreans: does the high/low model work? Business Communication Quarterly, 61/4: 9–22.

Ting-Toomey, S. (1985) Toward a theory of conflict and culture. International and Intercultural Communicative Annual, 9: 71–86.

Triandis, H.C. (1975) Culture training, cognitive complexity and interpersonal attitudes. In R. Brislin, S. Bochner and W. Lonner (Eds), Cross-Cultural Perspectives on Learning, pp. 39–77. Beverly Hills, CA: Sage.

Triandis, H.C. (1994) Recherches récentes sur l'individualisme et le collectivisme; Les Cahiers Internationaux de Psychologie Sociale, 23 (3): 14–27.

Ulijn, J. (1994) The Anglo-Germanic and Latin concepts of politeness in cross-atlantic business communication. A matter of cultural differences in power distance? Duisburg: LAUD. Series C: Languages for Specific Purposes, Paper No 28.

Usunier, J.-C. (1992) Commerce Entre Cultures. Une Approche Culturelle du Marketing International. Tome I. Paris: Presses Universitaires de France.

Usunier, J.-C. (1996) Marketing Across Cultures. London: Prentice Hall.

Vázquez-Orta, I.-S. (1995) Summary of "A Contrastive Study of Politeness. Phenomena in England and in Spain". Duisburg: LAUD, Series B: Applied and Interdisciplinary Papers, Paper No 268.

Victor, D.A. (1992) International Business Communication. New York: Harper Collins.

Vuysje, H. and Van der Lans, J. (1999) Typisch Nederlands. Vademecum van de Nederlandse Indentiteit. Amsterdam Antwerpen: Contact.

Watson, O.M. (1970) Proxemic Behavior. Mouton.

Weiss, S. and Stripp, W. 1996 (1985) Negotiating with foreign business persons. An introduction for Americans with propositions on six cultures. Duisburg: LAUD, Series B: Applied and Interdisciplinary Papers, Paper No 270.

# Chapter 21

# Intercultural Issues in Management and Business: The Interdisciplinary Challenge

**Gerhard Fink**
*Vienna University of Economics and Business Administration,
Vienna, Austria*

*and*

**Wolfgang Mayrhofer**
*Vienna University of Economics and Business Administration,
Vienna, Austria*

## ORGANISATIONS AS PROBLEM SOLVING SYSTEMS – A RESOURCE BASED VIEW OF THE FIRM

Organisational science offers many different ways of determining the core characteristics of organisations like firms, administrative units, hospitals, multinational corporations, etc.: they can be regarded as open, socio-technical systems with a close link between the company and its environment combining different kinds of resources to reach certain goals; they can be seen as micropolitical arenas where actors with a varying degree of power bases try to reach their goals and interests through power struggles and games; they can be conceptualised as organisms that develop within the opportunities that the environment offers – the list of possibilities could be continued (for an overview see, for example, Scott, 1986; Kieser and Kubicek, 1992). In general, organisations are one, maybe even *the* key characteristic of modern society. There are strong arguments that the number and density of organisations as well as their importance for business and everyday life is unique in human history (Kasper and Heimerl-Wagner, 1996).

One fruitful way of looking at organisations is to conceptualise them as problem solving social systems consisting of communication that are an answer to the needs of different markets. Figure 21.1 shows the core elements of a resource based view of the firm.

A resource based model of the firm consists of various core components (for a more detailed view of this concept see Nolte, 1999). *Organisational strategic assets* contain all those elements that organisations can use in order to create customer value. *Organisational resources* are of potential use for the organisation and include all those factors which are available for the organisation. In a broad categorisation, one can differentiate between physical resources, e.g. location, equipment, financial resources, e.g. capital structure, credit lines, and intangible resources, e.g. human resources, organisational culture. Transforming various organisational resources into customer benefits is the core task of management. This is done through combining and aggregating various types of existing resources into *organisational capabilities*. These capabilities have a profound effect on the processes of the organisations because they co-ordinate actions and are influencing as well as rooted in the basal, "deep" layers of the organisational structure. *Core competencies* are the link, the intersection between organisation-specific strategic assets and customer benefits, in other words: between the internal sphere of the organisation and the external market. They are a result of managerial efforts to convert organisational capabilities into customer benefits in order to create a sustainable competitive advantage. Through the feedback of the sales market the internal processes of the organisation creating customer benefits out of existing resources via organisational capabilities and core competencies is shaped and modified.

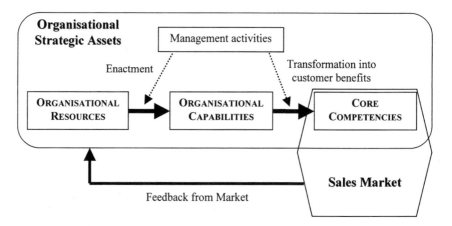

**Figure 21.1**  Basic model of a resource based view (modified from Nolte, 1999: 19).

# ADDING COMPLEXITY – DIVERSITY AS A STRATEGIC ASSET

The resource based model of the firm as presented above can be enlarged through a cultural perspective in at least two ways. Firstly, an organisational culture perspective focuses on the "soft" and "hidden" aspects of organisational processes beyond "visible", "hard" elements. Secondly, national cultural variety adds complexity to the various organisational processes. Therefore, we first describe the importance of organisational and national culture in organisations (The Role of Culture in Organisations) and then present an enlarged culture sensitive resource based model of the firm (Culture and Resource Based Management).

## The Role of Culture in Organisations

Since more than two decades organisational culture is one of the core concepts in analysing organisational processes and finding adequate ways of managing organisations. The academic as well as the practitioner literature has been discussing various aspects of this phenomenon (see, for example, Pettigrew, 1979; Louis, 1981; Deal and Kennedy, 1982; Fombrun, 1983; Smircich, 1983; Uttal, 1983; Allaire and Firsirotu, 1984; Maanen and Barley, 1984; Trice and Beyer, 1984; Schein, 1985; Kasper, 1987; Sackmann, 1992). One major reason for the academic and practical interest in this phenomenon was the experience that in spite of well developed and sophisticated functional-rational models and tools for managing organisations success is not guaranteed. On the contrary, counter intuitive phenomena, unforeseen effects of seemingly rational solutions are main drivers in looking for something beyond the technical and functional level. In addition to that, more flexible forms of working, an increasingly turbulent environment and a greater emphasis on team work make more traditional forms of co-ordination and control "from the top" less successful and less possible. Integrating organisational culture thinking and concepts into the managerial tool box promises a more successful "grip" on organisational processes. Deep layer phenomena like norms and values, unconscious assumptions, rites and rituals, ceremonies, etc. are regarded as possible tools for managing organisational behaviour since they are part of the organisational frame that directs actions and decision making. According to the results of an empirical research project by Hofstede et al, 1990, organisation cultures also reflect nationality, besides other given elements like, e.g. demographics of employees and managers (cf. ibid.: 311).

This leads to the second major source that stresses the role of culture in organisations is the intercultural management perspective. Given an increasingly international, even global business environment stimulating cross-border business activities the problem of interaction between members of different national and cultural origin becomes more prominent. Intercultural management tries to describe and explain organisational behaviour within a broad spectrum of national cultures, thus building a foundation for improving the interaction between various organisational actors/stakeholders (e.g. Adler, 1983; Phatak, 1992).

To get a better understanding why cultural differences are/can be so fundamental in the business area we have to take a look at the concept of culture and at some models for assessing different cultures. Depending on the scientific discipline, e.g. anthropology, psychology, sociology, business administration, or organisational behaviour, culture may be defined in many ways, emphasising different aspects. A good example for this diversity is given by the Kroeber and Kluckhohn (1952) who identified 164 definitions of culture (this also suggests that researchers are influenced by their own culture when working in this field. What we see is what we are culturally programmed to see (Apfelthaler and Karmasin, 1997)), discussed them and offered one of the most comprehensive and generally accepted definitions: "Culture consists of patterns, explicit and implicit of and for behaviour acquired and transmitted by symbols, constituting the distinctive achievement of human groups, including their embodiment in artefacts; the essential core of culture consists of traditional (i.e. historically derived and selected) ideas and especially their attached values; culture systems may, on the one hand, be considered as products of action, on the other, as conditioning elements of future action." (Kroeber and Kluckhohn, 1952, p. 32).

According to this definition culture is (see also Samovar and Porter, 1991: 47ff):

- Something that is shared by all or almost all members of some social group.
- Something that provides therefore orientation: understanding a culture may leads to expectations how group members might react in various situations without being aware of it.
- Something that the older members of the group try to pass on to the younger members.
- Something (as in the case of morals, laws and customs) that shapes behaviour, ...or structures one's perception of the world.
- Something that is learned and as such it is possible for a person confronted with another culture to adapt to the new culture.
- Something that is interrelated which means that the various facets of culture should be understood in their context and studied as an entity.

In the context of this chapter it is important to examine the relationship between culture and organisations. Research within cross-cultural management therefore attempts to identify how culture influences organisations as well as managerial functions and actions. Culture seems to have an impact on the micro-variables, such as people's behaviour, and also on the macro-level for example on technology or organisational structure. But the abstract and complex nature of culture makes it difficult to identify and analyse this phenomenon. A variety of models have been proposed that examine groupings of cultural values. (e.g. Thomas, 1996; Hofstede, 1980; Trompenaars, 1993; Keller, 1982). Each approach provides somewhat different insights; thus each can be useful on its own or in combination with other models. In essence, however, it has to be stressed that cultural models can only provide a simplified way to examine cultures. All cultures are far more complex than these models suggest, and it is important that this complexity is taken into account.

Crucial in the area of intercultural management is the issue of acculturation, i.e. "changes that occur as a result of continuos firsthand contact between individuals of differing cultural origins" (Redfield et al, 1936 in Ward, 1996, p. 124). At the level of the individual, acculturation plays an important role during expatriation. When organisational members are sent on a temporal job assignment into another country, they make acculturation experiences. A number of models have been developed to describe the psychological and social processes (e.g. Mendenhall and Oddou, 1985; Mendenhall et al, 1987; Tung, 1988; Brewster, 1991; Black et al, 1993; Mayrhofer and Brewster, 1995; Schlossberg, 1981; Allen and Vliert, 1984; Nicholson, 1984; Adler, 1985; Nicholson, 1990; Thomas, 1996; Mayrhofer, 1993; Ward, 1996) as well as organisational goals and consequences (e.g. Mayrhofer, 1996; Gunz, 1989) that are linked with such a change. During mergers and acquisitions cultural phenomena in both the sense of organisational and national culture play an important role for the success of this operation (Nahavandi and Malekzadeh, 1988; Schnapper, 1992). Likewise, within international joint ventures acculturation problems are crucial (Lane and Beamish, 1990). At the macro level, acculturation phenomena also can occur. For example, the theory of collective culture shock analyses the processes at the national cultural level in transition economies with special reference to post-communist countries (Feichtinger and Fink, 1998, 1999).

## Culture and Resource Based Management

Given the role of culture in organisations as briefly outlined above, the resource based view of the firm is influenced in two ways. Firstly, organisational culture influences all the internal processes of the organisation. In other words, organisational efforts to create customer value through the transformation of resources into customer benefits are embedded into the culture of the organisation. Secondly, cultural and national diversity adds an additional layer of reality to resource based management activities through increasing the complexity of these activities by making available more differentiated resources as well as sales markets. This leads to an enhanced, culture sensitive resource based model of the firm. Figure 21.2 shows the core elements.

The culture sensitive resource based view is grounded in the perception that avoiding cultural shocks and mistakes in international intercultural management is not enough. Assimilation, tolerance, and cultural awareness are insufficient, if not restrictive approaches to the intercultural issues confronting international firms (see also Holden in press).

When different cultures promote different qualifications (qualities) a new corporate culture which integrates a large array of different sources of knowledge and of cultural difference into a corporation is superior to a corporate culture based in a single national culture only. This is the challenge of cross cultural management! Cross cultural management makes international firms perform better, not because problems of cultural difference and acculturation are avoided. Avoiding problems which do not arise in firms based on a single national culture would just equal the chances of an international with a national firm. Cross cultural management makes international firms perform better than national firms, because it allows the tapping of more, better and cheaper resources than any national firm can exploit, to reach better market opportunities and to

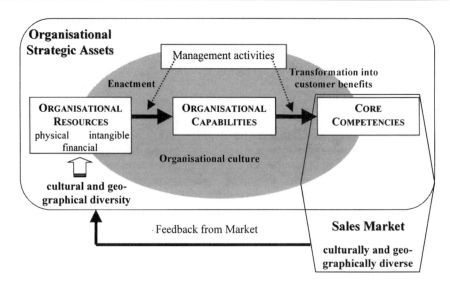

**Figure 21.2**   Culture sensitive resource based view of the firm.


grow larger than others. Large firms have a better capacity to reduce risk and to cope with shocks (Fink et al., in press).

In addition, it is essential to note that the cultural and geographical diversity inherent in organisational resources as presented in the culture sensitive model above can be used in quite different ways. If one follows the idea that international management (Boddewyn 1999) is always linked – to a greater or lesser degree – to intercultural issues, then four basic options can be distinguished (see Ward, 1996 for a similar distinction in the context of cultural adaptation). Using an integration strategy, the various units of an organisation operating across national and/or cultural borders use all the existing resources according to the degree of their comparative advantages. An assimilation strategy defines one or few unit(s) as dominating and the available resources of the 'minor' units are fed into the pool of resources of the dominating units and the former units are dependent on the resources of the dominating ones. On the other hand, a separation approach would not make very much use of the larger spectrum of resources available but would mainly depend on the domestic resources of each unit. Finally, within a marginalisation approach Unit 1 is not interested in devoting any significant resources to Unit 2, but also not interested in the resources of Unit 2. Figure 21.3 illustrates this argument.

We strongly argue that an integrative approach provides the adequate basis for superior performance of international compared to domestic companies. All other modes of operation do not make full use of the available diversity of resources and thus lack efficiency.

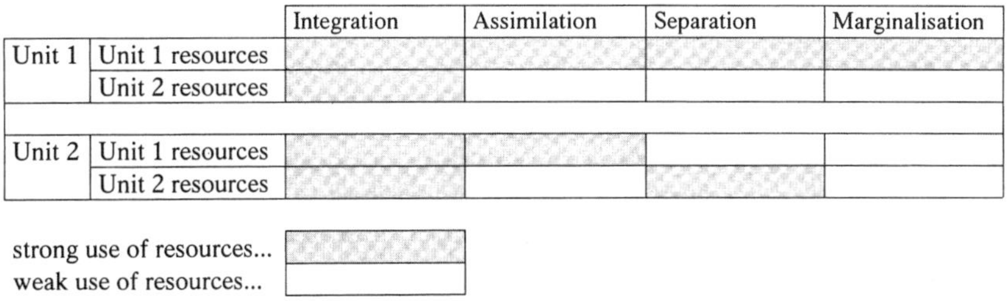

| | | Integration | Assimilation | Separation | Marginalisation |
|---|---|---|---|---|---|
| Unit 1 | Unit 1 resources | ▨ | ▨ | ▨ | ▨ |
| | Unit 2 resources | ▨ | | | |
| | | | | | |
| Unit 2 | Unit 1 resources | ▨ | ▨ | | |
| | Unit 2 resources | ▨ | | ▨ | |

strong use of resources... ▨

weak use of resources... ☐

**Figure 21.3**   Use of resources within a culture sensitive resource based view of the firm.

# MANAGEMENT IN A DIVERSE INTERNAL AND EXTERNAL ENVIRONMENT – THE INTERDISCIPLINARY CHALLENGE

The additional layer of reality enhances organisational complexity and makes an inter-disciplinary approach to organising, i.e. management, necessary. In essence, this means that disciplinary multitude is needed to cope with the diversity involved in management across borders issues and to achieve a full(er) understanding of the phenomena investigated.

## Contributions of Scientific Disciplines

A variety of disciplines offers major contributions to the culture sensitive model of resource based management. However, the contribution of these disciplines to the understanding of the relevant phenomena vary in terms of relevance and focus. In general, most important contributions from a business perspective can be expected from management science, economics, psychology, and sociology. In addition, for specific aspects in cross-cultural business activities additional perspectives prove valuable, e.g. linguistics in the area of intercultural negotiations.

### *Management*

At the core of management sciences is the organisation and its internal and external processes (for core issues in management see, for example, Steinmann and Schreyögg, 1991; Eckardstein ct al, 1999). Management thinking covers all processes and conditions that are necessary to transform raw materials through an input-throughput-output transformation into goods in a broad sense, including services and non-material results like ideas, etc. The core activities within the value chain of the organisation consist of input logistics (e.g. inspection of incoming shipment), production (e.g. assembling of parts), output logistics (e.g. dispatching of goods), marketing (e.g. sales personnel) and customer service. In addition, supporting activities like procurement, technological and process management, human resource management and organisational infrastructure contribute to the core activities (Porter, 1985). These activities refer specifically to the management activities in the model presented above that transform resources into customer benefits.

In the international arena, these processes become more complex because of the different countries and cultures involved (see Perlitz, 1995; Czinkota et al, 1994). Each process is affected. Take for example the are of human resource management. International HRM, too, has to provide the organisation with an adequate number and type of personnel, at the right time and location. However, in addition to that, the specifics of the respective countries involved in HR matters and various types of employees, i.e. members of the mother organisation ("home country nationals/expatriates"), from other countries ("third country nationals") and locals ("host country nationals") do play a role. The interplay of the functional, the country specific and the employee oriented dimension results in a new complexity which is a core characteristic of international HRM. More and more complex tasks, a higher risk and uncertainty of decision making and a wider scope of decisions involving many parts of an employee's life (e.g. Brewster and Burnois, 1991; Brewster and Hegewisch, 1994; Dowling et al., 1994; Briscoe, 1995; Mayrhofer and Brewster, 1995; Scherm, 1995; Shenkar, 1995; Brewster et al., (in press).

## Economics

Economic policy is setting the stage for business activities. Competition policy determines market organisation. Monetary policies have an impact on price setting (inflation) and exchange rates, and together with government tax and debt policies strongly influence interest rates, exchange rates (prices of foreign goods on the domestic market) and business prospects (growth rates). Plenty of information is provided as a public good by international organisations, governments, interest groups or by government financed research institutes. Regular reports by the OECD, the IMF, and the UN Economic Commission for Europe are of particular importance.

While large firms usually employ their own experts to assess business prospects and the impact of government policies on product and financial markets (availability of financial instruments, cost of finance) medium and small firms usually depend on outside experts (banks, auditory firms). Smaller firms are usually more vulnerable to changes in business conditions and government policies (for an overview see Czinkota et al, 1994; Schoppe, 1991).

## Psychology

Communication between (groups of) individuals in a specific context is one of the core contributions that psychology has to offer (Triandis, 1980; Brislin, 1990; Triandis, 1993; Thomas, 1996). In the context of the culture sensitive model of resource based management communication issues emerge especially during the enactment of culturally and geographically intangible resources into organisational capabilities, the trans-

**Table 21.1** Scientific disciplines and contribution to culture and business issues

| Discipline | Core issues in the light of a resource based view |
| --- | --- |
| Mass communication theory | Communication with sales market; transformation into customer benefits in different countries/cultures; highly dependent on media |
| Anthropology | Develop the culture concept that is essential to understand organisational behaviour in a geographical and/or cultural diverse setting; informs about "dos and don'ts"; |
| Linguistics | Intercultural negotiations during the enactment of resources towards organisational capabilities and at the interface between the organisation and the sales market |
| Historical science | Sheds light on the development of cultural and geographical diversity as part of the context of the firm |
| Law and history of law | Framework for internal and external organisational processes; mediating between culturally and/or geographically different frameworks |
| Philosophy, science of sciences, econometrics, statistics | Support the formulation and testing of hypotheses, laws and theories about the field |

formation of the latter into customer benefits – in a broader sense: into strategic assets – and the feedback from the market.

Communication among human beings takes place at four different levels: the biophysical level (senses and affects like crying or laughing), the motorial level (shape and attitude of the body, mimic and gestic), the vocal level (language, melody, noise) and the technical level (application of various media). Various forms of communication at the biophysical level are inherited. However, most forms of communication are acquired by acculturation. These forms of communication depend on culture, society and groups and can be changed by the society or group over time at least to some extent.

Messages consist of four components: mere information, self-presentation of the sender, appeal to the recipient, and information about the relations between sender and recipient (Thun, 1981; see also Watzlawick et al, 1982). Problems with communication emerge (noise, disturbances) if sender and recipient put different emphasis on the four levels of message content. Such disturbances are enhanced when different cultures have established different rules for senders and recipients of messages.

Communication stimulates specific reactions in individuals: thinking and sensing. Interpersonal communication requires that there is an active sender of messages (communicator) and a recipient. By help of communication a feeling of belonging together is generated. Groups, organisations or societies will be set up and developed. Interactions or transactions between members of groups, organisations or institutions take place. By communication information about the environment will be transposed into knowledge. Without intermediation neither intra- nor interpersonal communication is possible. The human system of nerves and senses, and technical means (recorders, transmitters, and receivers) are employed.

## Sociology

Actions in organisations acquire specific significance through the (cultural) context, i.e. the (cultural) frame of reference. This frame is necessary for actors to interpret and evaluate the behaviour of individual and collective actors (for the concept of collective actors see Coleman, 1986). Knowledge and mastering of rules and norms that are constitutive elements of this frame is a core prerequisite for moving within a cultural context.

Cultural sociology offers a multilevel perspective reaching from the individual to the societal level. This perspective conceptualises culture as a concept necessary to make sense of action and includes the interdependencies between various levels. From the perspective of the firm, its concepts are of special relevance for analysing the context within which the firm operates as well as the tight pattern of (cultural) rules and norms that govern organisational behaviour. Thus, culture functions as a frame of reference for behaviour.

## Other Disciplines

A variety of other disciplines also contribute to the understanding of the core business processes within the framework presented above. Table 21.1 contains the most important other disciplines and highlights their core contributions.

## Closing the Interdisciplinary Gap – An Exploratory Journey

Using an example, we show how a "truly" thorough analysis of managerial activities in an intercultural context requires a synergetic use of various disciplinary angles. To do this, we start with a small case example that illustrates the culture sensitive resource based view of the firm as discussed above.

A family owned, medium sized German company produces various types of adhesive tapes for industrial customers. The product range includes special tapes for packaging machines, covering tapes and various carpet tapes for specific surfaces. The company is very successful in its German home market and has acquired a stable market share even *vis-à-vis* giant competitors like BASF. Key characteristics for the company are well developed production know how and flexible production methods, a comfortable ratio of equity to total assets that allows the company to be largely free from pressures of lenders and a stable ownership situation since the daughter of the founder as well as her husband are well integrated into the management of the company and continually developed as successors of the company owner. The workforce mainly consists of German workers with a high amount of skilled workers and a substantial number of foreign workers at the shop floor level. In addition, some employees at the professional level come from abroad. A key success factor of the company are very intensive and personal customer relationship efforts undertaken by the salesforce of the organisation and the great flexibility of the company in terms of produced quantity and special orders. In line with the strategic plan of expanding operations with neighbour countries, the company decides to enter the market in specific regions in Austria and the Czech Republic. To prepare this move, a project group is created to prepare and accompany this project. The project group consists of five members out of the relevant department and functional areas, respectively, including two technical engineers from production, one member each from the marketing and the sales department and the assistant to the owner manager. The latter is of Austrian origin and has been with the company for five years. One of the technical engineers is Czech and has recently joined the company. The assistant of the owner manager is the assigned head of the project group and has ample experience in project management. It is his task to manage and channel the group processes. The first milestone for the project group is a decision about the regions in the Czech Republic and Austria where the company will try to enter the national market and how this entry – starting with some sales staff – is done. The questions that have to be answered in order to prepare this decisions include an analysis of the infrastructure, the industry structure and the financial status of the industries, the work force structure and the kind of competitors in various regions of each country. In addition, the legal framework especially in terms of start-up regulations, flow of capital and work permits has to analysed.

In the terminology of the culture sensitive resource based view of the firm this situation can be rephrased as follows. The company owns a great variety of resources in various areas. Especially important are financial resources, e.g. the high amount of equity capital, physical resources, e.g. well developed production facilities with good transportation infrastructure, and intangible resources, e.g. acquired know how, tacit and explicit technical knowledge, tacit cultural knowledge through a culturally diverse workforce. Some cultural diversity is built into the company by the diversity in the workforce. The project group is a specific management activity designed to transform (some of) the organisational resources into organisational capabilities and, further on, into core competencies. The main task of the project group is to assess whether the company can – based on the existing *repertoire* of organisational resources – build organisational capabilities that allow the company to enter culturally and geographically distant sales markets. The core competencies of the company in the national context – customised products in terms of quality and quantity, immediate and flexible response to customer demands, good customer relationship – shall be created through transforming the organisational capabilities into core competencies in two new countries. The project group itself builds heavily on intangible organisational resources, especially on the technical and cultural knowledge available through the members of the group. The questions that have to be addressed to reach the first milestone of the project focus on various aspects of the foreign sales markets in Austria and the Czech Republic as well as the institutional framework, e.g. legal regulations, labour market, or market structure. The various disciplines mentioned above can contribute descriptive, explanatory as well as prognostic elements when applied to this example.

Out of the management sciences, a variety of aspects are relevant. Knowledge around the choice of location, usually linked with the founding of a new subsidiary, can be used as a broad frame to guide the step into the new markets. More specifically, international marketing considerations identify issues like target-market selection and locally responsive yet organisationally compatible product, pricing, distribution and promotional policy as important. In addition, when opting for entering a market or not, various options of organisation and control in international operations play a crucial role. The use of various combinations of bureaucratic and/ or cultural mechanisms of co-ordination and control play an important role even in the relative simple case of having some sales people working in the foreign country without having a plant or joint venture there. The organisation-environment-interaction is regarded as a key element of successfully managing foreign operations. Therefore, the various elements mentioned in the example above, e.g. institutional framework, e.g. legal regulations, labour market, or market structure, have to be included into these considerations.

In this respect, other disciplines provide additional insight. Law provides comparative analyses of various legal systems in different countries. These analyses not only cover different legal provisions, but, even more important, shed light on the different historical roots of the legal system and the guiding principles that operate at the latent level and govern action, right/wrong differentiation and the use of the legally underdetermined "grey areas". Special importance has to be paid to the evolving area of legal regulations relevant for cross-border transactions and transcending national boundaries. Especially legal regulations based on EU law, e.g. in the area of capital movement, will be of relevance in the example mentioned above. In addition, specific subsidies granted from the EU for specific regions, might be of interest.

Sociological analyses not only take a macro view but also transcends across various levels of analysis. Cultural sociology deals with the genesis and development of national cultures and also provides insight into the relevance of national (and partly organisational) culture for the behaviour of individuals, groups, and organisations. In the example above, sociological concepts deepen the analysis of the national context, the culture in the countries involved, the relevance of the specific environment for organisational and individual behaviour, and the conflicts that are potentially involved by spreading out ones own business activities into "foreign territory".

Psychological concepts in this example are especially helpful in the area of communication, mass communication and motivation. Intercultural communication phenomena will be relevant for the work of the project group as well as for possible future co-operation with persons in the foreign environment, either locals or people familiar with the local situation. The benefits and dangers of multicultural work teams, especially the greater variety of ideas on the one side and the difficulties of reaching a common frame of reference on the other side can be mentioned here. Referring to mass communication, advertising and, in a broader sense, marketing, can be mentioned as relevant areas. The design of a compensation system that fits the motivation of employees is a crucial issue. The international context adds an additional element to these considerations because country and/or culture specific phenomena have to be taken into account. For example, the motivating forces can be quite different in various countries. In countries like the Czech Republic with a quite low wage level financial incentives play a different role than in a comparably "wealthy" context.

Also more "peripheral" disciplines can contribute to a thorough analysis in this example. Historical science can provide valuable insight into common ground and differences between Austria and the Czech Republic, thus providing information which can be used in the field of marketing or recruitment. In a similar way, linguistics generates information about the role of culture during different phases of negotiation talks (e.g. Rathmayr, 1998). Thus, the various negotiations that are linked with the entry of a new market and the building of a new operation are a core issue in this respect. Anthropological considerations centre around various images of man and can provide typologies of different images prevalent in various regions of the world. Considerations about leadership issues can profit from such concepts.

# FUTURE DEVELOPMENTS

It would be too far reaching to claim that a single person should be aware and master all management relevant knowledge generated dynamically by numerous disciplines and sub-disciplines. There are substantial difficulties to integrate knowledge provided by different scientific disciplines. Depending on contexts different fields are of different importance. As the scientific disciplines develop knowledge mostly independent from business needs they pursue different research questions which require different methodologies to find appropriate answers. Thus, scientific disciplines have no common language (they lack meta valency) and there are communication problems between disciplines. Communication among scientific fields and with business organisations is only possible if findings are translated into common language with all the consequences as lack of precision and enhanced risk of misinterpretation and misunderstanding.

Firms (business organisations) can only exist when observing the economic constraint: expenses must not exceed revenues. Thus, processes to gain information and to integrate it into management relevant knowledge are also under a time and cost constraint. The fact that the knowledge generated by the various disciplines is readily available in huge scientific libraries and millions of published articles constitutes a constraint for business organisations to tap this knowledge. There is an enormous overflow of excess information which makes it very difficult to find the "right information". Thus, enhanced by the economic constraints, techniques to prevent information overflows are permanently applied.

In four fields firms have learned to rely on external experts: tax advisors, lawyers, bankers and advertising agencies, or at least to acknowledge the importance of specialised knowledge to be integrated into a firm's (business organisation's) decision making. Apparently these four fields lend themselves more easily to be delegated to specialists. Firms (business organisations) have learned how costly it can become not to integrate this knowledge into their organisational capabilities.

By contrast, personal communication can not be delegated. With rapidly progressing internationalisation of firms (business organisations) to become better by exploiting more and cheaper/ better resources a rapidly increasing number of firms is in the process of learning to identify resource gaps and gaps in organisational capabilities to be transformed into core competencies.

Given the rapid pace of internationalisation it is becoming worth while for psychologists, sociologists, linguists, anthropologists, historians and philosophers to improve their own capabilities how to provide well tailored knowledge for international managers to make them more efficient in tapping international resources.

# REFERENCES

Adler, N.J. (1983) A typology of management studies involving culture. Journal of International Business Studies: 29–47.

Adler, N.J. (1985) Cross-cultural transitions: entry and re-entry. In D.W. Myers (Ed), Employee Problem Prevention and Counseling. Westport, CN:, Greenwood, pp. S.207–S.225.

Allaire, Y. and M.E. Firsirotu (1984) Theories of organizational culture. Organization Studies, 5(3): 193–226.

Allen, V.L. and Vliert, E.V.D. (Eds) (1984) Role Transitions. New York: London, Plenum.

Apfelthaler, G. and Karmasin, M. (1997) Cultural theory and cross cultural management. Approaching a new Approach. Wien, Unpublished working paper.

Argote, L. (1999) Organizational Learning: Creating, Retaining and Transferring Knowledge. Dordrecht: Kluwer Academic.

Brewster, C. (1991) The management of Expatriates. London: Kogan Page.

Brewster, C. and Burnois, F. (1991) Human resource management: a european perspective. Personnel Review, 20(6): 4–13.

Brewster, C. and Hegewisch, A. (Eds) (1994) Policy and Practice in European Human Resource Management. The Price Waterhouse Cranfield Survey. London: Routledge.

Brewster, C. Mayrhofer, W. and Morley, M. (2000) Challenges in European Human Resource Management. London: Macmillan, in press.

Briscoe, D. (1995) International Human Resource Management. Englewood Cliffs, NJ: Prentice Hall.

Brislin, R.W. (Ed) (1990) Applied Cross-Cultural Psychology. Newbury Park, CA: Sage.

Coleman, J.C. (1986) Die asymmetrische Gesellschaft. Weinheim: Beltz.

Czinkota, M.R., Ronkainen, I.A. and Moffet, M.H. (1994) International Business. FortWorth, TX: Dryden.

Dasgupta, S. and Tao, Z. (1999) Contractual incompleteness and ortimality of equity joint ventures. Journal of Economic Behaviour and Organization: 391–414.

Deal, T.E. and Kennedy, A.A. (1982) Corporate Cultures – The Rites and Rituals of Corporate Life. Reading, MA: Addison-Wesley.

Dowling, P.J., Schuler, R.S. and Welch, D.E. (1994) International Dimensions of Human Resource Management. Belmont, CA: Wadsworth.

Eckardstein, D.V., Kasper, H. and Mayrhofer, W. (Eds) (1999) Management. Theorien – Führung – Veränderung. Stuttgart: Schäffer-Poeschel.

Feichtinger, C. and Fink, G. (1998) Post communist management: towards a theory of the collective culture shock. Journal of Cross Cultural Competence and Management, 1(1).

Feichtinger, C. and Fink, G. (1999) The collective culture shock in transition countries - theoretical and empirical implications. Leadership & Organization Development Journal, 19(6): 302–309.

Fombrun, C.J. (1983) Corporate culture, environment and strategy. Human Resource Management, 22(1/2).

Gunz, H. (1989) Careers and Corporate Cultures. Managerial Mobility in Large Corporations. Oxford: Blackwell.

Hofstede, G. (1980) Culture's consequences. Beverly Hills, CA: Sage.

Hofstede, G., Neuijen, B., Ohavy. D.D. and Sanders, G. (1990) Measuring organizational cultures: a qualitative and quantitative study across twenty cases. Administrative Science Quarterly, 35: 286–316.

Kasper, H. (1987) Organisationskultur. Über den Stand der Forschung. Wien: Serviceverlag.

Kasper, H. and Heimerl-Wagner, P. (1996) Struktur und Kultur in Organisationen. Personalmanagement, Führung, Organisation. Wien: Ueberreuter, pp. 11–108.

Keller, E.V. (1982) Management in fremden Kulturen.Ziele, Ergebnisse und methodische Probleme der kulturvergleichenden Managementforschung. Bern: Haupt.

Kieser, A. and Kubicek, H. (1992) Organisation. Berlin: de Gruyter.

Kroeber, A.L. and Kluckhohn, F. (1952) Culture: A critical review of concepts and definitions. Peabody Museum Papers, 47(1).

Lane, H.W. and Beamish, P.W. (1990) Cross-cultural cooperative: behavior in joint ventures in LDCs. Management International Review, 30: 87–102.

Louis, M.R. (1981) A cultural perspective on organizations: the need for and consequences fo viewing organizations as culture bearing milieux. Human Systems Management, (2): 246–258.

Maanen, J.V. and Barley, S.R. (1984) Occupational communities: culture and control in organizations. Research in Organizational Behavior, 6: 287–365.

Mayrhofer, W. (1996) Mobilität und Steuerung in international tätigen Unternehmen. Stuttgart: Schäffer-Poeschel.

Mayrhofer, W. and Brewster, C. (1995) In praise of ethnocentricity: expatriate policies in european multi-nationals. Paper presented at the Annual Academy of Management Meeting, Vancouver.

Nahavandi, A. and Malekzadeh, A.R. (1988) Acculturation in mergers and acquisitions. Academy of Management Review, 13(1): 79,-90.

Nicholson, N. (1984) A theory of work role transitions. Administrative Science Quarterly, 29(June): 172–191.

Nicholson, N. (1990) The transition cycle: a conceputal framework for the analysis of change and human resource management. In G.R. Ferris and K.M. Rowland (Eds), Organizational Entry. Greenwich, CN: JAI: pp. S.209–S.264.

Nolte, H. (1999) Organisation. Ressourcenorientierte Unternehmensgestaltung. München, Wien: Oldenbourg.

Perlitz, M. (1995) Internationales Management. Stuttgart: Jena, Fischer.

Pettigrew, A.M. (1979) On studying organizational cultures. Administration Science Quarterly, 24(4): 570–581.

Phatak, A.V. (1992) International Dimensions Of Management. Boston, MA: PWS-Kent.

Porter, M.E. (1985) Competitive Advantage. New York: Free Press.

Rathmayr, R. (1998) Die Thematisierung von Kultur in argumentativen Phasen interkultureller Verhandlungsgespräche. In T. Berger and J. Raecke (Eds), Slavistische Linguistik 1997. München: Sagner, pp. 177–194.

Sackmann, S.A. (1992) Culture and subcultures: an analysis of organizational knowledge. Administrative Science Quarterly, 37: 140–161.

Salecker, J. (1995) Der Kommunikationserfolg von Unternehmen bei Mergers & Acquisitions. Bern: Haupt.

Samovar, L.A. and R.E. Porter (1994) Communication Between Cultures. Pacific Grove, CA: Wadsworth & Brooks, Cole.

Schein, E.H. (1985) Organizational Culture and Leadership. A Dynamic View. San Francisco, CA: Jossey-Bass.

Scherm, E. (1995) Internationales Personalmanagement. München, Wien: Oldenbourg.

Schlossberg, N.K. (1981) A model for analyzing human adaptation to transition. The Counseling Psychologist, 9: 2–18.

Schnapper, M. (1992) Multicultural/multinational teambuilding after international mergers and acquisitions. In N. Bergemann and A.L.J. Sourisseaux (eds), Interkulturelles Management. Heidelberg: Physica, pp. S.269–S.283.

Schoppe, S.G. (Ed) (1991) Kompendium der internationalen Betriebswirtschaftslehre. München, Wien: Oldenbourg.

Scott, W.R. (1986) Grundlagen der Organisationstheorie. Frankfurt a.M.: Campus.

Shenkar, O. (1995) Global Perspectives of Human Resource Management. Englewood Cliffs, NJ: Prentice Hall.

Smircich, L. (1983) Concepts of culture and organizational analysis. Adminstrative Science Quarterly, 28: 339–358.

Steinmann, H. and Schreyögg, G. (1991) Management. Wiesbaden: Gabler.

Stumpf, S. and Thomas, A. (1999) Management von Heterogenität in Gruppen. Personalführung: 36–49.

Thomas, A. (1995) Die Vorbereitung von Mitarbeitern für einen Auslandseinsatz. In T.M. Kühlmann (Ed), Mitarbeiterentsendung ins Ausland. Göttingen: Hogrefe, pp. 85–118.

Thomas, A. (Ed) (1996) Psychologie interkulturellen Handelns. Göttingen: Hogrefe.

Thomas, A. (1997) Untersuchungen des psychologischen Dienstes der Bundeswehr. München: Bundeswehr.

Thomas, A. and Hagemann, K. (1992) Training interkultureller Kompetenz. In. N. Bergemann and A.L.J. Sourisseaux (Eds). Heidelberg: Physica, pp. S.174–S.199.

Thun, F.S.V. (1981) Miteinander reden – Störungen und Klärungen. Reinbek: Rowohlt.

Triandis, H. (Ed.) (1980) Handbook of Cross-Cultural Psychology. Boston, MA: Allyn & Bacon.

Triandis, H.C. (1993) Cross-cultural Industrial and Organizational Psychology. In. M.D. Dunnette (Ed), Handbook of Industrial and Organizational Psychology. Palo Alto, CA: Consulting Psychologists Press, pp. S.103–S.172.

Trice, H.M. and Beyer, J.M. (1984) Studying organizational cultures through rites and ceremonials. Academy of Management Review, 9(4): 653–669.

Trompenaars, F. (1994) Riding the Waves of Culture. Understanding Diversity in Global Business. Chicago, IL: Irwin.

Tung, R.L. (1988) The new expatriates: managing human resources abroad. Cambridge, MA: Ballinger.

Uttal, B. (1983) The corporate culture vultures. Fortune, 108(8): 66–72.

Ward, C. (1996) Acculturation. In D. Landis and R.S. Bhagat (Eds), Handbook of Intercultural Training. Thousand Oaks: Sage, pp. 124–147.

Watzlawick, P., Beavin, J.H. and Jackson, D.D. (1982) Menschliche Kommunikation. Bern: Huber.

# Chapter 22

# Towards an Innovation Culture: What are its National, Corporate, Marketing and Engineering Aspects, Some Experimental Evidence

Jan Ulijn
*and*
M. Weggeman

*Department of Organisation and Management Science,
Eindhoven University of Technology, Eindhoven, The Netherlands*

Two important pioneer studies in the early eighties have led to an increased importance of culture research within a business context. First there was the work in 1980 by Hofstede on national cultures (NC) operating within the corporate culture (CC) of a Knowledge/Technology Intensive Organisation (KTIO: IBM). Second there was the discovery by Peters and Waterman in 1982 that culture is an important organisation design variable for successful organisations to attain their objectives. According to Arthur D. Little's 1997's Global Innovation Survey 669 firms across ten industrial sectors around the world report that their most critical concern is technological innovation. As a result they place high strategic priority on innovation, but few feel that they are effective innovators. It appears to be difficult to align activities in line with the mission and the vision of the company to operate effective cross-functional processes.

This chapter reviews some of the empirical evidence gathered since about the elements of an innovation culture. In the first section we will discuss how relevant an innovation culture for business development is and what is suggested as the ideal innovation management process. The next section presents some theoretical background and definitions and a few experimental assessment methods leading to some first empirical findings in the third section. The final section will conclude from this evidence how to champion innovation culture with some theory-based recommendations for managers. The chapter will end with a few future research questions important to support an effective organisational climate to increase the innovation performance of a firm.

# BUSINESS RELEVANCE OF AN INNOVATION CULTURE

What is the business perspective of research into Innovation Culture? If innovation and strategic vision is a vital competence of the Euromanager (Hogg, 1993), how to reach business success then? The Belgium multinational Bekaert explains as a background for their product innovation strategy of the future: *Innovation is a continuous effort of tapping into the minds of all employees.* A survey of the European Foundation of Quality Management (Nov. 97) indicates indeed that both Leadership/management and Employees' mindset and cultures (82.8 and 60.9 percent) are the main innovation levers. Since this is not only the case for KTIO's, but also for SME's (Small and Medium-sized Enterprises), it comes as no surprise that the European union (DG XIII) has launched an action plan in 1996 to foster the innovation culture of European SME's.

A study by the Bundesministerium für Wirtschaft (1997) indicates that the innovation barriers for KTIO's and SME's are different on aspects, such as legal constraints, the need of capital, the costs of innovation and the market risks: SME's might have lower costs, but they run into higher market risks. KTIO's might use their market contacts in return for which SME's could receive support from R&D to a mutual benefit. Some of the KTIO's try to use the small scale, personal and informal SME characteristics, as the following example illustrates.

How does 3M try to realise a corporate innovation culture? The company is mainly a production company, not typically the ideal environment for professionals. However 3M considers innovation to be vital to its existence and for this reason, would not think of contracting-out research work. The mission states: "30 percent of 3M's annual sales comes from products less than four years old". How can they stimulate eight thousand researchers to share and develop knowledge? 3M's 60,000 products are spread over the market groups but this does not apply to the underlying technology.

- There is a company-wide database that is used intensively.
- There are 33 company-wide technology platforms where researchers with common interests meet each other.
- Researchers are encouraged to spend a lot of time developing personal networks to create his or her own co-operative relationships and friendships.
- 15 percent of the professional time can be spent on further investigation into own pet projects in which pals can be involved (Friday afternoon research). If a researcher wishes to invest more time and money in a project, he just has to find sponsors from anywhere within the organisation.

The nice thing about the 3M example is that classic training forms are hardly used for the exchange and development of professional knowledge. There are still traditional training programs but they are of a different kind: teaching the researchers the unwritten rules and the informal ways to get things done in the hostile world of mainstream business culture and industrial culture.

Nicholson (1998) presents unique introspection evidence in this context from the staff vice president of 3M in St. Paul (Minnosota) about how to create an innovation climate. Innovation can spur growth, but growth cannot be commanded. Dick Drew, the inventor of masking tape, has ever said that one of the harbingers of innovation is management's awareness that it cannot order creativity, but it can only create an environment in which creativity flourishes by doing four things:

- Set a goal for innovators to achieve.
- Encourage innovators.
- Recognise innovators.
- Reward innovators.

There are some simple and fundamental rules to do so:

- Do it now.
- Keep the process going.
- Teach innovation.
- Hire creative people.

Mistakes, that will turn off innovation faster that you ever can turn it on, are:

- Creating a *rigid* command and control.
- Saying something the *wrong* way.
- *Punishing* somebody for failure.
- Operating in a mode of *command-and-control*, empowering employees to do as they are told.

Nicholson (1998) concludes that *informality* plays an important role in creating a good climate for innovation. A collegial climate is important, because innovation in an organisation depends mostly upon the sharing of information. The use of academic titles, as it is often the case in Dutch universities (to impress both peers and outsiders) is in this sense counterproductive. Informality exemplifies a climate of close, friendly and encouraging co-operation. How does this relate to cultural differences across national, corporate and professional borders?

In fact, KTIO's have a special problem in breaking away from red tape, bureaucracy and idea killing procedures and most of them have to be innovative in order to survive. This necessity, dictated by the environment in Western high-income countries, creates at least two major headaches for the management of these organisations: (1) the mini-misation of the costs of product life cycles that are becoming increasingly shorter and (2) the reduction in the time-to-market. Both of these management concerns provide strong arguments for the case for developing an organisation that is pre-eminently suitable for the realisation of rapid innovation. This brings Twiss (1986) to argue that the critical factor of survival and growth of such firms should lead to an effective innovation management. A key in this seems to be how to measure innovation performance and how to identify the effective strategies to attain the goals set?

Kleinknecht (1993, 1996) has not only outlined some indicators, but also tested their validity and reliability. It became clear that the very popular patents counting is only one factor to measure the innovation performance of KTIO's. Moreover, Kleinknecht and also Miles (1994) demonstrated that the innovation performance of the growing service sector could not use such an indicator. Other indicators, such as profit margins, market share, on time launch, and percent of revenues from new products or service would make the output of Figure 22.1 concrete. This same figure might depict how an ideal management process might work. Wheelwright and Clark (1992) did a very meticulous analysis of product development in different practical cases, to conceptualise a development strategy. This strategy included pre-project and aggregate project planning, cross-functional integration between marketing, engineering and manufacturing, organizing and leading project teams and tools and methods to test prototypes in cycles. They used the metaphor of the funnel to learn from projects how to build a development capability of a firm.

In the initial stage we added the fountain of creative ideas from individuals anywhere in the firm (see Neuijen, 1992) on the basis of their tacit or explicit Technology Push (TP) knowledge. The right organisational climate for the fountain should encourage the curiosity of individuals to cherish their creativity. In this stage there is a risk of divergence of too many unrealistic drops of ideas, so a funnel of teambuilding makes sure that best ideas are identified, accepted and developed or designed until a

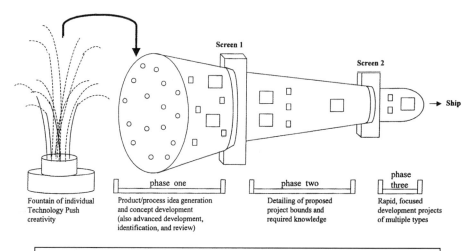

| Fountain of individual Technology Push creativity | Product/process idea generation and concept development (also advanced development, identification, and review) | Detailing of proposed project bounds and required knowledge | Rapid, focused development projects of multiple types |

- In this innovation development funnel, the front end (phase one) is expanded to encourage more and better idea generation. Following an initial screening, the best of those ideas are then detailed and analyzed (phase two), ready for a go/no-go decision. At screen 2, the approved projects are staffed and moved toward rapid introduction through a focused effort (phase three).

**Figure 22.1** The ideal innovation management process: From the fountain of individual TP-creativity with risk of divergence, tacit and explicit knowledge through the converging funnel of production constraints and MP to a team-based innovation performance result.

first screening in a first phase. The second phase proposes more detailed project bounds made ready for a go/no-go decision leading to a phase 3 where approved projects are staffed and moved toward rapid introduction through a focused effort until the actual shipment of the products. What would be the right innovation culture to makes this fountain and funnel work?

# THEORETICAL BACKGROUND AND DEFINITIONS: FROM BUSINESS PRACTICE TO RESEARCH QUESTIONS

Before we go into the theory of what might support the ideal innovation culture, we have to define some related concepts on a common sense or dictionary-type base, such as: Innovation, Knowledge, Management and Culture. Whereas ones' personality starts to develop thanks to a genetic transmission (Poortinga et al, 1990), which decreases over a life's time, the cultural transmission takes over and becomes more and more important, because of the constant exposure of the individual to his/her social environment. This predicts automatically the order and intensity of the different cultural layers to come, as outlined by Hofstede (1991): National Culture (NC), Professional Culture (PC) and Corporate Culture (CC). People are born in a NC context, acquire a certain PC, in particular, starting from the age of 18 or earlier depending on the educational level and then are exposed to the CC of a first employer. This time line might explain that values acquired first remain to be the strongest towards the end of one's professional life including one's PC. In following the order NC, CC and PC we try to conceptualise innovation culture beyond its constituents of a mere description in words to an operational level, for which experimental evidence is presented later in this chapter.

## Innovation, Knowledge, Management and Culture

The English word innovation literally means newness or difference. Innovate means make changes, introduce new things (Oxford Advanced Learner's dictionary, 1993). So, we can interpret the word innovation in business as creating newness or difference in the way an organisation doing business. According to Nagel (1998) innovation is a broad concept, that includes both technological (product and process on strategic and operational levels) and non-technological aspects. It is a successful market introduction of a knowledge-intensive renewed or improved product, process or service. This implies that knowledge and innovation management are related concepts in a KTIO. Since knowledge is more than data and information (see Davenport and Prusak, 1998) and is both tacit and explicit (see Nonaka and Takeuchi, 1995), fostering an innovative climate in a firm would include that aspect of the human resources available as well. Hence, management of technical innovation could be defined as *the planning, administration and evaluation of all activities directed to the successful introduction of that innovation into the market place*, as defined above, *including its knowledge aspects*. This type of management should be clearly differentiated from operations or logistic (supply chain) management, being also an indispensable element in the actual final innovation performance result. For the moment we define *Innovation Culture (IC)*as: *all principles on the way that an organisation operates that will raise the opportunities on creating profitable newness or difference in doing business.*

What is culture? The definitions and analyses of the concept of culture have been overwhelming since Kroeber and Kluckhohn (1963) who report 164 definitions. It is a matter of many disciplines, such as history, linguistics, literature, anthropology, sociology, psychology and more recently also economics, business and management science with all their different approaches and methodology. Moreover, culture has been applied to all kinds of differences between groups of people, such as nation, ethnicity, gender, generation, region, religion, profession, and organisation. This is not the place to deal with this issue at length, we refer for details to Ulijn with Kumar (2000) and Ulijn with St. Amant (2000) and try to summarise the essential here.

The definition of Hofstede (several sources, see bibliography) who sees culture as behaviour of people based upon a mental programming and its relation with language, is very attractive. The iceberg (Selfridge and Sokolik, 1975) and onion (Hofstede, 1991) metaphors illustrate well what has been suggested by Schein (1991, 1999) and Hofstede (1980, 1991) for cultures. The iceberg consists of the explicit top of artefacts, an under sea level of implicit written rules and procedures and an ever deeper under sea level with unwritten rules, norms and values and unspoken and unconscious rules of behaviour. The onion explains the same in its metaphor with layers at the outside, inside and a core with the norms and values. The idea of a mental programming, differentiating one group of people from another as in layers of an iceberg or in onion may guide us in examining possible effects of NC, CC, SC and PC on the innovation performance of a firm in the following sections. The five different cultural dimensions discovered by Hofstede may serve as a tested analysis framework for the importance of innovation. They are Power Distance Index (PDI), Uncertainty Avoidance Index (UAI), Individualism vs. Collectivism (IND), Confucian Dynamism Index (CDI) and Masculinity vs. Femininity (MAS). CDI looks at acceptance of change and perseverance and MAS divides the achievement and success with caring for others and quality of life (see for complete definitions of those dimensions Hofstede, several).

## National Cultures

As a contribution to research in global strategic management Adler and Ghadar (1990) developed an international strategy within the product life cycle from the perspective of people and culture with consequences for R&D, manufacturing, marketing, and finance. They hypothesise a four phase process:

- A domestic high tech start, initiating the innovation which would be rather insensitive to NC.
- A phase of growth and internationalisation where NC becomes critical.
- Multinationalisation, where NC's are just lined up and cultural sensitivity would be low.
- Globalisation where the NC interactions become mutual and very intensive.

On the basis of a review of studies Dunphy and Herbig (1994) claim that 30–50 percent of a society's innovative capacity would be influenced by NC. Much of the remaining variance among countries might be traced to structural differences, such as ease and acceptance of free entrepreneurship, size of the market and flexibility of the bureaucracy and social system. This would rate the US, the UK and then the other Anglo countries among the most innovative, as a kind of Anglo village market. Hofstede (1980, 1991) characterised this kind of NC of the Anglo world through the following scores on three dimensions: low Uncertainty Avoidance and Power Distance Indexes (UAI and PDI) and a high Individualism (IND). A low UAI makes culture an alluring companion for the CEO in village market companies (Jackofsky et al, 1988), such as in the US, UK, Sweden, Denmark and Hong Kong, where there are less task structure, fewer written rules, greater willingness to take risks, and less ritualistic behaviour. Shane (1997) used this dimension with PDI and IND to explain difference in styles to champion innovation and to infer consequences for American managers when they approach other markets than the village one in the world. This would hold true already for Europe where the Latin South would have a greater task structure, more written rules, more specialists, less willingness to take risks and more ritualistic behaviour.

In Europe it is a common saying that in new product development, one should ask French or Italians to design, Germans to manufacture and British (and Americans) to market. Looking at Figure 22.1 the Latin creativity of Italian and French design from an individual genius might be the beginning of a collectivistic teamwork in innovation. The studies by Gerybadze (1999) and Debackere (1999) pinpoint the bearing of new technologies on the organisation of innovation projects and the role of R&D for global corporations in managing technology competence centres in Europe. Europe is still needed on a global scale and Germany can act as an innovation lever through a well oiled machine to manufacture for the Anglo-Germanic village market located in North-West Europe and the Latin market in the South and outside Europe. If North and South co-operate together in creativity and innovation, it might be that the high PDI of the Latin countries according to Hofstede's findings is not a real handicap. The same might holds true for Central and Eastern Europe where upcoming new European Union (EU) members offer cheap labour and a large R&D potential for innovation (Russia). Both the Baltic Republics, Poland and the Czech Republic have more or less medium UAI and PDI's, whereas Hungary has with Austria and Denmark among the lowest PDI in Europe and a high UAI, similar to Slovenia and Russia. The economic changes in this part of the world are still turbulent which will have an influence on the development of their management styles, as is well recorded by Holden et al (1998).

In the case of Oriental cultures, Tatsuno (1996) tries to explain the success of recent Japanese innovations by the creative fusion of the Japanese group culture, for instance, in the case of the Sharp company. The Japanese are not just imitators and Just in Time-freaks. Creativity leads to quality- conscious-and consensus-based innovation. Before 1994 the West was only concerned how to make Japanese-led companies their customers (Holden and Burgess, 1994). Now it tries to learn from a Japanese innovation strategy through tacit/implicit, rather than explicit learning (Nonaka and Takeuchi, 1995 and Weggeman, 2000).

What about the innovation values of other parts of the world not mentioned yet, such as non Japanese Asia, Latin America or Africa, are they lost? Timmer (1999) finds evidence for the catch up hypothesis proposed by Gerschenkon (1962) in studying economic figures of Asian manufacturing companies in China, India, Indonesia, South Korea and Taiwan in 13 sets of products from 1963 to 1993 food, textile and rubber to machinery and equipment. Is there only a Western way to innovate? Would a high PDI or UAI in Latin Europe and America, and in Africa automatically imply innovation failures? The Japanese example seems to contradict this. This would lead to:

> Research Question (RQ) 1: What would be the effect of NC on IC, is there a difference between West and East, North and South?

To what extent are the Hofstedian dimensions PDI and UAI keys, IND (as opposed to Collectivism) in the West, CDI (Long Term Orientation) in the (Far) East?

## Corporate and Sector Cultures

The notion of corporate culture overlaps with NC, but is also distinct from it. The organisation culture is defined as the collective behaviour pattern that arises from the set of values that a group of people perceives as being a guideline for their activities. As suggested by Peters and Waterman (see above) it is rather action oriented. This action orientation of CC raises the question what can be changed and how quickly, if, for example, innovations would require that. Looking at Hofstede's Symbols, Heroes, Rituals, and Values as different layers of the onion metaphor, this would be also the order of decreasing ease to change. Values are deeply rooted, but probably in NC and even PC more so than in CC, in particular, when a lifetime employment with one firm tend to disappear. Symbols, such as logos, language and media use, humour, slogans, dress are much easier to change than style of meeting, lunches, use of the phone and values about what to (dis)approve.

Do firms and whole sectors innovate differently? What is their relation with their NC? The above distinction of low UAI and PDI for innovation makes its easy to use the same dimensions to get of values grouped together around four types of CC (see Figure 22.2 for details). We just summarise here (see for more details Bratatjandra, 1999; Ulijn, 2000; Ulijn and Kumar, 2000).

1. The *clan*, village market, adhocracy, open result oriented, pragmatic, the Grecian god Dionysus, egalitarian, and person-oriented. This would correspond to the Anglo-Nordic NC's, low on UAI and PDI.
2. The *guided missile*, well oiled machine, professional and normative, a project culture tuned into tasks, egalitarian, the Grecian goddess Athena, high UAI and low UAI, frequent in German speaking countries, such as Germany, Austria, Germanic Switzerland.
3. The *family*, closed system, employee-oriented, parochial, the Grecian god Zeus, low UAI, but high PDI, a lot of Asian cultures follow this CC-style.
4. The *Eiffel tower or pyramid of people*, job- and process-oriented, bureaucracy, the Grecian god Apollo, high UAI and PDI, values reflected in Latin NC's.

The way people run the company is apparently influenced by their NC. An example

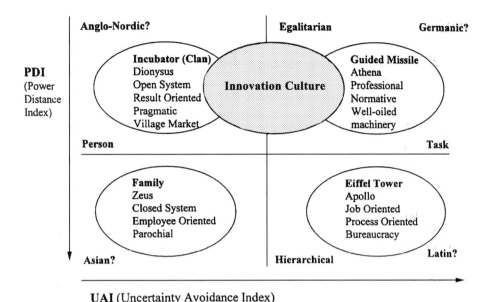

**Figure 22.2**  Possible position of Innovation Culture within a combined National and Corporate Culture framework based upon Hofstede et al. (1990), Handy (1991), Schneider and Barsoux (1997), Trompenaars and Hampden-Turner (1999), and Ulijn (2000).

for this is the differences between German- and French companies. German companies are usually strict on the work procedure and give priority to the reliability of the products. French companies, on the other hand, are more centralised, and prioritise analytic ability and technology superiority. Generally, French companies have an Eiffel/Apollo CC where hierarchy and bureaucracy are the important characteristics. This is mostly because this CC fits the best their Latin culture, which has a high PDI and a high UAI. This way NC affects CC to some extent.

Although Hofstede's main focus is on NC, he has done some comparative research in a later study with Ohayv, Sanders and Neuijen (1990) in both Dutch and Danish SME's about CC. This research suggests that CC and NC have at least two dimensions in common which give a possibility not only to relate NC and CC, but also to provide possible scales for a hypothetical construct, such as innovation culture. Important dimensions of innovation culture are Uncertainty Avoidance and Power Distance Indexes (UAI and PDI). The assumption is that both KTIO's or MNC's (Multinational Corporations) and SME's might have a high rate of technological innovation performance, if they have a low UAI and a low PDI. The critical question here again is: Would firms from the Anglo-Nordic village market (low on UAI and PDI) have the exclusive innovation capacity as hypothesised? What about the Asian family or tribe (low on UAI and high on PDI), the Germanic well-oiled machine (high UAI, low PDI) and the Latin traditional bureaucracy (high on both)? What about the role of other dimensions, such as collectivism and long term orientation? Are there several ways to innovative Rome, at what pace?

Since, in particular, the organisational climate of KTIO's is relevant for fostering innovation from the idea of R&D to the shipment of the goods to the customer, some aspects are reviewed here. According to Mintzberg (1979) a KTIO can be seen as either a Professional Bureaucracy or an Adhocracy. The dominant organisational element is in both types: the operating core, the workfloor where the professionals carry out their duties. Therefore the CC of a KTIO is most influenced by the culture of the operational core and not that of the top management team.

Frohman (1998) examines the relation between CC and innovation in detail and proposes three CC's:

- A paternalistic CC, corresponding to the above Family culture.
- A highly individualistic CC, combining the clan and the Eiffel tower.
- A CC based upon teams, which relates to the project and participative management culture of the guided missile: all noses in the same direction.

In particular, the last one seems to be helpful to bring a set of lose innovation ideas into the funnel of manufacturing and marketing the possible new products or services. In this CC, everybody is supposed to be part of a team, because teams are "the way things get done". Frohman argues, however, that elements of other CC's might also contribute to build an innovation culture to avoid that things go overboard in revering those in power of the team. To get innovation at all levels, a new type of culture has to be built in the organisation. In this new culture, the individuals' energy and ideas need to be focused on achieving challenging organisational goals, using teams as a vehicle. Innovation effort will obviously fail when goals and directions are made only by a few people in the top, such as in a family or Eiffel tower culture. The team values link up nicely also with MAS dimension of Hofstede: how to deal with relationships with others, caring for yourself vs. caring for the others and the compromise between the two. This leads to:

> RQ 2: What would be the effect of CC on IC, is the guided missile the most appropriate for innovation, what about elements of other CC-types: the clan, the family and the Eiffel tower?

Do sector cultures innovate differently from each other? In a study by Verweij (1998) on SME's in different European countries, the sectors of mechanical and electrical engineering and machine building differ strongly in functional and product centralisation. The machine building sector still prefers functional structures, whereas electrical engineering firms focus mainly on the product. Sector culture delineates clearly the transition to PC, since a set of CC's of companies operating on the same market of products and services have a lot in common because of this. It is obvious that extremes as a bank and an ICT-firm would differ, because of different PC's attributing to their SC. Therefore we will come to PC now.

## Professional Cultures

What are the different views of different professions on innovation? An organisation usually consists of people from different PC's. An organisation, where employees just focus on their professional area in implementing their tasks, does not fit to the IC that is required to cope with markets demands. Within one firm innovation is often a source of confusion: Marketing, R&D, Finance, Design, Production and last but not least the customers might have different concepts of the same new product in mind (see Funny Business by Barsoux, 1993).

In Figure 22.1 we have delineated a sort of ideal innovation management process. Wheelwright and Clark evidence that the more common reality, when the individual project results are disappointing on timing, budget and performance, is a loosely managed process. The funnel concept forces the individual "inventors" and the different functions to think and act as a team on realising innovations in common projects. What is their specific PC and how to make it manageable in an IC? What is PC? The term profession is taken to mean a job with a designated professional body, which attempts to regulate access to the job and professional liability. In the following sections engineering is reviewed with a focus on R&D, design, manufacturing and planning and   other sources of knowledge are dealt with, such as Marketing and Finance and their relation with engineering.

## *Engineering, the Main Source of Knowledge Management?*

Obviously in all knowledge and technology intensive enterprises, large, medium-sized or small, technology is an intricate part of their culture. Dussauge et al (1992) discuss for firms, such as United Technologies, Texas Instruments, Dupont de Nemours and Ford how both CC and PC use technology as a symbol, sometimes a myth in rituals and rites, such in team work and consensus of the employees "standing and learning around that exciting piece of new equipment". Strategic technology management that has to integrate product technology into global business strategies in the 21st century cannot do without culture and knowledge management. How are engineers acting as professionals in such a context? Is it different from other professions?

When seeking to become a member of an organisation, an R&D/knowledge worker usually looks for one in which he can realise as many of his personal aims as possible. Consequently, it is good policy for a KTIO to enter into an association with knowledge workers whose aims are largely in accordance with those of the organisation. An active relationship between an individual and an organisation is a result of the ties that bind that individual to that organisation. A relationship in which the employee demonstrates great personal commitment in order to help the organisation to achieve its aims. The interdependent relationship between knowledge worker and organisation, as is so often found in daily practice, can best be characterised by the term "freedom in commitment". Obviously this overall picture of the professional applies well to the individual R&D and Design worker in the beginning of the creation process of a new product. The engineering function of production as a next step can only do the job in teamwork. A marketeer might be another individualistic professional.

## *Other Sources of Knowledge, such as Marketing and Finance and their Relation with Engineering*

The mutual perception and stereotyping of the different functions towards each other might lead to conflicts, as Gerhard et al (1998) show. Within one culture they could ascertain different resolution modes related to the whole iceberg of culture in managing conflicts between the functional units in innovation projects. Let us compare some of the functions involved.

*Engineering and Marketing*   One of the authors' (Ulijn) training experience (based upon Biemans, 1993) gives anecdotal evidence that different types of engineers, economists and international business graduates in international MBA-classes quickly forget their NC descent when working on common management problems. In mutual perception exercises it appears that opinions of marketeers about engineers are quite common and NC independent. They have no sense of time, service or competitive advantage, do not worry about or underestimate costs, hide in the lab, think that the client should adapt and that standardisation and technology are sacrosanct, continue developing a product without planning. Engineers tend to stereotype marketeers as well. They want everything always NOW, are always in a hurry and impatient, they are aggressive, demanding and unrealistic, promise more than they can guarantee with a product, have no sense of technology, no trust in engineers and are not interested in their problems and focus on unrealistic profit targets.

When people in an organisation are strongly influenced by these prejudices, they will have an impression that it would not be very efficient to work together with people from another PC. Sometimes, they can even have a feeling that people from another PC are creating an obstruction for them in implementing their tasks. These prejudices would have a negative impact on the innovation effort of the organisation. In today's market, the engineers need to get input from the marketeers on issues such as the customer's needs. The marketeers, on the other hand, also need to know what technology is available and what could be developed from it in order to satisfy the customer's needs. This kind of communication and sharing of ideas will help an organisation a lot in developing innovative products and an innovative marketing strategy.

Why do those conflicts occur? The studies by Weinrauch and Anderson (1982) and Viviane and Christopher (1998) on engineering-marketing conflicts lead to some possible reasons.

- Differences in tasks, goals, and objectives of the two functions.
- Polarisation of behaviour, with marketing wanting customised products and engineering wanting to manufacture standardised product.
- Stereotyping of personality traits.
- Overestimating the competition and changes in the business environment.
- Ignoring differences in the power and organisation of the two functions.

To allow efficient communication and sharing of ideas, this stereotyping of personality traits or prejudices between two PC's essential for innovation should disappear.

*Manufacturing and Marketing*   Crittenden et al (1993) argued that conflict between marketing and manufacturing functions usually arises from the need to manage diversity in such things as:

- The number and the breadth of products.
- Customisation of products.
- Product quality.

According to these authors, there are some organisational factors that play important roles in these conflicts, such as:

- Communications between engineers and marketeers (lack of networking).
- Organisational structure.
- Reward systems.

Innovation management has to deal with this possible source of conflicts as well.

*R&D, Marketing and Manufacturing*   Xie et al's (1998) study considers new product development as a source of conflicts across three functions in the East (Japan, Hong Kong) and the West (US, UK) from the perspective of 968 marketing managers in those countries. Although is difficult to generalise over the external factors, type of product, etc. It seems that a sequence of different conflict resolution methods works best and that in any of those countries the avoidance method would have a negative effect on new product success. In a KTIO and KTI-SME marketing has to deal with at least two types of engineering functions in a firm as possible sources of conflict.

*Planning and Manufacturing*   In a study interviewing 41 managers and 85 planning and marketing employees within 11 firms Nauta and Sanders (2000) found that in negotiation about problems, high flexibility and customer service would need a flexible organisational structure, hence a guided missile approach and a not a pyramid of functions.

In conclusion, innovation might seem mostly related to the R&D function (TP), but the relation with other functions, such as marketing should be well established to realise a real MP. In the R&D sector of the industrial business, there is a natural transition for engineers from academia to industry. You have to be creative, your research topic is the boss, there is little flexibility on methodology, etc. The transition from the engineering culture to the market-oriented culture, on the other hand, is more difficult. Marketing/sales requires another culture. In this area, client is the boss. You have to be flexible and make concessions. This overall PC discussion brings us to the following research question:

RQ 3: What is the possible effect of different PC's, such as engineering and marketing on IC?

Given the roles of the Hofstedian dimensions in NC and PC (see RQs 1 and 2), is there a special PC dimension in IC, to be labelled as Innovation Drive (IDR), as a mix of MP and TP, where marketing relates to finance as the economic function and R&D to manufacturing as the engineering function? This possible new cultural dimension gets also support from CC, as Koene concludes from his review of quantitative culture studies (1996) and is confirmed by the funnel metaphor of innovation management in Figure 22.1: Organisational innovativeness is needed to realise administrative efficiency in a results orientation through an employee orientation, openness, communication and co-operation. This occurs also across NC borders. Schwartz (1994) concludes from his personality psychological effort to reduce the five Hofstedian dimensions into four, that the one of openness to change is characteristic for countries, such as France, Germany, Japan, The Netherlands, and Switzerland. This again contradicts the Anglo-Nordic village market idea that only a low PDI and UAI contributes to innovations, since France and Japan are high on both! What would be the elements of a global innovation culture?

## Innovation Culture

A global culture starts with the integration of NC and CC. The research discussed so far allows us to come to Figure 22.2.

From a situation where innovation will fail because of individualism, we can conclude that teamwork is necessary in IC to create a profitable newness for their company. In a culture that is strongly based on teams, it may, however, be the case that there is a small group in the team that has a powerful social force. This situation will force people to give up these ideas in order to keep themselves being a part of the team and, hence, be disadvantageous for the whole innovation management process for which new and different ideas are very important. Based on the known dimensions of CC, an IC should have the characteristics of an open system, teamwork that is characterised with low power distance, and clear goals to give directions in implementing the tasks. People are open for ideas and also open in sharing their ideas. This will support the communication between individuals and at the same time it will stimulate the creativity in developing new ideas. This open system will then have to be guided with a clear defined goal (task-orientation). This way IC combines the Anglo-Nordic clan and the Germanic guided missile.

The position of IC in a guided missile project culture has received some strong recent empirical evidence (Cobbenhagen, 1999) from 63 medium-sized enterprises from low to high tech firms selected by innovation consultants in 35 sectors. 59 percent of the innovation front runners organised their innovation processes as a project matrix or team. 69 percent of the pack members had an Eiffel tower, pyramidal, functional organisation or matrix. Three questions are left:

1. Is there still innovation hope for the Asian family and the Latin Eiffel tower? Cobbenhagen confirms only the position of NL in a Germanic (not so much Anglo-Nordic) NC.
2. The funnel idea of Figure 22.1 seems to need a guided missile culture, but is this appropriate for the individualistic creativity before the funnel is going to operate? The need of a clan-like open system would contradict this. In the following section we will connect this to the effect of personality on IC.
3. The Eiffel tower gives at least full identity to the different PC's. How would they

integrate in any of the other IC-options? A hypothetical intersection and integration of P, NC, CC, SC and PC in an IC is discussed below. The methodological issue of practical and theoretical assessment of the different parts of an IC and the whole is also discussed.

## The Role of Creativity and Personality (P)

On the definition of creativity, Mumford et al (1997) tries to get consensus by concluding from the theories from eight authors. *These theories hold that the combination of existing concepts, or the reorganisation of elements within an existing concept, give rise to the new ideas or approaches that are the hallmark of creativity.* Creativity, as the first individual step towards teamed up innovation, is compatible with a high IND and a low PDI (see Shane, 1992) and, therefore, seems to be rooted in a CC and NC having those values. In a loose NC, such as of the US, however, not all firms might share those values, whereas in a tight culture, such as Japan that has a medium IND and PDI, but a high CDI they would. Shane suggests that MNC's, therefore, should have at best their R&D labs in Western countries, but the same loose, individualistic and non-hierarchical cultural values do not lead automatically to coherent team work in any US-firm that would wish to innovate. The variety of personalities and their creativity could lead to innovative chaos. Professionals need to be managed to avoid and handle conflicts. A conflict management model, such as the one by Thomas (1976) includes five styles ranging from low to high assertiveness (2) and affiliation (2) and one compromise. The two dimensions used reflect more or less Hofstede's MAS, caring for yourself (high assertiveness) vs. femininity, caring for others (high affiliation). A team culture definitely needs to account for values, such as collectivism and femininity. All this means that all five Hofstedian dimensions are worthwhile to relate to IC, since they might have an effect on innovation performance.

## Intersection and Integration of P, NC, CC, SC and PC?

So far cultural models have used a varying number of dimensions from three to six. The hypothetical position of IC in Figure 22.2 uses a classic 2 × 2 framework combining NC and CC for the practical purpose of a start to include other factors of innovation, such as P and PC. P, as part from the fountain of ideas could be located as a connection to the upper left quadrant. The four quadrants may relate to the funnel of innovation management. Design, as being more closely related to R&D might have a clan aspect, production follows the characteristics of a guide missile. It seems as if this Anglo-Nordic/ Germanic approach is not enough. How to team up, how to use the expertise of all professions involved? How to deal with the different PC's, nicely separated in the pyramid of people? Overall Innovation culture might be a more a process and the outcome of the "ideal" interaction and intersection (see Figure 22.3) of CC, PC and SC or NC than a given construct beforehand, implying a dimension of Innovation Drive going from low (non-innovative) to high (strongly innovative).

So what kind of culture leads to innovation success? Innovation culture is something

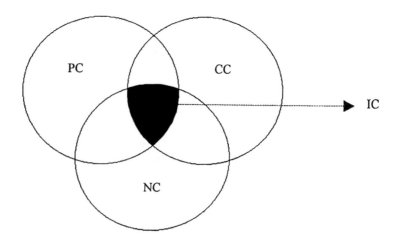

**Figure 22.3**  Innovation Culture (IC) as an intersection of Professional Culture (PC), Corporate Culture (CC), and National Culture (NC).

dynamic that is visible in human innovative behaviour, as was suggested in the definition given in the second section. When it comes to the choice of firms the comparison is made *ceteris paribus*: roughly no more than two culture types will vary, other factors, such as the innovation rate of projects and other culture types should be kept constant or under control. Innovation culture (IC) in the above sense is mostly the dependent or experimental variable: hence, compare two CC's within one SC, one CC across two NC's, two PC's within one CC, etc. After having outlined the possible effects of NC, CC and PC, the fourth research question can be formulated as follows:

RQ 4: What is more important in IC: NC, CC or PC?

Ulijn and Weggeman (2000) would argue that CC = f(NC) and PC is more important than most CC's, and will continue to get stronger. Because of the increasingly frequent switch of individuals between CC's, the employee will not root so quickly as, for instance, 20 years ago in Europe. The 1995 studies by Shane and Shane et al about innovation championing strategies suggests that NC's with a high UAI and a low PDI (mostly in the South and the East) would innovate through norms and rules to reduce uncertainty and seek cross-functional support for innovation effort. In doing so, the market, the PC of marketeers in a company and a more market-driven CC are keys next to the Western stress of R&D. MP might be even more so than TP. How should MP and TP work together? This brings us to:

RQ 5: What is the possible interaction between NC, CC and PC in IC?

Should the different PC's be integrated, only be differentiated or remain fragmented, as it is often the case? Martin (1992) offers those three options, but she does not present any evidence for a best bet in view of innovation yet. So far there are almost no precise analyses of the impact of the different PC's on a CC's success.

## Experimental (Scientific) and (Practical) Assessment Methods

The dominant belief in figures and quantification to make industrial engineering and management science a "hard science" (top of the iceberg) makes it difficult to measure something like innovation culture, which is definitely located in the bottom of it. Should we keep it "soft", as mainstream cultural researchers from anthropology and history have done, or should we follow Hofstede's example to reach a rather advanced stage of quantification, when it comes to assess cultural values? As Ulijn (2001) has argued for innovating international business communication the validity and reliability of culture studies for business practice can be increased by using both qualitative case study work and mere statistical verification of hypotheses by quantitative work with methods from experimental psychology and sociology. It seems, however, as it is the case of innovation culture, that we are still in the stage of conceptualising first by suggesting the right research questions (as tried in this overview) where quantitative data can help us well. From that perspective there should be no contradiction between the "hard" and the "soft" part of culture research methods. A combination would increase the ecological validity.

Given the fact that our five research questions deal with the differentiation and integration of culture elements in IC, Hofstede's questionnaire seems to be an excellent starting point, since it may refer to both NC and CC. We will, however, adapt it to our IC research question within the context of given case study and add the IDR dimension to it to focus on the supposed important role of PC in IC.

# SOME EMPIRICAL FINDINGS

The present state of research has allowed us only to formulate five research questions, which might lead later to testable hypotheses. To deal with them on measuring the possible different effects of NC, CC and PC and their intersection and integration, we choose the context of a small Dutch enterprise (Tedopres) of 80 employees. Tedopres introduced an innovation, called AIM (Advanced Information Management) in the ICT-software sector with an American license on the European market. The innovation makes it possible to manage all information flows needed for businesses around technical equipment and their use by their customers over the Internet with constant updates, answers to information demands, and trouble shooting. Tedopres employs Dutch and Indonesian engineers for development and marketing with the possibility of founding another firm in Indonesia in the near future. In the next section we can only summarise it (see for more details Bratatjandra, 1999).

## From an SME Firm (N = 42): AIM, an Innovative ITC Product as an Example

This study tried to gather some answers to the first two research questions in the NC × CC framework of Figure 22.2 using the five Hofstedian dimensions. To handle RQ 3, we proposed a new dimension; Innovation Drive. All six dimensions together then try

to address RQ 4 and RQ 5. The method, materials, design and statistical analysis used
are presented below, followed by the results and discussion and a conclusion.

## Method, Materials, Design and Statistical Analysis

This study makes it possible to get a first glimpse of a construct of innovation drive on
the basis of the five Hofstedian dimensions and an additional one on the mix of TP and
MP. Since we stated that innovation on the global scene would not only focus on PDI
and UAI, we included also innovation elements of the other dimensions, by assessing
the two sides of the iceberg.

Fifteen Indonesian engineers, just graduated from major technical universities in
Indonesia and 15 experienced Dutch employees of Tedopres including both engineers
and sales people filled in twice a pilot questionnaire consisting of 60 items in random
order related to the five Hofstede dimensions and Innovation Drive (IDR) (see Appendix). This was first done at the start of the training period of the Indonesian engineers to
be involved in the design and the production of the new AIM product and 6 months later
at the middle of that period to record changes in their culture perception. All items were
as much as possible contextualised by Bratatjandra, who is an electro-technical engineer with an Indonesian/Chinese background around the innovative ICT software
product at stake here. Other questionnaires devised dealt with the expectation of six
Tedopres managers towards the Indonesian engineers, active in the development of
innovation and to marketing aspects. The Indonesian engineers were all males. For the
sake of comparison only male Dutch technical and sales people were selected as
respondents. The overall business purpose of this study was to see the differences
and the similarities of the two NC's: Dutch and Indonesian to determine possible
conflicts or potential points of co-operation. The repetition of the same questionnaire
with an interval of 6 months allowed to get an impression about the possible shift of
these two NC's as a result of the interaction between the two NC's. For scoring five
point-Likert scales were used, just as Hofstede did. The nature of the data and the
exploratory character of this study did not make it possible or necessary to compute
more than simple statistical means and standard deviations. This analysis sufficed to get
an impression on the research questions formulated within only an East-West setting of
innovation.

## Results and Discussion

The overall result was that the ideal position of both Design and Production parts of the
innovation of this Dutch firm (Tedopres) could be located in the CC × NC setting of
Figure 22.4. This could be done through the perception of both Dutch and Indonesian
(TPD = Tedopres Dutch and TPI = Tedopres Indonesian) employees of present state as
recorded through the two rounds of survey and the desired state expressed by the six
Dutch top managers of this firm (Top Management Team). The desired ideal place for
this firm according to the opinion of the six members of the Top Management Team
(TMT) seems to be for the Design part in the top of the iceberg, related to the person

with a low UAI and PDI. It has the CC of a clan, a loosely related culture of islands of expertise differing in importance and size, as is suggested by the above literature. Production should have clearly a guided missile character with a project management aspect focussing on the task. All noses should be in the same direction in an egalitarian way. There is a shift towards a higher UAI here to guarantee the breakthrough of the innovation to become ready for the market. There is a tendency, however, that 6 months of interaction give them a feeling that a higher PDI and UAI is needed, which would not be in line of the Western ideal of Innovation Drive. Is this a sign of another Asian road to innovative Rome? Looking at the standard deviations, however, the Dutch become more united on the position of their firm and the Indonesians less. It might be that after 6 months there is more confusion and a longer exposure of the two NC's towards each other would show real opportunities for East-West co-operation in innovation.

Looking at RQ's 1 and 2, it is surprising to see that Indonesia here is not located in the (Asian) family quadrant of Figures 22.2 and 7.4, but in the (supposed) Latin quadrant. The above confusion might explain the need of clear directions and leadership in this innovation management process of this particular case. Whereas PDI and UAI say something on both RQ's 1 and 2, the other dimensions might give further suggestions about aspects of IC, outside the Western concept of an ideal innovation culture in an

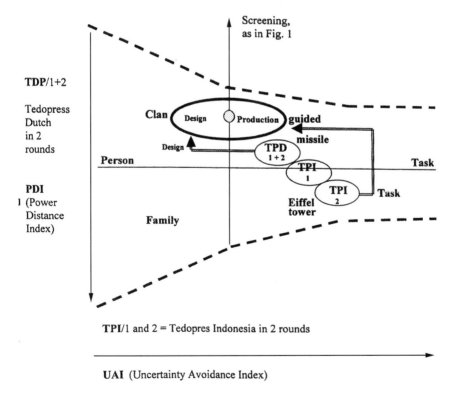

**Figure 22.4**   Position of an innovative firm in the funnel from design to production on the way out to market performance.

NC × CC setting. The IDR dimension reflects on RQ 3, where the TP × MP interaction and balance is introduced. Again the Indonesians get more divided about their opinions by increasing standard deviations, even for the "Asian" CDI, where the Dutch grow in unanimity, as both cultures do for IND! On MAS and IDR the Dutch get more divided. The Hofstede data show the biggest divergence between Dutch and Indonesians on IND (80 vs. 14), the latter ones being far more collectivistic (the family), then on MAS (14 vs. 46), the Dutch having much more feminine values. Although we have no CDI values for Indonesia, they can be expected to be higher than the Dutch score of 44. In terms of the team spirit needed in the innovation funnel of Figure 22.1 this difference in East-West values might reinforce co-operation in a complementary way: the Dutch femininity with the Indonesian collectivism, but what happens in the context of this innovative AIM product?

To substantiate RQ's 1, 2 and 3, we just review the differences and the similarities of opinions between the two culture groups towards items that belong to the six dimensions (PDI, UAI, IND, MAS, CDI, and IDR) (see Appendix).

*Power Distance (PDI)*    In this dimension, both the Indonesian engineers as the Dutch employees of Tedopres agreed on the items related to reducing the uncertainty and the problems in implementing their tasks. These items consist of statements as:

- Hierarchical line should be respected to maintain good work relationships (1).
- Having two bosses should be avoided (2).
- The importance of order/rank to give every one the appropriate place (10).

This situation might decrease the chance of miscommunication and misunderstanding since everybody has to follow the same well-defined rules.

On the other hand, there are also some differences, such as the Dutch employees underestimating the importance of status in a work situation (6). In Oriental societies, status is important as an appreciation of people's work. So, it is recommended to provide that a Western company grants the status to Oriental employees they deserve and take this status into account in dealing with them. A second difference is that the Indonesian engineers expect their manager to have precise answers to most of the questions that may arise about their work more than their Dutch colleagues (4). When a manager only demands for a certain result, the Indonesian engineers might loose their confidence and respect for the manager, which would make them feel uncomfortable to follow the direction given by him/her and tend to resist to it. In this situation, the Indonesian engineers would get an impression that communicating with their manager would not be a beneficial activity. As a result, the latter ones would have difficulties (confusion) in implementing their tasks.

*Uncertainty Avoidance (UAI)*    Towards this dimension, the Indonesian engineers and their Dutch colleagues agreed upon the importance of detailed job description (1) and a well-defined function for everyone (2). Both groups also found that rules should be flexible and adjusted according to the situation (7).

On the other hand, the Indonesian engineers found that any kind of conflict will decrease the efficiency and the effectiveness of the organisation (10). The Dutch people usually are used to set up a description of tasks based on a negotiation. When the Dutch start negotiating, they would begin with demanding large tasks that should be finished in a short period of time, which leads to overcommitted, conflict avoiding Indonesian engineers. As a result, they would get some difficulties in completing a project properly.

*Individualism (IND, as Opposed to Collectivism)*   The Indonesian engineers and their Dutch colleagues agreed upon one item in this dimension. They all agreed that relationships between managers and employees should be morally based (6). Further, the Dutch employees agreed upon the importance to consult their colleagues in making a decision (1). This belief can support the communication between them and the Indonesian engineers since the Indonesians belief that decisions made by groups are usually of higher quality than decisions made by individuals (2). Finally, the Indonesian engineers belief that an ideal organisation should look like a family (10) where policies and practices are based on loyalty and sense of duty (5). The Dutch employees, on the other hand, would prefer to have their private life (9) and they found promotion should be based on the market value rather than on loyalty (10).

*Masculinity (MAS)*   Both the Indonesian engineers and their Dutch colleagues agreed on the following items of this dimension:

- (3) One should have a need for achievement and excellence.
- (5) It is important to have a challenging task to do, from which you can get a personal sense of accomplishment.
- (9) A fair clear-cut target is important to create work motivation.
- (10) It is important to have a job with an opportunity for high earnings.

On the other hand, both groups reject the items:

- (1) It is not important to have sufficient time left for your personal life or family life.
- (6) Performance ambition is more important than quality of life and serving others.

In this dimension they agreed on so many items that the occurrence of a complication between the two cultures should not be expected.

*Confucian Dynamism (CDI)*   In this dimension, the Indonesian engineers and their Dutch colleagues agreed upon the importance to build long-term relationships with their customers by increasing the customers' satisfaction. Both groups agreed on:

- (1) Building a good relationship is more important than to get one good short-term deal.
- (2) Business strategy has to be adjusted according to the change of environment.
- (3) One should be flexible in the negotiation with customers in order to develop a good relationship with them.
- (4) Satisfied customers are more important than short-term profits.
- (8) In selling a product, after sales services are important to maintain good relationships with customers.

*Innovation Drive (IDR)*   In this dimension, both groups have a more or less similar opinion. Both groups believe that a good product can create demand in the market (7) and disagree upon the assumption that customers can not look ahead and define their future needs (5). At the start the Indonesian engineers agree on and with the statement: *The success of an innovative product in the market is strongly dependent on the technology used by R&D to develop it* (8). This is replaced after 6 months of interaction with the Dutch by a stronger role for R&D: *Innovation is a question of technology push rather than market pull* (3). In this case, we see that the PC of the Indonesian engineers has a significant influence on the way they see the importance of marketing. The fact that the Dutch employees are more market-oriented can be explained by their marketing background and their experience in dealing with customers.

What is the validity of the used six dimensions for a construct as IC based upon the five RQ's all together? Later analyses of this data (Ulijn and Weggeman, in prep.) show that we have to be careful. The tool used handles well the effects of NC and CC on IC. For each dimension, three to six items out of a total of ten are accepted by the Dutch and even five to six by the Indonesians. The most intercultural agreement deals with CDI, an Asian value, and the least on PDI. The Dutch reject eight and the Indonesians four out of the 60 items. Is this because we seem to have formulated the questions in enough neutral or even positive way? This works well for the five Hofstedian dimensions, but the nature of the newly proposed IDR is not convincing yet. The Dutch accept one and reject two items and their Indonesian colleagues accept one and reject another on which both groups agree with as a general conclusion: Both R&D and Marketing are essential for innovation and one cannot ask to the customer what innovation s/he needs. Is this because both NC's agree on this or is it because our research tool does not discriminate enough to find any differences between any NC's at all? Hence, further work is needed to build a valid and reliable Innovation Drive dimension as part of IC.

In sum, both NC's agreed in so many items, including the marketing need for innovations that no complication between the two cultures should be anticipated, apart from the cultural gaps to be covered as shown in Figure 22.4. The difference in PC between Dutch (more market experience) and Indonesian (fresh engineering graduates of a top level) might explain that the Dutch employees believe that *Market research is important in developing an innovative product and cannot based upon available technology only* (8) on which the Indonesian engineers, on the other hand, still have divided opinions. The question remains whether the level of Innovation Drive of the Indonesians would change after they have more work experience in the West and interaction with their Dutch colleagues. Ulijn (2000) discusses this issue with respect to the time dimension hidden in CDI: Who will adapt to whom? A mutual adjustment might take place within a global IC.

## Conclusion

Does a higher PDI and UAI than the ones of the Hofstede sample make a firm less capable of innovation in the Western sense? Figure 22.4 shows TPI in a Latin Eiffel tower position, whereas the Indonesians themselves see the ideal organisation as a family with loyalty and sense of duty. Is this a problem for innovation? There is, of course, still a way to go to overcome communication gaps, develop trust, etc. to reach an IC that has a clan culture for the Design part and a guided missile culture for the Production part. In the funnel metaphor of Figures 22.1 and 7.4 the Asian and Latin values might even support the creativity and teamwork needed, as it were the bottom of the iceberg, the Western IC being in the top. What about the role of PC in those processes? All culture quadrants should have an element of MP, the guided missile and the Eiffel tower, being probably the most TP, but innovations never happen through MP alone. Good strategies result from a combination of market scouting and technology gate keeping. The role of marketing should be more researched in future studies than it was possible in this one.

Irrespective of a NC background, as can be seen in Figure 22.4, there is some intercultural agreement about the importance of MP for innovation success. Engineering as part of the Production which involves the Indonesian engineers, and marketing as part also of the Design department, where mostly Dutch work, will have to co-operate. The IC of this firm would have open communication, freedom to experiment, lessons to learn from mistakes and a market-orientation for the Design part. The Production part of IC should have well-defined procedures, formality, technology oriented expertise and well-defined individual job and function descriptions. Although IDR seems not to have addressed in a valid way yet RQ 3 and it is difficult to disentangle the role of NC, CC and PC in their integration and interaction both, RQ's 4 and 5 should make room for a team or co-operation culture for which a proper organisational climate has to created.

## What is the Right Innovation Climate?

To give an example of the right organisational climate where synergy is sought through co-operation between different CC's coming from different sectors to establish affective ties, driven by a professional interest and challenge, we present the Dutch example of a television program for children (Klokhuis), a museum (the one of Archaeology in Leiden), a KTIO (Philips), a privatised Dutch institute of applied technology (TNO) and a British university (the one of Manchester). This example was covered in the press and has led to an innovative service product by the Leiden museum of Archaeology and TNO. What was the creative idea of the beginning of the funnel of Figure 22.1?

Klokhuis (apple core) is an award winning popular television program, which tries to explain relatively complex matters in a simple way to children. One of such matters was an item on mummies, which are kept in the Archaeological Museum, in Leiden. While Klokhuis was preparing the item they decided that only the outside of the mummy would not explain very much. On the other hand, opening up the mummy was, of course, no alternative because of its destructive character. Then it occurred to one of the museum officials that people at Philips Medical Systems would be able to "look inside" the mummy by using CT-scan technology. Philips complied with the request and delivered a set of two-dimensional cross-sections of the mummy. To the mind of Klokhuis, this would not appeal sufficiently to children. Philips, in turn, knew a research group at TNO who by using a computer coupled to a kind of sculpturing robot is able to convert the CT-scan data sets into a three dimensional model in wax. This resulted in a partly tissued skull and skeleton with holes in strange places due to a lack of data. Klokhuis thought children would be frightened by the view of such a partly complete human being. So, TNO knew a scientist at the University of Manchester who is specialised in reconstructive post-mortem surgery. After he had applied his reconstructive skills to the wax-model, Klokhuis was satisfied and broadcasted the item. People at the museum and at TNO are now thinking of defining an integrated service based on this unplanned new combination of existing bodies of knowledge.

What is the best organisational climate to foster such spontaneous teaming up for innovation? How to encourage R&D workers to develop affective ties with their firm to be creative as a source for successful innovation? Vermaak and Weggeman (1999) present evidence from 351 scientists in medicine and health care of the Maastricht University in The Netherlands about their satisfaction and irritation level. This study was based on an earlier analysis by Weggeman (1989) on the need for professional management in KTIO's. One positive conclusion which can be drawn form this study and the "Klokhuis" example involving a British R&D worker, is that KTIO's (including universities) have to strive to reach goals derived from a collective ambition in an open networking climate. This climate should contain an outside world that encourages people to be relatively open minded, honest and collegial. Political behaviour and social games as sources of irritation is unnecessary to foster an organisational climate in which employees feel secure and at home to be highly creative and innovative.

## CONCLUSIONS AND HOW TO CHAMPION INNOVATION CULTURE: SOME RESEARCH-BASED RECOMMENDATIONS FOR MANAGERS AND FURTHER RESEARCH

Championing innovation involves management across cultural borders not only of nations. Corporations and professions, such as engineering and marketing also bring their values to the process on innovation management, given the creativity and ideas at the start. This process of intercultural teaming up and co-operation involved, appeared to have a representative metaphor in that of a fountain and a funnel proposed by Neuijen and Wheelwright (see Figure 22.1). Individual TO-creativity with risk of divergence should converge into a shared tacit and explicit knowledge through production and market constraints towards a team-based innovation performance result. This is not to deny the importance of the personality of the innovator.

Once a Dutch SME wants to use the potential of creativity and innovation of Indonesian engineers, what is the role then of the different cultural factors and their interaction and integration? It seems there is no single way to innovative Rome. The Western combination of an Anglo-Nordic clan and a Germanic guided missile culture (see Figure 22.2) might only represent the top of innovation culture iceberg, the market-oriented design part in a clan, the production in a guided missile. The Asian family, such as the one of Indonesian engineers can support the guided missile and the Latin Eiffel tower the creativity of the individualistic French, Italians, etc. as the bottom of the iceberg: how to deal with feelings, how to network and how to use implicit knowledge. Interesting enough the Dutch study indicates that the cultural preferences of the Indonesian engineers go toward a Latin and not an Asian combination of high uncertainty avoidance and power distance. The other dimensions researched (collectivism, presumed feminine caring for the other) and so called Confucian long term orientation provide enough common ground for the co-operation process needed for innovation, at least in this case of an SME where there is a natural solidarity in doing things together. Our attempt to develop a special dimension Innovation Drive, which would integrate the innovation attribute of at least to key professional cultures: engineering (as in R&D and production) and marketing, appeared not be valid and reliable enough. How to combine Technology Push and Market Pull, or better Technology Pull, as Allen (1993) proposes, since the market can never tell to businesses what new product they should develop. The technology of the core competence of a KTIO should pull on the creativity of knowledge workers to realise an innovation, which the market accepts. This way the funnel process of ideal innovation management can be seen as a two-level operation, one in the top of the iceberg (Northern and Western) and one in the bottom (Southern and Eastern). A true innovation culture would teach then how to handle the real obstacles of the top and the hidden pitfalls and virtual opportunities in the bottom within the funnel from design to production on the way out to market performance. With respect to the nature of innovation culture based upon a first empirical study in a Dutch SME, we may confirm as a result of RQ's 1–5 that this construct is at least based upon some overlap and intersection of three deeper cultural layers: NC, CC and in particular PC, the last one including some fit between TP (Engineering) and MP (Marketing).

The survey by Shane (1997) of 4000 managers in eight organisations and 32 countries, in comparison with the Hofstedian values of PDI, UAI and IND allowed him to give answers to questions of innovation championing, such as:

* How to deal with rules, procedures, norms and the hierarchy of an organisation?
* How to get others in the organisation to support innovation?
* How to monitor the innovation process?
* What should be the composition of an innovation team?

He found that the 32 countries respond differently to those issues. Chile would not work outside the rules, the UK, the US and Zimbabwe would (1). Chile and Zimbabwe would make a strong appeal to the organisation as a whole, Finland and Germany would appeal to outsiders as well (2). France would closely monitor the innovation process, Germany, the UK and the US would not (3). In Germany all members of the innovation team would be treated as equals, not in Japan and Chile (4). Shane concludes that NC is far more important than CC, SC, PC, gender work or championing experience. The Hofstedian dimensions of masculinity and confucianism were not involved, why not? Although this is an impressive body knowledge, it is not sure if recommendations for championing innovation in countries, such as (in an alphabetical order) Canada, Chile, France, Germany, India, Japan, Malaysia, Mexico, The Philippines, Taiwan and the UK are sufficiently substantiated by his data.

More research is needed to what the above "Western" concept holds true for other parts of the world. How do our findings presented above relate do this? They certainly support some of the do's and don'ts listed above. If we were to change the culture of a KTIO, what should be done to relate knowledge and innovation management? We think indirect measures can be taken or should be avoided to handle the sources of satisfaction and irritation of knowledge workers in KTIO's, in particular, because of the scale of such organisations. What remains to be researched? A lot! Damanpour (1991) and Gopalakrishnan and Damanpour (1996) recommend on the basis of a number of reviews of innovation research that new studies should consider different dimensions and variables, such as the individual, organisational and environmental and include measurement of innovation using not only technical, but also organisational and administrative aspects. Both longitudinal and multidimensional studies are recommended to relate innovations to organisational effectiveness. The empirical evidence presented here is certainly of a multidimensional kind and accounts for organisational and slightly individual aspects, but it restricts to one case involving only Dutch and Indonesians in one firm and to one questionnaire devised to knowledge workers of one university in one sector. Our recommendations are, therefore, also based upon anecdotal evidence from consultancy and the literature, including some additional empirical studies. The research questions formulated, however, still need more analyses and should lead to testable propositions and hypotheses on various topics.

### Acknowledgements

This chapter is the results of bringing different approaches around innovation culture together. This would lead easily to an overdose of information. We thank the editors of this book to push for some restriction for which the authors have to thank the following persons: Sven Bakkes, MBA, a graduate from Maastricht University (International Business) and researcher at the Department of Organisation Science of the Eindhoven University of Technology and Martijn Lanenga, an industrial engineering student at the same university. They both helped us in editing this piece by valuable comments and summarising an earlier much longer version.

## APPENDIX A. THE 60 ITEMS USED IN THE PILOT CASE STUDY TO DETECT POSSIBLE ELEMENTS FOR AN INNOVATION CULTURE

### Power Distance Index (PDI)

1. The hierarchical line should always be respected in order to maintain good work relationships.
2. An organisation structure in which certain subordinates have two direct bosses should be avoided at alt costs.
3. The main reason for having a hierarchical structure is so that everyone knows who has authority over whom.
4. lt. is important for a manager to have at hand precise answers to most of the questions that his/her subordinates may raise about their work.

5. Most employees have an inherent dislike of work and will avoid it if they can.
6. Status is important to show the level of authority.
7. In an organisation, high centralisation is needed to get the implementations of tasks under control.
8. A large corporation (with a large distance between the hierarchical levels) is generally a more desirable place to work than a small company.
9. Older people are more experienced and should be respected.
10. Order/rank in an organisation is important in order to give everyone his/her appropriate place.

## Uncertainty Avoidance Index (UAI)

1. When the respective roles of the members of a department become complex, detailed job descriptions are a useful way of clarifying.
2. The more complex a departments activities are, the more important it is for each individuals function to be well defined.
3. Authorities in an organisation are there to give security to the employees.
4. Rules and formality are necessary to structure life.
5. A Corporation should have a major responsibility for the health and welfare of its employees and their immediate families.
6. It is important to have the security that you will not be transferred to a less desirable job.
7. Rules should not be changed even when people think it is in the company's best interest.
8. In an organisation, one should be more task-oriented (consistent) than interpersonal-oriented (flexible) in his/her style.
9. Security of employment is a necessity.
10. Most organisations would be better off if conflict could be eliminated forever.

## Collectivism/Individualism (IND)

1. It is important to consult your colleagues in making a decision.
2. In an organisation, decisions made by groups are usually of higher quality than decisions made by individuals.
3. It is important that every employee represents him/herself as a part of the organisation more than as an individual.
4. Ideally, one should support one's colleagues in the work situation.
5. Policies and practices in work organisations should be based on loyalty and sense of duty.
6. Relationships between managers and employees should be morally based.
7. Promotion should be based more on loyalty and seniority than on market value.
8. One should always try to fulfil one's obligations to organisation, family, and society.

9. The private life of an employee is properly a matter of direct concern to his company.
10. An ideal organisation looks after their employees like a family.

## Masculinity/Femininity (MAS)

1. It is not important to have sufficient time left for your personal or family life.
2. Status is important to show off success.
3. One should have a need for achievement and excellence.
4. In an organisation, successful achievers should be rewarded in the form of wealth or status.
5. It is important to have challenging tasks to do, from which you can get a personal sense of accomplishment.
6. Performance ambition is more important than quality of life and serving others.
7. To be assertive and achievement-oriented is more important than maintaining good interdependence relationships with others.
8. Work environment should provide chances to excel and strict accountability is needed to show your degree of achievement.
9. A fair and clear-cut target is important to create work motivation.
10. It is important to have a job with an opportunity for high earnings.

## Confucian Dynamism Index (CDI)

1. Building a good long-term business relationship is more important than to get one good short-term deal.
2. Business strategy has to be adjusted according to the change of environment.
3. One should be flexible in the negotiation with customers in order to develop a good relationship with them.
4. Satisfied customers are more important than short-term profits.
5. One should persist toward results, which can not be readily achieved.
6. One should use the available resources sparingly.
7. In an organisation, the obligations have to come before rights.
8. One should have willingness to subordinate oneself for a purpose.
9. In selling a product, after sales services are important to maintain good relationships with customers.
10. It is more important to look for the utility of new information than the consistency of it.

## Technology Push/Market Pull > Innovation Drive (TP/MP > IDR)

1. A technology-driven innovation strategy is better than a market-oriented one.
2. An innovative product has to be promoted to the market instead of developed based on market research.

3. Innovation is a question of technology push rather than market pull.
4. An innovative product can not be developed based on a market research, it has to be developed by R&D based on the available technology.
5. Customers can not look ahead; we can not ask customers for their future needs.
6. High-tech products sell themselves.
7. A good product as a result of R&D research can create demand in the market.
8. The success of an innovative product in the market is strongly dependent on the technology used by R&D to develop it.
9. A strict division between R&D and Marketing departments is important in developing an innovative product.
10. The R&D department knows how technology will fulfil market needs better than the market knows what they need from the technology.

# REFERENCES

Adler, N.J. and Ghader, F. (1990) International strategy from the perspective of people and culture. In A. Rugman (Ed), Research in Global Strategic Management, Greenwich, pp. 179–205.

Allen, Th.J. (1993) Managing technical communications and technology transfer: distinguishing science from technology. In Th. Allen (Ed), Managing the Flow of Technology. London: MIT Press.

Barsoux, J.L. (1993) Funny Business. London: Cassell.

Biemans, W.G. (1993) Relaties en samenwerking zijn essentieel voor succes bij productontwikkeling. IM Business Marketeer Blad.

Bratatjandra, G.H. (1999) Transition to innovation culture: a case study about an innovative product of Tedopres (AIM). MBA-thesis, TSM-Business School, Enschedé, The Netherlands.

Cobbenhagen, J. (1999) Managing Innovation at the Company Level: a study on non-sector-specific success factors. PhD-thesis Maastricht, The Netherlands: University Press.

Crittenden, V.L., Gardiner, L.R. and Stam, A. (1993) Reducing conflict between marketing and manufacturing. Industrial Marketing Management, 22: 299–309.

Damanpour, F. (1991) Organisational innovation: a meta-analysis of the effects of determinant and moderators. Academy of Management Journal, 34: 555–590.

Davenport, Th.H. and Prusak, L. (1998) Working Knowledge: How Organisations Manage What They Know. Boston, MA: Harvard Business School Press.

Debackere, K. (1999) Technologies to Develop Technology: The Impact of New Technologies on the Organisation of Innovation Projects. Antwerp/Apeldoorn: Maklu.

Dunphy, S. and Herbig, P. (1994) Comparison of innovative capabilities among Anglo-Americans countries: the case for structural influences on innovation. Management Decision, 32 (8): 50–56.

Dussauge, P., Hart, S. and Ramanantsoa, B. (1992) Strategic Technology Management: Integrating Product Technology into Global Business Strategies for the 1990s. Chichester: Wiley.

Frohman, A.L. (1998) Building a culture for innovation. Research Technology Management, 41 (2): 9–12.

Gerybadze, A. (1999) Managing Technology Competence Centers in Europe: The role of European R&D for global corporations. Antwerp/Apeldoorn: Maklu.

Gerhard, B., Amelingmeyer, J. and Specht, G. (1998) Managing conflicts between the functional units in innovation projects, contribution to the 5th International product development conference, Como, Italy.

Gerschenkon, A. (1962) Economic Backwardness in Historical Perspective. Cambridge, MA: Harvard University Press.

Gopalakrishnan, S. and Damanpour, F. (1996) A review of innovation research in economics, sociology, and technology management. Omega, 25 (1): 15–28.

Handy, Ch. (1993) Gods of Management: The Changing Work of Organisations London: Business Books.

Hofstede, G. (1980) Culture's Consequences: International Differences in Work Related Values. Beverly Hills: Sage.

Hofstede, G. (1991) Culture and Organisation: The Software of the Mind. New York: McGraw-Hill.

Hofstede, G., Neuijen, B., Ohayv, D. and Sanders, G. (1990) Measuring organisational cultures: a qualitative and quantitative study of twenty cases, Administrative Science Quarterly, 35: 286–316.

Hogg, B.A. (1993) European managerial competences. European Business Review, 93 (2): 21–26.

Holden, N.J. and Burgess, M. (1994) Japanese-led Companies: Understanding How to Make Them Your Customers. London: McGraw-Hill.

Holden, N., Cooper, C. and Carr, J. (1998) Dealing With the New Russia: Management Cultures in Collision. Chichester: Wiley.

Jackofsky, E.F., Slocum, J.W., Jr. and McQuaid, S.J. (1988) Cultural values and the CEO: Alluring companions? Academy of Management Executive, 2 (1): 41–50.

Kleinknecht, A. (1993) Testing innovation indicators for postal surveys. In A. Kleinknecht and D. Bain (Eds), New Concepts in Innovation Output Measurement, pp. 1–9. London: Macmillan.

Kleinknecht, A. (1996) New indicators and determinants of innovation. In A. Kleinknecht (Ed), Determinants of Innovation: The Message from New Indicators, pp. 1–11. London: Macmillan.

Koene, B.A.S (1996) Organisational Culture, leadership and performance in context: trust and rationality in organisations. PhD-thesis, Maastricht, The Netherlands.

Kroeber, A. and Kluckhohn, C. (1963) Culture: A Critical Review of Concepts and Definitions: Papers of the Peabody museum of American Archaeology and Ethnology. New York: Knopf.

Krogt, T. van der (1981) Professionalisering en Collectieve Macht: Een Conceptueel Kader. Den Haag: Vuga.

Little, A.D. (1997) Global Innovation Survey. Cambridge MA.

Martin, J. (1992) Cultures of Organisations: Three Perspectives, Oxford: Oxford University Press.

Miles, I. (1994) Innovation in services. In M. Dodgson and R. Rothwel (Eds), Handbook of Innovation, pp. 243–256. Aldershot: Edward Elgar.

Mintzberg, J. (1979) The Structuring of Organisations. Englewood Cliffs, NJ: Prentice Hall.

Mumford, M.D., Whetzel, D.L. and Reiter-Palmon, R. (1997) Thinking creatively at work: organisational influences on creative problem solving. Journal of Creative Behaviour, 31: 7–17.

Nagel, A. (1998) On Strategy, Innovation and Technology (non published paper). Eindhoven University of Technology.

Nauta, A. and Sanders, K. (2000) Interdepartmental negotiation behaviour in manufacturing organisations. International Journal of Conflict Management, 11(2): 107–133.

Neuijen, J.A. (1992) Diagnosing organisational cultures: patterns of continuance and change. Groningen: Wolters Noordhoff. PhD-thesis, University of Groningen, The Netherlands.

Nicholson, G.C. (1998) Keeping innovation alive. Research Technology Management, 41 (3): 34–40.

Nonaka, I. and Takeuchi, H. (1995) The Knowledge-Creating Company: How Japanese Companies Create the Dynamics of Innovation. New York: Oxford University Press.

Peters, T.J. and Waterman, R.H. (1982) In Search of Excellence: Lessons from America's Best Run Companies. New York: Random House.

Poortinga, Y., Kop, P. and van der Vijver, F. (1990) Differences between psychological domains in the range of cross-cultural variation. In P. Drenth, J. Sergeant and R. Talens (Eds), European Perspectives in Psychology, 3: Cross-cultural Psychology. Chichester: Wiley.

Schein, E.R. (1991) What is culture? In P.J. Frost, L.F. Moore, M.R. Louis and J. Martin (Eds), Reframing Organisational Culture, pp. 243–253. London: Sage.

Schein, E.R. (1999) The Corporate Culture Survival Kit: Sense and Nonsense About Cultural Change. San Francisco, CA: Jossey-Bass.

Schneider, S.C. and Barsoux, J.L. (1997) Managing Across Cultures. London: Prentice Hall.

Schwartz, S. (1994) Beyond individualism/collectivism: new cultural dimensions of values. In U. Kim, H.C. Triandis, C. Kagitcibasi, S.C. Choi and G. Yoon (Eds), Individualism and Collectivism: Theory, Method and Applications, pp. 85–119. Thousand Oaks, CA: Sage.

Selfridge, R. and Sokolik, S. (1975) A comprehensive view of organisational management. MSU Business Topics, 23 (1): 46–61.

Shane, S.A. (1992) Why do some societies invent more than others? Journal of Business Venturing (JBV), 7 (1): 29–46.

Shane, S.A. (1995) Uncertainty avoidance and the preference for innovation championing roles. Journal of International Business Studies, 26 (1): 47–68.

Shane, S.A., Venkataraman, S. and Macmillan, I. (1995) Cultural differences in innovation championing strategies. Journal of Management, 21 (5): 931–952.

Shane, S.A. (1997) Cultural differences in the championing of global innovation. In R. Katz (Ed), The Human Side of Innovation, pp. 296–303. New York: Oxford University Press.

Tatsuno, S.M. (1996) Created in Japan: From Imitators to World-Class Innovators. New York: Harper.

Thomas, K. (1976) Conflict and conflict management. In M. Dunnette (Ed), The Handbook of Industrial and Organisational Psychology. Chicago, IL: Rand McNally.

Timmer, M.P. (1999) The dynamics of Asian manufacturing: a comparative perspective, 1963–1993, PhD-thesis. Eindhoven University of Technology, The Netherlands.

Trompenaars, F. and Hampden-Turner, Ch. (1999) Riding the Waves of Culture: Understanding Cultural Diversity in Business. London: The Economist Books.

Twiss, B.C. (1986) Managing Technological Innovation. London: Pitman.

Ulijn, J. (2000) Innovation and global culture: time is money or time to get connected in an East-West communication? Paper submitted to Technology and Innovation Management Division, Academy of Management Toronto 2000 Conference: A new time (August).

Ulijn, J. (2001, in press) Innovation and international business communication: can European research help to increase the validity and reliability for our business and teaching practice? Outstanding Research Lecture contributed to the 1999 Los Angeles ABC Convention (3 Nov. 1999), to be published in JBC-Journal with comments by Lanar Reinsch and Iris Varner.

Ulijn, J. and St. Amant, K. (2000) Mutual intercultural perception: how does it affect technical communication, some data from China, The Netherlands, Germany, France and Italy. Technical Communication, 47 (2): 220–237.

Ulijn, J. and Kumar, R. (2000) Technical communication in a multicultural world: how to make it an asset in managing international businesses, lessons from Europe and Asia for the 21st century. In P.J. Hager and H.J. Scheiber (Eds), Managing Global Discourse: Essays on International Scientific and Technical Communication, pp. 319–348. New York: Wiley.

Ulijn, J. and Weggeman, M. (2000) Innovating the corporate strategy: what would be the mission for international business communication? Contribution to a special issue of the Journal of Business Communication on Strategy, Innovation, Culture and Communication.

Vermaak, H. and Weggeman, M. (1999) Conspiring fruitfully with professionals: New management roles for professional organisations. Management Decision, 37 (1): 29–44.

Verweij, M.J. (Ed) (1998) Small and medium-sized enterprises in European perspective: Results from the BETTI database, Utrecht: Berenschot. (www.bettibench.com).

Viviane, S. and Christopher, T.S. (1998) Conflict between engineers and marketeers. Industrial Marketing Management, 27: 279–291.

Weggeman, M. (1989) Is the professional self-managing or is there really a need for professional management? European Management Journal, 7 (4): 422–430.

Weggeman, M. (2000) Kennismanagement: De Praktijk (Knowledge Management: The Practice). Schiedam: Scriptum.

Weinrauch, J.D. and Anderson, R. (1982) Conflicts between engineering and marketing units. Industrial Marketing Management, 11: 291–301.

Wheelwright, S.C. and Clark, K.B. (1992) Revolutionizing Product Development: Quantum Leaps in Speed, Efficiency, and Quality. New York: The Free Press.

Xie, J., Song, X.M. and Stringfellow, A. (1998) Interfunctional conflict, conflict resolution styles, and new product success: a four-culture comparison. Management Science, 44 (12): 192–221.

# Section VI

# The Future of Organizational Cultures

## William H. Starbuck

This section of the Handbook discusses the potential future of organizational cultures. The chapters assert that the organizations that survive and perform well will be the ones that develop cultures that suit their challenges.

In "Where Are Organizational Cultures Going?", Philippe Baumard and William H. Starbuck lay groundwork for the remainder of this section. They discuss the processes that guide the evolution of organizational cultures, and they survey some of the more inertial trends that are likely to influence organizational cultures over the near-term future. These trends encompass changing norms about proper behaviour in organizations, changing distributions of people around the world, changing distributions of economic activities around the world, rising educational levels almost everywhere, ever-increasing computational power and telecommunication capacities, changing norms about organizational membership and work locations, and changing norms about inter-organizational relations. Baumard and Starbuck propose that, inverting the pattern observed during the 20th century, the 21st century may make organizational cultures key determinants of organizational structures, and hence of strategic behaviour.

Modem technology is offering opportunities to change working conditions. One of these proposed changes is the use of technology to create "awareness systems" that enable workers to monitor each others' behaviours even though they are far apart. Thus, close collaboration can span vast distances. In "Collaborative Insight or Privacy Invasion?" D. Harrison McKnight and Jane Webster observe that the ways workers react to awareness systems depends on the climates of trust within their organizations. In organizations with low-trust cultures, workers are likely to perceive awareness systems as invading their privacy. Consequently, organizations that intend to install awareness systems should first strengthen their trust climates. However, people around the world have been becoming more sceptical about institutions for forty years, and so organizations are finding it harder and harder to generate intraorganizational trust.

Differing birth rates, wealth differentials, and globalisation are leading organizations to incorporate more and more diversity. In their chapter, "In diversity is there strength?" Narayan Pant and Kulwant Singh argue that this diversity will have both positive and negative effects on organizational effectiveness. However, the overall result, they predict, will be that organizations with low diversity are going to find survival difficult, and they will be supplanted by organizations having high diversity. Especially in complex environments, the most effective organizations will tend to have elaborated cultures as well as high diversity, and their success will elicit imitation.

Telecommuting has been proliferating rapidly in societies that have strong support for telecommunications. In "Culture In-The-Making in Telework Settings", Roger Dunbar and Raghu Garud contemplate the implications of telecommuting for organizational cultures. They maintain that telework cultures promote different values, norms, behaviours and symbols than do on-site work cultures. Specifically, telework cultures support work performance rather than stable social relations and shared identities. One result is that norms of interaction become topics for continuing negotiation between employees and employers. Another result is that employees gain freedom to exhibit more diversity.

Modem telecommunications technology also enables organizations to develop and co-ordinate inter-organizational coalitions that co-operate closely without actually merging. In "Organizational Culture and Imaginary Organizations", Bo Hedberg and Christian Maravelias discuss the issues posed by interfirm coalitions and firms that have many free-lance individual collaborators. These "imaginary organizations" pose governance issues, as no traditional hierarchies dictate how members should share profits or influence. Hedberg and Maravelias argue that the success of imaginary organizations depends on their leaders' abilities to build trust, to foster respect, and to make exchange mechanisms transparent.

# Chapter 23

# Where Are Organizational Cultures Going?

**Philippe Baumard**

*IAE Aix-en-Provence, Puyricard, France*

*and*

**William H. Starbuck**

*New York University, New York, USA*

## RHYTHMS OF CHANGE

This section of the Handbook focuses on the future …a topic that holds endless fascination for human beings. Many of the discussions in the popular media speculate about future events. Academics achieve wide fame by offering imaginative predictions about future wonders or disasters. Corporations pay large fees to obtain forecasts about economic trends and societal changes.

The future is also a topic on which no one has demonstrated reliable expertise. Research about forecasting indicates that a prediction is almost certain to be right if it says that trends will continue for a few more time periods, and that a prediction is almost certain to very wrong if it says that trends will continue for many time periods. Also almost certain to be wrong are attempts to predict the times (turning points) when trends will shift abruptly.

The chapters in this section argue with amazing consistency that organisational cultures are going to be focal determinants of success: The organisations that do well in the future are those that develop cultures that are appropriate for their challenges.

Like most social phenomena, organisational cultures normally change slowly and current trends tend to persist. As well, organisational cultures also have properties that make them difficult to predict over long periods. Like prices, opinions, and governments, organisational cultures are determined by social construction, by interactions between people. People tell each other stories, and they negotiate with each other about the effectiveness and legitimacy of values, beliefs, and rituals. Although these interactions generally produce small incremental changes in organisational cultures, they do sometimes produce large dramatic changes.

Organisational cultures often stimulate changes in themselves. Cultures not only foster agreement and cohesion within organisations, they also create differentiation and conflict among organisational members (Martin, 1992). Cultures almost always endorse the values and beliefs of some subgroups while ignoring the values and beliefs of other subgroups. The devalued subgroups thus gain incentive to protest or oppose. Likewise, as cultures clarify some beliefs and rituals, they also create ambiguity about the beliefs and rituals that they ignore. This ambiguity harbours opportunities for innovation or deviance. One obvious example is the Protestant Reformation, which occurred because dissident members of the Roman Catholic Church believed that their Church was allowing improper rituals and accommodating improper beliefs. When the Church ignored the dissidents' protests, they founded new churches that were more in accord with their beliefs. Another example is the revolution that took place in the Free University of Berlin during the late 1960s. In this case, students asserted that professors had been allowing students insufficient voice in the control of the university and that curricula reflected professors' conservative political views.

A study by Jönsson and Lundin (1977) suggests that social construction produces waves of enthusiasm for successive modalities. Jönsson and Lundin observed small Swedish firms as they developed over time. The members of the firms showed increasing enthusiasm for a specific idea as more and more members understood the idea and saw its merits. But eventually, the idea's limitations became visible and enthusiasm for it waned. Eventually, a new idea would appear and begin to gather support.

As a product of social construction, an organisation's culture is not a demonstrable fact and rarely is there consensus about its character. Organisations' leaders often try to influence the definitions of culture that prevail in their organisations (Kunda, 1992). For instance, Hewlett Packard has de-emphasised rules and hierarchical controls and has sought to enlist members' strong commitment to its corporate mission statement, whereas Glacier Metals de-emphasised members' responsibility for corporate goals and specified their roles in very detailed documents (Brown, 1960; http:// www.hp.com/abouthp/corpobj.html). These differing concepts of desirable culture diffuse geographically and evolve over time, as organisational members explore different ideas and address different issues. Thus, Japan's economic success during the 1960s and 1970s induced many North American and European companies to try some Japanese ideas about organisations (Ouchi, 1981; Nonaka and Takeuchi, 1995).

Some contemporary trends in the ways people interact today, and how they will interact tomorrow, challenge current knowledge about organisational cultures. Changes are occurring in all of the main components of culture. One of the clearest trends has been a decreasing emphasis on traditions and hierarchical status as determinants of proper action and an increasing emphasis on markets as determinants of proper action (Williamson, 1975). Rather than references to traditions or authority, references to profitability and productivity support the rationales of issues such as corporate govern-ance, work-team designs, and compensation schemes. A second trend, coupled with the first, seems to have been rising cynicism with regard to organisational socialisation programs, organisational ceremonies and the statements of hierarchical superiors (Kunda, 1992). For instance, employees often view charismatic leadership as patern-alism rather than as strong vision and unity of direction. This latter trend may be related to rising educational levels among workers and to the layoffs that have accompanied market-driven events such as acquisitions and market-justified fads such as downsizing and re-engineering.

# PLUS C'EST OLA MÊME CHOSE, PLUS ÇA CHANGE

A few issues derive from organisations' hierarchical structures and they have been pervasive in organisations in very diverse societies and as far back as written evidence extends (Rindova and Starbuck, 1997). Everyone who lives or works in a hierarchical structure has to confront issues of dominance and subordination. Of course, the people on higher levels generally find their roles more satisfying than do those lower down. One of the very oldest documents is a Mesopotamian shard that says, "There are men who support wives; there are men who support children. Kings are men who do not even support themselves". But it may well be that superiors spend more of their time worrying about the issues that arise from hierarchies. In particular, superiors tend to pay much attention to methods of motivation and surveillance: How can they induce subordinates to comply? How can they assure themselves that subordinates are behav-ing as desired?

What makes these issues of hierarchy especially interesting is that (a) they present intractable "problems" and yet (b) organisations keep trying to "solve" these problems. The problems are intractable because they arise from the very fact that organisations are organised; organisations place restraints on the actions of their members. Even highly egalitarian organisations, where group discussions determine goals and methods, sometimes compel members to perform tasks they dislike. To alleviate these problems, organisations have to become less organised, less what they are supposed to be. Thus, organisations are intrinsically paradoxical.

It takes no special insight to predict that future organisations will try to solve the problems of hierarchy. Because people do not happily accept the restraints imposed by organisations, they are endlessly seeking ways to mitigate them. Superiors want to receive respect and admiration as well as obedience; subordinates want higher status and more autonomy. One result has been a continuing parade of management fads and fashions, each promising to "solve" the problems of hierarchy, and each bringing disappointment when people realise that the problems still exist. The "friendly super-vision" of the 1930s was replaced by "democratic management", which gave way to Management-By-Objectives and "considerate leadership", which were replaced by Quality Circles, which was generalised to "team building" during the 1990s.

Organisational culture has consistently played a central role in these fashionable solutions. The solutions have attempted to alter organisational cultures so as to assuage various symptoms. But the cultural changes have been rather superficial, and one effect has been to make organisational cultures themselves rather superficial. The solution attempts may also have elicited cynicism about the power and meaningfulness of organisational culture.

Because organisational cultures tend to be rather inertial and because subcultures tend to develop autonomously, they tend to cause problems for temporary organisations. From 1995 to 1998, Electronic Data Systems built a temporary organisation to organise the information system and ticketing for the World Cup. More than 40 percent of the computer engineers employed in this temporary organisation were volunteers such as retired computer scientists and young trainees. Teambuilding involved social events that brought together the regular employees and the volunteers. Then, after the World Cup concluded in 1998, the temporary organisation was dissolved. One result was that the managers of this temporary organisation needed psychological support for six months because they suffered from feelings of abandonment and chronic depression. They had put all their energy and commitment into an organisation that had disappeared as soon as it was deemed no longer necessary. As organisations rely more and more on "disposable" and "project driven" subcultures, they create similar problems within themselves.

There have also been efforts to employ technology to make hierarchies less visible or less personal. The mass-production conveyor affords one example; just-in-time inventories afford another. Many firms monitor their employees' uses of e-mail and Internet access. The ensuing chapter by Harrison McKnight and Jane Webster, "Collaborative Insight or Privacy Invasion?" discusses the use of telecommunications technology to co-ordinate group work, especially collaboration between colleagues who are separated by large distances. McKnight and Webster point out that employees' reactions to awareness systems depends on the climate of trust within their organisation. Organisations that want to install awareness systems need to strengthen their trust climates first, or else their employees will perceive the new technology as invading their privacy.

# PERSISTENT TRENDS IN ORGANISATIONS' ENVIRONMENTS

Organisations are going to confront many external pressures for change over the next decades. Most of these pressures do not yet exist and are impossible to foresee. However, it does seem possible to identify a few trends in population and technology that are likely to persist.

## Population Trends

Population trends tend to be inertial because birth rates and death rates change slowly. However, regions exhibit large differences in birth and death rates. Currently, birth rates in Africa are nearly three times those in North America and Europe. As a result, the United Nations is forecasting large changes in regional populations by 2050, as shown in Figure 23.1. According to these forecasts, the populations of Europe, Japan,

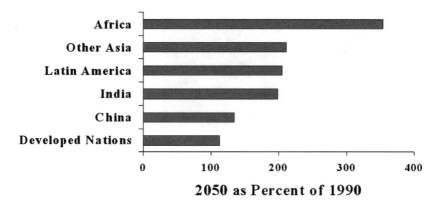

**Figure 23.1**  Population increases, 1990–2050 (source: United Nations).

and North America will increase very little, whereas the populations of South America and Asia will double, and Africa's population will more than triple. (The UN made these forecasts before there was publicity about the AIDS epidemic.)

One implication of these population trends is that almost all of the new jobs will be created outside Europe, Japan, and North America. Indeed, from 1985 to 2000, roughly 600 million new jobs were created world-wide and only five percent of these jobs were created in Europe, Japan, and North America. Three consequences are already apparent. First, increasing numbers of people are seeking to migrate from developing to developed countries. As time passes, these pressures are likely to escalate. Second, many new organisations are being formed in the regions where workers are readily available. Transoceanic travel more than tripled from 1985 to 1998; transoceanic communications multiplied 28 times from 1986 to 1997. Third, organisations that have headquarters in the developed countries are globalising. Not only are multinational firms opening new facilities in the developing regions, these firms are internationalising their executive ranks and they are starting to deny that they have specific national identities.

These population changes are being reinforced by changes in the distributions of economic activities. Throughout the twentieth century, the more developed countries shifted employment from manufacturing and farming and toward services. Many of the service jobs, especially in the latter part of the century, emphasised knowledge or expertise more than physical labour. The developing countries have been shifting employment from farming toward manufacturing, but they still devote much labour to farming.

The predicted population increases and economic shifts appear likely to accentuate the differences between the rich and the poor, the educated and the uneducated. Knowledge-based work requires more education and pays higher wages than does physical labour. Figure 23.2 shows forecasts by the World Bank: These forecasts say that people in upper-income or upper-middle-income nations will fall from 24 to 18 percent, whereas people in low-income nations will rise from 59 to 64 percent. Wars grow more prevalent as more people struggle to share limited resources, as has already

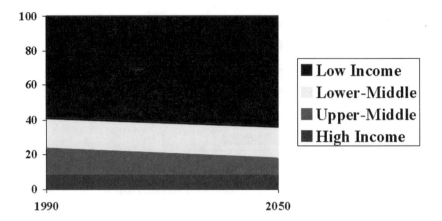

**Figure 23.2**  Population forecasts, 1990–2050 (source: World Bank).

been happening in Indonesia and central Africa. Globalising companies will tend to avoid regions that have the warfare, the regions with very fast population growths. Thus, the most disadvantaged regions may become even poorer.

Globalisation and migration pressure firms to encompass diverse cultures, customs, religions, and languages. In addition, changing expectations about gender and ageing are pressing organisations to accommodate females and older people. In the year 2000, eighty percent of US women between 25 and 54 years of age are employed and the other twenty percent are unemployed only temporarily. In the US, the years between 1970 and 1990 quadrupled the numbers of women, African Americans, and Hispanics in management positions.

Several studies have argued that heterogeneity among members of an organisation correlates with heterogeneity in that organisation's internal cultures (Carroll and Harrison, 1998). However, where this relationship holds, its implications are moot. The ensuing chapter "In diversity is there strength?" by Narayan Pant and Kulwant Singh, considers the implications of increasing intraorganisational diversity. They argue that organisations are going to incorporate more and more diversity and that this diversity will have both positive and negative effects on organisational effectiveness. One result, they predict, will be that organisations with simple structures are going to find survival difficult.

Rising educational levels are making organisations flatter and middle management less valuable. With more education, workers not only need less supervision, they become more resistant to direct supervision and more sceptical about hierarchical authority. In 1990, the average American manager supervised seven people. This number is expected to triple by 2010. Of course, resistance to supervision raises issues of motivation and surveillance. Firms have been dealing with these issues by substituting work teams for supervisors. Teams supervise each other even more closely than do hierarchies, yet educated workers generally find teamwork less objectionable (Katzenbach and Smith, 1992). It may also be that organisations will become more accepting of

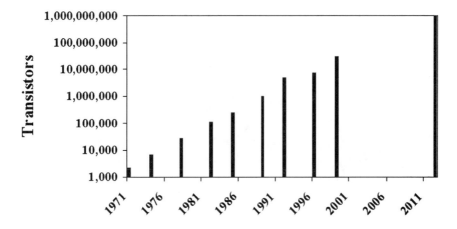

**Figure 23.3** Transistors on one chip, 1971–2012 (Intel's forecasts for 2001 and 2012).

antithetical processes and diversity as components of teamwork: Many professional firms are advocating that their members' heterogeneity fosters organisational cultures that support new ideas and flexibility.

## Technology Trends

As Figure 23.3 shows, the numbers of transistors on a single microprocessor chip has been growing exponentially and forecasts say this doubling will continue for at least the next decade. This growth has meant that computation speed has been doubling every 18 months, the amount of computation done with one unit of energy has been increasing about 30 percent per annum, the cost of circuitry has been decreasing 40 percent per annum for 40 years, and the sizes of memories have been increasing more than 40 percent per annum. Communication capacities have also been growing even more rapidly. The capacities of optical fibers have been doubling yearly, and the capacity for wireless communications has been doubling every nine months.

Although it may appear that computers and modern communications devices are everywhere, their impacts have only begun. Figure 23.4 shows estimates of the percentages of the world population that were using computers, e-mail, or the Internet between 1990 and 1996. Of course, the Internet was a very new concept in 1996 and it is concentrated in North America and Europe. In large firms, much intra-firm communication occurs via Intranets, which only began to be introduced in 1998.

These technological changes are having effects both within and between organisations. First, organisations have access to more data more quickly, which creates opportunities for surveillance from afar. The practice of "competitive intelligence" is becoming easier and more productive. Second, supervisors can monitor the activities of subordinates who are distant, organisations can spread geographically, and organisations can safely become more interdependent without actually merging. The boundaries between organisations are growing weaker, and co-operative relations between orga-

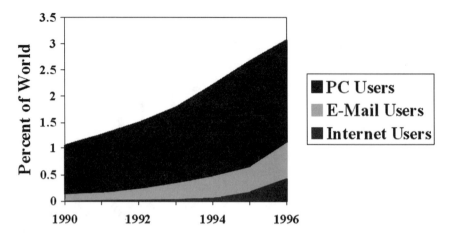

**Figure 23.4**   Worldwide computer users (source: Morgan Stanley Research, 1996).

nisations are growing more complex. Third, communications are replacing physical travel and direct supervision. This tends to substitute workgroups for hierarchies, and it is fostering telework.

The substitution of workgroups for hierarchies is illustrated by an experiment that began in 1999. STMicroelectronics is one of the ten largest makers of semiconductors with 29,000 employees in Europe, North America, and Asia. In 1999, the management of STMicroelectronics decided to facilitate the sharing of knowledge by encouraging employees to create on-line communities. These communities were intended to introduce flexibility and to cut across hierarchical chains. One result was that managers operating within the hierarchy felt that they were being by-passed. Also, STMicroelectronics provided a software tool that assumed that each community might include (a) facilitators, (b) "authors" who could write messages, (c) "readers" who could only read messages, and (d) "guests" who could only view some public documents but could not participate in discussions or read all documents. The people designated as "facilitators" were senior managers, so they gained influence while many lower-level managers lost influence (Lauféron, 1999).

The ensuing chapter "Culture In-The-Making in Telework Settings" by Roger Dunbar and Raghu Garud considers the implications of telecommuting for organisational cultures. Dunbar and Garud argue that telework cultures use values, norms, behaviours and symbols mainly to support work performance rather than stable social relations and shared identities. As a result, employees exhibit more diversity, and they regard norms of interaction as being subject to continuing negotiation.

Employees are also using telecommunications to protest management practices, and they are using the Internet to unite employees who are far apart and to enlist support from external constituents. For instance, Ubi Soft is a software firm with over 1000 employees in 16 countries. As a French company, it must conform to French laws regarding employment practices. During 1998, young employees of Ubi Soft began to express their unhappiness about the "archaic methods" and "paternalism" of the top management in their firm. Among other complaints, they said that their firm had no personnel department and that management had intentionally kept each workgroup small enough to exempt the company from the legal requirement to allow employees to form a union. In mid December 1998, six anonymous employees created a website for a "virtual labor union" named Ubi Free (http://www.multimania.com/ubifree/Index2.htm). They used this website to communicate with the other employees and to publicise their complaints about their employer. The website attracted considerable attention from the French press, and especially from on-line periodicals. Initially, the president of Ubi Soft refused to respond to this protest and he declined to be interviewed by the press. However, by early February, the firm had made substantial changes and Ubi Free declared victory. The creators of Ubi Free remained anonymous throughout the entire process.

The ensuing chapter by Bo Hedberg and Christian Maravelias, "Organisational Culture and Imaginary Organisations" discusses the issues posed by interfirm coalitions and firms that have many free-lance individual collaborators. Imaginary organisations pose issues of dominance, governance, and equitable profit sharing. Hedberg and Maravelias argue that the success of imaginary organisations depends on their leaders' abilities to build trust, to foster respect, and to make exchange mechanisms transparent. These are culture-building tasks, so culture becomes the focal point of leadership skill.

With distant work and tele-surveillance, belonging to an "organisation" is more a contractual agreement than a psychological and emotive involvement. Collateral with the changes in communications and computing have been changes in modal employment relations. Instead of open-ended and non-specific employment relations, more and more workers now have detailed contracts that are limited in time and that impose specific requirements on both workers and employers. Insofar as they define desired outputs and time schedules, contracts make it easier to manage relationships that span long distances and several time zones. Hedberg and Holmqvist (2000) have predicted that the world economy is making a dramatic reorientation towards an "economy of volunteers". In this envisaged economy, transaction cost economics elicit involvement and compliance by technical experts who dislike organisational hierarchies and entrenched authority. Project-oriented teams of these technical experts incorporate diverse participants, some of whom hold temporary contracts with the organisation while others hold long-term membership. As a result, these teams might not react positively to an imposed "organisational culture". The project-oriented teams need to combine cultural elements from their members' different backgrounds.

In spatially dispersed organisations, the rules for co-operation and co-ordination tend to become the essential skeleton of the organisation itself. The extended members do not look upon their organisation as a physical realm, but as a set of conventions that facilitate workflows and efficient action. Institutional trust is not founded on organisational hierarchies, but on the perceived productivity of co-operative relations. This means that organisational cultures become more central to organisational effectiveness, for it is cultures that frame the rules for co-operation and co-ordination and the processes of social construction that evaluate co-operative relations.

Also in spatially dispersed organisations, diversity rises. Members have less of the types of socialisation and homogenisation that depend on face-to-face interaction, and they have greater latitude for individuality, regionalism, and nationality. This decreases the importance of common values, conformity to norms, and obedience to direct supervisors, but co-operation is still possible as long as members have convergent aspirations and visions. This implies that organisational cultures need to emphasise aspirations and visions rather than face-to-face socialisation and homogeneity of values and norms.

The members of spatially distributed organisations tend to seek social appreciation in communities that spread far beyond the borders of their organisations. They seek appreciation within networks of friends and relatives, and they form subcultures that spread across several organisations and that may be more important to them than their focal organisation. These communities encompass more aspects of their lives than the strict duties of their work contracts so work and leisure infiltrate each other. It is difficult to articulate dissents and to organise revolutions against amorphous communities that are not distinct stable social systems, and community members can easily escape imprisonment in a single culture by moving to alternative communities. Thus, these community cultures are less prone than organisational cultures to stimulate opposition to themselves.

# FASTEN YOUR SEAT BELTS AND HOLD ONTO YOUR HATS

We may well be witnessing a significant inversion in the paradigm organisations need to follow in order to survive. The twentieth-century paradigm said that strategy should come first: The desired strategy should determine organisational structure, and culture is largely a consequence of structure (Chandler, 1966). The twenty-first century paradigm may be that organisational culture should come first: The desired culture should determine organisational structure, and strategy is largely a consequence of structure.

Certainly, there are signs that some twentieth-century organisations are finding the pace of change too rapid and the New Economy mysterious. In high-tech, knowledge-based industries, "junior" personnel may have much more expertise than their hierarchical superiors and hence they may challenge their superiors' authority. Young experts may also find their roles more satisfying than do their superiors, who are struggling to control a world they know they do not understand. Young experts may also be able to leave their employers and to start new ventures. People in the lower levels (i.e. in the new small ventures and start-ups) find their roles more satisfying than those of people in the upper level of the organisation.

Anticipating such problems, some firms are maintaining separation between more traditional organisations and high-tech new enterprises. For example, when the French company Vivendi acquired Cendant Software in July 1999, Jean Marie Messier, the CEO of the Vivendi, sent executive scouts to "assess the R&D portfolio in games and entertainment" of Cendant. The first contacts with Cendant's authors and creative staffs were awkward for the institutionally trained French executives. They came back to their Parisian headquarters expressing feelings of disorientation and puzzlement. The R&D done for Cendant's entertainment software was quite unlike that done for Vivendi's past products. Messier decided that Cendant had better remain an autonomous subsidiary.

In this turn-of-the-century period, the old and new are coexisting and creating inconsistencies. The newer organisational forms are using technologies that link people working in different cultures and settings to pursue shared goals. Meanwhile, more traditional firms are adopting temporary forms to deal with new market conditions. The chapters in this section discuss some of these inconsistencies, as structures and strategies come to rely more and more on the coherence and togetherness created by cultures.

# REFERENCES

Brown, W.B.D. (1960) Exploration in Management. New York: Wiley.

Carroll, G.R., and Harrison, J.R. (1998) Organisational demography and culture: insights from a formal model and simulation. Administrative Science Quarterly, 43(3): 637–667.

Chandler, A.D. (1966) Strategy and Structure: Chapters in the History of the Industrial Enterprise. Garden City, New York: Doubleday.

Hedberg, B. and Holmqvist, M. (2000) Learning in virtual organisations. In M. Dierkes, A. Berthoin Antal, J, Child and I. Nonaka (Eds), Handbook of Organisational Learning and Knowledge. Oxford: Oxford University Press.

Jönsson, S.A. and Lundin, R.A. (1977) Myths and wishful thinking as management tools. In P.C. Nystrom and W.H. Starbuck (Eds), Prescriptive Models of Organisations, pp. 157–170. Amsterdam: North-Holland.

Katzenbach, J.R. and Smith, D.K. (1992) The Wisdom of Teams: Creating the High-Performance Organisation. Boston, MA: Harvard Business School Press.

Kunda, G. (1992) Engineering Culture: Control and Commitment in a High-Tech Corporation. Philadelphia: Temple University Press.

Lauféron, M. (1999) OLC@STMicroelectronics. Knowledge Management Network Meeting, University of Aix-Marseille III, May 1999.

Martin, J. (1992) Cultures in Organisations: Three Perspectives. New York: Oxford University Press.

Nonaka, I. and Takeuchi, H. (1995) The Knowledge-Creating Company: How Japanese Companies Create the Dynamics of Innovation. New York: Oxford University Press.

Ouchi, W.G. (1981) Theory Z: How American Business Can Meet the Japanese Challenge. Reading, MA: Addison-Wesley.

Rindova, V. and Starbuck, W.H. (1997) Distrust in dependence: the ancient challenge of superior-subordinate relations, with Violina P. Rindova. In T.A.R. Clark (Ed), Advancement in Organisation Behaviour: Essays in Honour of Derek Pugh, pp. 313–336. Dartmouth.

Williamson, O.E. (1975) Markets and Hierarchies, Analysis and Antitrust Implications: A Study in the Economics of Internal Organisation. New York: Free Press.

# Chapter 24

# Collaborative Insight or Privacy Invasion? Trust Climate as a Lens for Understanding Acceptance of Awareness Systems

**D. Harrison McKnight**
*Information and Management Sciences Department,
Florida State University, Tallahassee, FL, USA*

*and*

**Jane Webster**
*Department of Management Sciences,
University of Waterloo, Waterloo, ON, Canada*

*If, as it is said to be not unlikely in the near future, the principle of sight is applied to the telephone as well as that of sound, earth will be in truth a paradise, and distance will lose its enchantment by being abolished altogether*

(Mee, 1898, p. 345).

## INTRODUCTION

Despite this prediction from more than 100 years ago, distance still acts as a barrier to collaboration in organizations. With the increasing reliance on distributed teams in organizations, and the growing numbers of temporary and virtual organizations (Hardwick and Bolton, 1997; Jarvenpaa et al., 1998; Turoff et al., 1993), organizations continue to explore methods for improving collaborative connections between distant employees. One such solution, awareness systems, represents a type of electronic monitoring that provides information on distant colleagues' availability or actions. However, we propose that a climate of trust in organizations will be crucial to the acceptance of such emerging technologies.

Although awareness has been broadly conceptualized in the human–computer interaction literature, it is generally considered to be "the likelihood of actions by one user being noticed by another" (Rodden, 1996, p. 90), or "information pertaining to who the users are, what groups they belong to, and what access they have to the data" (Hall et al., 1996, p. 142). Awareness monitoring systems, implemented in organizations such as NYNEX and Xerox (Lee et al., 1997a), have been designed and tested for the purpose of improving collaborative connections, rather than for monitoring employee performance. For example, periodic video snapshots of a distant co-worker's work area might help in determining when that co-worker is available or busy (Whittaker, 1995), or viewing the state of tasks on a distant co-worker's computer might aid in merging independently-developed software components (Simone and Bandini, 1997). However, some research has suggested that awareness systems (designed to improve cooperative working relationships) may actually have the unintended consequence of making privacy more salient to employees, resulting in lower system acceptance (Webster, 1998).

The question may be asked, "what is the moderating variable that leads one person to interpret an awareness system as a helpful tool and another person to interpret the same system as an invasive threat to privacy?" Some evidence exists that the pre-existing levels of trust between parties might determine how an awareness system would be interpreted. For instance, research has demonstrated that feedback is more effective in influencing a worker's performance if the worker trusts the feedback giver (Earley, 1986; Lawler, 1971; Lawler and Rhode, 1976). Further, the use of an awareness system is, in a sense, an act of self-disclosure, a willingness to share information about oneself. A significant body of literature has found that trust enables information sharing (e.g. Bromiley and Cummings, 1995; Lewis and Weigert, 1985a; McGregor, 1967; O'Reilly, 1978; Sherif, 1966; Zand, 1972) and self-disclosure (e.g. Altman and Taylor, 1973; Wheeless, 1978). This research underscores how vital a trusting climate is for sharing information about oneself – especially private information. Thus, in this chapter, we propose that a climate of organizational trust, or the general likelihood that people within organizations are willing to depend on others, will represent a key influence on acceptance of awareness systems. In addition, the relationship between trust and power balance and the effects of power balance on system acceptance are discussed.

The remainder of the chapter is organized as follows. The next section describes awareness monitoring in more detail, and distinguishes it from performance monitoring. The following section focuses on trust climate as a key explanatory factor for awareness system acceptance. The chapter concludes by drawing implications for research and practice.

# AWARENESS MONITORING SYSTEMS

Awareness monitoring represents an emerging application that organizations are beginning to explore, and on which the human–computer interaction (HCI) academic community has focused considerable design efforts (e.g. Lee et al., 1997a,b; Proceedings of CSCW (Computer Supported Cooperative Work), 1996 and 1998). For instance, such awareness systems might monitor: an employee's keyboard, mouse, and chair for activities (Honda et al., 1997), movements in a work area through motion detectors (Kuzuoka and Greenberg, 1999), or muffled speech in a co-worker's area (Hudson and Smith, 1996). HCI researchers view awareness as one of the most important design features for collaborative applications (Johnson and Greenberg, 1999; Lee et al., 1997b; Mariani, 1997; Palfreyman and Rodden, 1996; Simone and Bandini, 1997; Tollmar et al., 1996). For instance, these researchers have argued that awareness is necessary for collaborative work because there is an "expansive body of literature stressing the importance of awareness and availability of action" (Palfreyman and Rodden, 1996, p. 131).

Awareness systems have been developed in order to improve connections between employees in distant locations and in virtual organizations. Their developers have argued that employees who are physically separated do not have the same opportunities as co-located colleagues for informal interactions (Johnson and Greenberg, 1999). These developers propose that awareness systems can help improve communication by simulating informal face-to-face interactions through providing information on distant colleagues' availability or actions. For instance, Kraut and Fish (1995, p. 705) described the use of video in maintaining awareness between distant sites:

> People also use video for benign surveillance – to maintain awareness of what their colleagues are doing even when they are not immediately communicating with them. In the video telephony field experiments, users maintained long-lived calls to 'public' places – lobbies or lunch rooms, for example – just to know what was going on at remote sites or set up specialized applications to receive this background information as freeze-frame images. Researchers report that this use allowed spatially separated work groups to 'feel like we're part of the same group'.

Awareness systems generally are categorized into one of two types, peripheral or activity awareness systems. Peripheral (also called passive, pre-attentive, presence, or background) awareness systems provide employees with the ability to initiate opportunistic connections (Whittaker, 1995), or as Kraut and Fish (1995) termed it above, "benign surveillance". They often utilize audio or video connections between sites (Zhao and Stasko, 1998). For instance, Whittaker (1995) outlined three types of desktop videoconferencing awareness features to help initiate connections between distant employees: (i) a glance, which allows an employee to briefly look into a co-worker's area; (ii) an open link, which maintains a persistent channel between two physical locations; and (iii) periodic snapshots (freeze-frame images) of co-workers' areas. This peripheral awareness is said to allow employees to determine when co-workers are available or busy, save time in tracking down and traveling to their co-workers' offices, and foster closer working relationships (Adler and Henderson, 1994).

Activity (sometimes called detailed task, shared workspace, shared document, or synchronous groupware) awareness systems provide information on co-workers' computer desktop activities. For instance, activity-based awareness systems might allow an employee to monitor the state of computer-based tasks in which a co-worker is or has been engaged (Mariani, 1997), enable employees to share an information repository (Simone and Bandini, 1997), or support employees in jointly writing a document through a shared text editor (Rodden, 1996).

An awareness system might be implemented as one feature of a larger application (such as freeze-frame images as part of a larger desktop videoconferencing system; Webster, 1998), or as a stand-alone application (such as an open link between public spaces; Kraut and Fish, 1995). Figure 24.1 provides an example of a stand-alone peripheral awareness system called Portholes; every 5 min, this system provides both video snapshots and measures of movements in co-workers' offices.

Since awareness systems are emerging technologies, most research has focused on technical issues around their design and development (e.g. Johnson and Greenberg, 1999). Although others have begun to develop models of collaborative awareness (e.g. Rodden, 1996), these are technical models concerning the design of awareness systems, rather than behavioral models of employee reactions. Further, most implementations of

**Figure 24.1**   A peripheral awareness system.

monitoring systems, as well as modeling of employee reactions to these systems, have focused on performance-based monitoring.

Electronic performance monitoring has diffused widely in organizations and is continuing to grow. The number of US employees monitored is difficult to pin down, but is estimated to be over 26 million (Alder, 1998). Electronic performance monitoring is utilized in a wide range of industries, from utilities to airline reservations (George, 1996). For instance, performance monitoring applications might take the form of call centers using telephone monitoring to ensure the quality of customer service (Laabs, 1992), insurance companies employing computer-based monitoring to count completed transactions (Grant and Higgins, 1991), supervisors assessing employees' work through real-time and archival videos (Griffith, 1993), or public utilities tracking field vehicles through global positioning satellites (Borthick, 1997).

The same underlying technologies are used for both performance and awareness monitoring systems – for example, observations of employee locations through electronic sensor badges or "active badges" may be used by management to monitor employee performance or by employees to receive awareness information on group members (e.g. Harper, 1995). It is the intent of the monitoring system that distinguishes between them. That is, during performance monitoring, supervisors monitor subordinates for the purpose of evaluating their performance, whereas during awareness monitoring, peers monitor peers for the purpose of improving collaboration. Further, employees generally do not choose to be monitored for performance (involuntary usage), while employees do choose whether to be monitored for awareness (voluntary usage).

Although awareness systems are just beginning to emerge in organizations today, there is the potential for significant diffusion originating from the HCI community. Thus, it is important to study those factors affecting awareness system acceptance.

# ACCEPTANCE OF AWARENESS MONITORING SYSTEMS

What affects employee acceptance of awareness monitoring systems? Although a variety of factors, such as the design of systems and individual characteristics, could affect acceptance of awareness systems (see Webster, 1998), this chapter focuses on one key influence, organizational trust climate. Researchers have argued for some time that organizational context issues such as climate are important to the use and adoption of technology (e.g. Boynton et al., 1992; Davis et al., 1989; Hart and Saunders, 1997), and in particular have called for further examination of the relationship between organizational climate and acceptance of monitoring systems (e.g. Ambrose and Alder, in press). By organizational climate, we mean shared employee perceptions of practices and procedures of the organization, including what behaviors are expected and rewarded (Ruppel and Harrington, 1998). This broad construct has been dimensionalized to include perceptions of: autonomy, cohesiveness, fairness, pressure, innovation, recognition, trust, and support (Koys and DeCotiis, 1991).

## The Organizational Trust Climate

We define "trust climate" as the general likelihood that people within organizations are willing to depend on others. Although trust climate is only one dimension of organizational climate, Strutton et al. (1994) found that five out of their six psychological climate measures were significantly correlated with trust climate. Hence, trust may be a central aspect of the organizational climate, just as trust is often seen as central to an interpersonal relationship (e.g. Golembiewski and McConkie, 1975). Scholars have recently recommended that trust should not be treated as a unitary construct (e.g. Rousseau et al., 1998). Hence, this chapter primarily treats trust as a multi-dimensional set of concepts, each of which may form an indicator of the climate of trust in an organization. By using this approach, we can "zoom in" on trust climate aspects at various levels of analysis.

Researchers have examined trust at three distinct levels of analysis: individual, interpersonal/intergroup, and institutional/cultural. At the individual level of analysis, propensity or disposition to trust (e.g. Mayer et al., 1995) is the most common construct. Disposition to trust means the extent to which one is willing to depend on others across a broad spectrum of situations and persons. At the interpersonal or intergroup level, the most common trust constructs are trusting beliefs (i.e. that the other party is competent, honest, or benevolent) and trusting intention (i.e. that one intends to depend, or is willing to depend, on the other party). At the institutional/cultural level of analysis, two constructs have been defined (McKnight et al., 1998): situational normality (the belief that success is likely because things are proper or favorably ordered; Baier, 1986; Garfinkel, 1963; Lewis and Weigert, 1985a), and structural assurance (the belief that success is likely because structural conditions like guarantees, regulations, and procedures are in place; Shapiro, 1987a; Williamson, 1993). Together, situational normality and structural assurance constitute what is called system trust (Luhmann, 1991) or institution-based trust (Rousseau et al., 1998). While, for simplicity, we have defined interpersonal and structural concepts as cognitive beliefs, it should be noted that each of these concepts will contain an affective component (see Cummings and Bromiley, 1996 for evidence).

Each of these three types of trust forms a separate indicator of an aspect of the overall organizational trust climate (Table 24.1). A given organization may have a preponderance of those with high or low disposition to trust, or somewhere in between. An organization with mostly high disposition to trust individuals would be considered to have a positive *disposition to trust climate*. The sum of the trusting beliefs and intentions among parties (groups and individuals) in the organization indicates the likelihood that they will believe that the other party possesses trustworthy attributes. An organization with mostly high trusting beliefs and intentions among individuals and groups would be considered to have a positive *interpersonal/intergroup trust climate*. The sum of situational normality and structural assurance beliefs (institution-based trust) indicates the extent to which known situations and structures, such as employee-friendly policies and procedures, assure that one will succeed in the setting. Institution-based trust climate has more to do with how one feels about the organizational structures than with personal relationships. An organization with mostly high

**Table 24.1** A multi-dimensional typology of trust climate types

| Trust climate types | Level of analysis | Trust constructs | Object of trust | Domain of explanatory power |
|---|---|---|---|---|
| Disposition to trust climate | Individual | Disposition to trust: faith in people; trusting stance | People generally | Unfamiliar people in new situations |
| Interpersonal/ intergroup trust climate | Interpersonal/ intergroup | Interpersonal/ intergroup trust: trusting beliefs; trusting intention | Specific persons or groups | Known specific people in regular, repeated situations in an organization |
| Institution-based trust climate | Institutional/ cultural | Institution-based trust: situational normality; structural assurance | Situation and structures of the organization | Known situations and structures within an organization |
| Overall trust climate | Institutional/ cultural | Trust climate | Organization | Organization |

institution-based beliefs would be considered to have a positive *institution-based trust climate*. These constructs each contribute a distinguishable aspect of the climate of trust of an organization. *Disposition to trust climate, interpersonal/intergroup trust climate,* and *institution-based trust climate* constitute the overall trust climate of an organization. *Overall trust climate,* defined earlier, has itself been theorized and measured as a construct by others (e.g. Koys and DeCotiis, 1991). Therefore, we also list *overall trust climate* as a separate type of trust in Table 24.1.

All three sets of detail-level trust climate constructs are important in order to specify what leads to awareness system acceptance. The last column of Table 24.1 indicates that each set of constructs is best at predicting or explaining a different domain. The *disposition to trust climate* constructs indicate the likelihood that trust will be extended in novel situations, such as when a new manager is hired or a new vendor is selected (Johnson-George and Swap, 1982). Disposition to trust is salient here because the parties have little or no interpersonal or situational information on which to make a trust judgment, so they must rely on their general disposition to trust (Mayer et al., 1995). The *interpersonal/intergroup trust climate* constructs indicate the extent to which trust will be extended among those interacting internally in regular, repeated business roles, inside and outside the organization. That is, interpersonal/intergroup trust is person-specific and ongoing in nature. By ongoing, we mean subject to wide changes. The *institution-based trust climate* constructs indicate the extent to which one will place trust in the situations and structures of the organization (not the people).

Based on McKnight et al. (1998), these dimensions of trust are proposed to interact with each other as shown in Figure 24.2:

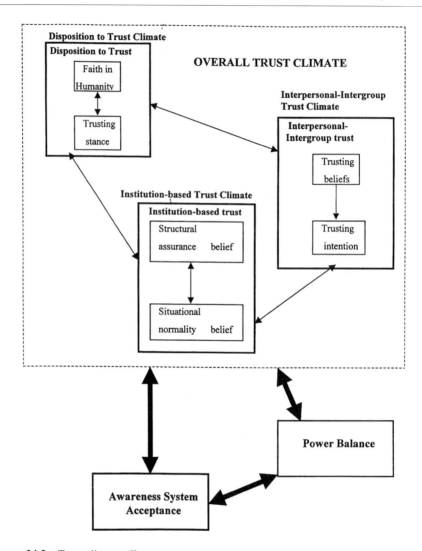

**Figure 24.2**   Trust climate effects on awareness system acceptance.

(a) disposition to trust relates to interpersonal/group in novel situations (e.g. Kee and Knox, 1970; Mayer et al., 1995; Rotter, 1980);

(b) institution-based trust relates to interpersonal/group trust by providing ongoing structural/situational assurances (Dasgupta, 1988; Lewis and Weigert, 1985b); and

(c) disposition to trust relates to institution-based trust by improving the odds that one will perceive the situation or structures to be favorable (McKnight et al., 1998).

# Effects of Trust Climate Types on Awareness System Acceptance

## *Disposition to Trust Climate*

The potential importance to awareness system adoption of disposition to trust is illustrated in the Lee et al. (1997a) study of "electronic portholes", or video snapshots of co-workers' areas. Assuring potential users of the benign purposes of the portholes was "effective with some of our users but others remain suspicious" (p. 389). High individual levels of suspicion usually indicate low disposition to trust. Similarly, Webster (1998) studied a desktop videoconferencing system that could provide periodic snapshots of co-workers' work areas. Some employees perceived that their work or personal activities could be monitored (by supervisors or others). In these two examples, it appears that individual disposition to trust differences affected how users viewed the system.

Researchers have found that disposition to trust has the most potential impact during the initial phase of some relationship or when considering someone or something one does not know well (Goldsteen et al., 1989; Rotter, 1971, 1980). Therefore, we propose that the disposition to trust climate will have its most pronounced influence on awareness system acceptance during the adoption phase, as the organization is investigating or being informed of the system, or during initial use, before people gain experience with the system. A high disposition to trust climate would be associated with greater adoption of awareness systems by encouraging low suspicion towards it. Further, a disposition to trust climate would only be salient if the other people involved in using the system are unfamiliar and the awareness situation is new. This is because interpersonal trust would mediate the effects of disposition to trust if the people are already known, and institution-based trust would mediate the effects of disposition to trust if the situation is already known (McKnight et al., 1998). Therefore, a disposition to trust climate will be salient to adoption or use of awareness systems in relatively few instances, such as when two different organizations that know little about each other propose to use the system together.

Disposition to trust may affect adoption in two ways (McKnight et al., 1998). First, one kind of disposition to trust (*trusting stance*) means that one forms a strategy to act as though other people (or technologies) are worthy and reliable – regardless of whether they are or not (Atwater, 1988; Luhmann, 1991). Trusting stance would encourage one to trust a new technology until it seems unwise to do so. Another kind of disposition to trust (*faith in humanity*) means that one believes others (known or unknown to one) to be typically reliable and benevolent (e.g. Rosenberg, 1957). Therefore, faith in humanity would affect awareness system adoption only to the extent that the people believe that those (currently unknown) people who might use the proposed awareness system will have their best interests at heart. A climate high in faith in humanity would encourage one to choose to adopt or use a new awareness system because it would suggest that the intentions of those using the system will be honest and benign.

## Interpersonal/Intergroup Trust Climate

Once one gets to know the people involved with the awareness system, the *interpersonal/intergroup trust climate* will be important to system acceptance (Ruppel and Harrington, 1998). Because this construct deals with specific people, it is important to determine who the group adopting the awareness system perceives to be using and controlling the system. If users perceive that management is using or controlling the awareness system, use will depend on the extent to which employees trust management. Ruppel and Harrington (1998) argued that management sets the tone for the overall trust climate. Koys and DeCotiis (1991) found that their support and trust constructs loaded together, providing evidence that trust and management support are closely linked antecedents of innovation. Harper (1995) found that some of those who did not want to wear activity badges distrusted management.

If the system is perceived to be used by people only within a department or other subgroup, then trust in those people will be essential. For example, the same group in the Harper (1995) study that refused to wear activity badges had a hard-wired video system that enabled internal group members to look surreptitiously into other group members' offices. When Harper (1995, p. 308) suggested to one employee that these systems were similar to activity badges, the respondent said, "No, of course they are not the same. Down here we all know each other so its not a problem invading each other's privacy over [the video system]. Of course its not the same. We trust each other." Membership in a particular group helps build what Shapiro et al. (1992) called "identification-based trust," as can proximity and shared values. Similarly, Culnan and Armstrong (1999, p. 106) proposed that people are less likely to perceive a procedure to be invasive of privacy when the procedure takes place "in the context of an existing relationship."

If people in another organization use the system, they must be trusted, making in-group, out-group issues important (McKnight et al., 1998). In-group members are generally trusted (Brewer and Silver, 1978), while those outside the group are not – particularly if they are potentially competitors (Sherif, 1966). Harper (1995) found very low levels of trust between two competing groups of corporate laboratory researchers. When one group advocated activity badges to other areas of the company, the competing group refused to wear the badges and vigilantly enforced non-participation among its members, claiming that the other group did not share their values.

Developing trust between out-groups is difficult. Social, ethnic and cultural similarity improve the chances for high trusting beliefs between out-groups (McAllister, 1995). But developing intergroup trust normally requires interaction time (Ring and Van de Ven, 1994), in which mutual feelings of security are tested and confirmed.

We speculate that trusting belief-benevolence and belief-honesty will influence awareness system acceptance more than will other types of trusting beliefs. Specifically, trusting belief-benevolence would assure one that others would not use awareness information against them. Trusting belief-honesty would assure one that the other person would not violate an implicit understanding to use the information properly. Trusting belief-competence would not be as influential, because privacy is the key awareness system issue.

If people within the organization have trusting beliefs in each other, they will be more creative, which leads to greater innovation (Ruppel and Harrington, 1998), and more organizational likelihood of adopting innovations. Trusting belief-honesty and trusting belief-benevolence of peers would be especially helpful because they minimize the risk that people will be hurt by others in the group (Ruppel and Harrington, 1998).

Based on the above discussion, we propose that the more positive the interpersonal/intergroup trust climate, the higher the likelihood that an awareness system will be adopted and used within the organizational setting.

## Institution-Based Trust Climate

The *institution-based trust climate* will also affect awareness system adoption. For instance, Harper (1995, p. 301) noted that an employee said s/he willingly used an awareness system "because I trust the environment". The institution-based trust climate affects acceptance through structural assurance and situational normality. *Structural assurance* affects adoption by making the awareness system participant feel secure that the environment is (a) fair, (b) ethical, and (c) protective or forgiving. The fairness dimension of structural assurance is similar to the procedural justice construct (Lind and Tyler, 1988; Ambrose and Alder, in press), which has a positive influence on adoption (Hosmer, 1994). Awareness systems provide information to people about each other. If the environment is perceived to be fair, then one will not believe that such information would be used against them. Culnan and Armstrong (1999) found that communication of procedural fairness practices increased willingness to disclose private information.

The ethical dimension of structural assurance is important to awareness systems because the awareness system can be used for unscrupulous purposes. Therefore, one who believes the climate to be unethical would be insecure using the system. The Hosmer (1994) model says that ethical treatment of employees leads to innovation because it creates trust. Similarly, the Cullen et al. (1993) model delineates three classes of ethical criteria: benevolence (concern for the well-being of others), egoism (self-interested concern), and principled (applying the law or rules). The first two appear to be opposite poles of the same concept – belief in the benevolence of the organization's structures.

The principled ethical criterion is similar to the Shapiro (1987b) description of rules, regulations, and legal recourse that provide people with structural safeguards for interaction with awareness systems. These structures assure that the environment is protective. To the extent that adequate privacy laws are in place and properly enforced, both at the societal and organizational level, people can feel relatively secure with an awareness system. These safeguards at the structural level can act as functional substitutes for interpersonal trust (Silver, 1985; Zucker, 1986). Hence, structural assurance is most salient when the people involved are not well known. Such structures may also act as an auxiliary support to adoption, acting as "side bets" (Shapiro, 1987b, p. 204) that go beyond the support afforded by interpersonal trusting beliefs. They may also interact with trusting beliefs: because structural assurance measures enforce good behavior or deter bad behavior, they make it easier to have trusting beliefs about other people in the situation (Luhmann, 1988). In this vein, Harrington and Ruppel (1997) found that an ethical work climate led to a climate of trust, which, in turn, was related to commitment to innovation. Overall, we predict that a positive structural assurance climate, as part of the institution-based trust climate, will be positively related to adoption and use of awareness systems.

*Situational normality* will also support use of an awareness system. Situational normality operates through the assumption that things are going well. For example, in the 1986 NASA Challenger disaster, Starbuck and Milliken (1988) found that because things were going well, managers ignored or explained away evidence that rocket booster O-rings would erode during a low temperature take-off. Even negative evidence may be ignored when things are perceived to be succeeding. If an awareness system is put in place with everyone's backing, and everyone understands how it will be used and for what purpose, the system becomes part of the normal, everyday situation. The awareness system is therefore an expected part of the social system, such that everything is perceived to be proper or normal (Lewis and Weigert, 1985b). This would especially be true when users fully understand and believe in the valid purposes for which the system is being installed. For instance, Culnan and Armstrong (1999) argued that people are less likely to think information collection procedures are invasive when the particular information being gathered is relevant to the business being transacted (e.g. a credit card transaction). That is, when information seems natural to provide in the situation, system users are more likely to cooperate. In such cases, an aura of normality engenders support for system use.

On the other hand, when an awareness system first becomes a possibility, it poses an out-of-the-ordinary wrinkle. Hence, situational normality would, if not properly managed, decrease upon the introduction of an awareness system. While any new system that changes a person's job can be upsetting (Zuboff, 1988), an awareness system can be disconcerting by reducing or eliminating personal privacy – part of the normal situation on which a person relies. Garfinkel (1963) proposed that unless a person can rely on such basic situational factors as the sun rising and the consistent operation of gravity, life would be so scary that we would hardly dare get out of bed. Privacy when one wants it is one of those "givens" upon which we normally can count. Our daily efforts to put on a good appearance when around other people is part of this. We may have little bad habits (e.g. nail biting) about which we do not want others to know. With privacy, we can bite our nails without revealing our habit.

When such barriers are removed by use of an awareness system, our self-preservation mechanisms put us on constant emotional alert for what others may think. As one becomes used to the lack of privacy over time, an awareness system can become part of the normal situation again. However, some people (especially those with low disposition to trust) will probably continue on alert until convinced that others' awareness of their habits will bring no harmful repercussions.

## Power Balance Effects on Awareness System Acceptance

Power and control issues are also important to awareness system adoption (Benford et al., 1998). For one thing, a control climate may lead to unethical behavior, inducing negative structural assurance. Cohen (1993) pointed out that organizations sometimes put so much pressure on employees to meet corporate goals that they resort to unethical acts. This can also happen when goal-driven leaders exemplify that the ends justify whatever means are used or when "performance goals are excessively demanding" (Cohen, 1993, p. 347). An unethical environment provides little assurance, making employees less likely to use an awareness system.

As Figure 24.2 indicates, power balance and the trust climate relate to each other reciprocally, and each affects awareness system acceptance. Implicit in the following explanation is the assumption that people must interpret what the awareness system represents to them.

A power imbalance may affect whether the awareness system is perceived as a benign communication enabler or a not-so-benign behavior monitoring tool. Although this distinction could apply to lateral relations, it is most pronounced in the employee–management relationship. Strickland (1958) found that supervisors who watched their employees more frequently felt that the employees' good behavior was caused by the supervisor's monitoring. This decreased the supervisor's trust in the employee, leading to a felt need for additional monitoring. Thus begins a self-perpetuating cycle, or downward control–distrust spiral (Golembiewski and McConkie, 1975), as low trust leads to more monitoring (Bromiley and Cummings, 1995; Fox, 1974) and more monitoring leads to lower trust (Grant et al., 1988; Lingle et al., 1977; Mayer et al., 1995). Similar effects may occur among peers.

From the employee perspective, people are motivated to see the world as a predictable and controllable place, and those most threatened are most motivated to restore a sense of predictability (Mark and Mellor, 1991). The powerless must either trust in the powerful to use their power benignly, or live in constant fear (Lewis and Weigert, 1985b). Trust is decreased to the extent that power becomes imbalanced (Fox, 1974; Golembiewski and McConkie, 1975; Pfeffer, 1993; Smith, 1989; Solomon, 1960) because those low in power tend to question the benevolence of the more powerful.

Power imbalance is an issue to low power individuals, first, because it increases perceived risk, which causes them to pay more attention to the other person and to do more attributional analysis regarding them (Berscheid and Graziano, 1979; Kramer, 1996). More attention may reveal more flaws in the other person, and more attribution may transform those flaws into perceived unacceptable-for-trusting traits. Also, low power people are more uncertain than high power people about their standing, the adequacy of their rewards, and how fairly rewards are distributed (Kramer, 1996).

Power imbalance can change what people perceive to be the intentions of those advocating an awareness system. For example, Harper (1995) found that the two competing groups of employees possessed radically different views of activity badges. Harper argued that the social setting provided widely different systems of meaning behind the badges. One group saw the badges as a benign and helpful tool. The other group suspiciously saw the badges as a tool that would give management power to invade employee privacy. From this example: (a) perceptions of the intent behind the badges were what mattered; and (b) the power of management made one group worry enough to attribute negative intentions to management with respect to the activity badges.

Research has shown that a low power position can easily become one of fear and related insecurity or paranoia (Kramer, 1996), which perceived behavior monitoring would only tend to magnify. Low power positions can produce the kind of paranoia that engenders the "sinister attribution error", in which "the failure of a senior colleague to return a casual hello as they pass one another in the hall may prompt intense rumination about the cause or 'meaning' of the event ('Did I say something...that offended the person?')" (Kramer, 1996, p. 225). This is because one with low power depends so heavily on those with power (Kramer, 1996). Kramer (1996, p. 217) cited evidence that "distrust and suspicion often travel widely over the hierarchical landscape". He found significantly lower levels of trusting beliefs among students than among faculty. People who believe private information will be used to draw invalid inferences about their attributes would be more concerned about invasion of privacy (Culnan and Armstrong, 1999).

Awareness systems provide the person who uses them to view others with a modicum of power because the viewer can, at will, monitor or watch the other person, or at least track their whereabouts or activities. The person of whom others are aware loses the power to be invisible. The ability of a manager, for example, to monitor or track an employee gives the manager additional power and subjects the employee to a set of contingencies not previously open. It opens the possibility that the manager many abuse that power. This is even true, to a lesser extent, with co-workers. Even off-hand joking (such as suggesting that catching another doing something socially unacceptable could be used to "blackmail" them) can be unnerving. Such negative possibilities between groups engendered strong emotional responses in the Harper (1995) study of activity badges. To those in one group, activity badges shifted power to management, raising the emotion-laden perception that badges would be used by management to track employees: "They [the badges] make me furious" (Harper, 1995, p. 302). This disapproval led to sanctions and fear: "I would not wear one round here...I would get shouted at" (Harper, 1995, p. 305).

From the viewpoint of one who has control, Culnan and Armstrong (1999) theorized that those who perceive they can control the future use of information given to others are less likely to feel that their privacy has been invaded. They found that those who were told that the company which sought their private information observed fair information practices were willing to disclose in spite of a high level of concern for privacy. Applying this finding to awareness systems, those who feel they can control how their privacy information is used will be more willing to use the system in their office. High trusting belief-benevolence in those using or controlling the system is a key in overcoming the effects of power imbalance. Tyler and Degoey (1996) found that people reacted favorably to authority figures if they believed the authority figure had benevolent intentions. High trusting belief-benevolence would provide the low power person assurance that those with power would treat them properly (Kramer, 1996). Chalykoff and Kochan (1989) found that belief in the supervisor's consideration was strongly related to satisfaction with computer-aided monitoring. A combination of high levels of trusting beliefs and institution-based trust would also help overcome the fragility of trust-related behavior by providing a more substantial basis for trusting behavior (McKnight et al., 1998). When trusting beliefs are high, evidence that disconfirms those beliefs is often ignored (Good, 1988) or even reinterpreted and absorbed

(Holmes, 1991; Luhmann, 1991). This tendency will be strengthened when disposition to trust and institution-based trust are also high (McKnight et al., 1998). Hence, the multiplex of trust climate variables can help to ensure against imbalanced-power-driven negative attributions regarding an awareness system. The result will be attributions that the awareness system is a helpful technology, even when power is imbalanced.

## Coming Full Circle: Effects of Awareness System Acceptance on Trust Climate

While the discussion has so far focused on how the trust climate may affect awareness system acceptance, this section focuses on how acceptance may affect the trust climate. We assume in this discussion that if the awareness system is accepted it will be used by organization members. If it is used, the type of use could either help or hurt the trust climate, depending on whether use is positive or negative. By positive, we mean benign use; by negative, we mean malevolent or power-based use.

If the awareness system is used for spying on people, then, assuming such use is detected or suspected, the control–distrust spiral will begin, decreasing interpersonal and institution-based trust levels. How quickly this occurs will depend on how solid the trust climate currently is, how long before the negative use is detected, and how egregious the violation of trust is. If use is controlling but not malevolent, such as for monitoring behavior for input to reward systems, system use has an indeterminate effect on the trust climate. If use is perceived as controlling, the control–distrust spiral may be initiated. If use is not perceived as being control-oriented, the trust climate will not be harmed.

If the awareness system use is positive, use could reinforce or even improve the existing trust climate for several reasons. First, use of an awareness system might signal that things are okay in the trust environment. That is, people will probably perceive that if the climate were not trusting, then the system would not have been accepted. Hence, system use will reinforce perceptions that the climate is highly trusting.

Second, awareness systems may give teams a way to build trust that they may not have otherwise. Control theory research posits that people often use behavior monitoring of the other party to reduce perceived risk of transacting business with them (Ouchi, 1979). But this is difficult when team members are not located together. When used for benign behavior monitoring, awareness systems can provide a person with assurance that the other team member is pursuing the team project in a diligent way because they allow one to see where the team member is or what they are working on. Having a window on other team members helps one feel secure that they are acting properly, which would increase interpersonal trust levels.

Third, awareness systems may build trust indirectly by improving communication among parties. Awareness systems can facilitate communication between parties by allowing one to easily see when the other is available for a visit or phone call. The result of increased communication should be a more trusting climate, since communication builds trust (Golembiewski and McConkie, 1975). For example, a team leader may find it more convenient to give co-workers helpful or complimentary feedback if they can easily see, via the awareness system, whether the co-worker is available.

Finally, awareness system use may encourage an atmosphere of openness that is conducive to a favorable trust climate. Trust thrives in an atmosphere of openness and self-disclosure (Golembiewski and McConkie, 1975). Further, as people become more accustomed to the lack of full privacy over time, their suspicions and inhibitions should decrease, and they should therefore become more trusting of others over time. Finally, if people do not have the ability to hide their behavior, they are more likely to act in trustworthy ways. Thus, the openness aspect of awareness system use should enhance the trust climate.

## IMPLICATIONS FOR RESEARCH AND PRACTICE

This chapter has proposed that the organizational trust climate will be crucial to understanding acceptance of emerging collaborative technologies, such as awareness systems. Awareness monitoring systems have been the subject of focused attention from the human–computer interaction community; however, most research has centered on technical issues around their design and development. Although others have begun to develop models of collaborative awareness (e.g. Rodden, 1996), these models are technical ones concerning the design of awareness systems, rather than behavioral models of employee reactions. In this chapter, we have made a start towards the development of such a behavioral model by proposing that awareness system acceptance will be affected by the multiplex of trust climate variables – disposition to trust, interpersonal/intergroup trust, and institution-based trust – as they interact with issues of power balance.

This chapter extends research on climates of organizations and electronic monitoring. For instance, the ethical aspects of organizational climate have received little empirical attention (Banerjee et al., 1998) and have been largely ignored in the monitoring literature (Ambrose and Alder, in press). Further, this chapter augments previous research on computer-based monitoring: as mentioned earlier, the majority of research on computer monitoring has been applied to performance appraisal (e.g. Ambrose and Alder, in press; George, 1996; Masterson and Taylor, 1996), and researchers have called for extensions to situations in which monitoring occurs for other than performance reasons and to situations in which the supervisor is not the monitor (Masterson and Taylor, 1996).

In the development of our predictions concerning trust climate variables, we did not distinguish between different types of awareness systems. But, as described earlier, not all awareness systems are the same. Peripheral awareness systems are more likely to be video-based, for instance incorporating snapshots of the employee, while activity awareness systems are more likely to be focused on the employee's desktop. Employees may view video-based awareness systems as more personally-focused, and thus more invasive (Webster, 1998). We also did not distinguish between different types of tasks for which awareness systems are used. However, for some tasks, such as space shuttle control, nuclear power plants, and air traffic management, real-time collaboration is key – for example, these systems may use background audio, called voice loops, to monitor communications throughout the operation (Watts et al., 1996). In such situations, awareness systems may be critical to maintaining collaboration. Therefore, our predictions concerning the relationships between trust variables and acceptance of awareness systems also may depend on both the designs of awareness systems and the tasks for which they are used.

Researchers should extend our model presented in Figure 24.2 to include other influences on awareness system acceptance, such as the design of these systems and application tasks. Additionally, the few studies that have addressed employee reactions to awareness systems point to some of the same employee concerns around privacy that have been found for performance monitoring systems (Lee et al., 1997a; Webster, 1998; Zhao and Stasko, 1998). That is, awareness features (designed into systems to improve cooperative working relationships) may actually have the unintended consequence of making privacy more salient to employees, resulting in lower system acceptance. Thus, past research on performance monitoring also will help to inform such a model (e.g. see Ambrose and Alder, in press).

As organizations move towards the use of more distributed teams and relationships, collaborative support systems, such as awareness systems, will continue to diffuse within organizations. However, a question remains: are awareness systems necessary for distributed, collaborative work, or can more traditional communication technologies, such as e-mail and telephone, provide the connections needed by distant employees – without raising the specter of privacy and trust? This remains an important area for future research.

Given that trust represents a central role in the acceptance of awareness systems, we now turn to some of the mechanisms that organizations can use to develop a positive trust climate.

## Mechanisms for Building a Positive Trust Climate

The overall trust climate is built through several mechanisms. Norms for organizational trusting develop over time (Currall and Judge, 1995). Rituals, long-term group membership, and goal congruence develop the common understanding and shared assumptions that build a strongly-trusting culture (Baier, 1986; Ouchi, 1979). Trust development can also involve role expectations between parties (Gabarro, 1978). Positive information sharing and conflict management also engender trust (Barber, 1983). Setting up and following employee expectations would maintain or improve the trust climate, improving the chances that awareness systems will be successfully adopted. Internal competition structures tend to breed low trust among high-discretion employees as they compete for approval or preference by their superiors (Cohen, 1993; Fox, 1974). In a network view of organizations, indirect connections between people, such as through gossip, strengthen the intensity of group trust (Burt and Knez, 1996). Rumors about the intentions behind the awareness system will therefore affect the overall trust climate.

Trusting beliefs tend to build to high and robust levels slowly, but are fragile enough at first to turn toward distrust relatively quickly (e.g. Worchel, 1979). The key to maintaining trust between people is positive interaction that shows no betrayal of that trust. Similarly, as an awareness system is used over time, consistently positive experiences with the system will tend to reinforce the trusting choice to continue to use the system. Once people are comfortable using the system, they become less attentive to abuses and less critical of various uses of it. In this way, trusting the awareness system enough to use it becomes a self-confirming cycle unless a major, visible abuse occurs. On the other hand, even one or two abuses of the information provided by an awareness system would lead to disuse of it by the specific individuals affected and by those in the affected individuals' sphere of influence.

Because the system may give some parties added power over others, specific structural methods of reducing the perceived risk of this power imbalance should be used, such as detailed procedures and regulations regarding the use of the system within the organizational context. This would be especially helpful in a low trust climate, in which people will want highly legalistic assurances before proceeding (Sitkin and Roth, 1993).

## Final Thoughts

Trust in institutions at the societal level will also influence the organizational trust climate. Over the past four decades, trust in almost every institution (and their leaders) has significantly decreased to historically low levels, both in the US (e.g. Mitchell, 1996) and in other nations (Pharr, 1997). Rotter (1971) warned that a continued trust decline would lead to serious problems for society. Some have blamed the decline on the decrease in interpersonal trust, while others have cited the influence of an increasingly negative press corps (Orren, 1997). While each may be true, as more instances of malfeasance by corporate managers occur and are reported, management is increasingly pictured as self-serving instead of caring about employee concerns like privacy. The popularity of the Dilbert cartoon strip, picturing management as an exploiter of workers, exemplifies the increase in cynicism toward managers and corporations. The growth in institutional skepticism at the societal level, along with the growing tendency for workers to leave, makes it harder for a trusting climate to develop within an organization. This decrease in overall trust provides a less than desirable backdrop to the acceptance of awareness systems in organizations.

## ACKNOWLEDGEMENTS

We would like to thank Jennifer Williams and David Zweig for their helpful comments on an earlier version of this chapter.

## REFERENCES

Adler, A. and Henderson, A.A. (1994) Room of our own: experiences from a direct office share. In B. Adelson, S. Dumais and J. Olson (Eds), Proceedings of the CHI '94 Conference on Human Factors in Computing Systems, pp. 138–144. Boston, MA: Association for Computing Machinery.

Alder, G.S. (1998) Ethical issues in electronic performance monitoring: a consideration of deontological and teleological perspectives. Journal of Business Ethics, 17: 729–743.

Altman, I. and Taylor, D.A. (1973) Social Penetration: the Development of Interpersonal Relationships. New York: Holt, Rinehart, and Winston.

Ambrose, M.L. and Alder, G.S. (in press) Designing, implementing, and utilizing computer performance monitoring: enhancing organizational justice. In G.R. Ferris (Ed), Research in Personnel and Human Resource Management, Vol. 18. Greenwich, CT: JAI Press.

Atwater, L.E. (1988) The relative importance of situational and individual variables in predicting leader behavior: the surprising impact of subordinate trust. Group and Organization Studies, 13: 290–310.

Baier, A. (1986) Trust and antitrust. Ethics, 96: 231–260.

Banerjee, D., Cronan, T.P. and Jones, T.W. (1998) Modeling IT ethics: a study in situational ethics. MIS Quarterly, 22: 31–60.

Barber, B. (1983) The Logic and Limits of Trust. New Brunswick, NJ: Rutgers University Press.

Benford, S., Greenhalgh, G., Reynard, G., Brown, C. and Koleva, B. (1998) Understanding and constructing shared spaces with mixed-reality boundaries. ACM Transactions on Computer–Human Interaction, 5(3): 185–223.

Berscheid, E. and Graziano, W. (1979) The initiation of social relationships and interpersonal attraction. In R.L. Burgess and T.L. Huston (Eds), Social Exchange in Developing Relationships, pp. 31–60. New York: Academic Press.

Borthick, S. (1997) Remote access moves beyond email. Business Communications Review, January: 41–46.

Boynton, A.C., Jacobs, G.C. and Zmud, R.W. (1992) Whose responsibility is IT management? Sloan Management Review, 33(4): 32–38.

Brewer, M.B. and Silver, M. (1978) Ingroup bias as a function of task characteristics. European Journal of Social Psychology, 8: 393–400.

Bromiley, P. and Cummings, L.L. (1995) Transactions costs in organizations with trust. In R. Bies, R. Lewicki and B. Sheppard (Eds), Research on Negotiation in Organizations, Vol. 5, pp. 219–247. Greenwich, CT: JAI Press.

Burt, R.S. and Knez, M. (1996) Trust and third-party gossip. In R.M. Kramer and T.R. Tyler (Eds), Trust in Organizations: Frontiers of Theory and Research, pp. 68–89. Thousand Oaks, CA: Sage.

Chalykoff, J. and Kochan, T.A. (1989) Computer-aided monitoring: its influence on employee job satisfaction and turnover. Personnel Psychology, 24: 807–834.

Cohen, D.V. (1993) Creating and maintaining ethical work climates: anomie in the workplace and implications for managing change. Business Ethics Quarterly, 3(4): 343–358.

Cullen, J.B., Victor, B. and Bronson, J.W. (1993) The ethical climate questionnaire: an assessment. Psychological Reports, 73: 667–674.

Culnan, M.J. and Armstrong, P.K. (1999) Information privacy concerns, procedural fairness, and impersonal trust: an empirical investigation. Organization Science, 10(1): 104–115.

Cummings, L.L. and Bromiley, P. (1996) The organizational trust inventory (OTI): development and validation. In R.M. Kramer and T.R. Tyler (Eds), Trust in Organizations: Frontiers of Theory and Research, pp. 302–330. Thousand Oaks, CA: Sage.

Currall, S.C. and Judge, T.A. (1995) Measuring trust between organizational boundary role persons. Organizational Behavior and Human Decision Processes, 64: 151–170.

Dasgupta, P. (1988) Trust as a commodity. In D. Gambetta (Ed), Trust: Making and Breaking Cooperative Relations, pp. 49–72. New York: Blackwell.

Davis, F.D., Bagozzi, R.P. and Warshaw, P. (1989) User acceptance of computer technology: a comparison of two theoretical models. Management Science, 35: 982–1003.

Farley, P.C. (1986) Trust, perceived importance of praise and criticism, and work performance: an examination of feedback in the United States and England. Journal of Management, 12: 457–473.

Fox, A. (1974) Beyond Contract: Work, Power and Trust Relations. London: Faber.

Gabarro, J.J. (1978) The development of working relationships. In J. Galegher, R.E. Kraut and C. Egido (Eds), Intellectual Teamwork: Social and Technological Foundations of Cooperative Work, pp. 79–110. Hillsdale, NJ: Lawrence Erlbaum.

Garfinkel, H. (1963) A conception of, and experiments with, "trust" as a condition of stable concerted actions. In O.J. Harvey (Ed), Motivation and Social Interaction, pp. 187–238. New York: Ronald Press.

George, J.F. (1996) Computer-based monitoring: common perceptions and empirical results. MIS Quarterly, 20: 459–480.

Goldsteen, R., Schorr, J.K. and Goldsteen, K.S. (1989) Longitudinal study of appraisal at Three Mile Island: implications for life event research. Social Science and Medicine, 28: 389–398.

Golembiewski, R.T. and McConkie, M. (1975) The centrality of interpersonal trust in group processes. In G.L. Cooper (Ed), Theories of Group Processes, pp. 131–185. London: Wiley.

Good, D. (1988) Individuals, interpersonal relations, and trust. In D. Gambetta (Ed), Trust: Making and Breaking Cooperative Relations, pp. 31–48. New York: Blackwell.

Grant, R.A. and Higgins, C.A. (1991) The impact of computerized performance monitoring on service work: testing a causal model. Information Systems Research, 2: 116–142.

Grant, R.A., Higgins, C.A. and Irving, R.H. (1988) Computerized performance monitors: are they costing you customers? Sloan Management Review, Spring: 39–45.

Griffith, T.L. (1993) Teaching big brother to be a team player: computer monitoring and quality. Academy of Management Executive, 7(1): 73–80.

Hall, R.W., Mathur, A., Jahanian, F., Prakash, A. and Rassmussen, C. (1996) Corona: a communication service for scalable, reliable group collaboration systems. In M.S. Ackerman (Ed), Proceedings of the ACM 1996 Conference on Computer Supported Cooperative Work, pp. 140–149. New York: Association for Computing Machinery.

Hardwick, M. and Bolton, R. (1997) The industrial virtual enterprise. Communications of the ACM, 40(9): 59–60.

Harper, R.H.R. (1995) Why people do and don't wear active badges: a case study. Computer-Supported Cooperative Work, 4: 297–318.

Harrington, S.J. and Ruppel, C.P. (1997) What is an innovative climate and how does a manager support one? Paper presented at the Diffusion Interest Group in Information Technology (DIGIT) Workshop, Atlanta, GA.

Hart, P. and Saunders, C. (1997) Power and trust: critical factors in the adoption and use of electronic data interchange. Organization Science, 8(1): 23–42.

Holmes, J.G. (1991) Trust and the appraisal process in close relationships. In W.H. Jones and D. Perlman (Eds), Advances in Personal Relationships, Vol. 2, pp. 57–104. London: Jessica Kingsley.

Honda, S., Tomioka, H., Kimura, T., Oosawa, T., Okada, K. and Matsushita, Y. (1997) Valentine: an environment for home office worker providing informal communication and personal space. In S.C. Hayne and W. Prinz (Eds), Proceedings of the International ACM SIGGROUP Conference on Supporting Group Work, pp. 368–375. Phoenix, AZ: Association for Computing Machinery.

Hosmer, L.T. (1994) Why be moral? A different rationale for managers. Business Ethics Quarterly, 4(2): 191–204.

Hudson, S.E. and Smith, I. (1996) Techniques for addressing fundamental privacy and disruption tradeoffs in awareness support systems. In M.S. Ackerman (Ed), Proceedings of the ACM 1996 Conference on Computer Supported Cooperative Work, pp. 248–257. New York: Association for Computing Machinery.

Jarvenpaa, S.L., Knoll, K. and Leidner, D.E. (1998) Is anybody out there? Antecedents of trust in global virtual teams. Journal of Management Information Systems, 14: 29–64.

Johnson, B. and Greenberg, S. (1999) Judging people's availability for interaction from video snapshots. In R.H. Sprague Jr. (Ed), Proceedings of the 32nd Hawaii International Conference on System Sciences, Maui, HI (CD-ROM). New York: Institute of Electrical and Electronics Engineers (IEEE).

Johnson-George, C. and Swap, W.C. (1982) Measurement of specific interpersonal trust: construction and validation of a scale to assess trust in a specific other. Journal of Personality and Social Psychology, 43(6): 1306–1317.

Kee, H.W. and Knox, R.E. (1970) Conceptual and methodological considerations in the study of trust and suspicion. Journal of Conflict Resolution, 14: 357–366.

Koys, D.J. and DeCotiis, T.A. (1991) Inductive measures of psychological climate. Human Relations, 44(3): 265–285.

Kramer, R.M. (1996) Divergent realities and convergent disappointments in the hierarchic relation: trust and the intuitive auditor at work. In R.M. Kramer and T.R. Tyler (Eds), Trust in Organizations: Frontiers of Theory and Research, pp. 216–245. Thousand Oaks, CA: Sage.

Kraut, R.E. and Fish, R.S. (1995) Prospects for video telephony. Telecommunications Policy, 19(9): 699–719.

Kuzuoka, H. and Greenberg, S. (1999) Mediating awareness and communication through digital but physical surrogates. ACM CHI '99 Video Proceedings and Proceedings of the ACM SIGCHI '99 Conference Extended Abstracts. New York: Association for Computing Machinery.

Laabs, J.J. (1992) Surveillance: tool or trap? Personnel Journal, June: 96–104.

Lawler, E.E. (1971) Pay and Organizational Effectiveness: a Psychological View. New York: McGraw-Hill.

Lawler, E.E. and Rhode, J.G. (1976) Information and Control in Organizations. Pacific Palisades, CA: Goodyear.

Lee, A., Girgensohn, A. and Schlueter, K. (1997a) NYNEX portholes: initial user reactions and redesign implications. In S.C. Hayne and W. Prinz (Eds), GROUP '97, Proceedings of the International ACM SIGGROUP Conference on Supporting Group Work, pp. 385–394. Phoenix, AZ: Association for Computing Machinery Press.

Lee, A., Schlueter, K. and Girgensohn, A. (1997b) Sensing activity in video images, CHI '97 Extended Abstracts, pp. 319–320. New York: Association for Computing Machinery Press (also available at: http://www.fxpal.xerox.com/papers/lee97/).

Lewis, J.D. and Weigert, A.J. (1985a) Trust as a social reality. Social Forces, 63: 967–985.

Lewis, J.D. and Weigert, A.J. (1985b) Social atomism, holism, and trust. Sociological Quarterly, 26(4): 455–471.

Lind, E.A. and Tyler, T.R. (1988) The Social Psychology of Procedural Justice. New York: Plenum Press.

Lingle, J.H., Brock, T.C. and Cialdini, R.B. (1977) Surveillance instigates entrapment when violations are observed, when personal involvement is high, and when sanctions are severe. Journal of Personality and Social Psychology, 35: 419–429.

Luhmann, N. (1988) Familiarity, confidence, trust: problems and alternatives. In D. Gambetta (Ed), Trust: Making and Breaking Cooperative Relations, pp. 94–107. New York: Blackwell.

Luhmann, N. (1991) Trust and Power. Ann Arbor, MI: University Microfilms International.

Mariani, J.A. (1997) SISCO: providing a cooperation filter for a shared information space. In S.C. Hayne and W. Prinz (Eds), Proceedings of the International ACM SIGGROUP Conference on Supporting Group Work, pp. 376–384. Phoenix, AZ: Association for Computing Machinery.

Mark, M.M. and Mellor, S. (1991) Effect of self-relevance of an event on hindsight bias: the foreseeability of a layoff. Journal of Applied Psychology, 76(4): 569–577.

Masterson, S.S. and Taylor, M.S. (1996) The broadening of procedural justice: should interactional and procedural components be separate theories? Paper presented at the Academy of Management Meetings, Cincinnati, OH.

Mayer, R.C., Davis, J.H. and Schoorman, F.D. (1995) An integrative model of organizational trust. Academy of Management Review, 20: 709–734.

McAllister, D.J. (1995) Affect- and cognition-based trust as foundations for interpersonal cooperation in organizations. Academy of Management Journal, 38: 24–59.

McGregor, D. (1967) The Professional Manager. New York: McGraw-Hill.

McKnight, D.H., Cummings, L.L. and Chervany, N.L. (1998) Initial trust formation in new organizational relationships. Academy of Management Review, 23(3): 473–490.

Mee, A. (1898) The pleasure telephone. The Strand Magazine, XVI(44): 339–345.

Mitchell, S. (1996) The Official Guide to American Attitudes: Who Thinks What About the Issues that Shape Our Lives. Ithaca, NY: New Strategist.

O'Reilly, C.A. (1978) The intentional distortion of information in organizational communication: a laboratory and field investigation. Human Relations, 31(2): 173–193.

Orren, G. (1997) Fall from grace: the public's loss of faith in government. In J.S. Nye Jr., P.D. Zelikow and D.C. King (Eds), Why People Don't Trust Government, pp. 77–107. Cambridge, MA: Harvard University Press.

Ouchi, W.G. (1979) A conceptual framework for the design of organizational control mechanisms. Management Science, 25: 833–848.

Palfreyman, K. and Rodden, T. (1996) A protocol for user awareness on the world wide web. In M.S. Ackerman (Ed), Proceedings of the ACM 1996 Conference on Computer Supported Cooperative Work, pp. 130–139. New York: Association for Computing Machinery.

Pfeffer, J. (1993) The costs of legalization: the hidden dangers of increasingly formalized control. In S.B. Sitkin and R.J. Bies (Eds), The Legalistic Organization, pp. 329–346. Thousand Oaks, CA: Sage.

Pharr, S.J. (1997) Public trust and democracy in Japan. In J.S. Nye Jr., P.D. Zelikow and D.C. King (Eds), Why People Don't Trust Government, pp. 237–252. Cambridge, MA: Harvard University Press.

Ring, P.S. and Van de Ven, A.H. (1994) Developmental processes of cooperative interorganizational relationships. Academy of Management Review, 19: 90–118.

Rodden, T. (1996) Populating the application: a model of awareness for cooperative applications. In M.S. Ackerman (Ed), Proceedings of the ACM 1996 Conference on Computer Supported Cooperative Work, pp. 87–96. New York: Association for Computing Machinery.

Rosenberg, M. (1957) Occupations and Values. Glencoe, IL: Free Press.

Rotter, J.B. (1971) Generalized expectancies for interpersonal trust. American Psychologist, 26: 443–452.

Rotter, J.B. (1980) Interpersonal trust, trustworthiness, and gullibility. American Psychologist, 35: 1–7.

Rousseau, D.M., Sitkin, S.B., Burt, R.S. and Camerer, C. (1998) Not so different after all: a cross-discipline view of trust. Academy of Management Review, 23: 393–404.

Ruppel, C.P. and Harrington, S.J. (1998) Fostering an innovative climate, first presented at the Diffusion Interest Group in Information Technology (DIGIT) Workshop, Atlanta, GA, 1997. Unpublished revised manuscript, University of Toledo.

Shapiro, S.P. (1987a) The social control of impersonal trust. American Journal of Sociology, 93: 623–658.

Shapiro, S.P. (1987b) Policing trust. In C.D. Shearing and P.C. Stenning (Eds), Private Policing, pp. 194–220. Newbury Park, CA: Sage.

Shapiro, D.L., Sheppard, B.H. and Cheraskin, L. (1992) Business on a handshake. Negotiation Journal, 3: 365–377.

Sherif, M. (1966) In Common Predicament: Social Psychology of Intergroup Conflict and Cooperation. Boston, MA: Houghten Mifflin.

Silver, A. (1985) "Trust" in social and political theory. In G.D. Suttles and M.N. Zald (Eds), The Challenge of Social Control, pp. 52–67. Norwood, NJ: Ablex.

Simone, C. and Bandini, S. (1997) Compositional features for promoting awareness within and across cooperative applications. In S.C. Hayne and W. Prinz (Eds), Proceedings of the International ACM SIGGROUP Conference on Supporting Group Work, pp. 358–367. Phoenix, AZ: Association for Computing Machinery.

Sitkin, S.B. and Roth, N.L. (1993) Explaining the limited effectiveness of legalistic "remedies" for trust/distrust. Organization Science, 4: 367–392.

Smith, H. (1989) The user-data processing relationship: a study in power and attitudes. In J.I. DeGross, J.C. Henderson and B. Konsynski (Eds), Proceedings of the 10th International Conference on Information Systems, pp. 257–269. Boston, MA: International Conference on Information Systems.

Solomon, L. (1960) The influence of some types of power relationships and game strategies upon the development of interpersonal trust. Journal of Abnormal and Social Psychology, 61: 223–230.

Starbuck, W.H. and Milliken, F.J. (1988) Challenger: fine-tuning the odds until something breaks. Journal of Management Studies, 25: 319–340.

Strickland, L.H. (1958) Surveillance and trust. Journal of Personality, 26: 200–215.

Strutton, D., Pelton, L.E. and Lumpkin, J.R. (1994) The relationship between psychological climate and salesperson–sales manager trust in sales organizations. Journal of Personal Selling & Sales, 13(4): 1–14.

Tollmar, K., Sandor, O. and Schomer, A. (1996) Supporting social awareness at work. Design and experience. In M.S. Ackerman (Ed), Proceedings of the ACM 1996 Conference on Computer Supported Cooperative Work, pp. 298–307. New York: Association for Computing Machinery.

Turoff, M., Hiltz, S.R., Bahgat, A.N.F. and Rana, A.R. (1993) Distributed group support systems. MIS Quarterly, 17: 399–417.

Tyler, T.R. and Degoey, P. (1996) Trust in organizational authorities: the influence of motive attributions on willingness to accept decisions. In R.M. Kramer and T.R. Tyler (Eds), Trust in Organizations: Frontiers of Theory and Research, pp. 331–356. Thousand Oaks, CA: Sage.

Watts, J.C., Woods, D.D., Corban, J.M., Patterson, E.S., Kerr, R.L. and Hicks, L.C. (1996) Voice loops as cooperative aids in space shuttle mission control. In M.S. Ackerman (Ed), Proceedings of the ACM 1996 Conference on Computer Supported Cooperative Work, pp. 298–307. New York: Association for Computing Machinery.

Webster, J. (1998) Desktop videoconferencing: experiences of complete users, wary users, and non-users. MIS Quarterly, 22: 257–286.

Wheeless, L.R. (1978) A follow-up study of the relationships among trust, disclosure, and interpersonal solidarity. Human Communication Research, 4(2): 143–157.

Whittaker, S. (1995) Rethinking video as a technology for interpersonal communications. International Journal of Human–Computer Studies, 42: 501–529.

Williamson, O.E. (1993) Calculativeness, trust, and economic organization. Journal of Law and Economics, 34: 453–502.

Worchel, P. (1979) Trust and distrust. In W.G. Austin and S. Worchel (Eds), The Social Psychology of Intergroup Relations, pp. 174–187. Monterrey, CA: Brooks/Cole.

Zand, D.E. (1972) Trust and managerial problem solving. Administrative Science Quarterly, 17: 229–239.

Zhao, Q.A. and Stasko, J.T. (1998) Evaluating image filtering based techniques in media space applications. ACM 1998 Conference on Computer Supported Cooperative Work, pp. 11–18. Seattle, WA: Association for Computing Machinery.

Zuboff, S. (1988) In the Age of the Smart Machine. New York: Basic Books.

Zucker, L.G. (1986) Production of trust: institutional sources of economic structure, 1840–1920. In B.M. Staw and L.L. Cummings (Eds), Research in Organizational Behavior, Vol. 8, pp. 53–111. Greenwich, CT: JAI Press.

# Chapter 25

# In Diversity is There Strength? Ruminations on Changing Faces in Business

**Narayan Pant**

*and*

**Kulwant Singh**
*Department of Business Policy,*
*National University of Singapore, Singapore*

## INTRODUCTION

Few issues possess as much potential to incite heated, passionate debate as do attempts to increase diversity in social groupings. People who will view the 20th century from a distant future may well conclude that the signal achievement of this century was the widespread overt acceptance that all people should be equal in the eyes of law. Yet there exists little consensus among academics, legislators and businesspeople as to how global societies can get from this overt acceptance to workplace environments free of discrimination based on gender, race, religion or language, among others.

Organizations feature as major battlegrounds for conflicts between differing views on how to achieve goals of diversity, if only because social actors earn their livelihoods in them. In countries such as the US, explicit laws have mandated appropriate levels of diversity along dimensions of race and gender among others in important organizations such as universities, government agencies, and business organizations. In Singapore, attempts to maintain harmony among different ethnic groups include mandated levels of diversity in individual housing estates, while in Malaysia, national policies aim to increase the share of national income of disadvantaged groups through increased participation in business and education. In countries as diverse as Germany and Australia, business-driven demands for skilled migrants have been stymied by concerns of increased diversity and the resulting impact on national culture.

Organizational cultures arise from the norms, values and underlying beliefs of the individuals who constitute organizations (Beyer, 1981). Increasing diversity in organizational memberships therefore increases variety in bodies of norms and beliefs that inform organizational cultures. However, there exists little evidence to indicate whether the resultant changes in organizational cultures will have positive or negative effects on their effectiveness.

This last issue commands more than passing academic interest in Asia. Values and cultures unique to Asian environments (Clegg and Redding, 1990; Nakane, 1984; Redding and Hsiao, 1995) receive much credit for the success of Asian firms and countries over the last few decades. Yet as these very firms have ventured abroad, their management has by force of circumstance, if not legislation, become more diverse. Such firms need to know whether introducing professional doctrines and cultures into their companies will compromise their success. Similar challenges face corporations originating from other homogeneous cultures that find it necessary to operate in new and different parts of the world.

The future of organizational culture will be inextricably intertwined with trends of increasing diversity within organizations. In some instances, extant cultures will resist raising diversity levels, which will in turn stem trends toward greater diversity. Elsewhere, the attraction of potential increases in economic benefits might cause organizations to raise levels of diversity, with subsequent changes in organizational cultures.

The performance effects of these different trends in culture and diversity will be moderated by the environmental conditions within which organizations operate (Richard, 1999). In complex environments (Dess and Beard, 1984) that place multiple causally interlinked demands on organizations, the greater internal variety created via increased diversity will widen the range of organizational responses to environmental demands (Ashby, 1956). In addition, the institutional legitimacy (DiMaggio and Powell, 1983; Meyer and Rowan, 1977) conferred on organizations with relatively higher diversity levels will provide firms with moral and legal advantages relevant to such complex environments.

The following section will briefly outline salient approaches to diversity in the literature on organizations. The third section will illustrate common characteristics of organizational cultures that help us understand how cultures interact with diversity. The fourth section outlines some emerging trends in the evolution of diverse organizational environments. The penultimate section discusses potential interactions between diversity and organizational culture and proposes that future benefits or otherwise from these will follow closely upon the nature of environments in which they might occur. The final section will, in closing, reiterate conclusions about possible interactions between diversity, culture and performance in some foreseeable futures.

# DIVERSITY

The perception of diversity arises in the absence of perceived similarity among the members of a social group (Triandis, 1995). Virtually any social group will likely experience perceptions of diversity. In groups where members share the same ethnicity, the presence of a minority of women or members of another age group generates perceptions of diversity. Education levels, socioeconomic status and professional training, among many others, represent dimensions that create perceptions of diversity.

This paper focuses on perceptions of diversity that arise due to cultural variations among members of social groups. People who share cultural backgrounds possess and use mutually understood channels of communication facilitated by shared language, place of origin and temporal co-location (Triandis, 1972). Other shared characteristics that commonly cause people to be classified as sharing common cultural backgrounds might include "physical type (colloquially called a race) ... same descent from particular ancestors (ethnicity), same gender, [and] age" (Triandis, 1995, p. 13) among others.

Some studies on diversity have examined how "non-traditional" groups have progressed – as percentages of new hires, in promotions to upper levels of management, and in procuring equal compensation (Barnum et al., 1995; Cox, 1991; Kossek et al., 1996; Marini, 1989; Morrison and von Glinow, 1990). Most of these studies concluded that minority groups continue to face discrimination, and that programs aimed at facilitating the increase of diversity need to continue. Consequently, some other studies examined the effectiveness of different programs in promoting diversity and achieving compliance with legal and ethical guidelines on diversity (Gottfredson, 1992; Hitt and Keats, 1984; Rosen and Rynes, 1995; Thomas, 1992).

Rules and legislation alone will likely not further the cause of diversity in organizations. Rather, lasting change will importantly depend on organizational appreciation of the correlation between greater diversity and the quality of work life. Studies in this perspective examined improvements in the quality of work life through acceptance of and support for non-traditional groups (Barry and Bateman, 1996; Larkey, 1996; Tsui et al., 1992).

Diversity will have an impact on organizational effectiveness both at the work group and firm levels. At the work group level, increased levels of diversity change the nature of interpersonal processes and hence influence group effectiveness (Cox et al., 1991; McLeod and Lobel, 1992; Watson et al., 1993). Over time, diverse groups can match or exceed performances produced in less diverse groups. At the level of the firm, diversity influences competitive advantage (Cox, 1993; Cox and Blake, 1991; Fernandez and Barr, 1993; Richard, 1999; Thomas, 1990; Wright et al., 1995) possibly by increasing the range of feasible behaviors examined by the firm.

## The Importance of Diversity and Effectiveness

North American and European interest in diversity stems from the need to manage issues associated with the increasing presence of minority ethnicities in these societies (Johnston, 1991). Researchers focused principally on legal issues premised on principles of equity, fairness, and procedural justice. The influence of diversity on organizational effectiveness receives little emphasis because pressing legal issues leave no place for such considerations. Yet, theorists generally favor increasing diversity to produce more responsive and adaptive workforces and workplaces, for the intrinsic rewards of being right, and to gain favorable publicity for organizations (Jackson and Alvarez, 1992; Korn et al., 1992; Milliken and Martins, 1996; Morrison, 1992; Nemeth, 1986).

In Asia, academics and managers face other pressing concerns pertaining to diversity. In Southeast Asia, business organizations tend to be disproportionately owned and managed by individuals of Chinese ethnicity (Backman, 1999). In countries with minority Chinese populations, both governments and shareholders benefit by ensuring adequate representation in organizations of the majority communities. Even in Singapore, where people of Chinese origin constitute the majority, the government manages relationships between the races to avoid repeats of race riots that took place in Singapore in the 1960s.

Yet, culturally homogeneous workplaces probably yield benefits too. Chinese business people reportedly share sets of norms and values that make for easy communication and allow them to contract with one another in the absence of formal instruments to enforce the contracts (Clegg and Redding, 1990). Tacit assumptions and codes deeply embedded in language and other cultural systems will be hard for outsiders to assimilate and use, thereby reducing outsiders' organizational usefulness in such contexts.

Yet, even such organizations have started assimilating people of different cultural backgrounds into their organizations. This has been driven – in Singapore at least – by the explicit recognition that the skills and experience necessary to manage organizations successfully in newly competitive and otherwise changing environments might not be readily present in local markets (Straits Times, 1999, 2000). The following sections will attempt to unravel these varied effects of diversity on culture and organizational effectiveness.

# ORGANIZATIONAL CULTURE

The discourse on organizational culture has taken widely varying forms in the course of its development (Allaire and Firsirotu, 1984; Kilmann et al., 1986; Meyerson and Martin, 1987; Peters and Waterman, 1982; Schein, 1984, 1985). The ensuing review focuses on some ways in which culture has been seen to affect organizational behavior and, in consequence, organizational effectiveness (Denison, 1990; Dunbar et al., 1982; Kotter and Heskett, 1992; Saffold, 1988).

## Culture and Conduct

Allaire and Firsirotu (1984) effectively catalogued the widely divergent lenses used by researchers to examine organizational culture. A common strand in these ostensibly divergent approaches pertained to the close correlation between culture and behavior. Thus, Geertz (1973) theorized that culture "programs" behavior and provides rationalizations for pragmatic needs (Kreiner, 1989). Schein (1985) developed this thesis further and proposed that values formed the foundations of culturally specific and visible behaviors and artifacts.

Values commonly held in a social grouping act as powerful determinants of behavior. The greater consensus there exists over a given value, the less likely that the value will change (Allport, 1961; Shils, 1961). Lachman et al. (1994) termed values that resist change as core values since they have disproportionately greater influences on behavior. Core values have stronger influences on strategy formulation and implementation (Pant and Lachman, 1998) than peripheral values.

Similarly, the extent to which culture influences behavior varies (Gagliardi, 1986), but not based solely on the strength of the values that underlie culture. Even organizations that form out of an inflexible commitment to a single value might permit widely divergent cultures. Religious organizations, for instance, devoted to the support of the same set of scriptures or manifestation in supreme beings might permit cultures that varied from semi-bureaucratic to the free-spirited.

Rather than consensus around values, then, the degree of elaboration of a culture will determine its resistance to change. The degree of elaboration refers to the extent to which artifactually, sociologically and psychologically the elements of the culture act as guides for organizational behavior (Saffold, 1988). Less elaborated cultures provide guides for behavior in fewer contexts as opposed to more elaborated cultures.

Cultural components develop as organizations test theories about how to achieve desirable outcomes. When particular theories repeatedly appear to explain favorable outcomes, the behaviors associated with them acquire positive value in their own right (Gagliardi, 1986). Eventually, the theories are forgotten and the values persist, creating institutionalized behaviors (Meyer and Rowan, 1977) associated with yet another fragment of organizational culture.

As more and more of these beliefs, values, and behaviors become institutionalized, individual elements of the cultural edifice pose increasingly greater resistance to change. In elaborated cultures, each component of the cultures becomes connected with more and more links to other parts of the cultural structure. Changing individual parts potentially threatens many other parts connected with the edifice leading to enormous resistance. Thus, the more elaborate a culture, the greater the resistance it poses to change.

## TRENDS THAT WILL AFFECT DEVELOPMENTS IN DIVERSITY AND CULTURE

Four major extant trends will continue to place demands on organizations' adaptive processes in the future. First, the decades-long trend toward greater globalization and increased competition will persist as many more economies receive the benefits of closer integration into the global economic environment. Reciprocal and multidirectional agreements will continue to facilitate the cross-border operations of both traditional and new multinationals.

This will inevitably increase levels of diversity as expediency in the form of cheaper costs for firms that engage in global sourcing for their members encourages others to

follow. Also, firms that understand multi-country and multi-ethnic customers, employees and shareholders better will be rewarded by better access to markets, again encouraging others to raise levels of diversity.

In the face of such increasing globalization, organizations will have to work much
harder to define themselves to their customers and thus positioning will become
increasingly important in a world of proliferating choices for customers. Internally,
organizations will work harder to define their identities and competencies in order to
attract and retain new, global, and potentially more mobile human assets. Organizational culture will play a key role in limiting the net costs of retaining such assets
(Camerer and Vepsalainen, 1988).

Two important consequences of the first trend will serve to reinforce it as part of a
positive feedback loop. First, the growing visibility of successful first world corporations and the people who work for them will lead to heightened desire among managers
and practitioners in other parts of the world to emulate the principles that appear to have
led to their success. In all likelihood, Weberian bureaucratic principles will emerge as
the norm in organizational conduct with their associated emphasis on rationality, rule-
based conduct and uniformity of application. These principles will in turn make diversity more palatable by exposing the rules along which people will associate, granting
them informed choice in their associations. Once again, the cultures of organizations
will have to evolve in ways that support this evolution towards "Western" principles,
and yet maintain a sense of respect for the peculiarities in business conduct in different
environments.

Clearly such changes cannot come about without the consequent lowering of the
risks involved for corporations that need to make fairly fundamental changes in their
character. Alavi and Shanin (1982) observed that subsistence farmers refrain from
adopting new farming techniques as the risks of failure for them would be too high,
whereas more well-off farmers were willing to try new techniques. Similarly, in the
context of globalization, the broader distribution of development and wealth will render
firms from different countries more likely to experiment with new forms and ideas.
Hence, the trend towards the spread in development will of itself lower the barriers to
firms trying greater diversity and indeed more evolved organizational culture.

The final new trend that will almost certainly impact both diversity and culture stems
broadly from various attributes of what commentators have called the "new economy".
The increasing availability of technologies that render communication easier thereby
reducing the disadvantages of distance will forever change the nature of organizations
as individuals come to forge new and customized contracts of association with them.
Yet increasing pressures on cost and operational efficiency will circumscribe the potential options available to corporations as they face wider and potentially stronger competition. The inefficiencies implicit in biases in the employment of human capital will
tend to be exposed more easily and tolerated less in such high velocity environments
(Bourgeois and Eisenhardt, 1988).

The foregoing trends have been in existence for some time now and will likely not
peter out any time soon. On the contrary, attempts to incorporate China into the global
trading system and to bring about similar kinds of economic development in Africa

indicate that the trends may be sustained. The following sections will discuss the implications of these for developments in organizational culture.

# DIVERSITY, ORGANIZATIONAL CULTURE AND ENVIRONMENTS

The foregoing trends suggest that organizations of the future will almost inevitably face more diverse contexts than those existing today. However, the extent to which they choose to reflect this diversity in their own makeup will still be largely a matter of choice for them. The following paragraphs will present a contingency model of organizational effectiveness incorporating diversity, culture and environments.

## The Benefits of Diversity

Organizations will, in future, receive two broad kinds of benefits from increased diversity in their memberships. The first arises from access to a wider pool of human resources and hence improved individual and group processes. In complex environments, organizations will find that increased internal diversity improves the effectiveness of their interaction with their environments (Ashby, 1956; Lumpkin and Dess, 1995; Weick, 1979, pp. 188–193). Employees who share cultural backgrounds with important stakeholders will provide organizations with improved means to communicate with them (Jackson and Alvarez, 1992). Also, greater employee diversity will provide organizations with access to wider ranges of culturally specific cognitive and learning abilities (Welch and Welch, 1997), which will be beneficial at times of environmental change (Boeker and Goodstein, 1991).

The second benefit is of an institutional nature (DiMaggio and Powell, 1983) and arises from the perceived advantages of being seen to be doing the right thing in an increasingly multicultural world. Institutional advantages will typically be highest in environments that themselves possess high levels of diversity. Awards and recognitions that flow to organizations that effectively manage diverse memberships serve to raise their profile in ways that stakeholders perceive to be valuable (Figure 25.1).

## The Costs of Diversity

As variety in the cultural backgrounds of employees increases, organizations will require more explicit norms and procedures where tacit ones might have sufficed, making for greater organizational complexity (Perrow, 1984; Weick, 1979). Even with explicit behavioral injunctions, variances in behaviors within the culture or between sub-cultures (Martin and Siehl, 1983) will increase the potential for organizational conflict (Milliken and Martins, 1996). Managing effectively in such an organization will require greater integration efforts, thereby increasing coordination and management costs.

Greater variety in norms and assumptions in different parts of the organization would encourage the development of more elaborate cultures that would in turn be more

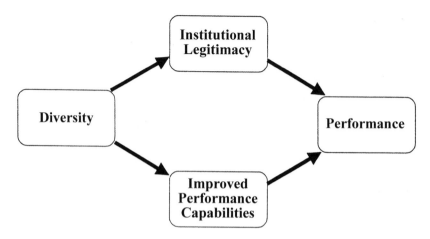

**Figure 25.1** A conventional view of the diversity advantage.

resistant to change. In relatively homogenous cultures, there would be lesser need for the organizational culture to specify codes of conduct explicitly as tacit norms might suffice. Hence, though greater diversity may increase group and unit responsiveness, the net effect of greater variety within organizations might result in more elaborated cultures that would eventually reduce flexibility.

## Diversity and Organizational Culture

The presumption that the benefits of diversity will overcome its costs underlies much of the diversity literature (Morrison, 1992; Nemeth, 1986). However, this literature often presumes that the benefits from diversity can actually be realized. But as Figure 25.2 depicts, the relation between diversity and organizational effectiveness will be contingent upon the nature of the environment in which organizations function and their cultures.

Figure 25.3 shows four possible combinations of culture and diversity that will become commonplace. The "functional axis" depicts combinations of culture and diversity that have adapted to one another. Increasing levels of diversity require cultures that have elaborate programs for behavior in a wide array of contexts since members with diverse backgrounds cannot depend on tacit rules of conduct. Thus, high levels of diversity and elaborated cultures will form a "complex fit". At the other extreme, homogeneous organizations display high levels of shared understandings that can work effectively using tacit rules prevalent in the wider culture, thereby forming a "simple fit". The following section discusses possible interactions between diversity and complexity and their implications for organizations in the future.

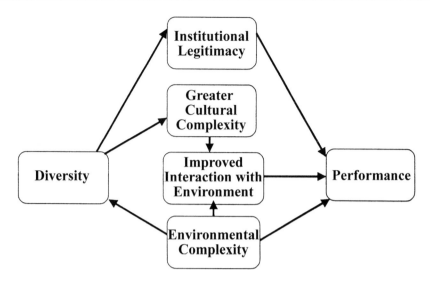

**Figure 25.2**   Contingent advantages of diversity.

## DIVERSITY AND CORPORATE CULTURE – FUTURE INTERACTIONS

Increased globalization, general improvements in prosperity in different parts of the world and the virtual expansion of business boundaries will mean that levels of diversity in organizations will increase, if not uniformly. Consequently all four of the possible combinations of diversity and culture depicted in Figure 25.3 might come to hold in different organizations. The following paragraphs examine closely the perfor-

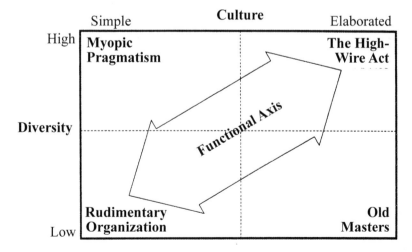

**Figure 25.3**   Interactions between corporate culture and diversity.

mance implications of each of the four combinations for organizations that might face different kinds of environmental conditions in the future.

## Low Diversity with Simple Culture – Rudimentary Bureaucracy

Rudimentary bureaucracies will in the future constitute a diminishing breed, their growth prospects limited, their customers deserting, and their business paradigms crumbling in the face of energetic global entrepreneurship. Today, these organizations can be seen everywhere in a newly resurgent Asia, with largely homogeneous family-owned businesses still following business practices premised on broader cultural norms of reciprocity and associative rationality. Thus far, such organizations have largely functioned in environments approximating the Emery and Trist (1965) "placid-clustered" environment where simple strategies aimed at extracting revenue from identifiable, clustered sources have served them well. In such environments business decisions can be determined by the degree of cultural affinity perceived for the business partner, rendering it almost a virtue to accord closely with traditions and norms common to large segments of the Overseas Chinese (Chang and Holt, 1996; Redding and Hsiao, 1995).

Few such simple environments will survive. The influences of multilateral institutions, the exigencies of global trade, and the increasingly confident demands of customers with choices will create complex environments with multiple powerful institutional stakeholders (Dess and Beard, 1984). With the demise of simple environments rudimentary bureaucracies will also decline.

## Elaborated Culture and Low Diversity – the Old Masters

Like "gentlemen's clubs" of the 19th and 20th centuries, the Old Masters have survived for decades, quietly certain in the cultural superiority of their highly evolved ways. The high levels of elaboration in the cultures of these organizations contain careful guidelines for behavior that evolved with their experiences of different environments. Yet low levels of diversity indicate their origins and histories in low diversity cultures.

These organizations usually dominated environments for long periods, developing elaborate cultures that helped them evolve with environments that changed along relatively certain paths over the years. However, the very elaboration that led to their success until this point will likely reduce their effectiveness in the future (Miller, 1990) in the face of rapid and less predictable environment changes.

There will soon be very few environments that will afford these Old Masters the comfort of their low diversity, elaborated cultures. Previously regulated environments including those of protected utilities will face even greater pressures to permit open competition. Previously protected markets not least in developed countries such as Japan will see competitors from different countries adopt seriously competitive positions. Hence, these organizations will face two sets of pressures. First, their elaborated cultures will prove to be relatively rigid in the face of environments that have changed possibly quicker than any changes they may have encountered in the past. Second, the major difference from any changes they may have encountered previously will be the increasing presence of equally viable and possibly fleet-footed competition that can take advantage of their present distress. In these "disturbed-reactive" environments (Emery and Trist, 1965), elaborated cultures will represent a hindrance to performance.

## High Diversity Simple Culture – Myopic Pragmatism

These organizations will demonstrate an admirable pragmatism towards the issue of diversity. From their perspective, greater diversity will imply simply access to greater pools of human resources. However, this pragmatism could confound attempts to build elaborated cultures. In the medical, accounting, consulting, and other knowledge-based professions, the "ownership" of rent-generating knowledge by key individuals proves to be the key organizing principle. Consequently, organizations tend to adopt "cultures" common to the professions that recognize this knowledge, rather than any unique cultural elaboration in individual organizations.

However, the proliferation of such knowledge in intensive firms will make it increasingly difficult for them to trade on the basis of their professional knowledge alone. This proliferation will create environments with several similar organizations, or disturbed reactive environments in which individual firms will benefit from unique positioning of their services (Starbuck, 1993). A key ingredient that will facilitate this positioning will be increasingly elaborated culture.

## High Diversity Elaborated Cultures – the High Wire Act

The preceding segments suggested that first, elaborated cultures that had developed in the absence of diversity would resist diversity even though it might improve effectiveness. As a consequence "Old Masters" as a breed of organizations will be under threat in the future. In addition, the myopic pragmatists who embraced diversity in order to improve effectiveness will face environmental pressures to adopt elaborated cultures.

Collectively, these two findings will suggest that high diversity, elaborated culture organizations will display the greatest effectiveness in the increasingly complex environments that will unfold in the future. High levels of diversity will provide them with both institutional legitimacy in environments that scrutinize them closely and access to functional internal variety. Elaborated cultures will permit the internal differentiation necessary to support unique positioning and explicit guides for behavior made necessary by increased diversity.

This complex high wire act will assist future organizations to manage the loud and powerful demands of diverse stakeholder groups, an act made easier by the presence of a diverse employee base (Morrison, 1992). The normative advantages of conforming to social expectations of diversity will in turn provide breathing room from what might otherwise be difficult demands.

## Implications of These Interactions

Briefly, the foregoing interactions implicitly suggest the existence of a dynamic grounded in organizational effectiveness that will drive organizations through the archetypes described above until they evolve high wire acts of their own. Eventually, the effectiveness of elaborated cultures with high levels of internal diversity in complex environments (Ashby, 1956; Fredrickson, 1984; Lawrence and Lorsch, 1969; Lumpkin and Dess, 1995; Weick, 1979) will encourage others to evolve in this direction.

Other combinations of diversity and organizational culture will likely prove less effective because of the direction of evolution in organizational environments. The global evolution of complex environments with multiple demands on organizations will necessitate increasing levels of diversity. These levels of diversity will in turn require explicit and elaborate guides for conduct given the absence of shared social contexts.

## Diversity and Corporate Culture in the Global Context

The global business environment will continue to display greater variety, diversity and complexity than most domestic environments. Firms that have operated in relatively diverse and complex environments will prove more adept at negotiating the global environment than firms from less complex environments. For instance, since US firms come from environments where managers gain experience in introducing and managing diversity (Fernandez and Barr, 1993), they ought to enjoy competitive advantages in international operations relative to, for example, Japanese firms that originate in culturally more homogeneous environments.

Firms from culturally homogenous environments could compensate for this homogeneity by embracing diversity along other, perhaps non-visible, dimensions (Milliken and Martins, 1996). Diversity along the latter will improve firms' abilities to deal with environmental complexity, thereby enhancing performances (Korn et al., 1992). Some large Norwegian firms such as *Norsk Hydro* deliberately introduce diversity into their organizations by using individuals from diverse backgrounds to provide inputs into decision-making. In one instance, the company hired a social anthropologist to investigate the effects of displacement among tribal people in India before deciding whether to make an investment that would cause the displacement.

Other avenues for firms to compensate for homogeneous backgrounds will include aggressive recruitment of staff from outside their societies. ABB, with roots in Sweden and Switzerland, for example, has a complex corporate culture that allows it to adapt to the many different environments in which it operates. Though this complexity is based on more than personnel diversity, extensive and long-term global hiring policies have played an important part in the organization's success in global operations (Guyon, 1996). In Asia, managers from India and the Philippines find themselves actively recruited for their willingness and ability to work in different countries (Yip, 1998), which are derived in part from their origins in diverse cultures. Diversity in the membership profiles of multinational organizations from even homogeneous cultures will increase dramatically in the near future.

The future success of ethnically Chinese firms in the countries of Southeast Asia (Backman, 1999) will depend largely on their ability and willingness to adopt not just greater diversity but corporate cultures commensurate with that diversity. Today, many of these firms continue to be run by their founders – often first generation immigrants from China – or by their immediate family members. Several have hitherto proven reluctant to hire managers from outside the immediate families or clans of the founder-owners.[1] Previously, these firms achieved success often from understanding the sources of power in the economy and "influencing the structures of the industry in which they operate to create privileged franchises" (Chu and MacMurray, 1993, p. 118). The Indonesian firm Sampoerna – run by the son of the founder – deliberately sought foreign managers from the US, UK and Australia among others to run the company. However, the absence of a corporate culture and systems that could utilize these managers meant that many of the advantages of this diversity could not be realized.

This section appears to suggest that there may be no place for low diversity or non-elaborated cultures in the world. In the long-term this will probably be true, but the near-term will present firms with transitional periods where pockets in environments render elaborated cultures dysfunctional. In the *Norsk Hydro* example discussed earlier, the local joint venture partners were incensed at the idea that a foreign firm might tell them how to deal with their own indigenous people. From the local perspective a foreigner ought to jump at the opportunity to invest in a potentially lucrative development. From *Norsk Hydro*'s perspective, short-term gains were not a sufficient justification to sacrifice what the firm believed in, and what they were convinced their own partners would come to believe in, in due course.

# CONCLUSION

This chapter has painted a fairly positive scenario of the future of the world. Barriers to trade will fall, cross-border movements of goods, services and people will grow, and income levels will increase generally across the world. Given such a world, the kinds of organizations we will see will likely reflect the benign nature of such an environment. The principal hypotheses made in this paper have to do with likely combinations of diversity and culture that might come to prevail in the future and the effectiveness levels of these combinations.

In the past, organizations with low levels of diversity and simple cultures have proved effective in environments of the placid-randomized kind (Emery and Trist, 1965). Few such environments will survive any length into the future. The rules of cross-border trade appear to be heading for inevitable liberalization. In such a world,

---

[1] An extreme example of the insularity of these groups is provided by the CP Group, a Thai Conglomerate MNC with 1998 sales of approximately US$7 billion. As with many family groups, the CP Group preferred to recruit managers from its own dialect group, if family members were not available. When it needed managers to staff its new Indonesian ventures, CP undertook recruiting in one of the few pockets of Teochew dialect members in Indonesia. This group, however, was located in a remote, obscure, non-industrial city on the island of Borneo, Pontianak (Backman, 1999). The equivalent may be for leading German firms seeking to expand into Silicon Valley to recruit from Frankenmuth, Michigan, the small town in the US mid-west which was founded by early German migrants.

organizations explicitly designed for simple environments will find pockets of survival shrinking rapidly.

Organizations with elaborated cultures but low diversity and those with high diversity but simple cultures will also likely prove to be transient stages of organizational evolution. Though the former may indeed be the product of slow evolution in culturally homogeneous environments, changes in the competitive natures of their environments will force them to adopt increasingly higher levels of diversity. In the case of the latter, the pragmatism implicit in high levels of diversity will prove to be unsustainable as the presence of several similar organizations forces internal and external differentiation.

In short, diversity will likely not enjoy a first-order relationship with organizational effectiveness. The relationship between diversity and effectiveness will depend on the interaction between diversity, the degree of elaboration of organizational culture and the stage of evolution of organizational environments. Nonetheless, given that the global environment in totality will likely increase in complexity, the increase in internal capabilities introduced by diversity will only become more valuable. The new challenges for global organizations will include managing increasingly valuable diversity with the inevitably greater rigidity of the complex corporate cultures that will evolve along with it.

# REFERENCES

Alavi, H. and Shanin, T. (1982) Introduction to the Sociology of 'Developing Societies'. London: Macmillan.

Allaire, Y. and Firsirotu, M.E. (1984) Theories of organizational culture. Organization Studies, 5: 193–226.

Allport, G.W. (1961) Pattern and Growth in Personality. New York: Holt, Rinehart & Winston.

Ashby, W.R. (1956) An Introduction to Cybernetics. Englewood Cliffs, NJ: Prentice-Hall.

Backman, M. (1999) Asian Eclipse. Exposing the Dark Side of Business in Asia. Singapore: Wiley.

Barnum, P., Liden, R.C. and DiTomaso, N. (1995) Double jeopardy for women and minorities: pay differences with age. Academy of Management Journal, 38: 863–880.

Barry, B. and Bateman, T.S. (1996) A social trap analysis of the management of diversity. Academy of Management Review, 21: 757–790.

Beyer, J.M. (1981) Ideologies, values and decision making n organizations. In P.C. Nystrom and W.H. Starbuck (Eds), Handbook of Organizational Design, Vol. 2, pp. 166–202. Oxford: Oxford University Press.

Boeker, W. and Goodstein, J. (1991) Organizational performance and adaptation: effects of environment and performance on board composition. Academy of Management Journal, 34(4): 805–826.

Bourgeois III, L.J. and Eisenhardt, K.M. (1988) Strategic decision processes in high velocity environments. Management Science, 34(7): 816–835.

Camerer, C. and Vepsalainen, A. (1988) The economic efficiency of corporate culture. Strategic Management Journal, 9: 115–126.

Chang, H.-C. and Holt, G.R. (1996) An exploration of interpersonal relationships in two Taiwanese computer firms. Human Relations, 49(12): 1489–1517.

Chu, T.C. and MacMurray, T. (1993) The road ahead for Asia's leading conglomerates. The McKinsey Quarterly, (3): 117–126.

Clegg, S.R. and Redding, S.G. (1990) Capitalism in Contrasting Cultures. New York: Walter de Gruyter.

Cox Jr., T. (1991) The multicultural organization. Academy of Management Executive, 5: 34–48.

Cox Jr., T. (1993) Cultural Diversity in Organizations. Theory, Research and Practice. San Francisco, CA: Berrett-Koehler.

Cox Jr., T. and Blake, S. (1991) Managing cultural diversity: implications for organizational competitiveness. Academy of Management Executive, 5: 45–55.

Cox, T.H., Lobel, S.A. and McLeod, P.L. (1991) Effects of ethnic group cultural differences on cooperative and competitive behavior on a group task. Academy of Management Journal, 34: 827–847.

Denison, D. (1990) Corporate Culture and Organizational Effectiveness. New York: Wiley.

Dess, G.G. and Beard, D.W. (1984) Dimensions of organizational task environments. Administrative Science Quarterly, 29: 52–73.

DiMaggio, P.J. and Powell, W.W. (1983) The iron cage revisited: institutional isomorphism and collective rationality in organizational fields. American Sociological Review, 48: 147–160.

Dunbar, R.L.M., Dutton, J.M. and Torbert, W.R. (1982) Crossing mother: ideological constraints on organizational improvements. Journal of Management Studies, 19: 91–108.

Emery, F.E. and Trist, E.L. (1965) The causal texture of organizational environments. Human Relations, 18: 21–32.

Fernandez, J. and Barr, M. (1993) The Diversity Advantage: How American Business Can Out-Perform Japanese and European Companies in the Global Marketplace. New York: Lexington.

Fredrickson, J. (1984) The comprehensiveness of strategic decision processes: extensions, observations, future directions. Academy of Management Journal, 27: 445–466.

Gagliardi, P. (1986) The creation and change of organizational cultures. Organizational Studies, 7: 117–134.

Geertz, C. (1973) The Interpretation of Cultures. New York: Basic Books.

Gottfredson, L.S. (1992) Dilemmas in developing diversity programs. In S.E. Jackson (Ed), Diversity in the Workplace: Human Resource Initiatives, pp. 279–305. New York: Guilford Press.

Guyon, J. (1996) World citizens: at ABB globalization isn't just a buzzword, its a corporate culture. The Wall Street Journal Europe, October 1: 1.

Hitt, M. and Keats, B. (1984) Empirical identification of the criteria for effective affirmative action programs. Journal of Applied Behavioral Science, 20: 203–222.

Jackson, S.E. and Alvarez, E.B. (1992) Working through diversity as a strategic imperative. In S.E. Jackson (Ed), Diversity in the Workplace: Human Resources Initiatives, pp. 13–29. New York: Guilford Press.

Johnston, W. (1991) Global work force 2000: the new world labor market. Harvard Business Review, 69(2): 115–127.

Kilmann, R., Saxton, M. and Serpa, R. (1986) Issues in understanding and changing culture. California Management Review, 28: 87–94.

Korn, H.J., Milliken, F.J. and Lant, T.K. (1992) Top management team change and organizational performance: the influence of succession, composition, and context. Paper presented at the annual meetings of the Academy of Management, Las Vegas, NV.

Kossek, E.E., Zonia, S.C. and Young, W. (1996) The limitations of organizational demography: can diversity climate be enhanced in the absence of teamwork? In M.N. Ruterman, M.W. Hughes-James and S.E. Jackson (Eds), Selected Research on Work Team Diversity, Washington, DC: American Psychological Association.

Kotter, J.P. and Heskett, J.L. (1992) Corporate Culture and Performance. New York: Free Press.

Kreiner, K. (1989) Culture and meaning: making sense of conflicting realities. International Studies of Management and Organization, 19(3): 64–81.

Lachman, R., Nedd, A. and Hinings, C.R. (1994) Analyzing cross-national management and organizations: a theoretical framework. Management Science, 40: 40–55.

Larkey, L.K. (1996) Toward a theory of communicative interactions in culturally diverse workgroups. Academy of Management Review, 21(2): 463–491.

Lawrence, P.R. and Lorsch, J.W. (1969) Organization and Environment. Homewood, IL: Irwin.

Lumpkin, G.T. and Dess, G.G. (1995) Simplicity as a strategy-making process: the effects of stage of organizational development and environment on performance. Academy of Management Journal, 38: 1386–1407.

Marini, M.M. (1989) Sex differences in earnings in the United States. In W.R. Scott and J. Blake (Eds). Annual Review of Sociology, 15: 343–380.

Martin, J. and Siehl, C. (1983) Organizational culture and counter-culture: an uneasy symbiosis. Organizational Dynamics, 12(2): 52–64.

McLeod, P.L. and Lobel, S.A. (1992) The effects of ethnic diversity on idea generation in small groups. Academy of Management Best Papers Proceedings: 227–231.

Meyer, J.W. and Rowan, B. (1977) Institutionalized organizations: formal structure as myth and ceremony. American Journal of Sociology, 83: 340–363.

Meyerson, D. and Martin, J. (1987) Cultural change: an integration of three views. Journal of Management Studies, 24(6): 623–647.

Miller, D. (1990) The Icarus Paradox. New York: Harper Business.

Milliken, F.J. and Martins, L.L. (1996) Searching for common threads: understanding the multiple effects of diversity in organizational groups. Academy of Management Review, 21(2): 402–433.

Morrison, A. (1992) The New Leaders: Guidelines on Leadership Diversity in America. San Francisco, CA: Jossey-Bass.

Morrison, A.M. and von Glinow, M.A. (1990) Women and minorities in management. American Psychologist, 45: 200–208.

Nakane, C. (1984) Japanese Society. Harmondsworth: Penguin.

Nemeth, C.J. (1986) Differential contributions of majority and minority influence. Psychological Review, 93: 23–32.

Pant, P.N. and Lachman, R. (1998) Value incongruity and strategic choice. Journal of Management Studies, 35(2): 195–212.

Perrow, C. (1984) Normal Accidents: Living with High-Risk Technologies. New York: Basic Books.

Peters, T. and Waterman, R. (1982) In Search of Excellence. New York: Harper & Row.

Redding, S.G. and Hsiao, M. (1995) An empirical study of overseas Chinese managerial ideology. In S.G. Redding (Ed), International Cultural Differences. Brookfield, VT: Dartmouth. pp. 183–196.

Richard, O.C. (1999) Racial diversity, business strategy and firm performance: a resource-based view. Paper presented at the annual meetings of the Academy of Management, Chicago, IL.

Rosen, B. and Rynes, S. (1995) A field survey of factors affecting the adoption and perceived success of diversity training. Personnel Psychology, 48: 247–270.

Saffold III, G.S. (1988) Culture traits, strength, and organizational performance: moving beyond "strong culture". Academy of Management Review, 13(4): 546–558.

Schein, E. (1984) Coming to a new awareness of organizational culture. Sloan Management Review, 25(2): 3–16.

Schein, E. (1985) Organizational Culture and Leadership. San Francisco, CA: Jossey-Bass.

Shils, E.A. (1961) Center and periphery. In The Logic of Personal Knowledge: Essays Presented to Michael Polanyi. London: Routledge & Kegan Paul.

Starbuck, W.H. (1993) Keeping a butterfly and an elephant in a house of cards: the elements of exceptional success. Journal of Management Studies, 30: 885–921.

Straits Times (1999) Foreigners needed for global race. August 20: 42.

Straits Times (2000) And then there were 66 MDs… February 22: 1.

Thomas Jr., R.R. (1990) From affirmative action to affirming diversity. Harvard Business Review, 2: 107–117.

Thomas Jr., R.R. (1992) Managing diversity: a conceptual framework. In S.E. Jackson (Ed), Diversity in the Workplace: Human Resource Initiatives, pp. 306–317. New York: Guilford Press.

Triandis, H.C. (1972) The Analysis of Subjective Culture. New York: Wiley.

Triandis, H.C. (1995) A theoretical framework for the study of diversity. In M.M. Chemers, S. Oskamp and M.A. Costanzo (Eds), Diversity in Organizations, pp. 11–36. Thousand Oaks, CA: Sage.

Tsui, A., Egan, T. and O'Reilly III, C. (1992) Being different: relational demography and organizational attachment. Administrative Science Quarterly, 37: 549–579.

Watson, W.E., Kumar, K. and Michaelson, L.K. (1993) Cultural diversity's impact on interaction process and performance: comparing homogenous and diverse task groups. Academy of Management Journal, 36: 590–602.

Weick, K.E. (1979) The Social Psychology of Organizing. Reading, MA: Addison-Wesley.

Welch, D.E. and Welch, L.S. (1997) Being flexible and accommodating diversity: the challenge for multinational management. European Management Journal, 15(6): 677–685.

Wright, P., Ferris, S.P., Hiller, J.S. and Kroll, M. (1995) Competitiveness through management of diversity: effects on stock price valuation. Academy of Management Journal, 38: 272–287.

Yip, G. (1998) Asian Advantage. Reading, MA: Addison-Wesley.

# Chapter 26

# Culture in-the-Making in Telework Settings

**Roger Dunbar**

*and*

**Raghu Garud**
*Stern School of Business, New York University,*
*NY, USA*

## INTRODUCTION

Teleworking possibilities are opening up quickly with the advent of portable computing and Internet technologies (Hedberg et al., 1977). Portable computers offer employees an opportunity to work any time, anywhere. Indeed, information technologies have enhanced employee productivity (Lohr, 1999) as Internet connections at remote locations enable instantaneous access to current data (Sproull and Kiesler, 1991). Employees are able to work from their car, hotels or airplanes and out of other firm's offices and from their homes. The ability to telework provides employees with an opportunity to utilize their time more efficiently and results in greater effectiveness (Dunbar and Garud, 1998).

While telework demonstrates that employees do not have to be located in corporate offices in order to get work done, many employees are still tethered to corporate offices. Organizations could have their employees work through telecommuting arrangements. Such a step would significantly change work organizations for it would institutionalize the idea that employees are neither necessarily nor primarily based in corporate facilities. While workers might be based in home offices, a more flexible view of telecommuting (i.e. telework) would see them as based wherever their work takes them (Raghuram et al., 1998). While some managers and employees find this notion natural and attractive, others find the idea of working continually untethered and "out there" as ambiguous and disconcerting.

Alvin Toffler (1991) discussed the idea of the "electronic cottage" in his book, "The Third Wave" and these early ideas about telecommuting continue to intrigue. Some managers are attracted to telecommuting because they believe it will enable their organizations to directly reduce real estate costs and indirectly increase work productivity. But telecommuting also terrifies some of these managers for they cannot see how traditional control methods will work when most of the time they will not have face-to-face contact with their employees (Wiesenfeld et al., 1999).

Workers who anticipate working in a telecommuting arrangement also have mixed reactions. Some look forward to the extra freedom they will have to explore new ways of doing things and to improve their performance. Others fret about the meaning of corporate membership and identity if they have no physical place they can call their own in corporate facilities (Wiesenfeld et al., in press). Nevertheless, many teleworkers are enthusiastic advocates for teleworking arrangements. They argue that telecommuting eliminates long, traffic-bound commutes, forced captivity in Dilbert-like cubicles, and inflexible and rigid workdays. They report the result is not only increased work productivity but also an improved quality to their personal lives (Dunbar and Garud, 1998).

Several corporations have experimented with telecommuting systems by either allowing or requiring selected employees to give up their corporate office space and to work either from home offices or other locations (Dunbar and Garud, 1998). Some of these efforts have proven to be very successful. Others have proven difficult to implement and some efforts have been abandoned. Academics and consultants have conjectured about the potential organizational and social hazards of telecommuting arrangements (Turner, 1998).

Yet even as these discussions continue, Wall Street's demands for increasing performance strongly encourage the diffusion of cost-reducing initiatives that can lead to productivity improvements (Dunbar and Garud, 1999). As organizations downsize, cut costs and seek ways to become more flexible, customer-oriented and productive, telecommuting arrangements may seem enticingly available solutions to help firms meet these continuing pressures (Raghuram et al., 1999).

For both management and workers, however, this new way of working implies significant cultural change. This is because most corporate work cultures are designed to support face-to-face work activities as these take place at or near firm facilities. A culture supporting telecommuting activities must support activities that do not take place within corporate facilities but are distributed across different locations where face-to-face interaction between firm employees is minimized. It is not surprising that telecommuting success varies, that different issues arise in different organizations, and that different reactions can occur in response to teleworking programs. A teleworking culture reflects the aims of the host organization's culture and the types of telecommuting initiative it designs and supports.

We begin by considering how cultures have developed and evolved in response to technological changes over the years. We describe how when a host organization plans a telecommuting initiative, it establishes a stage for change and new developments at all levels of its corporate culture (Martin, 1992). We then focus on the sorts of culture that emerge as telework supports employee knowledge development. The resulting telework culture centers on the work that people do and is highly dynamic. As teleworking cultures are likely to increasingly characterize organizations, we conclude by speculating how they may be conceptualized, studied and understood.

# CULTURAL RESPONSES TO TECHNOLOGICAL CHANGE

In order to exploit the possibilities associated with new technologies, people must often significantly change their cultural beliefs concerning how work should be organized. While in most situations some usually welcome the new possibilities, there are also usually others who resist and prefer to stick to established ways of doing things. An example would be Wedgwood's utilization of mass production pottery technology back in the 1760s (Langton, 1984). To utilize this new technology to improve pottery quality and productivity, Wedgwood needed employees who followed rules that facilitated mass production. This was a new idea at the time and local laborers were not used to having behavioral constraints that determined how they had to work. Many strongly resisted the imposition of bureaucratic discipline. Wedgwood responded by imposing stiff fines for transgressions and creating a supervisory career structure that rewarded those who consistently followed his rules by giving them physically less demanding work and higher pay. Eventually, he attracted a factory workforce that accepted mass production rules. The new work culture emphasized supervised rule adherence and was epitomized by the idea: "you are paid to do, not to think".

While these types of supervisory practice curtailed human creativity, they harnessed machine productivity. The new cultural framing defined work as activities determined by a fixed system of meaning, i.e. mass production work required employees to obey and not to question the rules. Encouraged by the productivity gains that this system of understanding accomplished, the architects of a fixed view of work continued to explore how a logic based on more refined divisions of labor might further increase productivity. Eventually, much mass production work became completely meaningless to the workers who were supposed to implement it and many viewed it as exploitative. This generated strikes, violence and sabotage along with a crisis of meaning that shifted power from management to labor unions and required managers to reconsider their cultural belief systems concerning work. A new management culture emerged based on the idea that more meaningful work experiences would improve work performance. This led to recommendations advocating increased worker participation in determining work-related activities (e.g. Likert, 1967), work designs that promoted more meaningful work experiences (e.g. Hackman and Oldham, 1975), and so on.

Just as the introduction of mass production techniques, automobiles and machine tools all served to change work cultures in recent centuries, the advent of information technologies sets the stage for a new round of cultural change in 21st century work places. In order to improve performance using earlier technologies, managers and entrepreneurs stood back, identified underlying work dimensions, and then manipulated structural designs in ways that were expected to improve work performance. The essence of telework technologies, however, is that they extend the human mind, liberating rather than limiting thoughts and ideas. One cannot stand back and identify different underlying dimensions for at the moment we are very limited in our knowledge of how the human mind works. We do know that the human mind can quickly redefine divisions, dimensions and variables and then link them together in new ways (Watzlawick et al., 1974). The aim of new technologies is to extend these mental abilities and their impact. The slogan of the 21st century work culture might be "you are paid both to think and to do".

The places where technology-extended minds may take people are inherently changing and indeterminate. Working with computer technology, people are not only in contact with others who think in different ways about different things but they also often change what and how they think about work matters as they find new material and information coming to hand. While the content of a work culture may be centered on specific tasks, an ongoing change process also emerges as participants continually renegotiate and redefine the system of meaning they work with in this context. A firm can suggest role-related normative expectations for how those involved should generally behave, but the knowledge that telework generates tends to evolve and change quickly and in ways that are not controllable (Tsoukas, 1996).

# THE IMPACT OF TELECOMMUTING ARRANGEMENTS ON ORGANIZATION CULTURES

Established organizations have been depicted as having relatively identifiable, stable cultures that vary along specific dimensions (Hofstede et al., 1990; Schein, 1992). Martin (1992) suggests that such dimensions can be understood in different ways and she identifies three perspectives that define alternative views of organization cultures. One perspective highlights the shared norms, beliefs and behaviors that comprise organization cultures. It is usually argued that these shared understandings develop over time as a result of face-to-face interaction and shared experiences. O'Reilly (1989) argues that these shared understandings define a cultural basis for organizational integration and control. Another perspective, however, highlights inconsistencies and differences in these norms, beliefs and behaviors that develop because different tasks require the support of alternative subcultures characteristic of different organization areas. Depending on how the skills, tasks and relationships supported by such subcultures are consistent with overall organization needs and priorities, so subculture norms, beliefs and behaviors become intertwined with organizational power and politics issues (Salancik and Pfeffer, 1977). Martin's third perspective focuses on the unique ways individual organization members interpret the specific norms, beliefs and behaviors comprising a firm's culture. From a top management functional perspective, fragmented views may not seem important and they may be perceived to constitute a problem. In fact, fragmented views provide an organization with the internal variety needed to recognize value in opportunities for change and adaptation along with the flexibility needed to develop and support such initiatives.

A top managerial decision is usually required to authorize a telecommuting initiative. Top management justifications for a telecommuting initiative typically emphasize the shared values and priorities characteristic of a host organization's culture. They might mention the corporate need to reduce costs by cutting firm real estate holdings, for example, or the need to forge closer relations with customers, or a desire to support the development of firm knowledge. These criteria may justify a telecommuting initiative and they can be used to define and constrain the overall cultural context wherein the telecommuting initiative is actually implemented.

A corporate decision to embark on a telecommuting initiative is a significant change for a host culture for it divides the organization into those who will work inside and those who will work outside. This split establishes a clear distinction around which new status assessments and emphases on specific cultural dimensions may develop. The importance of the units who telecommute will be interpreted in terms of their relation to organizational priorities and operations, the way in-house and telecommuting individuals are treated, the career opportunities that are opened or closed, and so on. In this way, telecommuting initiatives may come to be regarded as either new opportunities or changes that most employees try to avoid.

The culture that develops among teleworkers reflects overall firm objectives in assigning telecommuting work. If the organization is focused exclusively on cost reduction, for example, the telecommuting assignments may involve routine work and technology may be used simply to send and return assignments. In such an organization, those who work inside corporate facilities are likely to feel they have the preferred status and those working outside are likely to feel they have been transformed into a source of cheap, out-sourced labor. In contrast, if an organization makes telecommuting assignments with the intent of developing the firm's human capital faster, telecommuters may be seen to be among the firm's privileged who enjoy a preferred status and use technology in new and creative ways.

Depending on the overall objectives in making telecommuting assignments, individual teleworker reactions and interpretations can be expected to vary and generate different types of telework culture. As a teleworker interprets the new arrangements as simply a cost-reduction tool, they are likely to see the firm approach as isolating, alienating, exploitative and devoid of human sensitivity. Extrinsic rewards, i.e. financial incentives, may be the only justification for doing such work and such rewards are also not likely to do much in terms of building a positive teleworking culture. On the other hand, as teleworkers anticipate and enjoy the relative independence and flexibility associated with their telecommuting role, they may feel positively empowered and intrinsically motivated by the new work arrangements and develop unique cultures supportive of their work activities.

# CONTRASTS BETWEEN ORGANIZATION AND TELECOMMUTING CULTURES

The *ground* on which a host organization culture is built includes specified locations, determined tasks and bounded social units. One can see and identify such units and use structures and dimensions to describe such social and physical spaces. In contrast, the *ground* on which telework culture is built centers on individuals with computers working intensively on assigned tasks. Relative to the ground where host organization cultures are built, the ground on which a telework culture develops is less visible and also more work-oriented.

The *figure* on which host organization cultures focus includes the values, norms, behavior and symbols that establish and confirm enduring meaning, stable relations, and a shared identity for organization members who enjoy regular face-to-face interactions. The *figure* on which telework cultures focus includes the values, norms, behaviors and symbols associated with ongoing computer work performance. Depending on whether the host organization defines work performance for the telecommuting assignment in narrow or broad ways, so telecommuting cultures differ. Teleworking cultures are necessarily spurred by the work to be done, and then mediated by the individual needs and dispositions of teleworkers to the extent that they also interact with the interlinked diversity that is found on the Internet. Cultures develop to guide and assess task evolution, to determine what is inappropriate behavior, and to help interpret the meaning of telework interactions as different perspectives become juxtaposed with one another.

These contrasts in *ground* and *figure* suggest how host organizational cultures relate to and also differ from telework cultures. Host organization cultures are physically identifiable and socially based and much of the management-related literature emphasizes stable dimensions and meanings that are associated with such units and provide a basis for an enduring organizational identity (Albert and Whetten, 1985). Telework cultures may be constrained or provoked depending on how the host organization culture interprets and supports the telecommuting possibilities. While management cultures tend to highlight shared understandings of social contexts and social controls, telework cultures focus on task interpretations and assessment. Such interpretations and insights are both determined and also vary with the task domain.

A host organization's objectives in implementing telecommuting along with the nature of the work are critical in determining the telework culture that develops. We would conjecture that if firms assign telecommuters only routine tasks with the objective of reducing overall firm costs they will have great difficulty implementing a supportive and involving telework culture. This is despite the fact that top management under pressure to meet financial performance targets may see the telework option as appealing. For unless employees have other important life interests beyond the workplace that telecommuting helps them attend to, e.g. spending more time with their children, we believe employees will resist such assignments and management will also not trust telecommuters to do such tasks. As we believe a telecommuting approach is not a reliable or effective way to do routine work, we will not explore this idea

further. Instead, we will examine the telecommuting culture that develops as organizations seek to promote, support and develop their teleworkers' intellectual capital.

## TELEWORKING CULTURE AS A PROCESS TO HARNESS INTELLECTUAL CAPITAL

New information technologies are a big boon to those engaged in intellectual work.
This includes just about anyone who is engaged in work that has implications for
organizational strategy and planning. This includes a rapidly growing employee population within the American corporate workforce. New information technologies make it
possible for these employees to work at a distance from other intellectual workers as
virtually together they grapple with strategic issues.

Lacking the same degree of physical contacts as co-located workers, such teleworkers are likely to rely on e-mail to communicate with one another. In these situations,
the overall emerging network content reflects a combination of individual user initiatives acting in conjunction with the innumerable other links and interaction possibilities
characteristic of virtual communication. How should one conceptualize culture in such
communities where communication is mediated primarily by exchanges around specific tasks using electronic means rather than face-to-face communication? A useful
starting point may be McLuhan's insight that the medium is the message (McLuhan
and Fiore, 1967). E-mail is dynamic in the sense of requiring high user involvement and
interaction to be an effective tool. Within an e-mail context, culture necessarily
emerges as an evolving process that is both input and output for teleworkers' activities.
While the digital content of the process is indeterminate, the content is continually
being influenced but never controlled by individual teleworkers as through their interaction it evolves and changes.

In this view, teleworkers' values, norms and beliefs are continually emerging
through a constant process of negotiation among the members of e-mail networks.
The composition of this network is individually based, always open and potentially
changing. As a result, task boundaries also tend to become porous and evolving.
Culture becomes dynamic and represents the partial and temporary set of agreements
teleworkers have reached concerning a network's current values, norms and beliefs. It
offers a common ground to foster interactions amongst the various distributed agents
involved in task work. Culture becomes the input, the ongoing medium and also the
outcome of the interactions. Culture is continually being negotiated and continually
evolving in telework environments. McLuhan's quote, ''To define is to kill, to suggest
is to create'', seems a good way to describe the process (quote from Stéphane Malarmé
as reported in Levinson, 1999, p. 28).

Several facets of e-mail and related mediums used to connect participants drive
culture as a process. One facet is ease of use. It takes little effort to turn on a computer
and send an e-mail and there is no need to be physically and temporally co-located with
others. Electronic and phone messages await teleworkers, a facet that renders telework
a phenomenon that allows employees to be truly distributed over time and space. It also
makes it easy to add members to a working group. All it takes is that the person's name

is added to a mailing list. This facet generates several outcomes that affect teleworking cultures, i.e. there is both an acceptance and also an expectation of fluid memberships along with porous and evolving network boundaries.

Fluid membership comes about because of the ease and frequency with which members can be added to or deleted from groups. Porous boundaries are a corollary to fluid membership. Boundaries are porous because members may join and also leave a network group after they have made their contributions. Moreover, at any point in time, teleworkers may in fact be members of several groups (Lucas and Garud, 2000). Consequently, teleworkers' experiences from one work group impact processes in other groups. In this way, porous boundaries imply mutual influence patterns by social and economic agents who as individuals may link two or more evolving groups together. Rather than using the term ''boundaries'' to explore processes associated with groups that conduct task business using e-mail and the web, it may make more sense to think of persons as being either relatively close to or distant from the center of a dynamic network of relationships. Further, what is ''the center'' is continually redefined in each group (Starbuck, 1976). The same individuals may be at the center in some aspects of task development and on the periphery so far as others are concerned. Such a perspective further drives us to think of culture as an evolving process reflecting individual influence efforts that are differentiated around particular task activities. Culture emerges as a result of a task process where conventional organizational boundaries no longer have to exist.

Another property of the e-mail medium of exchange is that it generates content in its very use. Specifically, as teleworkers exchange e-mail, more information of their interactions and of their relationships is generated in the record that remains. This information is accessible and retrievable thereby leading to an ever-expanding base of information accessible to network members about their interactions with one another. The e-mail record becomes a trace of evolving understandings that have led to the developing culture.

Expanding information content along with fluid membership and porous boundaries impact culture as a process. To appreciate this, let us examine a routine exchange of information between members of a traditional group that are now teleworking. The output of such exchanges is information that is continually stored and updated. Members of a group have to make sense of this information. They do so by applying their individual interpretive schemes (Dunbar et al., 1996). The result is often different conclusions about the meaning of the same data. Indeed, e-mails trigger sequences of responses as teleworkers attempt to clarify and negotiate the meanings they generate from the expanding data. At some point, most networks agree that they need to develop understandings concerning how to summarize, simplify and clarify the understandings they have accumulated and these negotiated beliefs and norms become important aspects of teleworking cultures.

In sum, teleworkers embark upon continual exchanges of information through e-mail. As the numbers of people involved grows along with the intensity of the activity as reflected in the number of e-mails and as the discussion also broadens due to a lack of boundaries, the whole process can become overwhelming. Norms of interaction emerge that are designed to maintain work focus and control overload as this develops between teleworkers. These norms may include rules for how and when to respond to e-mails, the topics that it is legitimate to raise in a particular group, membership issues, the use of signals to communicate message urgency, and the like. They may also include cultural understandings as to when e-mail use is appropriate and when other media are required such as the phone, fax, and face-to-face meetings in order to clarify, coordinate and exchange sensitive and strategic information.

Even as norms facilitating interaction emerge amongst a group of teleworkers with different interpretive schemes, there is still no possibility that a stable cultural state will emerge because of the fluid memberships and porous boundaries. Consider what happens when a new member is added to an ongoing e-mail exchange network. On the one hand, the new member has to be brought into the conversation. The new member can achieve this by examining the records and asking questions of clarification. But once this is done, new members will impact the ongoing processes just like established members as they bring their own interpretive schemes into the mix and as their contributions also shape the evolving norms of interaction governing ongoing processes. Indeed, for members of an ongoing group and for its newcomers, differences in interpretive schemes and norms of engagement become all the more salient as they are juxtaposed with one another setting in motion a fresh round of interactions.

New processes are also generated by porous group boundaries. Members of a group may simultaneously be members of other groups with their own processes in place for sense-making and norms for facilitating interactions. After all, the information technologies that make telework possible also make it possible for teleworkers to be members of multiple groups. As groups mesh with one another through teleworkers who take on the roles of boundary spanners, processes in one group begin influencing the processes in another. As what seems to have worked well in one group is tried out in another, so group processes change and new cultural understandings are negotiated and further evolve.

How do collective values shape these fluid processes? Even these values emerge as a result of a continually negotiated process. In traditional work groups, values are often considered to be stable representing implicit or explicit collective aspirations or output goals. Because of its emergent nature, the members of a telework group are often not sure what is going to emerge from their efforts and so they only evolve to an understanding of what is not acceptable to the collective based on what is inviolate at an individual level. Defining such values as a ''noxiant space'' preserves teleworkers' flexibility to evolve in many directions for these communication boundaries suggest only what is unacceptable. As the members of teleworking groups are also members of multiple emerging groups, it is more likely that collective values represent the ''noxiant spaces'' within which each specific group evolves in its own unique way.

This issue is apparent in the way Hatim Tyabji of Verifone governed his virtual enterprise by setting in place processes designed to enrich ethical values and principles (Garud and Lucas, 1999). In defining the stable values of a host organization culture, Tyabji suggested that Verifone would ''create and lead the transaction automation industry worldwide'' and his firm would be close to customers and respond quickly to their needs. To achieve these broad goals, Verifone mobilized many cross-functional teams, many of which had members in different locations relying on e-mail and other means for communication. While team tasks were defined, how they would achieve these tasks was usually not defined and members relied on each other's individual ideas to determine what should be done. Teams posted both progress and problems on corporate networks and as situations arose, sought help from across the company. As other groups had solutions, they were immediately shared. Members of Verifone who had worked at other corporations reported that the response speed that these arrangements made possible often astounded them. But speed also generated tension, misunderstandings and the need for face-to-face interactions to complement e-mail messages as it was felt that these matters could not be resolved by e-mail. To make sure the mutual understandings and trust needed for rapid responses were always in place, Tyabji estimated that a third of Verifone's employees were always on the road having "off-line" meetings and he found that he himself was on the road most of the time (Garud and Lucas, 1999).

In traditional groups, individuals are likely to identify strongly with specific group values. This proposition is implicit in the notion of communities of practice (Brown and Duguid, 1991) and associated constructs such as legitimate peripheral players who eventually gravitate toward the center of a group (Lave and Wenger, 1991). In contrast, in telework groups where employees are quite likely to be members of more than one practice community at the same time, identification processes may become multimodal (Garud and Lant, 1998). By this we mean employees can shift their identification from one group to another depending upon the specific group that they are operating in at any particular time. Notions of evolving work identities replace notions of stable organizational identities. To the extent that their identification lies within the value space that has been negotiated by a teleworking group, an individual is likely to be a strong participant. To the extent that identification lies outside, the value space itself is likely to be something that is currently being negotiated by the group. Persistent mismatches may result in muting the extent to which an individual contributes to a teleworking group.

These observations suggest how and why culture in telework settings is a process that is always in-the-making. People with different interpretive schemes are always negotiating the meanings associated with the information they are exchanging. The norms of interaction between these teleworkers are in a continual state of flux, especially because of the porous boundaries and fluid membership that technology allows. Moreover, teleworkers continually negotiate the value spaces within which they will feel comfortable working and being associated with one another.

With this perspective it is possible to see how teleworkers gravitate towards an integrated, differentiated and individual view of culture that is work-centered rather than organizationally-centered (Martin, 1992). It is important to note that the sense of integration occurs around the processes associated with work cultures in-the-making rather than around the stable content specified by containers such as host organization cultures. Ironically, a view of culture as a stable content, a perspective that was probably appropriate in many organizational settings in the past, will probably impede the possibilities of organizations benefiting from telework where culture as a process allows participants to create and modify their cultures in an emergent way.

# CONCLUSION

Telecommuting assignments represent a decentering of organizations. They make it possible for employees to work any time and anywhere. In comparison to organizational cultures that emphasize stability and center around physical locations to which employees have to travel every day to accomplish their tasks, cultural values, norms and beliefs in teleworking situations emphasize change and continuing negotiation and evolution.

In centered organizations, cultures define what is positively valued. In decentered organizations, the focus is on the work to be done. As it is often less clear how it can best be done, so it is less clear what should be positively valued and so this remains a perpetually open issue. On the other hand, the sorts of behaviors and communications that are to be avoided are often clear within a teleworking group, i.e. what are considered to be "noxiants" by teleworkers. Most often these involve communications that move the focus away from work to be done.

Norms define how organization members are expected to interact. In centered organizations, there is often widespread agreement about the norms of interaction. But as organizations are more decentered, diversity emerges and interaction norms become subject to a continuing negotiation process. Beliefs reflect member interactions with their work tasks, at least for now. As organizations are decentered, so interactions between work tasks can become more locally sensitive but they may also become more idiosyncratic. As organizations emphasize environmental sensitivity, so conflicts between member beliefs, organization norms and even its values may emerge. As a result, organizational culture necessarily becomes an emergent process.

Teleworking culture in-the-making suggests emergent structuration processes and semiotic structures that provisionally define meaning. We think that to better understand culture in teleworking situations, therefore, these approaches to organizational understanding may prove useful. Giddens (1979) uses the term structuration to suggest that there is always a duality in our understandings of technology and strategy, for evolving structures linking the two are both the medium and also the outcome of the actions taken. Extending this observation to telework culture, the values, norms and beliefs that emerge are both the medium and outcomes of the actions taken and the interactions that go on between telework group members.

Similarly, semiotics (Eco, 1979) offers the potential of a finer understanding of how these structurational processes emerge. Specifically, values, norms and beliefs tend to become salient when they are juxtaposed against alternative values, norms and beliefs. The porous boundaries and fluid memberships of most teleworking groups ensure that participants are often placed in a juxtapositional state, thereby ensuring that negotiations continue and structuration processes shape a transitory culture that enables and encourages future interactions.

Melding structuration and semiotics may provide a powerful way to study emerging cultures as processes in telework contexts. In such contexts, it is important to appreciate the fluid and kaleidoscopic nature of group membership that such an approach to work opens up. Group boundaries and memberships can remain fuzzy and usually they also continually evolve. Those who are currently active members influence group cultural evolution by helping shape the work that is pursued. Group culture also retains a memory that includes past evaluations. The past can easily be made present for those using electronic mediums for it provides a record that informates, i.e. creates more information by continuing to use the medium (Zuboff, 1988). In this sense, the past is also not static but also subject to continuing reinterpretation.

As different people with different priorities and perspectives engage with one another, each teleworker interprets the data available in their own way. Different views inevitably arise. As members post and respond to messages, they set in motion a sequence of interpretations, emphases, contrasts and contradictions that serve to make their own positions and those of other members more salient. The process compels teleworkers to articulate what was tacit and desired and to confirm what is not acceptable if they are to respond to evolving concerns. Telework culture is the system of understanding that then evolves.

In bringing together structuration and semiotics one realizes that rapidly evolving teleworking cultures may in fact be very fragile and also fast-moving and they may require new perspectives if they are to be understood. As Gold (1980, pp. 83–84) suggests:

> Cultural evolution has progressed at rates that Darwinian processes cannot begin to approach. Darwinian evolution continues in Homo sapiens, but at rates so slow that it no longer has much impact on our history. This crux in the earth's history has been reached because Lamarckian processes have finally been unleashed. Human cultural evolution, in strong opposition to our biological history, is Lamarckian in character. What we learn in one generation, we transmit directly by teaching and writing. Acquired characteristics are inherited in technology and culture. Lamarckian evolution is rapid and accumulative. It explains the cardinal difference between our past, purely biological mode of change, and our current, maddening *acceleration toward something new and liberating – or toward the abyss*.

(Italics added)

Given such a conceptualization, one can visualize that the crisis of meaning that happened with the cultures associated with old technologies may also happen with the cultures associated with new information technologies. Specifically, teleworking cultures could evolve with such rapidity and momentum that another crisis may develop. Rather than the crisis of alienation and meaninglessness that was created with mass production systems, the new crisis might be one of boundarylessness and burnout emerging as distinctions between work and play are blurred and teleworkers are seduced and succumb to the embrace of an electronic prison.

# ACKNOWLEDGEMENTS

The authors thank Bill Starbuck for his helpful suggestions.

# REFERENCES

Albert, S. and Whetten, D.A. (1985) Organizational identity. In L.L. Cummings and B.M. Staw (Eds), Research in Organizational Behavior, Vol. 7, pp. 263–296. Greenwich, CT: JAI Press.

Brown, J.S. and Duguid, P. (1991) Organizational learning and communities of practice: toward a unified view of working, learning, and innovation. Organization Science, 2(1): 40–57.

Dunbar, R.L.M. and Garud, R. (1998) Best practices in the virtual workplace. Stern Business, Summer: 15–17.

Dunbar, R. and Garud, R. (1999) Value creation through new technologies in financial service firms. In E. Melnick, P. Nayyar, M. Pinedo and S. Seshadri (Eds), Creating Value in Financial Services: Strategies, Operations and Technologies, pp. 289–302. Dordrecht: Kluwer Academic Press.

Dunbar, R.L.M., Garud, R. and Raghuram, S. (1996) Deframing in strategic analyses. Journal of Management Inquiry, 5(1): 23–34.

Eco, U. (1979) A Theory of Semiotics. Bloomington, IN: Indiana University Press.

Garud, R. and Lant, T. (1998) Navigating silicon alley: kaleidoscopic experiences. Working paper, New York University.

Garud, R. and Lucas, H. (1999) Virtual organizations: distributed in time and space. Working paper, New York University.

Giddens, A. (1979) Central Problems in Social Theory. Los Angeles, CA: University of California Press.

Gold, S. (1980) The Panda's Thumb. New York: W.W. Norton.

Hackman, J.R. and Oldham, G.R. (1975) Development of the job diagnostic survey. Journal of Applied Psychology, 60: 159–170.

Hedberg, B., Dahlgren, G., Hansson, J. and Olve, N.-G. (1977) Virtual Organizations and Beyond: Discover Imaginary Systems. Chichester, Wiley.

Hofstede, G., Neuijen, B., Ohayv, D.D. and Sanders, G. (1990) Measuring organizational cultures: a qualitative and quantitative study across twenty cases. Administrative Science Quarterly, 35(2): 286–316.

Langton, J. (1984) The ecological theory of bureaucracy: the case of Josiah Wedgwood and the British pottery industry. Administrative Science Quarterly, 29(3): 330–354.

Lave, J. and Wenger, E. (1991) Situated Learning: Legitimate Peripheral Participation. Cambridge: Cambridge University Press.

Levinson, P. (1999) Digital McLuhan. London: Routledge.

Likert, R. (1967) The Human Organization: its Management and Value. New York: McGraw-Hill.

Lohr, S. (1999) Computer age gains respect of economists. New York Times, April 14, Wednesday, Business/Financial Desk.

Lucas, H. and Garud, R. (2000) New organization forms and work groups. In T. Griffith (Ed), Research in Managing Groups and Teams. Greenwich, CT: JAI Press.

Martin, J. (1992) Cultures in Organizations: Three Perspectives. New York: Oxford University Press.

McLuhan, M. and Fiore, Q. (1967) The Medium is the Message: an Inventory of Effects. New York: Bantam Books.

O'Reilly, C. (1989) Corporations, culture, and commitment: motivation and social control in organizations. California Management Review, 31(4): 9–25.

Raghuram, S., Garud, R. and Wiesenfeld, B.M. (1998) Telework: managing distances in a connected world. Journal of Business and Strategy, 10: 7–9.

Raghuram, S., Garud, R. and Wiesenfeld, B.M. (1999) Factors contributing to the success of teleworkers. Working paper, New York University.

Salancik, G. and Pfeffer, J. (1977) Who gets power – and how they hold on to it: a strategic-contingency model of power. Organizational Dynamics, Winter.

Schein, E.H. (1992) Organization Culture and Leadership, 2nd Edn. San Francisco, CA: Jossey-Bass.

Sproull, L. and Kiesler, S. (1991) Connections: New Ways of Working in the Networked Organization. Cambridge, MA: MIT Press.

Starbuck, W.H. (1976) Organizations and their environments. In M.D. Dunnette (Ed), Handbook of Industrial and Organizational Psychology, pp. 1069–1123. Chicago, IL: Rand McNally.

Toffler, A. (1991) The Third Wave. New York: Bantam Books.

Tsoukas, H. (1996) The firm as a distributed knowledge system: a constructionist approach. Strategic Management Journal, 17(Winter Special Issue): 11–25.

Turner, J. (1998) Will telecommuting ever get off the ground? Stern Business, Summer: 18–21.

Watzlawick, P., Weakland, J.H. and Fisch, R. (1974) Change: Principles of Problem Formation and Problem Resolution. New York: W.W. Norton.

Wiesenfeld, B.M., Raghuram, S. and Garud, R. (1999) Managers in a virtual context: the experience of self-threat and its effects on virtual work organizations. In C.L. Cooper and D. Rousseau (Eds). Trends in Organizational Behavior, 6: 31–34.

Wiesenfeld, B.M., Raghuram, S. and Garud, R. (in press) Communication patterns as determinants of organizational identification in a virtual organization. Organization Science.

Zuboff, S. (1988) In the Age of the Smart Machine: the Future of Work and Power. New York: Basic Books.

# Chapter 27

# Organizational Culture and Imaginary Organizations

**Bo Hedberg**[1]
*School of Business, Stockholm University,
Stockholm, Sweden*

*and*

**Christian Maravelias**[1]
*School of Business, Stockholm University,
Stockholm, Sweden*

## IMAGINARY ORGANIZATIONS

"We are not building a company. We are building an industry." (Dr. Pehong Chen, CEO and founder of BroadVision, Calif., commenting on his "extended organization"

In a changing business world, many new enterprises are characterized by partnerships, networks, shared resources and objectives that coordinate many separate actors (Bengtsson et al., 1998; Hamel, 1991; Inkpen and Beamish, 1997; Larsson et al., 1998). In addition, many old companies transform themselves to become more focused,

---

[1] Bo Hedberg is professor of management and Christian Maravelias is a PhD candidate at the School of Business, Stockholm University. Both are members of the research program on "Imaginary Organisations" and have published books and several articles on related subjects. Postal address: School of Business, Stockholm University, S-106 91 Stockholm, Sweden. Tel.: + 46-8-16-1550(vx); fax: + 46-8-15-30-54; e-mail: boh@fek.su.se, chm@fek.su.se, URL: www.fek.su.se/forskn/imorg/.

outsourced, and cooperative. Concepts such as federative organizations and network organizations are sometimes used to describe these new patterns of organizing. The *virtual enterprise* has emerged as a summarizing concept.

The term "virtual organizations" captures the idea of collective value-creation in partnerships. The term is typically used to refer to systems which are inter-linked by advanced information technology (Arnold, 1998; Grenier and Metes, 1995), and it mostly refers to rather temporary constellations (Goldman et al., 1995; Hale and Whitlam, 1997). Although many talk about virtual organizations, few definitions can be found. Zimmermann (1997: 2) tried to describe the reality behind the term:

> The term 'virtual' usually stands for something that is seemingly existing despite the lack of some distinguishing attributes. Thus, for example 'virtual reality' or 'virtual products' do not have any physical structure. They are only existing in computers. For the observer the reality product is 'existing in the mind, especially as a product of imagination' (…). The term 'enterprise' generally associates a bounded and durable object, consisting of people and buildings and basing on a legal framework. Accordingly a virtual enterprise is an enterprise which is lacking some structural characteristics of real enterprises, but nevertheless functions like an enterprise in the imagination of the observer.

This chapter explores the role of organizational culture in virtual enterprises, henceforth referred to as *imaginary organizations.* Imaginary organizations are systems where networking partners coordinate their activities through shared missions and visions, and by means of platforms of information technology, trustful relationships, and gain-gain economies. Although imaginary organizations mostly consist of a number of independent legal units, they behave as *one* organization and they *exist and are manifested in the imagination of their leaders.* (Cf. Zimmermann, above). Imaginary organizations are typically formed in situations where markets are turbulent, requirements on production are changing, and where resource combinations must be very flexible. They strive to be client-driven. They establish cultures of sharing between partners. They are typically knowledge-intensive, and they exploit the great opportunities of the relationship revolution that modern information technology brings about (Hedberg et al., 1997).

> The perspective of the imaginary organization refers to a system in which assets, processes, and actors critical to the 'focal' enterprise exist and function both inside and outside the limits of the enterprise's conventional 'landscape' formed by its legal structure, its accounting, its organigrams, and the language otherwise used to describe the enterprise. (Hedberg et al., 1997 : 13).

# BALANCED-TO-LEARN AND BALANCED-TO-LAST

Our ongoing empirical research (Maravelias, 1999; Hedberg and Holmqvist, 1999) indicates that imaginary organizations rarely are intended to be temporary. On the contrary, they are built-to-last and designed to be flexible enough to adapt to market changes and to reorganize when needs for competencies shift. Market mechanisms between actors and loose couplings between partners provide balances between open-ness and closed-ness, between discretion and control. Imaginary organizations are visibly scattered but functionally integrated. They lack some of the traditional unifiers of the modal enterprise, but they make extensive use of other coherent forces.

A crucial balance in organizational life is that between exploration and exploitation (March, 1999). Successful organizations often become victims of their own success, lose curiosity, and become action generators (Starbuck, 1983). And organizations that explore and experiment run the risk of spending too little attention to their daily operations and necessary standard operation procedures. Thus, designs for sustainable organizations should attempt to balance exploration and exploitation. Networks are good at inviting diversity and at bringing in the environment (Brown and Duguid, 1991; Powell et al., 1996). Hierarchies are good at getting things done, implementing strategies and keeping on track. Our empirical studies (Maravelias, 1999; Holmqvist, 1999; Uggla, 1999; Hedberg and Holmqvist, 1999) suggest that imaginary organiza-tions are promising designs to encourage such balances (Figure 27.1). In recent times we have thus developed our definition above (focusing on blurred boundaries) to focus more on governance and on the balance between exploitation and exploration as the extended organization develops and matures. In doing so, we discover that it is rather our definition of *organizations* that is problematic. If we widen that concept to include *organizing where several organizations are involved*(the extended enterprise) the need for the epithet *imaginary*would be reduced. Thus:

> "(Imaginary) organizations are cooperative enterprises that attempt to balance exploitation and exploration through combinations of systems for vertical inte-gration with processes for interorganizational collaboration. A core unit assumes leadership through the elaboration of shared visions and elements of communal culture. Although information technology mostly serves as an important enabler, the social texture of trust-building processes, interdependencies and synergies, mutual respect and learning, together with transparent exchange mechanisms are what makes these loosely-coupled networks organizations." (Hedberg et al, 2000)

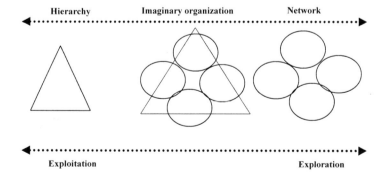

**Figure 27.1**  Balancing exploration and exploitation in imaginary organisations.

Organizations rely on a number of platforms in order to keep together (Figure 27.2). The *organizational structure* is one. In the traditional enterprise the structure mostly corresponds to the legal unit(s). In the imaginary organization, a number of companies, agents, and individual actors constitute the extended enterprise. The traditional industrial organization was held together through a strong *infrastructure of physical assets*; machinery, premises, flows of material, etc. The imaginary organization typically lacks these integrating structures. Instead, partners share infrastructure, outsource and insource, and often have very marginal tangible assets in their balance sheets. Intellectual capital (Edvinson and Malone, 1997), knowledgeware, and customer bases for CRM activities are new entries into these extended accountings.

All modern enterprises become increasingly dependent on *information technology*, and most imaginary organizations are highly reliant upon their IT networks, be they intranets or internet. The final integrating platform consists of the *organizational culture*. Every enterprise has some form of more or less coherent and explicit culture, but organizational culture *and cultures* play a very special role in enabling both homogeneity and heterogeneity in the imaginary organization, as we shall argue in this chapter. One reason is that some of the other integrating platforms, especially the physical infrastructure and the unified organizational structure, are lacking. However, this does not mean that imaginary organizations share one homogenous culture. In fact, the various subsystems have their subcultures, and cultural variety is an important requisite for learning and cross-fertilizing. The successful imaginary organization must manage to balance cultural variety and the sharing of culture so that a sufficient degree of control is maintained at the same time as requisite variety remains.

## SKANDIA AFS – A CASE IN QUESTION

Skandia AFS (Assurance and Financial Services) is a group of companies within the leading Swedish-based insurance company, Skandia AB. While the parent company was a fairly conventional insurance company until the early nineties, AFS is a highly

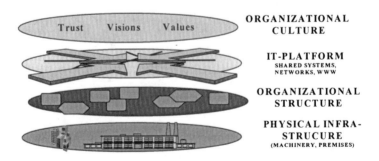

ORGANIZATIONAL
CULTURE

IT-PLATFORM
SHARED SYSTEMS,
NETWORKS, WWW

ORGANIZATIONAL
STRUCTURE

PHYSICAL INFRA-
STRUCURE
(MACHINERY, PREMISES)

**Figure 27.2**  Integrating platforms for the enterprise.

successful, rapidly growing, and very interesting imaginary organization which in less than ten years totally has redefined the Skandia Group. Skandia AFS now operates in twenty-nine countries on four continents outside Scandinavia. Ninety-five people make up the headquarters, and they are mainly located in Sweden and in Shelton, Conn., USA. An additional 3500 Skandia employees run the national companies. And these people engage around 105,000 partners in the various countries where AFS has established markets. The partners are money managers and financial advisers in the U.S. They other titles in other countries, and each national solution is slightly different. In Spain, for example, a savings bank (Intercaser) is integrated in the extended organization. Finally, some 1,7 million customers, or "contracts", form the outer circle of the imaginary organization, Skandia AFS.

Skandia AFS prospers from the growing concern of people in many countries that retirement systems and other welfare arrangements are endangered and may not deliver what they once promised. Therefore, families and individuals are increasing their savings, and Skandia is able to collect a portion of these savings and to place them with fund managers who promise to beat inflation. In short, Skandia AFS is a global savings organization with unit-link arrangements to tie those private savings to growth investments. (Figure 27.3).

Skandia AFS is an imaginary organization. The extended enterprise thus involves about 109.000 people of whom around 3600 are Skandia employees. Both sales and investments, most service delivery systems, and considerable parts of systems development and the provision of legal and tax expertise are handled by cooperating partners who *resource* the imaginary organization. Skandia AFS provides the overall leadership and couples or uncouples links within the network.

AFS defines its core competence as being "specialist in cooperation". In addition AFS provides the focal processes (product development, packaging, and administra-

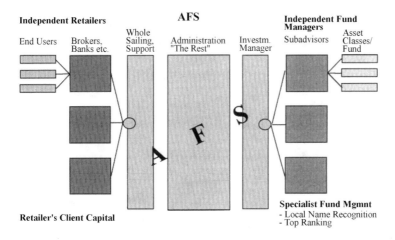

**Figure 27.3** Skandia AFS – a mediator between two global markets (AFS presentation material: with permission from the company).

tion) that interface with those of the fund managers and that support the activities of the financial advisers. Skandia thus focuses on the development and packaging of financial products and provides the infrastructure and the administrative backbone. Partners sell and distribute the products, and other partners invest the money and manage the resulting funds. The AFS concept is highly dependent on the ability of executives in the core organization to create, manage, and distribute knowledge throughout the imaginary organization. The company operates between a global market for savings and a global market for investments. The core-company acts as an exchange system between these two markets, as shown in Figure 27.3, above. Partners interact directly with clients (households) and present investment opportunities.

Information technology is a very important coordinator both within the inner system and the outer system of the AFS network. The national companies in twenty-seven countries are connected through a global area network (GAN) and intranets that facilitate both remote management and remote administration. A global management information system is another way to keep the world-wide organization together. The IT infrastructure also allows existing national companies to provide, e.g. back-office support for newly established subsidiaries. Thus, the back-office systems for the pioneer companies in Mexico and in Japan was initially run and managed from American Skandia in Connecticut.

AFS' CEO Jan Carendi says that in order to lead the imaginary organization he has to realize that he is managing a *voluntary organization*. His major task is to formulate a challenging vision, fast feedback on performance, and establish a "high-trust culture". Everyone in this organization should to be a "trustee" who deserves the trust of others and who trusts his/her collaborators. Trust is needed in order to glue the organization together. Trust is also a prerequisite for free flows of knowledge exchange. And knowledge-creation and dissemination of knowledge within the network is a primary strategy behind Skandia's rapid growth and proven ability to keep the partnership together.

The CEO spends a lot of time at the head offices or touring the world to the national companies in building interpersonal relationships. This process of establishing affective trust begins already in the very elaborate recruiting procedures where the CEO very often takes part. In a series of white papers, normally published in the company magazine New Horizons, Carendi attempts to build a boundary spanning business culture, create internal heroes, and underpin cognitive trust and trust that builds on performance. Several of these trust-building processes address both the inside and the outside world of AFS.

# THE ROLE OF CULTURE IN IMAGINARY ORGANIZATIONS

Although most of us have an intuitive understanding of the concept of organizational culture, few have succeeded in formulating a covering definition thereof. Thus, we mostly settle for fragments, which express the existence of culture, such as a common language, behavioral regularities, shared values, habits of thinking and acting, etc. Common to all of these expressions is the idea that culture is something which is shared or held in common within a certain social field (cf. Schein, 1992; Smirchic, 1983; Alvesson, 1993). Moreover, culture is taken to imply some level of structural stability within a social field. Culture is what prevails; it resists change and facilitates social integration because it lets individuals hold certain expectations about other people's behavior. Alvesson (1993) lists a number of metaphors for culture, such as "culture as blinders", "culture as world-closure", and "culture as dramaturgical domination".

We will use Schein's definition of culture (Schein, 1992: p. 12), as our point of departure:

> Culture is "a pattern of shared basic assumptions that the group learned as it solved its problems of external adaptation and internal integration, that has worked well enough to be considered valid and, therefore, to be taught to new members as the correct way to perceive, think, and feel in relation to those problems".

This definition describes culture as a social system with structural properties, which is functionally related to the environment. Culture appears as some form of social group, which is internally coordinated and to some extent adapted to its environment via a system of normative behavioral expectations. The culture of a social group is what distinguishes insiders from outsiders. Membership is based on the extent to which you conform to what is expected, and ultimately accepted, behavior of a member of certain social group (Luhmann, 1995).

How does the concept of culture differ when it is applied in an *organizational context?*We will assume that the formal nature of organizations is what distinguishes organizational cultures from cultures pertaining to cooperative groups in general. The formality of organizational structures and the principle of authority, which is implied, put constraints on membership roles and the behavior in organizations. Members must to some extent subordinate their personal beliefs, commitments, and wishes to organizational goals in order to be a member of an organization. And they must accept authority as the fundamental coordinating principle. This puts individual organizational members under particular pressure. It drives them to conform to the specific norms and expectations that relate to the role they play in the organization. They know that there are certain basic expectations they need to fulfil in order to remain as members of the organization. Hence, individual members *become aware* of the cultural traits that define the identity of the organization and that specify the criteria's of entrance and exit. In other words, organizational culture does not simply remain an implicit force that partly determines and coordinates individual behavior; it becomes a focused 'variable' that is taken into account when members construct their actions.

> Consequently, the principle of authority, which underlies organizational governance, functions as a homogenizing force. Leader's exercise of authority, e.g. specification of goals, allocation of scarce resources and rewards, promotion, etc. makes organizational members aware of the norms and values that underlies organizational behavior. It drives them to conform to the culture of the organization, which thereby tend to become more homogeneous and distinctly separated from the organization's environment (c.f. Katz and Kahn, 1978).

Many writers have argued that a strong corporate culture has a positive impact on organizational performance (c.f. Deal and Kennedy, 1982; Peters and Waterman, 1982). It has also been noted, however, that the character of an organization's culture is closely related to its abilities to manage environmental change (c.f. Alvesson, 1993). A distinct and strong culture helps to constitute an organization as a tightly-coupled system and might improve its capability to handle specific environmental circumstances. Yet, for the same reasons, its capabilities to adapt to changing environments might be hampered. These ideas are similar to Weick's (1976) proposition that adaptation and adaptability often are at odds with each other. Tight coupling (distinct cultures) tends to improve adaptation, while loose coupling (heterogeneous cultures with higher tolerance for ambiguity) tends to improve adaptability.

Hence, in turbulent environments where the requirements on production are changing and where resource combinations must be flexible, i.e. when adaptability rather than adaptation should be the focused term, a distinct organizational culture might become a paralyzing force.

How does the concept of culture differ when it is applied to the context of imaginary organizations? The participants within the imaginary organization depend on knowledgeable, skilled, and resourceful actors both outside and inside their formal domains. Each actor must continuously seek to maintain his position ("process edge" in Skandia AFS terms) as a vital partner within the alliance. In contrast to traditional – formally integrated – organizations, which risk substituting long term adaptability for short-term adaptation, participants of an imaginary organization are continuously reminded of the need for adaptability.

In the business networks that we have studied, partners are not only suppliers or customers, they are providers of expertise both in joint development projects and in ongoing activities. In this respect they are continuously involved in decisions of strategic importance. In comparison to traditional organizations, it is hard to find one definite center of an imaginary organization. On the one hand there are a number of small centers, one in each legal unit. Yet, on the other hand, since many strategic activities, such as product and service development, involve symmetrical contributions from several legal units, centers tend to emerge at the boarders between the legal units. In this way the authority of a traditional centralized group decreases while the authority (and discretion) of those actors who handle transactions that occur between the partner firms increases. In addition, actors are sometimes engaged in several networks. They co-operate in some and compete with each other in others.

These typical characteristics of imaginary organizations have significant implications for the role of organizational culture. *Firstly*, each separate organization within the imaginary organization will become less hierarchical. *Secondly*, it is difficult to distinguish between external adaptation and internal integration. Individual members develop loyalties, which pertain to the formal organization as well as to joint projects with partners. Hence, loyalties in imaginary organizations are fragmented. *Thirdly*, non-hierarchical structures and fragmented loyalties give rise to continuous reframing of participants' world views. The result of these three factors is that imaginary organizations build sources of conflicts and ambiguity (variety) into the structure of their interorganizational operations, but also they contain the potential for unlearning and adaptability.

The combination of symmetrical distribution of information and influencing powers and a balance between interdependence and autonomy and partly conflicting interests incite participants in imaginary organizations to form collegiums (c.f. Thompson, 1967) which make collective judgements (Thompson and Tuden, 1959). Moreover, imaginary organizations preserve moderate levels of dissent, partly as a result of conflicting views of means and ends relationships, keeps them in a state of 'unified cultural diversity'. In short: IO-cultures are semi-confusing cultures (Hedberg and Jönsson, 1978). The homogenizing forces, which are typical for traditional organizations, are counteracted by the multitude of nodes and centers in imaginary organizations. They become apt to handle turbulent environments. In line with Ashby's (1960) principle of "requisite variety" we have found that the semi-confusing cultures of imaginary organizations often offset traditional organizations tendency to reduce internal variety to a level that makes them incapable of adapting to the level of variety in the environment.

*Hedging against loss of control – the need for trust.* So far we have characterized Imaginary organizations as loosely coupled systems (cf. Weick, 1976, 1982). This means that they are neither tightly coupled, nor de-coupled. This loose coupling can keep the participants of the imaginary organization in a state of 'constructive confusion' that can facilitate adaptability. Yet, this characterization only points towards the potential positive advantages of loose coupling.

The lack of a legally sanctioned central authority, together with demand for high levels of expertise, imply that imaginary organizations repeatedly face the risk of losing control. Individual actors need to accept and manage high degrees of discretion and ambiguity, since authority is split between different legal units, and strategy formulation often occur at the boundaries between these different legal units. The leaders of an imaginary organization have limited ability to exercise direct control, since actors outside their official domains of authority handle strategic activities. These actors also often have such high levels of expertise and discretion that it is difficult for any leader to specify how matters shall be performed. The inability within imaginary organizations to build and maintain control through traditional bureaucratic and market principles (authority and price) creates a special need for trust in the overarching loyalty and expertise of its members. Trust becomes a substitute for explicit control mechanisms. This enables activities, which with low levels of trust would be perceived as too risky to pursue.

Hence, the role of organizational culture differs in some significant respects from organizational cultures. Acceptance of authority (and thus hierarchy of command) is institutionalized in traditional organizations and it constitutes the most fundamental and generic criterion for membership. Imaginary organizations, in contrast, need to establish trust, mutuality, and maintenance of complementary expertise. They also need to strike balances between interdependence and autonomy and between collective responsibility and self-interest.

*Predictable informality.* The importance of trust in imaginary organizations generates a need for individual members who are capable to win trust and to bestow trust.

Our studies have indicated that winning as well as bestowing trust is closely related to individual member's abilities to establish and maintain intimate relations that contribute to an informal professional climate (Holmqvist and Maravelias, 1998; Maravelias, 1999). In line with other studies on the underlying conditions of trust (Giddens, 1991; Luhmann, 1979), we have found that actors must be able to replace standardized – impersonal – expectations with such expectations that only he can guarantee to fulfil, if he is to prove worthy of the risk implied when trusting him. In order to win trust he must be able to establish and maintain a distinct professional identity, which is associated with him exclusively. Hence, an actor who does not 'dare to stick his chin out', will not be seen as an individual with a specific professional identity. He might rather become a predictable factor in the machinery. Yet he will not be trusted, because he will be perceived to conceal his personal opinions and commitments.

In this way imaginary organizations differ from classical conceptions of desired individual behavior in organizations. In Weber's view (1947) of the rational-legal bureaucracy, appropriate professional behavior was typically impersonal in that it followed the rules associated with each specific role in the organization. The personality of an organization member was best left at home. In imaginary organizations, however, where individual members – who might be members of different legal units – operate with high levels of discretion, coordination cannot be based on a line up and enforcement of explicit rules. Instead it must be based on trustful relations, which have been established gradually via individuals who are capable of proving not only their expertise but also their loyalty by acting in a manner which is best described as personal.

Imaginary organizations will at first glance appear as highly informal. However, there is a formality to this informality. Informal behavior, which builds trust among colleagues and partners, and which thus is to a degree predictable, is the real criterion for membership.

*Leaders as script-writers and directors of the play.* Imaginary organizations with loosely-coupled systems call for a type of leadership that departs significantly from classical bureaucratic principles. Since no singular organization within the imaginary organization can claim to have an official right to rule, the question of who is in charge typically remains ambiguous. The distribution of power in these decision-making processes varies with regards to the particular issue at hand and the different lines of expertise of the different participants.

Although strategic decision making processes are executed without an official central authority unit, our studies have shown that a special leading role often develops, which in most cases is adopted by one of the participating organizations. The unit which plays this role does not exercise authority in any direct sense. Rather, it functions as a form of 'script writer' that helps to set the stage for the others. It does so by continuously offering interpretations of the environmental conditions surrounding the imaginary organization, its internal characteristics including its strengths and weaknesses and distribution of roles, and in that connection, the strategic mission as well as fundamental values that needs to be shared by its participants.

The need for such a role goes back to the significance of maintaining mutual trust in Imaginary organizations. The formation and effective operation of collegiums, which transcend the formal boundaries of the separate legal units, presupposes that the participants find reason to trust each other's long term commitments. Since the multitudes of centers within an imaginary organization and the turbulent environments in which they operate give rise to ambiguity and shifting understanding of the joint situation, there is a constant risk that the cognitive frames and underlying values of the participants develop in different directions and become so dissimilar that mutual trust is undermined. The leading role as 'script writer' seeks to compensate for this risk by clarifying the underlying values of the imaginary organization and by conceptualizing – albeit on a general level – a joint situation in which each participant has a satisfactory role to play. The leader not only writes part of the script. He directs the play as well.

Hence, the organization which adopts this leading role articulates the intellectual platform of the imaginary organization and seeks to balance the sources of variety that are introduced in the form of uncertainties and ambiguities both by the environment of the imaginary organization and by its internal operation.

These observations have led us to conclude that leadership within imaginary organizations appears in a more subtle and indirect form as compared to traditional organizations; as a form of 'authoring' organizational texts rather than as exercising authority.

# SETTINGS WHERE IMAGINARY ORGANIZATIONS ARE LIKELY, OR LESS LIKELY, TO DEVELOP

Two major conditions appear to encourage the development of imaginary organizations.

One is uncertainty, or volatility, in the environment. When fashions change overnight, and many fashions co-exist simultaneously, garment manufacturers have to be very flexible and rapid to hit the market with their products. They focus on branding and logistics, and stay away from owning factories. Other conditions are lack of time, lack of people, lack of expertise, or lack of financial resources to support rapid organizational growth. The rapidly growing Skandia AFS lacked both time and the resources to build its on brand, or to organize its own sales forces, as the company entered twenty-nine new countries around the world in less than a decade. Oftentimes both uncertainty, need for flexibility, and lack of time and resources go together to drive the development of imaginary organizations. A final reason is sometimes also at hand. Since imaginary organizations differ substantially from traditional enterprises, their managers might find it difficult to persuade bankers to provide the necessary financial capital for growth. And when they fail to mobilize this traditional support, they bypass the bankers and proceed even further into imaginary organizing. When they cannot borrow money to build a factory, they partner with someone who owns a factory. When they hesitate to put new people on their payrolls, they line up with someone who already has many employees, or they cooperate with people who are self-employed.

Thompson (1967) distinguished between three modal types of core technologies in organizations: (1) sequential technologies (2) mediating technologies, and (3) intensive technologies. It appears from our research data that imaginary organizations are more common among the latter two categories. The role as mediator goes very well with imaginary organizing. The manager of intensive technologies builds a value constellation (Normann and Ramirez, 1993) around the client. Companies with sequential technologies tend to integrate upstream or downstream, and thus are less likely to develop imaginary organizations.

When futures can be predicted, when markets change rather slowly, when time and resources are sufficient for business development, and when economies of scale are more important than economies of reach (building relationships with a customer base), there is still a strong case to be made for traditional organizing.

## THE FUTURE OF IMAGINARY ORGANIZATIONS AND THE ROLE OF CULTURE(S) MANAGEMENT

Although the rate of change in our society is often exaggerated, there is every reason to believe that the need for flexibility and learning will increase in most organizations. To balance variety against the danger of losing control, and to shorten time-to-market and time-to-learn will be crucial success factors. Thus, to perceive and manage not only markets-as-networks but also organizations-as-networks will be increasingly important. We have found no instance so far where the traditional legal and institutional mechanisms for integrating strategic alliances have been able to apply and extend to more complex networks of interacting processes among interacting organizations. Instead, the *management of trust, respect, mutual performance, and transparency of exchange mechanisms*come across as crucial elements of the system which keeps imaginary organizations alive and growing while still maintaining some of these properties which constitute an extended organization and avoiding other mechanisms which often breed complacency and organizational inertia (Figure 27.4).

In order to be successful, leaders of imaginary organizations need to foster new relationships and mechanisms for interaction, distribution, and sharing which are capable of building firmness on relatively loose grounds, trust with few guarantees, culture out of diversity, and future where little or no common history exists. Fairness in

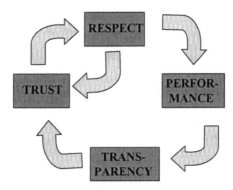

**Figure 27.4**  At the heart of the imaginary organisation – culture and leadership.

all human interaction is important. Trust comes from respect and trust breeds respect. Performance consolidates working relationships, but only in gain-gain situations and where transparency is so high that every actors can see that he gets his fair share, so that new levels of trust are established, etc. Imaginary organizations rely heavily on managers' abilities to build and manage such organizational cultures.

# REFERENCES

Alvesson, M. (1993) Cultural Perspectives on Organisations. Cambridge, MA: Cambridge University Press.

Arnold, O.(1998-03-06), Untitled, http://www.teco.uni-karlsruhe.de/ITVISION/

Ashby, W.R. (1960) An Introduction to Cybernetics. London: Chapman and Hall.

Bengtsson, L., Holmqvist, M. and Larsson, R. (1998) Strategiska allianser. Från marknadsmisslyckande till lärande samarbete, (In English: Strategic Alliances. From Market Failure to Learning Co-operation). Malmö, Sweden: Liber.

Brown, J.S. and Duguid, P. (1991) Organisational learning and communities of practice: toward a unified view of working, learning, and innovation. Organisation Science, 2 (1): 40–57.

Deal, T.E. and Kennedy, A.A. (1982) Corporate Cultures. Reading, MA: Addison-Wesley.

Edvinson, L. and Malone, T.W. (1997) Intellectual Capital, Harper Business.

Giddens, A. (1991) Modernity and Self Identity. Polity Press.

Goldman, S.L., Nagel, R.N. and Preiss, K. (1995) Agile Competitors and Virtual Organisations. New York: Van Nostrand Reinhold.

Grenier, R. and Metes, G. (1995) Going Virtual. Moving your Organisation into the 21st Century. Englewood Cliffs, NJ: Prentice Hall.

Hale, R. and Whitlam, P. (1997) Towards the Virtual Organisation. London: McGraw-Hill.

Hamel, G. (1991) Competition for competence and interpartner learning within international strategic alliances. Strategic Management Journal, 12: 83–103.

Hedberg, B., Baumard, P. and Yakhlef, A. (Eds) (in press) Imaginary Organising. Creative Management of Economic Realities. Elsevier, Amsterdam.

Hedberg, B., Dahlgren, G., Hansson, J. and Olve, N.G. (1997) Virtual Organisations and Beyond. Discover Imaginary Systems. London: Wiley.

Hedberg, B. and Holmqvist, M. (1999) Learning in virtual organisations. In M. Dierkes and I. Nonaka (Eds), Handbook of Organisational Learning. London: Oxford University Press.

Hedberg, B. and Jönsson, S. (1978) Designing semi-confusing information systems for organisations in changing environments. Accounting, Organisations and Society, 3: 47–64.

Holmqvist, M. (1999) Learning in imaginary organisations: creating interorganisational knowledge. Journal of Organisational Change Management, (5): 419–438.

Holmqvist, M. and Maravelias, C. (1998) Imaginary Organisations: Effective Partner Interactions Through Strategic Use Of Trust, Paper Presented at Beyond Convergence, 12th Biennial Conference, Stockholm, June 21–24, 1998.

Inkpen, A.C. and Beamish, P.W. (1997) Knowledge, bargaining power, and the instability of international joint ventures. Academy of Management Review, 22 (1): 177–202.

Katz, D. and Kahn, R.L. (1978) The Social Psychology of Organisations. New York: Wiley.

Larsson, R., Bengtsson, L., Henriksson, K. and Sparks, J. (1998) The interorganisational learning dilemma: collective knowledge development in strategic alliances. Organisation Science, 9 (3) 285–305.

Luhmann, N. (1979) Trust and Power. New York: Wiley.

Luhmann, N. (1995) Funktionen und Folgen formaler Organisation. Berlin: Vierte Auflage, Duncker and Humblot.

Maravelias, C. (1999) Trust-based-control, the example of skandia AFS. In B. Hedberg, P. Baumard and A. Yakhlef (Eds), Imaginary Organising. Creative Management of Economic Realities.

March, J.G. (1999) The Pursuit of Organisational Intelligence, Chapter 7: Exploration and Exploitation in Organisational Learning, pp. 114–136. Malden, MA: Blackwell Business.

Normann, R. and Ramirez, R. (1993) From value chain to value constellation: designing interactive strategy, Harward Business Review, 72, July–August, pp. 65–77.

Peters, T. and Waterman, R.H. (1982) In Search of Excellence. New York: Harper and Row.

Powell, W.W., Koput, K.W. and Smith-Doerr, L. (1996) Interorganisational collaboration and the locus of innovation: networks of learning in biotechnology. Administrative Science Quarterly, 41: 116–145.

Schein, E.H. (1992) Organisational Culture and Leadership. San Francisco, CA: Jossey Bass.

Smirchic, L. (1983) Concepts of culture and organisational analysis. Administrative Science Quarterly, 28: 339–358.

Starbuck, W.H. (1983) Organisations as action generators. American Sociological Review, 48: 91–102.

Thompson, J.D. (1967) Organisations in Action. New York: McGraw-Hill.

Thompson, J.D. and Tuden, A. (1959) Strategies, structures, and processes of organisational decisions. In J.D. Thompson et al. (Eds), Comparative Studies in Administration. Pittsburgh, PA: University of Pittsburgh Press.

Uggla, H. (1999) Managing bases of brand associations in the imaginary organisation. In B. Hedberg, P. Baumard and A. Yakhlef (Eds), Imaginary Organising. Creative Management of Economic Realities.

Weber, M. (1947) The Theory of Social and Economic Organisation. London: Oxford University Press.

Weick, K.E. (1976) Educational organisations as loosely coupled systems. Administrative Science Quarterly, 21: 1–19.

Weick, K.E. (1982) Management of organisational change among loosely coupled elements. In P.E. Goodman, et al (Eds), Change in Organisations, New Perspectives on Theory, Research and Practice, pp. 375–408, San Fransisco, CA: Jossey-Bass.

Zimmermann, F.O. (1997) Structural and Managerial Aspects of Virtual Enterprises, Http://www.teck.uni-karlsruhe.de/IT-VISION/vu-e-teco-htm.

# Author Index

# Subject Index